THE POWER OF FEASTS

In this book, Brian Hayden provides the first comprehensive, theoretical work on the history of feasting in prehistoric societies. As an important barometer of cultural change, feasting is at the forefront of theoretical developments in archaeology. *The Power of Feasts* chronicles the evolution of the practice from its first perceptible prehistoric presence to modern industrial times. This study explores recurring patterns in the dynamics of feasts, as well as linkages to other aspects of culture such as food, personhood, cognition, power, politics, and economics. Analyzing detailed ethnographic and archaeological observations from a wide variety of cultures including Oceania and Southeast Asia, the Americas, and Eurasia, Hayden illuminates the role of feasts as an invaluable insight into the social and political structures of past societies.

Brian Hayden is professor emeritus in the Archaeology Department at Simon Fraser University. His research focuses on the behaviors behind the artifacts in terms of societies, economics, rituals, and political organizations of past people, specifically in terms of the dynamics of feasting from an ethnoarchaeological perspective. He has worked with traditional people in Australia, the Maya Highlands, Southeast Asia, Indonesia, Polynesia, and British Columbia in order to learn about traditional technologies and how they are linked to the other aspects of cultures. He is the author of numerous articles and books, including *Archaeology: The Science of Once and Future Things*; *The Pithouses of Keatley Creek*; *Shamans, Sorcerers, and Saints: The Prehistory of Religion*; *Feasts* (with Michael Dietler); *Paleolithic Reflections*; and *Lithic Studies Among the Highland Maya*.

D1616695

The Power of Feasts

FROM PREHISTORY TO THE PRESENT

Brian Hayden

Simon Fraser University, British Columbia

CAMBRIDGE
UNIVERSITY PRESS

University Printing House, Cambridge CB2 8BS, United Kingdom

One Liberty Plaza, 20th Floor, New York, NY 10006, USA

477 Williamstown Road, Port Melbourne, VIC 3207, Australia

4843/24, 2nd Floor, Ansari Road, Daryaganj, Delhi - 110002, India

79 Anson Road, #06-04/06, Singapore 079906

Cambridge University Press is part of the University of Cambridge.

It furthers the University's mission by disseminating knowledge in the pursuit of education, learning and research at the highest international levels of excellence.

www.cambridge.org
Information on this title: www.cambridge.org/9781107617643

First published 2014

A catalogue record for this publication is available from the British Library

Library of Congress Cataloging in Publication data
Hayden, Brian.
The power of feasts : from prehistory to the present / Brian Hayden.
  pages   cm
ISBN 978-1-107-04299-5 (hardback)
1. Festivals.   2. Fasts and feasts.   3. Food supply – Social aspects.   4. Food supply – Political aspects.   5. Agriculture and politics.   I. Title.
GT3930.H39   2014
394.2–dc23   2013048106

ISBN 978-1-107-04299-5 Hardback
ISBN 978-1-107-61764-3 Paperback

Contents

Figures

Acknowledgments

This project has been a long time in the making, beginning around 1999. Over the intervening years, I have been extremely fortunate to have worked with exceptional people in the field, both as colleagues and as students, not to mention the many generous individuals in the villages where we worked and who shared their knowledge with us. Foremost has been the collaboration with Ralana Maneeprasert, who worked at the Hill Tribe Research Institute in Chiang Mai, as well as the administrative personnel of the Institute who facilitated our work together. Similarly, Stanislaus Sandarupa played a pivotal role in our work in Sulawesi, whereas Tran Quoc Vuong was instrumental in working with the hill tribes in Viet Nam and creating many fond memories. I regret that he did not live to see this publication. Mike Clarke and Ron Adams carried out the bulk of the field research in Thailand, Sulawesi, and Sumba, producing first-rate publications and documents on these areas. Suzanne Villeneuve was instrumental in encouraging me to pursue feasting research in Polynesia, and she carried out the bulk of the detailed data collection, again producing top-notch results. I am extremely fortunate to have had such a gifted and dedicated group of people helping me in the quest to find out about feasts in these societies. This book would not have been possible without them, and I will be eternally grateful to them. I would also like to thank the students in my early classes who were involved in starting me on the road to feasting. Far from least in my gratitude are the many people in the villages where we worked and the many government administrators who shared their time and knowledge and helped us all in our endeavors. Of course, such research would not have been possible without the financial support of a number of agencies, foremost of which was the Canadian Social Sciences and Humanities Research Council, the Simon Fraser University President's Research Fund and SSHRC Small Grants Fund, and the help of the Archaeology Department support staff. I would also like to acknowledge the helpful comments of anonymous reviewers of this manuscript.

1

Before the Feast

INITIAL CONSIDERATIONS

> *At the heart of science is an essential balance between two seemingly contra-*
> *dictory attitudes – an openness to new ideas, no matter how bizarre or*
> *counterintuitive, and the most ruthlessly skeptical scrutiny of* all *ideas,*
> *old and new.*
>
> – Carl Sagan, *The Demon Haunted World*

WHY STUDY FEASTS?

"Feasts." The word conjures up images of sybaritic self-indulgence or luxurious, lavish opulence and frivolity. In Industrial cultures, feasts are generally fun events that satiate our gustatory and social senses. They seem to have little practical benefit. They provide experiences outside our work and the drudgery of daily responsibilities (Figure 1.1). Feasts have undoubtedly always had such appeal. However, what you will discover in this book is that feasting in pre-Industrial societies had, and still has, far-reaching consequences in many other domains (Figure 1.2). In fact, up until the Industrial Revolution, there may have been no other more powerful engine of cultural change than feasts.

This book provides an initial synthesis of what archaeologists, ethnoarchaeologists, ethnographers, and historians know about the dynamics of feasting in pre-Industrial societies. Although ethnographers and historians have a long tradition of documenting feasts, sometimes in minute detail, they have not always been very diligent in probing the inner dynamics and benefits that are associated with feasts or in examining feasts from broader theoretical perspectives. Early colonial government administrators and missionaries were generally baffled by the enormous quantities of food and valuable gifts that seemed to be squandered at large tribal feasts. This behavior seemed antithetical to economic progress and particularly to company profits or government revenues. Governments often reacted by outlawing traditional

1.1. Although the term "feast" may conjure images of modern dinner parties and receptions like this one, in reality, feasts in traditional societies were quite different. (Photograph courtesy of Arlene Hayden).

1.2. Traditional feasts, such as this installation ceremony for a new village chief on the Polynesian island of Futuna, featured key individuals in the community or region and were quite formal affairs at which social relationships were consolidated and political debts were brokered. (Photograph by B. Hayden).

feasts like the potlatch of the Northwest Coast of North America and the major feasts in Indonesia and Vietnam. Classical archaeologists, profiting from a number of written accounts of opulent feasts, have a tradition of interest in the topic, especially the role of feasts in early Greek politics. Prehistorians, on the other hand, until the last twenty years, seem to have viewed prehistoric feasting as largely irrelevant to the more important issues of subsistence, trade, warfare, technology, and architecture (Hayden and Villeneuve 2011b).

In the 1980s and especially the 1990s, a number of key publications attempted to link pre-Industrial feasting with theoretically important issues in archaeology such as political complexity, social structure, inequality, domestication, the development of prestige technologies, and the creation of monumental architecture (Friedman and Rowlands 1977; Bender 1985; Dietler 1990; Hayden 1990). These theoretical connections provided a springboard for a vigorous new interest in traditional feasting behavior. One of the first results of this new interest was a mini-conference that I proposed to organize with Michael Dietler on theoretical aspects of feasting. Although our initial proposals for a workshop-style event were not supported by foundations that we approached, we did organize a symposium at the 1998 annual meeting of the Society for American Archaeology in Seattle. Since the publication of that symposium (Dietler and Hayden 2001), there has been an exponentially increasing rate of publications on the topic in archaeology around the world, including a number of edited volumes (e.g., Bray 2003a; Wright 2004; Kaulicke and Dillehay 2005; Aranda 2008a; Klarich 2010; Aranda et al. 2011). It is still possible to become familiar with the major publications in this rapidly developing area of research; however, this may not be the case a few years from now. Thus, it may be useful to pause briefly at this juncture in the development of feasting studies and take stock of what we know and how to best orient some future directions in studying feasting, either archaeologically or ethnographically. This is what I hope to achieve to some degree in the following pages.

This book is not meant to be a catalog of various feasting practices throughout the world, as many books on food and even feasting have been in the past. Rather, this book is meant to be a theoretical synthesis (supported by a sample of examples) of what has been learned over the past few decades. My approach is unapologetically comparative because I am interested primarily in understanding recurring patterns in the dynamics of feasts and linkages to other aspects of culture that are important to archaeologists. I will not dwell on the symbolism of foods or items other than to note their relative importance or value and to remark on some of the clearest examples of symbolic importance, as in the case of cattle in Chapter 5. It is the broad issues concerning sociocultural dynamics and change that are my focus.

In terms of prehistoric archaeology, there are a number of important reasons why researchers should pay close attention to any indications of feasting in their excavations and analyses, all of which we will explore in more detail in the following chapters.

- First, feasting constitutes a new kind of human behavior, one that probably first emerged in the Upper Paleolithic in a few favorable locations and only became more widespread in the Mesolithic/Archaic and Neolithic periods.
- Second, feasting is a type of behavior that can leave recognizable and diagnostic material remains in the archaeological record. In fact, their remains are eminently recoverable. Archaeologists just have to look for them.
- Third, feasting appears to be a major strategy used by ambitious individuals to achieve social, economic, and political advantages or dominance.
- Fourth, feasting can thus provide important insights into the social and political structures and dynamics of past societies.
- Fifth, feasting may have been intimately associated with the first specialized structures to appear in the archaeological record, often referred to as communal buildings or ritual structures.
- Sixth, feasting may provide the context, if not the underlying dynamic, for the development of a range of prestige technologies, including new food preparation and serving technologies involving pottery, brewing, the use of metals, record keeping, and calendrical and astronomical systems.
- Seventh, the domestication of plants and animals may be one of the most important prestige technologies to have been developed specifically for feasting contexts.
- And eighth, feasting systems arguably represent an entirely new phenomenon in the biological world in which surplus food can be converted into other desirable things or relationships in short spans of time.

For all these and other reasons (including gender roles, the creation of social identities, and understanding cultural symbols), it is important to study feasting. In addition to its academic relevance, feasting in most traditional societies is often the most valued aspect of cultural life. Participating in feasts elevates people from mundane everyday affairs, it panders to the senses, immerses the individual in social intercourse, animates ritual, and fosters fond memories. Traditional feasts epitomize the etiquette, dress, cuisine, customs, and rituals of village societies that are displayed or activated in few other contexts. The high value emically associated with traditional feasts is an important indication of why academics should deem them worthy of special attention.

This chapter discusses some background definitions, assumptions, and theoretical issues necessary for fully engaging in the discussions in the chapters that follow. This chapter can be viewed as a "primer." One of the most fundamental topics that should be addressed first is the general theoretical orientation of this study, namely paleo-political ecology.

THE PALEO-POLITICAL ECOLOGY PERSPECTIVE

My perspective on feasting is resolutely ecological. However, within the broad scope of the ecological paradigm are many varied subfields and theories. What might be referred to as "classical cultural ecology" has dealt almost exclusively with resource acquisition and how resource characteristics, such as resource density, size, seasonality, search time, processing effort, distance, and other factors, affected people's choice of resources, the strategies used to obtain them, and their influence on human behavior, especially competition, conflict, alliances, and even ritual life (e.g., Rappaport 1968; Suttles 1968; Vayda 1976; Yengoyan 1976; Wiessner 1982; E. Smith and Winterhalder 1992). As in animal ecology, the underlying issues were how energy could be captured, transformed, stored, and used for survival and reproduction. The process by which advantages were gained in these arenas operated via natural (or cultural) selection and adaptation. The production and use of surplus food was not given much consideration in animal ecology except as surpluses that might be stored for dearth periods (e.g., storage of nuts by squirrels or honey by bees) or incorporated via genetic adaptation over many generations in the form of physical displays of superior reproductive potential: the Zahavis's rather famous "handicap" or "show off" principle (1997), as illustrated by peacock tails or stag's antlers (Figure 1.3). Because ecology as a distinctive field first emerged in the

1.3. In biology, energy beyond what is required for basic subsistence is sometimes invested in showy physical features that have genetically evolved to attract mates or deter rivals, as with this peacock's plumage. Humans often do the same thing using material culture to "show off"; however, feasts go far beyond this basic type of adaptation. (Photograph by B. Hayden)

biological sciences, and because animals could not use more energy than they could eat, cultural ecology at first focused almost exclusively on the subsistence economy of human groups and ignored the status, or political, economy.

In more recent years, the study of the cultural use of resources to "show off" has been developed by human behavioral ecologists as "costly signaling theory." In this approach, costly displays are thought to convey signals primarily to competitors or adversaries to indicate the likely outcomes of any physical conflicts and thereby reduce the incidence of debilitating injuries or death (Wiessner 1989:60; Bliege-Bird and Smith 2005; Roscoe 2009). In earlier cultural and animal ecology studies, such costly displays were referred to as *epideictic* displays (Wynne-Edwards 1962:16; Rappaport 1968:195; 1999:83). Feasting in most societies certainly represents costly displays, with a number of different types of signals being transmitted, including the likely outcomes of conflict. However, as we shall see later, there is considerably more involved in feasting than the simple transmission of competitive signals.

In the ethnoarchaeological studies of feasting that I have been involved in, it became apparent that feasting in traditional societies was predicated on the production and use of surplus resources. Without surpluses, feasts would simply be unthinkable. Thus, potlatching on the Northwest Coast took place in times of abundance and increased in scale as wealth increased from the fur trade (Codere 1950). Similarly, in times of starvation, potlatching ceased (Niblack 1890). This aspect is dealt with in more detail in Hayden (1995:22–3; 2001b:247). Wiessner (2002b:234; Wiessner and Tumu 1998) has also shown how both socioeconomic inequality and feasting systems grew substantially in New Guinea as a result of the introduction of the sweet potato and the increased surpluses that this made possible. Feasting systems did not develop or thrive under stress conditions. It also became apparent during my fieldwork that feasts were being used to create debts and weld together political factions within or between communities. Similarly, on the Northwest Coast and Plateau, others have documented a strong relationship between food surpluses and population levels, wealth levels, and political complexity (Donald and Mitchell 1975; Hunn 1991:223–4). The same relationship has been documented in South Africa by Cashdan (1980) and in Polynesia, where Sahlins (1958:248–9) demonstrated a strong link between surplus production, redistributive economies (based on feasting), and inequality.

Equally important was the related use of feasts as a strategy employed by ambitious individuals to promote their own self-interests and to obtain power. Because these aspects fell outside the purview of classical ecology and signaling theory, I decided to refer to my own approach as "political ecology" (Hayden 2001a:27), or more precisely, "paleo-political ecology" because cultural anthropologists use a "political ecology" framework quite differently to study the exploitation of resources by modern-day elites (Wolf 1972; Bryant 1992; L. Anderson 1994;

Kottak 1999; Stott and Sullivan 2001). The goal of paleo-political ecology is to understand why surplus production takes place in traditional communities and especially how surplus resources are used to promote the self-interests of the producers and manipulators of surpluses in small-scale societies. It is, in many ways, similar to Herskovits's (1940:461–5) and Firth's (1959:480) "status economies," and Sahlins's (1972) and Earle's (1977, 1978, 1997) "political economies," as distinct from "subsistence economies."

The marriage of classical ecological concepts with political factors has perhaps been the single most significant development since the incorporation of ecological models in anthropological theory. Of course, in addition to ecological perspectives, there are many other approaches to explaining feasts. Early administrators and missionaries, as well as many ethnographers, viewed lavish feasting as simply part of distinctive cultural traditions that created their own internal logics largely divorced from economic reason or practical benefits. Thus, Rosman and Rubel (1971) argued that the potlatch of the North American Northwest Coast was the outcome of a particular social type of organization. Other anthropologists appealed to feasts as a means of gaining status, essentially a psychological gratification motivation. Others viewed feasts as wealth-leveling activities that the rich were pressured into hosting in exchange for status, thus maintaining egalitarian social structures (Carrasco 1961; Price 1972; Kirkby 1973:31). Communitarian or functionalist advocates view feasting as serving communal goals and promoting social solidarity (e.g., Saitta and Keene 1990; Potter 2000; Potter and Ortman 2004). However, even an astute ethnographer like Malinowski could not understand the rationale of these food exchanges from a functionalist perspective (Weiner 1988:126).

Cognitive, cultural normative, social, and psychological gratification explanations contrast markedly with ecological, political economy, or cultural materialist explanations. In terms of cultural ecological concepts, Rolf Knight was fond of stressing, in graduate seminars at the University of Toronto, that behaviors that are costly, persist over time, and are widespread can be expected to have adaptive benefits. Feasting exhibits all these characteristics in spades. In fact, various feasts often constituted the single most costly events ever hosted by most families or even entire communities in people's lifetimes. Feasting is certainly a widespread, almost universal behavior, and it has persisted for many thousands of years. Thus, feasting meets all of Knight's criteria for an adaptive behavior. However, from the existing firsthand ethnographic accounts, it was not at all clear what adaptive benefits might have been commensurate with the enormous expenditures of time, effort, and resources that typified many feasts. Appeal to enhancing individual status seemed an inadequate motivation for such lavish and costly expenditures. Some classical cultural ecologists like Suttles (1968) and Rappaport (1968) attempted to explain large feasts in terms of redistributing resources under conditions of pronounced local fluctuations or in terms of providing periodic protein consumption for large numbers of people. However, these interpretations have generally been discredited. As Niblack (1890) observed, feasting essentially ceases when food becomes scarce. It cannot have served a redistributive function when it was most needed. Thus, the following chapters focus on other practical, often implicit, benefits underlying the hosting of feasts. Before proceeding to these discussions, it is important to define feasts and set out some basic purposes for hosting them, as well as to establish a useful framework for classifying feasts.

DEFINITIONS

Feasts have been defined in a number of different ways by different authors. One commonly cited definition defines them as "forms of ritual activity that involve the communal consumption of food and drink," also as "public ritual events" (Dietler 2001:65,67,69). I find that there are some problems of vagueness with such a definition. For instance, do meals with one or two other people constitute "communal consumption"? In addition, despite Dietler's disclaimer, for many people, tying consumption to rituals implies that feasting only occurs in religious contexts, which would exclude many events generally viewed as feasting such as political support dinners, birthday parties, work feasts, and dinner parties. Although most of these events include "ritualistic" elements (as opposed to ritual activities), it is not entirely clear what constitutes a "ritual activity" or event, or why such a feature is essential to the definition of feasting. For Dietler, rituals may symbolically differentiate actions or purposes from everyday activities. To me, this use of "ritual" is too general and obscure, especially in relation to its generally understood meaning. Similarly, restricting feasting only to public events seems to exclude private parties and intimate meals. Given these ambiguities, I continue to prefer the definition that I originally proposed: any sharing of a meal including some special foods (i.e., foods not generally served at daily meals) between two or more people hosted for a special purpose or occasion (Hayden 2001a:28). This definition would exclude any communal meal simply held to feed large numbers of people, as in cafeterias. H. Leach (2003:452), Van der Veen (2003:411–2), Stasch (2012:360,371), and Hastorf (2008:1393) have all pointed out that unusual quantities of normal foods may also characterize feasts, especially "potluck" events. The definition of feasts might therefore be amended to read "any sharing between two or more people of a meal featuring some special foods or unusual quantities of foods (i.e., foods or quantities not generally served at daily meals) hosted for a special purpose or occasion."

Definitions proposed by some other authors exclude small-scale social gatherings involving individual households and close relatives from other households or even question the validity of distinguishing daily meals from feasts (Graves and Van Keuren 2004; Twiss 2012:8,23). This is counterproductive in my view. It may be useful to consider nuclear/extended family feasts as distinctive types of events from suprahousehold events; however, there is no rationale for eliminating them completely from analysis using a feasting framework simply because of their smaller size. Such a definition would exclude most of our Thanksgiving and Christmas dinners. This brings up the issue of how feasts can be usefully classified because there is a substantial range of variation in feasting behavior.

CLASSIFYING FEASTS

As with many archaeological phenomena, feasts can be classified in a bewildering variety of ways depending on individual interests, backgrounds, and the theoretical questions being addressed (see Hayden 2001a:35–40). Traditional anthropological descriptions have tended to classify feasts in terms of the emically recognized specific events associated with them: funerals, marriages, births, harvests, house building, and so on. Some analysts have classified feasts according to calendrical or seasonal events (New Year, solstices, harvests) versus life events (birth, marriage, death), to which one could add political events (such as interpolity alliances and village celebrations). Other approaches use the hosting social group (such as lineages, households, or communities) to categorize feasts. Others have examined them in terms of obligatory return feasts of equal or greater value versus nonreturn feasts (Perodie 2001:191). Still others, like Dietler (2001:76–88), emphasize the social relations involved in feasts, such as empowering (entrepreneurial) feasts for the acquisition or manipulation of influence and power, patron-role feasts (for legitimizing or helping to create sociopolitical asymmetries), work feasts (sometimes nonreciprocal labor contracts), and diacritical feasts (to display and reify concepts of ranked differences in the social order, hence events lacking reciprocal hospitality or debts). Many other distinctions can be used for classifying feasts, such as their size or auxiliary features (including, e.g., prestige gifts, dancing, religious rituals, heirloom displays, sport combats, or alcohol). However, there is no "right" classification for feasts (or most other phenomena). There are only more or less useful and insightful classifications – classifications that are better or worse for answering specific questions or dealing with specific issues.

Because my main interest is the relationship between feasts and community dynamics (including sociopolitical structures), I deal with feasts largely in terms of the social groups that host feasts and the types of benefits that they hope to gain from hosting them. I refer to these benefits as the underlying motives or purposes for hosting feasts. Examining feasts from this perspective might be considered a "formal" analysis (what practical benefits derive from feasts and what general forms they take), as opposed to "symbolical" analysis (focusing on the symbolic reasons for hosting events, such as curing or ancestor veneration; see Hayden 2001a:25). Various types of sociopolitical groups will be introduced in the following chapters,

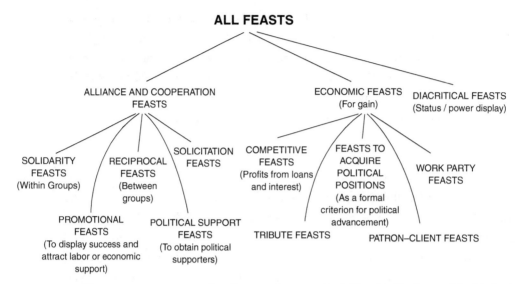

1.4. There are numerous ways that feasts can be categorized. The classification used in this book is represented here and is based on the underlying basic motive for hosting traditional feasts: solidarity within or between social groups, economic gain or advantage, and status or power display. Each basic motive can take a number of specific forms.

from nuclear households, to corporate groups, to bands, to special interest groups and communities. But the dominant purposes of feasts can be grouped under three basic types of benefits with a number of subvarieties, as illustrated in Figure 1.4. These are:

- Social Bonding:
  - Enhancing solidarity and effectiveness of social groups
  - Creating alliances between social groups
  - Bonding for warfare
  - Promoting or advertising group success and the desirability of affiliations
  - Acquiring political support and validating political positions through displays of that support
- Material/Economic Benefits:
  - Undertaking labor-intensive tasks
  - Extracting resources from community members (via tribute feasts, patron-clientships, royal life-event celebrations, touring feasts, harvest celebrations, secret society or temple events, or more subtle means)
  - Using feasts to invest in children or in exchanges
  - Compensating for transgressions or losses
  - Solicitation feasts
  - Investment (greater return) feasts
- Creation of Status Distinctions (diacritical feasts)

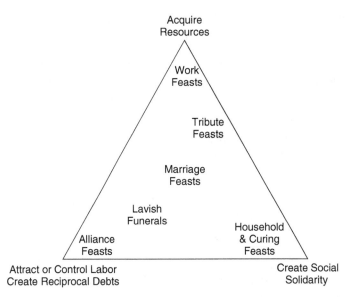

1.5. In reality, hosts and supporters often use feasts to achieve a number of types of benefits for themselves. Although one motive may dominate the organization of a feast, submotives can also be inferred and diagrammed with the use of a ternary graph based on three types of motives. Several examples of feast types are placed within this field to illustrate suggested mixes of motives.

POLYSEMY

Although pursuing one of the benefits just listed may constitute the main underlying purpose for organizing and hosting a feast, hosts often take advantage of these costly events to promote other goals as well. Almost everyone who has experienced traditional feasts has remarked on the fact that there are numerous facets to feasts with consequences for different social groups. In short, feasts are polysemous (e.g., Dietler 2001:78; Aranda 2008:117; Twiss 2008, 2012:8). Yet it seems that the dominant goals for hosting feasts largely determine the overall tenor and material manifestations of specific events. For example, it is true that lavish funerals bring together lineage members and reinforce lineage solidarity. Despite these solidarity aspects, the dominant character of these feasts is that of overtly competitive displays of material wealth organized primarily by individual households (but assisted by their supporters, especially lineage members). In contrast, feasts with dominant solidarity purposes often lack overt competitive displays involving wealth. The mix of motives involved in various types of feasts might be graphed as in Figure 1.5. Teasing out the various motivational components and combinations of specific events can be a difficult task requiring some finesse and insight but should be a productive area for future research.

For instance, it is not entirely clear to me what the dominant goal is for events described as "diacritical" feasts in stratified societies. Are diacritical feasts supposed to reify or naturalize concepts of differences between statuses or classes, or are the distinctive styles of consumption and cuisine more a by-product of attempts to advertise success and wealth in order to attract desired affiliations with similarly high-ranking individuals or social groups? An important point to note is that the "diacritical" interpretation of feasts in stratified societies rests on an *exclusionary* logic emphasizing boundaries, whereas it can be argued that *the most fundamental logic of all feasting is the sharing of food with others in order to create social bonds (or debts); that is, an inclusionary logic.* All feasts have limits and must in some sense be exclusive. However, I am not certain that the exclusion of people in a diacritical fashion has ever been the main underlying motive for hosting a feast in a pre-Industrial society. I would argue that without the inclusive sharing of food to create social bonds or obtain material advantages, feasts make no sense. *Food is provided at feasts in order to attract people,* not keep them at a distance. It is possible to have feasts with or without diacritical components, but a feast that does not attract people to form some type of social bond seems inconceivable, even for economic feasts that are ultimately dependent on the creation of a social bond for success, if only temporary. Some aspects of lavish feasts may certainly be used to create social solidarity and social identities, but the exclusion of others seems more like an incidental consequence of minor importance when compared to the more funda-mental social bonding logic for holding feasts.

EUPHORIA, SYNESTHESIA, AND THE ATTRACTION OF FEASTS

In sum, I argue that the essential aspect of feasts is the amassing of surplus food and other items in order to attract people and thereby gain some significant advantages. People come to feasts primarily because they receive "free" or highly valued foods – or at least food that they do not have to return in the immediate future. Because of this inherent logic, the amassing of surpluses to give away as food or gifts, or to put on display to impress guests, is an essential defining characteristic of all feasts. In general, surpluses in societies lacking enforcement cadres, such as police or standing armies, can only be amassed under conditions of abundance. Thus, feasts cannot be viewed as resulting from population pressure or stress conditions. Moreover, to attract as many, or as desirable people as possible, hosts generally pander to the popular tastes and desires for particular types of foods, especially fatty meats, starches, sugars, and alcohols, but also include many other gustatory specialties (soups, breads, large ripe fruits, chocolates, kava, and many more). As discussed in Chapter 3, the recurring cravings for some basic food types is probably the result of genetic adaptations that took place during our primate or early hominin period of evolution.

The goal of attracting people also helps explain an important characteristic aspect of most large-scale feasting: the sensory overloads and euphoric blurring,

1.6. Many people are drawn to feasts because of the prospect of experiencing a pleasantly altered state, or euphoria, which can even include synesthesia ("blurring of the senses"). Hosts may attempt to promote such sensations by providing copious amounts of alcohol or similar substances, rich food, colorful costumes, music, dancing, animal sacrifices, and rituals.

"union of senses" (Figure 1.6), or synesthesia (to stretch the term a bit) characteristic of larger events (Hastorf 2008:1391). These might profitably be analyzed from a phenomenological perspective. The use of sound, visual images, drama, animal (and sometimes human) sacrifices, dancing, and intoxication that all fuse together in an emotional amalgam make these events as sensually pleasurable, emotionally exhilarating, and memorable as possible. As Halpern (2000:11) has noted, "Pleasure has an important role in the healthy regulation of behavior, both physically and mentally," thus people gravitate toward situations that promise to provide pleasure, and feast-givers certainly try to make their events pleasurable experiences. The production of serotonin and oxytocin by many feasting foods and activities is undoubtedly important in creating feelings of euphoria and emotional bonds of closeness at feasts (Johnson 2003:73).

Many prestige technologies are enlisted, or even created, to enhance the pleasurable synesthesia of feasts, probably including the first use of metals, beads, tailored clothes, musical instruments, pottery, and elaborate architecture. The specific materials, styles, and creativity employed to achieve pleasing or impressive effects are potentially almost infinite. As a result, the larger feasting events in many traditional societies really embody the most spectacular aspects of those cultures and epitomize each social group's distinctiveness, creative style, and particular genius. The specific way that traditional social groups feast with their special foods, together with their material and performance styles largely define them and their cultures. Who participates, the foods, the etiquette, the dress, the events, the appeals to ancestors or spirits, dances, honor, gender roles, all combine to create what Sánchez (2008) and Aranda (2008:109–10) have called the "social identity" of families, kin groups, communities, and other social groups. In addition, as Polly Wiessner (1989:60) observed, people wanted to support and participate in successful displays because "Each individual stood to benefit from showing identity with a wealthy and unified group, in terms of promoting exchange and discouraging warfare." The very great tragedy in colonial history has been the frequent attempt to suppress traditional feasting on the grounds that it was economically regressive or represented "devil" worship. The result has often been the destruction of entire traditional cultural values – or what Tran Quoc Vuong, a Vietnamese ethnographer, referred to as "ethnic genocide."

AGGRANDIZERS

To understand why feasts began to appear relatively late in the archaeological record and why hosts wanted to attract people, I think it is necessary to recognize the role that aggrandizers play in community dynamics. The concept of aggrandizer is a critical one that deserves some discussion because it has been misinterpreted by some critics and will feature in many of the following discussions.

To begin with, it is worth noting that of all the Darwinian imperatives for survival, the pursuit of self-interest by organisms is the most fundamental. Self-interest is also considered the basis for market and government decision making (Lewin 1986) and has been explicitly used for a number of archaeological and anthropological models (see Wells 1984:36–7; Hayden 1995:23). Even Margaret Mead (1937:497) invoked the "will to power" in accounting for competition. In contrast, altruistic behavior is the most difficult to account for in terms of natural selection. Although scarcity and fluctuations in resources might induce early hunting and gathering communities to curtail the self-interested behaviors of their members (or at least channel them into avenues other than resource exploitation, e.g., into competition over marriage, ritual knowledge, or kin roles), such egalitarian communities were unlikely to eliminate expressions of self-interest entirely, even with systematic exclusion of individuals who would not refrain from overtly pursuing their own economically based self-interests (Hayden 2011a). In fact, there are a number of accounts in the ethnographic literature of self-centered individuals in egalitarian hunter/gatherer societies who intimidated and terrorized others to achieve advantages for themselves. Perhaps the most extreme case is that of an Inuit shaman who wanted to marry a woman in opposition to the woman's family's wishes. To fulfill his own desires, he killed the woman's family and others who opposed him (seven in all) and took the woman for himself (Campbell 1983:20,164–70). Accounts of killings from conflicts over women or elopements despite the death penalties for such behavior are not uncommon even in the Western Desert of Australia (I was told of several cases when I worked in the Australian Western Desert) or in !Kung or Hadza communities. These were clear examples of individuals who did not accept the "system" values that they had been brought up with and who had chosen options that favored their own emotional and reproductive interests, all at considerable risk. In the Western Desert, elopements and stealing one of the wives away from an elder were punishable by death, and couples had to flee for their lives, often with supporters of the aggrieved in hot pursuit. In North Australia, there was even an early account of a tribal Aboriginal who murdered for small economic gains (Love 1936:103–12).

In addition to this, I found that Aboriginal life, both now and in oral accounts of precontact life, was rife with factions and constant grievances being lodged against individuals for social infractions or infringements. Peterson (2006) makes similar observations for Australia. Internally, these societies were far from peaceful (Lee 1979:90–96; Knuckey 1991; Gat 2006:14–19,69). Allegations of violations of the egalitarian and other social ethics were constantly occurring, and communities were in constant need of vigilance and control over violators. Thus, it seems that at least some individuals who aggressively promoted their own self-interests existed in many, if not all egalitarian hunter/gatherer societies, but their behavior was systematically constrained (as indicated by Lee 1979:48–50; Wiessner 1996; and R. Kelly 1995), or they were eliminated from the community. Maintaining egalitarian socioeconomic systems was thus both difficult and costly (R. Kelly 1995). Wiessner (1996:187) summarizes the situation in the following terms: "As the many leveling mechanisms in forager societies imply, the tendency of individuals to seek status and influence is a current that runs through all cultures."

It seems that the extreme cases noted here were exceptional and that most people, most of the time, were, in fact, honoring the social norms of behavior, albeit sometimes grudgingly. What emerges from these and other ethnographic or sociological accounts of societies at all levels of complexity is that in all large human populations there is, and undoubtedly always was, a naturally occurring range of variability pertaining to the pursuit of self-interests. At one end were personality types who behaved extremely altruistically. In today's societies, extremely altruistic people devote their lives to helping the poor, they give away most or all of the money that they earn, and they even risk their lives for others by working in epidemic contexts or in conflict areas. They are the Mother Theresas of the world or the volunteers in Médecins Sans Frontières.

At the other extreme there are and were people with personalities who only think of their own self-interests or only think of others' interests when it is part of a

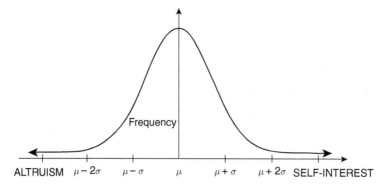

1.7. Like many other physical and personality traits, the extent to which people can be characterized as pursuing their own self-interests exhibits a normal or "bell-shaped" curve as illustrated here. At one extreme, there are very few people who only act to help others without regard for their own interest. At the other extreme, there are very few people who only act for their own selfish interests. Most people (the center of the curve) act for their own benefit much of the time but also act to help others much of the time. "Aggrandizers" are those people at the "self-interest" end of the spectrum.

scheme to advance their own benefits or advantages. In the extreme, they do not care what effects their pursuit of wealth and power have on other people. Thus, it was common for some entrepreneurs to develop industries that polluted or poisoned streams so that businessmen could make profits, to kill off native groups so that colonizing individuals could farm or mine the earth, to indebt factory workers, to scam the elderly of life-savings, to prostitute children or kin, and many other such kinds of behaviors. At the very extreme end of the spectrum, these people are referred to as "sociopaths" or "psychopaths": personalities who exhibit no emotional empathy for other people and seem to have no moral or social conscience, people who are frequently aggressive in the pursuit of their own advantages. In *Without Conscience*, Robert Hare (1993) makes the important point that sociopathic personality types occur in all societies, in all social classes, and in all kinds of family upbringings. He therefore concludes that there is (and presumably always was) an important genetic component to this type of personality. As with other genetically influenced traits, like height or weight, the distribution of behavior along the altruism–self-interest dimension of values seems to be represented by a bell-shaped curve, with some extreme cases that occur in any large population but with most people exhibiting moderate values (Figure 1.7). And, in fact, most people today prefer to devote most of their time and energy to achieving their own goals but are usually happy to spend time with others and to help others as well. Most people save or spend their earnings for their own projects and pleasures but also contribute to charities or make loans to friends in need or buy presents for others. The average behavior (the equilibrium point between communitarian helping of others and the pursuit of individualistic goals) may shift depending on economic or other conditions, but the important point is that the full range of behaviors has probably always been present in any large population. In evolutionary terms, both extremes may be adaptive under some unforeseen future conditions, and so the full range is maintained by selective pressures to draw upon if necessary under a range of different circumstances. However, the dominant values of a society are probably adapted to the prevailing or recent past circumstances.

Some criticisms of the political ecology approach pretend that I view all people as being driven exclusively by Machiavellian self-interest. This is far from the case. In fact, I try to describe the *full range* of people's personalities. What I do maintain is that individuals who aggressively pursue their own self-interests constitute a small but extremely powerful element in all populations. They constantly and aggressively push accepted values and social boundaries in order to promote their self-serving schemes. They are highly motivated to eliminate egalitarian or community constraints that curtail pursuit of their self-interests (as recently demonstrated by the refusal of banks and investment firms to accept more stringent regulations after the world economic downturn of 2008). I suggest that aggrandizers are probably responsible for many of the fundamental transformations of culture that archaeology has been able to chronicle over the past 40,000 years. As Margaret Mead is reputed to have said, "Never doubt that a small group of determined individuals can change the world. Indeed, it is the only thing that ever has" (http://www.interculturalstudies.org/faq.html#quote). However, she undoubtedly had a more utopian view of social change in mind.

Thus, we can expect that at least a few people who were highly motivated and determined to pursue their own self-interests (and change social norms to suit their own goals) occurred in all large populations, even in the most egalitarian cultures, and that they took risks to achieve benefits for themselves. These are the individuals that I refer to as "aggrandizers" or "triple A" personality types: ambitious, abrasive, aggressive, accumulative, aggrandizing people. Some aggrandizers are gifted and intelligent; some are dim and lack social abilities. But all are manipulative and implacably determined.

Today, individuals who cannot control their self-serving impulses are often incarcerated or confined in other institutional ways. In times of war or intense economic competition, their ruthlessness may be much more positively valued. But in normal times, people with less extreme expressions of this type of behavior often become successful in business and politics, and they constantly push for changes in policies (such as deregulations and tax exemptions) that will primarily benefit themselves or their associates. In the past, once technologies improved food production so that it no longer became necessary to rigidly enforce egalitarian behavior, individuals with triple-A personalities became freer to find ways to achieve their goals. On the basis of my own ethnoarchaeological research and readings, I have identified at least thirteen major strategies that aggrandizers use to achieve their goals in traditional societies. Feasts are by far one of the most common and powerful of these strategies, and the consequences are far-reaching. Other common strategies included the promotion of ownership of resources and produce, marriages obtained in exchange for wealth, wealth investments in children, claims for exclusive access to the supernatural (including ancestors), and the manipulation of allies and warfare. Many of these strategies were often cross-linked with feasts, and, as such, their success was also tied to the production of surpluses.

UNFAVORABLE AND FAVORABLE CONDITIONS FOR AGGRANDIZERS

Given these considerations, we come to what is perhaps the most important theoretical point of this book. In terms of unfavorable situations for aggrandizers, we can observe that the use of food resources under conditions of (a) scarcity, (b) fluctuations, and (c) easy overexploitation rendered any competition that was based on food resources self-destructive. Unfettered competition over limited resources could destroy resource bases in the past just as it has in recent years, as exemplified by the disappearance/near extinction of American bison, beaver, cod, moas, and many other species competitively hunted for food or profit. In the same way, exclusive control by some individuals over critical resources in times of famine would mean that many others might starve. Thus, private control over resources and competition using resources was prohibited in egalitarian societies where food availability was uncertain. The equilibrium point of social values in these types of societies appears to have been dramatically shifted toward communitarian (vs. individual) interests.

In contrast, under conditions of abundant resources that are relatively invulnerable to overexploitation (with appropriate technologies), it becomes possible to establish resource-based competition and to allow resources to be used to pursue strategies that enhance individual or group competitive advantages. As Cowgill (1975:114–5) has observed, social complexity appears to be stimulated more by the prospect of new opportunities rather than by hardships. In the case of agriculture, an almost endless ability to increase resource production was established, and I argue that it favored an escalating use of resource-based aggrandizer strategies in productive locations. However, among complex hunter/gatherer societies, too, such as those of the Northwest Coast of North America, the exploitation of abundant, rapidly reproducing plant and animal species such as fish and various plants with edible roots enabled many societies to create a similarly resilient resource base and to develop many aggrandizer strategies, although perhaps on less grandiose scales.

As previously noted, feasting is predicated on surplus production, and feasting probably constitutes the single most important way of utilizing surpluses to acquire other desirable forms of wealth and power, as will be documented in the following chapters. The resultant wealth and power, in turn, generally enables successful feast hosts to produce even greater amounts of surpluses (through additional marriages, increased control over labor, or acquisition of productive resource sites). Successful aggrandizer-feasters thus typically have multiple wives and large numbers of children (J. Hill 1984; Cronk 1991; Hunn 1991:205; Frayser 1985:252–6). Given the inevitable competition between aggrandizers and their insatiable desires, *successful feasting creates a positive "feedback" system* (a felicitous term, indeed) that spirals inexorably upward toward ever increasing production and the concentration of self-interests in the form of wealth and power. It is this positive feedback dynamic that relentlessly pushes food and related economic production to, or beyond, its tolerable limits in traditional societies, no matter what technology is employed or what innovations may occur. This enormous pressure to produce is dramatically documented in Andrew Strathern's film *Ongka's Big Moka* (Nairn 1991). As Firth (1959:480) observed:

The subsistence factor in the economy is inevitably the more stable. ...The status factor, on the other hand, is, by definition, expansive. Expansiveness, extravagance, exuberance, conspicuous display, prodigality. ...The status economy, in short, is always an economy of scarcity.

Ultimately, this is the most profound significance of feasting, for no other species in the world has the unlimited ability to transform surplus food production to promote self-interests in this way or to create increasingly complex forms of organization from immediate, competitive food acquisition. Species like squirrels and honeybees may store excess food (Vander Wall 1990), but they cannot use any more than they can consume other than via reproductively increasing numbers in the following generations, thereby entailing significant time lags, or via those gradual genetic adaptations over many generations that favor energy-consuming physical displays like elephants' tusks. In contrast, feasting and other surplus-based competitive strategies of aggrandizers (especially wealth-arranged marriages and investments in children) can convert *unlimited* amounts of surplus production into significant advantages for the producers within years, months, or even weeks after production. Thus, feasts really do constitute a new ecological paradigm on earth.

Prior to the appearance of feasting, human groups, even with their high intelligence and unique technologies, were not fundamentally different from other species in terms of resource use and demographic dynamics. Early humans may have vied with each other for mates or other advantages, but such competition does not appear to have been based on surplus food production. Early competition probably was based on physical strength, social cunning, skills, kinship support, or acquiring ritual knowledge (see Chapter 3). Any advantages gained from competition in these arenas resulted primarily from the ability to increase reproduction or perhaps from increased power in influencing group decisions. However, these advantages probably did not include the ability to directly use food to acquire personal benefits. In the following chapters, we will see just how aggrandizer strategies based on the production of food surpluses transformed earlier societies and created a new type of ecological system. Importantly, domination of group decisions, especially concerning the production and surrender of surpluses, could be manipulated and controlled by individuals with many spouses and adult offspring, hence aggrandizers typically have strived to obtain many wives and to have many children.

In addition to providing a good means of using surplus foods to achieve other benefits and advantages, feasts constitute ideal venues for aggrandizers to promote changes in cultural values and desired outcomes in small-community politics, social standards, or ideology. As noted previously, free food and the promise of pleasurable events will attract people. Dietler (2001), Wiessner (2001), Hastorf (2008) and others have emphasized the numinous qualities of feasts stemming from the effects of satisfying foods, drinks, social interactions, laughing, crying, singing, dancing, and the dramatic events such as the slaughter of animals, visual displays, and frequent lack of sleep. Feasts are meant to appeal to all the senses, to drown consciousness in synesthesious sensory-gustatory overloads, and to create states of euphorically altered minds. These authors also propose that social and emotional bonding is more effectively created under these conditions and that people become much more susceptible to suggestion – an idea supported by psychiatrists (e.g., Jilek 1982:24,28).

The invocation of supernatural entities is also a frequent feature of feasts that can be effectively used to consolidate or make sacrosanct key relationships that hosts wish to promote (Isaakidou et al. 2002:90). Thus, speeches extolling the virtues of ancestors, control over resources, the blessing of the gods, the magical powers of exotic objects, or the ability to provide desirable mates with surpluses are much more likely to be accepted and internalized by listeners when carried out at feasts than in other contexts. Moreover, feasts provide public contexts that are convenient venues for the introduction of new ideas or values to entire social groups and the witnessing of important gift-giving or social contracts (e.g., marriages, assumption of political offices).

Feasting is also effective in engendering changes in attitudes and values because of an apparent innate sense of obligation when people receive gifts, especially food. Giving food is well known by social psychologists to be effective in changing attitudes or obtaining compliance (Trenholm 1989; Perloff 2003). Thus, offers of free food or meals are frequently used by fringe cult proselytizers or fund raisers to obtain contributions of money and to recruit members because once individuals accept such offers, they feel some obligation to reciprocate or to acquiesce to requests from the donors. How much more would be the sense of obligation to honor seemingly innocuous requests from hosts when participating in their feast and consuming their food? Who could normally refuse a feast host's request to toast an honored ancestor or the family providing a highly valued bride even if obtained via a wealth exchange?

Feasts are also attractive strategies for aggrandizers because they can easily be constructed so as to make attendance conditional on reciprocal invitations that constitute debts that must be repaid. If I invite you to my feast, then it is understood that you must also host a feast and invite me, or our relationship is terminated. Once accepted, such invitations to feasts constitute tacit contractual agreements. And, once the principle of reciprocal debts is established, the stage is set for the creation of hierarchies and the acquisition of power via what Firth (1983) refers to as "indebtedness engineering." Feasts also are highly versatile. They can be held under many different pretexts, with variable sizes, predictability, and frequencies. However, some types of occasions are more suited for galvanizing public support (ostensibly for the good of kin or community groups) and raising emotions, as well as dovetailing with other aggrandizer strategies. Thus, funerals, acquiring military allies, ancestor veneration, marriages, decorations of lineage houses, and similar events are some of the most common pretexts for holding feasts. For all these reasons, they are ideal for the creation, reproduction, transformation, and concealment of power relations. Feasts can be manipulated to meld intense emotions with broader structures and ideologies of power (Dietler 2001:71; Wiessner 2001; Aranda 2008; Hayden 2009a). Because of the power of feasts, they can become intensely political.

Given all these characteristics, feasts are like sociopolitical and economic vortices. Similar to massive galaxies, feasts act as cultural black holes, with aggrandizing hosts at the center of the largest events surrounded by galactic quantities of economic materials spiraling into an insatiable event focus and giving off intense radiation as food and goods are consumed. The pull of materials into this maw creates an overarching structure in all that is within reach as it feeds off the matter and energy of others.

TRANSEGALITARIAN SOCIETIES

With the appearance of complex hunter/gatherer societies and the loosening of constraints on aggrandizers, a new type of society was created that was quite different from previous egalitarian hunter/gatherer societies. To distinguish these new types of societies, I refer to them as "transegalitarian" societies (see Hayden 1995, 2001b). This is a key concept that will be repeatedly used in this book.

I use the term "transegalitarian" to refer to societies that can be expected to produce some surpluses on a dependable basis, generally hold feasts or other competitive displays, recognize private ownership of products and resources, use food in competitive ways, use prestige items, and have a hierarchy of poor and wealthy families that do not form permanent classes due to the limited and unstable nature of surpluses (as opposed to societies with larger and more stable surplus production that results in permanent classes and political hierarchies). In contrast, in egalitarian societies like the !Kung or Western Desert Aboriginals of Australia, sharing is generally mandatory, and there is essentially little or no private ownership and no food-based competition or display. The definition of "transegalitarian" societies is fundamentally a social definition, with implied underlying resource conditions. The definition also entails many archaeologically relevant material consequences, such as the existence of prestige items, population densities that range from about 0.1 to 20 or more persons per square kilometer (Ames 2004:367), permanent architecture, various degrees of sedentism, storage facilities, and cemetery burials that can reflect pronounced wealth differences. However, transegalitarian types of societies are not strictly tied to any single form of subsistence. Thus, they can be based on hunting and gathering (complex hunter/gatherers), horticulture (or even agriculture), or on pastoralism. All such societies share the fundamental social characteristics just noted, but of course vary enormously in the magnitude, styles, and content of their expression.

ADDITIONAL CONSIDERATIONS

In setting out the basic conceptual framework for discussing feasts, I am acutely aware of the difficulties and dangers involved in trying to create general models based on the current limited amount of data, especially the lack of insightful and useful ethnographic data. The following chapters should thus be considered as a heuristic exercise in developing models that will certainly need to be refined in the future. However, the very great potential of feasting studies for developing new insights and explanations for cultural changes requires the development of at least some provisional models at this time to help guide future research. Several additional points warrant notice before proceeding to examine how the nature of feasts appears to be transformed from one level of sociocultural organization to another. First, it can be noted that food sharing is relatively common in other mammalian species, especially primates (see Chapter 2). To this extent, humans probably have some innate genetic proclivities to share food in specific contexts and for specific reasons, as well as entailing specific kinds of emotional reactions or mental states.

Second, humans have undoubtedly evolved specific reactions to the consumption of particular types of foods that can alter our emotional states and affect our sense of well-being. The most notable of these is the consumption of alcohol but also of great importance are other foods such as those rich in lipids or starches, sugars, caffeine, chocolate, kava, meat, a wide variety of herbs, and foods that trigger dopamine or endorphin release and result in feeling good (Curet and Pestle 2010). The innate appeal of some of these foods will be discussed as they become prominent features at various points in the following discussions.

Finally, as Monica Smith (2012) has emphasized, when hopeful aspirants host feasts, it always involves risks of failures. Like capitalist investors, feasters amass surpluses and use them in ventures that they hope will provide even greater future benefits. However, the outcomes are never assured. Businesses can go bankrupt, stocks can plummet, and feasts can fail to create the desired impressions. Etiquette can be offensive, food can be insufficient or of poor quality, gifts may be unwanted, disruptive violence is not uncommon, and there can be unpleasant digestive problems or even widespread food poisoning and deaths.

In the following discussions, I do not intend to focus in detail on the material, archaeologically visible correlates of feasting, although some salient observations will be noted. Dealing with material correlates of feasting is really more appropriate for an entirely separate volume devoted to the topic. Whereas Michael Dietler and I (Dietler and Hayden 2001:17–18) set ourselves the goal of studying *archaeological* feasting *systems* and their associated socioeconomic and political dynamics, dealing with full feasting systems of the past is complex and involved, so that delving into this topic would be unwieldy for the present volume. Elsewhere, I have attempted to develop a methodological framework for studying feasting *systems* using regional archaeological materials (Hayden 2011b). My goal in this book is to establish an interpretive framework of feasting systems based primarily on ethnographic materials and to present examples of archaeologically relevant interpretations. Thus, after an initial consideration of the adaptive nature of food sharing, especially in primates (Chapter 2), each chapter will deal with a general type of sociopolitical organization, beginning with simple foragers, progressing through complex hunter/gatherers, horticultural societies, and chiefdoms, and ending with states and empires. Each of these chapters will discuss the distinctive and some of the theoretical issues of interest for a type of organization. A number of ethnographic case studies from various regions of the world will be used to establish the general feasting patterns in each chapter, followed by relevant archaeological examples of interpretations and issues. Some of the more evident archaeological material indicators will also be mentioned. A special chapter will be devoted to the issue of domestication (Chapter 5), and a concluding chapter will examine feasting behavior in contemporary Industrial society.

I need to stress that this is only an organizational framework and is not intended to be any type of unilineal evolutionary model. As readers will appreciate, my repeated emphasis is on the various mixes of strategies that people used in promoting cultural changes, which resulted in various evolutionary pathways, as well as in some important continuities of feasting features across time periods and culture types.

With these thoughts in mind, let us examine the indications of food sharing among primates (Chapter 2) and then some forms of feasting, or proto-feasting, among simple egalitarian hunter/gatherers (Chapter 3).

2

Food Sharing and the Primate Origins of Feasting

by Suzanne Villeneuve

Food sharing is arguably the foundation from which feasting emerged, and it should be considered as one form of food sharing behavior. Food sharing among nonkin is viewed as one of the hallmarks of human evolution and a core feature of human societies (Gurven 2004; Stevens and Gilby 2004; Bullinger et al. 2013:51). It is considered by some to be the prime mover in social evolution from proto-hominids to modern humans in terms of its possible role in developing cooperation, sociality, sexual division of labor, morality, altruism, and perhaps human economic systems (Isaac 1978; Kurland and Beckerman 1985; Gurven et al. 2000a,b; Dubuc et al. 2012:73). Yet the roots of food sharing appear to go deeper and to have emerged among our nonhuman primate ancestors.

Food sharing with kin is relatively common in the animal kingdom (especially mother–offspring sharing), yet food sharing with *nonkin* among most nonhuman species is absent or very rare, although it does occur to some degree among some nonhuman primate relatives, particularly our closest ancestors, chimpanzees. Food sharing among nonkin does not appear to occur otherwise in the animal kingdom. Understanding why sharing food with nonkin occurs has become a major and controversial area of research. Like feasting, food sharing involves a fundamental paradox: why individuals give away valuable fitness-enhancing food resources (Gurven et al. 2000a:173; 2000b:264). In this chapter, I review some of the contending models regarding the underlying motivations and benefits of food sharing behavior, and I explore the implications of this for the evolution of feasting as one form of food sharing behavior. Some of the main points that are stressed in this review are:

- The explanations or models for food sharing among nonhuman primates and human foragers display a comparable range of motivations and benefits, as in feasting models.
- With some important exceptions, political models are some of the least explored explanations for food sharing among nonkin in primates. Yet

they are among the most important in terms of understanding the sharing of valued foods.

- Rare, highly valued foods play important roles in nonkin food sharing, whether among primates or foragers, or in feasting. These foods, especially meat, are critical elements in political strategies in these contexts.

Understanding food sharing at a more basic level can provide insights into the potential evolutionary trajectory of feasting and why this developed uniquely in our species, as well as how it has played a role in social adaptations and the development of complex societies.

EXPLANATORY MODELS OF FOOD SHARING

Why should individuals share food with unrelated individuals? Explanations proposed by primatologists and ethnologists tend to be used interchangeably between disciplines. This overview summarizes the main explanations and models from both disciplines to broaden perspectives of food sharing as a behavioral phenomenon. As in the explanations for feasting (Hayden and Villeneuve 2011b), early anthropologists and ethnographers lacked good theories for understanding food sharing. Early anthropological explanations for food sharing centered on cultural values such as strong sharing ethics and generalized reciprocity (e.g., Mauss 1924; Levi-Strauss 1969; Sahlins 1972). More recently, anthropologists have borrowed models from evolutionary biology and economics to develop testable predictions for the motivations and mechanisms involved in food sharing (e.g., Gurven et al. 2000a:173).

Primary issues for anthropologists or behavioral ecologists studying food sharing in human foraging groups and nonhuman primates involve under-standing why food is shared between nonkin, what motivations may underlie this behavior, and what benefits accrue to the sharer or recipient. In syntheses of food sharing explanations, some of the distinctions that have been empha-sized include (1) kin versus nonkin food sharing; (2) sharing for self-interested motivations versus group welfare; and (3) prosocial and active sharing in which the possessor initiates food transfer versus forms of sharing that are solicited or aggressive (Dubuc et al. 2012; Pruetz et al. 2012; Bullinger et al. 2013; Silk et al. 2013). The most common explanation of food sharing in primates is kin selection or nepotism, a situation that occurs when "individual acquirers can maximize their inclusive fitness if they direct resources to bio-logical kin who share a proportion of their genes with the acquirer" (Gurven et al. 2000a:174).

Social Explanations

Some of the social explanations for food sharing include "group augmentation" (Gurven et al. 2000a:174), immediate exchange for sex or for extended mating opportunities (Stanford 2011), and for grooming or other social favors (de Waal 1997).

Tolerated Theft and Sharing under Pressure

The tolerated theft (Blurton Jones 1984, 1987; Moore 1984; Winterhalder 1996a) and harassment or sharing under pressure models center on sharing for conflict avoidance (Wrangham 1975; Stevens and Stephens 2002; Stevens and Gilby 2004; Gilby 2006). Tolerated theft can involve solicitous behavior (Starin 1978; Jaeggi et al. 2008) or aggressive behavior (Fruth & Hohmann 2002; Stevens 2004; Jaeggi et al. 2010). To avoid conflict, the food possessor shares the food he or she possesses with the scroungers who have higher needs and are more willing to risk fight outcomes to obtain food. Thus, sharing in these circumstances involves a lower cost for the possessor. Similarly, sharing under pressure or due to harassment is viewed as reducing the cost of defending dominant status against rivals.

Hawkes (1992) suggests that the individual who has acquired food is tolerating theft in order to gain attention and support from those who have higher marginal value or needs. Sharing would in turn provide the food possessor with benefits of enhanced social alliances (with recipients) and/or access to future mates. Motivations behind tolerated theft sharing, under some circumstances, can thus potentially be correlated with the "reputation enhancement" model discussed later.

Reciprocity Models

The most common explanations of food sharing between nonkin are based on various forms of reciprocity under the umbrella of reciprocal altruism (Trivers 1971). The concept of reciprocal altruism was proposed to explain potential motivations behind food sharing that involve a cost to the provider, with the expectation that a benefit or return will result. Reciprocal altruism models take four basic forms: (1) tit-for-tat, (2) bargaining, (3) variance reduction, and (4) risk reduction reciprocity (RRR).

In tit-for-tat models, an individual who gives food to another expects to obtain a comparable gift in return from the recipient in a relatively short time frame. There is a relatively low level of trust involved, so that any failure to fulfill an expected return generally terminates the sharing relationship. The tit-for-tat model has been evaluated using a game (the prisoner's dilemma model) in which the failure to cooperate bestows more benefits than does cooperating with those who have cooperated in the past (Trivers 1971).

The bargaining model versions of reciprocal altruism allow the possibility of negotiation (Hill and Kaplan 1993). These models better explain how individuals choose to cooperate by incorporating decisions concerning the distribution of harvests based on the size of exchanges and expected returns. Individuals with higher needs have less bargaining power. The powerful or more dominant individuals can increase demands by playing competitors against each other and choosing to collaborate with those who offer the best deal (Gurven at al. 2000a). Under these conditions, the dominant individuals have greater ability to manipulate the subsistence base for their own gain.

The idea behind bargaining is similar to tolerated theft in that the more needy individuals will gain survival benefits through the transfer of food, whereas the more powerful or dominant (those who produce more) have less "need" and thus have greater bargaining power. As a result, the dominant individual will also obtain a social advantage by acquiring support from the "scroungers" and the needy who benefit from the production efforts of dominant individuals. This is similar to theories of human feasts, in which dominant individuals give away surpluses at feasts to obtain political or labor benefits while guests receive material benefits (food). This is also similar to the RRR model, in which part of the motivation behind sharing involves building exchange relationships to secure returns in the future when food is most needed.

Variance reduction models postulate that sharing assures that an adequate nutritional intake will be met daily, whereas producers who do not share but rely on their own food procurement have more variance or fluctuation in their daily diets and are less likely to obtain adequate food from day to day. Kaplan and Hill (1985) provide an example of variance reduction among the Aché foragers of Paraguay, in which hunters consistently give away more than they receive.

The RRR model is a type of reciprocal altruism in that individuals pool their food procurements and each then consumes relatively equal amounts, which in turn reduces individual variance in food intake. Two predictions underlie this model: (1) individuals are more likely to share difficult to acquire foods after procuring large amounts of food, and (2) by sharing larger amounts, the cost of transfers can be reduced (Bliege Bird et al. 2002). According to this model, the sharing of resources with nonkin increases the opportunity to receive shares during periods of shortfall (Bliege Bird et al. 2002:298).

Major environmental disasters, such as hurricanes in the Pacific, droughts, and epidemic diseases, are viewed as sources of variance in food availability that have been continually faced by individuals. Considering this, it would seem that RRR would be a significant contributing factor in motivations behind the development of food exchange patterns, especially in some specific ecological contexts.

Testing this model requires consideration of the amount of time between food transfers, the size of transfers, and the details of transfers between partners to assess whether individuals are acting out of long-term benefit for survival or more immediate needs.

The RRR model was tested among the Meriam in Melanesia where it was predicted that risk reduction approaches to food sharing would be important due to periodic extreme environmental factors like tropical storms. Bliege Bird et al. (2002) found no evidence to suggest that risk reduction was motivating food sharing. Instead, the authors proposed that sharing of resources operated as a means of advertisement to facilitate and maintain social relationships in terms of both alliances and mates.

General reciprocal altruism and tolerated theft models generate some similar predictions, notably that large, difficult to acquire foods will be shared more frequently than small, predictable foods. Neither of these models requires that exchanges completely balance out. To distinguish between reciprocal altruism and tolerated theft, the conditional transfer of food has to be accounted for. If the quantity that the first individual gives to the second individual depends on the amount the second individual gave to the first, then reciprocal altruism is more likely to be involved (Gurven et al. 2000a). Under this condition, the time between transfers should be short in order for the system to be maintained (Hawkes 1992). If the time between transfers is short, then the chance of repeated interactions or trust between individuals is low. This expectation suggests that the motivation behind food sharing is different from the RRR model because one must have the trust that reciprocity will occur during times of future need.

Reputation Enhancement

Because previous models of reciprocal altruism did not account for major aspects of food sharing (especially status, reputation, and relationship enhancement in some cases like the Meriam Islands), various researchers began exploring models focused on reputation enhancement. The reputation enhancement model (Gurven et al. 2000a) emphasizes the benefit implications of having a reputation for generosity, a feature of human behavior familiar to ethnographers working in traditional societies. The assumptions of this model are that an individual's motivation to share food (e.g., a chief's reputation for sharing) revolves around enhancing individual and/or family status, which in turn provides greater access to fitness enhancing resources, as well as practical and prestige benefits. A subsequent outgrowth of this model is referred to as *costly signaling theory*, although the focus here is on the avoidance of costly physical confrontations for mates and resources (Bliege Bird and Smith 2005; Hockings et al. 2007).

Political Models

Although considerable potential variation in food sharing is encompassed by the models or explanations just discussed (or combinations of them), few behavior ecology models deal directly with political dynamics. Reputation enhancement does to some degree, but not in enough explicit detail to understand the potential political benefits to sharing food. Other explanations that center more on political dynamics emphasize food sharing for coalition support among primates (Nishida et al. 1992; Mitani 2006) or food transfers due to dominant male coercion, which can be seen as similar to sharing under pressure (van Noordwijk and van Schaik 2009).

DISCUSSION OF MODELS

These explanations and models highlight the range of types of food exchanges that occur and the varied motivations, benefits, and contexts that are thought to characterize them. The range of food sharing that occurs among primates and simple foragers can be compared to the range of food exchange behavior that occurs in feasting in terms of the underlying motivations and benefits. For example, self-interested benefits versus group or prosocial benefits involving cooperation are the major distinctions made in both food sharing and feasting research (see Chapter 1). Moreover, as with much recent ethnoarchaeological research on feasting (as represented in this book), the more recent research on nonhuman primate food sharing heavily emphasizes the dominant role of self-interest in motivating food sharing (Bullinger et al. 2013; Silk et al. 2013:945), although, as in feasting studies, researchers have also emphasized the multiple purposes or advantages that food sharing generally involves. Thus, combinations of models or explanations are often used to study food sharing in different contexts (Winterhalder 1996b).

The major motivational categories recognized for feasting in this book (Chapter 1) include feasts for alliance formation and cooperation and feasts for economic gain. Alliance and cooperation feasts involve food sharing to create solidarity (within groups) and reciprocity or alliance (between groups). Other feasts are primarily held to acquire political supporters or to advertise, display, or promote the desirability of relationships with feast hosts. These feast categories and their underlying motivations can be compared to explanations and motivations proposed in food sharing studies (e.g., reciprocity models including risk reduction, alliance formation models, and reputation enhancement). In the classification used in this book, economic feasts types include solicitation and punishment feasts and competitive feasts. These involve direct economic gains, such as the ability to retain or acquire rights and resources in communities (in the case of solicitation or punishment feasts) or the promise of substantially increased returns on feast investments (in the case of competitive feasts). These can be compared to food sharing behavior in nonhuman primates involving solicitous food gifts to dominant individuals and perhaps exchanges for sex in which primate copulation is viewed as a type of commodity.

Political motivations and how these overlap with other models is perhaps the most fascinating aspect of nonhuman primate food sharing for understanding the evolution of feasting. In human societies, this aspect is highly developed, whereas in nonhuman primates it is rarely documented or dealt with (but see Nishida et al. 1992; Wrangham 1996). Nevertheless, the documented cases represent the first indication that such behavior can play a key role in primate social adaptations. Far more research is needed to determine the conditions under which political types of food sharing occurs.

If we consider feasting as one manifestation of a broader food sharing realm of behaviors, then it is possible to take advantage of the theoretical work undertaken from a number of different disciplines and perspectives. Ultimately, such a broader cross-cultural and trans-species perspective may help advance our understanding of human evolution, including why we developed cooperation and altruism, the full range of inequality and complexity, and many other human social character-istics. Of greatest relevance are the studies of closely related nonhuman primates, especially chimpanzees.

CHIMPANZEE FOOD SHARING

In some views, humans are often motivated by self-interest to share food, but they also sometimes feel a concern for the welfare of others and their immediate com-munities. This results in sharing beyond kinship and beyond strict reciprocity (Hill et al. 2011; Alvard 2012; Silk et al. 2013:945). In contrast, some of the more recent studies suggest that chimpanzees are much more strongly motivated by self-interest when sharing food rather than by the welfare of the group (Silk et al. 2005; Jensen et al. 2006; Yamamoto and Tanaka 2010; Bullinger et al. 2013). As Silk and House (2011; Silk et al. 2013) have argued, among chimpanzees the cost of helping is generally low so that if individuals were motivated by the welfare of others beyond their kin, then they would more often spontaneously offer food to others and respond more enthusiastically to solicitations.

Chimpanzee social structure plays an important role in food sharing behavior. Chimpanzees live in status-driven hierarchical male-philopatric societies in which males spend their time trying to rise in dominance rank (Stanford 2001:136). Research has shown that although chimpanzees preferentially share food with kin, they also selectively share some foods with nonkin. These studies suggest that sharing with nonkin generally involves reciprocating partners, the creation or maintenance of alliances, the reduction of harassment, or the creation of liaisons with potential mates (Silk et al. 2013:945). Foods are clearly not shared randomly. Small, reliable, or easily acquired packages of food tend to be rarely shared. When sharing does occur, it typically involves high-quality foods that are difficult to acquire or are highly valued, such as meat, honey, and high-calorie foods such as bananas, sugar cane, and hard to process nuts. However, the pattern of sharing varies according to the food resource involved (Nishida 1970; Goodall 1986; McGrew 1996; Mitani and Watts 2001; Dubuc et al. 2012). In all cases, the transfer of wild plant foods is relatively rare (Humle et al. 2008), although meat is more commonly shared.

Chimpanzees share meat on a frequent basis, primarily after hunting episodes (Stevens and Gilby 2004), although there is some variation in sharing patterns between groups. Meat is highly desired among chimpanzees, yet it is not required for their survival (Stanford 2001). Although males occasionally hunt in cooperative groups, meat tends to be shared in strategic ways (Teleki 1973; Goodall 1986; Nishida et al. 1992). After hunts, meat is first made available to the cooperating males in the hunt, especially the captor, although there is considerable discussion by researchers on the different criteria involved in meat distribution (Boesch 1994; McGrew 1996; Boesch and Boesch-Acherman 2000). In all events, most meat goes first to males. The distribution is controlled by dominant males even if they are not skilled hunters (Stanford 2001:136). When females do obtain meat from hunters, they generally pass their portion on to their offspring. Other studies have shown that, after initial distributions, meat can go to grooming partners, potential mates, and political allies (Mitani and Watts 1999, 2001; Hockings et al. 2007; Gomes and Boesch 2009; Dubuc et al. 2012).

Meat sharing may be highly political, as indicated by Nishida's (Nishida et al. 1992) often-cited research (e.g., McGrew 1996; Stanford 2001). In addition to being highly desired, meat is costly to acquire in terms of return for effort, and its distribution can be controlled (due to occurrences of small but divisible, high-energy, concentrated packets; see Melis et al. 2011:485). These characteristics make meat a potentially important resource for food sharing motivated by political concerns. In one example, the alpha male in Mahale's M-group distributed meat as if he were following these rules: (1) do not share with potential challengers to status (i.e., younger males), (2) do not share with the beta male (i.e., the closest rival), (3) do share with nonchallenging males (i.e., weak peers), (4) do share with old and influential males, and (5) do share with your mother, with your past and present consorts, and with old females. Similarly, studies in the Taï Forest (Côte d'Ivoire) and in the Kibale Forest (Uganda) have shown that males selectively transfer meat to other males that have previously transferred meat to them, as well as to males that support them in agonistic interactions (Mitani and Watts 1999, 2001; Boesch and Boesch-Achermann 2000).

It has been pointed out that the small quantities of meat involved, the high cost of their procurement, and their minimal contributions to chimpanzee diets do not correspond to what one would expect if this type of food sharing was motivated by concerns of risk reduction in food procurement or for supplying needed calories during times of resource shortages (e.g., Mitani and Watts 2001; Stanford 2001). In fact, hunting as a high-cost activity appears to occur predominantly when individual daily energy needs are being adequately met (Stanford 2001) and under what appear to be good resource conditions. Thus, although early studies explored whether meat was acquired to compensate for food shortages (e.g., Teleki 1973), more recent work has shown that this is not the case. Moreover, whereas some sharing of food among chimpanzees occurs for sex and grooming exchanges or is focused on kin, the behavior surrounding the sharing and distribution of special food resources such as meat appears to suggest a strong role of self-interested and political motivations, such as maintaining the social support needed for exercising dominant roles in groups.

DISCUSSION

Certainly, there are many differences between nonhuman primate food sharing and human feasting, and a number of important changes obviously took place during the course of evolution. For instance, humans were, and are, able to kill much larger animals than other primates, and they were able to transport much larger quantities of meat back to home bases for sharing, probably beginning in the Lower Paleolithic (Isaac 1978). In later prehistory, the use of storage technologies also created the possibility of amassing and using food surpluses in far more elaborate food sharing fashions. Thus, between nonhuman primates and humans, the scale of food sharing involved and reliance on it for developing political strategies are of different orders of magnitude. Interestingly, the use of tools by chimpanzees appears to be associated with increased sharing (Jaeggi and Schaik 2011). Whatever the causal relationship involved, this observation has interesting implications for early and later forager technologies and the trajectory of human food sharing/feasting behavior.

Despite these differences, there are also some important fundamental similarities that seem to have laid the foundations for human feasting behavior. In particular, it is possible to distinguish between more routine foods versus specialty types of higher cost foods. The sharing of nonspecialty foods between closely related kin in nonhuman primates might be compared to the generalized sharing of food that occurs within small (usually closely related) forager bands (see Chapter 3) or even in "potluck" style feasts that are meant to enhance group cooperation and solidarity.

A number of characteristics of both human and chimpanzee specialty foods make them especially well suited for use in political manipulation strategies: strong desires to acquire and consume specific specialty foods, costly procurement or processing, concentrated high-energy packets that are easily divisible, and restricted access to a few individuals or hierarchical ability to control access. Even more importantly, in both chimpanzee and human feasting studies, the procurement and sharing of specialty, high-cost foods does not occur under conditions of food shortage or nutritional duress, but only under conditions when normal subsistence concerns have been met. Both chimpanzee and human sharing of specialty foods appear to be costly supplemental strategies employed only when resource conditions permit luxuries such as food-based political manipulations. In this respect, the use of high-cost foods like meat for political purposes among chimpanzees can be compared to the use by humans of domesticates as feasting foods. As suggested in Chapter 5, early domesticates were high-risk, costly foods that only appear to be produced when normal subsistence was assured, and they were probably used primarily for sociopolitical maneuvering.

High-ranking or dominant political positions can, in turn, be used to organize other members of the group to increase the acquisition of specialty foods, as in hunting parties and feasting activities described in Chapters 4 and 6. Thus, the food sharing scenarios described by primatologists bear a number of striking similarities to human foragers and the feasting behavior in more complex types of social organizations. The range of explanations for food sharing among nonhuman primates and human feasters is very comparable at a general level. There is no single type of food sharing behavior but rather an array of different motivations, characteristics, and conditions that occur under the umbrella of food sharing. From this brief review, it should be apparent that far more research is needed to tease out many of the specific relationships and details of the many varieties of food sharing that occur among both nonhuman and human primates.

3

Simple Hunter/Gatherers

Everything that is not given is lost.

– Traditional Indian Proverb

All hunter/gatherers are not the same. Although they can be discussed from many different perspectives, for the purposes of this book, there appear to be two constellations of cultural traits that have very different impacts on the presence or absence of feasting behavior. At one end of an idealized spectrum are *simple hunter/ gatherers* (foragers) such as the Hadza who generally share food openly among band members, who maintain an egalitarian ethic and behavior concerning food resources, who prohibit private ownership of most or all food resources (and many other items), who prohibit any competition involving food resources, and who lack long-term storage and private wealth items. In contrast, *complex hunter/ gatherers*, such as those on the Northwest Coast of North America, produce and store surpluses, hold ownership rights over food and food resources, accumulate privately owned wealth, compete with food and wealth, and exhibit marked socioeconomic differences between individuals or families. Testart (1982:529–30) has shown a strong tendency for hunter/gatherers to fall into either the simple or complex side of this dichotomy.

Because many of these characteristics are related to resource abundance, it is not surprising that complex hunter/gatherer populations are denser than those of simple foragers and that they exhibit seasonal or full sedentism and larger community sizes, often ranging into the hundreds. Ames (2004:367) has suggested that there is a population threshold of around 0.1 people/square kilometer that divides simple from complex hunter/gatherers. I suggested the same break point (Hayden 2003a:125). Complex hunter/gatherers are transegalitarian societies and constitute the focus of Chapter 4, whereas simple hunter/gatherers are the subject of this chapter.

Given the discussion in Chapter 1 of feasting as predicated on the production of surpluses, one must wonder if feasts even existed among simple hunter/gatherers who are characterized as lacking storage or the production of surpluses. The characteristics of simple hunter/gatherers constitute the essence of Woodburn's (1982) description of "immediate-return" cultural systems in which food is consumed within a day or two of its procurement and in which politically assertive egalitarianism results in obligatory sharing of food and the deprecation of vaunted hunting successes, as well as sanctions against accumulating wealth or goods. Logically, one would not expect feasting to occur under such conditions. However, there are some archaeological and ethnographic observations that may require qualification of this notion or at least the recognition of a somewhat different kind of feasting that seems to occur among some simple hunter/gatherers. To appreciate some of the distinctive aspects of feasting-like behavior among simple foragers, it is necessary to discuss the importance of hunting and meat among these societies.

THE IMPORTANCE OF MEAT

As described in Chapter 2, there are probably deep primate roots for the use of food sharing, especially of meat, to create social bonds and political support. Although this is an episodic and dyadic behavior for the most part among nonhuman primates, for simple hunter/gatherers it is universal, obligatory, and part of normal routine. If one does not share food with other band members, one is no longer considered part of the community. Food sharing creates social solidarity and identity that may be largely taken for granted, given its pervasiveness, but which is nevertheless a powerful bonding force (Sharp 1994:269). Food sharing enhances cooperation and ensures that no one has exclusive access to critical subsistence resources. Precisely when during the Pleistocene obligatory general sharing of food became central to human cultures is open to some debate. Glynn Isaac (1978) argued that the bone accumulations associated with Oldowan tools 1–2 million years ago constitute good evidence that food sharing (at least of meat) was taking place on a broad scale by that time and that the basic forager social organization had been established. Others argue that the hunting/gathering lifestyle did not emerge until the advent of anatomically modern humans, about 100,000 years ago (Binford 1985; R. Klein 1989; Gamble 1999; Stiner et al. 2000:57; Kuhn and Stiner 2001; Dunbar 2003; Russell 2012:144–55).

Whenever it happened, hunting of medium and large-sized mammals eventually became important, together with the sharing of food and the sexual division of labor associated with hunting. There are divergent views on why hunting and meat became such a central factor in hominin subsistence, including simple diet breadth diversification, the caloric contribution of high-risk plus high-payoff strategies, the enhanced reproductive advantages that successful hunters obtained, status advantages, and the ability to hold groups together for cooperative breeding advantages

(Hawkes 1991; Wiessner 1996, 2002a; Stanford and Bunn 1999; Wood and Hill 2000; Hildebrandt and McGuire 2002; McGuire and Hildebrandt 2005; Ugan 2005). Whatever the ultimate reason that meat became a staple in the human diet, it is clear that by ethnohistoric times meat was almost, if not completely, universally valued by hunter/gatherers, as well as by other cultures (H. Abrams 1987; Tannahill 1973; Hawkes et al. 2001; Hawkes and Bird 2002). It is important to qualify this statement, however, because it was not all hunted meat that was emicly prized. It was only meat in a certain condition: meat with high fat content. Game animals are generally quite lean, with less than 4 percent body fat, and often considerably less (Eaton et al. 1988:70,108). As Speth (1990) and Speth and Spielman (1983; also Hayden 1981:535–6) have carefully documented, the protein in meat was almost useless for metabolism in the absence of adequate amounts of fats, lipids, or starches. This accords well with my experiences on hunting trips in Australia, where shot kangaroos could be left to rot in the bush if they were judged to have insufficient fat. The first thing that Aboriginals with whom I hunted did was to open the ventral cavity to determine how much fat was on the inner organs. This is also precisely the same concern displayed by hunters in Woodburn's (1966) film, *The Hadza*. When hunter/gatherers and even horticulturalists complain of having hunger, it is usually not because they lack sufficient calories, but because they do not have as much meat as they would like to have (Neitschmann 1973; Simoons 1994:5; Russell 2012:155). This hunger for meat may even go back to prehominin times because chimpanzees also seem to relish fresh meat and organize hunting expeditions to obtain it (see Chapter 2).

Because of the survival and/or reproductive benefits of fat-rich meat, it is perhaps not surprising that people would have evolved a genetically based taste for fat-rich meat, as well as for the lipids, starches, and/or sugars that were necessary to metabolize meat proteins. Kessler (2009) documents the stimulating, even addictive effect that fats and sugars have on the brain to create excited moods, and H. Abrams (1987) together with Beidler (1982:5) consider our taste for sweets to be genetically based as well as shared with other primates. Perhaps sweet-tasting lipids became part of our genetic propensities due to their association with mother's milk (Falk 1991:763-4; Albion 2005). Salt is another critical item for which we have an innate attraction and one that is necessary for proper metabolism. These are important points for understanding the choices of foods used in feasts the world over and in cultures far more complex than simple hunter/gatherers. In fact, as a number of paleonutrition books have pointed out, it is undoubtedly our genetic attraction to rich, starchy, sweet, and salty foods that has created many of the health problems of Industrial societies in which such foods are very affordable and available in abundance (Eaton et al. 1988; H. Walker 2003; David Kessler 2009).

Irrespective of modern consequences, the key point for simple foragers is that meat (fat-rich meat) was highly prized (Hayden 1981:394–7). Moreover, the image of early hunter/gatherers being satiated with generous portions of big game meat as daily fare does not seem to be realistic. Lee (1979:242) and others have noted that the incidence of successful hunts is actually quite low even in game-rich environments such as the African savanna. In the case of the !Kung, individual hunters killed an average of only 2.5 large antelope per year, with an overall average of only 0.6 large sized animals per man per year. The Hadza only kill one medium or large animal for every 45 days they go out to hunt (Hawkes et al. 2001:686–7). Thus, the killing of large sized animals for most simple hunter/gatherers outside the arctic and subarctic regions tends to be an unusual or special event, and eating fat-rich meat from large game appears to be relatively rare. Given this situation, it is easy to imagine why the killing of a medium or large sized animal might be some cause for formal celebration and communal eating. To varying degrees, this is what the ethnographic and archaeological records indicate for some groups. For other groups, killing a large animal may be reason to celebrate and even bring in other groups to share abundance, but there does not appear to be any formal eating event. Some of the simplest examples have been documented from Australia.

NON-FEASTS

While I was studying how stone tools were manufactured and used in the Western Desert of Australia, I was struck by the lack of anything that I could recognize as a feasting event among the Pintupi and other groups that I worked with (Hayden 2003b). The same was true of all the documentary films that I was able to view, including Tindale's early films of large tribal ritual gatherings. There were ceremonial occasions, but the provisioning and consumption of food was simply not a focus of interest. People ate together, but more as they would in a cafeteria. There were no speeches, no public displays of food or gifts, and no orchestrated distribution of food. Initiated men often retired to somewhat isolated places to pass the day in "ritual" or in conversation, crafts, or sleeping; although they often brought food to share among themselves to these locations, the context was casual and the food seemed to be more incidental to the gathering than any focus.

In a similar vein, Nicolas Peterson (personal communication, 2002) wrote to me that he had never seen anything in his extensive field work that he would call a feast. As he and others note, there are accounts of large quantities of food in the Australian literature (sometimes referred to as feasts), such as the bogong moth swarms in New South Wales, bunya nut harvests in Queensland, and beached whales, but these events do not appear to be coordinated or special collective meals.

Peterson notes that even when meat is used as payment to older men for initiating younger men "the meat is eaten individually ... shared among the men, each of whom eats as an individual and is not oriented to others; there is no formal beginning and end to the eating or emphasis on the collective nature of the meal in the sense we think of a collective meal or feast." These are simple meals, resembling daily meals, and are lacking in ceremony. Elsewhere in Australia, passing references are made to feasts as part of ceremonies (e.g., Davenport 2005:6), but no details are provided. In cultures where feasting is significant, ethnographers generally devote considerable attention to them. This does not seem to be the case with ethnographic observations of simple hunter/gatherers in Australia.

In the Great Basin, too, Steward (1938:237) reported that "among the Northern Shoshoni there seems to have been no major festival in aboriginal days." He does report "festivals" among the Western Shoshoni that were only held at times of communal hunts (rabbit or antelope drives), when small groups who rarely saw each other during the rest of the year came together mainly to dance, gamble, socialize, and, in some areas, undertake religious rituals. However, Steward never mentions "feasting" per se, nor does he indicate that meals were anything more than the ordinary communal sharing of food which one might compare to the kin-based sharing of food among chimpanzees described in Chapter 2.

James Woodburn (1966) also recorded the existence of separate men's camps. Like the Australian examples, these were simple gathering areas lacking structures about 100–200 meters outside the main camp where the best parts of large-game kills would be consumed by the initiated men in what might be referred to as a "meat feast" but that again apparently lacked most of the connotations of a proper "feast." It is nevertheless interesting that in both the Australian and the Hadza case, as well as in the instances about to be described, the best parts of game animals were reserved for men of higher status.

Although such celebrations may technically fit the definitions of feasts that I and others have proposed, it is clear that such events do not share many of the salient characteristics of feasts in transegalitarian and more complex societies. There are probably a number of reasons for this minimalist expression of feasts among simple hunter/gatherers.

- First, sharing food with many people outside the immediate family is a routine activity rather than a special occasion.
- Second, simple hunter/gatherers do not store food over the long term. Thus, they do not accumulate surpluses that can be used to attract people to special events, although they often do take advantage of seasonal abundances to invite other groups to join host groups in general exploitation of those abundances.

- Third, there is little or no tolerance for aggrandizing behavior in simple egalitarian societies, thus eliminating much of the motivation for acting as a host for a feast. Those who provide meat or other food for others are publicly derided for any boasting (Lee 1979; Wiessner 1996).
- Fourth, aside from some seasonal occurrences of predictable abundance, food procurement, especially of meat, is an opportunistic endeavor with unpredictable results. Thus, in the absence of storage, planning a feast – especially where other groups are to be invited – is difficult.
- Fifth, there is very limited or no ownership of procured food or food resources. Hunters may "own" the animals they kill (e.g., Wiessner 1996), but they are obligated to give most of the meat away, whereas the procurement of food resources in general is available to everyone.

MEAT FEASTS

Despite these considerations, there are a number of observations indicating that some simple hunter/gatherers may have had events that were more similar to feasts in the full sense of the term. In Australia itself, there are a number of reports of "feasts," especially events that were provisioned by communal net hunts that generally produce more meat more reliably than encounter hunting by individual hunters (Satterthwait 1987:619–21; Builth 2002). These hunts could produce surpluses that supported gatherings of several thousand people who typically used the events to engage in ceremonial activities together. However, it is still not clear from these accounts whether consuming these foods was anything more than communal eating, similar to events described by Peterson. Moreover, Satterthwait argues that the use of nets was a form of intensified food production. This is probably true because it is a more costly means of procuring meat than encounter hunting and could lead to overexploitation in some situations (Hayden 1981). Even more tellingly, Satterthwait associates this more complex hunting strategy with environments where resources were abundant and competitive social dynamics were involved (Satterthwait 1987:626–7). These are characteristics of transegalitarian complex hunter/gatherers. Without more information, it seems possible that these accounts of feasting from Australia may actually be from groups that were complex hunter/gatherers – the subject of Chapter 4. There certainly appear to have been complex hunter/gatherers in the better environments of Australia, such as the southeast (Lourandos 1985, 1988; Builth 2002; Ross 2006) and parts of Arnhem Land (Owens and Hayden 1997).

Several Canadian hunting/gathering groups provide similar quandaries for interpreting accounts of feasts. In these cases, however, there are some excellent descriptions from early contact observers of more complex and formal types of meat feasts. In particular, the capture of any prized animal (especially those with high fat content, such as bear, beaver, and moose) was an occasion for a "meat feast" among many Algonkian Mistassini, Montagnais, and Naskapi groups. Some of these feasts were participated in only by men and took place in specially constructed shelters (*shaputuan*) where some ceremony accompanied the consumption of prized animals and men could reaffirm important social relationships (Hallowell 1926, in Clermont 1980:102,106). Other "feasts" seem to simply represent a formalized sharing of a prized animal killed by the hunter, who, in accord with the traditions of some other simple foragers, did not receive any meat himself (Wiessner 1996). Spring aggregations seem to have supported a larger version of the band-level meat feast for some groups (Clermont 1980:102).

One of the most graphic descriptions of an early Montagnais bear feast was recorded by Nicolas Comeau at Godbout, Québec:

> [N]o women are allowed to be present, and special wigwams were built for the occasions. Moreover, places inside the tent were assigned according to age or rank as hunter. The chief helped himself first and passed on to next man in rank. . . . After everyone had eaten until he could stand no more, pipes and black plug tobacco were brought forth. What was left was quickly taken by women for their meal. (Speck 1935:105–6)

Speck also records detailed protocols for determining the sex and status of individuals who could butcher bears and who could consume various parts, with the head and right arm always going to the oldest (presumably highest ranking) men. This pattern of the right foreleg going to the highest ranking community member is curiously found in a number of transegalitarian societies around the world, such as the horticultural Southeast Asian Hill Tribes described in Chapter 6. The portion of kills reserved for initiated men's private consumption at the men's camp among the Hadza ("God's meat") is similarly an entire leg (Barnard and Woodburn 1988:17). It is also interesting that women are often excluded from consuming fatty meat, and sometimes any meat at all during menstruation (Roth 1899:113–4; Teit 1900; Speth 1990:161). The sharing protocols for the meat that was set aside for the initiated men may well serve to consolidate relationships between individuals or affirm their relative roles in the community. However, it is entirely unclear as to whether these relatively elaborate meat feasts simply reaffirmed inequalities already established on the basis of age, sex, kinship, and ritual knowledge, as suggested by Clermont (1980:102), or whether they could have been used to actually create inequalities.

In more recent times, Tanner (1979:163–70) describes surplus-based feasts among the Mistassini Cree. He states that these differ in eleven ways from regular meals. The most important features relate to the surpluses in feasts; the special recognition of the status of each participant (their seating position, their roles, and the portions of meat they receive); the offerings made to spirits; the drumming, singing and dancing; the restrained and respectful demeanor; cleanliness; special feasting structures that are sealed during feasts; clockwise movement of food and items; full accounting and proper disposal of all ("sacred") food; the dominant role of men in hosting, organizing, and cooking; and the serving of special foods prepared by special cooking methods that emphasize the importance of fat and sweets. Tanner (1979:177–8) also notes that each family owns its own stored supply of meat and that the old men are given ritual credit for the surpluses. These are *not* typical behaviors among most simple hunter/gatherers. One must wonder whether these descriptions represent changes in feasting behaviors due to effects of world economic interactions (as suggested by Leacock [1954] for family hunting territories), possible influence from contact with complex hunter/gatherers or horticulturalists farther to the south, the possible existence of genuinely complex hunter/gatherer societies in the Algonkian sphere, special conditions created by the need to store meat for the long winter months in the Subarctic and Arctic, or whether these kinds of feasts simply form part of the natural variation of simple hunter/gatherer feasting behavior.

There are several indications that the basic form of these Algonkian meat feasts are not recent developments. In Tanner's (1979:163) descriptions, it would appear that the Algonkian meat feast was primarily used to reaffirm and reinforce the existing social structure and associated social values and behaviors. The great efforts made to emphasize the sacredness of the proceedings, together with the dire consequences (bad hunting luck and starvation) said to result from anyone doing something "wrong" at a feast, attest to its major role in this respect. "If nobody did anything wrong at a feast, then they would kill plenty of game." Such feasts resemble social solidarity or social control feasts, although equality between participants is not a key feature, but is rather affirmation of different social roles. Finally, some of the earliest descriptions in the area, such as those of Jean de Brébeuf in 1636, describe essentially the same features of feasting, including the high value of bear meat because of its high fat content (Axtell 1981:146–50).

At least in some groups with better resources, Algonkian meat feasts probably evolved into characteristic transegalitarian feasts. Charles Bishop (1998:252–60) in particular has documented the occurrence of quite large feasts resembling potlatches with more than 2,000 people attending and 50,000 francs worth of prestige items given away among more southern Algonkian hunter/gatherers where territoriality; larger, more sedentary groups; storage; chieftaincy; and unilineal totemic groups appeared to have developed before European contacts. He noted relatively egalitarian groups in northern Quebec, but inequalities gradually increased farther south. In the most extreme cases, nonsubsistence property was owned by kin groups and was used in trade and alliance making. This property was controlled by elders and used in highly ritualized exchanges that created inequalities

(Bishop 1998:252–3). Feasts were required to validate new chiefs, and those who supported successful candidates through contributions of labor and materials expected subsequent benefits in the form of trade items and undoubtedly other help (Clermont 1980:103; Bishop 1998:260). This pattern resembles some of the Siberian complex hunter/gatherers to be discussed in Chapter 4 who established chiefdoms largely based on the trade in furs. Hides and furs were also central to trade among the southern Algonkians. Researchers sometimes seem to assume that all Algonkian hunter/gatherers lived in simple egalitarian communities. However, these observations, together with the substantial prehistorical depth of prestige goods exchange and funerary feasting going back to the late Archaic in the southern regions (Tuck 1976; Taché 2011), indicate that the feasting pattern is many millennia old, at least among the more complex Algonkian groups. There are several other archaeological indications that some kind of men's or meat feast occurred among possible simple foragers of Northeastern North America.

A number of structures interpreted as specialized Algonkian feasting facilities (*shaputuan*) have been excavated in Newfoundland and Labrador dating from 3,000 years ago to late prehistoric times (Pastore 1985, 1992:40–2; Loring 1989:49; 1992:445–53; Schwarz 1994, 1996) (see Figure 3.1). These elongated structures contained elongated hearths (1 × 4–5 meters) with extremely dense faunal remains, which in one case comprised a solid hearth mass of 7,800 calcined bone fragments (Figure 3.2; see Loring 1992:245, figure 6.3). Whether these structures were used by simple hunter/gatherers or complex hunter/gatherers is a matter of debate. The recovery of high proportions of exotic stone materials, including parts of a gorget

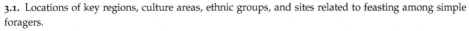

3.1. Locations of key regions, culture areas, ethnic groups, and sites related to feasting among simple foragers.

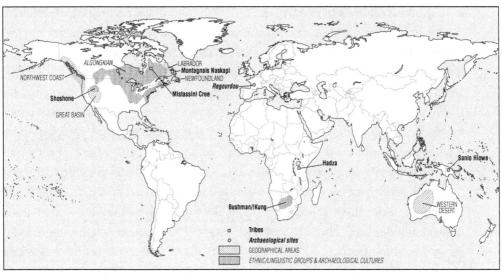

3.2. The central hearth (1 × 5 m) of the Algonkian ritual and feasting structure excavated at the Daniel Rattle site in Labrador by Stephen Loring. The hearth contained 7,800 calcined bones. (Photograph courtesy of Stephen Loring.)

and parts of celts (Loring 1992:253), makes it seem likely that these structures were used by more complex hunter/gatherers. I know of no other possible archaeological instances of feasting structures recorded from potentially simple hunter/gatherer societies.

Thus, a tentative case can be made for the absence of typical feasting among simple foragers because they generally seem to lack the production and storage of surpluses and/or competitive displays of food or prestige items. The few ethnographic observations of events resembling feasts among simple hunter/gatherers primarily involve parts of game put aside for consumption by initiated men or elders in their special men's camps. These can reasonably be viewed as opportunistic solidarity feasts for the initiated or older males of the group. Labrador, Newfoundland, northern Quebec, and the Arctic all have relatively cold climates where open air gatherings are impractical for much of the year. In these environments, it is conceivable that there may have been special structures erected and a substantial use of stored meat via freezing without the connotations of socioeconomic complexity that such features usually imply. Thus, it is possible that some meat feasts may have been part of the simple hunter/gatherer spectrum of variation developed under these special conditions. However, this is entirely speculative. In most ethnographic and archaeological cases, it is not clear whether these meat feasts resembled the initiated men's solidarity feasts of the Hadza and Australian Desert Aboriginals (being simply better documented or somewhat more elaborated versions) or whether they might be instances of feasts among complex hunter/ gatherer. The large scale, the use of prestige items, the importance of trading furs, the existence of family storage, and the competitive aspects of some of the ethno-historic cases seem to imply that many of the reported Algonkian events probably occurred among complex hunter/gatherers and should more appropriately be dealt with in the next chapter. However, the existing data are slim enough that these preliminary interpretations may have to be modified by future research.

COMPETITION IN SIMPLE HUNTER/GATHERERS

Of all the typical feasting characteristics that seem to be missing from men's meat feasts in Desert Australia and Africa, the use of food and prestige items in competitive displays is perhaps one of the most striking. Because the absence of competition appears to run counter to Darwinian expectations, it is worth under-scoring the fact that competition per se was not absent from most simple foraging societies, only competition based on food procurement (Sahlins 1958:1; Beteille 1981; Hayden 2011a). Under conditions of limited and fluctuating resources (including many game animals) that are vulnerable to overexploitation, competi-tion over food would only destroy the resource base and result in starvation. In contrast, competition over marriage partners, ritual knowledge, leadership in con-flicts between groups, status, and even kinship roles was often rampant (Keen 2006) but always disconnected from food procurement. Gat (2000, 2006:15–19,69,129–30) summarizes data on lethal violence among hunter/gatherers, which was wide-spread and generally fairly intensive, sometimes constituting fatalities of 10–20 percent or more of the male populations. "Within the tribe, women-related quarrels, violence, so-called blood feuds, and homicide were rife . . . some caused by suitors' competition, some by women's abduction and forced sex, some by broken promises of marriage, and most, perhaps, by jealous husbands over suspicion of wives' infidelity. Between tribes, the picture is not very different" (Gat 2006:69). Peterson (2006) paints a similar picture for life among Australian Aboriginals, and my own field work corroborates these accounts as well.

Kinship could also be a field of contention and competition. Whereas in Industrial cultures we may view kinship as clear-cut and unambiguous, in most traditional societies, including simple foragers, kinship was often a matter of negotiation and manipulation. Family names/surnames were rare or more often completely absent in all groups that I know of so that genealogical reckoning usually only extended back one or two generations. In Australia, mentioning the dead was taboo in many groups, and the use of Hawaiian kinship terms was used to refer to entire classes of individuals, rendering kinship recognition even more difficult. Thus, claims to residence or custodian rights over core locations within band territories could be easily manipulated. Chagnon (2000), for instance, has demonstrated how kin classifications among the Yanomamo could be modified and manipulated particularly when competition over marriageable women was involved.

Keen (2006) has written about the social and environmental constraints on the development of enduring inequalities in Australia. In like manner, the topic of constraints on the development of competitive feasting should eventually be addressed in more detail as a theoretical topic of importance. In addition to the mobility, egalitarian values, sharing imperatives, lack of storage, and lack of surplus already mentioned, it should be emphasized that there were generally a wide variety of economic and status-leveling mechanisms to ensure that no one gained economic advantages or contravened the egalitarian sharing ethics so essential for survival. These mechanisms have been discussed extensively by Wiessner (1996) and Blake and Clark (1999:58–61). They include demands for modest behavior by successful hunters; erasing any sense of debts from "gifts"; gossip, ridicule, accusations of sorcery; group fissioning; ostracism; and violence or even death. All together, such constraints, plus the egalitarian and obligatory food sharing ethic, must have limited the development of aggrandizers and competitive feasting, if not all feasting-like behavior (aside from initiated men's sharing of prime parts of large game) and all aggrandizer strategies, or at least those involving food resources and the use of surpluses. Some simple foragers in New Guinea, such as the Sanio-Hiowe (Townsend 1974), may be aberrant in this respect, and it is not clear if they have been misrepresented as simple foragers (with some domestic animals and garden plots!), if there were special resource conditions involved, or whether they may be devolved horticulturalists forced into marginal environments.

Aside from the prehistoric structures indicative of feasting among possibly simple Algonkian speakers in northeast North America, there are very few archaeological indications of feasts at this level of sociopolitical organization. The unique bear remains associated with a Neandertal burial at Régoudou in France may be the best candidate of a funerary feast from simple Paleolithic foragers (Hayden 2003a:108–14).

Although simple foragers may be limited to solidarity meat feasts to enhance solidarity between initiated or high-ranking men, the situation changes dramatically with the emergence of complex hunter/gatherers, a topic to which we now turn.

4

Transegalitarian Hunter/Gatherers

Our chief brings jealousy to the faces ... by ...
Giving again and again oil feasts to all the tribes ...
I am the great chief who makes people ashamed ...
I am the only great tree, I am the chief!
You are my subordinates, tribes ...
I am he who gives these sea otters to the chiefs, the guests, the chiefs of the tribes.
I am he who gives canoes to the chiefs, the guests, the chiefs of the tribes.

– From Benedict 1934:175–8

With the appearance of complex (transegalitarian) hunter/gatherers, we enter into an entirely different cultural realm – one that is not egalitarian and does not shy away from competition based on economic production to underwrite bids for greater influence and greater benefits. Feasts become the arenas for economically based competition and many other gambits for power, prestige, spouses, and capital. Feasts become the venues for social and political negotiations; feasts are the seat of village governments (Beynon 2000:31; Clarke 2001:163; 1998). At times, the importance of feasts, the array of different kinds of feasts, and the exalted importance of feasts become bewildering. There are lavish feasts for coming of age, for marriages, funerals, building houses, solstices, succession to political roles, and many other events. Nothing could be further from the behavior of the simple foragers that we saw in the preceding chapter. To understand the nature of and the reasons for this change, I discuss in further detail some of the characteristics of these societies and some of the ideas about why such changes took place. We then explore the principles on which transegalitarian feasting was based and some of the resulting characteristics, followed by a sampling of ethnographic and archaeological examples (see Figure 4.1).

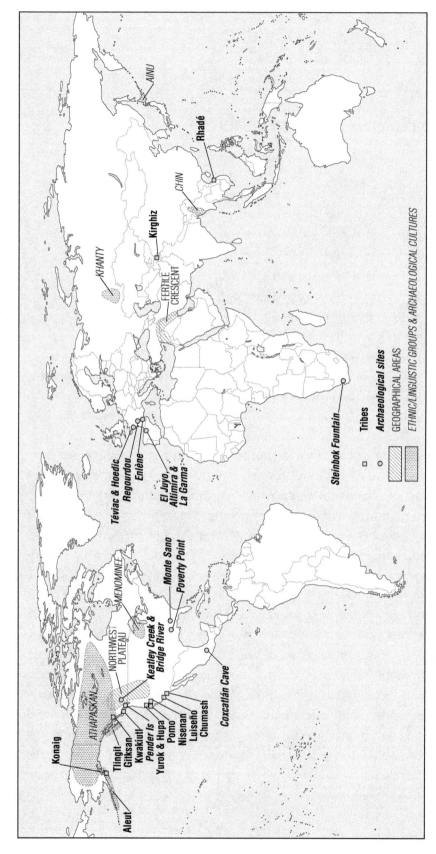

4.1. Locations of key sites, culture areas, ethnic groups, and regions related to feasting among transegalitarian (complex) hunter/gatherers.

AGGRANDIZERS AND THEIR STRATEGIES

As discussed in Chapter 1, aggrandizing personality types can be assumed to occur in all cultures. However, under resource conditions that require sharing and mutual help for survival, these personality types are placed on very short leashes and not permitted to engage in any competitive or self-aggrandizement behavior based on the use of economic (food) resources. In fact, any aggrandizing expressions or behavior is frequently viewed as threatening. Paul Roscoe (personal communication) adds that very low population densities also make it impractical to assemble or manipulate a significant following. It only seems to be under conditions of relative abundance that these tight constraints are loosened and some people are permitted to use surplus resources to try to benefit themselves and create hierarchies. Archaeologically, abundance appears to have been generated by technological improvements that enabled groups to harvest, process, and store quantities of rapidly reproducing plants, animals, or fish in areas where these occurred in abundance, at least seasonally. Such technologies appear to have first developed in a few special locations during the Upper Paleolithic but became much more widespread with the development of Mesolithic technological innovations involving the mass harvesting, processing, and storage of fish, grass seeds, nuts, and other types of foods.

However, for aggrandizer strategies to work, there is a price to pay. To involve other people in aggrandizer schemes, there has to be a carrot – or multiple carrots – to make others in the community want to become part of aggrandizer schemes and to produce surpluses to achieve those goals. This is similar to the banker's dilemma: how to get large numbers of people to hand over their surplus savings so that bankers could use them for their own benefit. The answer for the banker was simply to make it in the self-interest of many people by paying them a certain percentage of their surpluses as "interest." Of all the schemes devised and widely used by aggrandizers, feasting is perhaps the most widespread and powerful means of attracting other people and of converting surpluses into other desired goods or relationships. Other strategies included paying for spouses; polygyny; private control over resources, produce, and wealth; investments in children; requiring prestige items to consummate social pacts; and restricting access to the supernatural. Social scientists argue that support is difficult to obtain when people feel that it is being forced on them or when sanctions are seen as being motivated by greed or selfishness; but support is easily and productively obtained when people feel positive about their roles and relations with leading figures (Trenholm 1989:311–5; Fehr and Rockenbach 2003; Perloff 2003:247–62). Thus, it should not be surprising that successful aggrandizers are frequently charismatic and try to involve/entice people by giving them modest gifts or that many supporters viewed certain of their aggrandizer's successes as being in their own best interests

(Rohner and Rohner 1970:92). Nevertheless, there are sufficient observations of "despots" among complex hunter/gatherers who instilled fear into the hearts of their subjects by capricious acts of violence to indicate that people who were not swayed by the arts of persuasion were often cowed into compliance by other means including sorcery and physical force; these aggrandizers used both the carrot and the stick (Boas 1966:106; Le Gros 1985:51–1; Barbeau and Beynon 1987; G. MacDonald 1989; for despots in transegalitarian horticultural groups, see Chapters 6 and 8 and Ruyle 1973:616; Feil 1987:104–5; Lemonnier 1990:38; Roscoe 2000:90–2; 2002). In short, aggrandizers were master manipulators.

The upshot of this new dialectic, between ambitious aggrandizers with a freer rein and other community members, was a new type of society. New values and norms were adopted emphasizing private property, restricted requirements for sharing, debt obligations or contracts, the importance of ancestors, obtaining spouses based on wealth, the sociopolitical roles of prestige items, and other related new ideological concepts. Overt ostentation and boasting may still have been proscribed, but covert socioeconomic and political inequalities were tolerated. Ethnographers sometimes remark on the "masked" nature of inequality in transegalitarian societies. As Simeone (1995:xviii) observes of some northern Athapaskan groups, "People compete for power and prestige in the face of a cultural ideal that stresses cooperation and solidarity." Dietler (2001:79), too, notes the "self-interested manipulative nature ... concealed or euphemized by the fact that it is carried out through the socially valued and integrated institution of generous hospitality [which] may even be perceived by the participants as a leveling device" (see also Mauss 1924; Reay 1959; Trinkaus 1995:57).

However, it must also be recognized that not everyone who becomes a leader is necessarily a manipulative aggrandizer. Some ethnographers are persuaded that leaders often do act in the interests of their communities and have the best interests of supporters at heart. Although this is not generally what I have found in my own ethnographic work (e.g., Hayden and Gargett 1990), it is certainly true that community-minded individuals sometimes do get into positions of control. Some people inherit such positions or are asked to serve. However, the altruistic behavior of these individuals cannot be used to account for the origin or persistence of practices that essentially disenfranchise other members of the community, such as those just mentioned. In more modern terms, not everyone who was a slaveholder or supporter of apartheid was an aggrandizer, and many treated those under them in kindly or helpful ways, all the while defending the system as being in the best interests of everyone. No matter how good natured some slave owners or administrators of apartheid policies may have been, such institutions simply cannot be understood without invoking the motivations and actions of aggrandizers.

Ostentatious competition between leading factions within communities was permitted when indirect pretexts were used, especially at funerals or events for ritual purposes. There typically were (and often continue to be) a number of contending factions within transegalitarian communities so that the power base was diffused among a number of centers. The political structure was thus frequently heterarchical rather than hierarchical (Suttles 1958; Rautman 1998; Hayden 2001b:257), often taking the form of a number of nominally kin-based corporate groups (longhouses, great houses, lineages, or clans) governed by "elite" families with inheritance claims to the corporate resources and positions of control. Because this early form of socioeconomic inequality had to be based on attracting cooperative families, benefits tended to be widely distributed (Wiessner 1989:60), and large numbers of families were considered well-off, or at least as having some "elite" claims. This resulted in a roughly inverted socio-economic pyramid (Figure 4.2), which Suttles (1958:500–1) has likened to an inverted pear in shape. This corresponds entirely with my own experience with transegalitarian societies. Teit (1900:576) has similarly remarked on the unusual prevalence of "elite" or well-off families (one-half to two-thirds) in Interior complex hunter/gatherer communities, and the same is true of horticultural transegalitarian societies (see Figure 6.3).

The existence of factions within communities that were competing over control of resources, trade, labor, and other factors led naturally to elevated levels of conflict within and between these communities. Given this competitive tension in communities, if an individual did not have adequate backing of other community members, he could find himself under attack on valid complaints, trumped-up charges, or for infractions of the typically multitudinous community norms and taboos. Sociopolitical litigations tended to be legion in most transegalitarian societies. Life was often rife with brutality for those lacking strong allies, as many ethnographers have documented (e.g., Chagnon 1968; Condominas 1977) and as the thousands of bog bodies in Europe attest (Sanden 1996). Thus, it is not surprising that Otterbein (2004:74–5), Gat (2006:24–35), and Fry (2006:103–7) place the origin of warfare in complex hunter/gatherer societies, although Gat emphasizes earlier roots as well. I also think that many community taboos (which often seem overwhelming in number and capriciousness) may have been promoted by aggrandizers as a means of taking advantage of defenseless individuals or adversaries. With so many and varied taboos, no one could avoid breaking some of them at one time or another. When they did, the poor or weak could be severely punished whereas the wealthy and well-connected could get off with nominal or no punishment, as is especially evident in Chapter 6. The wealthy generally got their way. Thus, I think that having a strong support network in such litigious societies became a critical element for survival in transegalitarian communities, and feasting was one of the

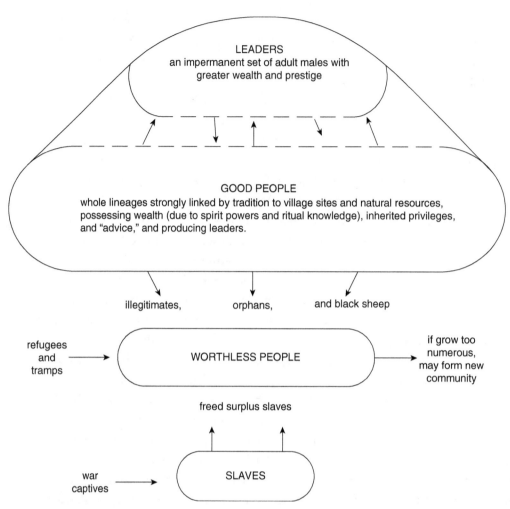

4.2. Wayne Suttles (1987) portrayed Coast Salish socioeconomic structure as an "inverted pear" shape, as illustrated here. This is similar to other transegalitarian societies such as the Hill Tribes of Southeast Asia (see Figure 6.3), but the complete opposite of typical socioeconomic "pyramids" of state-level societies with the elites forming only 10 percent or less of the population and the poorest forming the broad base of the pyramid.

most preeminent means of establishing and keeping strong support networks. How and why such societies developed from egalitarian foragers is a critical issue for understanding why elaborate feasting systems developed. Although I place a strong emphasis on the role of aggrandizers, their motivations, and their schemes, this is far from a universally accepted explanation for how such societies developed.

THEORIES OF FEASTING

When we purvey the literature on feasting, there are a number of frequently occurring kinds of explanations that address the question of why feasting tends to be so lavish. Explanations range from status acquisition to deterrent signals or symbolic capital, to political self-interest, to functional or communitarian models. I and Suzanne Villeneuve (2011b) have already explored many of these contending explanations, and they were briefly introduced in Chapter 1; however, a few more comments on some of these are appropriate at this point.

Redistribution and Resource Banking

There is a long and sustained ecologically based tradition in anthropology that maintains that "trade feasts," potlatches, pig feasts, and many other events at which large amounts of food were consumed were organized to even out regional resource abundances and deficits between groups. In this model, prestige goods are viewed as media for ensuring the flow of subsistence goods (Flannery 1968:107; J. Arnold 1995, 2001) while the elites are seen as benevolent managers (Ames 1995). Vayda (1967) sees the Pomo gatherings to exchange food surpluses for beads in these terms, as does Suttles (1968) and Oberg (1973:98) for the potlatch, and Jackson (1991) for the regional gatherings at Poverty Point. Halstead and O'Shea (1982, 1989) refer to this as "social storage," which I think is a misleading term that distorts the concept of storage. "Resource banking" might be a better term, as would be consistent with Codere's, Boas's (1966:77), and Oberg's (1973:98) comparisons of potlatching to investments. Jochim (2002) has drawn out the implications for this model of feasting versus others in terms of differing dynamics and expected material patterns. Although these ecologically based functional models continue to attract some advocates, most researchers and early ethnographers argue that the major feasts among complex hunter/gatherers had little to do with subsistence. The major focus of feasts was explicitly on status. In addition, prestige goods were generally *not* exchanged for subsistence items (Dalton 1977), and, when they were exchanged for wealth, this generally occurred *outside* the context of elaborate feasting, which begs the question of why feasts were necessary. Moreover, the many years of preparation and amassing of wealth for large feasts cannot be explained in terms of subsistence redistribution (Loeb 1936; J. Adams 1973:90–2; Ruyle 1973:605). The observation by Niblack (1890) that feasting essentially ceased on the Northwest Coast when food was scarce is also inconsistent with the idea that its role was to redistribute food to alleviate food shortages (Figure 4.3). In a more sophisticated version of the redistribution model, J. Adams (1973) has argued that the potlatch functioned to redistribute population to match resource rights and resource production on the landscape. His arguments are persuasive, but I suspect that this is more an auxiliary, perhaps unintended, consequence of the feasting system rather than its driving motivation. Harkin (2007:228), in particular, has criticized the idea that any conservation-motivated behavior was involved in feasting.

4.3. A potlatch given by a Quatsino chief c. 1900. Guests are seated by rank inside the structure. These individuals were those who benefited most from the potlatch system, rather than the common people who remained outside (see Figure 4.12). Both their attire and the surplus food consumed and given away indicate that potlatch feasts were not the products of resource-poor conditions. (Vancouver Public Library Ref. No. 14049A)

Status

In traditional ethnographies, acquiring status and prestige are among the most often cited motivations for hosting feasts. However, status and prestige are rarely defined; they are difficult concepts to deal with. At the most rudimentary level, prestige appears to be sought for the psychological gratification it provides to a person's sense of ego and self-identification. This is a very introspective, contemporary, or Western meaning of the word "status." When we look closely at what is actually meant by "status" or "prestige," as used in the original linguistic contexts of transegalitarian societies, the indigenous term frequently appears synonymous with or a consequence of wealth, power, and success (Izikowitz 1951:117,303; Barnett 1955;253; Clark and Blake 1989; Lemonnier 1990:47,49; Clarke 2001:163; Hayden 2001a:32–3; Perodie 2001). As J. Adams (1973:118) phrases it, the Gitksan "equates the social worth of people with the amount of food and wealth which they distribute publicly. ... To be given large amounts of goods is to be given a public estimate of one's ability to repay, and is, therefore, a sort of credit rating." For the Chin, Lehman (1963:195) puts it more bluntly, "Power over others (status) is thought of and acted out in terms of enforced hospitality, coercive feasting, and the like." I would argue that it is because those who possess wealth and power can put on lavish displays (whereas others cannot) that those who mounted inferior displays were obliged to yield (Roscoe 2009:72,102–3). It is unlikely that those who yielded did so out of deference to someone with prestige but lacking either wealth or power. Moreover, psychological gratification appears to have little to do with actual feast behavior. As Roscoe (2000:105) notes, even if status (in the Western sense) was not a consideration, leaders would fundamentally behave the same way because they are motivated by considerations of security, revenge, and reproduction. In the paleopolitical ecology model, aggrandizers seek power to satisfy many such desires, the least of which is perhaps prestige (in the Western sense). Thus, when viewed from a more emic perspective, acquiring "status" may be a motivation for feasting if status is considered as a synonym for wealth, power, or fighting strength or as a kind of credit rating or practical criterion for future investments and alliances (J. Adams 1973:118; Perodie 2001; Roscoe 2009).

Communitarian, Functional, Social Factors

From the communitarian perspective, it is community needs that determine what activities need to be carried out to maintain Durkheimian social solidarity and cooperation, especially for effective food production and defense (see Mauss 1924; Boas 1966:77; J. Adams 1973:110; Oberg 1973:98). In such models, leaders are not motivated by self-interest but by communal interests, service ethics, and by the adulation or "status" in the community that serving the community is supposed to confer. In the communitarian view, aggrandizers are not responsible for creating feasting or other institutions; these are created by community needs and consensus (Saitta and Keene 1990; Nassaney 1992; Saitta 1997, 1999; Kohler et al. 2012). In this scenario, ambitious individuals are kept on a short leash by the community using leveling mechanisms similar to those discussed for simple foragers. If necessary, economically successful individuals are more or less forced into public offices where they are obligated to distribute their wealth as part of public and administrative feasts (the "burden of the cargo" described by Carrasco [1961] and others). It would require a lengthy digression to provide a detailed critique of these models here. However, in brief, such models do not correspond to the ethnographic evidence or the archaeological patterning that one might expect (see Hayden and Gargett 1990; Hayden and Villeneuve 2010). Efficient management of community affairs leads one to expect centralized authority with the prestige, ritual, or other paraphernalia required for its exercise concentrated around single individuals in leadership positions. In contrast, as previously discussed, transegalitarian societies such as those in Northwest North America tend to be characterized by multiple loci of power within communities and relatively diffuse distributions of prestige items. Both of these features seem inconsistent with postulated communitarian dynamics. Moreover, once the community "need" has been met through establishing such roles, there is little logical reason why such societies should change. This is essentially a static, negative feedback (homeostatic) model. In contrast, the aggrandizer role in political ecology models produces a dynamic, positive feedback system in which there is constant pressure for change. Which of these outcomes best characterizes the archaeological record of the past 15,000 years?

Costly Signaling/Epideictic Displays/Symbolic Capital

In Chapter 1, I mentioned that it is fashionable among behavioral ecologists to explain excessive, often wasteful food consumption events and material displays in terms of costly signals that display the power of host groups and warn adversaries against any contemplated use of force (Bliege-Bird and Smith 2005). Such shows are often characterized as "symbolic capital," a term that seems misleading and is often imbued with more powerful and long-lasting effects than are warranted. In reality, as soon as groups fail to produce adequately impressive displays, their credibility plummets and they become targets for competing individuals or factions. It is not because leaders have not built up enough symbolic capital or because symbolic capital has gone bankrupt that they are sometimes deposed or killed, but simply because they are materially and sociopolitically weak and vulnerable. The costly signaling approaches do account for some types of promotional displays used in feasting, but to limit the motivations and purposes of feasts to these factors is far too narrow a view of why people give feasts (see Chapter 1 and Hayden 2009a:37). Instead of the preemptive *repelling* of physical conflicts, signaling in traditional feasting is much more frequently used to *attract* desirable partners for wealth exchanges, marital partnerships, political support, and military alliances. Even more importantly, such displays typically entail the giving of prestige foods and gifts with the unstated but implicit contractual understanding that such gifts must be repaid. They thus form a *reciprocal obligation*, the social bonding effects of which go far beyond any simple signaling value. Reciprocal obligations are the stuff on which complex social and political networks or organizations are founded, and feasting obligations are among the most important. Thus, lavish feasts go well beyond the importance of signals. In fact, sometimes lavish displays of wealth and food, far from having any desired deterrent effect, serve quite the opposite – they attract attention from belligerent groups and sometimes they provoke armed conflicts when one group cannot repay the constantly escalating debts. On the Northwest Coast and Interior, it was the richest communities that were most often raided for dried salmon, wealth items, and slaves (Cannon 1992; Schaepe 2006).

Like communitarian models, costly signaling theory is also handicapped by theoretical foundations that tie it to a static, negative feedback cultural dynamic in which positive feedback and resulting dramatic cultural changes are excluded (Codding and Jones 2007:350,354–5). Contrary to these static expectations of signaling theory, the political ecological approach expects the advantages that feasts confer to result in constant pressures to increase production and foment positive feedback changes. Ecologically oriented ethnographers of transegalitarian societies have remarked on these pressures in many areas of the world (see Chapter 5), and such pressures arguably account for the rapid rate of culture change documented in the archaeological record of the past 15,000 years wherever the resource base could support intensification.

During this time, the exponential changes in technology, demography, and social complexity can plausibly be attributed to the positive feedback effects of feasting (Hayden 1986, 2001a). It is also important to note that once some individuals in a population achieved differential success by adopting various aggrandizer strategies, other individuals would have been obligated to support or imitate them or become socioeconomically disenfranchised, often being relegated to evolutionary oblivion due to lack of ability to marry or reproduce. Thus, the paleopolitical ecology model predicts widespread participation in lavish displays, whereas signaling theory predicts that only the highest ranking individuals should participate in lavish signaling behavior (Codding and Jones 2007:353). Others have criticized the signaling interpretations of the ethnographic examples used by costly signaling advocates. Critics propose very different interpretations for the "signaling" behaviors cited (Hill and Kaplan 1993; Marlowe 1999; Gurven et al. 2000:195; Wood 2006). Thus, signaling theory may be useful in animal ecology. However, it creates a static model for human behavior and deals only with a narrow range of phenomena within the gamut of feasting effects and adaptive advantages. In contrast, the paleopolitical ecology model encompasses many more aspects related to feasting and politics. Costly signaling models do not account for the debts and political centralization associated with most feasting systems.

Aggrandizers

At some point between egalitarian foragers and modern Industrial societies, aggrandizers became dominant figures in promoting social changes that were to their own benefit in occupying positions of power from which they could exploit others. Exactly when this occurred is a matter of debate. However, from the paleopolitical ecology perspective, I suggest that it began with complex hunter/gatherers and that the changes that made complex hunter/gatherers so different from simple foragers were engineered by aggrandizers for their own benefit. They used the strategies mentioned previously, many of which were manifestly not in the interest of most members of any community. For instance, the establishment of wealth as a basis for obtaining a spouse, especially when combined with polygyny, was clearly disadvantageous for younger men at the beginning of their productive life and for men with poor or even modest resources (Meillassoux 1981; Ensminger and Knight 1997; R. Adams 2007b:195). Ancestor worship in which descendants were ranked in importance and inheritance rights according to genealogical criteria also disenfranchised most descendants. Nor was the use of wealth to restrict access to supernatural powers in the interests of most people.

These and other material-based strategies all benefited highly ranked wealthy individuals. Senior men and wealthy individuals could control the labor of their children by controlling the wealth needed for marriage and legitimate reproduction. Lineage heads could interpret the pleasure or wrath of ancestors in terms of the behavior or economic contributions that they wanted to impose on other lineage members. You could be accused of incurring an accident or falling ill because you did not contribute enough to the last ancestral feast so that your ancestor punished you. On the Northwest Coast, the spirits were portrayed as rewarding potlatch supporters (J. Adams 1973:119). Thus, it is not surprising that many commoners and junior lineage members who performed the bulk of the productive labor were not interested in maintaining the elaborate and costly feasting systems that they were forced to contribute to and that largely benefitted elders or the elite (J. Adams 1973:46,146; Beynon 2000:69,192; Perodie 2001:199). As described by Ruyle (1973:616), the potlatch was, in essence, a thermodynamic pump that created an upward energy flow benefitting primarily the elites, depending on their relative ranks (Figure 4.3).

Moreover, as earlier noted, many aggrandizers were not above using more forceful means, as indicated by the enforcement cadres of elites and the warrior despots that sometimes terrorized transegalitarian and more complex communities. Needless to say, terrorizing or beating up members of one's own community seems inconsistent with the idea that the people who initiated those actions were placed in positions of power in order to serve their community. As Cowgill (1975:514–5) has noted, the development of complexity is a function of the perceived advantages for the elites. It is not hardships or communitarian efforts to deal with hardships that stimulate complexity, but the prospect of new opportunities. It seems evident that surpluses were necessary to maintain the feasting systems (J. Adams 1973), that these systems primarily benefited the elite organizers, and that success in feasting was the basis of elite power (Dawson 1880:126; Ruyle 1973:610,616; Jewitt 1974:36–9,112–3; Perodie 2001:194; Harkin 2007:227). This is, in essence, what the paleopolitical ecology model maintains.

Although transegalitarian aggrandizers may not have had much direct power over people, I argue that they developed numerous manipulative strategies to take advantage of actual and potential surpluses, one of the most effective strategies being feasting. The kinds of relationships that I envisage are presented in Figure 4.4 (after Burley 1980:72). To justify taking other people's produce and labor (on various pretexts such as resources needed for marriages, rituals, ancestors, or group defense, i.e., "getting things done"), it must have helped enormously if some of what was obtained was returned or shared, thereby giving people the sense that they were getting something immediate and tangible in return for their contributions. However, if individuals became recalcitrant, more physical means could always be used.

Debates on the various theoretical aspects and motivations behind hosting feasts may go on for decades. Nevertheless, using paleopolitical ecology as a working premise for the present analysis allows the formulation of some tentative principles, assuming that aggrandizers were the major promoters.

GENERAL PRINCIPLES OF FEASTING

Obligatory Reciprocity and Debts

For feasts to function most effectively in manipulating others and building power bases, establishing some principle of obligatory reciprocity is essential. Although informants may not articulate such agreements very often, it seems that they are always tacitly understood. John Adams (1973:110) makes the point that invitations to feasts and gifts given in feasts were essentially reciprocal contracts. If one accepted an invitation to a feast and a gift, one was obligated to return something comparable or more. This, of course, was Mauss's (1924) major premise. Once the egalitarian sharing ethic (with generalized reciprocity) could be effectively altered, contractual reciprocity was a relatively natural principle that could be introduced, added on to, or even substituted for generalized reciprocity. As Rappaport (1999:132) maintained, breach of obligation is universally the most basic immoral act, and aggrandizers probably made all of their prestige gifts or feasts contingent on agreements for obligate returns in kind. They could then use these agreements and the innate sense of morality to forge their own power structures.

From an aggrandizer perspective, the primary goal of feasting invitations and gifts would appear to have been to create debts that could be manipulated and used either for sociopolitical support or to leverage resources and/or labor when needed. However, to get potential supporters to cooperate, the entire group also had to benefit, and so, feast organizers always stressed the group interests in both rhetoric and public outcomes. For close supporters, gifts or loans were repaid at par with no

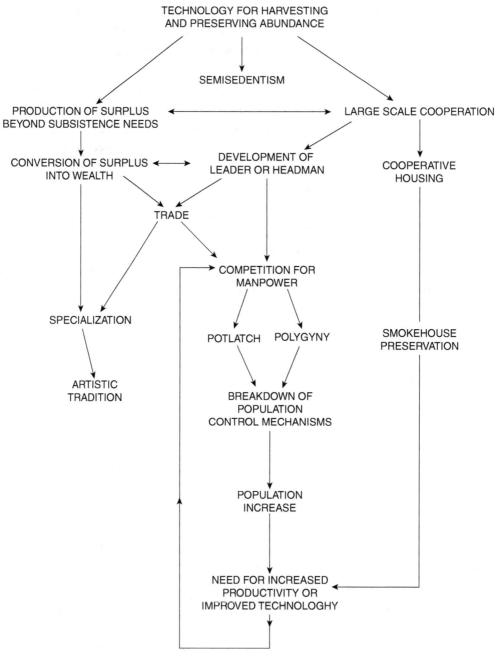

4.4. A diagram for the Northwest Coast culture pattern by Dave Burley (1980: figure 14) showing the relationship between surplus food production and the development of competition, leadership, feasting, and pressures for increased production.

expectation of any increase or interest accruing. This would correspond to the most natural and acceptable condition for making a loan. I give you the use of something that I own on condition that you return it, or an equivalent, to me in the future. However, once this principle was well-established, in some situations variable interest rates could be charged, especially on loans or gifts to nonkin or where borrowers were desperate for loans, as when they needed resources to marry, to avoid starvation, or to advance politically. Rates typically varied from 25 to 100 percent per loan event. As Walens (1981:13) explains it, the nobleman's success was achieved only through careful deployment of his food resources to create reciprocal obligations from people whom he fed. However, to be effective, such agreements required some kind of sanctions to control breaches, freeloaders, and cheaters.

Defaulting Consequences

It comes as little surprise, then, that people who defaulted on repaying loans were likely to be eliminated from the feasting system and would subsequently find it difficult to borrow (Ford 1968:19,171fn,194). However, defaulters could also lose ownership of their crests to the creditor, become the target of raids or open warfare, and in some groups might become enslaved, as with the Tlingit and a number of Californian groups (in addition to the cases cited by Perodie 2001:200–1; see Codere 1950:122–3; Kroeber 1953:32–3; Gould 1966:83; De Laguna 1972; Oberg 1973:118–9; Ruyle 1973:613; also, for horticulturalists, see Condominas 1977). Feuds were often generated over loans and debt payments among the Nisenan (Wilson and Towne 1978:393). And Olson (1954:240–1) reported that failure to perform dances or songs at feasts could result in beatings, whereas the breaking of taboos could result in killing the offender. In a similar vein, among the Luiseño, defaulting on debt payments could result in death of the debtor or war (Boscana 1933:69; Noah 2005:46–7). When asked in the film *Ongka's Big Moka* what he would do if a large feasting gift was not returned, Ongka stated that he would slit his rival's throat (Nairn 1991). Thus, we see that the simple contemporary niceties of declining a dinner invitation or attendance at some similar event scarcely represents feasting relations in transegalitarian societies. To refuse a feast invitation or gift in traditional societies, or to fail to reciprocate, was tantamount to a declaration of total social rupture: social and/or physical warfare. Once an individual entered the feasting system, he could almost never extricate himself from it. "Everyone who participates is linked together in cycles of indebtedness and of financial expectations" (J. Adams 1973:111). They inexorably sank deeper in debt, and those debts usually followed them after death and had to be paid off by their heritors, often giving rise to disputes (Ford 1968:171).

Private Property and Storage

All of these understandings and practices were based on an even more elementary new norm: the recognition of private control over resource sites, produce, and wealth. Without such a provision, general sharing would prevail, and individual efforts to accumulate or use resources for one's own benefit would be ineffective since everyone else could and did take advantage of individual initiatives, leaving the person who did all the work with little or no benefit for him- or herself. Claims to private ownership of gathered, fished, or hunted food appear to have been significantly reinforced by the practice of storage, which required substantial additional outlays of time, effort, and risk taking beyond the initial procurement of the foods. Moreover, storage led to habitual overproduction to hedge against losses and future uncertainties, and, when unused (as in most years), these surpluses could be put to other uses or they would be lost to spoilage (Testart 1982:527–8; Halstead 1989, 1990:151–6). Thus, storage fostered the development of feasts, prestige goods, costly marriage partners, and other economically based strategies of investment or benefit acquisition. It has also been suggested that storage arose from increased feasting needs to amass surpluses and that therefore storage capacity reflects feasting intensity (Morgan 2012:718,731).

Sanctification

Because obligatory reciprocity was so central to effectively manipulating the system, an aura of sacredness was established in many societies by invoking supernatural entities to witness the events and reward feast supporters but punish those who transgressed their obligations (J. Adams 1973:119). In a like manner, the community ideology was generally reconfigured to sanctify those who achieved success and wealth by portraying material well-being as a sign of supernatural blessing or power, often derived from ancestors. This is yet another example of an ideological concept that clearly benefited successful aggrandizers but was not very favorable for the poor or average person. It also masks the ambitious and sometimes exploitative nature of aggrandizers. Clarke (2001:163) summarizes this relationship nicely for a horticultural group, and it seems equally applicable to most transegalitarian groups in which ideological claims to political power are based on ritual potency. In these cases, "ritual potency" is usually demonstrated, or proved, by economic success.

Altering Attitudes and Ideologies

One of the goals of aggrandizers, in general, is to change attitudes, values, and community norms to enable ambitious individuals to pursue strategies that enhance their own self-interests and benefits. In general, the less secure people are in their sociopolitical positions, the more frequent and lavish their feasting displays seem to be (Randsborg 1982; Cannon 1989). As discussed in Chapter 1, feasts have a remarkable potential for achieving such ends. Thus, the organization of feasts frequently entails the creation of favorable emotional, altered, and/or synesthetic states of mind for the presentation of new values or the reaffirmation of those components important to the success of aggrandizer strategies. Also important in this respect are the public orations, expressions of gratitude, invocations of spirits, and expressions of values that generally occur once guests are adequately satiated and socially malleable.

Another way of making feasting events more impressive and lending an air of authority or sanctification to them in order to change guests' attitudes and values is through the involvement of high-ranking dignitaries or people perceived to be of high status from outside the community. Thus, today, at many large events, government officials, priests, and even visitors or ethnoarchaeologists from industrial centers become centerpieces in the guest lists and in seating arrangements. This principle has been expressed for the Tlingit, among whom the number of feast guests and their distance traveled was a source of prestige (Cooper 2006:154).

However, given aggrandizer motivations and goals, the agenda for changing attitudes, values, and ideologies would have been much more pervasive than the simple sanctification of feasts as reciprocal events. I have already alluded to the recognition of claims to private property and reciprocal obligations, and I will discuss the creation of corporate groups and the elevation of ancestors or animal spirits to powerful spiritual roles. These are sometimes graphically displayed for all to see, as on the totem poles in Northwest Coast cultures that record corporate elite totemic history and inheritances (see also the section "The Importance of Funerals"). Equally important are the conceptual transformations involved in requiring large amounts of wealth in order to acquire spouses or properly bury the dead. The establishment of secret societies also entailed major transformations in ideology and economic transfers. The equation of elite welfare with community welfare begins with transegalitarian hunter/gatherers, although this could be a double-edged sword when communities experienced difficulties and might lay the blame on their leaders. Additional ideological transformations involve the viewing of wealth as proof of spiritual power (or the power of one's ancestors) or the corollary that the spirits reward feasting supporters with material benefits, the denigration of those who decline to participate in feasting systems, the creation of multitudinous taboos, the concept that breaking of taboos threatens the spiritual health of the community and especially its leaders, and the claims that elites never undertake feasts or other endeavors for their own benefit but only for the good of their social group. Thus, it is a recurring rhetoric that leaders never use anything for their own ends, only for the good of their people (Beynon 2000:145; but see 69,192). As J. Adams (1973:46,96,113,118) notes, the elites always describe themselves as altruistic, helping, and redistributive; but in reality, they constitute an oligarchy that controls resources, protects each others' interests, excludes nonelites, and exploits commoners and slaves. At the chiefdom level, this disconformity between ideology and practice has been dramatically documented in the film *The Kirghiz of Afghanistan*, in which the chief argues that he only acts to help his people, whereas poor herders complain bitterly about how the chief exploits them (Nairn 1981). None of these ideological transformations from egalitarian forager ideologies is very intelligible in terms of communitarian, functional, or costly signaling theories. They are, however, understandable as the result of aggrandizers' strategies to increase their own self-benefits

Kin-Based Corporate or Support Groups

Although there can be and often are intense conflicts between close kin, there are generally also close bonds and mutual help relationships. Bloch and Sperber (2002), as well as sociobiologists, have argued that strong cooperative and mutual helping relationships among close kin are innate evolutionary dispositions for humans. It is therefore not surprising to find most feasting supporters being drawn from kinship networks. That being said, however, it should also be acknowledged that productive performance was also highly valued in many corporate groups sponsoring feasts. Thus, it was not uncommon for desirable workers or administrators who were unrelated by kinship to be brought into groups and given fabricated genealogies to fictitiously make them part of the kinship network and make them feel, or even believe, that they were members of a kin group with common interests.

Attracting People

As discussed in Chapter 1, the main goal of aggrandizers was to attract people so that they would want to participate in events, even if they were obligated to make some sort of contribution or future repayment. To attract specific people, benefits were promised and large quantities of normal foods and/or some specialty foods or preparations were obtained and proffered to special guests. In general, Hastorf (2003) argues that one criterion for choosing luxury foods was that they were difficult or costly to procure. But as H. Leach (2003:454) observes, common foods could become "fit for a feast" through being assembled in massive quantities, given added value as a result of labor-intensive preparations, selecting superior varieties, or prepared in numerous ways. Frequently, elaborate serving vessels accompanied these dishes, such as the elaborately carved bowls used in Northwest Coast pot-latches (Figure 4.5); the pedestaled bowls used by Torajans in Sulewesi (Figure 4.6); the large, often decorated gourds used by the Highland Maya (Figure 4.7); or

4.5. Wherever hosts want to impress guests, special serving dishes for food seem to become prominent parts of feasts. On the Northwest Coast, "grease bowls" for dipping food in fish oil became elaborate works of art (shown here) that displayed the wealth and abilities of corporate kinship groups and their elite administrators. (Photo courtesy of the Simon Fraser Museum of Archaeology)

4.6. In other areas, like tribal (and Neolithic) Southeast Asia and Neolithic or Bronze Age Europe, the importance of a guest's status was indicated by the height of a stemmed eating bowl, such as these wooden examples from the Torajan highlands in Sulawesi. Neolithic versions of these bowls were ceramic. (Photograph by B. Hayden)

4.7. Another form of special serving vessels is made from gourds. Although simple gourds are used even today among many Maya groups, specially decorated gourds such as those shown here were reserved for important guests. I was even told that, in earlier times, gourds with silver rims were used when an individual wanted to make a request of an important person. It is interesting to note how many cultures make special serving vessels out of perishable organic materials that would ordinarily leave no archaeological remains. (Photograph courtesy of John Clark)

the elaborately carved spoons and stirrers of the California Yurok (Figure 4.8; Kroeber 1953:plates 17 and 20). With a few notable exceptions, before pottery was developed, most such vessels were made of perishable materials, and many continued to be so constructed even after the introduction of pottery. However, in some cases, such as in the early ceramic traditions of the Maya and Southeast Asia, the ceramic forms imitated the earlier high-status organic serving vessels. In fact, given the widespread and long-lasting use of ceramic pedestaled forms in Southeast Asia as indexical of prestige, I suspect that the same was probably true elsewhere in the world where pedestaled forms occur.

As previously discussed, an entire array of other display kinds of prestige technologies were also usually developed for use in feasting contexts in order to attract and impress people. Prestige clothing, jewelry, elaborate ritual objects, masks, heirlooms, textiles, complex architecture, dramatic performances, demonstrations of supernatural feats, musical instruments and performances, body deformations or tattooing, and many other prestige materials probably were developed primarily for use and display in such contexts (Hayden 1998). The desire to impress special guests apparently often led to highly elaborate crafting and the establishment of part-time specialists, such as the carvers of the Northwest Coast and California.

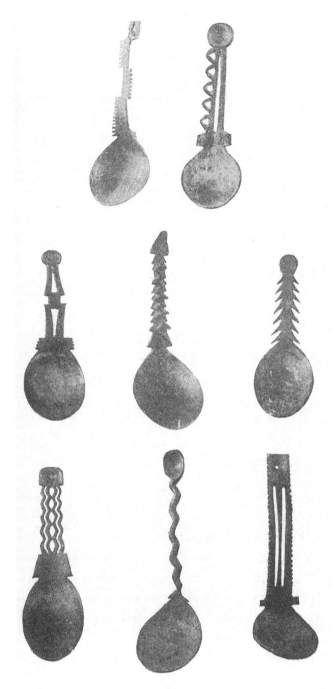

4.8. Occasionally, utensils used in the serving of foods were also elaborately decorated, such as these ornately carved antler spoons for eating acorn gruel among the Yurok Indians of California (see also Figure 4.21). Kroeber (1925:93) recounts that "Rich houses kept a store of fine spoons to bring out when they entertained dance guests." (Kroeber 1925:plate 20)

Denigration of Nonparticipants

In tandem with developing ways to positively attract people and induce them to support feasts, aggrandizers frequently developed negative sanctions for recalcitrant individuals who refused to support feasts either because they were disadvantaged or because they simply were not interested in working harder to produce the necessary surpluses to participate in feasting systems or become entangled in debts. Nonparticipating individuals were progressively marginalized and disempowered from community decisions due to the links between feasting networks and political decision making. They were also vulnerable to political or economic attacks, as well as to physical attacks by aggrandizer henchmen, in which they could lose property, freedom, or children, or be forced out of communities. Such individuals in transegalitarian hunter/gatherer and horticultural societies were subject to public ridicule and revilement by developing terms like "dead skin," "rubbish men," "lazy moochers," and "abominable people" (Shinichiro 1960:23; J. Adams 1973:73; Condominas 1977:342; Hayden 1992a:544,554; Yan 1999:103–4; Perodie 2001). These are terms that are uncommon among simple foragers or have no equivalents; they seem to reflect the emergence of a mind-set obsessed with preventing others from accessing wealthy individuals' private property (in sharp contrast to egalitarian sharing ethics). Again, these developments are intelligible primarily in terms of aggrandizer strategies.

Potential for Enlisting Support and Expansion

For feasting to be effective as a strategy to increase and control surplus production and to increase personal power, it would be important for the system to be capable of involving many people and to be expandable. There are a number of basic ways, already mentioned, in which feasts can be structured so as to make them seem to be in the self-interests of many individuals. Like bank patrons, everyone gets some benefits from contributing, even if the gain is often nominal: increased security, access to wealth through loans or investments, marriageability, "free" food, a channel for grievances, and some access to political power. Just like modern land developers pushing construction programs, organizers could always capitalize on the needs of – or benefits for – the community and on how feasting could meet those needs or contribute to those benefits. Some aggrandizers even provoked wars to pressure community members to support their self-benefit schemes (Sillitoe 1978). Thus, as many ethnographers have noted, aggrandizers received active support from their constituents who expected to benefit in one way or another from their leaders – and often did (Wiessner 1989:60).

Moreover, there is an unlimited variety of reasons – or pretexts – that could be invoked to hold feasts, most of which could be portrayed as benefiting the social group in one way or another. A wide range of sponsoring social units and numbers of participants can also characterize feasts, from small family events to corporate kinship celebrations, to regional gatherings. And feasts, by nature, can be easily expanded simply by inviting more people, giving more gifts, and holding more feasts. As well, feasts can be scheduled at various frequencies or various times depending on available resources. Moreover, if there are competitive advantages to be gained from feasting, the magnitude and the intensity of labor costs can always be increased beyond household resources through the system of debts and borrowing that is such an integral part of most feasting dynamics. This explains why some individuals or families among groups on the Northwest Coast and California gave away so much at potlatches that they could not live in comfort or eat wholesome food for some time afterward (Loeb 1926:292; Codere 1950:82; see also Chapter 6). Like modern-day ambitious entrepreneurs, ambitious feast-givers often borrowed as much as they could to invest in long-term future returns. However, in waiting for those returns to (hopefully) bear fruit, they were reduced temporarily to poverty because of the large debts that had to be paid off in the short term. A similar dynamic is clearly evident in the documentary film *Ongka's Big Moka* (Nairn 1991). Thus, for a variety of reasons, feasting is a remarkably flexible and expandable kind of system.

SOME CONSEQUENCES

A number of regularly recurring cultural and feasting aspects can be derived from the just described principles for transegalitarian feasting systems. Not all of these were probably intended, but many undoubtedly were.

Increased Power

The first consequence that I propose is that successful feasters actually achieved their goal through feasting and acquired more power (or at least influence) in their communities, if not in other communities as well. Directly or indirectly through debts, they controlled more resources than others, and, as Gopnik (2009:127) phrases it, "He who has the gold makes the rules" (a point elaborated by Hayden and Villeneuve 2010). Similarly, Roscoe (2009:72,102–3) notes that those who mounted inferior displays were obliged to yield. In addition, individuals who were more powerful and influential paid lower fines for transgressions and exacted higher compensation from the less wealthy or powerful in the community (Kroeber

1953:33). Among the Ainu, the rich and powerful could avoid severe physical punishments or exile for transgressions through pay-offs, and they sometimes even provoked quarrels with the less powerful in order to acquire their wealth (Shinichiro 1960:20–1). As previously mentioned ("Consequences of Defaulting"), the most extreme expression of this power took the form of debt slavery. This practice was also present in a number of horticultural transegalitarian societies, such as the Rhadé in Vietnam where, I was told, members of rich and powerful corporate kin groups paid only half the penalties or compensations of poor and unaffiliated households. If the rich paid fines or compensations for the poor, the poor became indentured servants to the rich.

Warfare

The elevated levels of competition for survival, reproduction, power, and standard of living benefits engendered considerable conflict. This competition, together with the potential consequences of defaulting on debts and the manipulation of conflicts in order to pressure community members into aggrandizer schemes based on economic production, all meant that warfare often increased substantially in transegalitarian hunter/gatherer societies. Based on information from cemeteries, in California and the Northwest Coast during the past 5,000 years, violent mortalities often reached 30 percent or more (P. Walker 1989; Cybulski 1992; Keeley 1996; Otterbein 2004:74–5; Gat 2005:24–35; Fry 2006:103–7).

Plethoras of Feasts

Another consequence is that aggrandizers found a number of ways in which feasts could be used to gain advantages. The variety of feast types thus proliferated to include various kinds of simple feasts in exchange for labor (work feasts; Dietler and Herbich 2001), feasts to establish desirable social relationships (including feasts to advertise the success of a group), feasts to create solidarity within a social group, and feasts to invest surpluses with the expectation of greater returns (as in stock markets). Of course, a number of these goals could often be combined within the organization of a single feasting event. Although a wide array of purposes and pretexts are employed by aggrandizers in formulating feasts, some occasions are far better suited to achieving their goals than others.

The Importance of Funerals

Of all the occasions for holding large feasts, funerals appear to be one of the most commonly employed. This is as true of complex hunter/gatherers as it is of horticulturalists, chiefdoms, and early states (J. Adams 1973; Clarke 2001; Perodie 2001; Hayden 2009a). For many groups on the Northwest Coast, the potlatch was fundamentally a funeral feast. The reasons why funerals have so frequently served as the venue for the most overtly lavish and competitive displays of wealth and success have often been rather mysterious. Why should people go to such extremes to honor a dead person who cannot acknowledge, appreciate, or reciprocate any of the efforts expended on his or her behalf? Ames (2008:55) refers to the long-held view in anthropology that the potlatch was economically irrational.

I have suggested that funerals provide one of the best opportunities for ambitious aggrandizers to promote their own interests for a number of reasons (Hayden 2009a). First, the ambition is masked: the event is nominally for the dead, not the host. Largely because of this feature, competitive displays of success on behalf of the deceased can be indulged in without severe sanctions. Thus, in many transegalitarian societies, funeral feasts tend to exhibit the most competitively ostentatious displays that occur in these communities. Second, due to the large scale and lavish expenditures, funeral feasts are often used as epideictic (signaling) displays that indicate to all guests the power of the host group, especially important after membership has been reduced by a death. Third, supporters and guests are in emotionally altered or disoriented states in which they are more likely to be susceptible to suggestions, open to reconfiguring relationships, conciliatory, and compliant with requests (Huntington and Metcalf 1979:114). Fourth, kin connections of the deceased and host can be used effectively to marshal support and resources. Fifth, the frequency of funeral events within a family or lineage is infrequent enough so that large amounts of resources can be amassed and expended for funerals, even if the event takes place several years after the actual death (via delayed interment or secondary burial). Sixth, because a wide array of kin and other supporters are drawn to funerals, they make excellent venues for establishing or reestablishing mutual support networks, including networks involving other communities. Seventh, construing lavish funeral feasts as a requirement for respectable households creates pressures on many families to produce surpluses and indebt themselves through borrowing, all to the potential advantage of aggrandizers. Eighth, lavish funerals can be used to establish the dead as powerful spirits to which only successful lineage heads have direct access. The stated goal of many funeral expenditures is to enable the deceased to enter "heaven" and become an empowered spirit that can dispense well-being (or punishments) on his or her descendants (P. Jordan 2003:217) or at least to make them happy (DeLaguna 1972:606; Ruyle 1973:616). The Kwakiutl maintained that the spirits only favored for initiations those with wealth (Codere 1950:6). In turn, wealth was portrayed as proof of spirit blessings. Such claims are usually accompanied by dominant roles of lineage heads in ancestral rituals and care of ritual paraphernalia.

Thus, genealogies become critical ideological features in many transegalitarian societies, as graphically displayed on Northwest Coast totem poles and as often recounted at length in feasts.

Funerals provide one of the best occasions for enacting aggrandizer agendas, and most major features of funeral feasts are intelligible in these terms. Feasts organized to create defense or offensive alliances constitute other situations that could be used to strongly motivate people to produce and contribute surpluses.

Cost and Frequency

In their attempts to impress guests with a group's wealth, hosts often encourage guests in alliances and competitive feasts to receive and eat as much as possible, even to the point of vomiting (Harkin 2007:226–7). Such lavishness of the larger feasts was extremely costly and, as a result, usually required anywhere from one to ten years of preparation, with the result that given individuals could rarely organize more than five to ten large feasts in a lifetime, even for funerals (McIlwraith 1948:243; DeLaguna 1972:606).

Numeration and Records

Most simple foragers that I am familiar with, in Australia and elsewhere, have numbering systems that go no higher than ten or, at the most, twenty (Overmann 2013). Beyond that, quantity is simply expressed in terms of "many." In contrast, most complex hunter/gatherers have numeral systems that reach well into the hundreds if not thousands. I suggest that this is due to the need for keeping track of the quantities of food items and other gifts received or given at feasts (see Chapter 6 and Hayden and Villeneuve 2011a). Because gifts were contractually reciprocal, some record of quantities would have been extremely beneficial, if not mandatory, given the complex transactions and debts created by the bewildering number of feasts and support gifts that characterized most transegalitarian hunter/ gatherers. As J. Adams (1973:111) says so succinctly, "indebtedness fosters elaborate record keeping." Scheduling of feasts could also favor the development of calendars and astronomical observations in some cultures in order to plan for feasts (Hayden and Villeneuve 2011a).

Effects on Carrying Capacity

One of the unintended effects of using feasting strategies, as well as other economically based strategies, may have been their influence on limiting carrying capacities due to the overproduction of surpluses used for nonsubsistence purposes. As previously mentioned, these resources make up the "political economy" described by Firth and Earle. Even among transegalitarian hunter/gatherers, the magnitude of the political economy could be very substantial. Ruyle (1973:615) indicated that between one-fifth and one-half of all food production on the Northwest Coast went to chiefs and was predominantly used for feasts. In horticultural and Polynesian chiefdoms, the amount could even be greater (see Chapters 6 and 7). In essence, the production for the political economy could create a buffer between resource availability and subsistence needs, or, in other words, it could maintain human population levels well below carrying capacity limits and therefore reduce the risk or frequency of starvation. Although transegalitarian groups were sometimes reduced to meager fares and endured hardships, actual accounts of starvation are rare. In fact, in my work in Mesoamerica and Southeast Asia, I was unable to elicit any oral history accounts of actual deaths from starvation, whereas accounts of deaths from starvation among groups like the Inuit or boreal forest hunter/gatherers are far from rare and constitute major preoccupations of many forager groups (Hayden 1981: table 10.21).

On the other hand, as discussed next, there were also strong pressures to increase the numbers of laborers and thus the number of children. How exactly these two antagonistic pressures balanced out is still a topic for investigation. The combination of the need to overproduce for feasts and the political economy versus the need to produce as many children as possible may account for the seemingly contradictory observations of people going hungry while producing abundances for feasts.

Intensification

Another paradoxical or counterintuitive effect of feasting involves intensification. Most archaeologists assume that resource stresses led to intensified food procurement techniques. However, populations were probably kept below carrying capacity and avoided real resource stress, but they nevertheless intensified food production as a (probably unintended) consequence of pursuing feasting strategies ("intensification" is defined in Chapter 5). A similar situation exists in Industrial societies where there is no perceptible starvation or population pressure, but food production continues to become ever more intensified. This is an important part of the positive feedback loop that many forms of feasting create. Wherever there is even a slight competitive element in feasting, the stage is set for people to try to produce more food. With hunter/gatherers, this may be achieved initially by working harder and longer, but increased food production can also be attained by obtaining more labor (more wives, children, or adjunct workers). Typically, having enough labor to take advantage of seasonally abundant foods constitutes the major bottleneck in procurement, processing, and storage. Thus, transegalitarian societies often emphasize human fertility (perhaps reflected in "Venus" figurines) and wealth-based polygyny. This can also create positive feedback reproduction relationships in which those with wealth can procure more wives and have more children who, in turn, produce more wealth. The upshot is that a few successful aggrandizers in transegalitarian communities can father the great majority of children. For instance, in one extreme example, Napoleon Chagnon (1979) reported that 95 percent of the children in one Amazonian village were descended from a single successful big man grandfather (see also J. Hill 1984; Frayser 1985:252–6; Cronk 1991; Hayden 2003b).

These labor solutions to production will eventually be limited by the existing technologies, and it is at this point that efforts can be expected to be made to improve food production by improving technologies or techniques of food production, even if these may be less efficient and more labor intensive. The main goal is to produce more food and thereby to obtain more benefits. Thus, large amounts of effort can be invested both in obtaining more wives with more children and in developing labor-intensive extraction or processing technologies, such as making nets for hunting and fishing (Satterthwait 1987); constructing deer fences, fishing platforms, or weirs (Figure 4.9); weeding, spading, or irrigating plant patches;

4.9. The use of more complex and labor-intensive technologies, such as these fishing platforms at Celilo Falls near The Dalles, on the Columbia River, enabled groups to obtain more food, support larger groups, and produce surpluses that could be used in feasts. The men in the foreground on platforms attend "set nets" while the man in the background on a scaffold is using a dip net. (Photograph courtesy of David Cole)

4.10. With large surpluses, some resources could be transformed into highly desired, more valuable types of foods such as alcoholic beverages, cheeses, and oils. Here, a dugout canoe is being used as a container for boiling up eulachon in water to extract the valuable oil from these fish. The skimmed off oil will be put in boxes or containers and later refined by heating in a pot or bucket. The resulting oil was a highly prized item featured in potlatches and in trade along the coast and into the Northwest Interior. Photograph taken at the beginning of the twentieth century at the Chilkat River. (Image No. 13991, American Museum of Natural History; photo by Blankenberg)

procuring, processing, and storing large seasonal harvests; extracting nut or fish oils (labor-intensive, highly valued foods; see Figure 4.10); and exploiting low-ranking (effort-demanding) foods such as grass seeds, lentils, or other species that yield poor calorie returns. I argue in Chapter 5 that the process of intensification, together with the increased demand for highly valued foods, led to the domestication of plants and animals, as well as to population increases.

ETHNOGRAPHIC EXAMPLES

To see how some of these relatively abstract or theoretical factors were manifested in real examples, a number of ethnographic accounts from various complex hunting/gathering groups are examined here. Many of the earliest accounts focused almost exclusively on the largest, most impressive feasts within communities. Where such large feasts were present, it can usually be expected that other, smaller, and less noticeable feasts were probably taking place at the household or lineage level, even if they have not been explicitly described.

In examining accounts of feasting in the literature, as well as in studying feasting in contemporary societies, the paleopolitical ecology approach places the greatest emphasis on actual behavior and results, rather than on symbolic, cognitive, or inner-discourse phenomenological aspects. In this respect, political ecology is similar to animal ethology studies that have the goal of understanding animal behavior in underlying adaptive terms, even if these may be long term. It also follows a well-established tradition in ethnography and cultural anthropology (Steward 1938, 1955; Firth 1951, 1959; E. Leach 1954:x,14; Lehman 1963; M. Harris 1979). From my perspective, what is most essential in cultural behavior is what people do, not necessarily what they think about what they do, or the various justifications they may use for what they do, or how aware they are of why they do what they do, or what subconscious motivations may be involved in directing their actions.

In the short run, some people's ideas may influence what they do, but in the broad scheme of things, and in the long run, to keep electricity flowing, to keep tigers away from flocks, and to establish a family must be dealt with in practical terms. It does not matter whether one's religious beliefs maintain that Sunday (or Saturday, or Friday) should be days of no work (and by implication, no electricity), or that tigers are supposed to have Christian souls, or whether the only available spouse is of the correct kinship relation. As discussed in Chapter 1, in examining feasting, I have assumed that people were generally seeking practical, adaptive benefits in hosting costly feasts. Although people may sometimes be able to accurately articulate such motivations, they can probably be more reliably inferred from a number of behavioral indicators such as:

- Who the hosts/organizers were, plus their socioeconomic and age characteristics
- Who the supporters were and what kind of contributions they made to events
- How many people attended, plus age and gender profiles
- Who the specially invited guest were and why they were invited
- The exclusivity of specially invited and other guests
- What gifts were distributed and to whom, plus reciprocity expectations
- Record keeping
- What nonreciprocal gifts were given away
- Total costs
- What ostentatious prestige items or acts were used or displayed
- Hierarchical versus egalitarian features (seating, serving, speaking, gifts)
- Whether the food was provided and prepared by the host or was provided potluck-style

- Food quality (prestige foods vs. filler foods)
- Conspicuous waste
- What other strategies were components of the event (marriage, defense, child investments, supernatural displays, etc.)

Even in contemporary ethnoarchaeological research, determining the exact nature of the resultant benefits from *specific* feasts can be difficult because they are often long-term advantages that are sought or they are the reaffirmation of already existing relationships and ongoing mutual advantages. Like investments in the stock market, there can be short-term benefits that are more easily monitored from daily trades or long-term strategies in which benefits may not be immediately obvious and are more difficult to gauge. Short-term benefits consist of feasts that consummate a marriage (but not the feasts of preceding years that were hosted to attract desired families into potential marriage alliances or that created close reciprocal bonds between those families), or feasts for harvesting the hosts' fields, or for going to war (but again, not the feasts of preceding years that established mutual support alliances between communities). Longer term benefits must be inferred from deductions based on behaviors at feasts and logical or expectable outcomes, much as in animal ethology studies. It is often difficult to identify or infer the long-term feasting advantages from existing ethnographies.

Archaeologically, the situation is somewhat different because there are usually no strong indications as to what cognitive features (aside from some very general notions, such as the importance of ancestors) may have been associated with feasts of the past. Thus, we are largely restricted to the more ethological behavioral remains of prehistoric feasts.

So, what were feasts like among historical and ethnographically complex hunter/gatherers? The most detailed corpus of literature is related to the Northwest Coast of North America and the justly renowned potlatch.

The Northwest Coast

It should be recognized that, in the Northwest Coast culture area, there was considerable variation between cultures, including their housing styles, degrees of hierarchy, feasting behavior, art, dress, and language (there were five language phyla or isolates including ten language families). However, to discuss all relevant variations would require an entire volume or more dedicated to that topic alone. Because the goal here is to provide examples of general feasting behavior, I use the academic deceit of pretending that there was more homogeneity that there actually was. Caveat lector.

It should also be recognized that the feasting described during the eighteenth and nineteenth centuries was heavily influenced by the new economic opportunities made available from the fur, fish, and other trade with Euro-Americans, combined with a substantial demographic collapse of native communities. The combined effects created a material and wealth glut that most scholars think made the feasting complex mushroom out of all proportion to prehistoric practices, much as the introduction of the sweet potato in New Guinea transformed the feasting complex there (Wiessner and Tumu 1998). Birket-Smith (1967:13,18,21,27) even thinks that the competitive potlatches were entirely a product of historical contact. Although this may be true of some extreme examples in which large amounts of wealth were destroyed in competitive bouts between rivals, I think it is unlikely that all competitive aspects of feasts were absent before contact. McIlwraith (1948:243) makes the same point, emphasizing that potlatches in early times took years to prepare, whereas in the 1940s, they could be financed with a season's earnings, but that their basic nature had not changed. Even if the historically recorded events were highly inflated, they still are likely to have emerged from preexisting practices that had established the basic structure of reciprocal feasting, resource ownership, socioeconomic inequalities (including slavery), secret societies, elaborate carvings, corporate longhouses, and other fundamental features. What the historical examples do usefully demonstrate is the trajectory that feasting systems tend to take when resources become more abundant. Thus, the precontact events may not have been as lavish as contact period records indicate, but their basic nature would probably still have been recognizable.

A number of authors argue that funerals or death celebrations were the universal reason for potlatches (Birket-Smith 1967:36; J. Adams 1973:51). However, as Perodie (2001:186–7) observes, the term "potlatch" is used in different ways by different ethnographers. At one extreme, potlatches may be equated with any kind of feast. At the other extreme, potlatches are defined only as funeral feasts or feasts at which wealth is given away. I will use the term in its more generic sense.

There was an amazingly wide array of situations for which feasts were held on the Northwest Coast. Births, namings, ten moons from birth, weening, menses, puberty, tattooings and piercings, coming out of seclusion, first events (e.g., first successful hunt), marriage, death, immunity from breaking some taboos, success at hunting or fishing, completion of a canoe or house, appeasement of evil spirits, clan events, women's events, elders' events, secret society initiations or celebrations, erasing insults or embarrassment, acquiring names or titles, accession to new roles, war, peace, allies, and undoubtedly other situations were all fêted with feasts (Dawson 1880; Krause 1956; Ford 1968; Oberg 1973; R. Jordan 1994). As Olson (1954:238) observed, "The ideal man looks for an 'excuse' to give a potlatch and almost any excuse will serve." How different this is from simple forager societies, but how similar it is to other pastoral or horticultural transegalitarian societies. How to deal with such diversity can be daunting; however, Perodie (2001) provides a good synthesis of the relative advantages of different categories of feasting in the southern part of the Northwest Coast. He divides his analysis into events for which no return is required (including solidarity, work party, and solicitation feasts), events for which an equal return is expected (including child growth, political support or office accession, and reciprocal feasts), and events for which greater returns are expected (competitive feasts).

NO RETURN FEASTS

Since wealth, status, and power depended on the labor needed to make owned resources productive, solidarity feasts provided the practical benefit of maintaining a cooperative, motivated work force within corporate houses (Ruyle 1973:615). Work party feasts had the obvious advantage of getting houses or canoes built, poles carved and raised, or tasks of similar scales completed. Solicitation feasts had the advantage of achieving someone's cooperation, but these were undoubtedly small in scale and were poorly documented. Jewitt chronicled the frequent feasts that the Nootka chief, Maquinna, attended several times a week (Marshall 2002:97). For the most part, these were presumably small house feasts for alliances or solidarity where he had affili-ations either through kinship connections or political ties. These were again poorly documented, although Ford (1968:52–4) describes many informal feasts among friends and kin whenever there was a catch of fish or other extra food.

EQUAL RETURN FEASTS

In contrast to informal solidarity feasts, the main recipients of more formal equal return feasts were elite individuals from outside the hosting social group (Figure 4.11), and the main goal appears to have been the establishment or main-tenance of a mutual support network involving other social groups. Elite guests were reciprocally invited to attend marriages, training, puberty, initiations, funer-als, or other important events involving elite individuals of the host and guest groups. The series of reciprocal feasts between intermarrying families exemplifies such equal return feasts. These feasts could go on indefinitely or be terminated after a few years. They solidified mutual support networks that, among transegalitarian societies, typically consisted first of all of kin, second of all of families that had intermarried, and third of all of other relationships, such as "friends." Individuals in these networks were approached for help or support in defense, holding feasts, borrowing, obtaining access rights to resources, factional disputes, or individual conflicts. Promotional displays of wealth and success were common at many reciprocal invitation feasts to impress guests and to reaffirm or create alliances in which resources could be shared and power wielded. In the case of naming,

4.11. Elite guests at potlatches generally tried to competitively impress their hosts and each other with showy clothes and ritual paraphernalia, such as these Sitka guests attending a potlatch at Klukwan to dedicate a new Whale House. (Image No. 159 by Blankenberg; American Museum of Natural History)

training, first events, or puberty celebrations of high-ranking children, feasts could also be venues for investing surpluses in the value of children so that, when they married, greater marriage payments could be received (Hayden 1995:44–5,54–5,59; Perodie 2001:198–9).

Funerals served as the main occasion for elite successors to take over the role of the deceased and to (re)establish political support. Partly for this reason, Harkin (2007:227) refers to feasts as the basis of chiefly power. Support at funerals could be in terms of simple reciprocity with equal return of support gifts, as among the Coast Salish (Barnett 1955:217,255) or perhaps more frequently with expected returns that demonstrated appreciation by increases of anywhere from 20 to 100 percent over the original gift (Codere 1950:78; Barnett 1955:258; Birket-Smith 1967:14–5,20,30,51,53,65,79; Ford 1968:18,55,110,170; Oberg 1973:118–9; Perodie 2001:199–200; A. Mills 2005:116). Succession to chiefly positions could be competitive and contentious, with quarrels often breaking out even at funerals. Conflicts at feasts focused on hereditary jealousies, as expressed in terms of accusations concerning unpaid debts, poaching on house territories, illicit sex, and sorcery (Ford 1968:71; De Laguna 1972:615; Bishop 1987:77). In spite of such disruptions, it was important for guests and hosts to demonstrate political support at these times. Numerous authors refer to the competitive aspects of the major potlatches, although it is not always clear that these were funeral events (Codere 1950; Barnett 1955:265; J. Adams 1973:33; Oberg 1973:97; Bishop 1987:77; Beynon 2000:17). Chiefs tried to outdo previous hosts in food, gifts, and property destruction in order to advance the interests of themselves and the elites of their clans. Thus, funerals were typically the most lavish displays in the Northwest and the quintessential pot-latches. They combined both promotional features and reciprocal gift exchanges among the invited elites. Where the aim was to create bonds of alliance rather than establish superiority, hosts were careful to tailor gifts to the estimated ability of the recipient to repay the gift, but it was unacceptable to refuse to accept a gift in a feast (Barnett 1955:257; Birket-Smith 1967:17; J. Adams 1973:93).

Similarly, to mask the ostentatiousness of the displays, or perhaps not to appear offensive to guests, hosts often appeared to be self-effacing at these events, not sitting or not even eating (Ford 1968:85; J. Adams 1973:52) – a behavior that is common in horticultural transegalitarian feasts (see Chapter 6, and Clarke 2001:152; Hayden 2001a:31). According to John Adams (1973:95,96), the explicitly stated hope of hosts was to at least break even between expenses and contributions, although hosts tried to outdo each other in the total amounts consumed and given. As documented in the Gitksan area (and as was likely the case elsewhere), one impor-tant reason for this competition was that whoever contributed the most to the funeral took the title of the deceased. A title conferred the management of the resources linked to that title, especially hunting territories. Everyone who contrib-uted to the funeral costs had some claim to reside in the corporate group house that owned the title and to use those resources (J. Adams 1973:35–6,73). Funeral contributors typically were from the new title-taker, his father's lineage and other kin, from houses that wanted to be affiliated with the new title holder, from the deceased person's children and spouses in his house, and from other families whose members took new names on the occasion of the funeral feast of the host (67–70). Other authors describe the host group simply as the "clan" of the deceased (Ford 1968:194–5; A. Mills 2005:77). If an individual needed to borrow food or wealth in order to augment his own contribution to the feast, these loans would involve the payment of interest of 20 to 100 percent, as noted above, unless the lender was a close family member.

About four years after the initial funeral feast, a similar feast could be held, at which time the bones of the deceased were reburied and a memorial (totem) pole could be erected for chiefs in their honor (displaying their totem ancestry) if resources permitted. Only the wealthy elites could afford the feasting costs asso-ciated with these secondary reburials (Teit 1900:336; Krause 1956:87; J. Adams 1973:52; Ostopkoawicz 1992:33). Such feasts usually required many years (five to ten) to produce all the food and wealth required, as well as making new invest-ments and calling in old investments (McIlwraith 1948:243; Olson 1954:237; DeLaguna 1972:606; Oberg 1973:121; Perodie 2001:207). All contributions from others had to be returned at subsequent funerals, and witnesses were paid to remember debts (often with the aid of tally sticks) or, in more recent times, account books (J. Adams 1973:45,72,111; Beynon 2000:122). In all cases, the chiefs received

4.12. As in most large transegalitarian feasts, there were separate areas for specially invited guests versus the generally invited populace. At this potlatch near Victoria at the beginning of the twentieth century, the general populace is gathered outside while the elites are conducting their affairs inside (compare Figure 4.3). (Vancouver Public Library 85849)

by far the largest and best food portions and gifts while lower ranking individuals received small or nominal amounts (Ford 1968:238; J. Adams 1973:66; Beynon 2000:134,183). This is an apparently universal pattern for high-ranking individuals that will be encountered in other chapters.

Also, typical of large-scale equal return promotional feasts, there were two kinds of participants: invited guests and spectators (Beynon 2000:70). The invited guests were only people with high positions who typically could receive gifts and/ or give contributions with expected returns of equal value or with added appreciated value (up to 100 percent; Ford 1968:193; A. Mills 2005:116). The spectators typically consisted of anyone who wanted to get some part of the food being distributed, usually the lower ranking members of a community who frequently were excluded from the elite focus of the feast inside houses (Figure 4.12). In some cases, commoners had very limited participation (J. Adams 1973:38). As is generally also true in horticultural societies, younger members of the host group prepared and served the food for the event (Ford 1968:193). Many members of corporate houses were commoner workers who were nominally "adopted" into the kinship group to maintain a fiction of kinship unity. They consisted of 8–13 percent of the corporate membership that Adams recorded (see also Ruyle 1973:615), and they would frequently move from house to house seeking the best work arrangements, although this was also true to some degree of elites seeking to improve their rights and benefits (J. Adams 1973:30,35–6,47, 97,101).

Funeral feasts were often conducted in buildings especially constructed for large feasting events, one early example being a structure 40 feet square with carved posts holding 200 guests (Bishop 1987:77; Beynon 2000), although it appears that feasts could be held in the main corporate houses as well. Such ceremonial houses, and even corporate houses that served as a group's ritual and feasting center, had to be properly fêted with an inaugural feast in order to be recognized as valid by the community (DeLaguna 1972:609) – yet another feature in common with many horticultural transegalitarian societies. Serving high-quality foods was a central feature in Northwest Coast reciprocal feasts that were meant to honor and impress guests. Prized foods included seal meat, long cinquefoil and clover roots, fish oil, bear grease, berry cakes, and dried meat (Boas 1921:1337; Drucker 1951:253; Ford 1968:51–2; Bishop 1987). Curiously, ethnographers rarely describe in any detail the elaborately carved serving dishes used at feasts. They are often simply referred to as "grease bowls," although the collections in museums of feasting vessels leave no doubt as to their high artistic and prestige value (Figure 4.5). Coordinated dances, singing, dramatic ritual performances using masks and robes, and painted faces were also major parts of these feasts.

Thus, depending on the specific community, funeral feasts could be primarily events to establish close ties with other social groups (usually clans in the same or other villages) by requiring a reciprocal return of gifts at subsequent funerals of guest groups (with no or nominal interest expected). This kind of rotation of feast hosts was probably particularly important in creating alliances for defense, as seems to have been the case among the Koniag, where a wealthy chief in each village would host an intercommunity feast each year, and the feast would rotate from village to village on a yearly basis (R. Jordan 1994:151–3). We will see this same pattern in the dynamics of consolidating Polynesian chiefdoms later in Chapter 7. Alternatively, especially under European contact economic conditions, funerals could be events of more aggressive displays in which gifts were distributed in the context of more ambitious agendas and return payments were expected to increase in value. This brings us to Perodie's third type of feast, those with greater returns expected.

COMPETITIVE FEASTS

The blatantly competitive feasts for which the Northwest Coast has achieved such renown were the most extreme form of feasting in the Northwest. They could develop out of many contexts: marriages, maturation celebrations, secret society initiations, insult reparations, rivalries, or intercommunity meetings. Preparations typically required five to ten or more years and involved enormous quantities of food and wealth: jewelry, canoes, boxes, masks, clothes, furniture, thousands of blankets. All gifts were expected to be returned in the next feasting cycle with double the amount initially given. The Kwakiutl exceeded all other groups in destroying large amounts of wealth at their rivalry feasts. They burned blankets, fish oil, and canoes, and sometimes killed slaves. The aim was to make rivals admit that they could not match or return the hosts' gifts and displays – essentially an admission of bankruptcy and inability to borrow enough resources or marshal enough labor to respond. Hundreds or thousands of people attended (Perodie 2001). In contrast to simple foragers, hosts were far from self-effacing, as the opening quote in this chapter demonstrates.

SECRET SOCIETY FEASTS

Finally, although all the feasts just described are intelligible in terms of relationships between elite administrators of corporate kinship groups and how they decided to use corporate or individual surpluses to maintain their positions of privilege, there was another complex of feasts that revolved around a very different social institution that merits particular attention: the secret societies or "dance societies." J. Adams (1973:119) suggests that there were inherent limits to the power that ambitious individuals could acquire within the structure of kinship-based corporate houses. Therefore, to increase power and wealth, it was necessary for those with ambitions to go outside the corporate house framework and develop other frameworks that were more wide reaching. I suggest that secret societies were established precisely to achieve these goals.

Secret societies were normally voluntary associations (at least for the higher positions) that were internally ranked, with initiations into successive ranks involving increasing costs and feast-giving (Johansen 2004). Secret societies typically claimed to possess powerful, secret, supernatural knowledge and rituals (their "secrets") that could benefit their communities but also could potentially threaten adversaries or noncompliant community members. Full knowledge of the society's esoterica was restricted to the highest ranking members of the secret societies who were normally from wealthy elite families. Thus, together with relationships to powerful ancestors and training as shamans, elites had claims of special access to supernatural powers (Ruyle 1973:617). In some regions on the Northwest Coast, each secret society in a community had its own special building for its rituals (Drucker 1941:201,220), although it seems that members could also give performances to show off their powers in public at funerals, intergroup potlatches, or other events (compare Beynon 2000:71–9; Drucker 1941:203,220). Elsewhere in the world, secret society public feasts might host hundreds or even thousands of people (see Chapter 6).

The *hamatsa* (cannibal) society of the Northwest Coast was probably the most famous example of a secret society. In their ideology, wild cannibal spirits threatened to possess community members and wreak havoc in the communities. Only the *hamatsa* initiates had the knowledge and power to control possessed people. This was demonstrated at every initiation (and at succeeding ceremonies), when the initiate became possessed and then was taught to bring his cannibal spirit under control. As payment for his initiation and for the return of initiates to normal states, the family of the initiate had to give a series of feasts to the higher ranking "shamans" of the society. These could be considered solicitation feasts pertaining to an exchange of knowledge for food and wealth. However, the actual initiation feast of a sponsor's child appears to have been the greatest potlatch of the sponsor's lifetime (Drucker 1941:208,212–4). The climax event was open to noninitiates as well as initiates, probably to advertise the newly acquired status and power of the new initiates. Thus, these lavish feasts appear to have been promotional in nature, although they conceivably could become competitive if major rivals were sponsoring their respective children. But they certainly seem to have advertised the wealth, success, and dramatic "supernatural" displays of the secret society members (which could then be attributed to their secret knowledge).

It is not clear from the accounts, however, whether the important gifts given at these major events required repayment, and, if so, whether it was generally at par or with interest. Secret societies undoubtedly requisitioned large amounts of food, wealth, and labor from members and their families and possibly others. The large initiation feasts open to larger segments of the community were undoubtedly a type of pay back for the substantial contributions that were exacted over the years. However, there were also series of feasts that appear to have been sponsored and organized by the society administrators (probably using society resources) exclusively for the membership of the secret society (Drucker 1941:220). These appear to have been essentially solidarity feasts for society members. From a feasting perspective, secret societies sponsored somewhat similar events to those of residential corporate groups with solidarity, promotional, and solicitation feasts to enter the society (but perhaps lacking true equal return or greater return feasts, an issue that needs clarification). However, in contrast to corporate houses, secret societies do not seem to have owned any food-producing resources, only supernatural knowledge, rituals, and paraphernalia. It is worth emphasizing that young children of wealthy elite families were often initiated into secret societies (Figure 4.13), as they were in the Medewiwin (Grand Medicine) secret society around the Great Lakes where four- to eight-year-olds could be initiated (Hoffman 1896:125,136–7).

This completes the overview of Northwest Coast feasting. Ruyle (1973:617) concluded that the basis of elite control in Northwest Coast societies was economic,

4.13. Young children of high-ranking individuals were often initiated into secret societies and fêted with some of the most lavish feasts to celebrate the event. Here, a proud Chilkat chief poses with his wealth and his young son, who wears a cedar bark ring that displays his status as an initiate of the *Hamatsa* secret society. Membership in this society was a key step in attaining power in the community and region. (Alaska State Library, Collection, Winter and Pond Collection P87–0010)

political, and ideological. Feasts played an important role in all three of these domains. Similar, although generally less extreme forms of feasting appear to have also characterized the better endowed groups in the Northwest Interior. Documentation is not as detailed for these groups as Coastal groups (see Teit 1900, 1909; Bishop 1987; Romanoff 1992). There are, nevertheless, some photographs of temporary feasting and ceremonial structures from the Columbia Plateau at the turn of the past century; these buildings are up to about 50 meters long and were used for funerary feasts and other ritual events (Galm and Masten 1985: figure 5.24). For a comparison to the Northwest Coast groups, we now turn briefly to some of the ethnohistoric accounts from California, southwest Australia, and Japan.

California

California was affected by European colonization much earlier than was the case in the Northwest Coast, where relatively independent native societies were still thriving until the birth of North American anthropology under Franz Boas. Thus, in general, there is not as much detailed documentation of feasting among the Californian or other groups as among the Northwest Coast groups. Since Arnold (1996, 2001), Gamble (2008), and others have presented a good case for the southern California groups such as the Chumash having been organized into politically, economically, and socially stratified chiefdoms, these groups will be dealt with as chiefdoms in Chapter 7. Most of the rest of the Californian groups appear to have been more or less similar to groups in the Northwest; that is, socially and economically stratified, but lacking intervillage political hierarchies. They are therefore considered here as transegalitarian societies.

Like Northwest Coast groups, funeral or memorial feasts for the dead (mourning ceremonies) appear to have been among the most important events for most Californian groups, although they were usually collective events with individual families staging separate demonstrations and gift-giving with general support from the rest of the community and its leadership. These were apparently also displays of community strength that demonstrated the desirability of establishing alliances between communities (Blackburn 1976:230). These events involved great expense and thus were only held every one to three years. In central California, at least three different communities were involved in mourning ceremonies: the hosts (collectively led by chiefs and mourning families), a group with which they exchanged wealth, and a group that exchanged reciprocal ritual services. People from a number of other communities in the region might be present due to the attraction of wealth exchanges, sometimes up to 2,500 or 3,000 people in all. Specialist washers, singers, dancers, and shamans were paid for their services at the mourning feasts. Any gifts presented to the guests had to be returned with 100 percent interest (Blackburn 1976:230–2). As in the Northwest, it took years of preparation for large mourning feasts, and the expenses of the events economically exhausted host households for some time afterward, leaving many families destitute (Loeb 1926:292). In some instances, spectators were expected to contribute to the costs of the feasts, of which a sizeable portion went to chiefs who often seem to have used such events to increase their resources (Blackburn 1976:235).

In addition to the funeral feasts that seem to have served alliance, promotion, and investment goals all at once, special cult-oriented feasts apparently served similar functions. The White Deerskin Dance of the Hupa in northern California is perhaps the best example of this. Wealthy families would organize this eight- to ten-day feast event that was largely used to display the wealth and success of various families (Goldschmidt and Driver 1943). One of the major displays of wealth consisted of large obsidian or flint bifaces (Figures 4.14 and 4.15). The nominal purpose of the event was a type of world renewal, specifically performed to wipe out evil brought to the community from the breaking of taboos (an advantageous piece of ideology for those making taboo rules and

4.14. The Hupa White Deerskin dance, ritual, and feast. The performers in the front are displaying obsidian wealth bifaces. The display of wealth is characteristic of competitive feasting. (Kroeber 1925:plate 3)

imposing fines for them). However, Goldschmidt and Driver (1943:128) note that the dominant activities were wealth display and entertainment, rather than world renewal. The event was overtly competitive to determine which social group could put on the best display, and, as one might expect of competitive contexts, it was also characterized by constant gossiping and quarreling (123). In essence, the event enabled ambitious big men to attract supporters and form supporting social groups to defend their self-interests, especially since social justice was largely a matter of threats and shows of force (130). In this regard, Morgan (2012:720) cites McCarthy to the effect that Mono "chiefs" gained and maintained power by throwing feasts.

Vayda (1967) has also examined trade feasts among the Pomo in the north, where food was exchanged for shell beads in a rotating fashion. He explained this behavior as a means of evening out unequal regional resource distributions, much like Suttles's interpretation of the potlatch. However, Vayda also recognized that ethnographers claimed these feasts did not serve any subsistence goal, but were hosted to establish and maintain social bonds between community leaders, therefore making them a type of alliance feast. For these and other events, specialist singers and dancers were "kept on a steady salary by the chief," who in turn received a substantial portion of the contributions collected at their performances (Blackburn 1976:237).

4.15. Examples of the Hupa obsidian wealth bifaces, perhaps the only ethnographic record of the wealth role of unusually large, well-made bifaces. (Kroeber 1925: plate 2)

A final point of similarity between the Northwest and Californian complex hunter/gatherers was the involvement of secret societies in feasting activities. In addition to the *'antap* and related secret societies in southern California (discussed in Chapter 7), the Pomo and neighboring groups in the north sponsored secret societies of which the *kuksu* was the most important; it was open only to elites (about 10 percent of the community were members, including some women). Many groups had special ceremonial pithouse structures near the centers of village, although apparently not the Pomo (Loeb 1926:270,356). Boys were fêted at around

4.16. Two of the finely made stone bowls from southern California apparently used prehistorically to prepare or serve feasting foods. Similar bowls were also used by Natufian complex hunter/gatherers in the Near East. (Photograph by B. Hayden, courtesy of the Dallidio Collection, housed at the San Luis Obispo Museum)

eight to ten years old and identified for future initiation into the secret society. Initiation was by costumed individuals representing animal spirits. It is unclear whether any detailed information is available on the costs, participants, and other characteristics of the feasts associated with these societies. They may have been generally similar to Northwest coast events.

There is little information on the use of the finely made and decorated stone bowls found in a number of California areas (Figure 4.16). At least Gamble (2008:183–6,245) and Noah (2005:48) consider the stone bowls to have been used primarily in feasts although I have not seen a definitive study on this issue. Such a study would be valuable for a number of reasons, not the least of which would be for identifying their specific uses and understanding why such an excessive amount of labor went into the production of these sometimes decorated artifacts.

Eastern Woodlands

Aside from the lavish feasts of some Algonkians mentioned at the end of Chapter 3, perhaps the most well-known feasts of predominantly hunter/gatherer groups like

4.17. An outside view of a Medewiwin structure used by the Menominee Indians for secret society rituals and feasting. These structures were only temporary and were rebuilt outside normal settlements when major events required large interior spaces. (Hoffman 1896:figure 5)

the Menominee and Ojibwa (some had small gardens) were those associated with the Medewiwin ceremonies described by Hoffman (1891, 1896), Ritzenthaler (1978:755), and Spindler (1978:715). This medicine society had all the characteristics of a secret society, and their feasts were events held outside their special ritual structures (for those who assisted and who often tried to look inside), as well as inside the structures (for initiates only) (Figures 4.17 and 4.18). A similar feasting and ceremonial pattern was widely used around the Great Lakes, including among the Winnebago, Ottawa, Potawatomi, Sauk, Fox, and Kickapoo groups. Many of these groups had hereditary elites, slaves, prestige goods (including copper items prehistorically), and other diagnostic characteristics of complex hunter/gatherers. Interestingly, children were sometimes initiated as young as four to eight years old (Hoffman 1896:125,136–7) and were loaded down with beaded décor and valuable medicine bags indicative of their families' very substantial wealth.

The Arctic and Subarctic

Some areas of the Arctic also supported complex hunter/gatherer groups with big men, stored surpluses, and elaborate feasts. The area around Bering Strait was particularly prolific in terms of whaling. Meat could be easily stored in cold cache pits, and socially stratified societies flourished there. Of the reported feasting events, there were large trade fairs in some locations with as many as 2,000 people participating in feasting, dancing, athletics, and trade (Burch 1988:105–6).

4.18. The interior of a Medewiwin structure where wealth was displayed by hanging it from central lines and dances occurred up and down the aisles. (Hoffman 1896:plate VI)

However, it is unclear to what extent these events constituted special meals or were organized around special food consumption.

Messenger (invitational) feasts were more clearly organized feasting events, specifically by wealthy men from different communities in special alliance relationships (R. Spencer 1959:210–12; Burch 1988). The main goal was to increase individual and/or group prestige by displaying success and to solidify alliances. Such feasts were only held after successful summer and fall hunts. "Food was amassed in quantity, but also were clothing, skins, pokes of oil, kayaks and umiaks, sleds, dogs, and the like" (R. Spencer 1959:212).

Of particular note were the feasting events that appear to have taken place in the special men's ceremonial structures especially used by whalers (the *karigi*). In these structures, the archaeological ground could be saturated with grease (Sheehan 1985, 1989). Exactly what the nature of the feasting was in these structures is somewhat vague, but the events may have been part of whaling secret societies similar to those among the socially complex Aleuts (Fitzhugh 2003:75). Crew solidarity and hierarchical command relationships would have been especially important for whaling crews. Conversely, the feasts in *karigi* may have been similar to Algonkian meat feasts described in Chapter 3. The grease impregnated soils seem to suggest that considerable food wastage occurred in contexts of conspicuous consumption tied to hunting successes and perhaps social rank.

Japan

Continuing westward along the Pacific rim, the Ainu of Japan and a number of Siberian groups were also renowned for their complex hunting and gathering societies and for complex feasting, especially their bear feasts. The Ainu resemble Northwest Coast groups in their strong reliance on marine foods, high population densities, degrees of sedentism, use of wealth items, polygyny, domestication of dogs, cemetery burials, and relative social complexity (Watanabe 1973).

Of all their feasts, the bear feast is of exceptional interest because it may play a key role in understanding the domestication of animals (see Chapter 5). Bear feasts were ideally hosted once a year by one or more leading families within a community (especially headmen's or high ranking families) who were apparently among the wealthiest because of the requirement of feeding a voracious bear for one or two years (Watanabe 1973:75). However, some communities could not afford to host such events every year and simply attended bear feasts at neighboring communities. Several hundred people could attend these feasts from surrounding related settlements (Ohnuki-Tierney 1974:92). Thus, bear feasts provided good occasions to display success and broker marriages or other alliances after assessing family wealth and support.

The bear was captured as a cub and raised for a year or two until it was killed for the winter feast (Figure 4.19). As discussed in Chapters 1 and 3, bear meat was greatly prized by most northern hunter/gatherers due to its high fat content. In many respects, these feasts were like potlatches. The film *Iyomande*, by Neil Munro shows honored guests wearing elaborately decorated garments. They sit together and are preferentially served bear meat and *sake* with specially prepared dumplings. Spectators appear to be lower ranked community members dressed less elaborately and remaining outside the host house.

Instead of honoring a deceased person as the focus of a funeral feast, the bear takes the place of honor, as in funerals for ancestors, and, like an ancestor, is implored to send benefits to the host and participants. As in funerals, this focus of ritual activity serves to deflect or mask the role of the hosts while at the same time justifying the advantages of the wealthy (who obtained material blessings due to the rituals that they performed for the bear – again similar in this regard to ancestral feasts and the claimed power of ancestors). And, in a similar fashion to funerals elsewhere, the host played a relatively subdued role (aside from his silent visual display of wealth) and was forbidden to consume any bear meat until well after the feast was over (Shinichiro 1960:23; Ohnuki-Tierney 1974:95). Elaborate serving vessels (lacquer ware, metal bowls), as well as other prestige items (swords, fine clothes, beer or *sake*), were conspicuously displayed, used, or consumed (Munro 1970; Ohnuki-Tierney 1974:92).

4.19. The bear feast was a common element in the feasting and ritual life of many complex hunter/ gatherers in Siberia and Japan. A young bear cub was captured and raised by a family with the means to feed it for one or two years. With great fanfare and public celebrating, the bear was sacrificed for a great feast and treated like an ancestor who was implored to send survivors many benefits. This image from Siberia shows the more secretive part of the ritual within the house of the host where specially invited guests would participate in the feast. (Image courtesy American Museum of Natural History)

Although it was not mentioned in accounts of the bear feast, one could expect there to have been reciprocal obligations to hold similar feasts and invite former hosts who expected to be served as honored guests. The competitive display of wealth is clearly shown in the documentary film by Munro, as are the public appeals to sacred powers (the bear), organized singing and dancing, and secret aspects (the butchering of the bear). The host seems anxious to demonstrate his success while at the same time entering into a reciprocal network. During the feasting season, sequential bear sacrifices (following recognized rankings) in allied communities could extend over a month (Watanabe 1973:76). Thus, in addition to displaying desirable family qualities for marriage or wealth exchanges, these feasts undoubtedly cemented intervillage alliances and provided the advantage of establishing indebted relationships beyond one's kin or community.

In addition to these regional feasts, there were also feasts to consecrate newly built houses (promotional feasts) and smaller household solidarity feasts to celebrate dead ancestors or family bear-meat feasts after the main bear feast event of the village (Neil Munro 1963:55,74–5,87,169–71; Ohnuki Tierney 1974:95). Funeral feasts among the Ainu were also mentioned (Ohnuki-Tierney 1974:66) but do not seem particularly notable. Village-wide feasts were organized for the first and last fish catches of the season (Wantanabe 1973:73), apparently to promote village solidarity and perhaps to reconfirm the status of the organizing headman or specialized fisherman.

Shinichiro (1960:23) reports that "chiefs" hosted drinking events in honor of the gods for neighboring groups. It is unclear from the description whether these were to create defense or other alliances. He also records feasts held at the chief's house for all household heads to honor ancestral deities (17). This may have been similar to a village solidarity feast or to Algonkian meat feasts, but details are lacking. As an incidental note, people who worked for others and had no wealth were despised as "abominable" individuals (23).

Siberia

The Khanty of western Siberia continue a rich heritage as complex hunter/gatherers that included an earlier lucrative role in the fur trade and even the development of fortified chiefdom centers (P. Jordan 2003). Today, they are not as politically complex, but they still lead a semisedentary lifestyle that includes supplying furs for middlemen, the use of spirit figurines, and the consumption of prestige foods, drinks, and goods. They also hold bear festivals, although less information seems to be available on this aspect of their lives. As with the raising of a bear cub for a feast, domesticated animals (reindeer, sheep, goats, and horses) appear to have been raised primarily for use as sacrifices in ritual feasts at sacred sites (P. Jordan 2003:125,278). Like the Ainu, the men providing the animals for feasts were those with the largest herds and thus appear to be the more wealthy individuals. Moreover, they provided animals with the claim that such sacrifices would give them "blessings" in the form of wealth and welfare (147). One may view these offerings as a means to justify the acquisition of wealth and diffuse criticism through some sharing of it at ritual meals. Special ritual meals were consumed by both men and women when groups aggregated near sacred sites about four times a year. Aside from the meat of domesticated animals, food included alcohol and elk heads. In a photograph depicting one such event (Figure 4.20), there are fewer than twenty people, including men, women, and children (P. Jordan 2001:97). This may be more similar to a solidarity feast or alliance feast between families, perhaps not dissimilar to Algonkian meat feasts where social ranks and roles were reaffirmed. In fact, Khanty gender and age ranks were emphasized in these feasts because lineage elders directed the event and only men were allowed to participate in some aspects (P. Jordan 2003:159,200). Ancestral feasts were also held at cemeteries, reaffirming the importance of lineage positions and the important effects that ancestors had on the living and hence the need to ensure that the dead were comfortable in the

4.20. A feast held by Khanty hunter/gatherers in western Siberia at the shrine of a local spirit steward of the forest. Gender and age distinctions are strictly observed, and offerings are made at the shrine, the small elevated structure behind the participants. (Photograph courtesy of Peter Jordan)

cemetery (217,222). An interesting feature of these events is the pouring of alcohol into a hole in the ground as an offering to the dead. This is a ritual motif that continues from complex hunter/gatherers through to Classic times around the Mediterranean.

Australia

Of note in Southeast Australia was the intensified capture of migrating eels by means of artificially constructed canals and ponds, sometimes several kilometers long (Lourandos 1980:225, 1985; Williams 1988:44–54; Builth 2002, 2006). These eels are oil rich, and so it is not surprising that special efforts were taken to procure them or that they should be featured as a feasting food for the complex hunter/gatherers of the region (2002). Unfortunately, little more information is available on their feasts, but they again demonstrate how much effort people were willing to put into the procurement of feasting foods.

Patterns

It is sometimes difficult to find much information on the full range of feasting among the less well-documented complex hunter/gatherers. Yet what can be gleaned from these and the better documented groups seems relatively consistent. In summary, the more common elements are:

- Private property
- Mutual contractual obligations to return invitations and gifts
- Potentially severe consequences for defaulting
- Wide ranges of events for holding costly feasts, including critical life situations (marriages, defense, funerals)
- Opportunities to display wealth in competitive fashions – especially at funerals – often delayed for months or years (resulting in secondary burials) to maximize resources used for these purposes
- Violence at feasts and warfare from economically based competition and defaulting on debts
- Ideological requirements to offer excessively lavish funeral feasts in order to empower the dead or make them happy so that they would send more prosperity to those who honored them (or at least justify their wealth)
- The denigration of nonparticipants
- A variety of ideological transformations favoring aggrandizer strategies
- Maintenance of a general egalitarian ideology in the face of pronounced socioeconomic inequalities and competition
- High costs of major feasts involving years of preparation, borrowing, and charging of interest rates
- Intensified food production for feasts
- Wealth exchanges
- Economically based polygyny (bride prices, dowries)
- Differential power in communities based on economic production and aggrandizer strategies to use surpluses
- The formation of corporate groups based nominally on kinship that host major feasts
- The development of frameworks to extend individual power beyond corporate groups (via secret societies, exchange networks, or war alliances)

ARCHAEOLOGICAL INDICATIONS

Are there any archaeological indications of these kinds of feasts among past complex hunter/gatherers? Although there are surprisingly few good examples from the Northwest Coast, given the intense feasting activity that we know took place there ethnographically, there are nevertheless a few instances comprising special food remains in elite houses at the Ozette site and animal or shellfish remains associated with burials (Ames 1994:222). Samuels (2005:206) also observes that

4.21. An elaborately carved antler spoon that accompanied one of the burials at the Pender Island site in the Northwest Coast. Roy Carlson thinks that these were for feeding the dead. They were also likely to have also been used in potlatches for the highest ranking living guests, perhaps in competitive bouts of consuming fish oil, as recorded ethnographically. (Photograph courtesy of Roy Carlson)

only elite houses at Ozette have central hearths. Central hearths may well have been used primarily for feasts. Elaborately carved antler spoons (Figure 4.21) were also part of the funerary materials at the Pender Island site, where Carlson (2011) thinks funerary rituals included feasting before 2000 BCE and where an impressive heap of burned shellfish appears to have been associated with burials (Carlson and Hobler 1993) (Figure 4.22).

In the Northwest Interior Plateau, large roasting features (up to 8 meters in diameter; see Figure 4.23) containing abundant fire-cracked rock associated with either animal bones or root remains were most likely used to prepare food for large feasts at the unusually large Keatley Creek site (Hayden and Adams 2004; Hayden and Mossop 2004). Fretheim (2009:382) found that root roasting pits only 1 meter in diameter would contain enough food for thirty to forty people. By extrapolation, 8-meter roasting pits would have contained food for 500 or more people. Cail (2011) reported the consumption of dogs at the Bridge River site and emphasized that these were likely a luxury food of the rich used in feasts due to their desirable high fat content (yielding more calories than deer) and the high cost of raising them (one kilogram of salmon per day). In fact, she compared dog production to the intensification involved in raising pigs in New Guinea. Wilson and Carlson (1980:39) and Blake (1974:36) have also documented unusual species (bear, elk, beaver, horse) in unusually dense concentrations of faunal remains in certain housepits that seem to represent the ethnographically described "potlatches" for this area.

4.22. At the Pender Island site, there was also striking evidence of feasting in the form of a thick mound of burned shell shown here to the right of the bottom three rungs of the ladder, apparently all deposited and burned in a single event. (Photograph courtesy of Rob Gargett)

In California, Hildebrandt and Rosenthal (2009) have shown that, beginning over 2,500 years ago, marine shellfish were transported more than 25 kilometers inland, probably reflecting feasting activities in interior areas. The unusually large and well-made stone bifaces such as those displayed as wealth items as part of the Hupa feasts may also provide archaeological indications of feasting contexts (Goldschmidt and Driver 1943). As already mentioned in the ethnographic section, the large stone bowls found in many parts of California were apparently used by the elites for feasting.

In the south of California, Maxwell (2003) and Fagan et al. (2006) have identified several feasting deposits on San Nicolas Island that are similar to other deposits in the region that were identified as feasting remains associated with mourning rituals or secret society (*'antap*) rituals. These deposits included hundreds of large abalone shells and thousands of animal bones. Hull et al. (2013:26–7,42–3) have expanded the number of identified mourning sites in Southern California but concentrated on the ritual rather than the feasting aspects at these sites. As is common, they attribute

4.23. Large roasting pits capable of roasting 2,800–3,300 liters of roots, occur at the unusually large winter pithouse site at Keatley Creek in the Interior of British Columbia and are spatially associated with ritual structures. This circular roasting pit (to the right of the pine tree) is almost 10 meters in diameter. They represent some of the best evidence for large feasts in the region c. 1,000–2,000 years ago. (Photograph by B. Hayden)

these ceremonies to "communal rather than personal or familial needs" in order to "recount group history and thus reinforce community identity." They try to explain the presence of large stone bowls as "suitable for public performance" and the purposeful destruction of wealth items at these sites in terms of "rules for handling power" and nebulous notions of "meaning attached to fragmentation" (42–3). However, from my perspective, these features were hallmarks of competitive displays of wealth and, like the White Deerskin Dance, were meant to benefit specific families or individuals rather than a community, although this undoubtedly was an auxiliary outcome.

In addition to these observations, Noah (2005:242–83) and Arnold (2001:51–2) have identified luxury foods in deposits 8 centimeters thick of whole abalone shells in an occurrence that extended more than 11 meters. The deposits from this one feast included one large swordfish, a tuna, four seabass, two bonito, seven barracuda, twenty-two rockfish, two fur seals, two sea lions, one dolphin, various birds, and a large sea turtle. These were mostly boat-captured, harpooned species and were associated with elite Chumash households. Noah interprets this deposit as representing a harvest and mourning feast. It certainly appears to have been some form of competitive display feast.

Elsewhere in North America, there are scattered indications of feasts in the archaeological record, particularly during the Middle and Late Archaic period characterized in many areas by complex hunter/gatherer societies. R. Saunders (2004), Russo (2004, 2008; Russo and Heide 2001), Marrinan (2010), Schwadron (2010), Sassaman (2010), and D. Anderson (2010) have all argued that the impressive ring-shaped shell middens (some more than 100 meters in diameter), near or off the southeastern coast of the United States, were formed from feasting activities of seasonally aggregated macrobands, with intrasite variations that reflect socioeconomic inequalities (Figure 4.24). Thompson and Andrus (2011:337) have provided important support for these views by demonstrating the occurrence of short-term large-scale processing of shellfish at these sites.

In the lower reaches of the Mississippi River Valley and other southern rivers, some Middle and Late Archaic communities also began constructing earthen mounds that have been suggested as similar aggregation and feasting sites (J. Saunders et al. 2005; J. Saunders 2010), the earliest being at Monte Sano (c. 5000 BCE). However, the most extraordinary Archaic mound site is Poverty Point (Figure 4.25). Jackson (1991) maintains that the impressive mound complex at Poverty Point (the second largest known in North America from any time period) was an aggregation and feasting site of complex hunter/gatherer societies (see Kidder et al. 2008). In addition to the exceptional mounds at Poverty Point, mounds also begin to appear in the Late Archaic in the Ohio and adjacent river valleys (Heyman et al. 2005, Claassen 2010) that are probably related to feasting for local or regional aggregations.

There is widespread evidence of increasing cultural complexity in the Middle and Late Archaic of many regions, including specialist production of stone beads and bone pins, exchange in exotic prestige items and regional inter-action spheres, mound construction, increasing violence, and large cemeteries. Many of these manifestations occur in rich ecosystems such as riverine, coastal, or wetland environments. One recurring element is evidence of feasting and prestige items associated with mortuary complexes (Jefferies 1997, 2004; Brooks 2004; Nicholas 2007; Robinson 2008; Taché 2008). This also occurs in the Late Archaic Northeastern American cultures, where the earliest pottery appears to have been used to produce labor-intensive fish oils for special events like feasts (Taché and Craig, n.d.).

More grisly evidence of unusual meals in the Archaic comes from the Mesoamerican site of Coxcatlán Cave, where remains of two beheaded children

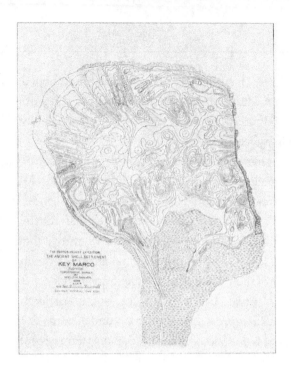

HOUSE'S HAMMOCK

DISMAL KEY
SE RING

WEST PASS

TURNER RIVER

KEY MARCO

SANDFLY KEY

RUSSELL KEY

DISMAL KEY

FAKAHATCHEE KEY

N

METERS

0   200   400   600

4.24. Impressive constructions of shells characterize some late hunter/gatherers in the Southeastern United States. A number of researchers, such as Margo Schwadron, argue that the impressive accumulations like those illustrated (note the scale) were largely the result of seasonal occupations of sites where feasting was held. Only the outline forms of these shell mounds are shown in this figure. (Schwadron 2010; Courtesy the American Museum of Natural History). The upper figure is a detailed map of Key Marco.

4.25. An aerial view of the ridge mounds and outlying circular mounds at Poverty Point, the most remarkable hunter/gatherer site in North America (comparable in scale with the efforts expended by hunter/gatherers at Göbekli Tepe in Turkey, described in Chapter 6). It is generally assumed that extensive feasting took place at this Archaic site. (Photograph courtesy of the USDA Agricultural Stabilization and Conservation Service; Aerial Photo CTK-2BB-125, taken November 11, 1960)

were found, one of whose skulls was charred and scraped (Drennan 1983). Based on later evidence of anthropophagy at cave or remote sites in the region and elsewhere in the world (discussed in Chapter 6), one can wonder if this could have been part of a secret society ritual feast.

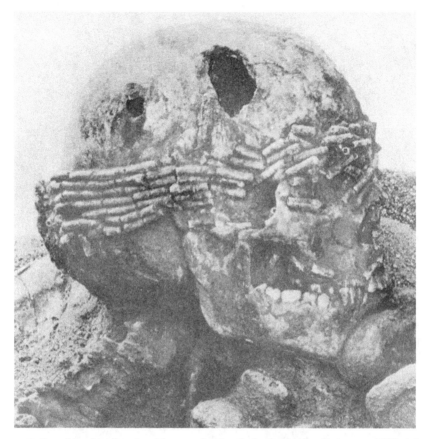

4.26. One of the dentalium headdresses adorning the body of a Natufian man at El Wad, in the Levant. As on the Northwest Coast of North America, Natufians appear to have considered dentalia shells as wealth, and the personal use of hundreds of these shells for decoration of a single individual indicates substantial wealth accumulation and inequalities in Natufian societies. (Garrod and Bate 1930)

Archaeological occurrences of the *karigi* feasting and ritual structures has already been mentioned (see Sheehan 1985).

I have summarized much of the archaeological evidence for feasting in the Epipaleolithic of the Fertile Crescent (Hayden 2004, 2011b; Hayden et al. 2012). This includes large hearths, hearths or special features with abundant animal remains, prestige serving and preparation vessels, special locations (especially burial caves or proximity to ritual structures), prestige items, "rich" burials that indicate socioeconomic inequalities (Figure 4.26), secondary burials (indicative of delayed final burials in order to amass as many resources as possible for competitive funeral feasts), storage facilities (Figure 4.27), and abundant natural resources in site catchment areas. There are enough indicators of feasting in this region that it has been possible for me to offer a reconstruction of a full range of basic Epipaleolithic feasting types and connect these with sociopolitical groups (Hayden 2011b). Corporately supported feasts appear to predominate in the archaeological

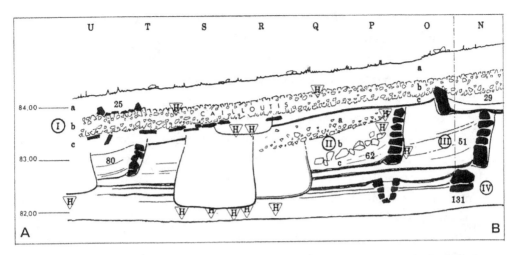

4.27. Storage facilities not only indicate recurring surpluses but also indicate private control over food products (and perhaps resource locations). Thus, the occurrence of Natufian storage pits like these at the Ain Mallaha site in the Levant contribute to the overall assessment of feasting conditions in the Natufian and other cultures. (Perrot and Ladiray 1988: figure 4; Archives du Centre de Recherche Français à Jerusalem)

record of this area and period, complemented by secret society feasts and possible village-level solidarity feasts or intervillage alliance feasts.

In Europe, there are a few rare indications of possible feasting behaviors in the Middle Paleolithic, such as the bear bones associated with the Neandertal burial at Régourdou (Hayden 2003a:108–15). Much more convincing evidence occurs in the Upper Paleolithic, where there is evidence for storage, seasonal or longer term sedentism, large hearths, unusually dense bone accumulations (especially in caves such as Enlène, La Garma, or El Juyo), carved spoons in bone or ivory, prestige goods, intentional breakage of prestige items, notations similar to records of potlatch debts, and possibly even human sacrifices (Conkey 1980; Bégouën and Clottes 1981; Beaune 1995:125,152,212; Oliva 2000; Soffer 2000:67–8; Formicola 2007; Hayden 2008:105–6; Hayden and Villeneuve 2011a:332). Perlès (1996:39) has noted that the areas where art flourished were also areas where highly organized and planned mass hunting occurred, which must have entailed surplus production and storage. It is also interesting that animals portrayed in most art were not the ones usually eaten but rather were animals that seem to have been depicted for special qualities, either gustatory (feasting) or symbolic (such as power animals associated with secret societies or shamanism). These observations lend themselves to interpretations of some form of aggregation (alliance) types of feasts in the case of the Pavlovian sites, Altamira, and El Juyo (Conkey 1980) and secret society types of feasts. Caves like Enlène and La Garma lend themselves to secret society interpretations due to the restricted access and accommodation of small groups of people, as well as by the presence of children (footprints and handprints), whose attendance is difficult to explain without some sort of initiation scenario (although obviously for a relatively exclusive set of children) (Owens and Hayden 1997). However, much more archaeological evidence needs to be analyzed from the feasting perspective in order to develop a more complete picture of Upper Paleolithic feasting.

Indications for feasts continue in the European Mesolithic with roasting pits that appear to occur at aggregation sites, presumably where alliances between groups were maintained (Fretheim 2009). Remains of funeral feasts were associated with status burials at Téviec and Hoëdic (Schulting 1996:338), and competitive feasts involving exotic prestige goods appear to have played important roles in establishing ranking within other communities (Zvelebil 2006:185). There are feasting remains, too, in cave contexts (Miracle 2002:82), possibly representing feasts of special sodalities like ritual groups. Something similar to the Ainu bear feast may also be represented by the Mesolithic remains of a bear that was apparently held in captivity for some time (Chaix et al. 1997), while Lewthwaite (1986) has argued that the first domestic animals adopted by Mesolithic groups were used for feasting.

In Japan, there are abundant indications of feasting in much of the Jomon period. The first appearance of plain pottery may, by itself, be an important indicator of the preparation of special foods for feasting, such as fish oils or nut oils (Hayden 2009b). As in the American Northeast, the recent recovery of aquatic animal or fish lipids from early Jomon pottery (Craig et al. 2013) would seem to support the suggestion that pottery in the region was initially developed for producing highly valued fish oils that were ethnographically used in feasts. The subsequent development of remarkably elaborate pottery (Figure 4.28), including spouted and pedestaled forms (some interpreted as used for serving alcoholic beverages), together with the increased sedentism and high population densities, the impressive storage facilities (Sakaguchi 2009), the lacquer ware serving cups, the exotic luxury foods, the large-scale mounds and monumental post architecture, the large centralized buildings with stone-lined hearths, and the considerable array of prestige items, all indicate a very complex society that indulged in a great deal of feasting that undoubtedly was expressed in many forms, although the details have yet to be established (Aikens and Higuchi 1982; Hayden 1990; Habu 2004).

Finally, Sadr (2005) has argued that groups of complex hunter/gatherers in South Africa used introduced sheep and pottery for feasting, much in the same fashion that Lewthwaite (1986) has argued for the same situation in late Mesolithic Europe. Jerardino (2011) also argues for a number of South African sites like Steinbok Fountain/Steenbokfontin Cave as having served as regional feasting sites for a number of hunter/gatherer groups about 2000–3000 BP.

Thus, all in all, there is abundant archaeological evidence for the occurrence of feasting among complex hunter/gatherers beginning in the Upper Paleolithic

4.28. The elaborate decoration on these "flame"-style Jomon pottery vessels indicate that they were used for preparing or serving some kind of special food or drink for special occasions. (Photograph by Tadahiro Ogawa, courtesy of the Tokamichi City Museum)

of Europe but becoming much more widespread during the Epipaleolithic/ Mesolithic/Archaic periods in Europe, the Near East, North America, Japan, South Africa, and undoubtedly other areas of the world as well. The archaeological evidence appears to reflect the patterns documented in the ethnographic record, although there may be some regional variations. Very few archaeologists who deal with any kind of hunting and gathering societies venture beyond basic descriptions of the material feasting remains other than obvious associations such as likely aggregation locations, ritual sites, or burials (Rosenberg and Redding [2000] and Taché [2008] provide the best interpretive analyses). Nevertheless, funerals emerge as very common venues for large display feasts indicative of potlatching types of events. Prestige ornaments and serving vessels appear in funerary or other contexts, whether domestic or ritual, indicating that feasting was not confined to specialized ritual locations, but was part of many households' activities, probably in the context of celebrating marriages, births, maturations, house embellishments, and funerals. Secret societies may provide yet another venue for the displays of wealth at feasts and status/power acquisition. There are important indications of feasting by ritual sodalities like secret societies (in caves and sometimes involving cannibalism or human sacrifices).

A range of new food-related technologies appear about the same time as feasting and are probably related to feasting, but all require more research. These include the first pottery, grinding stones, mortars, and probably brewing paraphernalia (Hayden 2004, 2009b; Hayden et al. 2012). Other prestige technologies also develop in tandem involving costly clothes and costumes, bone and shell jewelry, pocket-sized sculptures, mural art, and masterpieces of flintknapping. Together with these, there sometimes appear material signatures of competitive events involving the destruction of prestige items. Although archaeological details are often scant, it can probably be assumed that there were many smaller sized, household or lineage feasts held to promote solidarity in smaller social groups and that some larger feasts were hosted to create or maintain intergroup alliances. Major research programs await the study of the role of prestige items and storage as manifestations of feasting. At least a few researchers have suggested that large storage facilities were probably related to sponsoring feasts (e.g., Wilcox et al. 1981; Bahuchet and Thomas 1985:27; Seymour 1994; Twiss 2008). Much more documentation is required on the occurrence of faunal remains and on the contexts of special serving and food preparation vessels, as well as for the functions of early forms of "communal" or "ritual" structures. The apparent relationship of secondary burials to delayed and lavish funeral feasts should also be investigated more thoroughly.

That feasting emerges so strongly in the context of complex hunter/gatherers and is associated with intensified food production is highly significant and has some important implications for the domestication of plants and animals, a topic to which we turn in Chapter 5.

5

Domesticating Plants and Animals for Feasts

> For me, nothing is more basic than political-economic aspects of
> societies, and models that neglect them are as fatally flawed as
> would be models of climate that left out precipitation.
>
> – Cowgill (1998:122)

At the turn of the past century, the geographer Eduard Hahn (1896, 1909) suggested
that the motive for capturing and maintaining wild aurochs was to have a supply
available for sacrificial purposes. This suggestion seems to have been largely
ignored by archaeologists until Lewthwaite (1986) suggested that European
Mesolithic groups adopted domestic animals for feasting purposes (also see
E. Isaac 1962 for geography).

When I was teaching in 1988, however, I was unaware of these ideas. I came
to them via a different route. In a class on Mesoamerican archaeology, on a
pedagogical whim, I asked if anyone knew what the first domesticate in that
region was (see Figure 5.1). When students ran out of suggestions after naming
maize, beans, tomatoes, and squash, I smugly replied that according to the
information at that time, chili peppers, gourds, and avocados were the first
domesticates. Then I rhetorically asked what that implied for the then dominant
population pressure or other "pressure" explanations of domestication. None of
those foods seemed to be logical choices for domestication if one were running
out of food. At the time, I did not have an answer to my own question. It had
always been just one of those curious aspects of Mesoamerican archaeology.
However, having voiced the question stirred further thoughts. In my ethnoarchaeological research in Mesoamerica, I had recorded that chili peppers were
used almost exclusively for feasts in traditional Maya communities where I had
worked; however, I had not previously made any connection between this
observation and the first domesticates or the reasons for domestication. Other
thoughts followed in rapid succession. I had also recorded that large and

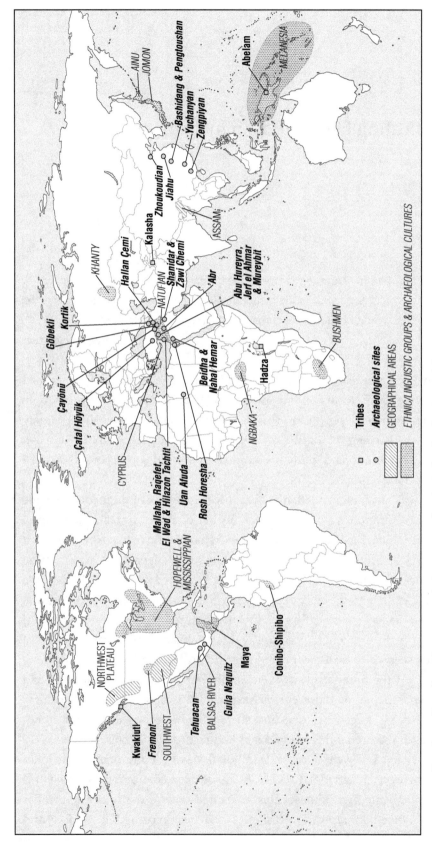

5.1. Locations of key sites, culture areas, ethnic groups, and regions related to feasting and domestication.

5.2. Unusually large gourds were used for important Highland Maya feasts such as the Fiesta de San Juan (at the summer solstice) in Chanal shown here. The gourds are held by specially woven supports and were used to serve *atole* (a special maize drink) to the most important participants. The desire to grow unusually large gourds for such events plausibly explains why gourds were one of the first plants domesticated. (Photograph by B. Hayden)

elaborate gourds (Figure 5.2) were used in Maya villages as special feasting containers for *atole*, the Maya ceremonial maize drink. And, of course, avocados still continue to be used as feasting foods all over Mesoamerica.

It was that class and my spontaneous question about the first domesticates that initially established the link for me involving feasting as a critical element in understanding cultural changes like domestication. In the following months, the more I considered the possible role of feasting as the main reason for domestication, the more the limited ethnographic and archaeological data seemed to fall into place. However, consulting the literature then available, I realized that feasting was a topic almost wholly ignored by archaeologists, and most ethnographers had not really tried to understand the internal dynamics of traditional feasting in terms that were useful to archaeologists or, for that matter, for understanding the potential role of feasts in domestication. Therefore, I decided to undertake my own program of ethnoarchaeological research on traditional feasting to better understand the conditions, motivations, benefits, dynamics, and material consequences of traditional feasts, including their effects on food production. The outcome of this research has never failed to stimulate and excite me. It has had ramifications far beyond anything that I could have initially imagined, as can be appreciated from the other chapters in this book.

Since that beginning, I have explored in much greater depth the possibility that feasting was the motivation behind the initial domestication of animals and plants. Although some of the details concerning which plants were first domesticated have changed with new discoveries, I have become more convinced over time that this basic scenario provides the best explanation for domestication, despite the staunch skepticism of other researchers (Keeley 1995; B. Smith 2001a; Zeder 2001; Cohen 2009; Piperno 2011). Because the issue of whether feasting was a major factor behind initial domestication is so pivotal, I devote this chapter to some of the more important points, although many additional details can be found in previous work (see Hayden 1990, 2004, 2009c, 2011b, 2011c, Hayden et al. 2012). The topic is complex, and there are many contending theories about why domestication took place. Thus, I begin this discussion by defining some key terms and mentioning some of the most popular explanations. We will then be in a position to examine a sampling of the ethnographic data related to feasting, and then some of the archaeological implications and observations.

DEFINITIONS

Cultivation and Domestication

Tabarev (2007:55) provides a clear distinction between domestication and cultivation that I adapt for present purposes: "*Domestication* is a biological process causing genetic changes and resulting in the emergence of new species of plants and animals which can exist and reproduce only under man's permanent control. The new species have all the qualities that are incipient in wild species and that have been selected for and augmented by man. *Cultivation* is a technological process."

Beyond this, definitions vary, with David Harris (1989) restricting cultivation to systematic tillage and land clearance and Peacock (1998:36–9; 2002) and R. Ford (1985) including a wider range of plant management techniques, specifically including digging and replanting, tending, tilling and weeding, sowing and transplanting, pruning, coppicing, and burning. Many of these Harris would consider as wild plant food production techniques. In most definitions, cultivation does not imply that the species being managed were necessarily domesticated.

Tabarev's distinction between biological and technological processes is useful; however, I suspect that most paleoethnobotanists would not go so far as to insist that initial domesticates were separate (non-interbreeding) species that could not reproduce without human assistance. Many domesticated plant species can reseed themselves and continue to reproduce. How effective they would be at competing with wild species is open to speculation. It is generally assumed that, eventually, it would be difficult to maintain some of the traits selected for by humans (large seeds, tough rachises, free-threshing); however, without experiments, this is difficult to determine. Certainly, after a prolonged period of selection and domestication, some plants like maize have been altered genetically to the point that they cannot reproduce without human assistance; however, it is doubtful that initial domesticates were this extreme.

Intensification. Cultivation and domestication can be viewed as two among a number of strategies that were used to intensify food yields. Most of the techniques used by hunter/gatherers initially appeared in the Epipaleolithic, Mesolithic, or Archaic periods. These included the firing of landscapes, coppicing nut and fruit trees, constructing weirs or "clam gardens" and drive lines, developing techniques and tools for the mass harvesting and processing of plant foods, cultivating wild plants, and using traps or nets to obtain a broad spectrum of animals. As one manifestation of intensification, it has generally been assumed that the origins of domestication were intimately related to the causes of intensification and that, if it were possible to understand why intensification occurred, we might be able to understand why domestication occurred. Thus, considerable attention has been focused on conceptualizing and analyzing intensification. The concept of intensification plays an important role in a number of theoretical discussions on domestication. However, it tends to elude clear definitions despite many attempts to define it, and efforts thus far have not provided many new insights into the origins of domestication. Morrison (1996:587) presents one of the more operational definitions in my opinion, and one that accords well with intuitive, commonsense notions of intensification: "In agricultural production, intensification proper, the process by which the yield per unit of land and/or labor of an existing resource base is increased (Tringham and Krstic 1990 [in Morrison 1996]), may take the form of increased investments in practices such as plowing, seed bed preparation, weeding, transplanting, manuring, or the construction of soil and water control facilities." Others, like Feil (1987:39), simply consider intensification as increased inputs to land in terms of capital, labor, or skills. However, increases in productivity may, but do not necessarily, involve increased labor costs (Lourandos 1985:389).

Intensification of resource use is generally thought to characterize complex hunter/gatherers and many horticultural or agricultural societies but is rarely mentioned, if at all, for simple hunter/gatherers. It is generally argued that, on their own, families will produce far less food than they are capable of (chronic underproduction) and thus they do not produce any significant surpluses unless induced to do so (Sahlins 1972:41,51; Stannish 1994:314). People may be induced to intensify production by increased population growth (Cohen 1977; Rosenberg 1998) or concentrations of population (as in urban areas), by need for trade (Jochim 2002), or by sociopolitical competition (H. Leach 1999) including the pursuit of wealth or other benefits (Testart 1982:528).

The anthropological and archaeological study of food procurement and use by hunter/gatherers has largely been modeled on animal ecological and behavioral ecological work over the past fifty years, as exemplified by optimal foraging theory. In these domains, the idea that social and political competition could create enough pressure to intensify economic production is one that rarely occurs (although see Zahavi and Zahavi 1997; Netting 1977:33–4). Nevertheless, there are enough observations in the ethnographic record to indicate that sociopolitical factors are often enormously important in creating resource intensification and may be the predominant precondition for intensification in general, whether among complex hunter/gatherers, pastoralists, or cultivators. For instance, Blackburn (1976:242) points out that, among Californian complex hunter/gatherers, "social factors involving the demands of an annual ritual cycle as well as reciprocal obligations of a social, economic, or political nature became the primary motivations for social action ... a socially catalytic necessity, stimulating the production, exchange, and consumption of economic goods." Ruyle (1973) and Perodie (2001) make much the same point for potlatching among the Northwest Coast hunter/gatherers. In the Northwest Interior, the high feasting value of chinook salmon and deer meat plausibly led to the construction of deer fences kilometers long and fishing platforms extending out over the rivers (Figure 4.9; Teit 1900:246,250; Alexander 1992:139–43). In Australia, where relatively complex hunter/gatherers developed in the southeastern and north central regions, Lourandos (1988:157) has documented resource intensification involving extensive canal systems and the production of surpluses (including wild yams, cereals, cycads, and eels) connected to social and ritual events. Similarly, Satterthwait (1987:627–8,619–20) noted that the labor intensive technique of net hunting in Australia was used only for feasts and that, in this context, intensification was socially and politically driven. In addition to these hunter/gatherer examples, African groups with extremely rudimentary cultivation, such as the Ngbaka, procure and store surplus meat not for subsistence needs but for feasts, and it is the need for surpluses for competitive displays in funeral, marriage, and alliance feasts that resulted in intensified hunting techniques (Bahuchet and Thomas 1985:27–8).

Among horticultural groups that raise animals, a strong link has been established between competitive feasting and the need for animals on the one hand (especially for marriage payments and feasts) and agricultural intensification to feed animals on the other hand. Hakansson (1994, 1995) has documented this for east Africa, and Feil (1987:40,55,59,265), Modjeska (1982), Blanton and Taylor (1995), M. Young (1971:257, 264), and Lemonnier (1990:68,140) have documented it for Melanesia, while Halstead (1990:154) similarly documented it in Greece. Netting (1977:33–4) argues that feasting and gifts were generally the stimulus for producing more than subsistence needs and that these systems were inherently expansionist and inflationary (an extremely critical point also made by Feil [1987:265], M. Young [1971:257], and Brookfield [1972], among many others). A similar view concerning production above household subsistence needs was earlier propounded by Herskovits (1940:461–7) in terms of a prestige economy. This concept was reworked by Sahlins (1972:101–7) in terms of a domestic versus political economy that was fundamentally driven by aggrandizers seeking power and wealth. On the face of it, it would seem that given the strong inflationary pressures created by competitive feasts, the only way for hunter/gatherers to respond to such pressures would be to adopt food production wherever possible, even if it resulted in more work and less efficient returns. Similarly, Firth (1959:480), Brookfield (1972, 1984), Spriggs (1990:178–9), Earle (1978:173; Kirch (1990, 1994), Junker (2001:297–8), and others have argued that agricultural intensification in the Pacific is almost entirely due to the demands of the sociopolitical system and feasting. Other horticultural groups in Southeast Asia and Melanesia push produc-tion to the maximum possible almost entirely for sociopolitical reasons rather than subsistence reasons (Izikowitz 1951:341,354; Modjeska 1982; Sherman 1990:304).

Archaeologically, the close link between intensifying social competition resulting in the creation of material sociopolitical monuments and the intensified production of resources (indicated by new technologies or storage abilities) is sometimes remarked upon (Lightfoot and Feinman 1982:66; Midgley 1992:481–2; Stannish 1994; Boyd 1996:209; Cowgill 1996); however, this has not been a major focus of attention. One important relationship that Grier (2010) has highlighted is the plausible impact that investments in resource intensification should have on justifying claims of ownership (see also Hayden 1994a).

EXPLAINING DOMESTICATION

There is a vast literature addressing the problem of why people began to cultivate and domesticate plants and animals covering at least ten or more independent locations in the world, all within a few thousand years of each other. After living as hunters and gatherers for over two million years, this is a remarkable conver-gence. Space does not permit even a cursory review of this literature. However, it is possible to focus briefly on several of the most popular explanations generally adopted by archaeologists, such as population pressure, climate change, and cog-nitive changes.

Population Pressure

Probably the most commonly encountered explanation for why people first domes-ticated plants and animals is population pressure in one form or another. Population pressure is also commonly invoked to explain a wide range of other cultural changes, from increasing cultural complexity to increasing violence. This is essentially a "push" explanation in which necessity is the mother of invention. This assumes that cultivation and domestication both entail more effort than the simple collection of wild plants or hunting animals. Although questioned by some, this premise seems to be borne out by Woodburn (1966) who, after discussing in his documentary film, *The Hadza*, how unpalatable most wild plant foods are, states, "The Hadza envy their neighbors for the good taste of their cultivated plants, but all the same do not consider it worth all the effort to produce them." Similarly, the Bushmen told Richard Lee, "Why should I farm when there are so many mongongo nuts?" (Lee and DeVore 1968). The same sentiment was expressed by Australian Aborigines: "You people go to all that trouble, working and planting seeds, but we don't have to do that. All these things are there for us. ...We don't have all this other trouble" (Berndt and Berndt 1970, in Harlan 2006). This is also a common assumption among most behavioral ecologists who rank cereal grains among the lowest plant species in caloric returns for effort invested and initially cultivated varieties lower still (K. Wright 1994:243–6; Winterhalder and Goland 1997; Barlow and Heck 2002:133–4). Paleoethnobotanists like Hillman concur that farming was hard work, with high costs creating lifetimes of toil, especially grinding grains (Hillman et al. 2001:387; also Moore et al. 2000:508; Willcox 2005, 2007). These anecdotal accounts are supported by cross-cultural analyses of simple hunter/gatherer workloads versus horticultural work loads for subsistence (Bowles 2011a,b). Thus, according to population pressure models, when populations increased through inherent growth to levels that could not be supported by wild resources, people were forced to intensify their exploitation strategies. They did this by initially exploiting a wider range of lower ranked species, and when this no longer sufficed, they began to produce food through cultivation, which eventually led to domestication (Cohen 1977, 2009).

This is an elegant and seductive theory. It is everything that a good theory should be. It is parsimonious, logical, contains easily understandable causality, it is powerful in its scope, and, at first blush, seems to accord with many archaeological observations of increasing population levels over time and increasing intensification just prior to the appearance of domesticated species. However, it has a number of fatal flaws (e.g., see Hayden 2000). Three factors are especially significant. First, the population mechanics simply do not work. Populations existed in Africa for over two million years with only a narrow bottleneck (the Isthmus of Suez) for excess population to escape. In contrast, all of North and South America were first inhabited by humans little more than 20,000 years ago – only one-hundredth of the time that Africa was inhabited. Yet, domestication occurred almost simultaneously in both the Americas and Africa. How could this be if population growth, and hence pressure, is assumed to have a natural, constant rate of growth?

The second factor is that the population pressure model leads us to expect that cultivation and domestication will occur under conditions of duress, where people are constantly coming up short of food. In contrast, as we shall see, most cases of domestication appear to have occurred in rich environments where people had enough surpluses to produce prestige items and settle in large sedentary communities with high population densities.

A third factor is that population pressure cannot account for the nature of many of the first domesticates, including dogs, gourds, chili peppers, and avocados. These cannot be viewed as being cultivated or raised to stave off starvation.

In addition to these general considerations, a number of archaeologists have failed to find evidence of population pressure involved in domestication or the agricultural intensification process or in the development of social complexity: in East Africa (Hakansson 2010:106), Polynesia (Brookfield 1972, 1984; Kirch 1975, 1990, 1991, 1994), Europe (Milisauskas and Kruk 1993; Meiklejohn et al. 1997:322; Koch 1998:179–80; Fischer 2002:367–81), the Near East (Asouti and Fuller 2013:331; see Hayden 2004:295, for additional citations), the Far East (Cohen 2001:274; Crawford 2011:342); Mesoamerica (Brumfiel 1976; Flannery 1986b:515), South America (Stannish 1994); North America (Lightfoot and Feinman 1982:66; Boyd 1996:209; Sassaman et al. 2006:561; B. Smith 2007:197; B. Smith and Yarnell 2009:6565–6), and elsewhere (Cowgill 1996; Junker 2001; Erickson 2006; Widgren 2007). In a similar vein, conflict and war are often viewed as the result of population pressure or population-to-resource imbalances. However, Cowgill (1979:59–60) has argued that "conflict *did not* escalate because of growing population pressure or subsistence problems," and R. Kelly (2000:135) maintains that "it is not a paucity of resources that provides conditions favorable to the origination of war but rather reliability and abundance." There are still more disconforming expectations between population pressure models and domestication that I have presented elsewhere (Hayden 1992b). The ethnographic data that we are about to examine only increases the disconformity between population pressure theories and real-world dynamics.

Climate Change

In addition to inherent population growth, another major cause of population and resource stress is climate change. Climate change can have many adverse effects ranging from increased regional aridity, to colder temperatures, to reduction in land areas due to sea levels rising, to reduced carbon dioxide in the atmosphere, to increasing risks for adequate food procurement, to rapid oscillations in climate that eliminate the environmental stability necessary for the development of agriculture (Balter 2007).

Of all the climate "triggers" proposed for the beginning of domestication, the effects of the Younger Dryas in the Near East have been the most persuasively argued (Hillman et al. 2000; Moore et al. 2000; Bar-Yosef and Belfer-Cohen 2002:56). The Younger Dryas downturn in temperature about 11,000 years ago preceded the appearance of the first *morphologically* identifiable domesticated forms of cereals in the region by a few hundred years. Once again, however, this interpretation is not without its problems. On a global basis, the climate change model fails to explain the differences in timing of first domesticates in some centers. As Bruce Smith (2007:197) points out, domestication in the independent hearth of eastern North America only occurred about 5,000 years ago, well after any disruptions that the Younger Dryas might have created (Stothert 1985; Balter 2007:1835).

Even in the Near East, Jacques Cauvin (1978:77–84) was an early critic of the climate change explanation of domestication, arguing that the climate data simply did not fit the proposed explanation and that social or ideological changes were more important, a stance defended more recently by Watkins (2010). An even more definitive refutation of the climate change explanation was published by Maher et al. (2011) who found no correlation between culture changes or domestication and climate changes in the Near East (see also Makarewicz 2012). Willcox (2005) and others have also pointed out that cereal abundance in the interior areas of the Fertile Crescent actually increased during the Younger Dryas and that people were traveling considerable distances (60 or more kilometers) even before that to obtain cereals, so that any slight increase in distance to harvest cereals in the Younger Dryas should not have had a major effect on subsistence. Weinstein-Evron (2009:112) similarly fails to see any significant change in the Natufian core area during the Younger Dryas. Moreover, most paleoethnobotanists now think that cultivation was the key step in food production, as well as domestication, and that this began before the Younger Dryas (Willcox et al. 2008; Willcox 2011). Although climate change may have had some role to play in initiating domestication in some areas, this role would seem to have been an auxiliary one rather than a primary cause.

Cognitive and Ideological Changes

Cauvin (1978) was one of the first archaeologists to propose that the Neolithic (defined by the production of domesticated foods) was the result of an ideological or cognitive revolution that sought to exploit and profit from nature. A number of other archaeologists have taken up this idea (Jennbert 1985, 1987, 1998; Hodder 1990; Watkins 1992, 2010; Whittle 1994), and Hahn might also have had similar thoughts. However, such explanations beg the question of why there should have been such a dramatic change in cognition or ideology at this time and in so many different places in the world within a few thousand years. Watkins (1992:69–72) has suggested that sedentism and storage led to population increases that resulted in social stresses that, in turn, created a need for a new ideology involving territorial ownership, which then gave rise to intensified resource production. However, it can be argued that this is ultimately a materialist scenario of causality rather than a cognitive one. For me, most cognitive explanations are unsatisfactory and create epistemological malaise. Marvin Harris (1979) has provided a trenchant critique of cognitive models. His view that ideology is simply used to justify what people want to do seems far more realistic.

Surplus and Feasting

The paleopolitical ecology explanation of domestication shares a few common assumptions with the push models. Notably, both approaches view prestige objects as serving social functions (although different ones), both consider risk reduction as important (in different ways), and both treat early domesticates as more labor intensive to produce than wild foods. There are a few archaeologists who would disagree with this last premise (Patricia Anderson 1999:119,122,131,138; Piperno 2011). However, untested as it is, the high labor cost, low productivity, and high risk of failures of early domesticates is a major assumption of most archaeologists – a topic that will be discussed further in the "Ethnography of Cultivated Plants" section. If we accept the high-cost premise for domesticates, it is unlikely that prehistoric people would have begun cultivation under normal conditions; they would either have had to be pushed or pulled into cultivating plants. The political ecology model postulates that there was a compelling pull factor that emerged in the Epipaleolithic. As discussed in the preceding chapter, once survival, reproductive, and quality of life benefits were linked to surplus food production through feasting, enormous pressures logically (and ethnographically) ensued that must have increased and intensified food production. This, in essence, is the argument that I wish to pursue. There are a number of possible variations on this basic scenario: early domesticates could have involved only luxury foods; early domesticates could have consisted only of nonfood animals and/or plants used for prestige purposes; early domesticates could have been some combination of the above, as well as plant staples (needed in large quantities for feasting fillers); early domesticates could have been produced in large surplus quantities for use in brewing; early domesticates could have been used to raise animals; or early domesticates could have been entirely staple foods (perhaps the least likely situation in this paradigm). Whichever of these variant models one chooses to pursue, the expectations of the general model contrast markedly with those of the pressure models in terms of expected environmental richness, cultural complexity, sedentism, evidence for feasting, the nature of the first domesticates, the minor role of first domesticates, and the long duration of that pattern (see Hayden 1992b).

This very brief introduction to some of the leading contenders in the explanation of domestication should provide enough critical awareness to appreciate the observations that follow.

ETHNOGRAPHY OF DOMESTICATED ANIMALS

The earliest recognized domesticated species of either plant or animal is the dog (Davis and Valla 1978; Tchernov and Valla 1997; Snyder and Leonard 2006). Although dogs were used for feasts among some groups and are associated with ritual contexts in other groups (M. Schwartz 1997), there is no indication that the earliest domesticated dogs were kept for their subsistence food value. It is rather assumed that they played a social role, probably as status items. There have been no attempts made to explain dog domestication in terms of population pressure. Rather, there are good ethnographic and archaeological examples of dogs being sacrificed as part of rituals (Jochelson 1908; Davis and Valla 1978; Crellin 1994; M. Schwartz 1997; Crellin and Heffner 2000). Moreover, the keeping and breeding of dogs seems to form part of a broader pattern of status display among complex hunter/gatherers. As Teit (1906:250), Post (1938:34), and Elmendorf and Kroeber (1960) recorded, elite families of complex hunter/gatherers in the Northwest Interior Plateau and in California sometimes captured animals in the wild and kept them as pets, including hawks, crows, geese, magpies, turkeys, foxes, coyotes, marmots, raccoons, deer, moose, bison, bears, wolves, and especially eagles. Erikson (2000) and Serpell (1996:49–52) provide additional examples. Because such animals were tethered to their owners, they had to be fed and thus represented costs that only the energetic and well-off could afford to maintain. As we saw in Chapter 4, among the Ainu, it must only have been wealthy households that could have afforded to keep and feed a bear for one to two years.

This was also generally the case with domesticated animals. The vast majority, if not all, ethnographically domesticated animals constituted luxury items used in ceremonial exchanges that only the "well-heeled few" could afford to keep since kept animals could consume 50–60 percent of a household's agricultural production (Waddell 1972:118; Modjeska 1982:62,74; Feil 1987:63; Lemonnier 1990:141; Nairn 1991; Barker 1992; Hakansson 1994, 1995). This is reflected in the typical distribution of animal holdings recorded by Falvey in Southeast Asian hill tribes (Figure 5.3). Domesticated dogs, too, such as those in Australia (Hayden 1975) and probably in the Northwest Interior were generally unable to forage effectively enough to provide their own food, especially in game-depleted areas around major settlements. I would suggest that all domesticated dogs were largely dependent

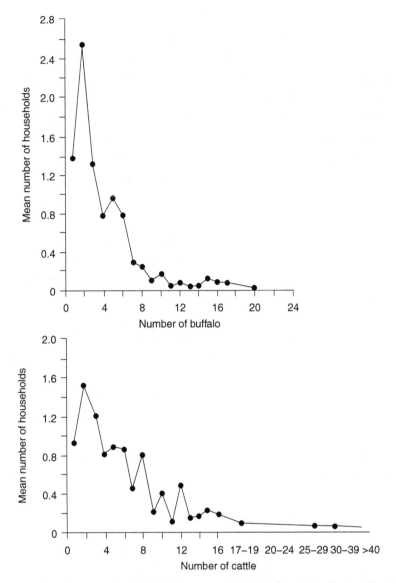

5.3. Among transegalitarian hill tribe communities in Southeast Asia, the typical pattern of livestock and swine holdings (the major form of wealth) is for the vast majority of households to have none or one or two animals whereas a very few households own ten to thirty or more animals. This appears to be a typical wealth distribution in most, if not all, transegalitarian societies. (Graph courtesy of L. Falvey 1977:34,35)

on their owners to be fed, as indicated by isotopic analysis of their diets (Snyder and Leonard 2006:452). As mentioned in Chapter 4, Cail (2011) concluded that raising dogs in the Pacific Northwest was a costly luxury dependent on intensified production similar to raising pigs in New Guinea. The "wool dogs" of the coast were even clearer examples of animals kept for prestige purposes (Schulting 1994; Snyder and Leonard 2006:461–2). Their fur was used for weaving some of the prestigious capes and blankets of the Northwest Coast. In the American Southwest, the only other domestic animal, the turkey, similarly appears to have been kept and domesticated initially for prestige purposes (the feathers), as were macaws at the time of European contact (Terrell et al. 2003:344–5; Natalie Munro 2006:467). These turkeys were also fed considerable amounts of maize (Rawlings and Driver 2010). Thus, the first domesticated animals appear to have been prestige items. Specially bred dogs continued to be important prestige items throughout the Iron Age, the Roman Empire, and have remained so down to the present.

This is an important observation because it sets the stage for understanding domestication in the context of a prestige display system that included foods. This system really only emerged with the appearance of complex hunter/gatherers (as discussed in Chapters 3 and 4). Although Woodburn (1988:57) probably had other kinds of causality in mind, it is significant that he, and others, too, have argued that domestication was unlikely to have developed among immediate-return (simple) hunter/gatherers, but that it really only made sense in the context of delayed-return (complex) hunter/gatherers. The same year, Runnels and van Andel (1988) also argued that the evolution of complex societies was the cause of agricultural origins. They argued that trade was the major causal link, whereas Woodburn simply argued that it was primarily the obligatory sharing of foods and other leveling mechanisms that inhibited any investment in long-term food production, such as that required by cultivation and animal rearing. Willcox (1998:35; 2005) similarly has argued that sedentism, storage, and complex social organization were prerequisites for domestication. Mace (1993) similarly found that the keeping of animals should be associated with increasing wealth. These arguments make a great deal of sense to me since they seem to describe transegalitarian hunter/gatherers. I would only add that the imperative to impress people in complex hunter/gatherer societies, especially via feasts and conspicuous displays, adds a powerful incentive to increasing the amount and quality of food produced.

Thus, for the first time in prehistory, complex hunter/gatherers in the Epipaleolithic/Mesolithic/Archaic – and perhaps the Upper Paleolithic – period began to raise and use animals for display purposes. Specially bred dogs also seem to have been part of the prestige displays to impress guests, as were specialty foods in large quantities that had to be reciprocated as part of contractual debts. Some feasting animals were procured in hunts shortly before feasts, but these were often an unreliable and uncertain source of meat needed to impress guests, especially since kills of large, desirable or rare game were relatively low-frequency events (see Chapter 3).

Feasts generally had to be scheduled months or years in advance. Fresh meat had to be procured shortly before feasts, otherwise it would spoil. One way of dealing with this situation was to smoke and dry meat, fish, or plants ahead of

5.4. Albino water buffaloes (*saleko*) with white-pink skin and blue eyes, such as the one shown here, are highly prized in the Torajan highlands and, like other domesticated animals, are exclusively used for feasts in most transegalitarian communities. They are worth up to ten times the value of a normal water buffalo. Careful breeding of such high-demand animals for feasts probably is simply a continuation of the processes that originally led to domestication. (Photograph by B. Hayden)

time. Another way of dealing with these constraints was, like the Ainu, to capture young animals in the wild and keep them for months or years while preparing for the specific feasts in which they would be consumed. Following Hahn, I would suggest that it is this last strategy that provides a key link to the domestication of animals. It is only a small step from capturing wild animals (and raising them for several years) to the practice of keeping and *breeding* animals on a more enduring basis that leads to the genetic changes that produced domesticated varieties. This process is still going on for feasting purposes in tribal societies, as demonstrated by the selective breeding of albino water buffaloes that are worth ten times the value of ordinary water buffaloes in feasts (Figure 5.4). Marshall and Hildebrand (2002) contend that the principal advantage that domestication of animals provided was the predictability of animal availability. However, such strategies would also have the advantage that animals could be fattened up prior to their sacrifice and consumption, and, as we have seen in Chapter 3, it is above all fat-rich meats that are relished most and that would have been most likely to impress guests. A number of ethnographers have noted that it is the fat content that is one of the prime objectives for people raising domestic animals, especially just before they are consumed, when they are often fed large amounts of food (Young 1971:230; Modjeska 1982:62,74; Feil 1987:45; M. Clarke 1996; Halstead 1998–9, 2007; Mainland and Halstead 2002:111).

Ethnographically, we have already seen in Chapter 4 that the Ainu and Siberian groups kept and raised bear cubs (as well as dogs; Ohnuki-Tierny 1974:92) for one to two years specifically to sacrifice for feasts. Fages (1937:50) also reported that some California groups captured, raised, and fattened bear cubs for eating "like pigs." Like the Ainu bears, DeBoer (2001:218) reports that wild peccaries, monkeys, tapirs, currasows, and even manatees were caught and raised as pets only to be fattened and sacrificed for the major Conibo-Shipibo feast events. Elsewhere, deer were raised and fattened for feasts (White 2001:94). Where resources were inadequate for keeping and breeding pigs in the Pacific, wild pigs were captured and reared for feasts (Baldwin 1990:243), and this practice is explicitly viewed as the "missing link" for understanding domestication. As noted in Chapter 4, the Siberian Khanty (considered to be complex hunter/gatherers) take this practice one step further by keeping and raising domestic sheep, goats, and horses for feasts (P. Jordan 2003:125,147,278). Cashdan (1980:117–8) further observed that among //Gana Bushman groups in South Africa that keep goats, these are eaten on ritual occasions. The Piik ap Oom in Africa also use domestic animals for feasts (Marshall and Hildebrand 2002:104). Sadr (2005) makes a similar case for the complex hunter/gatherers of South Africa, whereas López and Restifo (2012:1043) have noted that the intensified exploitation of camelids leading to their domestication was accompanied by increasing cultural complexity similar to that occurring in Natufian and Jomon contexts. Lewthwaite (1986) similarly argued that the adoption of domesticated ovicaprids by complex hunter/gatherers in Europe at the end of the Mesolithic was for feasting purposes. For the Kalasha of Pakistan, Parkes (1992:37) maintains that goat herding was "largely motivated by sacrificial feasting." On Cyprus, Vigne et al. (2011:256) have documented the importation of wild boars during Late Natufian times (c. 11,700 cal. BP) indicating that some sort of control was likely already taking place on the mainland. The brief appearance of genetically wild cattle on Cyprus at the beginning of the Neolithic, followed by their disappearance (Simmons 2004, 2007:236–42,257–9; Vigne et al. 2011), also seems to make most sense as the temporary importation and raising of captured young wild cattle (similar to the capture of bears) for the purposes of feast sacrifices.

When we look even further along the domestication spectrum (among tribal societies in which animals have been fully domesticated), we find a continuation of this same basic pattern especially for bovids, suids, and caprids, as will be documented in the next two chapters. Moreover, as Lemonnier (1990:59–60,141) points out for New Guinea, domestication for subsistence needs makes no sense at all since domestic pigs provide only 0.5 percent of the calories and 2–3 percent of the protein in diets, whereas raising pigs consumes 50–60 percent of the sweet potatoes that are grown (Waddell 1972:118), which are the main source of subsistence calories. In addition, Lemonnier remarks that if people needed protein, they would not be giving it away to others, especially in large quantities. Simoons (1994:260–1) similarly notes that feast hosts do not generally eat any of the meat that they have raised for the feasts, which makes no sense from a subsistence point of view but makes perfect sense from a political ecology perspective because the purpose of raising animals is to impress guests by giving meat away. That is, hosts abstain in order to maximize the amount that can be given away. Thus, Simoons (1994:245) concludes, in accordance with Hahn, that bovids were domesticated in Assam for feasting purposes. In addition to these considerations, to keep animals for any significant subsistence benefit would require very large herds, even just for their milk and blood products (Strathern 1971a:130). This consideration makes the domestication of animals by hunter/gatherers for subsistence purposes highly unlikely.

Following the work by Hakansson, Halstead, Young, Feil, Modjeska, Blanton, and others, an important principle can be suggested from some of these observations for understanding intensification and domestication. Notably, the major reason for intensification and domestication of mundane plant crops may not be for direct consumption in feasts but as a means of producing other valued foods and drinks for feasts, such as meat and alcohol. Moreover, the only reliable way to obtain fat-rich meat that would be particularly relished in feasts would be to raise animals and overfeed them.

Throughout Southeast Asia, tribal groups look on domestic animals as a means of investment. Large animals constitute the major form of wealth, and the same is true in rural Greece and probably Europe (Falvey 1977:22–3,38,40,86; Halstead 1990:152). Domestic animals are prestige items almost exclusively consumed in the context of feasts (Modjeska 1982:105; Feil 1987:63; Hayden 2001c). The same pattern is repeated in tribal Africa, India, Europe, Oceania, and the Near East, whether groups are traditional agriculturalists or pastoralists (e.g., Keswani 1994; Griffin 1998:35; Halstead 2007:28–9). Even in the much more developed societies of Europe, the "stock" market was originally where domesticated animals were bought and sold, and the piggy was the bank (Figure 5.5). My former wife was raised in traditional rural France where meat was only eaten at Sunday feasts with the extended family or at larger events. As far as I know, this was the general pattern throughout traditional rural Europe until recently. That domestic animals are only killed for feasts is one of the strongest relationships that I know of in all of anthropology; it is on a par with the incest taboo and the sexual division of labor. In fact, there is not one single ethnographic example of a traditional society that I know of where animals are kept primarily to provide meat for daily subsistence.

Throughout the traditional world, the general pattern is to rear domesticated animals as highly valued assets or prestige items. In most of these societies, domestic animals are absolutely required for important social transactions, especially

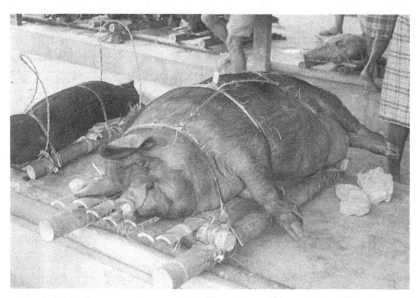

5.5. Excessively fat pigs are also highly prized for feasting in the Torajan highlands and most other Southeast Asian tribal communities. Using resources to raise pigs for important social transactions is considered like putting money in the bank – probably the symbolic origin of contemporary "piggy" banks. (Photograph by B. Hayden)

marriages and funerals. However, there are major costs and risks to raising medium- and large-sized domestic animals, including feed, management, unexpected animal mortalities, theft of animals, and claims against their owners for damages caused by animals, especially to crops. Therefore, as a rule, only well-off families can afford to keep and use domestic animals (Hayden 2001c), and this gives such families extremely important sources of leverage in traditional communities. The typical outcome is that a few families end up possessing large herds of animals whereas most families possess either no animals or only one or two (Figure 5.3; Falvey 1977; Barker 1992; Parkes 1992; Hayden 2001c). The implications for community dynamics and the creation of inequalities are far-reaching. For instance, in most transegalitarian communities, there were strong competitive pressures to produce and use surpluses (especially in animal forms) to achieve basic life goals such as marriage and proper burial. Yet most families were not capable of financing these events on their own and had to go into debt to procure them. As Keane (1997:57) characterizes the situation in Indonesia, "to maintain basic social relations with others, to sustain a decent reputation, and to avert the ire of ancestors one must have access to cattle and rice." Nairn (1991) makes a similar point in the documentary *Ongka's Big Moka* when Ongka explains that people can feed themselves and get by all right without pigs. But if people want to get ahead in life and marry, they must have pigs. Modjeska (1982:62,74) makes the similar point that domestic pigs are not necessary for subsistence; they are luxuries.

This situation naturally generates competition between individuals and families who want to marry desirable spouses, establish close ties with the most successful or powerful families, and occupy various positions of power or influence. Doing so is, to a large degree, contingent on one's ability to produce or procure domestic animals. As Thomas Hakansson (1994, 2010) has documented in East Africa, this competition can be extremely powerful and can actually result in the development of new techniques, such as irrigation to intensify agricultural production so that more animals can be raised to better compete in these social arenas – all in the absence of any detectable population pressure. The same is true for tribal Southeast Asia where the main motive for producing more maize and rice is to raise more pigs or other animals for feasts (Falvey 1977). Blanton and Taylor (1995), Lemonnier (1990:59–60,68;), Feil (1987:63), and Modjeska (1982:62,74) make similar observations in New Guinea, where they clearly identify social and political benefits as the fundamental impetus behind the production of yams to feed pigs for feasting purposes or exchanges rather than any subsistence need.

Thus, it would seem that there is robust support from ethnographies in many parts of the world for the proposition that animals were initially domesticated for feasting purposes. In view of this ethnographic patterning, it would seem that the onus is on behavioral ecologists or population pressure advocates to show why domestication of animals should be explained in terms of subsistence needs. Indeed, there are also significant archaeological indications that feasting was, in fact, the primary impetus behind initial animal domestication.

ARCHAEOLOGICAL EVIDENCE

I have already alluded to the European Mesolithic bear that was kept in captivity (Chaix et al. 1997), whether as a prestige display pet or for a ritual feast such as the Ainu held. Bahn (1980) has also argued for the keeping of horses by some Upper Paleolithic groups in Europe. The introduction of deer, cattle, and other animals to Cyprus at the dawn of the Neolithic, their consumption at ritual sites, and the subsequent disappearance of cattle (Simmons 2004, 2007:236–42,257–9) is puzzling if this was done for subsistence purposes, where the goal would have been to maintain and increase animal populations. However, if wild animals were being captured and brought over for feasting purposes in a fashion similar to Ainu bears, the introduction and disappearance of these animals makes perfect sense, especially given the high costs of procurement, transport, and presumably maintenance for certain lengths of time. If conditions resulted in fewer surpluses, it would undoubtedly have become too prohibitive to continue importing such feasting luxuries.

In a similar fashion, Gronenborn (1999) reported the occurrence of keeping a wild pig in Mesolithic Europe, and others (Zvelibil 1995; Rowley-Conwy and

Dobney 2007:142) conclude that pigs were probably imported or managed by some Mesolithic groups. Boars also appear to have been imported and raised in some Jomon communities from Early Jomon times, as well as on Okinawa (Matsui et al. 2002; Minaegawa et al. 2005; Kaner 2009:32–3). Lewthwaite (1986:61–2) and Sadr (2005) similarly argued on the basis of archaeological remains that ovicaprids were adopted by complex hunter/gatherer groups for feasting purposes, and other examples for camelids and chickens are provided by Stahl (2003). Indeed, the observation by Legge and Rowley-Conwy (2000:471) for the early Neolithic at Abu Hureyra, Syria, is perplexing from a subsistence ecology perspective. They state that "the first inhabitants kept small numbers of domestic sheep and goat. At that time the wild fauna of the region was still abundant, and the migratory animals were hunted on a large scale." However, if the purpose of keeping domesticated animals was to provide fresh meat from *fattened* animals for feasts, such behavior is entirely intelligible. Perhaps following Hahn's early lead, Jacques Cauvin (1978:116–7; see also Marshall and Hildebrand 2002:107) persuasively argued that the bull was an important symbolic animal before it was domesticated, recalling rather strikingly the role of the bear among the Ainu. Indeed, the baiting of bulls and their former use around the Mediterranean for mortuary feasts, and even their use in contemporary bullfights, bears a striking resemblance to the baiting and killing of the bear for the bear feast depicted in Neil Munro's documentary film, *Iyomande*. More recently, Bar-Yosef (1999:24), Russell et al. (2005:104; Russell 2012:233) and Twiss (2008:430–1) have endorsed the symbolic role of bulls in early Neolithic feasting and suggested that this was likely the main purpose behind their domestication. Goring-Morris and Belfer-Cohen (2011:68) have even suggested that the apparent depiction of halters on some pre-pottery Neolithic B (PPNB) figurines of aurochs (similar to Ainu halters used on bears) indicates that they were captured and kept for subsequent consumption at feasts. Louise Martin (1999:100–1) has made similar suggestions for the domestication of sheep and goats in the Near East, where domesticated forms appear while there were still many wild animals available. And, the evidence of penning ovicaprids 8,000–9,000 years ago at Uan Afuda, in Libya, prior to domestication in North Africa and Asia Minor, would seem to confirm this scenario (Garcea 2001:228, 2004:122,124,141–2).

There are also important indications that camelids in South America were domesticated to serve aggrandizer or elite prestige interests. In the northern Andes, Stahl (2003) documents the non-native importation of animals along routes controlled by elites who sought to acquire exotic resources, whereas Natalie Munro (2006) argues that domesticated turkeys were ritual offerings in the Southwest United States (presumably valued, like macaws, for their feathers). Domesticated animals were thus associated with elite prestige systems in these areas. Farther south, Yacobaccio (2004:239) made similar observations: "whatever the primary causes for camelid domestication in the southern Andes, it was part of the context of increasing social complexity that took place in the hunter-gatherer groups."

In northern Africa, Garcea (2004, 2006, 2008) and Marshall and Hildebrand (2002) document the earliest occurrence of domestic animals among ceramic-using hunter/gatherers with delayed-return economies (including an important role for aquatic resources), storage, relative sedentism, large settlements, large thick hearths, and social organizations conducive to resource intensification or cultivation, including the recognition of rights to resources and concepts of ownership – all necessary preconditions to herding. Garcea (2001:229, 2004:130, 2008:59) further maintains that early pottery was relatively rare and, rather than being used in domestic contexts, must have been used for special purposes and had important social symbolism in its use or in the foods that were produced from them. Similarly, she argued that the earliest domestic cattle were rarely killed and represented status items. Marshall and Hildebrand (2002:114) make the further point that pastoralists cannot afford to harvest more than 4–8 percent of their cattle herds, which would yield even fewer animals than a !Kung hunter would kill in a year. It would seem that herding provides even less meat than hunting in most environments, and when pastoralists kill an animal from their herd, it must be for an unusually important occasion, like a marriage. The economic and social characteristics of early Holocene Saharan societies in early domestication regions appear to correspond to complex hunter/gatherer types of societies, as predicted by the feasting and surplus/paleopolitical ecology model of domestication, and the use of ceramics and domestic cattle appears to correspond to their postulated initial use for feasts. Thus, there seems to be substantial archaeological support for the argument that animals were initially domesticated as part of strategies of aggrandizers to create social links and alliances and to impress others with displays of prestige items (including dogs, camelids, turkeys, and exotic animals), as well as to provide highly desired fresh meat to impress feasting guests. In fact, of the major contending models of domestication, the political ecology explanation is the only one that is consistent with the ethnographic observations on the keeping and raising of wild animals, and it is the only one that can account for the full range of animal domesticates. One of the more interesting hypotheses derived from this model is that we might expect early domestic animals to differ from wild animals in their levels of fat. This could be reflected in the cortical thickness of bones or in the structure of the cancellous bone cells where fats are produced.

In the following chapters, we will see many other examples of domestic animals being used in feasting contexts. However, at this point, it is important to examine the first plant domesticates in order to determine whether their management and production also plausibly resulted from feasting demands.

DOMESTICATING PLANTS

A curious distribution curve describes the numbers of traditional societies and their relative reliance on cultivated plants. Whereas all other sources of subsistence are unimodel, the curve for reliance on cultivated plants is bimodal (Figure 5.6). If cultivating domesticated plants provided advantages for subsistence, one would think that societies familiar with domestication would be eager to adopt cultivated plants and increase reliance on them, but this does not appear to be the case. Nor was it the case for one or more thousand years after the first appearance of domesticates. In fact, most groups used domesticates as a minor adjunct to their normal hunting and gathering subsistence and kept it that way for many generations. Why would they do that? This long period of low reliance on domesticates has been a source of fascination and puzzlement for most archaeologists and archaeobotanists (Cowan and Watson 1992:209; Crawford 1992; Chapman 1995:34,38; Willcox 1996:143,

5.6. The importance of farming in a cross-cultural sample of traditional societies throughout the world displays a curious bimodal distribution unlike other subsistence modes. There are a large number of societies with minimal reliance (10–20 percent) on farmed foods with another high peak of reliance over 50 percent. This distribution is difficult to understand if domestication provided clear benefits for communities but is expectable if domesticates were originally used in feast contexts and later for general subsistence after genetic improvements made farming more productive. (Williams and Hunn 1986: figure 3).

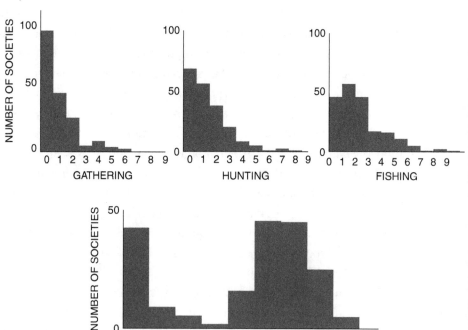

1999:494; B. Smith 2001b; Benz and Staller 2006:670–1; Asouti and Fuller 2013. As Harlan (2006) has mused, "If they were being forced into agriculture because of population pressure, they surely would not have taken 2000 yr to accomplish the job." If there was such dire need for additional subsistence resources, as population pressure advocates would have us believe, and if cultivation and domestication was such a breakthrough in subsistence procurement, why did it stall for so long at such a low level of importance? Even worse, why do some early Neolithic sites in the earliest hearths of domesticated plants seem to have no indication of using domesticated plants or animals at all (e.g., Göbekli Tepe, Jerf el Ahmar)?

One plausible answer is that early cultivated plants were inherently risky. In good years, they might produce good surpluses; however, in poor years, after a great deal of labor expended, the entire crop might be lost due to storms, insect pests, diseases, drought, poor temperatures, wild or domestic animal depredations, birds, rodents, spoilage, or theft during storage. Rodents alone can cause harvest losses of up to 92 percent, although the average is closer to 30 percent (Gregg 1988:97,134). As Bogucki (1999:197) and others (Flannery 1969:74; Gregg 1988:62–6,73,97,132–4,156,161) have argued, domesticates, by nature, are high risk, unstable products (see also Hayden 2011c; Hayden et al. 2012).

Moreover, initial yields must have paled in comparison with modern crop varieties (Flannery 1969:74; Rindos 1984:87–8; Gurven et al. 2010:50), whereas the required labor for clearing land of competing vegetation and root systems must have been far greater at the dawn of domestication given the stone tool technology then available rather than the steel tools used today. Bowles's (2011a,b) economic models indicate that hunter/gatherer caloric returns were 60 percent higher than cultivators, and he concludes that initial cultivation was uneconomical for subsistence purposes. Thus, initially, it is unlikely that cultivated domestic plants were relied on for subsistence needs.

In contrast, if the goal of cultivating plants was to produce a surplus whenever possible and to use that surplus for feasting purposes, this would involve no subsistence risk. The only risk involved would be of foregoing the ability to hold a feast in a given year. However, feasts can always be rescheduled, and, in any event, large ones require several years of planning. Thus, ambitious political or social plans may have to be deferred a bit, but subsistence would not be jeopardized, nor would sociopolitical plans be abandoned under normally variable circumstances. On the other hand, if the harvest was good, those households investing time and effort to produce it could reap great benefits through the hosting of feasts, marriage payments, acquisitions of prestige objects, and other resource-based aggrandizer strategies. Moreover, feasts are episodic so that foods used exclusively for feasting usually constitute a minor proportion of all foods consumed. I suggest that this is the meaning behind the unusual bimodal curve of societies relying on cultivation. The many societies in which cultivated foods constitute only 10–20 percent of the diet would be those transegalitarian societies in which food was cultivated primarily for feasting events, and thus domesticates constitute only a minor proportion of the total diet. Those societies in which cultivated foods constitute 50–70 percent of the diet (the other high point of the bimodal curve) would be societies in which genetic improvements in cultivated plant species reduced risks and increased productivity of cultivation to the point at which cultivation provided better and more reliable returns than did gathering wild plants: that is, conditions in which cultivated domesticated foods became economically worthwhile to use for subsistence rather than political purposes. Because genetic changes could be expected to take hundreds if not thousands of years, the transegalitarian pattern of low-level reliance on cultivated foods could be expected to have been stable for prolonged periods of time in most cases. In fact, this is precisely what has been repeatedly found in the major hearths of domestication of the world.

Thus, the paleopolitical ecology model of domestication featuring surpluses and feasting leads to a number of other distinctive expectations including that special foods used in feasts should be among the first domesticates (as well as plants and animals used in other prestige or feasting fashions; e.g., gourds, chilies, tobacco, *Cannabis*) and that cultivation and domestication should take place in the contexts of complex rather than simple hunter/gatherers. That is, initial domestication should take place in societies found in relatively rich environments where at least seasonal sedentism developed and at least occasional surpluses were being produced, stored, and used to create cultural complexity via some or all of the aggrandizer strategies previously mentioned. It should also be remembered that storage, by its very nature, leads to surplus production and subsequent strategies to put those surpluses to beneficial use via feasts or other production-based schemes (see Chapter 4).

In my opinion, these are the conditions which *do* occur immediately prior to the appearance of domesticated plants in most or all of the best studied and documented cases of early domestication, including the Near East (Hayden 2004, 2011b), China (Hayden 2003c, 2011c), Jomon Japan (Habu 2004), eastern North America (D. Anderson 2002:257; 2010), and Africa (Garcea 2001, 2004, 2008; Marshall and Hildebrand 2002:107,114). Situations in Mesoamerica and South America are still too poorly understood to assess the role of complex hunter/gatherers there. Tellingly, even critics of the feasting model like Zeder and Smith (2009) agree that early domestication occurred in the context of rich environments. Crawford (2006:91) reached the same conclusion:

Several features appear to be common to domestication around the world. .... Seed plants were the first to be domesticated ... *affluent people in large, permanent communities* near rivers and lakes were the first to domesticate plants. Another factor is lack of security in the environment, especially marked seasonality. (emphasis added)

In fact, this now appears to be a consensus position (Price and Bar-Yosef 2011:168). Flannery (1986c:314–5) has even quantified the resources that were available from Guilá Naquitz, a minor and peripheral early domestication site in Oaxaca, Mexico. According to his calculations, just 2.5 hectares near the site could have provided enough food for a family over a four-month period, whereas the 5-kilometer catchment area around the site could have yielded 195 tons of acorns, 673 tons of agave hearts, 1,923 tons of prickly pear fruit, and 4.7 tons of venison. Given this impressive abundance, it hardly seems that people needed to produce more food for subsistence.

Willcox (2005:539–40) makes a very similar point to Crawford's, going even further to suggest that:

Social considerations such as the accumulation of wealth, social stratification, ownership and exchange can no longer be ignored as incentives to cultivate. .... With increasingly complex village life and regional rivalry for access to wild stands, the adoption of cultivation near a village would be a distinct advantage.

Asouti and Fuller (2013) concur and even emphasize the importance of "communal food consumption" by suprahousehold groups in the development of cultivation and domestication. In contrast, Bruce Smith (2001a:220) sees no evidence for social complexity prior to domestication and views the first domesticates as "mundane, vulgar, subsistence food items." I discuss the issue of complexity later, but in regard to the special status of the first domesticated plants, a number of comments can be made about foods like cereals that are usually assumed to have always been staples used for subsistence. For instance, it is important to note that cereals do not appear to have played any discernable or significant role in prehistoric diets until the Mesolithic or late Epipaleolithic, when mortars and pestles and grinding stones first become common, together with the first clear indications of sickle polish on chipped stone tools. Why were cereals so late in being utilized as food? The standard behavioral ecological explanation is that they were time-consuming to collect, process, and prepare, and thus they were ranked lower than other plant foods and generally not used at all or only used under conditions of stress. Importantly, Gremillion (2004) argues that the very low rates of return of seeds used for food prehistorically in eastern North America made it unlikely that they were adopted under resource stress conditions or that technological innovation would have made much difference in their relative ranking. Barlow and Heck (2002) make a similar point for Near Eastern cereals, whereas Flannery (1973) characterizes the use of cereals as "third choice" foods for hunter/gatherers, enumerating a plethora of problems associated with their use.

An alternative explanation to the standard subsistence crisis view is that cereal grains may have been used exclusively as highly desirable foods in feasting contexts that did not appear in most areas until the emergence of complex hunter/gatherers in the Mesolithic or Epipaleolithic. The expenditure of extra efforts to impress feast guests with desirable, high-cost foods could have led to the inclusion of boiled cereals, bread, and/or beer. Flannery (1986a:17) makes the interesting observation that squash plants (among the earliest domesticates in the Americas) were probably not originally cultivated for their flesh, which is negligible and bitter, but for their seeds, which are rich in oil (see the Americas subsection of the "Archaeological Records" section). Harlan makes the same observation and adds the comment that "it seems certain that a few squash vines had very little if any effect on the economy of the Indians who grew them. The activity could hardly have affected the food supply significantly" (Harlan 2006).

Desirable Characteristics of Cereals

What could have been the characteristics of cereal seeds that made them so desirable as a food? First of all, as noted in Chapter 3, lipids and starches are generally in short supply for most hunter/gatherers. Cereal grains have an inherent appealing balance of protein (c. 15–30 percent), oils (c. 5 percent), and starches (75–80 percent). They also have a tasty flavor when boiled up, especially when combined with meat juices or other flavorful plants. The first use of cereals was probably as boiled whole grains or gruels. In some areas of Australia, cereals were highly prized and used for social occasions (Lourandos 1988:157). Readers can acquire some appreciation of these qualities themselves by obtaining kamut or wheat berries from a supermarket or health food store and boiling them up like rice. Although this may be simple using today's technology, dehusking and prolonged boiling of wild or early domesticated varieties would have been time-consuming and difficult with Epipaleolithic technologies (Meurers-Balke and Luning 1999), especially since metals and pottery were lacking. Thus, even boiled cereals (or, for that matter, any kind of hot soup with grease or oils extracted by boiling) were probably highly esteemed feasting foods, whereas more labor-intensive preparations of cereals, such as breads and beers, would have been even more valued. Making these value-added foods went well beyond what was necessary for simple subsistence, typically requiring hours of grinding every day. I suggest that the effort spent in making bread, not to mention its unique texture and taste, may have made bread an exceptionally highly valued feasting item for many Epipaleolithic complex hunter/gatherers in the Near East 15,000–11,000 years ago. As Young (1971:157,167,196,241) observed, the highest valued foods in feasts were those that involved the most labor to obtain or prepare.

This role of traditional bread continues today. As Paul Halstead once remarked to me, one can have a feast in Greece without meat, although it would be considered a very poor feast; however, a feast without bread is simply inconceivable. In many ways, bread in Europe and the Middle East plays the same role as rice in the Far East. A feast without rice in the Far East is equally inconceivable as European feasts without bread. The sacred nature of rice is legendary, but wheat was equally so in pre-Industrial Eurasia. In fact, wheat and rice are the only food plants in these regions that have souls like human beings that have to be properly honored with rituals (see Hayden 2011c). Like wheat, rice, especially archaic forms of rice like red rice or hill rice, has superb gustatory qualities that are almost completely lacking from the Industrial varieties of white rice that are the Asian equivalent of commercial white bread (versus, for example, French bread).

However, perhaps even more important than nutrition, taste, and effort, cereal (as well as milk) digests contain exorphins that resemble opioids in their effects on the human brain (Wadley and Martin 1993). Although the amounts are not great enough to produce a pronounced "high" under normal conditions of consumption, eating cereals can induce a sense of comfort and well-being, as anyone who has experienced rapture at the smell and taste of freshly baked traditional breads can attest to. Thus, cereals would have had an additional inherent attraction beyond simple nutritional satisfaction. The exorphin production from cereals provides another compelling reason to view cereal-based foods as highly desirable but costly feasting foods that would have attracted people to events where they were being provided. Wadley and Hayden (under review) argue that plants were largely selected for domestication due to their innate appeal to human tastes, whether for sugars, alcohol, exorphins, nicotine, or other psychoactive characteristics.

Brewing

Another possible reason for thinking that there may have been an overpowering desire to consume cereals as costly foods for feasts is that they can be transformed into beer. Braidwood (1953), followed by Katz and Voigt (1986) and McGovern (2003:10), among others, has suggested that brewing may have occurred in the Epipaleolithic of the Near East and been the driving force behind the domestication of cereals. Smalley and Blake (2003) make a similar argument for the domestication of maize in Mesoamerica, although they focus on the stalk juices as being the most readily fermentable element of the maize plant. Dietler (1990) and others (e.g., Arthur 2003; Jennings et al. 2005) have observed that beer and other alcoholic beverages are almost exclusively consumed in the context of feasts in traditional societies, and these are generally hosted by families wealthy enough to be able to use surpluses to make beer. In a recent assessment of these suggestions, I and several students (Hayden et al. 2012) have argued that the first ethnographic and archaeological indications of brewing occur among complex hunter/gatherers and that there are strong indications that brewing beer was probably occurring in the Epipaleolithic of the Near East. There is evidence of stone boiling technology, of pounding and grinding technology useful for making malt, of suitable groundstone and organic containers, of probable oil extraction and gruel preparations using the same preparatory procedures as brewing, of probable familiarity with fermented palm saps or fruit juices, and likely inoculation with yeasts of pounded grains from acorn preparations using the same mortars. If simple boiling of grains was the most efficient means of preparing cereal grains (with boiling practiced since the Upper Paleolithic), then the rather sudden increase in grinding stones in the Epipaleolithic may have been due to the need for grinding malt in newly developed brewing technologies of the time. In addition, there is ample evidence that many Epipaleolithic settlements were complex hunter/gatherer societies with relatively sedentary and dense population, stored foods, substantial feasts, prestige items, socioeconomic inequalities, corporate burials, and investments in children (see Hayden 2004, 2011b; Hayden et al. 2012). Although brewing does not seem to occur among any simple hunter/gatherers, it does occur sporadically among some complex hunter/gatherers, such as the Ainu and Jomon (Neil Munro 1963:69; Habu et al. 2001:13), some California groups (Fages 1937:22), and the complex hunter/gatherers of southeast Australia (Builth 2002:331). More recently, indications of brewing at the dawn of the Neolithic have been found at the pre-pottery Neolithic A (PPNA) sites of Göbekli Tepe, Jerf el Ahmar, and Tell 'Abr 3, with at least one case interpreted in feasting contexts (Yartah 2005:5; Haaland 2007:174; Stordeur and Willcox 2009:704–6; Dietrich et al. 2012). Moreover, the notion that brewing was well established by, and even before, the appearance of domesticated varieties of cereals is indicated by DNA studies carried out on European and Near Eastern yeasts. According to these results, yeasts used in brewing beer became distinct about 10,000–12,000 years ago (LeGras et al. 2007), which is about when domesticated cereals first begin to appear. All these factors make beer brewing a plausible, attractive motivation for the domestication of cereals. Indeed, making beer was a strong enough motivation to result in polygyny in some societies in which there was high demand for female labor to produce beer (DeBoer 1986:237; Dietler 1990:369).

Other Plants

Lentils were also one of the first domesticates in the Near East. Although there is no research that I know of indicating that lentils have any unusual psychotropic qualities, they do contain unusually high levels of proteins and starches, making them tasty and desirable (c. 25 percent protein; Weiss and Zohary 2011). However, wild lentils were unusually *un*productive as a gathered source of food, with an average of only ten seeds from each of the rare, widely dispersed plants and only about one out of ten seeds that viably germinated (Weiss et al. 2006:1609). This would have made gathering the seeds exceptionally time-consuming and trying to initially cultivate them remarkably unproductive – hardly something one would undertake if starving. Nevertheless, lentils are very rich tasting, and they are still a highly valued food in the region (as well as in India to the present day). They may well be viewed as a possible feasting food, as may the chili peppers and avocados mentioned earlier. Wild Asian rice (*Oryza rufipogon*) is yet another cereal that is exceptionally *un*productive to harvest or cultivate (see the "Archaeology" section below). As previously mentioned, risks of crop damage or failure would have also been high for cultivated cereals, including rice. In both the Near and Far East, the costs of clearing the native vegetation from adequately watered microniches would have been arduous (Hillman et al. 2001:387,390; Willcox 2005, 2007; Weiss et al. 2006:1609). Given all these theoretical disadvantages, what can ethnographic observations tell us about the origins of cultivation and domestication?

THE ETHNOGRAPHY OF PLANT CULTIVATION

As can be imagined, observations on incipient cultivation among historic hunter/ gatherers are few and far between. However, probably the most sensational research development of recent years in our understanding of complex hunter/gatherers has been the realization that some Northwest Coast hunter/gatherers also engaged in the cultivation of small, privately owned plots of land near the shore suitable for growing large clover roots and Pacific cinquefoil roots, both of which had high starch contents. Douglas Deur (2002, 2005) has been instrumental in bringing these facts to the attention of academic researchers, although Boas and Turner and Kuhnlein (1982, 1983) recorded similar observations much earlier. Of critical importance are the facts presented by Turner and Kuhnlein to the effect that gardens were labor inten-sive, bounded plots (often with boundary boards, rock accumulations, or fences), owned and guarded by individual elite families, and that the roots produced were primarily feasting foods (Figure 5.7). The large, starchy roots were considered so important that they were counted when presented at potlatches, presumably as a record of reciprocal debt. In fact, there were potlatches in which roots (and later potatoes) were the featured food. They were also used as part of bride prices and in prestige exchanges. They were a prestige food, considered as the "food of heaven." Only the elites ate the large roots (Deur 2005:297–303). Deur also argues that culti-vation was indisputable in the prehistoric period of the Northwest.

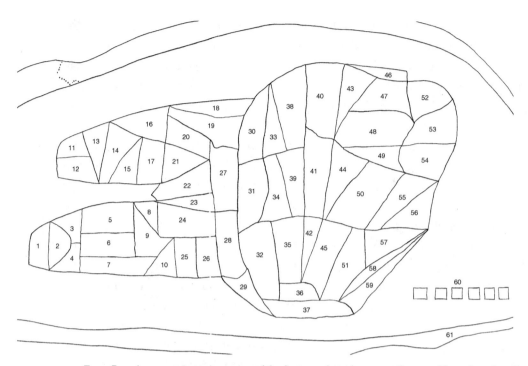

5.7. Franz Boas (1934:37, map 21) was one of the first people to document the use of formal gardens by native peoples on the Northwest Coast to grow clover and cinquefoil roots. His map of one of these gardens at the mouth of the Nimkish River is shown here. Until recently, ethnographers and archaeologists largely ignored this farming activity. However, it is a key demonstration of cultivation beginning among complex hunter/gatherers for the purpose of producing feasting foods by high-ranking households.

In addition to clover and cinquefoil roots, there are indications that the production of wapato was intensified and resembled cultivated crops (Darby 2005; Turner and Peacock 2005). Some groups also intensified shellfish production by creating or enhancing beach terraces known locally as "clam gardens" (Figure 5.8; Williams 2006), although no genetic changes seem to have resulted from this practice. Similar examples of intensified aquaculture have been recorded from the southern Siberian coast (Tabarev 2007). It is also known that a number of groups on the Northwest Coast and Interior kept tobacco gardens, again for the purpose of provisioning feasts (Teit 1900; J. MacDonald 2005:257). Although the occurrence of tobacco in the Northwest must ipso facto be viewed as a domesticate (used again for sociopolitical and feasting purposes rather than for subsistence) given its occurrence far out of its natural range, there is as yet no indication that any of the root crops can be considered as genetically modified or domesticated as a result of cultivation. Thus, the Northwest Coast societies provide prime examples of indigenous cultivation of morphologically wild plants used specifically for feasting purposes by complex hunter/gatherers. Of exceptional importance for the expectations derived from the paleopolitical model of domestication are the

5.8. Between pressures to produce more food for feasts and to feed larger groups of people, other resources became increasingly managed for intensified production. It has recently been recorded that clam beds were managed much like garden plots. Here is a classic clam garden form with a boulder wall used to retain finer sediments that form a beach terrace behind it to promote the growth of clams at Monday Anchorage on the Coast of British Columbia. (Photograph courtesy of Judy Williams and New Star Books, from *Clam Gardens*, 2006, p.117)

observations that this cultivation was conducted by elites for the purpose of producing desirable feasting foods.

Peacock (1998:46–8,57,113,121–2; 2002) has made similar arguments for the complex hunter/gatherers of the Interior Plateau of British Columbia, where mountain potatoes (*Claytonia lanceolata*) and other root crop patches were owned by elites and intensively worked in fashions that resembled cultivation. This stands in stark contrast to the views mentioned earlier of simple hunter/gatherers like the Hadza who thought that cultivated foods were simply not worth all the work involved. Thus, Woodburn and others' notion that cultivation is unlikely to occur among simple hunter/gatherers but can be expected to occur in complex hunter/gatherers is borne out.

If we move along to societies in which cultivation of domesticated plants is an established feature, some other relevant observations indicate that the fundamental reason for cultivation probably had not changed in many cases. For instance, Sand (1999:329) states:

what the ethnographic data clearly show is that the cultivation of surplus horticultural products in Oceanic societies plays a social rather than a food role, serving as a symbol of wealth in confrontations between antagonistic chiefdoms.

Bliege Bird and Smith (2005:228–9) add some important details by noting that the main reason for trying to increase the size of yams in many Melanesian societies is the political rivalry between ambitious men. Tellingly, the large yams (up to 3 meters long) are very labor intensive to produce (yielding only four pounds of yams per hour vs. the thirty-seven pounds per hour of normal yams), and they symbolize a man's industry and his potency. Such large yams are used in ceremonial reciprocal exchanges much like potlatch gifts, and these are accompanied by feasts, although the large yams are themselves "too valuable to be eaten" (228). Big yam men become high-status political entrepreneurs. Such yams demonstrate the ability to devote time to activities that are not directly productive. Kaberry (1942:96) emphasizes that, contrary to the assumption by many archaeologists (that cultivation and domestication were initiated by women), ambitious men are the ones who strive to produce the largest yams in gardens that they cultivate. Big men take credit for the yams produced in their clans due to their ritual knowledge, magical power, and organizational skills. In these cases, and throughout most of Melanesia and Polynesia, it is the men who were putting the most pressure on the food plant genome to transform it for feasting display purposes. Kyakas and Wiessner (1992:104) similarly note that, in New Guinea, it is the men who cultivate crops slated for feasts.

Kaberry's (1942:82–3) observations among the Abelam of New Guinea are even more instructive for the role of domesticates because she notes that cultivating crops requires a great deal of work effort; for almost half the year people subsist largely on wild resources, with yams and taro only being eaten on ceremonial occasions – that is, for feasts. This again emphasizes the special value of cultivated domesticated foods for people who rely on wild foods for their daily subsistence fare. In short, the limited data available from the ethnographic occurrences of incipient and limited domestication seem to support the notion that early cultivated foods were of unusual importance, cost, and value. Moreover, they appear to have been used preferentially or even exclusively for feasts and consumed primarily by elites or incipient elites. But domestication occurred long ago for the most part, and assessing the role of feasting in the domestication process is and must ultimately be a matter of archaeological testing of competing theories using field investigations.

ARCHAEOLOGICAL RECORDS OF EARLY DOMESTICATES IN FEASTS

The Near East

Because the most intensive research on the origins of domesticated plants has been conducted in the Near East, it is appropriate to begin there. As noted earlier, the premises of the paleopolitical model lead us to expect certain archaeological observations (rich environments, sedentism, feasting, prestige items including specialty foods and nonfood domesticates, lengthy minor use of domesticates). However, within this scenario, prestige objects or other prestige indicators need not be overly abundant, and no settlement/political hierarchy or hereditary inequality need exist at all. Most transegalitarian feasting societies do not exhibit extreme characteristics in these areas. The first domesticates are most likely to have been desirable food items, especially rare or difficult to procure or process in the first centers of domestication, although, as previously noted, alternative scenarios are possible.

I have summarized elsewhere the detailed evidence for the communities in the richer Near Eastern environments as having been complex (transegalitarian) hunters and gatherers replete with feasting and prestige items (Hayden 2004, 2011b). To briefly recapitulate, there are few if any indications of feasting or complex hunter/gatherer communities prior to the late Epipaleolithic in the Near East. However, with the late Epipaleolithic come a number of indications of transegalitarian sociopolitical organization, including cemeteries and pronounced inequalities in wealth (Figure 4.26). Even some children had hundreds or thousands of shell or stone beads, whereas other people may have been sacrificed at funeral sites that featured the first elaborate plastered facilities (Figure 5.9). Environments where large communities were located seem to have been exceptionally rich, with "endless

5.9. One of the most remarkable burial features of the Natufian culture was the large pit dug at Ain Mallaha with plastered walls, a number of burials (indicative of its use by a corporate kinship group), several layers of rock paving, abundant faunal remains, broken basalt pestles, and a slab-lined hearth on top of everything (center right), with a severed human head resting against the large hearth stone to the upper left, possibly indicating human sacrifice at this time. The burned human remains scattered over the floor of a Natufian ritual structure at Wadi Hammeh may also reflect the practice of human sacrifice and possibly cannibalism (Webb and Edwards 2002:118–9; see also Haimi, 1960, for Nahal Oren). Such elaborate burials indicate the transegalitarian nature of Natufian communities. (Perrot 1957:96)

5.10. The three stacked caprid bucrania shown here led Michael Rosenberg to infer that feasting had taken place at the Epipaleolithic site of Hallan Çemi. (Rosenberg and Davis 1992: figure 2)

vistas" and "vast supplies" of plant foods and mass kills of animals "in whatever amounts were needed" (Hillman 2000:366; Moore et al. 2000:480). Some environments were so rich that they apparently supported fully sedentary and growing communities. Numerous large and medium storage pits were excavated at Ain Mallaha (Perrot and Ladiray 1988:4–5,13–14) indicative of probable surpluses (Figure 4.27). In the Epipaleolithic, there are also a number of sites with unusually large hearths up to 7 meters in diameter. These only seem to make sense in terms of feeding large numbers of people (see Asouti and Fuller [2013] for an additional analysis of communal food preparation and consumption areas). Hearths over a meter or more in diameter occur at Mureybet, El Wad, Rosh Horesha, Beidha, Shanidar Cave, and to lesser extents at other sites. Such hearths are often associated with burials and interpreted as having been used for funerary feasts. In addition, specialty food animals and large quantities of faunal remains occur at Hilazon Tachtit, Hallan Çemi, Ain Mallaha, and Zawi Chemi Shanidar, sometimes even placed on display from feasts, as at Hallan Çemi (Figure 5.10).

Prestige serving and food preparation vessels are also well attested in the Epipaleolithic. Stone bowls or cups and "plates" often made of basalt imported from 60 to 100 or more kilometers occur in a number of Natufian, late Epipaleolithic, and PPNA sites near the Euphrates, as at Abu Hureyra, Jerf el Ahmar, Körtik, and

Hallan Çemi. Like some of the finely made basalt mortars in the "core" Natufian sites, these cups are often decorated with incised designs (Figure 5.11). Stone cups and plates are labor-intensive to make, especially compared to equivalents made of wood or bark. Therefore they make little sense as practical technological items, but they can be easily understood as prestige items meant to impress others at food events like feasts (see M. Klein 1997).

Even more impressive are the massive (up to one hundred kilograms) deep mortars found in the Natufian (Figure 5.12 – Rosenberg and Nadel, In Press). It is far from clear how such deep mortars could have been manufactured using stone tools, much less why they would have been manufactured (in preference to using wood) given the great amounts of time needed to quarry, transport, and manufacture these items. The unusually deep insides of some mortars seem to have no practical purpose in terms of processing grains or nuts, especially since stone tends to damage grains, resulting in difficulty separating husks from fragmented grains and thus engendering much greater losses than the use of wooden counterparts. Thus, there are good reasons for viewing these mortars (often associated with graves) as unusual and high-cost prestige items, possibly only used for preparing special foods in feasting contexts and sometimes broken at funerary rites.

One of the more common features of feasting among complex hunter/gatherers is that items of wealth (prestige objects) are displayed and often given to guests in the contexts of feasts. Such items can even be destroyed in intensely competitive feasts, and this may be why the large mortars associated with some Natufian burials were intentionally broken or breached. Prestige objects are relatively common in the richest late Epipaleolithic centers of the Near East, including imported dentalium shells (used by the hundreds on burial garments), stone beads (buried by the thousands with some individuals), the imported basalt bowls and mortars, deco-rated pebbles, imported obsidian, pierced canine teeth or bone pendants, shark teeth, bone sculptures, fox and leopard phalanges (indicative of pelts), raptor talons and wing bones (presumably used in costumes), dogs, jade, copper, malachite, and plastered or flagstone architectural features. Feasting often took place in special locations, and these are well represented in the late Epipaleolithic and associated with special community buildings (e.g., at Hallan Çemi, Ain Mallaha, Rosh Horesha; Figure 5.13) and at burial sites that are often located in or in front of caves and associated with bedrock or stone pipe mortars (e.g., Hilazon Tachtit, Shanidar Cave, Raqefet, El Wad; see Solecki et al. 2004; Munro and Grosman 2010; Yeshurun et al. 2013; Rosenberg and Nadel, In Press).

Secondary burials, common in the Late Natufian (Belfer-Cohen and Goring-Morris 2011:215), probably also reflect elaborate funeral feasts since the reason for waiting extended periods of time before final burial is generally to allow enough time to accumulate the maximum resources possible for competitive funeral feasts,

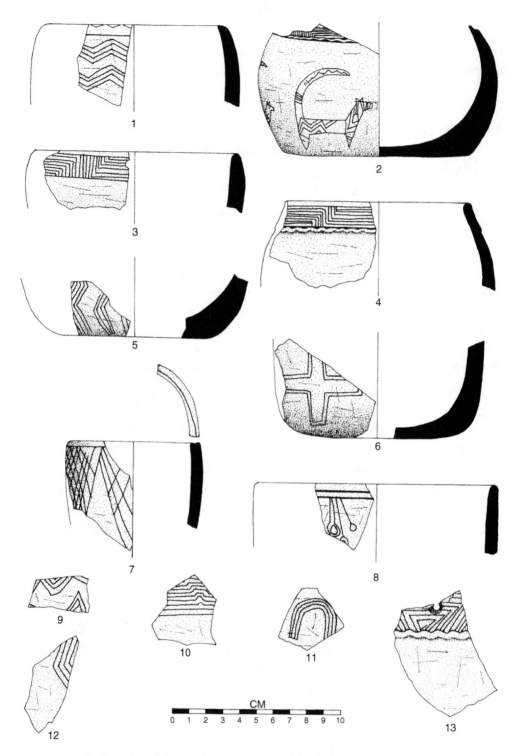

5.11. Finely made and decorated stone cups or small bowls from Hallan Çemi (shown here) and other Epipaleolithic or Pre-Pottery Neolithic A (PPNA) sites in the Near East also testify to the serving of some form of highly valued liquid to important guests at feasts, just before the domestication of plants. One of the most likely liquids to have been served is beer or other fermented drinks. (Rosenberg and Davis 1992: figure 8)

5.12. Some Natufian communities also imported basalt from distant sources (up to 80 kilometers away) and made large "mortars" and stone bowls similar to those made by California Indians (see Figure 4.16). The larger receptacles such as those shown here (c. 40–50 cm tall) from Jebel Saïdé in Lebanon, would have been large enough and narrow enough for effectively brewing beer, but could have also been used for crushing malt for brewing or for processing other nuts like acorns or pistachios. (Photograph courtesy of Bruce Schroeder)

even if grave goods do not accompany the body (Hayden 2009a). Thus, contra Belfer-Cohen and Goring-Morris (2011:215), secondary burials cannot be viewed as indicative of stress conditions, but of situations where surpluses were used in highly competitive fashions.

Despite the richness of foods surrounding major sites, the earliest documented centers for domesticated cereals seem to have been quite far from wild stands of the cereals used, at least 60–100 kilometers in the case of Muyrebet and Abu Hureyra (Hillman et al. 2001:389; Willcox 2007:27,32). Moreover, social complexity appears to have reached remarkable levels in the case of Göbekli Tepe, an initial Neolithic ritual site in Anatolia with monumental stone carvings featuring bulls and other powerful animals. All these sites lack any indication of domesticated animals or plants. Following Hahn's early lead, this led the excavators of the site to suggest that domestication may have arisen from ritual needs (Peters and Schmidt 2004:215), which presumably involved feasting. Jerf el Ahmar, in Syria, is yet another initial "Neolithic" site exhibiting complex ritual architecture including indications of human sacrifices but no domesticated plants or animals. It, too, is far from wild sources of cereals and would appear, on the face of it, to be fundamentally a community of complex hunter/gatherers. As earlier noted, both Göbekli and Jerf

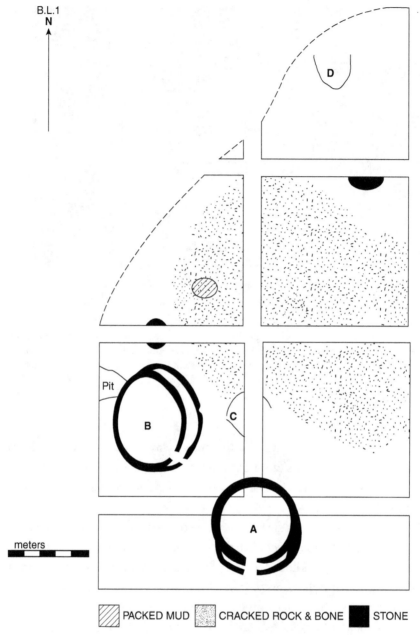

PACKED MUD ⬚ CRACKED ROCK & BONE ■ STONE

5.13. Two ritual structures were excavated at Hallan Çemi next to an open area with abundant faunal remains (black dots) that Michael Rosenberg has interpreted as produced by feasting activities. I suspect that high-ranking individuals may have consumed the best, boneless cuts of meat inside these structures while the general populace ate the bony elements outside. However, the ritual structures may have been reserved for nonfeasting aspects of the ceremonies, with everyone eating outside. An aurochs skull once hung on the wall of the southern structure but was found on the floor together with a variety of prestige items (Rosenberg 1994: figure 3) el Ahmar contain the best evidence for brewing yet found in the Neolithic (Stordeur and Willcox 2009).

Thus, all the expectations of the paleopolitical model of domestication seem well established in the Near East. The initial sites of domestication (as can best be determined) occurred in rich environments among at least seasonally sedentary, complex hunter/gatherers who exhibited socioeconomic complexity and feasting typical of transegalitarian societies. The initial domesticates appear to have been highly desired but labor-intensive cereals to procure and process that did not occur near the first sites of domestication.

With the domestication of plants and the beginning of the Neolithic, there is also a new emphasis placed on the creation of simple clay figurines, especially female figurines (Figure 5.14). These are small, simply made figurines for the most part, not pieces that can easily be conceived of as impressive displays or prestige items. In fact, many are intentionally broken and discarded in areas with everyday domestic refuse, although a few have been found in storage bins (Perlès 2001:262–3; Nakamura and Meskell 2009:226). They are common and widespread, with many households probably making them and discarding them over relatively short time frames, such as a few months or a year or two (Perlès 2001:263). The function of these figurines has often puzzled archaeologists and opinions vary as to whether they are goddess images, pin-up figurines, toys, instructional aids, used in curing rituals, or for other purposes (S. Clark 2009). According to Nakamura and Meskell, the symbolism represented in these figurines was oriented heavily toward signs of longevity, good health, access to food, and abundance as ideal states of being.

Using the historic, and still existing, European and Southeast Asian traditions of corn dollies and rice mothers/goddesses as a conceptual model, I would suggest that the Neolithic figurines might well have represented the "corn" (wheat) spirit of cultivated plots. In both the European and East Asian traditions, there was a spirit that lived in and animated the cultivated fields of grain – a unique feature not characteristic of other crops. As the grain was harvested, the spirit retreated until it was entirely contained in the last sheaf to be cut. In East Asia, this last sheaf was carefully curated until the next year and was typically shaped into the image of the rice goddess or more abstract wheat weavings emblematic of the wheat spirit (see Hayden 2003a,c, 2011c). In Europe, similar practices and beliefs took the form of "corn dollies" (Figure 5.15; Eliade 1958:335–6,341–3); in Japan, they were *shimenawa*; in Thailand, they embodied the spirit of Mae Sophop (Figure 5.16) or guardians of the granaries. After the harvest, these straw figurines were kept in the granary or household and were thought to confer abundance, protection, and good health on the members of the house for the coming year. After the crop was seeded in the following year, the old straw figures were burned or discarded, symbolically returning the spirit to the earth for regeneration.

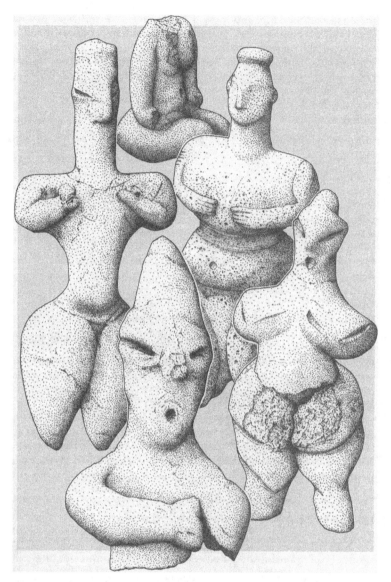

5.14. Neolithic female figurines such as these examples from early Neolithic Greece were widespread but enigmatic features of many households throughout the Eastern Mediterranean. They appear to have been used for short periods and then been broken and discarded together with household refuse. (Perlès 2001: figure 12.1, illustrated by G. Monthel)

I suggest that the clay figurines may have played a similar role during the Neolithic. This would explain their simple manufacture (like the straw figurines), their widespread occurrence, their symbolism involving abundance, and their casual and frequent discard in domestic refuse contexts (or occasional abandonment in granaries) after the grain spirit entered the field again with the new seedings. Similar figurines to those in the Near East and other archaeological material characteristics also occur in Europe.

5.15. One function of the Neolithic figurines that would account for most of their archaeological characteristics would be as representations of the grain spirit, thought to reside in the last harvested sheaf of grain and from which "corn dollies" were made similar to the one shown here. Throughout historical Europe, corn dollies were kept in the houses or granaries and thought to bring good fortune. They were burned or returned to the fields in the following spring. In Southeast Asia, similar figurines (male or female) are made and kept in granaries to protect the grain from malevolent spirits. (Owens-Celli 1997:86)

Europe

Because the domesticated crop complex spread from the Near East to Europe, the tradition of making harvest figurines may have diffused with it. Where European hunter/gatherers adopted the new food complex, it is worth briefly examining the characteristics of these societies to see if the conditions surrounding the diffusion of early domesticates resembled the original conditions in the Near East that produced the new food complex. In particular, the Mesolithic in Northwestern Europe has been shown to have been undergoing resource intensification well before the arrival of Neolithic crops. Intensification took the form of coppicing nut and fruit trees to increase their productivity, as well as the use of hoes and antler mattocks for

5.16. Like the grain spirits of European fields, there was a grain spirit in Southeast Asian rice fields, depicted here as Mae Sophop. As in Europe, only grain crops embodied such spirits. They required care and respect but, in return, conferred prosperity.

working the soil, weirs, basket traps, and probably nets, and the husbanding of wild starchy plant foods (Zvelebil 1994). The result was the emergence of complex hunter/gatherers during the Mesolithic in resource-rich areas, and it can be surmised that these groups probably engaged in potlatch-style feasting. When these groups came into contact with Neolithic immigrants, Van Gijn and Zvelebil (1997:7–8) argue that there would have already been a demand for a number of Neolithic products, especially prestige items or foods such as domesticated animal meat, polished adzes, and cereals, an argument supported by Rowley-Conwy and

Dobney's (2007) study of Mesolithic pig remains. All these items could have been good candidates for use in feasts because they were exotic and therefore would have been avidly sought after. In contrast, the basic subsistence economy would have been relatively unaffected by contacts for some time, perhaps for hundreds or more than a thousand years. Van Gijn and Zvelebil (1997) therefore see little difference between some of the resident late Mesolithic groups and the incoming Neolithic groups in terms of basic social structure and dynamics. However, in their view, eventually, the continual demand for new, more exotic valuables would have created a need for economic intensification and, ultimately, a transition to a new economic system. The process of Neolithization of Mesolithic groups in Western Europe would therefore primarily be driven by social intensification resulting from the exchange and consumption of Neolithic prestige items and foods.

Although the issue of the dietary importance of cereals is a contentious topic, a number of researchers support the conclusion that, in Northwestern and Central Europe at least, cereals were not major dietary items. Lidén (1995:411; 1996) examined the contribution of cereals to diets in Megalithic cultures of Sweden using stable carbon isotopes and concluded, "I would consider cereals as luxury or ritual products in the form of bread, beverages, or just as kernels rather than as an important dietary resource." Jennbert (1984:147; 1985, 1987) also thinks they were luxury items, especially consumed in the form of beer. Stafford (1999:13), Chapman (1995:38–9), and others (see Oswald et al. 2001:33–4) argue for a slow adoption rate and minor role of cereals among megalith builders of North and Western Europe. Much earlier, Kaelas (1981:88) referred to Neolithic foods as luxury items in Germany and Scandinavia and of little dietary importance because they required more effort to produce than collecting the wild plant foods, whereas Marciniak (2005:207–8) came to the same conclusion for domesticated plants and animals in Central Europe, suggesting that they spread in the context of feasting. Fischer (2002:349,372–3,376–7) came to the same conclusion for Denmark, where cultivation in the early Neolithic was very limited and unimportant in subsistence, and he viewed cattle and grain as luxury items probably used in feasts, with grain most likely consumed in the form of beer and bread. These views make sense in terms of the high risks associated with early cultivation, especially in European forests (Gregg 1988:156,161).

The conclusions about the type of society that would have had a use for, and be attracted to, domesticates (complex hunter/gatherers), the long-lasting relatively minor role of domesticates, and the prestige role of domesticates for special events, are precisely what the paleopolitical ecology model predicts should have been the case. Given the pattern thus far, it will be instructive to compare the Near Eastern and European cases with the Far Eastern center of cereal domestication involving rice.

China and Japan

Some critics of the feasting and surplus model of domestication claim that rice was a mundane, vulgar subsistence food never being used as a luxury food (e.g., B. Smith 2001a). Therefore, it was argued, the feasting model of domestication was not credible. In view of such claims, I decided to investigate this question in greater depth. I had ethnoarchaeological experience with Southeast Asian hill tribes, and I was impressed with the fundamental role that rice played in their culture, especially their feasts. I suspected that key features involving the initial domestication of rice had remained relatively unchanged in some of these groups, especially since the cultivation of hill (swidden) rice was much less productive than irrigated paddy rice and was probably the earliest form of rice cultivation. Essentially, it seemed to me that although technology had improved with the use of metals, marginal groups like the hill tribes had been able to subsist in increasingly marginal environments where the production of cereals remained approximately on a par with the likely production levels of grains in early Neolithic societies. If this was true, the dietary and cultural roles of rice might also be similar to the way early Neolithic groups dealt with rice. In any event, the role of rice in tribal societies with traditional social organizations is arguably more similar to early prehistoric societies than contemporary industrial or even intensive lowland paddy agricultural societies. The detailed results of my investigation are available elsewhere (Hayden 2011c), but a few key points can be highlighted here.

A number of important technological innovations appeared in the Chinese "Mesolithic" (about 15,000–10,000 years ago) including the first pottery, grinding stones, bone tools, ground-edge axes, hoe-shaped stone tools, bone hoes and spades, bone drills, pierced stone disks (for fishing or digging stick weights), harpoons, and possible shell sickles. It appears that some groups had the technology to extract abundant resources from favorable environments, especially where water resources were plentiful. Dugout canoes that are materially documented by 8000 BP but are probably older and, at the site of Yuchanyan, there was a wide array of animals used (twenty-eight species) in addition to fish, waterfowl and birds (twenty-seven species), shellfish (thirty-three species) nuts, and other plants (forty species). The presence of pottery so early is important because it is considered an indication of increased, at least seasonal, sedentism and because pottery may have been used to prepare specialty foods such as fish oils, nut oils, soups, or beers that would have been especially important in feasts (Hayden 2009b). There are also indications at the site of Zengpiyan that pigs may have been raised for funeral feasts during the Chinese Mesolithic, even if their skeletal morphology was still wild. Social complexity appears to have been increasing in the Chinese Mesolithic, as indicated by the first appearance of shell beads, perforated tooth necklaces, and bone needles at several burial sites. Cemeteries also appear for the first time, such as Zengpiyan and the Upper Cave at Zhoukoudian. Thus, in favorable localities, it would appear that complex hunter/gatherers developed in the Far East just as they had in the Near East. These developments became even more elaborated in the following Pengtoushan/Bashidang culture (c. 9000–7500 BP) with permanent architecture, more refined and more common pottery, larger permanent settlements, an array of prestige items (beads, pendants, bone flutes, incised shell rattles, turquoise, and other grave goods), and even defensive ditches and walls. This is the first time that rice grains are found in any quantity, although authors are divided in their opinions as to whether the rice was wild or domesticated. If it was largely or entirely wild, as maintained by Fuller et al. (2007, 2009) and Crawford (2006), then the Pengtoushan/Bashidang cultures begin to look quite similar to the late Epipaleolithic complex hunter/gatherers of the Near East at sites like Abu Hureyra or even Jerf el Ahmar in terms of sedentism, permanent architecture, resource exploitation, prestige goods, and socioeconomic complexity. The production of alcohol has even been documented at a contemporary Chinese site (Jiahu) further downstream along the Yangzi River (McGovern et al. 2004).

Also important is the fact that wild rice was remarkably unproductive as a plant food (yielding only about 1.3 grains from each panicle). In part due to its low seed production, which is spaced out over time (Lu 2006), wild rice would require between 8.7 and 10.2 hours every day to gather, husk, and cook for a meal. In contrast, experimental gathering took only two to three hours to obtain other wild foods for daily fare consisting of wild yams, bamboo roots, and shellfish (142–4). Even more telling is the fact that the sites where the earliest evidence of domesticated rice occur all fall at the margin or even outside of the natural distribution of rice so that, at best, wild rice plants would not have been very plentiful (Figure 5.17). Thus, although wild rice may have been relished for its natural good taste and nutrition or perhaps for its ability to produce alcoholic beverages, it would have been very costly to procure and prepare in the heartland of rice domestication. However, in the early hearths of domestication in the Far East, the natural characteristics of wild rice would have made it an excellent feasting food for any complex hunter/gatherers or later cultures. I suggest that this is why there has been such an enduring emic tradition throughout East Asia focused on the importance and value of rice, just as bread continued to be valued for feasts in Europe. Even up until historic times, the production of rice was a risky undertaking, and few families could produce as much as they wanted to consume. For example, even the historic elites in China used rice primarily for ceremonies, which included feasts (Ho 1969:27). The same pattern is found throughout most of island and mainland Southeast Asia, including the Philippines (R. Adams 2001; Junker 2001).

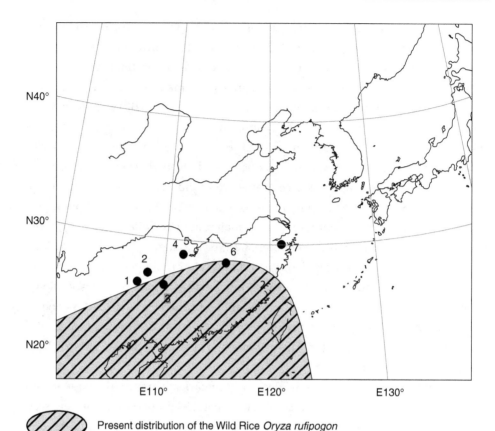

N40°

N30°

N20°

E110°   E120°   E130°

Present distribution of the Wild Rice *Oryza rufipogon*

● Earliest rice farming sites

1   Liuzhou Dalongtan Liyuzui site, Guangxi zhuang Autonomous
2   Miaoyan site, Guilin, Guangxi zhuang Autonomous
3   Yuchanyan site, Dao County, Hunan Province
4   Bashidang site, Hunan Province
5   Pengtoushan site, Hunan Province
6   Xianrendong site and Diaotonghuan site, Jiangxi Province
7   Hemudu site, Zhejiang Province

5.17. A key feature of early domesticated grains like rice and wheat is that the regions of first domestication were generally close to or beyond the zones of natural occurrences, as illustrated in this distribution map of wild forms of rice and the earliest sites where domesticated rice has been claimed (sites 3–7). (Yasuda 2002: figure 15)

Rice came late to Japan, approximately coeval with the arrival of the Yayoi culture and populations from the mainland c. 2000 BP. However, thousands of years before, the indigenous complex hunter/gatherers of Japan, the Jomon, had already imported luxury foods to the Japanese archipelago. Peaches, paper mulberries, lacquer, and wild boars do not appear to be native to Japan but begin to appear by Early Jomon or later deposits (Esaka 1986:226). The other early domesticates in Japan hardly can be considered subsistence staples but make much more sense as feasting condiments or as simple prestige displays. These include the bottle gourd, the dog, mung beans, hemp, colza (for oil), shiso mint, and burdock plus small later amounts of millet and barley that Habu (2004:71–2) links to feasting. It is difficult to construe the Jomon as anything less than complex hunter/gatherers given their large settlements, large-scale storage, elaborate cemeteries, sedentary lifestyle, production of elaborate pottery, many prestige objects, monumental architecture and mounds, stone features, exotic imports (amber, jade, cinnabar, shells, obsidian, asphalt), and luxury items (lacquered wares and decorative pieces, earrings, pendants, bone hairpins, shell bracelets and ornaments, even phallic stone scepters; Habu 2004:182–3,221–38).

The Americas

Many of these same features occur in the centers of domestication of eastern North America, and they warrant at least a passing mention. The first evidence for cultivation or domestication appears in the late Archaic period (Gremillion 1996), around 5,000 years ago (or up to 7000 BP for managed, "semi-domesticated" bottle gourds; Doran 2002:14–18). The first domesticates consist of bottle gourds (*Lagenaria*) and squash, probably cultivated for their use as large (possibly decorated) display containers (Figures 4.7 and 5.2) for liquids or grease (in the case of gourds; Doran 2002) or for their oily seeds in the case of squashes (Flannery 1986a:6,17; D. Anderson 2002:254; Taché et al. 2008). Chenopods, sunflower, and marsh ivy were cultivated later, followed by the introduction of maize. As described in Chapter 4, there is also considerable evidence that by 5000 BP or earlier, Middle and Late Archaic communities in environmentally productive areas were developing increasingly complex socioeconomic systems using exotic or local prestige goods produced by specialists and mounting elaborate funeral ceremonies at recognized cemeteries involving funeral feasts (Charles and Buikstra 1983:126,140; James Brown and Vierra 1983:165–6; D. Anderson 2002:257, 2010; Brookes 2004; Taché 2008), sometimes even erecting mounds for ceremonies possibly related to funeral rites (Knight 2001; D. Anderson 2010). In fact, D. Anderson (2004:293) argues that the appearance of these types of societies probably preceded the first appearance of mounds. James Brown (1983:7) describes plant domestication as taking place among "affluent" midwestern foragers, a point on which even Bruce Smith concurs (Smith 2007:197; Smith and Yarnell 2007). Thus, transegalitarian complexity was developing either before or in tandem with the first domesticates in eastern North America. Although it is easy to see how increased complexity (including feasting) could have created pressures to develop domestication, as Harlan said, it is difficult to see how a few domesticated squash plants could have had much, if any, impact on cultural complexity – that is, unless they were part of a prestige food system already in place, as indicated by the gourd use in Mesoamerica previously discussed.

In general, the first North American domesticates appear to have played little if any role in overall subsistence, and this situation persisted over hundreds, if not thousands, of years even into Hopewellian times (Webb 1998:743; Knight 2001; Yerkes 2005, 2006; Pluckhahn et al. 2006:272; also Diehl 1996 for the Southwest). Even more importantly, after their introduction, domesticates like maize and tobacco appear to have been cultivated in small quantities and were primarily associated with elites or ritual contexts, such as platform mounds (Nassaney 1992:126; Fritz and Kidder 1993; Wymer 1994; Lindauer and Blitz 1997:186; Knight 2001:327–8; Coltrain and Leavitt 2002:474; Reber 2006:244–5). The Fremont elites did it, the Hopewellian and Mississippian elites did it, the elites along the South American Pacific coast did it. All the early maize using elites seem to have done it. They all used maize as a special food. Although maize was introduced as a domesticate relatively late in some regional sequences, it seems reasonable to assume that the role it played in Woodland societies would have been similar to indigenous domesticates. Thus, it is of additional interest that a number of researchers in the field have suggested that maize was a powerful instrument in the negotiation of shifting socioreligious patterns (Johannessen 1993:188) or as initially being important in ceremonialism (Wymer 1994; Webb 1998:743). Even earlier, in the Late Archaic, Sassaman et al. (2006:561) argue that changes in technology including the early adoption of pottery, pit storage, carinated bowls (and presumably early domesticates) were not due to climatic stress or population–resource imbalances but to the increasing costs of intensified ritual activity. The same relationships appear to have continued into historic times beyond the northern limits of maize cultivation, where boreal forest hunting and gathering societies went to great lengths and distances to obtain maize from horticulturalists farther to the south. These efforts were not to procure maize for subsistence purposes. Its primary value appears to have been symbolic and social – as a luxury food, involved in "gift giving, reciprocity, ritual feasts and ceremonies" (Boyd and Surette 2010:129).

In Mesoamerica, very little archaeological research has been conducted in the Central Balsas drainage, which is currently viewed as the most likely hearth of domestication for maize (Piperno 2011). However, the original role of maize may be reflected in its first appearance in neighboring areas. For instance, throughout early coastal southern Mesoamerica, there was a general pattern "of a relatively low-yield primitive maize variety being adopted by Early Formative communities (or perhaps even earlier by Late Archaic populations), not as a subsistence crop but, rather, as an exotic commodity for use in specialized activities such as competitive feasts" (VanDerwarker and Kruger 2012:528). VanDerwarker and Kruger note that when more productive forms of maize became available, it was able to become a staple food, without, however, losing its status in specialized rituals. In addition, Smalley and Blake (2003) have argued that the initial motive for domesticating maize may have been because of demands for making alcoholic beverages from its stalk juices, a practice still followed in various parts of Mexico. They note that, in addition to the high labor costs of growing and processing maize, it has several dietary deficiencies and would be unsuitable for use as a lone staple. As has been noted earlier, in traditional societies, alcohol appears to be consumed exclusively in feasting contexts and therefore any indication of brewing or alcohol consumption can be considered indexical of feasts in archaeological contexts. In addition, Smalley and Blake note that the earliest ceramic forms resemble gourds and were probably used to hold special liquids, like fermented juices or maize drinks.

In South America, it is well established that maize was used by the Inca to marshal labor and essentially run their empire via work and other feasts (Morris 1979; Jennings et al. 2005; Staller 2006). Tykot and Staller (2002:674) extend this pattern back to the initial introduction of maize into the northern Andes by suggesting that maize "spread initially as a primary ingredient for the consumption of fermented intoxicants rather than a solid food staple." Maize also tends to be found in ritual contexts in South America, indicating its use in feasting. Benz and Staller (2006:670–1) document its minimal importance to early agricultural economies but its widespread occurrence in early ceremonial contexts. They go so far as to conclude that "in its early stages, maize was primarily a ritual plant used to make fermented beer or *chicha* that was consumed in the context of gift giving, ritual feasts and religious ceremonies ... it initially is associated with elite and ceremonial contexts almost exclusively." Logan et al. (2012) confirm this pattern for the first use of maize in the Titicaca basin. The same was also true during Chavín times (Burger and van der Merwe 1990). By the first millennium CE, elites were consuming significantly more maize (probably as beer) than others (Ubelaker et al. 1995). In sum, as Ikehara et al. (n.d.) have argued, maize was adopted due to political considerations, not subsistence needs. Modern maize requires four times more land to produce a calorie than manioc requires, and prehistoric maize varieties were even less productive. Moreover, producing maize beer requires 4.8–26 times more cultivated land than manioc. Hence, where agricultural land was at a premium, as on the coast, Ikehara et al. think that maize must have been produced by the affluent and played a critical role in social control and the development of hierarchies. Maize use is, in fact, strongly associated with political complexity throughout Andean prehistory (see Chapters 6–9). Ikehara et al. suggest a similar feasting role for manioc before the introduction of maize.

But even before the appearance of maize in South America, bottle gourds (as net floats or, perhaps more likely, the cultivation and selection of larger varieties as display containers for serving or storing oils or greases) and squash were domesticated plants (c. 2200 BCE). They, too, occurred primarily in ritual contexts (Duncan et al. 2009). Even earlier (c. 6000–4200 BCE), groups on the northern Peruvian coast were constructing mounds, indicating that they had developed relatively complex socioeconomic societies and that they were engaging in "incipient horticulture" using several species of cultigens including squash, peanuts, and quinoa, although it is not clear whether these displayed any domesticated morphological characteristics (Dillehay et al. 1989:749).

What do the preceding patterns of contexts for early domesticates reveal about the initial reasons for domesticating plants?

DISCUSSION AND SUMMARY

What all the preceding observations indicate is that ethnographically and archaeologically, the first domesticates appear to have played important roles in feasting. The case is especially strong for domestic animals, to the point that, when archaeologists find remains of domesticated animals in prehistoric contexts, they should be asking themselves "What kind of feast does this represent?" rather than "Does this indicate feasting?" Although some of the modern forms of the plant domesticates may have now become the "vulgar" staves of life – major caloric staples for billions of people – the early yields of the wild forms and initial domesticated forms of these modern staples hardly seem to have been calorically attractive. Wild rice, in particular, is remarkably unproductive. Other cereals require considerable processing to render them edible and thus have low caloric returns. The earliest cultivated maize from the Tehuacan Valley is estimated to have produced only sixty to eighty kilograms or less per hectare, whereas modern subsistence farmers consider anything less than 200–250 kilogram per hectare as not worth the effort to plant (Flannery 1973:297–8). These are all a far cry from the 100:1 returns achieved by Sumerian farmers (Liverani 2006:6), and such returns could hardly have been anticipated at the dawn of domestication. Rather, people had to contend with unusually low returns, replete with high risks of partial or complete failures and crop losses.

From traditional ecological perspectives, considering the substantial distances people often traveled to procure cereals or to procure and raise animals like bears and aurochs, it is difficult to make economically rational sense out of such behavior unless people were on the verge of starvation. On the other hand, the feasting model ties a wide range of archaeological and ethnographic observations together and makes sense of unanticipated outcomes, such as the bimodal distribution of reliance on domesticates and the overseas transport of wild animals and their subsequent disappearance. Feasting provides the motive, the energy, and the tangible benefits to the effort-demanding cultivation and domestication of unrewarding plants or costly and difficult-to-raise animals. It provides the reason for intensification. It accounts for the early domestication of nonfood plants and animals such as bottle gourds, dogs, turkeys, tobacco, and hemp. It accounts for the long delay of any significant impact on subsistence in all the independent centers. It makes sense in the context of prestige and other technologies: the dentalia, the mortars and grinding stones, brewing, fire-cracked rocks, ritual, new procurement technologies, storage, intensification, the entire range of aggrandizer strategies, higher population densities, and more. Instead of developing *separate* explanations for the domestication of nonfood species, food species, and incidental food species, these can all be brought together under the umbrella of a single theory of domestication. Herskovits (1940:461–5), Sahlins (1972:101–7), Earle (1978:173), and others have argued that the dynamics of "political economies" are quite different from the dynamics of normal subsistence economies. Although optimal foraging theory, behavioral ecology, and other models have dealt very effectively with subsistence economies among hunter/gatherers, they have failed to deal with, or even to acknowledge, the importance of political economies. The main imperative in political economies is to establish sociopolitical networks of debt and support by gifting prestige objects, including prestige foods, and by mounting impressive displays. To impress actual or potential partners with hosts' socioeconomic power, ambitious individuals try to invest as much effort and labor into the procurement or production of prestige objects as they can afford. In contrast, the goal in practical technologies is to minimize the amount of effort expended to make tools or perform tasks. Thus, the logic of prestige technologies is diametrically opposed to practical technologies and turns its energy dynamic upside down (Hayden 1998). I suggest that the same thing is true of subsistence foods versus prestige foods used in feasts, where the most highly valued foods are the most labor intensive to procure or prepare (e.g., Young 1971). People used as much time and resources as they could to create prestige items, and they did the same thing for feasting foods: they cultivated and made substantial efforts to improve them. It cannot be coincidental that prestige technologies develop just before or at the same time as domesticates first appear, even though the traditional view has always been that agriculture made social and technological complexity possible. This is clearly not the case in the Jomon, the Northwest Coast, Eastern North America, or the Natufian, where the prestige technologies of complex hunter/gatherers appeared before domestication.

The development of political and prestige economies represents an entirely new dynamic that emerged in the world for the first time late in the Pleistocene. This new dynamic created unlimited demands for resources due to the competition for benefits associated with surpluses used in feasting and other resource-based strategies to promote the self-interests of the ambitious. There could never be enough prestige items or food, the entire system was highly inflationary, and the boundaries of potential production were constantly being stretched (Hakansson 1994, 1995).

I have developed these insights from direct experiences in traditional villages. The power of feasts can probably best be appreciated from actual experiences in traditional villages rather than from archaeological excavations or analyses undertaken by the "hard science" practitioners who like to vaunt their white coats but who are reluctant to venture into real tribal communities. People do not engage in feasting when they are hard pressed by subsistence needs nor do they start experimenting with risky, unproductive, and uncertain cultivation or domestication when they are hard pressed by subsistence needs. Like the chimpanzees described in Chapter 2, people need to be assured of adequate subsistence before they begin investing large amounts of time and effort in risky propositions for highly desired foods that might not yield anything in any given year.

In addition to the specialty prestige plants that were domesticated, it may be that the production of some more staple or even "vulgar" plant foods were also intensified or cultivated to provide surpluses to feed animals raised for feasts, to brew beer, or to provide enough feast "filler" foods for large events, much as salmon and shellfish were the dominant feasting foods for Northwest Coast feasts, in contrast to the hunted meat, oil, and starchy roots that were the most prized foods consumed by the most important guests. This is the same logic that continues to guide food provisioning in contemporary feasts in which there are some less expensive filler snacking foods and more valued main course foods.

It should be emphasized that once a feasting system was established, the system would have been extremely resilient. Once aggrandizers managed to obtain benefits and power for themselves and supporters through establishing ownership rights to food resources, the uses of prestige items, bartering for marriages, and restricted access to the supernatural, they would have defended these gains using every means possible against any erosion due to economic or environmental downturns. Even if it was necessary to abandon some of these claims temporarily due to climate or other economic setbacks, aggrandizers would have clung tenaciously to their hard-won benefits and worked relentlessly to restore their positions of privilege by intensifying production even more, inventing new technologies, going greater distances to procure the most desirable foods for feasts, and probably beginning to grow the required foods locally to supplement what could not be obtained by travel or trade, even though cultivated crops demanded considerable efforts.

The paleopolitical ecology model also predicts that the internal dynamics of feasting systems would eventually sow the seeds of transformation of many luxury foods resulting in their conversion to mundane, even vulgar subsistence foods. Because individual resources were limited, but individuals strove to put on the most impressive displays that they could afford, it could be expected that aggrand- izers would have attempted to minimize actual costs while maximizing display appearances. One obvious way to achieve this would have been through develop- ing technologically more efficient ways of harvesting and processing luxury foods. Another way would have been to try to improve cultivated production through seed selection that enhanced size or other desirable characteristics, such as those that facilitated harvesting or processing. If these strategies were sustained over many generations, the ultimate result would have been the debasement of the cost of luxury foods to the point at which they could compete with and even supplant almost all other wild foods in terms of return rates and diet breadth ranking.

This process is still going on today and can be chronicled in any modern food store. Historically, white bread or cake (using refined labor-intensive flour without husk or bran) was reserved only for the European elites. Today, due to technological improvements, white bread has become the banal plague of modern meals. Chocolate, once reserved for Mesoamerican elites, is now the bane of overfed multitudes. Oversized, out-of-season fruits and vegetables that once only graced the tables of kings and nobles have become everyday fares. Fat-rich meats formerly used only for special occasions or for the highest ranks of society are now common- place for all but the poorest, to the extent that they now clog the arteries of large segments of the population. Beer and wines that played special roles in feasts and rituals for elites have now become the profane intoxicants of households through- out the Industrial world. In short, our modern eating habits largely are the result of – and reflect – the luxury foods of the past. Technology and genetic manipulation have made them cheap and commonplace. Thus, when some archaeologists object to the feasting model of domestication because they think the early domesticates were mundane, vulgar, subsistence foods, we should pause to wonder if our contemporary views are not obscuring past realities that we have forgotten or are only dimly conscious.

With the establishment of the first cultivation systems, even on small scales, we enter into the traditional realm of horticulture, that is, transegalitarian gardening societies. In some of the more remote areas of the world where they sometimes persisted down to the present, such societies maintained or enhanced the fine art of feasting and politics. This is the topic of the next chapter.

6

The Horticultural Explosion

> Neailena of Foloyi ran amuck in his fury at being given "food for nothing." Foloyai is not Ainaona's fofofo, nor are they fictionally related ... Kaniyowana was roundly defeated by several pigs. In the main contest, Kwalauya won in taro but lost in bananas.
>
> – Young 1971:219

With the emergence of cultivation and domesticated species of plants, a new chapter in cultural development opens. However, this chapter does not read, as the traditional textbooks would have it, with agriculture as *the* major watershed in cultural evolution. The major watershed occurred with the appearance of complex (transegalitarian) hunter/gatherers. Virtually all of the cultural innovations traditionally attributed to Neolithic cultures actually first appeared before agriculture or domestication arrived on the scene. Pottery, ground stone tools, sedentism, storage, population densities that were often greater than one person per square kilometer (with the worldwide average density for swidden horticulture of 5.6 people/square kilometer; Watters 1960), large villages with permanent architecture, heterarchical organization, monumental architecture, burial mounds, competitive feasting, all of the most common aggrandizer strategies, cemeteries, socioeconomic inequalities, secret societies, ancestor worship, prestige items, and even the use of native metals are often still considered to be hallmarks of the Neolithic, but *all occurred first in complex hunter/gatherer societies.*

The main point is that aside from the use of domesticated species (often as very minor components of subsistence), *there are no fundamental differences between most complex hunter/gatherers and horticulturalists*, despite what some archaeologists and ethnographers may imagine (e.g., Whittle 1994, 1996). A number of researchers have commented on this basic similarity (Testart 1982; Price and Brown 1985; Shnirelman 1992; Arnold 1996; Roscoe 2002), but the observation seems to have gone largely unnoticed by many archaeologists. Nevertheless, the fundamental similarities in the dynamics of these cultures, whether complex hunter/gatherers or horticulturalists or pastoralists, is why I refer to them all as *transegalitarian cultures*. And, as may well be expected from the overall similarity of transegalitarian cultures, there is a strong continuity and similarity in feasting expressions, dynamics, and behavior between what was documented for complex hunter/gatherers in Chapter 4 and what we will be observing in this chapter on horticultural societies (see Figure 6.1).

Conversely, the introduction of food production in the form of cultivation and domestication did *ultimately* have some effect on cultural complexity and feasting behavior, but I think this occurred long after horticultural societies became established. In my conception, the initial production of food with cultivation and domestication probably only enhanced the feasting fare, so that initial effects on cultural complexity were minimal. However, as we saw in the preceding chapter, as the technology of cultivation improved (with irrigation, manuring, spading, weeding, and the ability to clear forest cover) and as people improved the productivity of various species by selectively planting seeds or vegetative parts with the most productive or easily processed characteristics, food production eventually began to become more cost-effective for subsistence purposes than did collecting wild foods. It was at this point that it became possible to increase amounts of surpluses and to produce much greater amounts of food. Whereas hunter/gatherers were limited in the amount of surplus that they could produce from the natural biota, horticulturalists could always increase the amount of food and surplus they produced by modifying their environments via the clearing and planting of more cultivated area and by investing more energy in the area worked via irrigation, weeding, fertilizing, and excluding competing species (Figure 6.2).

This was the real meaning of horticulture. It did not change the nature of society, but it did make it possible to intensify social, economic, and political features that had already been established by complex hunter/gatherers. Aggrandizers in horticultural societies could eventually produce more surpluses, hold larger and more costly feasts, create more debts, and engineer somewhat more political control. Cultivation rather than rearing animals may have been the major means used to augment feasting abilities for the first several thousand years perhaps because raising animals was more costly than cultivating plants (and it still is). However, at some point, domestic animals became the repository of family wealth, and their consumption was only deemed appropriate for special occasions when they would be used to make a social investment, such as in marriages, alliances, and political factions. Even pastoralists rarely consume their animals except for special events but rely instead on their milk and blood or the high exchange value of domestic animals for agricultural products. The descriptions of feasting dynamics to come should thus seem familiar although there are, to be sure, local variations.

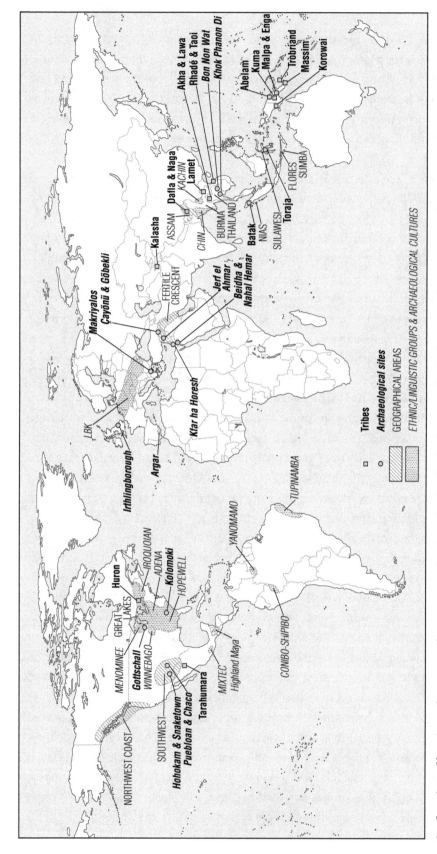

6.1. Locations of key sites, culture areas, ethnic groups, and regions related to feasting in transegalitarian horticultural societies.

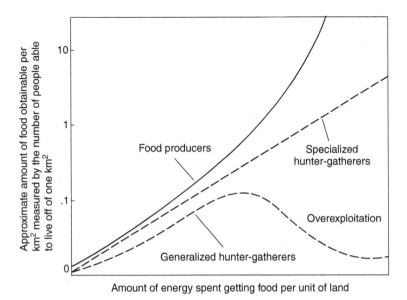

6.2. The amount of food that individuals can obtain by working more hours changes dramatically with the advent of farming. If foragers increase the amount of time they spend getting food in a given area, they will eventually deplete their wild resources, resulting in diminishing returns for increased work. Complex hunter/gatherers generally depend on resources such as grass seeds or fish that are difficult to overexploit with traditional technologies so that there is a regular incremental gain in yields in relation to the hours spent working. On the other hand, the more effort that farmers put into their fields (fertilizing, irrigating, weeding, mulching), the more food can be produced. (Hayden 1993: figure 7.4)

GENERAL FEASTING PRINCIPLES

The basic feasting principles that can be identified among transegalitarian horticultural groups are virtually identical to those of transegalitarian hunter/gatherers. Surpluses were essential for feasts. As Tooker (1964:64,72, ftn. 21) observed, there were many feasts when the fishing was good. Private property and control over sites with the best resource production were key ideological foundations. Among the Batak, "the drive to produce above need is set in motion by individual seekers of power or wealth. ... The desire to accumulate surplus is undeniably motivated at times by the desire to give a feast – to improve one's chance of future success, as well as to acquire or validate prestige" (Sherman 1990:304). As we shall see later, others make the same point and describe domestic animals as luxury products used for ceremonial occasions but unnecessary for subsistence. Amassing the desired surpluses generally entails borrowing resources and the creation of debts as well as storage of resources, and, at least in some cases, feasting may be the major reason for storage (see Chapter 4). However, even when used as a means of reducing subsistence risk, storage creates strong pressures to hold feasts or invest unused production in domestic animals (to be used in feasts). As mentioned in Chapter 4,

Testart (1982:527–8) and Halstead (1989; 1990:151–6; Halstead and O'Shea 1989) discuss the overproduction that storage entails due to risks of losses and the quandary of what to do with such surpluses in years when risk factors fail to materialize. Many aggrandizers must have found ways to use surpluses to advance their own benefits, especially via loans at high interest rates, invitations to feasts that indebted guests, and high marriage prices.

Loans of such surpluses typically carried the same range of interest rates as those in complex hunter/gatherer societies. For unrelated individuals, and sometimes kin, this was usually 50–100 percent per loan, sometimes compounded yearly (Head 1916). Loans between kin or other supporters of a given feasting network often had no or low interest charges to pay (Monaghan 1990:770). The amount of surplus production consecrated for use in feasts is rarely mentioned for trans-egalitarian hunter/gatherers, although we may suspect that it was substantial given the number and frequency of feasts recorded by Jewitt (Marshall 2002). For horticultural groups, there are a few more estimates. Waddell (1972:118) states that 60 percent of sweet potato production and 50 percent of overall food production was fed to pigs, all of which were used in feasts, together with more sweet potatoes and other foods. Roscoe (2012) used reports from a number of groups in New Guinea to estimate that adults spent 8–18 hours per week raising pigs, all of which were for feasts and ceremonies. On a similar scale, Dietler (2001:81; 1990) and others (Arthur 2003:517; Barth 1967:161) document the use of 25–50 percent of grain production being used to brew beer, all of which would have been consumed in feasts together with other foods. In roughly comparable terms, Stevenson (1943:115) reported that Kachin surpluses ranged from 600 to 1,600 pounds of grain per household, the great bulk of which would have been destined for feasting. Archaeologically, Bogaard et al. (2009) have estimated that households at Çatal Höyük stored 50–100 percent more than they needed for subsistence, and this excess was probably used mainly for feasting. Thus, it would appear that the total amount, or cost, of food produced for horticultural feasts could be of surprising proportions, amounting to half or more of all food production, probably stretching voluntary production capacity close to its limit. Even with this large proportion devoted to feasting, hosts strived to provide ever more by borrowing and abstaining from eating to put on better displays at feasts. Monaghan (1990:760) provides an excellent discussion of this system in terms of maximizing feasting food via prior reciprocal loans that acted to store surpluses with other families, maximize the labor pool for food preparation, and make surpluses available when needed. By this means, households hosting feasts only directly supplied 12–23 percent of the food consumed.

Many of the foods used in ceremonial exchanges and presumably in feasts, at least for high-ranking individuals, were scarce items or costly to produce or acquire.

such as pigs (Modjeska 1982:74; Feil 1987:244; Lemonnier 1990:73). However, normal staples sometimes were used as fillers, in special preparations, or in the form of special sizes or varieties, as with taro and sago (Powdermaker 1932:240; Stasch 2012:60,371). Amassing the large surpluses required for the most important feasts typically required 5–10 years, or rarely 15 years (Young 1971:247; Wiessner and Tumu 1998:265–8) perhaps representing an upper time limit for practical reasons involving career spans and life expectancies.

Although some authors seem to imply that the simple act of giving confers superiority, status, and power on people, reality seems far different. As Chapman (1996:36), has noted, giving by itself does not lead to power. It is the contractual obligation to return the gift that creates power and "status." Monaghan (1990) views these mutual debts as creating a sense of community (as his Mixtec inform-ants expressed it). However, he ignored the rampant factionalism and struggles for political power that typify indigenous Mesoamerican communities and the roles that debts and feasting play in these contexts. I think he placed too much trust in the ideological rhetoric of his informants, which, like the expressions of "equality" in other transegalitarian communities, bears little relationship to actual behavior or motives. In Monaghan's study, this was evident in the paternalistic attitude of political leaders (768), and, as Monaghan himself says, "fiestas signal the economic and political potency of the household." Obligatory debts resulting from being an invited guest and recipient of gifts appear to be universal in transegalitarian feasts (Mauss 1924; Durrenberger 1989:106). If anything, they are even more pronounced in transegalitarian horticultural societies than in complex hunter/gatherer societies. Consequences for defaulting on contractual feasting debts are equally severe as those in complex hunter/gatherer societies and could lead to raids, warfare, or enslavement (discussed in Chapter 4; see also Kaberry 1942:86; Condominas 1977; Sillitoe 1978:260; Woodward 1989:124; Reay 1959). Refusal of a "gift" was tanta-mount to a declaration of war (Mauss 1924). The same basic strategies were used to attract people to feasts as among complex hunter/gatherers: abundant and lux-urious foods ("food of the gods"), prestige objects, songs, dances, costumes, drama (sometimes including human as well as animal sacrifices), and intoxicants (now almost universal), all creating kaleidoscopic sensual and emotional experiences for participants. Those who could not be attracted to participate were derided and ostracized with epithets similar to those reported in Chapter 4.

Emerging elites evidently found it prudent to avoid drawing too much attention to the increasing inequalities in power and wealth lest people opt out of their schemes. However, aggrandizers did their best to manipulate community norms and values in their favor using feasting venues. Edmund Leach (1954:87,263) found that all leaders wanted to change their social systems for their own benefit and often repudiated or broke existing norms and rules. In Leach's words, a leader is

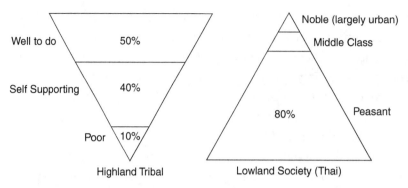

6.3. Hill tribes in Southeast Asia, like most transegalitarian societies with limited and unreliable surplus production, have a very different socioeconomic structure from the more stratified societies of the highly productive lowlands and most state societies. The familiar socioeconomic "pyramid" of state societies is essentially turned upside-down. The similarity with Suttles's independent characterization of Northwest Coast cultures (Figure 4.2) is remarkable. (Falvey 1977:41)

"an ambitious seeker after power who treats economic facts with greater respect than ritual theories." Feasts are excellent venues for achieving transformations of ideological values (Dietler 2001:79,82–3). They can be used to camouflage or legitimize asymmetries of power or to promote ideologies that normalize private property; use wealth to obtain spouses via wealth transfers; create claims of dangers from breaking taboos; and increase the powers of secret societies, ancestors, or the material blessings that come from hosting feasts and offering sacrifices to ancestors (e.g., Durrenburger 1989:107–8). In addition, Roscoe (2009) observes that aggrandizers in New Guinea continued to construct and manipulate kin-based support groups to underwrite feasting and other enterprises, changing genealogies as needed (E. Leach 1954:164; Lehman 1963:113; Feil 1987:156). "Great men" achieved power through their knowledge and skill in war, hunting, ritual, feasting, and art; "big men" achieved their goals through the social (and other) manipulation of others, especially via feasts and the conspicuous distribution of materials. They were manipulators par excellence, and noncooperating families generally became socioeconomic casualties (e.g., E. Leach 1954:182). The result was a socioeconomic pyramid that was inverted or, perhaps more accurately, pear-shaped, similar to the one for complex hunter/gatherers (compare Figure 6.3 with Figure 4.2; Falvey 1977), with most families being involved in feasting networks and thus being well-off, and fewer noncooperating and nonfeasting families ending up disenfranchised and poor. On the basis of African ethnographies, Webster (1990:346) argued for a similar socioeconomic structure for prehistoric Europe.

As among complex hunter/gatherers, foremost among the main transegalitarian feasting and competitive arenas were lavish funeral feasts at which alliances were brokered or renewed and ancestors were elevated in importance as useful tools to promote compliance with lineage heads' agendas as well as

6.4. Animal sacrifices at major feasts are perhaps the most dramatic aspects of large feasts and undoubtedly helped to attract many people to these events (as well as the prospect of eating meat from the sacrifices and other fine foods). They were also compelling demonstrations of the wealth and power of the host group because animals were the major form of wealth. The episode shown here took place in the central area of a funeral feast in the Torajan highlands. (Photograph by B. Hayden)

warranting the inheritance of resources by successive generations. Funerals or other pretexts constituted major venues for the competitive display of wealth and support (Figures 6.4 and 6.5) because overt competition based on wealth continued to be unacceptable (Wilk 1983; Dietler 2001:79,101). Funerals often

6.5. A procession of visiting guests at a funeral feast in the Torajan highlands. Such processions with coordinated clothing and gifts carried for display not only demonstrate the size and power of the guest group but their support for the hosting group. Note the surrounding temporary structures that were all constructed for the funeral feast and dismantled afterward. (Photograph by B. Hayden)

became stepping stones to local power (M. Clarke 1998, 2001; Weiner 1988). In fact, Izikowitz (1951), explicitly identified ancestral feasting among the Lamet in Laos as the main driving force behind surplus production, and the same was undoubtedly true in many other cultures. Fear of the dead could be an especially powerful tool in promoting aggrandizer agendas, and such fear would have been particularly easy to manipulate or augment to serve one's wishes. As Tyler (1973:134) says so well, "To neglect the souls of the departed is to take a great chance with supernatural vengeance and to place all members of the joint family in jeopardy. Because the ancestors are potentially dangerous, a man would be foolhardy indeed to fail in his obligations to them ... Without the sustenance derived from the offerings, the soul never attains heaven." To whose advantage was it to promote such beliefs? It would have been particularly easy to attribute any accident or illness in a family to individuals who failed to produce enough for feasts or to acquiesce to elders' wishes. Consequently, in most transegalitarian societies, it is the lineage elders with closest connections to the ancestors who hold most of the power and who negotiate affairs between each other and settle disputes (Skibo 1999:viii,5; Hayden, in prep). Elders' control was additionally enhanced where they could institute high marriage prices that few junior lineage members could afford on their own.

Because of this internal hierarchical control, corporate kinship groups frequently played strong sociopolitical and economic roles, whether united under a
single roof or dispersed into nuclear family households but nevertheless strongly
networked as a major community force. The overall result of lineage power groups
was the frequent political organization of communities as heterarchies with a
number of power centers in each settlement. Several ethnographers remark on
the necessity of holding feasts in order to maintain corporate kinship groups
(e.g., Modjeska 1982:83; Sherman 1990:304; Stasch 2012:379–80; for an archaeological perspective, see Ensor 2013). Of additional significance is the position of
lineages rather than households as the primary power brokers and competitive
units in many societies (Clarke 1998, 2001:148; Ensor 2013). This aspect can obscure
expected material patterning in the archaeological record: a poor person may be
buried lavishly because his lineage is powerful and the extended family uses his
burial to display their rank; a lineage head owning a house with exotic ritual
paraphernalia may not be wealthy himself but able to draw on other well-off
lineage members; and very productive wealthy households may not be the most
powerful families within a lineage.

Wherever the resource base was productive enough, marriage prices and elaborate feasts were frequently used as strategies by aggrandizing kinship heads to
advance their agendas. This forms a major theme in transegalitarian horticultural
societies. The best documentation of how elevated marriage prices were used by
elders to indebt unmarried and newly married men (sometimes for life) and control
their labor comes from horticultural and pastoral transegalitarian societies (e.g.,
Kaberry 1942:89; Stevenson 1943:19,106; Izikowitz 1951:100,140; Yanagisako 1979;
Meillasoux 1981; Modjeska 1982:56–8, 67–8; Feil 1987:160; Lemonnier 1990:14;
R. Adams 2007b:184–7,198). These same authors, along with others (e.g., Sherman
1990:292), emphasize that women in these societies are viewed as and treated like
valued goods that are conferred on others to establish debts and exchanges, just as
female family members were used as prostitutes by elites on the Northwest Coast to
obtain European goods and finance potlatches.

The escalating value of children for creating wealth exchanges and debts also
provides the motive for using various techniques to enhance the value of children
for marriage, including special training, body deformations (e.g., neck elongation,
foot binding, sloped crania, elaborate labrets, tattoos, or scarring), and maintenance
of virginity or sexual cleanliness via circumcisions or other surgical interventions
(e.g., Schlegel 1991). As the value of women increased in this fashion, so, too, did the
status and importance of the highest valued women from wealthy or high-ranking
families, so that they sometimes played important roles in society. In addition,
their value was enhanced by conferring elaborate costumes and jewelry on them
(generally at maturation feasts), which they presumably were buried with if they

died before marriage (Figure 6.6). This transegalitarian strategy of investing in children to establish wealth-based alliances and thereby increase control is the real meaning behind wealthy subadult burials rather than the usual assumption by archaeologists that such burials are indexical of stratified inherited status or chiefdoms (Mainfort 1985; Hayden 1995). *Wealthy child burials can occur in transegalitarian societies before the development of any classes or stratification.* In transegalitarian societies, there is no necessary inheritance of status or socioeconomic stratification, although this can occur and, even where it does not, there appears to be a strong tendency for advantages and training to be passed from father to son (Rosman and Rubel 1971:132; Strathern 1971b:120,171,210–12; Young 1971:77; Feil 1987:120,278–9; Lemonnier 1990:44–5). Lemonnier (1990:18,25,108) also emphasizes the important change in cultural dynamics and structure that occurs with the adoption of prestige items (including pigs) as substitutes for human lives – either lives lost through violence or through marriage (see also Chapter 4 of this volume and Modjeska 1982:56).

Wealth exchanges similar to potlatching constitute another aggrandizer strategy in horticultural societies that is usually combined with some form of feasting, either as an auxiliary feature of large feasts or as the main focus, with feasting occupying a subsidiary role. Frequently, luxury foods constitute part of the wealth that is exchanged, and it can be assumed that these foods were consumed in feasting fashion to commemorate the exchange event even if the foods were eaten in individual households. Gregory (1982:19,43,48) and Lehman (1963:73,196) emphasize the exchange features of the Chin and Kachin and other groups, noting that, like reciprocal feasts, the goal of gift exchanges is to establish a relationship between the participants (including control and domination in some cases). A person bestows a gift to secure a relationship, not because he wants a thing. *Debts from valuable gifts and feasts "ensure the continuity of the relationship"* (E. Leach 1954:152–3). The goal is to acquire as many gift-debtors as possible, not to maximize profit, although the more profits one can make, the more debts one can create. The contracts represented by debts continued to be frequently bound by supernatural sanctions (e.g., E. Leach 1954:179). Gregory (1982:20) quotes Mauss to the effect that gift exchanges flourish most in societies where the clan hierarchy is unstable and changeable, and, according to Kirsch (1973:28–9), the same seems to be true of feasting (see also Parkes 1992:43). Birket-Smith (1967:39), too, noted that powerful chiefs gave fewer feasts. Thus, the Kula exchange network flourished in the Trobriand Islands where chieftainship was weakest and resembled big men societies (Gregory 1982:201). These observations tend to support archaeological assumptions that lavish public displays vary in opulence due to the stability or instability of sociopolitical positions in social groups (Randsborg 1982:135; Cannon 1989).

6.6. Above: Three children from Mount Hagan in New Guinea who have been given wealth in the form of shell jewelry, undoubtedly to enhance their value as marriage partners and the amount of wealth exchange that can be obtained from marriages between families. Below: A Mount Hagan girl dressed for marriage wearing part of her bride-wealth in shells. (Connolly and Anderson 1987:141,249)

In addition to the similarities between transegalitarian hunter/gatherer and horticultural societies just noted, horticultural feasts also exhibit all the potential for expansion that complex hunter/gatherer feasts do. There is an almost unlimited variety of pretexts for hosting feasts (e.g., Powdermaker 1932:238). A key feature of importance for subsequent political developments was probably the secret society feast held to impress the wider community, or even a number of communities, with up to 400 people attending and 300 pigs being slaughtered (Speiser 1996:71,386). In addition to the ideological transformations promoted to form these societies, taboos and rules seem to have been developed in profusion in many societies accompanied by ideological claims that breaking such rules endangered the entire community or, in particular, its leaders who had to be compensated.

One factor that does appear to be new on the scene is the occurrence of destructive socioreligious movements or annihilation cults as described by Wiessner (2001) and Blanton and Taylor (1995:139) in New Guinea. These cults appear to emerge when the level of debt and obligation in a feasting system becomes so overwhelming for individuals that the only way most people can see to avoid crushing debts is simply to abolish the entire system (under the guise of religious edict or inspiration) and start from zero again. These cults are accompanied by massive destruction of wealth together with a strong affirmation of egalitarian ethics and egalitarian potluck types of feasts. Although the best ethnographic observations that exist come from horticultural societies, it is unclear whether this may be due to unique inflationary developments of the feasting system that resulted from contact with Industrial cultures and the introduction of new more productive cultigens, or whether this is a cyclical pattern that may have been a regular, if transitory, feature of most transegalitarian societies, including complex hunter/gatherers, but for which we simply lack historical documentation or recognition due to a lack of observers in the right places at the right times. Certainly, as noted in Chapter 4, there were numerous community members in complex hunter/gatherer societies who thought the traditional feasting systems were a waste of resources and who resented being pushed into supporting those systems.

There is also more explicit documentation among horticulturalists that warfare was used and manipulated by aggrandizers for their own ends, even to the extent of arranging murders to provoke wars (Strathern 1971b:79; Sillitoe 1978; Lemonnier 1990:95; Wiessner and Tumu 1998). Obviously, the need to defend one's community is best served by acquiring allies, but potential allies must be hosted in feasts and any injuries or deaths that allies sustain in conflicts involve compensation, as does the re-establishment of peaceful relationships, all of which requires the production and surrender of surplus goods and prestige items. As Roscoe (n.d.) has observed, big men use community interests and all their charms and powers of persuasion to advance their own agendas. But when this does not always work, they might resort to using intimidation and physical force (judiciously!) to get their way. Big men were often former warriors and physically powerful; and they could be ruthless in getting their way, sometimes using henchmen to do their dirty work.

The social and material consequences of the horticultural feasting system were also very similar to the outcomes of feasting in complex hunter/gatherer societies. Specialty foods and preparations were used almost exclusively in feasts, particularly the consumption of meat and alcohol. It is also interesting that some of the high-status foods and preparations from hunter/gatherer feasts appear to carry over into horticultural feasts, even when technological improvements such as pottery may have lowered the costs of production and preparation. In addition to alcohol and meat, soups continued to be important preparations even into early state periods (Waley 1996:319), and breads made from refined flour may have been as well. There is a plethora of feasts in most horticultural societies, and they become ever more costly, continuing to result in the intensified production of selected resources. As with complex hunter/gatherers, competition, especially to put on lavish funerals, led many families into temporary (and sometimes perhaps permanent) destitution and impoverishment (Talbot 1923:142; Stevenson 1943:132; Trigger 1969:110; Hampton 1999:115; Dietler 2001:82; Stasch 2012:371). This frequently vicious competition and the inevitable inabilities for everyone to meet all their feasting debts plausibly resulted in the increased levels of violent conflict typical of horticultural transegalitarian societies (Keeley 1996; Gat 2006; Fibiger et al. 2013). Where surpluses could be produced in considerable abundance and more reliably, aggrandizers managed to acquire greater power within their communities. Systems of numeration to deal with the escalating scale of debts became more widespread, as in the case of the Batak and Torajans who have scribes recording the names of guests and gifts received or given (Figure 6.15; E. Leach 1954:146; Monaghan 1990:760; Sherman 1990:299; Hayden 2009a). Various groups may also have developed relatively precise calendrical reckoning for scheduling feasts.

Summary

Thus, transegalitarian societies share many basic structural social and feasting features with transegalitarian hunter/gatherers. Although not all these traits may occur in all transegalitarian communities, they tend to become more common as the levels of surpluses increase and transegalitarian sociopolitical organizations become more complex. In summary (but there are undoubtedly more), they include:

- An ideology of private property and household control over prime resources as well as an egalitarian ideological façade masking obvious inequalities in wealth and power

- Dependence of feasting on production of large surpluses (overall costs stretched to maximum voluntary limits)
- Storage and consequent strategies to use surpluses in feasts
- Obligatory or contractual debts from participating in feasts
- Lengthy periods of accumulation and investment before major feasts (typically up to 5–10 years)
- Borrowing to enhance the magnitude of feasts, often to the point of temporary impoverishment
- Potlatch-style wealth exchanges, with the use of prestige items and foods to certify social pacts (at feasts) and as payments for human lives
- Potentially severe consequences for defaulting on feasting debts
- Elevated levels of conflict and violence-related mortality, as well as the occasional use of force by leaders to obtain their goals
- Disenfranchisement of nonfeasting families and a resulting inverted socioeconomic (or pear-shaped) pyramid
- Auxiliary (synesthetic) features used to attract people to feasts
- The use of recording devices or paid witnesses to keep track of gifts, contributions, and debts, as well as the use of astronomical observations or calendars for scheduling feasts
- Aggrandizer attempts to alter community norms in self-serving ways (often using feast venues)
- The promulgation of numerous taboos and rules with different scales of enforcement and justice for rich and powerful versus the poor and unaffiliated
- The predominant role of corporate "kinship" groups (with fudged genealogies) under the dominating control of elders
- Strong tendencies toward heterarchical political organization in communities with councils of elders wielding power
- The use of ancestors to consolidate power, together with using lavish funeral feasts, in part, to display the spiritual potency of the dead
- Elevated marriage costs and investments in children, especially for creating wealth exchanges and debts (via marriage)
- Powerful secret societies with public feasts to impress their communities

ETHNOGRAPHIC MODELS AND OBSERVATIONS

There is a vast anthropological literature on horticultural feasting in New Guinea alone, not to mention the rest of Melanesia, tribal Southeast Asia, Africa, and the New World. Some of the traditional documentation is superb (e.g., Strathern 1971b; Young 1971; Wiessner and Tumu 1998). Because many of these societies were impacted by Industrial cultures relatively recently, it has also been possible to conduct ethnoarchaeological studies on traditional patterns of horticultural feasts, such as those of R. Adams (2001, 2004, 2007a,b) and M. Clarke (2001). The result is a much more complete ethnographic record on feasting than has been possible to establish for hunter/gatherers. The following ethnographic accounts of the feasting complexes in various cultures may seem somewhat redundant and detailed, almost like a catalog. However, I feel that it is important to document these recurring patterns to emphasize just how coherent and strong the patterns are in transegalitarian societies. I trust that readers will bear with me in this endeavor or pass on to more general discussions. Along with these data come a range of ideas and interpretations on the nature, function, and purpose of horticultural feasts. Many of these were initially addressed in Chapter 4. However, several proposed archaeological models based on horticultural feasts warrant more attention here due to their historical role in bringing the attention of the academic community to the importance of feasting. The discussion by Friedman and Rowlands (1977) and later by Bender (1985) are particularly important.

Friedman and Rowlands and Other Theoretical Constructs

As was typical of much structuralist-Marxism in the 1970s, Friedman and Rowland's framework for interpreting tribal cultures focused on the way that social structures determined economic production and how social forms had their own internal laws of development largely divorced from economic or environmental considerations (Friedman and Rowlands 1977:202–3). They, I think correctly, argued that the early or tribal political (surplus) economy was driven by competition between lineages and that it was inherently expansionist and intensified resource production because economic production was used to underwrite the competition (207). However, they view this competition in terms of "prestige," although they used the term in a special sense. They maintained that prestige was "very different than in our own society," being the social value attributed to the ability to produce and dispense wealth (notably at feasts), including women (brokered as wives to other lineage). There was no attempt to link this feasting system to any practical benefits other than an internally generated social feedback loop in which greater production led to more feasts, more prestige, and more wives, which led to more children and more labor to increase production. How or why such a system became established was never satisfactorily addressed. In a parallel ideological fashion, feasting empowered ancestors who then were believed to bestow blessings in the form of abundant crops and animals on the lineage. Therefore, they argued, ideology drove the feedback loop as well. For Friedman and Rowlands (207), "Economic activity in this system can only be understood as a relation between producers and the supernatural ... because wealth and prosperity are seen as controlled directly by supernatural spirits ... an extension of the lineage structure."

The resultant model was rather convoluted and laden with obfuscating jargon. Nor was it entirely consistent internally because status was supposed to be gained by giving wives away, which should have depleted high-status lineages of women, thus reducing their labor force and productive ability. Conversely, if lineages actually had used the wealth that they gained (either from their own production or from giving women as wives to other lineages) to acquire wives, then their status should have been lowered. In short, the entire central emphasis on brokering of prestige leads to contradictions and confusion. If Friedman and Rowlands had linked feasting to environmental conditions and the acquisition of practical benefits, their contribution would have been much more useful. Irrespective of these theoretical differences, they did place feasting at the theoretical forefront of archaeology concerning resource intensification and economically based competition. From a geographical perspective, Brookfield (1972) had earlier made similar arguments about sociopolitical competition leading to agricultural intensification in the Pacific. Bender (1978, 1985), later picked up Friedman and Rowlands model and suggested that it might apply to understanding the domestication process. More recently, Ensor (2013), using a political economy framework, has squarely placed surplus production at the center of constraints over competition for marriage alliances and thus on marriage and kinship systems.

Before looking more closely at some ethnographic examples of horticultural feasting, it might also be worth noting that the "redistribution" economic model of horticultural rank societies as espoused by Fried (1960:720), Service (1962, 1975), Sahlins (1972), Rappaport (1968), and others – which is still widely endorsed by many archaeologists – is fundamentally flawed. This is yet another reason for abandoning the concept of "rank" society since the term is closely linked to functionalist redistribution. In addition to the critiques of the functionalist school noted in Chapter 4 (in which potlatches and feasts were viewed as means of redistributing resources that varied from place to place and time to time), Sherman (1990:300–1) has noted that, in some cases, hosts received more gifts than they distributed and therefore feasts concentrated resources rather than redistributing them. He also points out that "it is difficult to consider the feasting system as the mainstay of ... 'subsistence guarantees' ... the contribution of feast meals to subsistence of the needy could never have filled more than a minor portion of their needs." As Dietler (2001:84) and Gilman (1981:3) have argued, the feasting system cannot be considered adaptive in the functionalist terms of redistributing food. To construe it as such is to misunderstand the fundamental dynamics of the system. Fried's characterization of "rank" society economies was a useful stepping-stone in the development of cultural evolutionary theory; however, I think that we have progressed well beyond these notions and that these older concepts need to be put away at this point.

Other theories that attempt to account for feasts among horticultural societies cover the same basic gamut as previously discussed. These include feasting for social solidarity or social cohesion, or, as Powdermaker (1932) expressed it, "for impressing upon the individual the sentiments of his society," although she also acknowledged the role of feasts in creating relationships, in facilitating trade, and in politics. Woodward (1989:123,126,134) viewed feasting as fundamentally motivated by status competition, although, he, too, acknowledged its importance in obtaining seats on village councils and the fact that wealth was necessary to host feasts that conferred "prestige," which in turn created the supernatural basis for fertility that, in turn, resulted in wealth. Durrenberger (1989:108–9) similarly emphasized the role of feasts in "showing honor," presumably in the same vein as establishing prestige. Roscoe (2012), too, argues that prestige competition is the driving motivation behind feasting, although he explicitly links the objective of obtaining prestige to the acquisition of social power, which in Melanesia is also strongly linked to the creation of military alliances and war reparations. In other publications, Roscoe (2009) recasts the ultimate causality of feasting in terms of signaling; that is, feasts as deterrents to physical contests between groups or factions vying for control, resources, and power. This more political perspective is endorsed by Weiner (1988), Parkes (1992), and Hefner (1983) who view feasts as tools used for political domination or at least to create sociopolitical bonds. Lehman (1989) is one of the few field researchers to have perceived that feasting was often used for creating economic security (the economic safety nets described by Michael Clarke [2001] and Ron Adams [2004, 2007b]). Ensor (2013) attributes feasting and prestige items to the need for reproductive security (marriage) and the competition for this security that the production of surpluses permits. Although I think this is certainly true, other factors are also involved. Only a few attempts have been made to attribute feasting to wealth leveling motivations (e.g., Hefner 1983; Woodward and Russell 1989:14,16–8), and these, I think, can be discounted on the basis of previous discussion concerning the benefits acquired via feasting.

ETHNOGRAPHIC REALITY

Melanesia

There is an embarrassing richness of classic ethnographies from Melanesia dealing with feasting and other aspects from an amazing variety of transegalitarian societies, and it is impossible to adequately deal with them all in this context. A number of books could be written on comparative Melanesian feasting alone, and I apologize in advance to the many authors whom I have not been able to cite in selecting examples from this intellectual feast for the present discussion. The following discussion does not deal with the impressive variability between groups in New Guinea. It only highlights some of the more interesting features from a selection of societies.

Wiessner (personal communication) has stressed that ceremonial wealth exchanges such as the *tee* and *moka* do not involve feasting at the actual wealth distributions of live pigs; however, there is a subsequent phase of the event in which great amounts of food are both consumed and taken home. Feil (1987:249) documents an impressive twelve pounds of meat consumed per person at ceremonial exchanges of wealth with anything left over being smoked and carried away. This seems commensurate with the 700 pigs and 25-foot-high masses of food reported by Roscoe (2009) to have been presented at some New Guinea feasts every five to six years. It is not clear whether meat taken would be shared with other members of the lineage or consumed only by the nuclear family. In fact, most ethnographers are surprisingly vague about the actual consumption of foods at special events like wealth exchanges, cult events, funerals, marriages, or other occasions. There are even very few documented ground plans showing where such events took place or where the meat and food was prepared for group distribution and/or consumption. Hampton (1999) provides some of the few plans available, whereas a few ethnographers like Powdermaker (1932) refer to communal cook houses but provide no further details. In instances that I have observed in Southeast Asia, I and my coworkers have endeavored to document as many of these details as we could, from special constructions, to cooking areas, to butchering and trophy displays, to discard patterns (Figures 6.4, 6.5, 6.7, 7.7, 7.10, and 7.11). Of special importance, in addition to the large amounts of food that were consumed at funerals and other events were the substantial amounts of food (like the leg of a water buffalo) that were given to special guests, such as allied lineage heads. These meat gifts were taken to the recipient's household afterward and presumably consumed with or subdivided and given to close associates. Not all members of a household or lineage attended most feasts. Feil (1987:255) estimates that only 60 percent of sponsoring group members actually participated in the events sponsored by their group, while women often were systematically excluded from ritual events including feasting. Taking food back to households therefore enabled the feasting event to be extended to include more people, even if they were not physically present at the more public displays. I refer to this practice as "cascading feasting."

To what extent some of the Highland New Guinea wealth exchanges should be considered cascading feasts, and to what extent they are simply wealth exchanges without feasting is unclear. There could be variable mixes and emphases on feasting

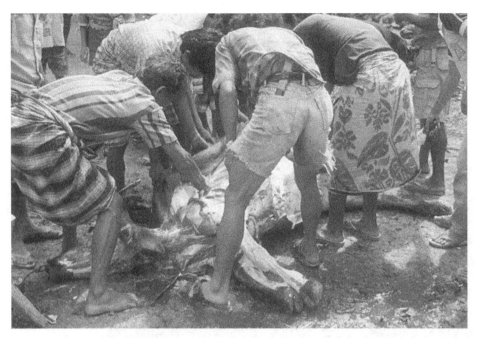

6.7. Some of the aspects frequently omitted from standard ethnographies include observations that are of great concern to archaeologists, such as butchering patterns (above) and discard locations of bones behind the abandoned temporary funeral structures (following page). These observations were made in the Torajan highlands. (Photographs by B. Hayden)

versus wealth exchanges. However, both aspects seem to involve the same kind of debt dynamics, and it is rare to find pure wealth exchanges without some form of feasting. Strathern (1971a:132) has indicated that some type of feasting involving pig consumption occurred as part of funerals, marriages, and cult (secret society) events. He also has implied that feasting occurred for curing or spiritual threats, as part of the payment of fines, and at dance occasions sponsored for clan epideictic displays. Wiessner would add war reparation events with food also taken home.

The Kuma

Having made these general observations, we pass on to some specific examples. For me, one of the most archetypal, quintessential, and insightful studies that epitomizes the dynamics of transegalitarian societies in general was carried out by Reay (1959) among the Kuma in the New Guinea Highlands. Here, clans controlled land, and competition between them was a major social and economic feature of society. Clan solidarity was often touted in appeals for support. However, Reay also recorded intense individual maneuvering for self-benefits, especially to acquire food and wealth (and, in particular, women and pigs) that conferred power within and between clans (23,57,192). According to Reay, leaders often paid lip service to

6.7. (cont.)

clan solidarity while self-restraint was a mask for shrewdness that covered flagrant
departures from altruism; leaders gave goods away in public but hid their most
valuable items; they had to seem to be generous and fair, but they obtained
advantages for themselves; there was a ruthless calculation of ultimate advantages
motivated by greed; they outwardly displayed conformity to social rules and clan
solidarity, but they saw themselves as above social norms and used social conventions for their own advantage; self-interest dominated their behavior; most people
were often short-sighted and materialistic in trying to achieve goals; moral

principles only applied to some people (not aggrandizers); and rapacious rivalry created instability (110–1,129–30,191–2). Wohlt (1978) similarly observes that big men had to convince their supporters that they acted in the interests of supporters, despite the fact that big men covertly acted in their own interests. More blatantly, Roscoe (2009) observed that big men could be pushy and nasty, but used charm, flattery, oratory, supernatural claims, gifts, and any other means necessary to achieve their goals. The ultimate result was relatively pronounced inequalities in power, wealth, rewards, and costs (Reay 1959:191).

The commonly promoted values of older brothers having authority over younger brothers and their need to act harmoniously appeared to be frequently rejected by younger brothers, as were the taught values of arranged marriages and wifely subordination by young women (Reay 1959:74,97,113,192,202). Women who rebelled from arranged marriages threatened the system of balanced payments between clans and therefore were put under great pressures to conform, sometimes resulting in suicides. Other values promoted by aggrandizers included the denigration of people who did not produce surpluses as "rubbish men" (24). The dead were portrayed as dangerous and vengeful, and all important rituals were the concern of men (133,156,201). Much ritual activity was directed toward the increase of fertility (131,157). These examples demonstrate how social values can support or further the vested interests of aggrandizer lineage heads (and presumably were developed and promoted by aggrandizers) but are not necessarily accepted automatically by everyone in their communities, even when taught such values from an early age. I have found that when received values contravene basic self-interests, they are rarely followed blindly, whether these are social norms or ideas about the supernatural or the putative sacredness of leaders.

Feasting was a major part of the strategies that aggrandizers in Kuma society used to promote their own advantages. To make this strategy work, aggrandizers promoted the production of surpluses to host feasts and give away wealth to create contractual debts (Reay 1959:96). Records were kept of these debts by careful mental accounts, as well as with the aid of vines and knots that indicate the kind and size of the goods involved (88,98,111). Defaulting on debts resulted in suicide or the kidnapping of children who were held for ransom or, in other cases, it resulted in war (Reay 1959:107,198; also Knauft 1990:277; Lemonnier 1990:96,118). Clan leaders generally paid for wives for junior members, but the debt had to be repaid with interest, up to 300 percent in some groups (Reay 1959:97–8; Lemonnier 1990:152). In this respect, it is not surprising that wealth items were primarily used for bodily decoration and to enhance sexual attraction (Figure 6.6). High-cost marriages resulted in a stream of income beginning with betrothals and continuing with marriages and births of children that husbands could never completely pay off. This seems to have been an obvious strategy by aggrandizers to acquire advantages as wife providers, as well as a means of control through the debt financing of others' wife purchases. There were also many disputes that arose in which clan leaders could play key roles, all with a view of promoting their own interests. Disputes were especially common involving women, theft of pigs, and damages that pigs did in gardens (Reay 1959:22,113).

The basic tenets of feasting were that sharing food created an identity of interests. Food was never shared with enemies or strangers. Similarly, gifts – especially food, pigs, and valuables – were used to maintain, create, or change social relations (Reay 1959:86,111). "Food has an intimate place in all formal procedures. . . .Withdrawal expresses enmity and suspicion." When given with pomp, food emphasized the separateness of groups by exalting the host (i.e., competitive or promotional feasting); when given informally, food dissolved group separateness (i.e., solidarity feasting; 95). Reay (1959:90–2) stated that the basic food sharing unit was the subclan (and nominally the clan), implying that there were a number of feasts at this level, although these were not described. A number of clans ate together at marriages and funerals, implying some sort of social alliance or identity of interests between them.

The creation and maintenance of a close social bond was clearly the goal of feasts hosted between trading partners (Reay 1959:107). As stated by informants, the goal of the much larger nut feast was to reaffirm and create close social ties between clans that had intermarried. The nut feast was a reciprocal event given between clans at three to seven year intervals. Sweet potatoes were not featured, but peanuts (an introduced crop largely replacing scarcer pandanus nuts) were amassed in enormous quantities (60,000 cubic feet of them in one instance). There was conspicuous waste of food and considerable contributions from allied clans. Thus, aside from the emic assertion that such feasts were to create bonds between clans, there seems to have been a strong competitive undercurrent that may have reinforced the value of such alliances for the participants, but may also have served to shed poor allies and seek out better ones (86–9).

It is less clear what the goal was for other large feasting events. These consisted of pig ceremony feasts held ostensibly to increase fertility once every generation. Boys were initiated at these feasts, and special longhouse structures were built for preparing the pigs for such feasts (Reay 1959:94,102,157,170). Presumably, these feasts helped to create community solidarity or to attract people to live in the village because village size was critical in defense, which probably accounts for the competitive display elements (Kaberry 1971:66–7). In one of these events in 1954, 2,000 pigs were killed. Although the number may have been inflated by modern economics and technology, even at contact, one of the Melpa tribes staged a one-day pig feast in which 700 pigs were killed yielding more than twenty tons of meat (Ross 1937, in Roscoe 2009, 2012). In this area, large pig feasts were held every five or six years.

Although not all ethnographers reported details on raising domestic animals, at least Clarke (1996 fieldnotes) obtained accounts of giving large amounts of food to pigs in the final attempt to fatten them for a feast. Young (1971:230) also referred to the need to raise "fat" pigs for feasts (see also Chapter 5). Such behavior would seem to indicate that the production of fat-rich meat was one of the major concerns in keeping and breeding animals. Such large feasts also required special areas (ceremonial grounds) and special structures (Wiessner and Tumu 1998:420–1). At these large feasts, there was so much meat that some of it ended up rotting and being thrown away (419,422), as was also the case with the Kuma (Reay 1959:88–9) and undoubtedly most groups trying to impress others. This was sheer conspicuous consumption because pigs were wealth that was never used for everyday subsistence (Kaberry 1959:40). Similarly, in a number of groups, the large yams that were indexical of abundance and the magical potency of individual gardeners were sometimes left to rot as conspicuous displays, for only the most powerful could afford to destroy wealth in this fashion (Young 1971:162,168,195). Speeches at such events were highly egocentric, with organizer aggrandizers loudly boasting of their own achievements and great qualities (Nairn 1991; Wiessner and Tumu 1998:421) and arranging impressive displays of the food they had organized to distribute and of the gift distributions that they were going to supervise – similar in many respects to Northwest Coast potlatches.

The Abelam

Kaberry (1971:40) has added interesting comments about the plant foods used in feasts among the Abelam of New Guinea. There, leadership was largely dependent on the ability of men to produce a surplus of fine and prestige yams for feasts or sometimes simply as wealth displays. Growing unusually large yams, up to 3 or more meters long, was labor intensive and involved the preparation of special gardens as well as considerable horticultural knowledge and claims to the possession of special garden magic. These long yams were emblems of manhood; they were exclusively prestige items and not eaten (ibid., also often the case among the Massim; Young 1971:195). This is an important point in terms of the potential special nature of a species that otherwise had a relatively routine role. The simple identification of "yams" in an archaeological context could not reveal the special prestige role of the very large variety or the feasting roles of the finer varieties. The same is true of taro in Polynesia, where irrigated taro is considered far superior to swidden taro, although morphologically the two would be difficult to distinguish in an archaeological context from starch grains or tissue remains.

Among the Abelam, as among the Kuma, we also find many of the fundamental characteristics of transegalitarian societies. There was competition between clans to attract members who were relatively mobile and sought the best benefits from affiliating with different clans, no matter what the emic or genealogical ideal (Kaberry 1971:58–9). There was also strong competition between villages to attract members because large village populations were important factors in defense (66–7). These factors seem to be essentially similar to the clan longhouse feasts of the Korowai, as described by Stasch (2003:379–80). Kaberry (1971:60) also reported that as men approach marriageable age, they became much more sensitive to their rank within their clan, as well as to the relative rank of their clan, specifically in respect to arranging the best marriage possible for themselves. However, as elsewhere, the wealthy elders controlled the necessary resources for marriage and tried to increase the value of clan children through feasts via wealth investments (61). Small and poor households had little or no surpluses and were forced to borrow from the wealthy for funerals, curing rituals, subsistence, or other events requiring feasts. Kaberry has documented the usual conflicts within and between communities and the high variability of surplus production, so that exchanges between villages exhibited great flexibility depending on the year's production in any given village (50,66–8). Elders occupied important roles in public affairs, especially in settling disputes and taking responsibility for dependents, whereas the big men of the clan provided the organization and financing of events with elders' approval (51–2). The big men were the entrepreneurs of Abelam society. Importantly, Kaberry (38,55–6) documented the *Tamberan* secret society with its impressive (competitive) ceremonial structures and major initiation feasts that attracted representatives from a number of surrounding villages. The lavish events and structures appear to have been meant to attract military allies, partners, or more residents. On the coast, Roscoe (2012) estimated that the construction of such competitive spirit houses required 3,500–10,000 person days (on a par with many megalithic structures in Europe).

The Massim

Michael Young (1971) has provided many similar kinds of observations for the Massim of New Guinea and added other important general statements and observations. Key for understanding feasting in general were his conclusions that food was highly valued and used in creating or maintaining social relationships, that abundance served as the basis for power (and often jealousy), and that feasting only occurred in good times rather than in times of famine when populations dispersed. Paradoxically, people giving feasts often abstained from eating before feasts in the midst of this plenty. This is entirely comprehensible within the political ecology paradigm of feasting (and as documented for complex hunter/gatherers), as a tactic to increase the surpluses that hosts could use in feasts and wealth exchanges for sociopolitical ends (160–1). In accord with another political ecology premise, eco-logically poorer areas with less productive potential had less developed feasting systems (146,155,173,260). In general, Young has noted that competitive feasting was highly inflationary in terms of food production and labor acquisition; feasting was the main stimulus to the production of surpluses and ultimately resulted in a general increase in the standard of living (257,264). The highest valued foods were those that were the most labor intensive produce and/or prepare; in this case they consisted of extra large yams and domestic pigs (wild pigs were unacceptable as feasting foods or for wealth exchanges –157,167,196,241).

In Massim society, the main role of the big man was to coordinate food exchanges and feasts, and he bore the responsibility for the full amount of debts incurred by his sponsoring group (78,200). Young observed that although there was a great amount of food consumed at the major events, there was no unified feasting event. Rather, there were public speeches, dances, singing, and giving of food, but the food itself was taken away to be eaten by smaller groups of kin and supporters (204,235). Thus, whether these events should technically be referred to as "feasts" or not is somewhat uncertain. They are, nevertheless, clearly related to feasts since food is a central component and all the other auxiliary activities are essentially identical to feasting events. To get others to participate and contribute to major feasts, big men had to make the overt goal of feasts a demonstration of group strength, wealth, and power for defense and attracting desirable partners (i.e., by appealing to the common self-interests of participants). But, covertly, the under-lying motivating goal of big men was generally their own personal "prestige," self-interest, and dominance, and there was intense competition within clans for these positions of dominance (250–2,257). Not surprisingly, then, clan representatives displayed the wealth of the clan and occupied high-status seats at major events (on platforms), ate high-status foods, and consumed high-status intoxicants (betel). The clan representatives were usually the clan big men, and the maintenance of lineages and clans was achieved primarily through pig exchanges and feasts that required surplus production (Modjeska 1982:83; Sherman 1990:304).

Big men promoted themselves as possessors of powerful garden magic (and often sorcery) and performed spells for the gardens owned by clan members (Young 1971:80,89) – undoubtedly to be able to claim some rights over clan produce and perhaps to thwart competitors with claims of magical powers. Big men had more gardens, grew more large yams and taro, had more wives (to increase production), had to be exceptional gardeners, and, like most aggrand-izers, were extremely individualistic and jealous (89,92,108,170). To achieve their goals, they produced more and gave away more than others. When persuasion did not work, however, they resorted to more forceful tactics (Lemonnier 1990:39). Most (90 percent) of their supporters were from their own clan; they feigned poverty when convenient and displayed wealth when they felt it was safe to do so. They used natural misfortunes for their own benefit, claiming that their supernatural powers were responsible, and they used insignificant offenses as pretexts to challenge rivals and marshal supporters for feasting events (Young 1971:94,112,185,247). As elsewhere in New Guinea, there was a pronounced tendency for big man positions to be passed from father to son, but this was not institutionalized (77).

Young focused on the two largest types of feasts among the Massim, the *abutu* and the pig festivals, although he intimated that there were also smaller feast types that he did not describe. Briefly, the *abutu* refers to food given to shame someone. This could be either an enemy rival big man in another village or someone from another clan within the village who was accused of insulting or wronging a member of another clan, often involving adultery or wife stealing. Clans frequently used disputes for their own political ends or to advance land claims. *Abutu* were organized by big men competing for "prestige" and occurred about once a year in any given village. The aim was to shame a rival by giving so much, especially in the form of large yams, that rivals could not pay back the gift (Young 1971:190,194,207,211). Young (1971:256) also cited a number of examples of comparative competitive feasts from Melanesia. From an ecological perspective, I suspect that the underlying goal of these events was to attract labor, supporters, marriage partners, and military allies by displaying success and desirability.

An important organizational detail for these events has been provided by Young (1971:197) when he described how supporters were recruited. When a leader wanted to hold an *abutu*, he invited all the people he wanted to involve as supporters to a meal – what I would call an auxiliary meal to the main feast. *If an individual accepted this invitation to share food for the purpose of planning a feast, he could not refuse to support the organizer. It constituted a contractual agreement.* This is the same way that large feasts were organized in the areas where I worked in Southeast Asia and was probably common among most transegalitarian societies. Similar strategies or techniques were probably used for organizing other events such as raids, although these details are rarely provided.

After special gardens were planted to underwrite the future feast and supply the necessary surpluses, and the gift of a large yam was accepted by the target rival, a date was set for the *abutu* exchange and feast. The first day of the eventual feast, the recipients of the first food volley hosted the entire village with pork. Key supporters of the respective big men received the largest amounts of pork. Feil (1987:247) similarly notes that the best meat portions were given to allied groups, although a great deal of pork was consumed by the producers, too. The next day, the second volley of food was given away as a return payment by the previous recipient, followed by a few residual food give-aways over the next days. Accounts were kept of transactions (Young 1971:199,201). The public disbursement of food was accompanied by many self-aggrandizing speeches that sought to put down rivals, sometimes leading to violence (198,202,244). Groups and big men that were cleanly defeated in such competitions had to eventually pay off all outstanding debts before they could compete again, and they did not usually feast again with the same rival (205). The debts incurred in this fashion could take years of hard work to pay off.

The other major feast of the Massim was the pig festival. These were major food exchanges between clans within a single village involving reciprocal debts between clans. They were again organized by big men who used the events, as well as the *abutu*, as a means of aggrandizement and coercion (Young 1971:247). Pig festivals were held in cycles of four to twelve years depending on the number of clans in a village. Each festival was actually composed of a series of periodic gatherings featuring food give-aways, with nightly dancing and singing by fires that lasted anywhere from a few months up to three years, although they generally lasted one to two years depending on the surpluses available (Young 1971:230,234). Rival clans received the largest food gifts, as well as insults, and food gifts were used to publicize grievances in a sensational way as well as to reward helpers and supporters who had to be generously repaid (240,244). Like lavish funeral feasts, the main goal appears to have been to acquire political power and prestige within the village (232). Preparations required the planting of extra gardens for prestige and filler crops and the raising of fat pigs (Young 1971:230,241; Feil 1987:179). Other goals of the pig festivals were to demonstrate clan strength, wealth, power, and dominance, even if temporary (Young 1971:252), presumably again for the purposes of maintaining that power within the community and attracting supporters to make that power possible.

The Enga

Another major occasion for feasts was the hosting of what Wiessner and Tumu (1998:265–8) refer to as "Great Ceremonial Wars." These were confrontations organized by leaders, *kamongo*, from participant tribes primarily for the purpose of generating social ties, exchanges, and for displaying strength and wealth. However, the creation of ties and exchanges resulting from war compensations for the dead (about thirty pigs per death; Modjeska 1982:87) seem to have been equally or more important. These ceremonial wars occurred at intervals of ten to fifteen years due to the enormous costs involved, and they lasted for weeks or months with feasts, dancing, and socializing occurring almost nightly (87). The general atmosphere seems to have been festive, like a game, with the few combatants actually killed considered to have died for a good cause (the exchange of wealth). Once the respective antagonists had amassed sufficient wealth to host the feasts and pay for compensations, almost any pretext for war would do, including settling outstanding debts or the theft of even a single stalk of sugar cane, or the purported exploits of peeping toms. If no suitable pretext was immediately available, the organizers could revert to bribing individuals to commit homicides in order to provoke the conflicts. The feasts associated with these events appear to have had alliance-affirming functions for the collaborating tribes. However, with the establishment of colonial rule, these ceremonial wars were eventually suppressed and their function subsumed under the *tee* cycle.

Melanesian Overview

On the basis of extensive oral histories, Wiessner and Tumu (1998) concluded that before the introduction of the sweet potato in New Guinea (about 250 years ago), there was little agricultural surplus in the highlands, and feasts were predominantly based on hunted marsupials that were used for funerals and ceremonies for the ancestors and/or the spirit world. As expected from political ecology models, as production increased after the introduction of the sweet potato, so did the magnitude, variety, and frequency of feasts together with ceremonial exchanges of wealth, although considerable variation also developed depending largely on the relative agricultural productivity of the local environments (Feil 1987:234–8).

Ethnographers like Weiner (1988:43–8,117,134–5) working on the coast, have stressed that funeral feasts with their associated gift exchanges appeared to dominate social life. Women worked for months to accumulate wealth to give away at funerals, including making thousands of bundles of nonutilitarian fibers. This was critical for the demonstration of lineage strength, which was, in turn, critical for brokering political power within and between communities. As among complex hunter/gatherers of the Northwest Coast, benefits appear to have accrued primarily to lineage leaders as indicated by the complaints from junior lineage members in New Guinea that funerals were too much work (Weiner 1988:49,120; compare Beynon 2000).

As Young (1971:256,264) and others (e.g., Feil 1987:277) emphasize, prior to colonization, feasting was only one strategy used to achieve political goals. Physical violence and warfare were alternative strategies that were frequently resorted to or used in conjunction with feasts by aggrandizer leaders. The magnitude of reliance on such strategies can be judged by estimates of overall mortality from warfare in New Guinea reaching 30+ percent and possibly even 50–60 percent – rates comparable to Amazonian transegalitarian societies (Keeley 1996:90; Roscoe 2009). Although not all ethnographers have reported details all of the time on all of the aspects critical to understanding feasts in Melanesia, enough of them have reported enough details enough of the time to form a relatively coherent composite picture of the most important dynamics of feasting

in this important area. These include (1) intense sociopolitical pressures to produce surpluses for competitive display feasts at the kin group or village level in
order to attract marriage partners, military allies, or new members; (2) manipulation of the system and group interests by leaders for their own benefits; (3) the
contractual debts established by hosting and participating as an invited member
in feasts; (4) contingency of hosting a feast on adequate economic production;
(5) the emphasis on maximizing displays and debts in feasts to the point of
conspicuous waste or spoilage, paradoxically coupled with personal privation
and crushing debts from borrowing; and (6) the use of solidarity feasts within social
groups to maintain cooperation and integration, especially important given high
rates of nonparticipation (e.g., c. 40 percent). In these and other respects, precolonial
tribal society in Melanesia was relatively similar to Southeast Asian feasting systems,
and a brief review of some of the feasting features in Southeast Asia will highlight a
number of these similarities.

Southeast Asia

Although there have been many accounts of feasting in transegalitarian tribal
societies of Southeast Asia, probably the most detailed and useful accounts have
been recorded by members of my own ethnoarchaeological program of research
(Hayden, in prep.), in particular, the work of Ron Adams (2001, 2004, 2007a,b)
and Michael Clarke (1998, 2001), focused intensively on the feasting dynamics of
the region. These studies cover both relatively low-surplus producing communities like the Akha hill tribes in Thailand, as well as relatively abundant surplus
producers verging on chiefdom organizations such as those of central Sulawesi.
In both areas, funerals constitute the single most prominent, and most costly,
types of feasts. To obtain a rough idea of the relative levels of surpluses in
different areas, it is possible to compare the maximum costs of the largest feasts.
The maximum surpluses that we recorded in the Akha area consisted of nine
water buffalo and a horse sacrificed for a headman's funeral (plus rice, condiments, and alcohol). In contrast, the largest funeral that we recorded in the
Torajan area of Sulawesi involved the sacrifice of 200 water buffalo and countless
pigs, as well as copious amounts of rice and alcohol.

The Akha

The Akha have a wide range of feast types (Figures 6.8 and 6.9) ranging from family
solidarity feasts (e.g., ancestral and newborn feasts), to lineage solidarity/alliance
feasts (e.g., curing, butchering, and work feasts), to village solidarity feasts
(e.g., harvest, gate rebuilding, honoring the Lords of the Earth, and New Year's

6.8. One of the most common types of feast among the Akha is a "curing" feast. As shown here a child is having a string tied around his wrist for spiritual protection by the officiating shaman. Interestingly, these feasts are often held for people who are not really sick, but by anxious parents. This indicates that the real motive is to reinforce social ties between the participants and the host. (Photograph by Mike Clarke)

feasts), to promotional feasts for specific households or lineages (e.g., feasts held to celebrate weddings, new house constructions, funerals, or menopause; Clarke 1998, 2001:151–3). There are also feasts of social control, perhaps involving some degree of exploitation, such as feasts imposed as penalties to be given by individuals who have transgressed social norms or been responsible for damages to others' property or persons. As Clarke (2001) describes the situation, "Akha life is rife with feasting," ranging from small household events to village or regional feasts. As with complex hunter/gatherer feast hosts, Akha hosts of large promotional feasts are usually self-effacing, and Stasch (2012:374) has observed the same among the Korowai in New Guinea. Members of prosperous and strong lineages incur lesser penalties than do poor and unaffiliated residents, something I have also documented among the Rhadé hill tribes of Vietnam, where the rich lineages incurred only half the fines and compensations that others had to pay. In addition, if the rich paid the compensations for the poor, the poor became indentured servants to the rich. The lineages are the major competing social groups within the villages, and feasts provide the contexts for negotiating power and outcomes between lineages. In this respect, Clarke compares Akha feasting to Occidental parliamentary institutions. I suspect that this pattern is fairly representative of most hill tribes in the area, as well as of many other low-surplus level transegalitarian societies.

6.9. At Akha wedding feasts, the most important guests (lineage and political heads) eat inside the host's house, seated on elevated platforms, as shown here. Helpers eat on the floor while wives eat in a separate room inside. The bride is secluded by herself and does not participate in the main feast; in fact, she plays an inconspicuous part in the feast, indicating that it is above all the relationship between the families and lineage heads that is of most importance at in these events. (Photograph by B. Hayden)

Some of the key features of interest for archaeologists include the display inside or outside houses of the skulls, mandibles, or horns of valuable animals (particularly bovids and pigs) sacrificed for important feasts (Figure 6.10). Another feature is the holding of small, medium, and even relatively large feasts (marriages and funerals) at the homes of the hosts, where important guests eat on platforms inside the houses while low-ranking guests eat outside (Figures 6.9 and 6.11). The rotation of feasts between households, as well as the gifting of joints of meat to special guests, which are taken away and consumed at guests' homes (with bones discarded in their household toft areas), acts to randomize the spatial distribution of faunal remains throughout the villages. The activity of dogs and other scavengers further contributes to this randomization of discarded bones. Thus, in terms of material spatial patterning, faunal remains from many household feasts may mimic theoretical faunal distributions from meat consumed as daily subsistence fare. For details of Akha feasts and the sociopolitical structure, consult Clarke (1998, 2001).

Lawa

Kunstadter (1966:69) has provided additional details for the Lawa and probably most other hill tribes in terms of the many resources and the amount of labor that were required to build houses – all largely obtained through work feasts. As noted in other groups, rights to land depended more on residence with the land-holding corporate group rather than on descent, no matter what the emic rules or kinship

6.10. Above: A very widespread tradition throughout Southeast Asia, Assam, and probably Neolithic Europe was for the sponsor of important feasts to commemorate the feast by displaying on or in their houses the trophy parts of the animals sacrificed. Here, the bucrania of water buffaloes are displayed on the outside wall of an Akha headman's house who organized village feasts. Feast sponsors also often place pig mandibles on racks inside their houses. Both instances can also be viewed as a kind of record keeping. (Photograph by B. Hayden) Below: This practice probably accounts for the display of bucrania inside Neolithic structures such as those at Çatal Höyük where important feast guests seated on platforms (as in Figure 6.9) would have been reminded of the success and power of the hosts by the bucrania. (Mellaart 1967: figure 54)

6.11. As in many large "public" feasts, attendance at marriage feasts is open to everyone in the community; however, only the specially invited guests eat together inside while the general guests eat outside, as shown here at the same Akha marriage depicted in Figure 6.9. (Photograph by B. Hayden)

ideology might be (69,73). Interestingly, Kunstadter also recorded the amalgamation of several villages for defense, much like a confederacy (65), and we can expect that such political arrangements were accompanied by solidarity or alliance feasts, as recorded by Ron Adams in Sulawesi. As was also common in the region, swidden lands were held in common as corporate property by the village or kin group, whereas highly productive land with costly improvements, like irrigated paddies, were privately owned and produced the largest, most reliable surpluses, which were used primarily for feasting (65,69). This is an expected pattern from the domestication model discussed in the preceding chapter.

The Dafla

On the fringes of this hill tribe culture area, Simoons (1968) has partially documented similar feasting patterns for groups in Assam, northeastern India. He described many of these groups, such as the Dafla, in archetypal transegalitarian terms of land use, prestige item use, jewelry worn by women, the supreme value of domestic bovids and their use in feasts or exchanges, bride prices and the role of women in exchanges, disputes (especially over women and debts), marked differences between rich and poor, the variable fines for transgressions (in the form of atonement feasts by rich vs. poor individuals), the great importance and cost of funerary and marriage feasts (as promotional events), and the role of the ancestors (50–5,96). In fact, as may be frequently the case, at marriage feasts, the bride and groom appeared to be of secondary, or even incidental, importance compared to the payment of the bride price and the exchanges between corporate group leaders. There were also periodic community solidarity feasts every four or five years to which everyone contributed in order to buy a *mithan* (the local domesticated bovid).

In richer regions with substantial irrigated paddies, there were also ritual alliances between a number of villages (four in one case) that were cemented by periodic intervillage feasts and exchanges that rotated among the allied villages (Simoons 1968:1–3,77). In some areas, there were even intervillage councils to settle disputes. These groups may have verged on incipient chiefdom organizations (83). Aspiring members of strong village councils had to give costly feasts to support their bids for positions (82). Among other things, disputes arose from defaulting on debts and were settled by kidnapping relatives and holding them for substantial ransoms or by the competitive destruction of wealth at feasts (70,186). Warfare was endemic in the region until recent times, and there were special purification feasts and rituals for men who had killed an enemy (92), possibly to promote and elevate the importance of such individuals. As among the Akha that Clarke lived with, there were household solidarity feasts to ancestral or other spirits about once a month and there were agricultural feasts for clearing, fencing, weeding, harvesting, and droughts. There were also community hunting festivals with feasting (76,93–6).

The Naga

Among the Naga, Simoons (1968:112,128) related that individuals gave feasts to transfer life forces from successful and wealthy hosts to stone or wood monuments that village members could then access and use to increase their productivity. This seems like a rather transparent justification for other underlying feasting motives, which Simoons refers to as "economic and political benefits." Simoons does not specify what these feasting benefits were, other than obtaining seats on village councils, for which substantial wealth to supply the *mithans* used in the feasts was required (140–1,151,170–1). These were the renowned "feasts of merit." There were four levels of feasts of merit in some groups. *Mithan* or cattle were required for all of them, as well as varying quantities of rice beer, pigs, cocks, and rice. The village clan members were the primary guests, and the dragging of stones to be erected were features in some areas (one cattle for every 3 miles for a medium-sized stone that was 8 feet long and 3 feet wide). Completing the four-level cycle gave the host the right to become a priest and wear a special type of cloth that undoubtedly carried with it economic and political advantages, although this was unstated (126–8). Ancestors could only enter heaven and become powerful forces via the giving of feasts of merit for them. This was the justification for making funeral feasts much more elaborate than the poor were able to afford (148–9).

The Chin

Some of the feasting groups in Assam and Burma that Simoons has dealt with verged on chiefdoms and may have even cycled between transegalitarian and chiefdom organizations depending on local resources and other factors, as among the Kachin described by E. Leach (1954). However, the more "democratic" variants of Chin groups documented by Stevenson (1943) and Lehman (1963) were classic transegalitarian communities in the region and provide another good example of the role of feasting in this culture area. They were ruled by councils of elders with headmen, priests (often the same as headmen), and blacksmiths as the leading figures. Each elder in the council represented a lineage or kinship group or village sector, and those who had given the requisite number of feasts of merit became members of the village council (Stevenson 1943:18,90,138–9). Members of the village council received a number of substantial economic benefits, as well as being able to make all the major decisions for the community. The village council constituted the main meat-consuming group at village sacrifices; they received payments from individuals who cut thatch from community lands as well as part of any litigation settlement or fine; and they could collect grain and liquor from each household for community projects or festivals. As the most influential men, they also retained the use of the best fields for themselves, and the rich were usually polygamous (82,84,87–8,152,160–1). The quantity of meat consumed at village feasts was considerable: one year, one village witnessed sixteen feasts that in total involved fourteen mithans and forty-nine large pigs. The headmen, priests, and blacksmiths received additional benefits in the form of two days of free labor per year from each household. In addition, the headman had his house built for him by the community; erected carved posts to commemorate the feasts that he had organized; received a share of all feasting meat and a leg of any hunted animal; a share of any salt, wax, or grain produced; and he made decisions on the allocation of community land (20,37,68,82–3, plate facing 118).

   Lehman (1963:73–4,79,83,103,113,123,142,144,151,166,203) elaborates a model of Chin political organization in which obtaining imported prestige goods provided the underlying motivations for creating centralized political authority that engendered trading and raiding to secure these goods. Agricultural surpluses were used in exchange for exotic items that were then circulated via feasts of merit backed by local mithan production. Traditional power and hostilities were based on trade.

Military alliances were created primarily between lineages by means of costly intermarriages, with stronger lineages obtaining the highest prices for women given in marriage. The higher the price paid for the women of a lineage, the higher the lineage rank, although genealogical reckoning was also considered and a constant source of conflict, genealogical manipulation, and litigation. Bride prices were not so much for the brides as they were paid to establish alliances between kin groups – alliances that had to be constantly reaffirmed via feasting participation and support, probably to be sure that an ally's fortunes and strength had not diminished. The poor also sought the protection of the powerful and became indebted servants. Gateway communities with monopolies on trade were particularly warlike. Lehman describes developments of chiefly power as stemming not from conquest (although this is postulated for the past) but from land acquisitions from bride price payments and continuing payments of affiliation ("tribute"). As was typical of many functionalist and systems-oriented anthropological studies of the time, Lehman (104,108,154) viewed the centralization of power as benefiting "the entire society" by increasing trade and making imported goods available. It is difficult to reconcile such views with the blatant exploitation of slaves or indebted servants or with the excessive concentration of wealth in the hands of a few families that owned the vast majority of valued land. Political ecology models centered on aggrandizer motivations seem more realistic than system-serving models.

Feasts of merit were so common among the Burmese Chin hill tribes that Stevenson (1943:137–8) has described them as the cornerstone of Chin economic organization because they consumed most of the surplus production and were a "shortcut to temporal power." These feasts required great effort and wealth to host, therefore necessitating kin support and participation. Household heads used the wealth of the household for feasts of merit, and lineage leaders were always among wealthy feast performers (Lehman 1963:90). Feasts of merit were explicitly promotional in nature, meant to celebrate or advertise individual success and prosperity, although the outward purpose for them was stated in terms of enhancing the "natural fertility" of the rich (and obtaining fertilizing *mana* from the dead) or of storing wealth in the afterlife for the host. They could feature much conspicuous consumption and waste, including the sacrificing of pregnant mithans, the fetuses of which were placed on top of houses wrapped in costly blankets (Lehman 1963:180). They were also highly competitive in nature, even involving hosts trying to force special guests who had also given feasts of merit to consume excessive quantities of food and drink using assistants armed with sticks (Lehman 1963:178–9, figure 30; Simoons 1968:170–4) recalling the forced eating at some Huron feasts (Tooker 1964:74). From a political ecology perspective, one would expect some substantial benefits to be associated with highly competitive feasts. In economic terms, Stevenson has mentioned that hosting feasts of merit led to protection and work contributions from the headman, the blacksmith (who forged weapons and tools), and kin, plus an increased share of meat at the feasts of others and an increased bride price for the host's daughters. Because the public and competitive consumption of food with distributions of property was used to establish "status" and political power, feasts of merit have sometimes been compared to potlatches (Lehman 1963:179).

Other feast types in the region bear even stronger similarities to competitive potlatches. The *lisudu* was held when individuals or kin groups wanted to settle disputes by competitive destruction of wealth, with the loser giving up possession of his land and other important possessions (Simoons 1968:175–6). Still other types of feasts were similar to those recorded by Clarke among the Akha, including agricultural feasts, feasts for curing, feasts to end feuds or establish peace, feasts for fines, and feasts to propitiate the dead so that they would not adversely affect the living (176–86). In addition to village-wide feasts, there were the familiar "household" feasts that comprised events for the entire patriclan in order to appease their ancestors and promote prosperity, as well, presumably, as smaller nuclear family feasts such as birth feasts (Stevenson 1943:128,158–9). Together with feasts of merit, marriages and funerals provided the pretexts for the major feasting events hosted by individual households in conjunction with kin groups (19,106,121,130–3). The groom's father and his kin provided the substantial wealth necessary for the marriage, thereby indebting the groom for life. An important observation by Lehman (1963:100) is that bride prices varied from village to village as a function of the amount of wealth available, once again emphasizing the critical role of surpluses in the development of social and political practices. For funerals, people tried to outdo each other in wealth displays. Thus, funerals always led to borrowing and generous meat gifts to major kin supporters and village officials. As elsewhere, lavish funeral displays often led to temporary impoverishment.

There were also some distinctive forms of feasting in some Chin villages. Stevenson describes the "Feasters Club" and the "Hunters Club." Membership in the Feasters Club conferred "great economic and social benefits," and only people who had hosted a feast of merit could join. In many respects, the structure and dynamics of the Feasters and Hunters Clubs were similar to secret societies, although they lacked the "secret" supernatural rituals that were used to justify the wielding of temporal power. Like secret societies, the Feasters Club was internally ranked, with the cost of the feasts (in 1943) ranging from 15 to 250 rupees in 1943. Meat was distributed at feasts according to rank. The head of the Feasters Club received the hind leg from all feasts, and the high ranks were given the best beer, supplied in great abundance (60–150 pints of beer per feast for some individuals). If the beer was of inferior quality or if there was not enough, fines were imposed on the feast-givers (Stevenson 1943:136,139–45,147). Hence, there was considerable incentive to supply as much beer as possible at these feasts. The Feasters Club also hosted an annual dinner with contributions from all members; however, it is not clear whether this was a public event open to everyone (a promotional feast) or whether it was only open to members (a solidarity feast). Moving up in the ranks of the Feasters Club led to membership on the village council and entitled members to attain the Plain of Heaven when they passed on (24). As for the Hunters Club, little information is available on it other than the fact that it also was ranked and that membership attracted economic opportunities as well as participation in more hunts, feasts, and agricultural benefits, perhaps the principle one being the amount of beer consumed together with the sacrificed domestic meats used to celebrate successful hunts (134–5). Simoons (1968:153) also mentions that members of the Hunters Club engaged in competitive boasting. It can be assumed that only relatively wealthy individuals could afford to fête their hunting successes in this fashion.

The basic dynamics of Chin villages were similar to that seen in other regions of Southeast Asia. Large domesticated bovids (*mithans*) were the main form of wealth, although less than a quarter of the households owned bovids and only a few households owned the vast majority of these; every endeavor above the subsistence level required surpluses (households often producing 600–1,600 pounds of surplus grain) although crop failures were common, leading to a periodic reliance on jungle foods; grains were the only crop that could be used to fulfill obligations for weddings, feasts, payments, and brewing; corporate kin groups were the main power groups and competition between them was elevated, as was endemic warfare between groups; help from kin and supporters was required for large feasts; spirits were thought to control material prosperity and often asked to "give us the goods"; substantial animal sacrifices were required for the dead to enter the "Plain of Heaven"; there were punishments for spiritually endangering the village due to a variety of prohibitions; and loans to nonkin typically carried interest rates of 100 percent per annum – loans to kin resulted in simple reciprocal debts (Stevenson 1943:44,47,107,121,133,147,151,156,175–6; Lehman 1963:77,82,89,179).

The Kachin societies reported by Leach strongly resembled the basic characteristics of the Chin as just described. To iterate some key points from Leach (1954:21,72,90,152–3,164,179,182,194), swidden agriculture produced only unreliable surpluses with frequent rice deficits, meat was only eaten at feasting sacrifices, offenses resulted in debts, mutual relations were based on debts to ensure continuation, there was often blatant manipulation of genealogies, contractual exchanges (debts) were bound by supernatural sanctions, families without "status" were open to sorcery and other accusations, and competition was often "vicious." Such competition usually belies a scramble for important benefits such as reproduction, defense, and quality of life.

There were a number of important material correlates of feasting in the region. Lehman explicitly discusses feasts as a major means of converting agricultural surpluses into political power that controlled the circulation of prestige goods and land. With the introduction of cash economies, markets, and wage labor, the feasting system collapsed. Stevenson (1943:120–1), too, observed that feasts were the means of "transmuting" goods, labor, and management into social, economic, and religious privilege. There was a "great keenness" to progress in the feasting ranks, indicating that the rewards of hosting feasts were commensurate with the expensive obligations that they entailed. The material signatures included the use of metal (probably bronze) bowls for cooking meat (generally only prepared for feasts), the construction of large sacrificial structures or porches for the domestic animals used in feasts, the use of bovid skulls from feasts that were placed on hosts' graves, the fertility symbolism of horns and their placement on headdresses or their use for drinking rice beer, the elaboration of house decoration as a function of the number and types of feasts (with crossed bamboo elements on top of the roof representing bovid horns and displayed exclusively as the privilege of the highest levels attained in feasts of merit), special clothes and jewelry being reserved for those who had given feasts of merit, and, of course, the erection of megalithic commemorative stones as part of major feasts of merit (55,85,196–203). Headmen or other feasters of merit were also able to erect carved posts representing each feast that they had organized (Stevenson 1943: plate facing 118, Lehman 1963:178, figure 32).

Bull (or other animal) fights were also held to increase fertility (Stevenson 1943:190), as was probably the case in the Mediterranean Classic and pre-Classic world, even continuing up to the present. Also of relevance for archaeological models of domestication is Simoons' (1968:245) view that bovids were domesticated in the region for sacrificial purposes (per Hahn's original thesis) and that this was probably also the case in the Near East. He has further suggested that the prominent role played by cattle at Çatal Höyük was likely related to a fertility cult (also expressed in Neolithic Danubian cults with goddesses and bulls representing gods) and that the cross on Halafian figures was a fertility symbol (248–55).

The Torajans

When we look at tribal villages in island Southeast Asia, we find many of the same characteristics as among mainland hill tribes. For example, in Sulawesi, Ron Adams (2001, 2004) has described the feasting complex for a remote, traditional Torajan village that still practices subsistence agriculture and holds animist rituals. Feasts predominantly relate to three issues: solidarity within socioeconomic groups, promotion of social groups for exchange or alliance purposes, and mar-shalling labor. The solidarity feasts (including "curing" feasts, life cycle feasts, agricultural feasts, and calamity feasts) are the most frequent and involve potluck-style food contributions at the household, village, or confederation level. Use of prestige items or prestige displays are relatively limited. In contrast, promotional feasts (especially funerals and feasts to elevate the importance of households) are largely provisioned by a specific household or kinship group (usually involving contributions from kin and other supporters as well as heavy borrowing). Promotional feasts feature the use, display, and gifting of prestige items and foods. Reciprocal debts are created by inviting specific guests and bestowing gifts on them as well as by accepting (or soliciting) major contributions for the feast, especially pigs or water buffaloes. Copious amounts of rice and meat are provided to large numbers of people, and heirloom textiles are exhibited together with jewelry and other prized possessions.

As an indication of the greatest quantities of surpluses that could be achieved in this area, the most costly funerals provided sixteen water buffaloes and more than thirty-six pigs to feed more than 1,000 guests, but these were unusual events, and the most common "wealthy" funerals involved nine to ten water buffaloes and about twenty-four pigs together with the erection of stone megaliths (Figure 6.12; R. Adams 2001:82; 2004:65). As in most other Southeast Asian societies, funerals were the primary venue for competitive displays of productivity, support, and wealth (Figure 6.4). Labor was largely recruited via work feasts in which valued food and drink was exchanged for help in building houses, creating irrigation ditches, or other projects. Wealthy households tended to invest more in feasting than others, and this feasting, in turn, provided them with recognition of their ability to marshal large amounts of food and labor and of their desirability for wealth, marital, and defensive (political) exchanges or alliances. This desirability usually translated into a broader network of supporters that could help in times of economic or political need, whether for hosting feasts, engaging in major work projects, defending political or economic interests, or obtaining privileged access to marriage partners, resources, or positions of importance (R. Adams 2004:75–6). Feasts in this area were also critical in the past for holding together military defensive confederations of villages; however, these confederations did not exhibit any chiefdom-like intervillage hierarchy of control but involved collaboration between independent villages with transegalitarian characteristics.

Sumba

One other example of a transegalitarian society in island Southeast Asia, this time at the complex end of the transegalitarian spectrum, is provided by Ron Adams's

6.12. Here is one section of a Torajan megalithic memorial ground with a wood structure from which meat was distributed to guests. Megaliths were erected at great cost (mainly in animals sacrificed) in order to confer more spiritual power upon a dead family member. The dead could then send more material blessings to their living descendants or could be used by families to justify their greater wealth and the displays of it for all to see. Although large funerary feasts were held on these grounds, the dead were not usually buried here, but in near proximity. (Photograph by B. Hayden)

(2007b) study of villages in the west end of Sumba Island in Indonesia. These societies, as well as a few other island polities in Indonesia, are rather unique in that they still have a vibrant tradition of erecting megalithic monuments over the graves of important and wealthy individuals (Figures 6.13 and 6.14). Adams concludes that they exhibited a number of indications of "proto-chiefdom"-like sociopolitical organization. Traditionally, there was a hereditary class of nobles as well as slaves (c. 20 percent) and a regional feasting system among allied clans (*kabihu*; 93–4). Thus, they provide some interesting background for the discussion of feasting in chiefdoms in the next chapter.

Some of the familiar transegalitarian characteristics of West Sumban villages include the limited and variable surpluses (R. Adams 2007b71–4); the high value of domestic animals, which were only used for feasts (R. Adams 2007a:350; 2007b:72, 271–6); endemic warfare; the occurrence of kin-based corporate groups controlling land and owning central corporate lineage houses serving as loci for corporate feasts, as well as the residence for the head of the corporate group with his family and as the storage location for corporate wealth (R. Adams 2007b:80–85); high prices for obtaining brides (used as a means of controlling labor; R. Adams

6.13. In Western Sumba (Indonesia), megalithic tombs were erected by wealthy and ambitious families, with much the same logic as the megaliths in the Torajan area. Erecting an imposing megalithic tomb for a dead family member was usually a necessary precondition to acquiring power within one's clan. (Photograph by Ron Adams)

2007a:351; 2007b:196–8); the existence of support networks primarily for political and military allies (and power) rather than for subsistence purposes (R. Adams 2007b:172); disputes over inheritance, infidelity, marriage payments, tomb building, reburials, theft, herding, borrowed animals, irrigation, use of land without permission, or *defaulting on feasting debts* (60,62,70–1,88,100–3,229,255); and the existence of an inner circle of power composed of the most authoritative individuals (*rato's*) within clans (89,119,182–3). Rice was used for feasts, whereas cassava and maize formed the daily staples (58–9).

Adams has also supplied additional important details not always mentioned by other ethnographers. Perhaps most importantly, he noted that investments in clan feasts were necessary for an individual to have a voice in clan affairs and that defaulting or excessive delays on loans could result in delisting from corporate kinship rituals and genealogies, or even enslavement (R. Adams 2011, 2007a:350; 2007b:70–1,78,90). Similarly, lack of support (including feasting support) for clan leaders could lead to withdrawal of clan support from delinquents, exclusion from clan events, or expulsion from the corporate kinship group (R. Adams 2007b:90,131). People who failed to contribute to feasts on the Island of Flores (also with megalithic traditions) lost title to clan lands (virtually all land; 258), and the same could be expected on Sumba. The same logic extended to any ancestor who failed to send prosperity to supplicants. The tombs of such offending ancestors were

6.14. Although some people wonder how the large stones of megalithic tombs or the pyramids could have been moved with traditional technology, the reality was not very mysterious. It was and is a relatively simple matter given enough manpower, although the manpower had to be compensated with the slaughter of a water buffalo for each day's work. This early twentieth-century photograph from Sumatra Island (Indonesia) illustrates the procedure. The technique Ron Adams recorded was the same in Western Sumba. (Schnitger 1939)

broken apart and those ancestors were removed from lineage genealogies, thereby losing any ritual honors or sacrifices (Barbier 1988).

Large animals were loaned only for feasts and used in sociopolitical manipulation as well as for increasing the power of the stock owners (R. Adams 2007b:68). Feasts and tomb building provided a number of important benefits to their hosts. Successful hosts and tomb builders acquired improved access to the inner circle of clan power and its associated benefits, such as acquisition of cash crops, shielding from litigation or fines, generous terms for loans (sometimes never repaid), support for political positions, provision of the wealth needed for marriage, and support during sickness or accident or during food shortages (228–31). The renown of one's clan was considered an important factor in acquiring desirable marriage partners. Only the most successful feast hosts (the wealthiest and most capable) became members of the clan inner circles (118). In the megalithic cultures of Nias Island, winners of competitive feasts also dominated and exploited the losers (243). Feasting was strongly correlated with wealth, tomb building, and the level of marriage expenses.

Given these characteristics, it should not be surprising to find that the major focus of feasting activity was based on corporate kinship groups. Major feasts hosted by individual households had to be sanctioned by the head of the clan and were traditionally at least partly held at the main corporate kinship house, which was larger and more elaborately constructed and decorated (with bucrania and pig mandibles from previous feasts) than normal houses (R. Adams 2007a:350; 2007b:81–4).

Other Areas

The Melanesian and Southeast Asian examples provide some of the best available documentation on feasting and associated characteristics in transegalitarian horti-cultural societies. There are a number of other good accounts from elsewhere in the world. The Kalasha agropastoral groups in the Hindu Kush Mountains, for instance, engaged in feasting in very similar ways to Southeast Asian groups. Despite a superficial egalitarian ethos, there were major wealth differences between households. Ownership of animals was largely confined to the wealthiest house-holds who used them as a means of controlling younger and poorer members of their kinship groups or community, resulting in what Parkes (1992:39) refers to as a "latent gerontocracy." The wealthiest patriarchs used surplus production to engage in prestige feasts that Parkes compared to Southeast Asian feasts of merit. Funeral feasts again constituted the major venue for competitive displays of production and support. A minimal funeral required more than 450 kilograms of wheat (and the considerable labor to grind it into flour and make bread), 75 kilograms of cheese, and the slaughter of several goats. More prestigious funerals involved two to three times these amounts and upward of twenty goats. Commemorative feasts for high-ranking individuals (similar to commemorative potlatches on the Northwest Coast) were held about a year after the funeral and could require 4,500 kilograms of wheat and 60 cows (40).

Promotional "feasts of merit" were relatively uncommon, although they could be combined with other events such as the giving of dowries to daughters. Nevertheless, they involved more than 1,000 kilograms of wheat, 100 kilograms of cheese, and upward of 60 goats. Of particular note was the importance of bread and cheese in these events, indicating their status as prestige foods (see the discussion of bread in Chapter 5). Parkes did not indicate whether reciprocal debts were created as part of these feasts, but he did emphasize the extravagant display of gowns, turbans, jewelry, and other "festally achieved emblems of rank" including thrones for the hosts (Parkes 1992:42). In related groups, such feasts were preconditions for effective political leadership, and they were associated with quasi-chiefly governments. Among the Kalasha, Parkes has noted that the sponsors of major feasts had usually retired from political life, but he also observed that major feasts were "overtly associated with local factional politics" and could be decisive in a particular faction acquiring political power. Thus, the elder patriarchs might not have held feasts for themselves, but held them to support their candidates for political positions, similar to the dynamics of lineages as the major power holders in Southeast Asian hill tribes. Importantly, Parkes has suggested that there have been different periods of highly intensive competitive feasts and that these appear related to periods of political struggles between factions for the control of leadership (43).

When we turn to South America, Napoleon Chagnon (1968:105–13; Chagnon and Asch 1970) has detailed the feasts held by the Yanomamo for making peace and creating military alliances between villages. Headmen organized these feasts and planted larger gardens to help provision them. They hosted about one hundred visitors and served soups from large wood troughs. Hunts were organized to obtain meat worthy of the feast, and men were dressed up with their finest display plumage in order to perform and to acquire admiration. Exchanges of gifts helped to cement these alliances. Chagnon has also noted that such feasts not infrequently involved real fights and violence (117), a characteristic also noted in Southeast Asia by Condominas (1977) and others, as well as in South America and Mesoamerica (see later section).

Elsewhere in the Amazon, Warren DeBoer (2001) has described the fiercely competitive feasting that takes place in conjunction with the coming out and ritual excision of the clitoris of Conibo and Shipibo girls at the *ani shrëati* feast. One to five men were the core sponsors and organizers of the event, including fathers of the girls. Like other competitive display feasts, a lengthy preparation was involved, up to two or three years, and entailed the planting of more extensive gardens for the brewing of manioc beer and cane liquor. As the event approached, peccaries, monkeys, tapirs, curassows, and even manatees were captured, raised, and fattened to provide meat for the guests. New clothes and beaded decorations were made for the girls to be initiated, who were dressed in "dazzling" attire; a large guest house was constructed; and specially decorated large pots and beer mugs were used for brewing and serving. Guests were welcomed with music, followed by ritual confrontations and dancing, as is common among many groups when guests arrive from other villages. However, as also occurred elsewhere (e.g., the Caribs, Mnong, Massim; Kloos 1969:510; Condominas 1977; Young 1971), serious fighting was also prevalent, especially when the marriageable girls were presented to the assembled feasters and males competed to display their virility and desirability for marriage.

Farther afield, in the Tupinamba region of the Amazon, huge quantities of manioc and maize beer were consumed at weddings, rites of passage, funerals, councils of war, and to welcome visitors of renown, but especially to celebrate the death and devouring of captured enemies (Azevedo 2009). Feasts were also held to accomplish work, such as the clearing of forest. Very early accounts in the seventeenth century describe the binge drinking and packed longhouses that accompanied the sacrifice and consumption of enemies, with singing and dancing lasting for days. Both DeBoer (2001:221) and Azevedo (2009:117) have emphasized the multimedia kaleidoscopic nature of the events geared toward creating altered states of consciousness and frenzy that transformed individuals into supernatural beings in their own perceptions. In addition, the Yanomamo used drugs to achieve such goals. Among the Waiwai, feasts were held at the village leader's house, which was at the center point of the village – its *axis mundi* (Peter Siegel, personal communication). In spiritual power, numbers of wives and offspring, political power, and gender dominance, the Amazon was far from egalitarian (Chagnon 1979; Lorrain 2000).

In North America, the Southwestern pueblos are above all known for the feasts associated with the *katsina* and other religious cults (B. Mills 2004). These bear striking resemblances to secret societies (Johansen 2004). Mills (2004, 2007) has also described lineage feasts that seem to have been prominent. Due to high population densities and concentrated populations in villages, hunted meat was a scarce but valued commodity for feasts. As a result, a significant trade with surrounding groups centered on the exchange of meat for maize and prestige items (Speth 1990; Bamforth 2011:33).

In terms of interpretive theories of feasts, Potter (2000) has viewed almost all ethnographically described feasts in the Southwest as communal events serving to integrate the community (whether lavish weddings, baptisms, funerals, anniversaries of deaths, installation of political officials, special holy days, moiety ceremonies, *katsina* celebrations, or costly large-scale "curing" feasts). He thus has aligned himself with the communitarian (vs. hierarchical) school of thought on the nature of prehistoric pueblo society (e.g., Saitta and Keene 1990; Saitta 1999). He has viewed the large-scale of the events and large debts associated with the *katsina* cult as "obligations" to the community, perhaps a holdover from the "burden of the cargo" notions from Mesoamerica – a view that I think is mistaken given the socioeconomic inequalities in these societies and the benefits derived from hosting large feasts (see Johansen 2004; Hayden and Villeneuve 2010:97–8). In contrast, in an ethnographically based analysis of Hohokan feasting, surpluses, and symbolic crafts, Ensor (2013) has argued that competition over marriages by corporate descent groups waxed and waned in response to abilities to produce surpluses. He also viewed rituals sponsored by descent groups as overtly or covertly used to enhance marriage prospects. This is one, perhaps overly narrow, political economic scenario to which other political and economic motives can be added.

In Northeastern North America, the Feast of the Dead among Iroquoian speakers, as well as their Green Corn festivals, are perhaps the best known feasting events (Tooker 1964:134–7; Trigger 1969:107–12). The multivillage Feast of the Dead certainly served some community solidarity and alliance functions, but, as in so many other transegalitarian funerary feasts, these funerary feasts also appear to have been an opportunity for individual families to vaunt their wealth and material success by displaying and giving away prestige items accompanied by formal public announcements, with clan heads receiving most wealth (Trigger 1969:111). The Huron Feasts of the Dead commemorated all individuals of a particular social group who had died since the previous Feast of the Dead (usually at eight- to twelve-year intervals). These individuals were commemorated and reburied in a communal pit. Leaders stood high on platforms displaying the accumulated wealth and announced the givers, the recipients, and the amounts – a kind of public accounting. The total given in the name of the dead could be impressive: more than 1,200 announced items (including many fur robes) at one feast in 1536. Many of the beaver robes were cut up and the parts distributed, perhaps a form of wealth destruction similar to the cutting up of coppers for gifts at Northwest Coast potlatches. Many other robes lined the burial pit for those being commemorated. These were manifestly ostentatious displays of destruction of wealth as promotional features at such feasts (Tooker 1964). Thus, there appears to have been a strong competitive element based on wealth used to secure "friendships" and alliances at these feasts. Of note is the recurring secondary interment of individuals after a lapse of several years. This allowed families to accumulate as many resources as possible for the event. Typically, secondary burial has nothing to do with individuals dying far from their homes (as assumed by some archaeologists), but has everything to do with putting on lavish displays by wealthy families, an aspect well documented on the Northwest Coast and Interior, in the Torajan area, among the Kalasha, and many other groups.

Between such large multivillage feasts, there were also feasts to promote individual successes, especially in war, or for achieving political positions. Such feasts are recorded as employing thirty kettles (formerly ceramic pots?) used to cook up to thirty deer or bear or fish with representatives invited from surrounding villages (Tooker 1964:75). Tooker also mentions curing feasts, which possibly resembled Southeast Asian curing feasts used to create solidarity within lineages, and thanksgiving or harvest feasts. As in many Southeast Asian tribal feasts, hosts were relatively inconspicuous and often did not even eat (73).

The Green Corn feasts may have provided similar opportunities to enhance community solidarity or corporate solidarity, or to vaunt the successes of individual social groups. Around the Great Lakes, W. Fox (1997) has documented feasts of Thanksgiving in which dogs were killed following harvests, apparently to promote community status because messengers were sent to invite guests from other groups. Fox and Salzer (1999) have also reported that the most important ceremony among the Winnebago was the War-bundle Feast in which only the person who represented an important war spirit was allowed to eat a sacrificed dog; however, few other details were provided. Others indicate that the *Medewiwin* secret society feasts (described in Chapter 4) were the most important feasts in the Great Lakes area. Some of these groups cultivated small gardens whereas others did not, thus making the practices transitional between trans- egalitarian hunter/gatherers and horticulturalists.

Ancestor veneration and feasting at funerals is, of course, also prevalent throughout Mesoamerica in all levels of social organization. This may be because connections to ancient genealogies were critical to the maintenance of land rights and sociopolitical roles (Nash 1970; McAnany 1994:18). Monaghan (1990) provides an excellent analysis of the mechanisms and support groups involved in large-scale feasting in a Mixtec community, notably for funerals, weddings, and cargo posi- tions. However, he relies on the communitarian ideology of the community to propose a social solidarity motive for feasts and the debts that they create, and ignores the factional nature of these villages and feasting networks. Factional feasting support systems probably also occur in other peasant societies where violent conflicts have been suppressed by state authorities and local political power has been largely diverted to central governments.

Among other Mesoamerican groups such as the Tarahumara, work feasts con- stituted the major social events of communities. These feasts involved copious amounts of beer, and work projects were sometimes initiated solely to engage in feasting (McAnany 1994:71,111). These events often involved fighting, perhaps not surprising given the amazing quantities of beer often consumed and the lurching, staggering, blind drunkenness that accompanied the feasts, which sometimes even led to killings (Kennedy 1978:98–100). But beer was sacred and dedicated to the gods, and it was part of all curing, protection, rain-making, or other ceremonies (115,140–1). The limited social rank differences that existed were mainly based on wealth, which was dependent on surplus maize production (117). Beer drinking (feasting) networks constituted the primary social groups above the household level, and participants extended reciprocal invitations (120). Funeral feasts were comparatively simple affairs featuring only a goat, a chicken, and some beer (150). There are undoubtedly many other accounts of feasting among transegalitarian North, Central, and South American groups, as well as from Africa. However, a comprehensive review is beyond the scope of this chapter, and I thus pass on to consider some examples of archaeological documentation of transegalitarian horti- cultural feasts.

ETHNOGRAPHIC SUMMARY

To recapitulate, in addition to the common patterns noted at the beginning of the ethnographic section, it should be emphasized that feasting among ethnographic transegalitarian horticultural societies is a vast and complex topic due to the great number of these societies and the great diversity of feasts used. Nevertheless, some of the more apparent trends include the use of funerary feasts as the primary arena for competitive displays (and ingroup consolidation) by families and *especially corporate kinship groups*, especially lineages that vie for local political support and important marriage, exchange, or military alliances. Marriages, feasts of merit, and house building or house investitures are the next most important types of events used for these purposes. Other feasts, such as birth feasts, naming feasts, ancestral feasts, curing feasts, and many other types serve essentially to promote solidarity within families or corporate kinship groups and to establish mutual support and safety nets. Still other feast types serve to enhance the value of children for marriage exchanges or to undertake large work projects such as building houses or large monuments. Still other feasts are given to obtain favors or as penalty payments for social transgressions. Regional feasts may also occur when a number of communities are coalescing into defensive or proto-chiefdom confederation-like arrangements. Secret societies, too, hold public and private feasts to promote their own interests.

One of the most evident tendencies is for competitive feasts to outperform solidarity feasts (in size, prestige gifts, and amount of meat) and to require extended preparation periods to plant special gardens, raise animals, call in debts, borrow resources, and, in general, oversee the underwriting of such major events. Typically the most competitive feasts involve one to ten years of preparation, whether the occasion is a funeral, a feast of merit, a coming of age, the arranging of ritualized conflicts, or other justifications. Due to the creation of contractual debts at these events and the complex web of debts generated, specialized record keepers or "witnesses" are frequently associated with these feasts (Figure 6.15). Traditionally, these record keepers often used some form mnemonic device, such as notched tally sticks, although these are frequently of perishable materials (Figure 6.16). These individuals are essentially paid to remember and validate what is owed to whom. It is also interesting to note that special structures are often, but not universally, built for ritual and feasting use in horticultural transegalitarian societies such as the Lacandon, Highland Maya, and some of the Southeast Asian hill tribes that I have visited (Figures 6.5 and 6.17). It would be an interesting exercise to determine whether there is any rhyme or reason to the construction of such special structures in some groups or the lack of them in others.

The sociopolitical context of most transegalitarian feasting tends to be heterarchical, with multiple kinship groups or factions wielding power and creating an inverted socioeconomic pyramid or, more accurately, a pear-shaped distribution

6.15. Large feasts such as marriages and funerals involve large-scale debts. With a multiplicity of feasts in a community, keeping track of debts can become a problem that many transegalitarian societies tried to solve by creating various kinds of record keeping systems or paying special "witnesses" to remember debts. At this Torajan funeral, two water buffaloes are being presented to the sponsor as support gifts, while two men write down the gifts in books. Note also the temporary structures in the background constructed solely for use at this feast. (Photograph by B. Hayden)

with the well-off families being in the majority. This is probably the result of the need by aggrandizers to garner a wide base of support and distribute benefits in order to make their strategies work. While aggrandizer-type leaders used all their powers of persuasion to get people to buy into their agendas, when necessary they were not adverse to using force themselves or through henchmen to get their way.

One of the far-reaching consequences of establishing debt and support networks through feasting is the social, political, and economic marginalization of nonparticipants. Only a small proportion of the households tend to be poor, and they are constantly derided as "rubbish" by aggrandizers apparently in attempts to promote the production of surpluses and participation in aggrandizer schemes. Poor people or nonparticipants in feasting become disadvantaged in any conflicts where wealthier households can draw on support from their feasting network. Wealthy households tend to receive nominal fines and penalties for social transgressions or offenses or to pay their way out of the most severe situations. Wealthy households can count on winning any dispute with a poor household and frequently seem to provoke disputes in order to appropriate the resources of the poor or even to enslave them. In addition, due to the strong competitive and social pressures to put on impressive displays at funerals or other feasts, the rich often became

6.16. Denise Schmandt-Besserat (1996) has argued convincingly that clay tokens like these from Susa in the Near East were record-keeping devices for loans or gifts of animals and other food stuffs from Early Neolithic times if not before. These would make the most sense as resulting from feasting debts. (Photograph courtesy of Denise Schmandt-Besserat)

lenders of wealth which enabled them to exploit debtors even further. Sandarupa (1996:13,20) has trenchantly observed that: "as the early Dutch missionary van de Loosdrecht noted, the mortuary ritual created the 'dispossessed' where in order to meet his sacrificial obligations at the death feast, a landholder pawned his land to get a buffalo, and this land could pass permanently from its owner's control to that of pawn holder ... Realizing the close interconnection of ritual order and socio-economic order, van de Loosdrecht explicitly attacked the social hierarchy, the inequality that was caused by excessive sacrifices at the death rituals. As he said, 'So long as the death feasts are not limited, the process will continue and the gap between deep poverty and great riches will assume still graver form.'" Thus, feasting plays a central role in the transformation of transegalitarian societies into hierarchical systems. I think the preceding observations convincingly show that the process is internally driven by a resolute minority of aggrandizers, and it is ultimately only constrained by the technological ability of the economic sphere to produce surpluses and the ability of groups to produce manpower.

ARCHAEOLOGICAL EXAMPLES

There is perhaps more written in the archaeological literature on feasting among transegalitarian horticulturalists than any other grouping of cultures. I thus restrict

6.17. In Vietnam, lineage structures like the one shown here are often constructed for honoring deceased lineage members. Typically, there are few if any artifacts inside the structures, which were used by high-ranking lineage males for feasting and rituals while lower ranking lineage members gathered and ate outside in the courtyard area, again illustrating the dichotomy in feasting locations between important participants versus support personnel. (Photograph by B. Hayden)

myself to briefly mentioning some of the more prominent examples that I am familiar with on a region-by-region basis. I apologize in advance for omitting the many good studies that I may have neglected to mention.

North America

Because of the work of a number of archaeologists in the Southwestern United States, a considerable amount is known about prehistoric feasting there. Following Longacre's (1964) and Hill's (1966) ideas about kivas and rituals being used to socially integrate coalescent groups into larger villages, Blinman (1989) was one of the first to specifically look at evidence for feasting in the Southwest and interpret archaeological remains from kivas and plazas as evidence for "potluck"-style feasts, hence of solidarity or community integrative types of events. However, he noted that prestige wares were concentrated in the highest ranked ritual structures and room blocks, which, in my opinion, is not consistent with expectations for solidarity types of feasts. The entire issue of whether prehistoric Puebloan societies were egalitarian and communitarian or hierarchical, with concentrated political power in some families, is a hotly contested topic in the Southwest. Blinman is clearly on the communitarian end of the spectrum, whereas Earle (2001) and others tend to view some of the prehistoric Puebloan societies as constituting chiefdoms. Potter (1997, 2000; Potter and Ortman 2004) largely follows Blinman's lead. He has argued for a number of different types of feasts in prehistoric pueblos, including work feasts and especially communally oriented feasts that integrated communities. He has downplayed the evidence for competitive feasts at some of the Chacoan Great Houses like Pueblo Alto, although the debate on how substantial any feasting was in the Great Houses continues (Plog and Watson 2012).

Potter has tried to place the motivating factors for holding feasts in the ritual sphere. I think this "tyranny of beliefs" approach is inappropriate given the wide range of beliefs and ideas that occur in contemporary, and presumably past, trans-egalitarian villages. For instance, Lehman (1963:175,207) observed that the Chin "profess indifferent faith" in reports about the gods and doubted that all people even believed in gods. Izikowitz (1951:321) reported that about 10 percent of the Lamet were agnostic or atheistic, and I found a similar proportion of skeptics among the Highland Maya villages where I worked. Reay (1959:131) even reported that most people in the Kuma area did not have a working knowledge of their own religious doctrines or myths, even though these were accessible. Thus, I have severe doubts about the so-called power of religious beliefs as a motivating force behind feasting in transegalitarian communities.

What Potter has documented are the unusual amounts of rabbits and hares in some structures (ethnographically these were hunted by communal groups before feasts), the large, sometimes exotic, pots associated with feasts, the prevalence of domesticated turkeys in public plazas, and significant differences in feasting evidence between communities. Along similar veins, Muir and Driver (2002) argued that communal hunts were only undertaken for ritual feasts; that is, to produce the large surplus quantities needed to feed large numbers of people. Deer and sheep were the most important ritual foods, although rabbits were hunted communally for feasts, too, and the meat was stored at the houses of ritual leaders. Whether these practices were part of communitarian or more competitive self-serving feasting strategies still needs to be determined.

Barbara Mills (2004, 2007) has explored the dynamics of Southwestern feasting in more detail, referring to the costly feasts required to make and use the *katsina* masks. The high cost could well indicate that these *katsina* societies were organized and run by the wealthy families or lineages and probably constituted secret societies, as suggested by Johansen (2004). In addition, however, "all important ceremonies" were attended with feasting. Mills has described the special roasting pits, structures for cooking, serving bowls, and faunal indicators of feasting. An interesting observation is the shift from decorating the interior of serving bowls to boldly decorating the exterior of bowls in the twelfth century (for larger village feasts) and then a reduction in size of many exterior motifs that occurred with a shift from partially enclosed plazas to enclosed plazas and more different types of ritual spaces, all of which she has related to the changing size of groups viewing the feasts. Small designs, in particular, she suggested, imply small, restricted, supra-household groups of feast participants after 1325 AD (B. Mills 2004, 2007). These are features typical not only of short lineages, but of secret societies as well. The occurrence of mask motifs on these vessels reinforces this interpretation of secret society feasting, especially because, as Van Keuren (2004) suggests, this and other imagery on these vessels could only have been produced and used by restricted and exclusive segments of the community. Schachner (2010:490–1) has more recently implicated the use of feasts as a means of establishing social differentiation especially between corporate groups vying for control over economic production and rituals, leading eventually to the establishment of Chacoan great houses. The restricted size of most kivas also argues for a limited number of exclusive partic-ipants in rituals and feasts. Ethnographically, this seems more consistent with the creation of social divisions and the concentration of political powers for a select group rather than the promotion of social solidarity for entire communities or community segments.

In the Hohokam area, the intensity of feasting as indicated by large ovens and storage facilities at Snaketown; and Pueblo Grande has been interpreted by Ensor (2013) as related to competitive marriage struggles between corporate descent groups. Grimstead and Bayham (2010:861) have documented what was probably a work feast within an elite Classic Hohokam compound apparently associated with the intentional destruction of one of the buildings, perhaps as a closure ceremony. However, they explicitly view such an event as a "strategic sociopolitical manipulation of power" to further elite interests.

Shifting to the Southeast, Lindauer and Blitz (1997:186–7) published a seminal analysis of feasting associated with platform mounds in both early (Hopewellian c. 100 BCE–800 CE) and later (Mississippian) sites. They argued that large-scale feasting and food storage took place at these mounds based on the concentrations of food remains at the mounds featuring high-utility meat elements; the large sizes and food functions of ceramics associated with the mounds, including highly decorated, ostentatious serving vessels; the spaciousness of mound tops and struc-tures; and the use of massive hearths. They also noted that maize and tobacco seeds were confined to mound contexts, indicating a role as elite ceremonial foods. Although the main thrust of their interpretation was to view mound construction, use of prestige objects, and feasting at the mounds as socially integrative and communitarian, I would suggest that it is more realistic to view these aspects as strategies used by aggrandizers for forging self-interested alliances and manipulat-ing community surplus production.

James Knight (2001) has also had a long-standing interest in the evidence for feasting associated with early platform mounds from about 100 BCE to 700 CE (primarily Hopewellian era features). The many postholes, including large posts meant to impress viewers; the lack of clearly defined structures; the size and openness of design; concentrations of ceramics, deer remains, and domesticated plant remains; and the use of hearths and exotic artifacts (including ceramics) all seem to imply some intercommunity or interkinship rituals and feasting. Gift giving also seems to have characterized these events, which would be expected in any alliance transactions. Knight (2001:327) has estimated that 100–200 people probably attended feasts at these mound sites, whereas the villages associated with them consisted of only six to eight houses (about 30–60 people), thus indicating intergroup gatherings presumably to create alliances. It is also significant that only some villages were associated with mounds, thus implying regional gathering centers. As in the study by Lindauer and Blitz, and in sync with the discussion in Chapter 5, maize appears to have only been used for special purposes and to have been restricted to the wealthier and more powerful members of the feasting community (327).

Similar patterns occurred in the upper reaches of many of the major river systems, notably in the Ohio River Valley. There, Abrams (2000) documented a number of Adena period burial mounds (c. 500–100 BCE) that exhibited large cooking features (2 meters in diameter). These appear to have been used to cook large amounts of meat. Unlike the mounds farther south, these mounds were also used for burying selected members of the community and for funerary rites. The size of some mounds indicates that ten to thirty small hamlets had participated in their construction, made contributions to funerary feasts, and interred their prominent members therein. Thus, as in the Southeast, it would appear that major intercommunity alliances were being forged at rituals with feasts that were held at the major mound centers – perhaps even proto-chiefdom types of confederations similar to those recorded by Ron Adams in the Torajan and Sumban areas of Southeast Asia. Smaller mounds appear to have served local hamlet purposes, perhaps for lineage or local community competitive displays and/or solidarity events. Both Seeman (1979, 1986) and Shryock (1987) have drawn attention to the dense faunal remains found at Adena and Hopewell sites, especially in features under burial mounds, seeming to indicate a hosting of intervillage funerary feasts just prior to the construction of the mounds.

Somewhat later, the Ohio Hopewell communities appear to have established full-blown charnel houses replete with funerary feasts (Seeman 1979:40). The special structures for processing of the dead had floors that were strewn with bones of deer, elk, bear, turkey, and raccoon, as well as abundant broken pottery associated with food preparation and storage. The structures were also associated with substantial roasting pits. All these patterns fit with the elaborate funerary feasts documented in ethnographic transegalitarian societies, as well as with chiefly societies, as will be seen in the next chapter.

Pluckhahn et al. (2006) have extended this research to Kolomoki, Georgia, where excavations at one of the nine Middle Woodland mounds (c. 350–750 CE) yielded indications of small-scale feasts involving minimal prestige items. The overall interpretation is that these were primarily solidarity feasts for relatively small kinship groups such as lineages that used the mounds as ritual centers.

Extending the scope of the survey even farther north, to the Northeast, reveals that lavish funeral feasting in the context of multigroup gatherings was also prevalent among Early Woodland and later societies there. Karine Taché (2011) has probably done more than anyone else to explore the evidence for and significance of funeral feasting from Late Archaic to Early Woodland times. She has argued for the use of early ceramics in terms of preparations of specialty foods for feasts (e.g., nut oils, soups, fish oils; Taché et al. 2008) and has documented their association with burials, prestige items, indications of storage, large cooking hearths (up to 2 meters in diameter), and occurrences of highly valued fauna in graves, as well as feasts at residential sites that imply other nonmortuary, household-based types of events even if their specific nature cannot be determined at this point. In all cases, ethnographically, the most extravagant feasts were funeral feasts, and this appears also to have been the case prehistorically. Taché explicitly relates the mortuary feasting practices to emerging elites that headed corporate trading groups in the region and used feasts to broker trading alliances or marriages as well as to enhance their economic or political benefits.

In later prehistoric times, ossuaries occurred at some Iroquoian sites confirming the ethnographic accounts of the Feast of the Dead, which might have developed as more elaborate forms of earlier Woodland and Late Archaic funeral feasts. Trigger (1976) has discussed a number of ossuary sites in the Huron area, and William Fox (1988) interpreted a 1.4-meter diameter pit containing a massive deposit of fish bone above which were scattered human remains at the early Iroquoian Elliott site in Ontario as a funerary pit that was preceded by a funerary Feast of the Dead (Salzer 1998).

The Gottschall site (in Wisconsin) produced evidence of another major feast involving five deer and a dog, which Salzer (1998) interpreted as remains from a "War-bundle Feast." In ethnographic accounts of the Ho-Chunk in Wisconsin, these events focused on single individuals of power associated with other important allied members. Similarly, W. Fox (1997) has documented ritual structures around the Great Lakes that he identified with thanksgiving feasts as described for the Central Algonkian groups, although it is not clear whether guests were from within the community or from other communities. These feasts featured dogs, ducks, squirrels, and bear; and Fox (19) suggested that a number of pre-Iroquoian sites contained remains of similar feasts. Interpretations of the function of these feasts has not gone further.

Europe

European archaeology has provided perhaps more archaeological documentation of feasting among horticultural transegalitarian and chiefdom societies than any other region in the world. This is especially true of the Neolithic period, although increasing emphasis has been devoted to the topic by Bronze Age archaeologists. Some of the most significant documentation and interpretation of Neolithic feasting behavior has been carried out by Paul Halstead in Greece. At the 50-hectare Neolithic site of Makriyalos (c. 5000 BCE) in Macedonia, one remarkable large borrow pit (originally about 500 square meters) was filled over a short period with an estimated 1,000–2,000 animals (almost half sheep and goats, a third pigs, and a fifth cattle with additional dogs and nondomestic animals; Pappa et al. 2004:33–4). The quantity of meat represented by these animals was estimated to have been more than 10 tons, an amount that could have fed 700 people for an entire year. The individualized pottery cups discarded in the same deposit appeared to represent more than 200 people, or, if shared by several people, more than 1,000 individuals (36–7). The unusual diversity in styles of ceramic cups indicated that participants in this unparalleled Neolithic feast probably came from a number of locations in the surrounding region. At a more general level, Perlès (1992:149) has observed that the circulation of pottery in the Greek Neolithic seems closely linked to social interaction and alliances between closely related groups and individuals. Although the ceramic assemblage at Makriyalos was dominated by serving vessels and cups, cooking vessels were also represented, presumably used by family-sized social groups. Thus, the family, community, and regional scale appear to be represented by this (perhaps extended) event. As is common in archaeology, the authors interpreted the large-scale feasting at this site in terms of needing to increase social solidarity within the community and reduce social tensions. They have stressed the overall ceramic uniformity as indicating the lack of "diacritical" aspects of feasting, although they suggested that the scale of the event was more indicative of chiefly feasts meant to garner political support, with considerable potential for competition between families or communities in providing animals, the scale of which may have decimated some herds. However, in contrast to the waste that occurred later in palatial Minoan feasts, Halstead (2007:42) did not see the same conspicuous ostentatiousness in bone processing in most Neolithic deposits. At Makriyalos, Pappa et al. (2004:41) have suggested that the pursuit of symbolic capital may have been important but also alluded to the importance of cementing social relationships on a regional scale.

Although I would question the usefulness of invoking "symbolic capital" or the reduction of social tensions to explain the feasting remains at Makriyalos, the notion that such large-scale feasting may have been to acquire allies or even to develop proto-chiefdom political structures (as documented by R. Adams 2007a,b) seems reasonable and is certainly commensurate with the size of the settlement at Makriyalos. Pappa et al. (2004) also noted an association of human skeletal elements with animal bones in various pits and perimeter ditches that seemed to indicate funeral feasting, perhaps on a community-wide basis similar to the Iroquoian Feasts of the Dead. As we shall see, this is a common feature in many Neolithic regions, and lavish funerary feasts form a leitmotif of transegalitarian societies in this region as well as in most others. In earlier work, Halstead (1989; Halstead and O'Shea 1980) developed the idea that the surpluses resulting from storage likely entailed the development of "social storage" including debts and, presumably, feasts, in the Neolithic of Thessaly. Although much of his discussion of the role of "social storage" parallels the role of feasts discussed here, Halstead did not specifically focus on feasts in his earlier work, but his theoretical modeling of the effects of physical storage (especially as it leads to overproduction and strategies to use surpluses) are certainly useful for understanding the origins and dynamics of transegalitarian feasting.

In the Southeast European Neolithic, Narissa Russell (1993) has focused on the faunal evidence for feasting. Although much of her analysis dealt with faunal indicators of feasting, she also linked feasting with exchange, ritual, and the struggle for power and control of production (61). She also emphasized that the use of wild animals like the aurochs in feasts may have been primarily for symbolic reasons. In Central Europe, Arkadiusz Marciniak has explored feasting evidence in the Linearbandkeramik early Neolithic Danubian cultures as part of his social zooarchaeological investigations. He has argued for the consumption of large amounts of food, especially in the form of cattle, which constituted 90 percent of faunal remains at many sites and were predominantly found between longhouses Marciniak (2001:107–8; 2004:133–5; 2005:207–8). As is common in archaeological interpretations of feasts, he then inferred that these must have been communal events that helped to create community identity and solidarity in an egalitarian context, although, in a somewhat contradictory note, he later emphasized the apparent competitive nature of these feasts (presumably between communities). This was in contrast to Sherratt (1995:15–16) who argued that feasting in the early Neolithic involved only high-status, wealthy individuals.

Marciniak (2001:108) interpreted the predominance of axial parts of cattle and pigs in the faunal remains as an indication of communal eating rules, even going so far as to argue that "early cattle and pig exploitation was not meat focused." Such views are difficult to swallow given that the head and horns are highly symbolic faunal elements in many transegalitarian cultures. They are frequently treated

differently and used for symbolic displays during and after feasts hosted by individuals or social groups trying to impress others (and may have been ritually
deposited in pits, which is where most of the Danubian elements were found). In
contrast, legs are prime meat-bearing elements that are often given to important
(high-status and powerful) guests who take them away from feasts for consumption at their homes or in other contexts. If cattle and pigs constituted wealth in Early
Neolithic societies (as in other transegalitarian societies), and their consumption
was indexical of competitive displays or destruction of wealth, their occurrence in
feasts probably also indicates that wealthy elites dominated or promoted those
events, even if the general community was participating on a nominal level. These
observations suggest to me that the patterning of Early Neolithic feasts documented
by Marciniak is more intelligible in Sherratt's terms of nonegalitarian hosts and
important invited guests. In Denmark, the burial of adults with pig mandibles from
up to thirty-four individuals is more indicative of individualistic competitive feasting displays during this time period (Rowley-Conwy and Dobney 2007:142). Large
numbers of peripheral guests may have attended the Neolithic feasts in which cattle
were killed, as is typical of many ethnographic cases in which anyone who wants to
attend a major event receives at least a small portion of meat although such casual
guests do not form the core of important feast guests who eat the prime cuts.

On the other hand, there are definitely ethnographic instances of community
feasts at which bovids were obtained for community consumption. These feasts
were apparently organized to increase community solidarity, such as those documented by myself, Mike Clarke (1998, 2001), and Ron Adams (2007b). It would be
worthwhile to develop more criteria for differentiating between these two possibilities. I would begin by suggesting that the sheer magnitude of some feasts precludes
their role as communitarian events. The village solidarity feasts that I am familiar
with involved single bovids sacrificed for the feast, which contrasts markedly with
the 5–20+ bovids sacrificed for competitive mortuary feasts in the same villages.
Thus, it seems that large amounts of meat, large numbers of animals, and occurrences
of prestige items should be indexical of competitive contexts. Russell (2012:388) also
suggests that displays of trophy faunal elements like bucrania indicate competitive
elements in feasts. Consistent with many other transegalitarian groups with domestic
animals, Marciniak (2001:108; 2004:135,138) concludes that meat (especially domestic
animals – and Marciniak would add domesticated plants) made up a very small
portion of the diet, and one may presume that they were prestige foods only
consumed at feasts. This pattern is intelligible in terms of suggestions made in
Chapter 5 concerning the initial and subsequent use of domesticates as feasting foods.

As we shall see in Chapter 7, when communities begin to compete with each
other for securing alliances and building political networks, the magnitude of
feasting almost seems to know no limit aside from the ability to produce, and the

locations of these feasts are, incidentally, the ceremonial centers of the chiefly polities, each of which takes a turn at trying to out-feast the others (e.g., Figure 7.5). This dynamic is similar to Patton's (1993:66,124–5) use of Friedman and Rowland's model of competition between communities via feasting and monument building in order to demonstrate which family was the closest to a clan ancestor, had the strongest claim to political power, and hence could get higher bride prices and more women, resulting in larger social groups. Indeed, some of the smaller megaliths in Europe appear to have been constructed by local kin groups at a transegalitarian level of organization (Renfrew 1983; Hedges 1984). It seems clear that periodic feasts to memorialize important dead lineage members were held for numbers of people outside megalithic tombs, with some food consumption by a more exclusive group of individuals also taking place inside the tombs. Given the blatant display characteristics of the tombs themselves, it would be surprising if these feasts were not promotional and competitive, with important members of other, probably allied, kin groups invited as special guests. Sherratt (1991) has presented indications that psychotropic substances such as opium poppies and cannabis were probably involved at least in the inner sanctum ceremonies. Ethnographically, some of the more complex transegalitarian groups also erected megalithic monuments (R. Adams 2004, 2007b; Adams and Kusumawati 2011). However, the largest prehistoric constructions, such as Durrington Walls, Stonehenge, and Avebury (where most of the evidence for feasting has been recovered), were almost certainly the product of chiefly organizations and are dealt with in the next chapter.

Before leaving the transegalitarian herding and horticultural societies of Europe, it is worth pausing for a moment to examine their manifestations during the Beaker and Bronze Age. Even though some of these groups were undoubtedly involved in chiefdom-level political organizations, many others appear to have remained organized at the simple big man level of independent communities and are discussed here. For these periods, most of the emphasis on feasting appears to come from the Iberian Peninsula (with several recent volumes on feasting; Aranda 2008; Aranda et al. 2011).

In the Iberian Peninsula, Gonzalo Aranda has documented the use of bovids in funeral feasts, and he has begun to model the sociopolitical dynamics involved. He has argued that sumptuous funerary feasts hosted by Bronze Age elites of the Argar culture in the south were used to reaffirm and contest social positions through the creation of debts and support groups, thus advancing vested interests. In concert with paleopolitical ecology models, he has viewed the primary role of these feasts as holding together political factions, the creation (or contestation) of political power, and as reflecting social conflicts (Aranda and Esquivel 2006, 2007:115; Aranda 2008a, 2008b:109–10,112–9, 121; Aranda and Montón-Subías 2011). The consumption of bovids was associated with elite burials, whereas ovicaprids were consumed with lower ranked individuals, and no meat consumption appears to have taken place at burials of the lowest status individuals. Although participation in large-scale feasts could promote a sense of belonging to a specific social group, accepting food from hosts could also promote acquiescence in asymmetrical power relationships. Social identity of groups was undoubtedly produced in the process, as emphasized by Sánchez (2008, 2011). Armada (2008) has also drawn attention to the high-status feasting implications of Bronze Age cauldrons and meat-hooks.

Rojo-Guerra et al. (2006) have documented in detail the use of beer in Bell Beakers and bowls, as well as their relatively standardized volumes and prestige-like qualities (fragility, thinness, decoration). They have postulated that Beaker ceramic sets were used by elite members of societies in their feasts and that each ceramic "kit" could serve between three and eight people in a ritual. As Garrido-Pena (2006:86–8; Garrido-Pena et al. 2011) has argued, these ceramics were unlikely to have been used in everyday domestic meals but were most likely used in Beaker competitive feasts between aspiring leaders. The similarity of styles and ritual over relatively large regions is indicative of high levels of interaction between the elites of regional centers (92). Garrido-Pena has firmly placed these funerary feasts and rituals in the context of transegalitarian social dynamics and identifies them as a key strategy for the acquisition and maintenance of power.

A number of these ideas (e.g., beakers as prestige wares used for drinking beer by elites in regional interaction spheres) were also mentioned briefly by Shennan (1986:135) for Central and Northern European Bell Beaker cultures. Similar notions have been expressed for the menhir statues in the Swiss valleys, where it is thought that feasts were required to erect menhirs and that power was determined largely by the ability to give feasts (Saulieu 2004:65).

In England, one of the most notable examples of funerary feasting was excavated at the Irthlingborough Barrow, where 184 cattle skulls were associated with a rich Beaker period burial (Davis and Payne 1993). At Buckskin Barrow, a rich feast has been documented inside a staked circle, with remains of a bonfire and joints of meat strewn on an inner platform. Since there was a central pole but no indication of a burial, Allen and Applin (1996) suggest that this may have been something like a harvest feast, thought to have occurred in the autumn around 2000 BC. However, these excavators, like those at Irthlingborough Barrow, do not go beyond such identifications to address the modeling of feasting dynamics.

The Near and Far East

Attention is beginning to focus increasingly on evidence for feasting among some of the early horticultural societies of both the Near and Far East. Probably the most comprehensive overview of the topic for the Pre-Pottery Neolithic (PPN) of the Levant has been assembled by Katheryn Twiss (2008). She has been largely concerned with the material correlates of feasts, but has also noted that many feasting foods such as pigs, aurochs, cattle, and cultivated crops were so labor-intensive or difficult to acquire that domesticated animals probably were never slaughtered simply to supply a meal (422–3, 428,430). She has even ventured to suggest that "intensification of cattle feasting might have been a key factor in the animals' domestication" (437). In addition, she has observed a close association between feasting and the first ritual structures occurring in the PPN, although she has neglected to mention the major storage rooms in the ritual building at Jerf el Ahmar as well as the cooked human heads associated with it (see Stordeur and Abbès 2002:553). The almost completely subterranean structure at Jerf el Ahmar, with its elaborate benches exhibiting engraved headless figurines was very possibly the meeting place of a secret society.

As consistent with the prevailing outlook in the Near East, Twiss has viewed the PPNA communities as being essentially egalitarian with "little need for feasts to bring the small communities together" (Twiss 2008:426,436), a view that I think is contradicted by the remarkable and rather exclusive opulent ritual structures at Gobekli, Jericho, Körtik Tepe (Ozkaya and Coskun 2009), and Jerf el Ahmar, as well as by the human sacrifices, the evidence of select ancestor worship, and the many prestige objects at these sites. In fact, the lack of elaborate grave goods in general is a very poor argument for the lack of socioeconomic differentiation. According to Feinman and Neitzel (1984:57) only 16 percent of the ethnographic societies displaying socioeconomic inequalities express inequality in the form of grave goods. Twiss's assertion that "At the origins of agriculture, it appears unlikely that the ability of feasts to communicate both social integration and social differentiation would have been important," is unfounded in my opinion, given the evidence from Natufian sites discussed in Chapter 4. It should be emphasized that the predominance of secondary burials in Late Natufian and PPNA sites (Belfer-Cohen and Goring Morris 2011:215) is probably indexical of competitive, elaborate funerary feasts because, ethnographically, secondary burials seem to result from the need to amass huge quantities of resources over several years for final burial (Hayden 2009a). Secondary burials can hardly be interpreted as indicators of stress, as Belfer-Cohen and Goring-Morris have suggested. Where Twiss has ventured into notions of causality, she has relied on the regionally popular notion that increasing size of settlements and increasing economic diversification in egalitarian societies created socially divisive stresses that needed to be overcome to hold communities together (Twiss 2008:427,436–7). Thus, in her view, funeral feasts were community solidarity events (437) rather than the competitive corporate arenas that are so abundantly documented ethnographically. These interpretations have also been adopted by Asouti and Fuller (2013), who document further evidence of feasting at many of the major sites during the PPNA and early PPNB periods.

Paradoxically, Twiss argued on the one hand that feasts reduce social stresses and integrate communities, and, on the other hand, that "feasts enhanced social divisions" thereby increasing "the need for integration and further feasting" (Twiss 2008:426–7,436). In addition to this perplexing interpretation, there is absolutely no support for her notion that "Feasting became a leveling mechanism" or that feasts became "increasingly explicitly diacritical" in the PPNB (436). All these internally contradictory statements create something of a theoretical quagmire. I much prefer to view the PPN pattern of feasting as fundamentally similar, if not identical, to the feasting system established by the Natufians (described in Chapter 4), only becoming more grandiose in scale. The main components of this were competitive corporate kinship-based funeral feasts (and probably marriage or house feasts), secret society feasts, communal ritual solidarity feasts (minimally involving all heads of corporate kin groups), and probably household and lineage solidarity feasts, as well as intercommunity alliance feasts.

Twiss has chronicled the increasing evidence for storage, larger site size, human remains, botanical remains, and feasting remains in the PPNB. She views stone bowls (similar to those in the Epipaleolithic) and the first fleeting appearance of pottery as serving ritual or feasting functions (Twiss 2008:430–1). I think this is very reasonable. Following more traditional outlooks in archaeology, Rosenberg (2008) has interpreted these stone vessels simply as household domestic wares that were not involved in feasting. In my opinion, this is an unrealistic view. These stone vessels make no sense as ordinary domestic wares due to their high quality and the time investment involved in their manufacture. Like Twiss, I think they are only intelligible as feasting serving wares meant to impress important guests. Twiss also reports abundant hearth and faunal remains as associated with ritual structures at village sites such like Beidha and Yiftahel (in plausible village council or secret society meeting and feasting locations), as well as at remote ritual sites such as Nahal Hemar cave (where 40 percent of the fauna were from cattle), or at Kfar HaHoresh, a mortuary and feasting complex where cattle remains were also abundant (Goring-Morris and Horwitz 2007). Nahal Hemar is a prime candidate for a secret society ritual center, especially given its isolated location, small size, and stone masks, whereas Kfar HaHoresh has been interpreted as a regional burial site for select individuals, I suspect either as part of a corporate kinship group or secret society, but there are other possibilities. Goring-Morris and Horwitz estimate that the 500 kilograms of meat represented by the eight wild aurochs associated with one burial could have fed 2,500 people. However they underestimate the quantity of meat that can be consumed by individuals at traditional feasts (up to 12 pounds per person instead [Feil 1987:249] of the 200 grams used by Goring-Morris and

Horwitz – see previous discussions), and they do not take into consideration the fact that large joints of sacrificed animals at funerary feasts are generally given to honored guests to take away with them as gifts that require return payments in the future. This may well have been the case at Kfar HaHoresh, as indicated by the fact that only 356 bones from all these animals were recovered (i.e., only 25 percent of the bones that should have been present from the eight animals).

Gorring-Morris and Horwitz have made another interesting observation that such a number of aurochs would imply either a large communal hunt or the management of raised wild animals similar to the raising of bear cubs for feasts by the Ainu. I suspect that these authors emphasize the large potential numbers of people at such feasts in order to support their interpretations of communal tasks (including lime plastering of burial areas and the erection of public edifices) that they claim would enhance group integration as well as provide venues for the exchange of exotic items. At Kfar HaHoresh, these included stone axes, stone bowls, palettes, malachite, pendants, obsidian, turquoise, greenstone, cinnabar, and sea-shells. I tend to view the location and labor-intensive aspects of this burial site as more appropriate for elite purposes than community integration, although they may have integrated the participating elites helping to consolidate their power.

Twiss has also documented feasting remains (primarily pigs, ovicaprids, and cattle) associated with burials at other sites such as Basta, Ain Ghazal, and Atlit Yam. The same mortuary feasting pattern appears to continue on at Cayönü and on into the Halafian ceramic Neolithic at Domuztepe in southeastern Turkey, where mortuary feasts were yet again viewed as "a means of integrating large numbers of people" (Kansa and Campbell 2002:13), a recurring theme also used by Bogaard et al. (2009) to account for indications of feasting at Çatal Höyük. However, the scale of these feasts fits better with the characteristics of competitive funeral feasts between families and lineages discussed earlier in this chapter.

Twiss (2008:435) has noted that the scale of feasting appears to have increased steadily through the PPN, with relatively small (without specific estimates) events in the PPNA. Of considerable interest is her suggestion that storage capacity at these sites is directly related to feast sizes (see also Morgan 2012:718,731). If this turns out to be a generally valid relationship, it could provide a valuable technique for quantifying and comparing feasting behavior between locations and time periods. However, the relationship between storage volume and feasting frequency and/or size requires further documentation. Twiss has also noted that the use of more and larger animals should be related to larger scale feasting, which, as I have observed appears to be a general principle that seems relatively well documented from a wide range of cultures. She also observed that ritual and feasting room sizes (only 38–45 square meters) indicated that only a subset of the feasters used these struc-tures (435). This is consistent with my own ethnographic observations from

Southeast Asia, where high-ranking lineage members occupied the interior of structures while lower ranking individuals gathered and ate outside.

Moving out from the PPN core, Russell and Martin (2005:97; Russell et al. 2005) have observed faunal indications of feasting with cattle and equids at Çatal Höyük but have not explored wider implications. Ian Hodder (2006) has elaborated the theoretical implications of the evidence from this region, finding indications of work feasts, initial feasts, community-wide feasts, multihouse feasts, and house foundation and house abandonment feasts (60,63,172). He cited large-scale animal processing at Musular as evidence for community feasting (or perhaps intervillage events), and he has emphasized the dominant role that feasting appears to have played at Çatal Höyük and the region around it. Hodder has also extended the theoretical implications of this evidence. In addition to the usual references to increasing prestige and community integration, he has suggested that there was social competition, that feasting and associated rituals were attractive forces that brought people together in early Neolithic agglomerations, and that feasts were instrumental in acquiring social power (together with capturing wild animals and the veneration of ancestors; 57,63,204,236). He has noted, too, an association of obsidian with feasts and gone so far as to support suggestions that cattle may have been domesticated for feasting purposes (172,255). To his credit, Hodder views most of these developments as originating before the Neolithic (236). Most of these views appear eminently sensible to me, especially within the overall framework that Hodder constructs of the major roles of corporate kinship groups and ancestor worship. Certainly, the elaborate prestige items at the site, as well as the larger more decorated houses with multiple (selective) burials, the skull (ancestor) cult, and the decorated bucrania, all amply testify to important surpluses, socioeconomic inequalities, and feasting typical of transegalitarian societies, much as Hodder and Meskell (2012) may wish to deny such implications. As argued earlier, socioeconomic inequalities need not be materially elaborate for them to exist or for major aggrandizer strategies, including feasting, to be important in village dynamics.

From my ethnoarchaeological work in Southeast Asia, it seems probable that the household "shrines" at this site, replete with decorated walls and bucrania, were the locations for lineage feasts and rituals with lineage heads and their allies sitting on the platforms as high-ranking hosts and guests (Figure 6.9). The "kitchen" and storage areas associated with these shrines were probably, above all, feasting food preparation areas. Hodder admits that bucrania were possibly placed on display to demonstrate the number and richness of feasts hosted by the household or lineage, but he is reluctant to accept this (Hodder 2006).

Surprisingly, relatively little attention has been devoted to archaeological indications of feasting in Far Eastern pre-state archaeological assemblages, and almost all of it focuses on funeral feasting. Kim (1994) has summarized much of the evidence for feasting associated with Neolithic burials in China and has related such feasting to the creation and distribution of "funds of power" in which feasts were given to create asymmetrical relationships in which some individuals could not reciprocate equivalent gifts, especially in the form of pigs and prestige items (120). I doubt that "funds of power" were built by such asymmetrical gifts or feasts. Rather, the ethnographic record seems to indicate that funds of power in transegalitarian societies were generally created by structuring symmetrical reciprocal gifts and feast obligations while manipulating the debts so created.

Kim has provided abundant ethnographic and historical documentation for the ideological, ritual, and economic importance of pigs and displays of pig trophy bones in East Asia, as well as noting that the differential occurrence of pig skulls in burials reflected the economic status of the deceased (121). Elaborate ornaments were carved out of pig tusks and may have been used as symbols of power in Neolithic China (Kim 1994:123). Kim has viewed pig control as the basis for the ability to give feasts and therefore the basis of power and authority. Kim (123) also mentioned in passing that pig bones were abundant in settlements, but does not discuss any implications for feasting of these remains.

In Southeast Asia, Charles Higham (1989:71–80; 1994, 2011) has recovered similar associations between high-status burials (spectacularly accompanied in some cases by tens of thousands to hundreds of thousands of shell beads and many food bowls) and elaborate feasting at the sites of Khok Phanon Di and Ban Non Wat in Thailand dating to the late Neolithic (c. 2000 BC) and Bronze Age, respectively. Feasting is evident from the abundant hearths and faunal remains of articulated pig limb bones as well as cattle, chicken, and fish bones associated at Khok Phanon Di with mortuary structures and graves. Higham has placed these apparently competitive funerary feasts squarely in the context of transegalitarian communities and strategies to obtain political power that were undoubtedly active during these periods.

Latin America

One of the few treatments of feasting in pre-state village societies in Latin America that I am aware of is Joyce and Henderson's (2007) examination of feasting in an early Honduran village dated to c. 1150 BCE. Here, as in other early village sites, *tecomates* (gourd-shaped ceramic vessels for drinking liquids; see Figure 6.18, compare with Figure 4.7) constituted one of the earliest forms of pottery (see also Clark and Blake 1994:25), followed by bottle and bowl forms. Clark and Blake (1994:25) have suggested that *tecomates* were used for competitive feast displays by individuals seeking to increase their personal advantages,

6.18. The earliest pottery forms in Mesoamerica (shown here) imitate large, elaborately decorated gourds such as those shown in Figures 4.7 and 5.2; they were used for feasts. The implication is that early pottery was developed to enhance serving displays at feasts (or to produce specialty foods for feasts). A similar phenomenon appears to be represented in Jomon pottery (Figure 4.28). (Photograph courtesy of John Clark)

whereas Joyce and Henderson (2007:649) have argued that the use of bottles and bowls for the consumption of chocolate (including alcoholic chocolate drinks) at feasts was related to emergent sociopolitical complexity, although details of how this transpired in this particular case have not been elaborated. Clark and Blake (1994), Clark and Gosser (1995), and Smalley and Blake (2003) have all emphasized the likely importance of fermented maize or chocolate drinks as part of feasts in early Formative societies of the region, although their discussions have generally not delved into the wider dynamics of such feasts.

Archaeological Discussions

In terms of material patterns, there are a number of interesting observations. At a general level, it is interesting to see a few instances (Chin, Kachin, Kalash, Kula, Hohokam; see also Birket-Smith 1967:39; Kirsch 1973:28–9; Gregory 1982:20) in which political instability engendered more lavish material and feasting displays as Cannon (1989), Randsborg (1982), and others (see Chapter 7) have suggested should happen. Along similar lines, B. Arnold (1999:73) has argued that the attempts of lower ranking individuals to increase their positions by materially emulating elites can be viewed as creating the driving force behind the need for elites to develop new forms of prestige items, resulting in the stylistic and technological changes that occur archaeologically and historically in prestige items. Another driving force behind cultural change was undoubtedly the stresses involved in keeping track of escalating levels and complexities of feasting debts, with gifts of support typically coming from dozens of individuals for a single large feast. These stresses must frequently have led to the development of material record keeping devices and counting systems ranging into the hundreds and thousands. When recovered archaeologically, such systems should be considered in feasting terms (see Hayden and Villeneuve 2011:344–6).

In other theoretical domains, it has become fashionable to argue that the structure of material space (together with proscriptions and prescriptions for its use) conditions people's outlooks and social interactions by creating "body memories" (Turnbull 2002; Hodder and Cessford 2004). However, E. Leach (1954:15) observed that most social structure was not evident in daily behavior of the Chin and that it only became manifest in ritual events. Similarly, elsewhere in Southeast Asia, Adams (2005) observed, as did I and Clarke (1998:52), that during normal daily routines, children or others indifferently used or played on ancestral tombs or platforms reserved for high-ranking participants at feasts. The special use of these features was only apparent at relatively infrequent ritual or feasting events. Peter Jordan (2003:194–200) made the same types of context-dependent observations among the Khanty of Siberia. Thus, the "body memory" theory of conditioned social action seems to owe more to intellectual reverie than ethnographic reality.

In terms of feasting remains, I am convinced that they are generally well-represented in most transegalitarian domestic contexts; however, they are rarely recognized as such by archaeologists due to a number of factors. Meat gifts from feasts were usually taken home, and the rotating nature of many small or medium-sized feasts tended to randomize the distribution of feasting faunal remains throughout communities, thus mimicking everyday meal discard patterns. In addition, it is difficult to archaeologically distinguish many prestige varieties of species and preparations from ordinary varieties (e.g., large yams or irrigated taro vs. ordinary varieties). Given this situation, identifying feasts at the household level is probably better accomplished by taking account of the nature of the fauna and flora (where distinct prestige species clearly occur), specialized types of artifacts for the preparation of prestige foods (such as beer), size and type of ceramics or serving vessels, the occurrence of prestige items, the display either in or on houses of special skeletal parts from animals killed for feasts (usually skulls, bucrania, or mandibles), the presence of any record keeping items, size of hearths or earth ovens, amount of storage, and other such indicators. Unfortunately, there is great variability in the materials used for both common and prestige serving wares, ranging from simple large leaves, to basketry, to gourds, to wooden dishes sometimes with elaborate shapes or decor, to fine ceramics, and stone bowls. Obviously, not all of these materials would be preserved archaeologically, so that absence of special serving vessels archaeologically does not necessarily indicate absence of feasting. It is also unclear at this point whether there is a threshold of surpluses beyond which prestige types of serving vessels (in whatever medium) are generally made for honored guests. However, at least in the case of Northwest Coast carved bowls, the Torajan pedestaled bowls, and the highly decorated beer vessels of the Conibo, we can say that serving vessels were elaborated in the context of substantial surpluses and competitive feasts.

Thus, it is hoped that the more promotional types of feasts held in domestic contexts (e.g., for marriages, house feasts, curing, feasts of merit, penalty payments, solicitations, and child investments) can be identified archaeologically, although small solidarity feasts such as those held within households or even for lineage solidarity may be more difficult to detect. Work feasts are sometimes detectable due to the incorporation of remains into the fill of buildings or under monuments. References are sometimes made to nonmortuary types of feasting in the archaeo-logical record (as at Kolomoki, Makriyalos, Çatal Höyük, Hopewell mound feasts, and kiva or lineage feasts in Pueblo sites), but these are often not placed within an overall feasting framework or model.

By far the most common type of feast recovered archaeologically is the funerary feast. This accords nicely with the ethnographic pattern. Funerary feasts are prom-inent archaeologically largely because parts of the feasts are often shared with the deceased and occur as grave goods or in nearby features, as well as the fact that the events often involve many people and unusual types or quantities of food, and the remains are usually in distinctive geographic or cultural places on the landscape removed from habitations. At the transegalitarian level, secondary burials per se should generally be assumed to have been undertaken in order to hold as lavish mortuary feasts as possible. Similarly, the occurrence of rich grave goods with transegalitarian subadult burials should be assumed to reflect feasts given when they were living to elevate their worth for marriage prices, and *not*, as is generally assumed, as indicators of ascribed status characteristic of stratified societies. Maximum levels of wealth invested in children in this way, as well as in funeral feasts, are probably reasonable proxies for the overall amount of surpluses gener-ally capable of being produced by social groups in specific communities.

The clear documentation of costly funerary feasts in so many instances is a valuable anchor for understanding past socioeconomic dynamics. The ultimate meaning of mortuary feasts may still be a matter of debate (see Hayden 2009a and comments). Many of those who deal with these topics view elaborate funer-ary feasts as indications of attempts to create community solidarity due to the stresses accompanying the development of larger settlements. From my perspective, the portrayal of lavish funeral feasts as serving exclusively or primarily to reduce social tensions or to create social solidarity is to uncritically adopt the public rhetoric of the organizers of such events or Rousseauian idealism. Although funerals undoubtedly helped create solidarity within corporate groups and their alliance networks, it is more realistic to view these ostentatious events as competitive strategies used by the ambitious to acquire power and by the less ambitious to fend off depredations. In fact, there appears to be a major divide in archaeological interpretations of feasts between those who view virtually all feasts as functioning to integrate communities (e.g., Twiss, Goring-Morris, Potter, Marciniak, and others) versus those who view feasts as promoted by aggrandizers seeking to enhance their own power and benefits and who use various feasting strategies to achieve these goals (e.g., contractual and reciprocal feast invitations, work feasts, marriage feasts, feasts to enhance the value of children for marriage, penalty feasts, and others – as proposed by Dietler, Bradley, Aranda, Garrido-Pena, Rojo-Guerra, and myself). The ultimate result of these latter strategies is divisiveness, strife, and inequality in communities rather than solidarity. Which outcome has characterized community developments from the past to the present (keeping in mind that some minimal degree of communal benefit must accrue to everyone in a community)? I would suggest that ethnographic transegalitarian communities everywhere are riven with strife, jealousies, competitive struggles and often even fighting at feasts.

In any event, it is important to distinguish between solidarity feasts and other more competitive or manipulative types. I have suggested that communal feasts should be characterized by relatively modest amounts of valued foods, whereas competitive feasts should be much more lavish, involving many more animals, much more meat, and more prestige objects. Russell (2012:377–91) has an excellent discussion of many of these issues, and further suggests that the display of trophy parts of animals indicates some competitive component in feasts. I have additionally also suggested that the intentional destruction of wealth is only comprehensible in terms of competitive feasts. I think that these aspects are clear in the ethnographies of transegalitarian societies and that they become even clearer in examining the ethnographies of chiefdoms, a topic to which we now turn.

7

Chiefs Up the Ante

Ah, the glorious ancestors – Endless their blessings,
Boundless their gifts are extended ...
We have brought them clear wine; They will give victory.
Here, too, is soup; well seasoned, Well prepared, well mixed

– From Waley 1996:319

Although the term, "chief," has a long history of use in the English language designating persons of authority, the concept of a "chiefdom" is a relatively recent development in anthropology. Oberg (1955:477,484) seems to be the first to have used the term to describe regionally integrated tribes under higher authorities in the lowlands of South and Central America. In his definition, he emphasized the paramount chiefs who controlled districts and other villages via a hierarchy of subordinate village chiefs who had judicial powers to settle disputes, punish offenders, and requisition men and supplies for war (although they lacked permanent armies). Oberg also insisted that surpluses were necessary for political development (in particular chiefdoms) together with class stratification. Service (1962, 1971:134,144–5, 159), Fried (1967:117), and Sahlins (1958) picked up this concept and redefined it so that in their definitions the core function of the chiefdom organization, and the basis of chiefly power, became economic redistribution (see Figure 7.1).

There have been other views on the fundamental nature of chiefdoms so that defining chiefdoms can become contentious. Moreover, there is considerable variation between chiefly societies in size, power, privileges, and other characteristics. However, the concept of a level of sociopolitical complexity intermediate between transegalitarian societies (with independent villages) and full-blown states (with multilevel political hierarchies, standing armies, and urban centers) is a useful one for research purposes. From my perspective, I find definitions of chiefdoms that stay close to Oberg's original concept to be the most useful for archaeologists

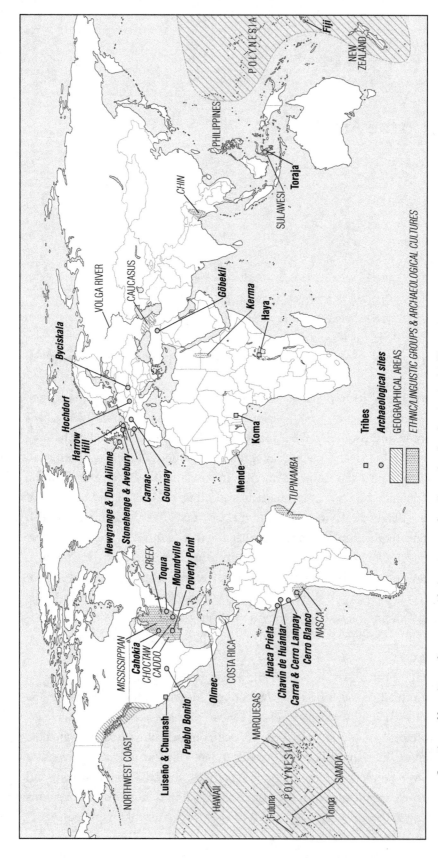

7.1. Locations of key sites, culture areas, ethnic groups, and regions related to feasting in chiefdoms.

Map labels:

POLYNESIA
Fiji
NEW ZEALAND
PHILIPPINES
CHIN
Toraja
SULAWESI
VOLGA RIVER
CAUCASUS
Byciskala
Göbekli
Kerma
Haya
Hochdorf
Harrow Hill
Newgrange & Dun Ailinne
Stonehenge & Avebury
Carnac
Gournay
Koma
Mende
CREEK
Toqua
Moundville
Poverty Point
MISSISSIPPIAN
Cahokia
CHOCTAW
CADDO
Olmec
COSTA RICA
TUPINAMBA
Huaca Prieta
Chavín de Huántar
Carral & Cerro Lampay
Cerro Blanco
NASCA
NORTHWEST COAST
Luiseño & Chumash
Pueblo Bonito
MARQUESAS
HAWAII
Futuna
POLYNESIA
Tonga
SAMOA

Legend:
Tribes
Archaeological sites
GEOGRAPHICAL AREAS
ETHNIC/LINGUISTIC GROUPS & ARCHAEOLOGICAL CULTURES

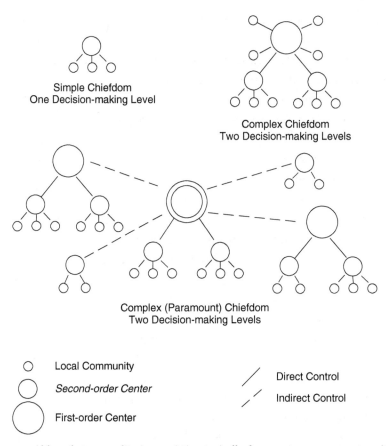

Simple Chiefdom
One Decision-making Level

Complex Chiefdom
Two Decision-making Levels

Complex (Paramount) Chiefdom
Two Decision-making Levels

○ Local Community

◯ *Second-order Center*

◯ First-order Center

╱ Direct Control

╱ Indirect Control

7.2. Although transegalitarian societies typically have autonomous communities, chiefdom-level political organizations exhibit hierarchies of settlements, as shown here with dominant control or influence from the community where the paramount chief resides. (D. Anderson 2001: figure 1)

(see H. Wright 1977, 1984; D. Anderson 1994a:5–6; Junker 1999:66). That is, chiefdoms are considered to be societies with a two- or three-tier settlement (political) hierarchy in which one community (and its chief or chiefs) dominate or exert some degree of control over various activities in other settlements (Figure 7.2). Social anthropologists have emphasized a number of other critical domains, such as social stratification, economic stratification, and political stratification (Miller and Boxberger 1994). According to these social criteria, there are probably many ethnic groups in which leaders are called "chiefs" that do not qualify as chiefdoms in the archaeological sense, including the Northwest Coast Indians, Iroquoian groups, and many minor Polynesian groups on atolls. Sahlins (1968:24) provided yet another perspective, maintaining that "A chiefdom is not a class society . . . it is not divided into a ruling stratum in command of the strategic means of production or political coercion and a disenfranchised underclass." Aside from his divergent views from other anthropologists (e.g., Miller and Boxberger 1994), Sahlins entirely ignores the existence of a slave class in the vast majority of societies considered as chiefdoms and even in many of the more complex transegalitarian societies. In contrast to Sahlins, Service (1971:134,144–5) refers to chiefdoms as having "broad *strata*" with "pervasive inequalities" (see also H. Wright 1984:42–3; D. Anderson 1994a:5–6). Irrespective of these social distinctions (which are difficult to monitor in the material record), among archaeologists, Beck (2003:642) sees a general consensus along the lines that Oberg originally proposed and that H. Wright (1977) and others have endorsed; that is, polities based on several levels of political hierarchy (see also D. Anderson 1994a:7–9).

There are also many ways of subdividing chiefdoms that researchers such as Sahlins, Goldman, Earle, Howard, and others have advocated. For my purposes, I find Beck's (2003) distinctions between constituent (simple) and apical (complex) chiefdoms to be most useful because simple chiefdoms seem to reflect early stages of the development of chiefdoms whereas "complex" chiefdoms seem more elaborated and evolved. In Beck's terms, "simple constituent chiefdoms" exhibit regional integration in some realms, but local village leaders maintain considerable autonomy, only ceding a portion of their authority to the regional center or chief for specific ceremonial or military occasions (Beck 2003:643,656; see also Kirch 1975:83; Frimigacchi 1990:173; Earle 1997:169). Such chiefdoms appear to be based on persuasive political affiliations and are characterized by "endemic competition between local leaders to attract new followers" including raids and skirmishes intended to undermine the support base of rivals rather than achieve territorial conquests (see also D. Anderson 1994a:19–20). This characterization certainly seems to fit the chiefdoms that I dealt with on Futuna Island and as described by Nicholas Thomas (1990) for the Marquesas Islands, by Junker (2001, Junker et al. 1994) for the Philippines (see below), and by Blitz (1993a:183) for Mississippian chiefdoms. In contrast, complex (apical) chiefdoms such as those of Tonga, Hawaii, and Samoa, are usually associated with territorial conquests in which a conquering chief places his close supporters in charge of conquered territories, uses more overt secular force to retain chiefly power, and maintains that all authority of village chiefs derives from the paramount chief – a characterization endorsed by D. Anderson (1994a:19–20). It is important to stress that chiefdoms do not necessarily have a single hierarchical head. Lehman (1963:146–7) specifically emphasizes that some chiefdoms were run by councils in an internal heterarchical arrangement. Thus, archaeologically there may be no single outstanding chiefly residence in a paramount community, but rather a number of them.

In considering such typologies, it may also be useful to view some societies as "proto-chiefdoms" as suggested in the previous chapter (and as dealt with further later). Many societies sometimes described as chiefdoms by ethnographers were probably proto-chiefdoms or complex transegalitarian societies, such as most Northwest Coast groups, the Huron, Sumban societies, some simpler megalithic cultures, and others. In archaeology, the issue of whether regional settlement or ritual centers should be considered chiefdoms, proto-chiefdoms, or complex trans-egalitarian polities is still unresolved concerning many Neolithic, Bronze Age, and Iron Age communities, hence the somewhat ambiguous treatments of some groups in Chapters 6 and 7. Nevertheless, studying proto-chiefdoms may help us under-stand how and why chiefdoms emerged from transegalitarian contexts. Aside from definitional problems, the underlying issue for understanding the cultural dynamics of chiefdoms and how these may impact feasting behavior is the means used by some aggrandizers or groups to exert control over communities besides their own and what specific domains were included in such control. This is a topic to which we now turn.

MODELS OF HOW CHIEFDOMS DEVELOP

Within the cultural ecology paradigm, a number of different types of theories have been proposed to account for the development of chiefdoms. One theory proposed by Wittfogel (1957) suggested that it was the control of critical resources such as irrigation water that led to the concentration of power in the hands of small groups of elites. Other ecologically oriented researchers have proposed models in which chiefdoms emerged as a response to population pressure. However, as Earle (1989:84), Rousseau (1979), Junker (1999), Andel and Runnels (1988:243), and others have noted, there are a number of examples of chiefdoms with low population densities and virtually no indications of population pressures. Because land does not appear to be scarce and "population pressure" appears to be absent, labor is argued to be the critical resource in these cases. In a similar vein, Webster (1990) argued that labor was the key bottleneck in building political hierarchies and that prospective elites competed to gain control of the available labor.

In yet other ecological models similar to the potlatch models discussed in Chapter 4, chiefs and the chiefly feasts that they hosted were postulated to have served an important functionalist/ecological role of redistributing food resources among participating communities, for example, fish from shore settlements for yams from inland settlements (Sahlins 1958, 1972; Fried 1960:718–20; Service 1962, 1971, 1967:117; Sanders and Price 1968; Rathje 1972). However, as Firth (1959:501,508) argued, "to think of the great intertribal food distribution as utili-tarian is to invert the traditional Polynesian concept. The aim of the hakai is not to nourish, but to exalt ... The feast had to represent excess." In addition, Earle (1977, 1987) demonstrated that the redistribution of basic food resources and other practical goods generally took place directly between communities (i.e., outside the

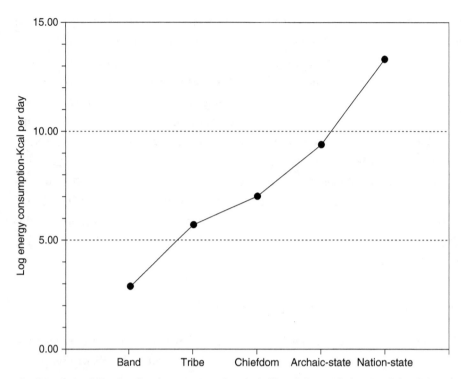

7.3. Because traditional political systems are largely held together with feasting "glue," the costs of creating and maintaining larger and more complex political systems increases exponentially as the number of people in the administration rapidly increases together with the escalating costs of feasting foods and gifts required to maintain political debts and loyalties. Terry Rambo (1991: figure 10.3) has graphed this relationship here.

compass of chiefly activities), so that redistribution does not seem to have been the underlying ontological dynamic of chiefdoms (see also Peebles and Kus 1977). Sahlins (1958) and Earle have argued that there is a strong relationship between island food productivity in Polynesia and political complexity. This indicates that the ability to produce surpluses was a key factor in the development of chiefdoms.

This observation makes sense in terms of Rambo's (1991; see also Tainter 1988; Scarborough and Burnside 2010:330) observation that increasing political complexity requires exponential increases in energy consumption at every step (Figure 7.3). These underlying conditions dovetail with political ecology models in which aggrandizers employ a range of surplus-based strategies to concentrate as much power in their own hands as possible. In these models, prestige goods and foods are required to motivate administrators and others to participate in the political hierarchy (to grease the political machine), and, as the system grew, the number of participants and the number of prestige items needed to motivate them grew exponentially. Ambitious aggrandizers had to find and somehow appropriate the surplus resources to fuel this political system; thus, they were limited in their acquisition of power by the amount of surplus that could be produced and controlled. Whereas Fried (1960:720) thought that redistributive networks emerged as "random social mutations" that subsequently spread due to their adaptive value for everyone, other researchers viewed the driving force as self-interested profitable control over materials and labor (D. Anderson 1994a:5–6,17). For instance, Sahlins (1968:88–90) sometimes characterized chiefs and big men as ambitious individuals who used gifts to create obligations through "harnessing their [supporters'] production to his ambition." Hill and Clark (2001) argued along similar lines, although they viewed aggrandizers as acquiring power through the creation of debts and inequalities via feasting and competitive sports that involved costly wagers rather than through warfare or resource shortages. In their view, surplus production had to exist to underwrite these strategies (see also Clark and Blake 1994).

Still other ecological explanations for the emergence of chiefdoms involve the competition for marriages (Clarke 1998:98; Ensor 2013) or the demographic circumscription of groups resulting in warfare that would then lead to political complexity (Carneiro 1981). Although there may be a germ of truth in this latter argument, it does not explain why some groups such as those in New Guinea or Amazonia never developed chiefdom-level political organizations despite what appears to be thousands of years of occupation, presumed population growth, and warfare, whereas other areas developed political complexity within a few centuries of initial colonization (as in Polynesia) – so rapidly in some areas, in fact, that chiefdoms were hardly perceptible in the archaeological record before state-level polities appeared (Yoffee 1993, 2005). Still other areas such as Southeastern North America developed chiefdoms but never became more complex. I want to suggest that the most likely reason for these differing rates of development and levels of stability in political complexity were ultimately determined by the ability of various environments and technologies to produce the sustainable surpluses required for successful long-term functioning of chiefdoms or more complex types of organization. The feasting complex was probably one of the most costly and distinctive features of the chiefly political organization. Although data are sparse, estimates of total production devoted to feasts constitute an impressive 20–60% (Hayden and Villeneuve 2010:119). Beer production for feasts alone could range from 20–43% of all calories consumed in a number of communities (references in Hayden et al. 2012; Garine 2001:191–2,201). However, before exploring the political ecology of chiefdoms in greater detail it is worth discussing several other theories concerning chiefdoms and the conditions that gave rise to them.

As noted in the previous chapter, Friedman (1975:170–4; Friedman and Rowlands 1977) made the critical link between feasting (hence production) and social differentiation. However, rather than ecology, economic production, labor, material benefits or ownership of land as the factors responsible for chiefdom development, he portrayed competition between social groups and individuals in terms of prestige and claims of descent from founding ancestors who conferred sovereignty as the ultimate cause. In a rather convoluted Marxist analysis, Friedman and Rowlands (1977:211) postulated that it was control of the "imaginary conditions of production" (the system of ideas) that linked one lineage and its head to the founding ancestor of the entire region and thus formed the basis of power.

This was similar to Pauketat and Emerson's (1997, 2008) views of how major centers emerged from a tribal matrix. These authors viewed the creation and control of rituals with unusually powerful psychological effects as the underlying force responsible for the acquiescence or submission of entire regions to the wills of a small elite in control of the rituals and the paraphernalia needed for them. In a similar vein, Vaughn (2005) has proposed that chiefs in the Nasca region of Peru obtained their power from the control of symbolically laden pottery used in feasting, rather than from any economic or productive base such as the ability to produce surpluses for feasts. Such cognitive theoretical scenarios have also been proposed by Helms (1994:58–9; 1999), Lewis-Williams and Pearce (2005:165–7,248,288), Joyce and Winter (1996), and others for the basis of power in chiefdoms. However, given the high costs of buying into such ritual systems, together with the religious agnosticism of 10–20% of the individuals in "tribal" societies documented by others as well as in regions where I have worked (see Chapter 6), I seriously doubt that claims for exclusive control over rituals or anything else related to religions would have constituted a sufficient inducement for significant segments of a regional population to give up their labor or surpluses to self-appointed ritualists. Nor does it seem credible that such systems could be long-lasting, especially when rivals or other factions could make counter claims, develop competing ritual systems, and produce alternate symbols or ritual paraphernalia. Earle (1989:85–6; 1997) observed that control based only on ideology and/or militarism was unstable and would continue to fragment due to competition. Moreover, how could the chief manage to convince everyone else that he and his lineage were the closest to a founding ancestor and that other lineages therefore owed him tribute and labor, especially when distant genealogies were notoriously subject to manipulation and reinterpretations (Brumfiel 1994:35–7; Junker 1999:137,142; see also Chapter 6)? Certainly, chiefs make such claims to *justify* their privileged positions, especially at the lower end of complexity (D. Anderson 1994a:20), but it is difficult to see these claims to supernatural or genealogical knowledge as the real basis of power (contra Aldenderfer 2010) without compelling practical consequences to back them up. The corpulence of many chiefs noted by Sahlins (1968:26–7; Kirch and Salins 1994:57; Kirch 2001:177–8) was the materialized testament to the underlying chiefly control over surpluses and labor.

From a political ecological perspective, and in concert with social anthropological views on kinship of the past 40 years (Ensor 2011), it is rather the ambitious aggrandizers' control over surpluses and the use of surpluses to advance aggrandizer power (especially using feasts) that seems to be of critical importance for the initial development and persistence of chiefdoms. As Friedman and Rowlands (1977:213) later somewhat contradictorily acknowledged, "The developmental situation of the chiefdom depends very much on techno-ecological conditions," even though they abjured any causal relation between technology and social forms. Friedman and Rowlands did argue that "control over certain kinds of valuables is in itself a source of prestige and power" (214), although they probably had ritually symbolic items in mind rather than prestige goods or foods. One of their most important insights was that the "tribal system" is inherently expansionist, demanding ever more alliances and exchanges, hence surpluses. I would simply add that the feasting system per se, as established in transegalitarian ("tribal") societies was inherently expansionist and logically led to more complex political forms of organization, like chiefdoms, wherever the ability to produce sufficient surpluses was present. To iterate Rambo's (1991) and Scarborough and Burnside's (Scarborough and Burnside 2010; see also Earle 1977) estimates, the surpluses required to unify an entire region under centralized political authority constituted an order of magnitude above the surplus amounts required to keep tribal feasts and alliances between independent villages functioning.

A very different view of chiefdoms is provided by communitarian proponents who view chiefdoms as kindred and religious-based, peaceful, and voluntarist, with chiefs constantly expending all of their resources for community interests and feasts, thereby often reducing themselves to poverty (see Earle 1997:109; Hayden and Villeneuve 2010:105–8). Confronted with the specter of political leaders systematically impoverishing themselves to the point of destitution, communitarian proponents suggest that wealthy individuals were obligated by the community to take on costly leadership roles via the power of cultural values and the conveyance of prestige to the selected individuals for public services rendered, similar to the idea of the "burden of the cargo" in native Mesoamerican communities. This, of course, ignores the well-documented, intense, and often violent competition in chiefdoms between individuals vying for the positions, as well as the limited longevity of individuals who did manage to become chiefs (Earle 1997:140). Such competition and violence is far more characteristic of situations in which key positions are coveted for the wealth and power that stand to be gained from them, which indeed appears to have been the case in Polynesia (Hayden and Villeneuve 2010). It is true that in order to access these positions, ambitious individuals had to give away a large proportion of what they obtained, resulting in an internal contradiction between the desire to acquire materials for themselves and the need to give in order to access labor and support, as described by N. Thomas (1990:103). However, fundamentally, this is no different from the need of capitalist entrepreneurs to pay their workers in order to profit from their labor.

Lehman (1963:104,154) developed a slightly different version of the communitarian model in which regional organizations headed by chiefs came into existence to benefit their entire communities by ensuring access to prestige goods, metals, and other accoutrements of civilization. However, indebtedness, destitution, slavery, and the control of virtually all land by a few families seems out of all proportion to the supposed benefits of such a hypothesized arrangement. One thing that is fairly certain is that chiefly feasts were not "leveling devices" as some scholars have argued. Chiefly feasts were antithetic to leveling, but instead exalted hosts (per Firth 1959:508) and created profound inequalities. To emphasize a point made in Chapter 4, according to communitarian theoretical principles, one should expect little change in cultures except as required by major alterations in outside factors such as climate, population pressures, or warfare. This is due to the conservative constraints placed on ambitious individuals to serve community interests first and the resistance to change once basic needs are met for the majority of community members. On the other hand, the political ecology model that features aggrandizers is fundamentally unstable since ambitious individuals are constantly searching for innovative ways to expand their power and promote community production levels to the maximum possible. Such individuals actively push to change cultural systems to fit their expansionistic agendas (Earle 1977:227).

Thus, there are many different views on how chiefdoms should be defined, subdivided, and explained. It is beyond the scope of this book to try to resolve these broad and deep issues. However, there are many aspects of chiefdoms that fit well in the paleopolitical ecology theoretical framework. From my own fieldwork with Villeneuve in Futuna and on the Northwest Coast, I am convinced that placing the emphasis on the production, control, and use of surpluses to acquire benefits explains the drive to intensify production (e.g., via irrigation), the various strategies used to acquire power (especially those based on the use of surpluses), the high levels of competition for high political positions and between villages, the lavish feasts (especially funerary feasts), the monopolization of ancestral kinship and rituals by the elites, the construction of monuments for those purposes, many blatantly self-serving ideological characteristics, and the political instability of chiefdoms. It also obviates the issue of land or resources versus labor. Carneiro (1981:61) has aptly summarized the dynamics of chiefdoms:

By the selective distribution of food, goods, booty, women, and the like the chief rewards those who have rendered him service. Thus he builds up a core of officials, warriors, henchmen, retainers, and the like who will be personally loyal to him and through whom he can issue orders and have them obeyed. In short, it is through the shrewd and self-interested disbursement of taxes that the administrative machinery of the chiefdom ... is built up ... [T]he chief ... is an appropriator and a concentrator.

Sahlins (1968:88–90) similarly observed that chiefs and big men try to get people forever in their debt and use gifts to create obligations. Irrespective of the theoretical model favored, there appears to be a fairly widespread consensus that the major role of chiefs involves the organization of feasting, rituals, and warfare (see Hayden and Villeneuve 2010:129, and references therein). Chiefs use surpluses to carry out these functions as well as to construct impressive edifices, support specialists, entertain visitors, and to create an aura of awe surrounding themselves and, when absolutely required, to aid those in need – entailing the creation of more debts (Sahlins 1968:91). Given this basic framework, let us see how these dynamics translate into feasting behavior.

Continuities

Because chiefly strategies for obtaining power and influence were fundamentally derived from transegalitarian aggrandizer strategies, one could expect many continuities to exist from transegalitarian feasting practices to chiefdom levels. In fact, in simple chiefdoms, constituent villages exhibited a remarkable degree of autonomy in most domains and strongly resembled transegalitarian communities in their general sociopolitical dynamics. Just as Ongka spent most of his time arranging *moka*'s (Nairn 1991), chiefs seem to have spent most or perhaps all of their time in politicking, rituals, and feasting, trying to keep their fragile organizations together through perennial feasting debts and rituals, punctuated by military actions that had similar effects and that also created ever more debts. It only appeared to be for special occasions such as warfare and chiefly feasts that the supralocal political organization became activated and manifest (Hayden and Villeneuve 2010). Without having done a thorough literature review, I suspect that, in most chiefdom communities, corporate kinship groups were prominent and controlled important resources or other sources of power. They probably also vied with each other for political allies, lucrative economic control or relationships, beneficial marriages, and power. In the Polynesian chiefdom that I am most familiar with, the competitive lavishness of corporate kinship group feasts, the increased value of their offspring as established by maturation feasts (Figure 7.4), and the wealth exchanges at marriages are major means by which influence was acquired. Thus, corporate kinship feasts in chiefdoms bear strong similarities to corporate kinship feasts in transegalitarian societies, such as the potlatches of the Northwest Coast.

7.4. First communion feasts on Futuna have taken the place of traditional circumcision feasts as major occasions to display family wealth, success, support networks, and power in the form of gifts (above) and major feasts (below). They are fundamentally competitive promotional feasts that also enhance the value of children for future marriage arrangements and consolidate support networks. (Photographs by Suzanne Villeneuve)

In addition, as was also characteristic of some transegalitarian societies, there could be secret society feasts in chiefdoms such as the *Ekkpo* and *Poro* secret societies in Africa. In general, public feasting and rituals sponsored by secret societies could be used to promote the ideologies and agendas of the secret societies in their communities. With costly paraphernalia and impressive dramas or magical demonstrations, aided by copious food and drink, they could demonstrate the power of the secret societies as well as manifesting the secret society's links to supernatural realms and forces. By accepting the food and drink proffered by the secret society, community members tacitly indicated their consent and acquiescence to the ideological claims of the secret societies. The goal was to create an unequal balance of power. To do so, secret societies required a means of demonstrating their importance and power, notably via public spectacles. Since these feasts were ostensibly held to enable the secret society to protect the community, they could also be used as a means of leveraging food and other support from community members that would primarily benefit the secret society members. However, leaders of secret societies also needed to maintain the commitment and convictions among their own enlisted members and thus also needed to sponsor more intimate, nonpublic feasts restricted to society memberships or, in some cases, the highest ranks.

NEW FEASTING ELEMENTS

Village Feasts

The flexibility and fluidity of alliances between communities that constituted simple chiefdoms appear to have led to pronounced competition between communities (in particular, their elites) for support and relative positions within the ritual/warfare framework of these chiefdoms. This competition was manifested in lavish intercommunity or "intertribal," feasts in which chiefs from allied communities within the chiefdom alliance were the principal guests and recipients of gifts that entailed obligatory reciprocity. This was documented in the early accounts of Marquesan feasting (N. Thomas 1990:93) and in Futuna by myself and Suzanne Villeneuve relying on earlier accounts and our own observations (Figure 7.5; Hayden and Villeneuve 2010). In these cases, the paramount chief attended and received large quantities of food and wealth. Guest chiefs took food and wealth with them to their own villages or to supporters for redistribution and/or personal use. Special structures and facilities associated with large, open areas (plazas) frequently were required to accommodate the large numbers of people and large amounts of food distributed (Figures 7.5 and 7.6) whereas smaller versions were used at the local level (Figure 7.7). Although some special structures or facilities and

7.5. Villages and their elites compete with one another for influence and positions within simple chiefdoms. Thus, each village in the Futuna chiefdoms tries to outdo other villages to display its productive and manpower abilities in its annual village feasts to which other village chiefs and the paramount chief are invited. These specially invited guests feast inside a special village feasting and meeting structure (*fale fono*) and receive large food gifts (mainly the large pigs shown here and taro) that are displayed in the courtyard in front of the *fale fono*. Lower ranking individuals stayed at the opposite end of the courtyard. These gifts constitute binding debts that help to hold the chiefdom political structure together. Village elites also compete to build the most impressive churches (and formerly temples) for the same promotional purposes. (Image courtesy of RFO TV, Wallis and Futuna)

7.6. On O'ahu (Hawai'i), large temple enclosures (*heiau*) probably functioned in similar fashions to the *fale fono* on Futuna. The sometimes impressive sizes testify to the large labor pool controlled by chiefs and the power of their political organizations. The enclosure at Pu'u o Mahuka Heiau shown here is about 100 meters long, with a second enclosure of the same size below it. In all, they enclose almost a hectare in area. (Photograph by B. Hayden)

areas for feasting occur in transegalitarian societies, in chiefdoms, they are generally much larger and more evident due to the greater numbers of people involved in the largest feasts held, greater control over labor, and the space needed for displays or performances. Kirch (2001:175) reported one feasting and dance area that measured 175 × 25 meters in the Marquesas Islands, whereas on O'ahu the largest area covered almost a hectare. Where the landscape was significantly modified, these features could constitute monumental constructions. The chiefs of each host village vied with each other to give away as much as possible to other chiefs (presumably to achieve greater influence and power within the chiefdom – or to defend their positions against rivals), and they thus created reciprocal debts that effectively bound the chiefdom network of elites together. I suspect that if one village became too indebted and unable to meet return payments, they may have changed their allegiance to another chiefdom, thus eliminating their debt and possibly creating conditions for renewed warfare or at least political instability. In Mesoamerica, it appears that sports events, such as the ball game, were associated with feasts and were also major opportunities for competitive displays between constituent communities within chiefdoms (J. Fox 1996). In fact, Hill and Clark (2001) have gone so

7.7. A smaller, *fale fono* on Futuna with its associated refuse accumulation area over a nearby stream bank. (Photograph by B. Hayden)

far as to argue that competitive sports together with feasts were the main dynamic forces behind the creation of hereditary inequalities (as opposed to warfare or resource shortages as causal factors).

In addition to the competitive village feasts, there were events at which family, lineage, or clan heads, or local elites from all villages were expected to attend. Although the paramount chief organized and hosted these events, they were largely supported by "gifts" from corporate kin groups. In Polynesia and North America, the "first fruits" feasts, similar to Old World harvest feasts, constituted a major yearly feast in which large amounts of the first harvests were given to the paramount chief who, in turn, made contributions to elite supporters. It would appear that these feasts constituted important venues for controlling and collecting food resources (Peacock and Turner 2000:159; Hayden and Villeneuve 2010:116; Kirch and Green 2001:226,259). They were essentially tribute feasts at which everyone contributed a great deal, everyone ate a great deal, and the chiefly elites kept a great deal. Compared to transegalitarian feasts, chiefly "first fruits" feasts (as well as some other chiefly feasts) represent a quantum increase in the sheer scale of surplus production and gifting, as well as in the number of people fed (Figures 7.5 and 7.8). For example, one nineteenth-century feast in Fiji that probably was held to celebrate the "first fruits" involved 420 large pigs and 3,500 yams, of which 220 pigs and 1,500 yams went to the two joint paramount chiefs (Douaire-Marsaudon 1998:117,123). Similar or even more extreme accounts were reported for Tahiti and the Marquesas Islands, where up to 10,000 people were reportedly hosted at some feasts, while in Hawai'i a nineteenth-century description of a *preliminary* dedicatory feast for a new temple saw some 1,440 pigs baked and served primarily

7.8. The sometimes phenomenal amounts of food amassed for major chiefdom feasts was graphically recorded in this depiction of a scaffold erected in New Zealand for a chiefly feast. Food and gifts would be piled high on all levels of the scaffold which could reach up to 30 meters in height. (W. Yates, *An Account of New Zealand*, London. 1835)

to the priests prior to the "great feast" (Kirch 2001:179). Similar scales of feasting were reported on Tonga, where a chiefly feast in 1862 was said to have involved 150,000 large yams and 7,000 hogs (Goldman 1970:502,508; Oliver 1974:260; N. Thomas 1990:95; Stevens 1996:264–5,416).

Another new feast type involved paramount chiefs staging "touring" visits of communities in which the visited community was obligated to host the visiting chief with food, gifts, and entertainment as elite etiquette required, but which became, in essence, a type of tribute feast or taxation strategy (Earle 1977:225). One early account of such a touring visit described a Hawaiian chief and his entourage as "descending like a company of locusts ... pigs, dogs, fish, fowl have been slaughtered in large numbers" (Kirch 2001:178).

Touring feasts were probably also a means of reinforcing alliances and political control, as with some early Central European states (see the "Europe" section). In fact, feasts in general were probably a means of acquiring food and wealth for chiefs and elites – a kind of gloved taxation that could turn to plunder if villages did not meet expectations or demands (Sahlins 1968:26–7; Earle 1977:225; Kirch and Sahlins 1994:50–1). In complex chiefdoms, almost every chiefly meal became a feast so that chiefs ate meat and other prestige foods constantly and abundantly. In contrast, other classes rarely, if ever, had such foods (Shnirelman 1990:133; Kirch 2001). The notable weight that many chiefs vaunted (Kirch and Sahlins 1994:57; Kirch 2001:177) was a testament to such distinctions rather than to any knowledge of the supernatural realms.

In simple chiefdoms, the life stage feasts of chiefs and their families might not differ too much from life stage feasts of other wealthy lineage or corporate kinship group heads, although chiefs sometimes promoted their own importance via life-stage feasts. For example, in the Marquesas Islands, N. Thomas (1990:91) noted that the most important feasts were for the chiefs' family members' rites of passage. Kirch (2001:180) has argued that feasts at this level fostered a kind of Durkheimian social solidarity with chiefs giving feasts *for* the common people. As previously discussed, I am skeptical that this is a realistic explanation for feasting in simple chiefdoms. In complex chiefdoms, it seems relatively clear that we can see, perhaps for the first time consistently (aside from earlier funerary ceremonies), chiefly life stage feasts that became great public events and causes for general festivities and feasting, as well as occasions for the erection of monuments. These were new feasting elements that appear to be the beginning of a pattern of what Kirch (2001:179–80) has termed the "co-option" by elites of feasting practices (and the sharp reduction of feasting practices among commoners, especially domestic-level feasts), or the attempt to make all important community feasts revolve around the elites, and particularly the chief, as well as making every meal of the chief a feast. These events may correspond best to Dietler's notion of diacritical feasts, although there is still much more to investigate and debate on this issue, and I am dubious of such an interpretation. More realistically, chiefly feasts may also herald the formal appearance of what Dietler (2001) terms, "patron-role" types of feasts. Normally, special guests are of comparable sociopolitical status to a host and are obligated to return invitations to similar feasts and gifts as those given by a host. However, with patron-role feasts, there is supposed to be an asymmetrical obligatory return that mirrors an asymmetrical sociopolitical and economic relationship. In this situation, a much greater value (in terms of labor and energy) is given by a subordinate to an elite host in return for a feast and the support that it implies (protection or help when in need). Thus, elites give a feast and receive a return in a different form, typically labor, produce, military support, or other service. This situation resembles a work feast. However, work feasts typically are single events with no subsequent obligations, whereas patron-role feasts generally imply a lasting and binding relationship. I have not been able to clearly identify patron-role feasts in my own field work or in the literature that I am familiar with. However, they may typify some areas not intensively covered in my overview, such as Africa, and researchers should be alert to their possible occurrence. As far as I can tell, they do not appear to occur in most transegalitarian societies, or even in chiefdoms, although the gratis distribution of food to lower ranking guests in larger transegalitarian feasts may have served a similar role and been a precursor to patron-role types of feasts. Large-scale chiefly events may have been organized primarily for tribute collection purposes rather than for reifying patron-role relationships.

The effects of all of these increases in the scale and types of feasts was to create major pressures to increase and intensify food production to the maximum possible limits (Brookfield 1972; Earle 1977a, 1977b; N. Thomas 1990:101; Kirch 2000; Junker 2001). Such pressures were entirely divorced from, if not the antithesis of, population pressures (Earle 1978:183,192). In the few quantified estimates of the proportion of food production that was consumed by hosting feasts, ethnographers report fully one-fifth to three-fifths of the food produced (or salaries earned) was given away at feasts (Ruyle 1973:615; Hayden and Villeneuve 2010:119), similar to the proportions of production devoted to feasting in transegalitarian societies (Chapter 6). The demands for food production to underwrite feasting for sociopolitical goals was virtually unlimited due to the competitive nature of sociopolitical relationships and the critical role that food and wealth played in those competitions. As Firth (1959:480) noted over half a century ago:

The subsistence factor in the economy is inevitably the more stable. . . . The status factor, on the other hand, is, by definition, expansive. Expansiveness, extravagance, exuberance, conspicuous display, prodigality. . . . The status economy, in short, is always an economy of scarcity.

Earle (1977a, 1997:70–4), following Herskovits (1940), Stevenson (1943), Sahlins (1958, 1968:77,89, 1972:101,130), and Dalton (1971, 1977), has developed these notions in terms of his characterizations of "domestic" and "political" economies. Both Cowgill (1996) and Earle have emphasized the fact that the major advances in agricultural and productive technologies did not necessarily serve the public interests but rather served individual (elite) interests. The ultimate effect of intensifying the political economy to serve elite interests was to raise the ceilings on population densities to the maximum possible, thus creating the correspondences between levels of complexity and resource potentials noted by Sahlins (1958), Earle (1977b:227). and others.

Archaeological Correlates

Of some relevance to archaeologists is the observation that in some regions of Polynesia, the consumption of meat was at least supposed to be restricted to the elites. Although there were probably many exceptions to this emic view, significant differences in meat consumption probably did characterize chiefly elites and nonelites in many regions (Shnirelman 1990:133; Junker 2001; Kirch and O'Day 2003). Chiefs' residences were also frequently described as much larger and associated with much larger storage facilities than common houses, as in Polynesia and the American Southeast. As Wason (1994:141–8) noted, chiefs' households were often meeting locations as well as temples, including distinctive numbers of structures, platforms, plazas, barriers, and qualities of materials used. The monumental constructions at chiefly sites were also testaments to the chiefly or elite control over labor, achieved in large part through feasting debts (R. Adams 2007a,b). Chiefs also had special ceremonial clothing and prestige items (Shnirelman 1990:131). Of special note is the common creation of large formal plazas or gathering areas for dancing, displays, and feasting.

On yet a broader scale, Junker (2001:298; also N. Thomas 1990:87–108) has suggested that there also appears to be a strong relationship between the occurrence of intensive (competitive) elite feasting activities in archaeological chiefdoms and indications of escalating interpolity conflicts and human sacrifices. This makes sense in terms of Urry's (1993:75–7) observations that competition for land was often for its ability to produce feasting foods and not for subsistence needs or from population pressure. Following Thomas and Junker, she, too, views a main goal of warfare as the destruction of competitors' ability to produce foods for feasts. Long-distance trade (and perhaps the production of local copies of foreign imports) also appears linked to expanded feasting activities in chiefdoms (Junker 2001:296), as does craft specialization. In addition, Brumfiel (cited in LeCount), Le Count (2001), and Randsborg (1982:135) have all suggested that under unstable, competitive political conditions, the use and display of prestige goods (and presumably feasts) should flourish. This may be particularly true of labor-based chiefdoms (vs. land- or trade-based chiefdoms), which tend to be less stable in any case.

As intimated earlier, the new feasting elements in simple chiefdom organizations appear to revolve around the need to hold together disparate communities in a political organization under a titular political head, the chief. If the Futunan case is any indication, in simple chiefdoms, this appears to be achieved primarily through the reciprocal network of obligations created by rituals and feasting together with mutual military support between participating communities.

Proto-Chiefdoms and Complex Chiefdoms

R. Adams (2007a:93–114; 2007b:353–4) has studied what he considered to be types of political organizations that were intermediate between transegalitarian communities and chiefdoms in the Torajan highlands and in Western Sumba. In these areas, megaliths were erected as part of the funeral feasts of the most wealthy individuals and powerful clans. In the Torajan proto-chiefdoms (mentioned in Chapter 6), the principal new type of feast was a regional or district feast, sometimes hosted by different communities that formed a type of confederation for mutual defense. These confederation feasts were probably similar in size and general organization to the yearly village feasts described earlier in this chapter; however, the detailed information that Adams could collect on them was limited. In the Torajan case, these regional feasts were held only every seven years and tended to be hosted most often by the largest, most prosperous village of the confederation. Moreover, it is unclear to what extent competition displays may have characterized these feasts. In the Marquesas, early accounts of reported "intertribal" feasts held every seven years may have been similar in nature, although these were overtly competitive between villages, and important political details are lacking (N. Thomas 1990:93). They may have been similar to intertribal feasts described for Futuna (see below). In the Sumban case of proto-chiefdoms, small dispersed household clusters of junior branch members were politically and socially tied to ancestral houses in central villages where the clan heads resided and where all matters of importance in the clan were celebrated (R. Adams 2004, 2007a). Although this settlement pattern may superficially resemble a chiefdom, members of several different clans might be present in a village without any dominant political figure coordinating affairs for the entire community. In these cases, they constituted a heterarchical community organization. Members of the same clan often resided in different major villages as well. As in the Torajan area, larger, multiclan villages (and confederations) appear to have formed as defensive measures and lacked the integrative political characteristics of clearly recognizable chiefdoms. In the Sumban area, there seem to have been few differences from transegalitarian societies in the types of feasts hosted.

At the other end of the spectrum, the complex chiefdoms on the larger Polynesian islands and in Africa exhibited much greater centralized control by chiefly elites. However, aside from the scale of feasts and the elevation of chiefly family rites of passage to general feasting occasions, it is not clear to me how this affected the overall feasting repertory. This should be a topic for future investigation. But, for now, a few ethnographic examples of chiefdom level feasting complexes will help to illustrate the previous points.

ETHNOGRAPHIC OBSERVATIONS

Polynesia

Some of the most detailed descriptions in the world of chiefdoms and chiefly feasts come from Polynesia. In fact, as Pat Kirch (2001:169) observes, the literature is vast, suitable for a monograph on its own. Thus, it is here that we begin sampling the ethnographic observations pertaining to feasts in chiefdoms. In fact, the terms for "mana" and "taboo" (often used in conjunction with chiefs and feasting) derive from Polynesian languages. There is considerable variability among Polynesian chiefdoms, especially in terms of small-island, weakly developed chiefdoms versus large-island, highly complex chiefdoms. However, underlying this variability is a useful composite profile of Polynesian chiefs as characterized by Shnirelman (1990). He and others (Kirch 1975:83; Spriggs 1986:140; Frimigacchi 1990:173) state that the main role of chiefs was to organize feasts, rituals, and warfare. This observation alone provides an important clue as to the origins and initial raison d'être of chiefdoms. In their domains, chiefs concentrated food for feasts via the imposition of food taboos (up to seven years) before major feasts and enforced taboos with coercive measures (Spriggs 1986:14; N. Thomas 1990:93). In general terms, chiefs' power was closely connected to the wealth that they controlled; they also had their gardens tilled by commoners or servants; they participated in secret societies; they were exempt from heavy manual labor; they developed complex etiquettes and educational or training needs; they extolled their mystical strength ("mana") from supernatural connections; they claimed that surpluses proved the power of their mana and garden magic; they ate fish and meat more regularly than others; they could change social rules and customs at will to suit their own interests (resulting in frequent accusations of moral depravity); they established exclusively elite occupations for producing prestige objects and large canoes; they traveled extensively, thereby acquiring distant contacts, exotic materials, and deep knowledge of regional matters; they had multiple wives; and they were supposed to enter paradise and become powerful spirits after lavish funeral sacrifices were performed (whereas commoners had a poor afterlife, or none at all, being condemned to wander endlessly if their descendants failed to sacrifice at least a pig at their funeral).

On the basis of ethnoarchaeological work that I and Suzanne Villeneuve carried out in Futuna (Hayden and Villeneuve 2010) and on the basis of previous work of others in Polynesia, we compiled a basic outline of the dynamics of simple chiefdoms in the region. In addition to the general observations made up to this point, our overview indicated that chiefs and the powerful kinship groups that sponsored chiefs were able to consolidate enough support to secure the most productive land, goods, and labor. The political titles, including that of chief, were owned by specific kinship groups with the help of allied supporters so that the loci of power were ultimately corporate rather than individual. As a result, corporate kinship feasts continued to be extremely lavish, highly competitive affairs (Figure 7.4), at least perhaps until chiefs could consolidate enough power to undermine the power of corporate kinship groups, as suggested by Kirch (2001:177,180) for the Hawaiian (and perhaps other complex) chiefdoms encompassing 250,000 people and verging on state-level organizations. Early accounts on large islands with complex chiefdoms like Tonga describe basically feudal types of political organizations (Vason 1840:139–40,190–1).

On smaller islands with simple chiefdoms, like Futuna, although ownership of land was primarily vested in the corporate kinship groups, the paramount chief laid ultimate claim to ownership and helped resolve land disputes between kinship groups. The best (irrigated) land was owned almost entirely by elite individuals or kinship groups, thus giving them major advantages in terms of their ability to produce surpluses, host feasts, create debts, broker marriages and alliances, influence policies or beliefs, control prestige goods, finance wars, and access positions of power. Using these material advantages, I argue that chiefs were able to successfully manipulate public acquiescence, and to some extent belief, toward the acceptance of the ideological changes that chiefs and elites viewed as useful for themselves. I have compiled a list of beliefs and values that can be arguably viewed as fairly transparent ideological changes that elites promoted in the community to serve their own interests (Hayden and Villeneuve 2010:131). These include the purported power of ancestors to enforce behavior that supported corporate kinship groups and their leaders; the notion that all members within the chiefdom descended from a common ancestor to whom the chief was the most closely related, thus giving him a variety of rights; claims that individual, group, or community misfortunes result from social transgressions; wealth as a prerequisite for marriage; ideas about the sacredness of chiefs; the notion that powerful supernatural spirits reside in the bodies of elites; the angry nature of most deities that had to be propitiated through feasts and elaborate rituals; the idea that the prosperity of the land stems from the chief and that crop failures stem from enemies; concepts of mana and taboos; acceptance of the reciprocal and contractual nature of feasts and gift debts; claims that wealth-food consumption at funerary feasts was required for the dead to enter paradise and that the quantity of animals sacrificed determined the happiness or power of the dead; and the claim that warriors ascended to heaven if killed in battle. In essence, these concepts constitute an elite-centric vision of ideology that benefits elites. The promotion of these and similar values by the elite class, and at least the acquiescence of others, probably represents an important example of how the self-interest of a few aggrandizers could transform cultural norms if the appropriate leverage mechanisms were employed. It is difficult to believe that any of these cultural values originated out of communal interests, were really accepted or believed by the entire constituent populations, or could have affected economic production without additional means of "persuasion." Moreover, if these or other cognitive beliefs on their own had been effective in making people produce and surrender surpluses to chiefs (as claimed by Friedman and Rowlands, Pauketat and Emerson, Godelier, and others), then why did chiefs so often resort to more coercive means of enforcement?

In his study of Maori communities in New Zealand, Firth (1959:132–3) portrayed chiefs and the society in much the same way. Wealth was critical for holding chiefly positions (and as an indicator of social standing), and the chief was like a capitalist who accumulated wealth but used some portion of it for creating communal (corporate) infrastructure (irrigation, defense, public buildings) and to pay laborers (largely in the form of feasts) to produce food, prestige items, and constructions for the running of the chiefly organization. Chiefs' wealth was used primarily for their own "aggrandizement and influence" and they accumulated "considerable stores of wealth" to finance undertakings despite the "inroads of guests" and demands of supporters (298,304). Generosity was necessary for power and prestige, but it was predicated on rules of reciprocity (429). Chiefs put on superficial shows of generosity, but these displays hid underlying strong self-interests. Their gifts might appear free, but in reality there was always a payback, a constant insistence on reciprocity, an obligation of return, if possible with an increase (423). Chiefs used gifts and sponsored feasts for supporters to maintain allegiances and repay them for support (Figure 7.5). To underwrite projects and feasts, chiefs relied on production from their own abundant lands (worked by commoners, slaves, attendants, wives, their children, and themselves), gifts from groups seeking favors or to elevate their positions, war booty, and other feasts (especially in the form of first fruits and touring visits). Chiefs had to exhibit keen abilities to balance incoming gifts and debts with the liabilities incurred, especially because their support depended on their ability to satisfy the demands of supporters and the constant demands for "hospitality," help, and feasts. Sponsoring large feasts often "drained him of food supplies" (134,297–8). Chiefs who assumed office on the basis of kinship positions but who were incompetent administrators were given honorific ceremonial roles while the real organizational work was carried out by their more gifted supporters (132). Kirch (2000:263; see also Hayden and Villeneuve 2010) maintains that, in general, chiefs obtained a great deal of material support from feasts that served as a kind of tribute collecting system.

FEAST TYPES

Some of the earliest explorer accounts from Polynesia appear to describe large village or first fruits feasts, as well as funeral and marriage feasts (Vason 1840:108–9,163,147–51; N. Thomas 1990:87–104; Kirch 1994). These have been documented by ourselves (Hayden and Villeneuve 2010) and many others. Pigs, dogs, eels, birds, crayfish, humans, and taro featured as the most valued foods, with taro being grown specifically for feasts rather than for subsistence (Urry 1993:39–40, 66; H. Leach 2003). Taboos were placed on the consumption of key feasting foods such as pigs (sometimes for years before major feasts), pigs were fattened before feasts, and wars could be waged to obtain captives to sacrifice (J. Martin 1827:90, 342–5; Spriggs 1986:14; N. Thomas 1990:93; Kirch 1991:16). Highly competitive village or "tribal" feasts played a particularly prominent role in Futuna (Figure 7.5), in New Zealand at *hakai* feasts (Urry 1993:18,30–3), and in other simple chiefdoms such as the Marquesas (N. Thomas 1990:93). However, both on Futuna and in New Zealand, there were also unusually large, island-wide, interchiefdom feasts, the dynamics of which are somewhat vague. On Futuna, these island-wide events involved the two rival paramount chiefs and large numbers of people from their rival chiefdoms. Something similar may have occurred in the Marquesas, where a feast was reported with 10,000 participants – perhaps the largest reported feast gathering in Polynesia (N. Thomas 1990:95).

It is perplexing to try to determine why rival polities that were often at war with each other would gather together for a large feast with obvious competitive display elements unless everyone involved was using such events to assess or reassess the comparative worth of villages, chiefdoms, and potential alternative alliance configurations in a political mosaic that was constantly in flux. Firth (1959:319–34) called these events "intertribal" feasts and described them as literally overflowing with food. Food was amassed in rows, in stacks, on scaffolds, and probably exhibited in open pits (Law 2000). The largest recorded scaffolds were 90–100 feet (27–30 m) high and 64 m long (Urry 1993:36) (Figure 7.8). One feast reported by Firth was attended by 3,400 people from fifteen different "tribes," and the food was piled in rows 400 yards long, 7 feet wide, and 4 feet high. Law reports another feast that had an array of food a mile long. Urry (1993:42,93,95) further documented a feast that provided 109 tons of potatoes, 9,000 dried sharks, 100 large pigs, and large quantities of other starches. Other feasts were reported to have provided 20,000 dried eels, tons of sea fish, and 11,000 baskets of potatoes. Several feasts involved 3,000 participants, some of whom traveled 2,000 miles to attend the events.

These staggering amounts of food produced primarily for promotional displays resulted in large amounts of food wasted (often allowed to rot) ultimately to end up in huge middens (Firth 1959:332–2; Spriggs 1986:14). This, of course,

7.9. Food gifts at feasts could either take the form of whole animals, as in Figure 7.5, to be taken away and divided up, or as smaller portions of butchered animals and other foods given in baskets such as those shown here being prepared for guests at a relatively small feast for the installation of a new village chief on Futuna. (Photograph by Suzanne Villeneuve)

came at considerable cost to many villagers who were prohibited from eating these types of food for months or years prior to the big events, and, because they gave away so much, resulted in hunger or semi-starvation for months afterward, with people largely subsisting on wild fern roots (Firth 1959:332–3; Urry 1993:40–1,66). Recall that estimates of total production devoted to feasting range from 20% to 60%, although our data indicate that this probably varied considerably from household to household, with the higher levels of feasting expenses characterizing only the most ambitious and productive families or corporate groups. Characteristically, such lavish expenditures were one of the first indigenous practices to be suppressed by colonial governments (as of 1850 in New Zealand; Firth 1958:334).

Other feasts became essential for undertaking major elite activities, whether war, political support, harvesting, politics, marriages, or funerals (Kirch 1991:17).

7.10. Preparations for feasts require the coordination of a large number of support people for supplying the food and its transport, the butchering and cooking of animals, the preparation of special foods, the manufacture of serving or gift containers, determining specific gifts to be given according to rank, and the serving of foods. Here, one group of men shreds cocoanut meat as a delicacy for a feast on Futuna. (Photograph by Suzanne Villeneuve)

Firth (1959:311–4) was one of the few early ethnographers to broach the question of what practical benefits these feasts provided. Although according to some analysts, he appeared to have overlooked important sociopolitical implications of feasts in Maori dynamics (Urry 1993:29), he did perceptively observe that all feasts promoted some form of social bonding. However, he also identified economic feasts (essentially work feasts to build canoes, meeting houses, and to undertake similar projects), marriage feasts to bond together the families of the groom and bride, and intertribal feasts. He listed alliances, increased production, and political negotiations as benefits resulting from feasts, many of which were presumably between corporate kinship groups. As always, these systems were based on obligatory reciprocity between specially invited individuals or representatives of corporate kin groups or between formal exchange partners, and there were severe sanctions for not returning gifts (Firth 1959:417). This was the key to the creation of power. The initiator of the gift exchange usually was at an advantage because greater returns were expected (429). Firth (310) also developed a typology of feasts based on their intended emic purposes, which resembled in some respects the typology that I developed from ethnoarchaeological work on feasts in Southeast Asia, at least

7.11. Butchering is a major undertaking at most feasts, such as this one on Futuna, and the butchering patterns together with the association of specific bone remains with specific house structures provide archaeologists with important indications of activities and statuses. For instance, chiefs in many areas preferentially receive one of the forelimbs of sacrificed and hunted animals. (Photograph by Suzanne Villeneuve)

in terms of distinguishing practical economic goals from social bonding goals. Firth's typology consisted of feasts to:

- Celebrate important life events and integrate individuals into their social group
- Mark important economic or social events (harvests, New Year)
- Establish social links
- Achieve economic goals

Somewhat later, N. Thomas (1990:87–104) echoed similar perspectives in his insightful analysis of early Marquesan feasting. He, too, noted work feasts, feasts to organize war, harvest ("prosperity") feasts, and competitive tribal feasting including human sacrifices. However, he placed special emphasis on the reciprocal feasts between elites and the competitive promotional displays at funerals, tattooings, and circumcisions, all held apparently as part of intense competition between corporate kinship groups. Hosts vied with each other to display or augment their relative ranks at these events. N. Thomas (1990:89,96) considered feasting events as "crucial" and "central to the process of hierarchical reproduction in the Marquesas," as well as being "crucial to the pursuit of prestige and the overall dynamic of Marquesan society."

What these descriptions have left out are references to "touring feasts" in which the chief and his retinue, or representatives of the local deity, traveled from village to village to collect tribute, often exhausting a villages' food supplies (Earle 1977:225; Kirch 2001:178). In Hawai'i, villages that did not supply the requested amounts were plundered by the chief's forces (178). I also recorded similar accounts in the simple chiefdoms on Futuna, as did earlier observers (Hayden and Villeneuve 2010). Like the first fruits or harvest feasts, these touring feasts were essentially a form of taxation in which a considerable proportion of the resources were returned to the producing populace in the form of a feast while the elite administration also kept a sizeable amount (Hayden and Villeneuve 2010; Earle 1977:225).

Another feasting form that seems to have gone largely unnoticed involved feasts to inaugurate temples (as described earlier)and probably maintain them afterward. It seems likely that the requisitions for food to hold such feasts also served as a kind of taxation under the pretext of honoring or appeasing the gods. It may be that chiefs were still somewhat reluctant to place too many demands on their subjects for tribute to blatantly serve chiefly self-indulgence. By claiming that food requisitions were for the gods (but in reality were used by elites), they could at least claim that the food was not for their personal use. Among less complex Southeast Asian groups that sometime cycled into chiefdoms, Durrenberger (1989:115) observed that attempts to gain prestige via feasts that were too openly self-serving led to rejection. Thus, people used pretexts that were beyond reproach, such as curing the sick, honoring the dead, or appeasing the gods.

On Tonga, John Martin (1827:90,109–13,210–9,350–3) described the elaborate funeral and marriage feasts for chiefs and their families including human sacrifices, burials in large stone vaults closed with stones requiring 200 men to move, and attendance by 3,000 people. Whether these feasts or the quotidian meals of chiefs in the more complex polities of Hawai'i should be viewed as purely diacritical in Dietler's sense (as also suggested by Kirch 2001:178,180) or as serving a deeper promotional or bonding role as suggested by Junker (1999:314) is a matter of conjecture and debate, although I doubt that diacritical motives can account adequately for such events.

Thomas (N. Thomas 1990:97,101,104) also provided other important details in his analysis, such as the higher ascribed value of chiefs' crafts and gifts (vs. the lower value attributed to gifts from nonelites), the redistribution of received feast foods to supporters as rewards, and the undertaking of raids with the primary goal of destroying rivals' abilities to produce feasting surpluses, a situation also reported for New Zealand (Urry 1993:78) and the Philippines (Junker et al. 1994:323; Junker 2001). Significantly, Urry (1993:76) also stated that competition and conflict over land was not necessarily due to population pressure, but to produce prestige feasting foods. Production of food for feasts had to be planned well in advance.

Thus, in Polynesia, there appear to have been large feasts between competing chiefdoms, feasts involving competing villages within the same chiefdom, tribute feasts (in the form of harvest feasts, temple feasts, chiefly life-event feasts, and touring feasts), competitive feasts between corporate kinship groups (marriage, funeral, child maturation feasts), feasts for corporate solidarity, work feasts, and war feasts for allies.

Southeast Asia

Laura Junker is probably the person who has done most to research the historic accounts of chiefdoms and feasting in Southeast Asia, notably in the Philippines, and, as she observed, little comparative or integrative research had been previously conducted there. Beginning in the 1990s, she documented in increasing detail the low population levels in historic Philippine chiefdoms, the internal dynamics of chiefdoms, and the competitive use of feasts and displays of wealth central to the creation of political power (Junker et al. 1994; Junker 1999, 2001; Junker and Niziolek 2010). Her thorough syntheses of documents from the Philippines reveal a distinctive characteristic of the regional polities: simple chiefdoms that relied heavily on interpersonal relationships and debts as the basis of power rather than the ownership of the means of production (e.g., land, fishing sites, boats, or other resources, as common in Polynesian and African chiefdoms). This same interpersonal basis of political organization is also argued to characterize early states in Southeast Asia, including the Khmer Empire and Balinese kingdoms.

The reliance on personal relationships as the basis for political power in the Philippines is explainable in terms of the unusually low population densities and relative abundance of land that characterized the Philippines and many other areas of Southeast Asia. Why populations should have remained so low is something of a mystery, but numerous accounts leave little doubt that they were low (Rousseau 1979; Lehman 1989:96–9; Junker 1999:61) effectively annulling Carneiro's model for the development of political complexity based on circumscription and population pressures. As a result, feasts, gifts, debts, marriages, and the use of slave labor became the primary means of establishing prestige and power. Reciprocal gifts of food and wealth became the material glue of alliance building and constituted contractual agreements (Junker et al. 1994:317). Prestige and social rank were fundamentally equated with positions in the feasting system, together with the consequent debts and political power. Elite kin helped to physically enforce chiefly taboos and implement chiefly undertakings (Junker et al. 1994:311,323). In general, personal ties and debts are more difficult to transfer between generations than heritable property or resource rights. Thus, where chiefdoms emphasized personal relations to establish power, social rank was unusually fluid or unstable, and competition was strongly developed. As a result, it is not surprising to find that descent rules and genealogies were often manipulated to accommodate the new status of successful pretenders to power (Junker 1999:137,142).

Control of trade in prestige goods (largely via personal connections) and the manufacture of prestige goods was critical for the feasting and gift giving that created binding political debts and political power. Porcelain serving wares were especially prized for use in feasts. Therefore, warfare over the control of trade routes was endemic, even fatally involving the purveyors of prestige goods themselves, such as Magellan who was killed in the sixteenth century by getting involved in a trade dispute between chiefs. Bride wealth payments for elite marriages involved many animals (water buffalo and horses), metal gongs, weapons, and other valuables (Junker 1999:299), and ambitious men sought to marry numerous wives.

Feasts were described by the Spanish chroniclers as the cornerstone of social, political, economic, and religious life, and, on the basis of their observations, Junker (1999:314) was able to identify three distinct purposes for the feasts described: (1) to celebrate life events of the elites (birth, maturation, marriage, illness, death) that were used to engage kin and supporters in reciprocal exchanges and debt relationships, (2) to organize occasional elite events (generally work-types of feasts for the construction of a chief's house, or for raids, alliances, and trading expeditions), and (3) to marshall labor or collect tribute at critical points in the agricultural cycle (314). Most of the recorded feasts were sponsored by elites and held in or adjacent to their spacious homes, apparently capable of sheltering several hundred people. Elites may have borne the brunt of the costs, but they expected contributions from all of the specifically invited guests, as well as tribute from subordinates or slaves of the host (Junker et al. 1994:313,323; Junker 1999:317–8). Valuable animals were sacrificed; large quantities of meat, rice, and alcohol were consumed; and costly gifts were presented to the elite guests reaffirming mutual support relationships. Agricultural feasts occurred sufficiently frequently that they probably constituted the key context in which food was collected as tribute. Communal agricultural labor was also organized for the production of chiefly surpluses.

Overtly competitive feasts (challenge feasts), in which rival chiefs tried to destroy each other by giving so much that their opponents were essentially bankrupted, occurred at times but were probably relative rare (Junker 1999:322–3). However, there were many less extreme forms of competition exhibited in other feasts, such as those where the guest chiefs tried to outdo each other with boasts of noble ancestors and accomplishments as well as providing ever more impressive wealth and food (up to 70 water buffaloes and 180 chickens) at funerals and rights of passage, as also occurred in Futuna (Polynesia). Succession feasts typically involved all the chiefs from surrounding districts coming together presumably to ratify and sanctify the position of the new chief. Competitive boasting and displays at feasts allowed the honored guests to gauge the relative strengths and weaknesses of various chiefs, whereas the competitive drive to produce ever more must have led to intensified food production as well as increasingly devastating raids on resources (e.g., debarking fruit trees, smashing weirs) and the capture of slaves in order to undermine the ability of rivals to amass the resources needed to hold impressive feasts (Junker et al. 1994:323; Junker 2001). Given this competitive atmosphere and the consequences that feasting performances could have for the acquisition of power and wealth, it should not be surprising that contentious disputes often erupted during feasts between rival elites, ending sometimes in armed battles, just as in many transegalitarian societies (noted in Chapter 6). In fact, almost all of the characteristics and functions that Junker describes could equally well apply to many transegalitarian societies described in the preceding chapter.

Junker (1999:324) took exception to my speculations that competitive feasts were probably not as important in chiefdoms as in transegalitarian societies where power was less institutionalized (Hayden 1995:64). This was an early impression of mine and may still be true for complex chiefdoms that rely to a great extent on secular force to maintain chiefly authority (D. Anderson 1994a:19–20). However, even in the case of complex chiefdoms, Anderson (50–2) has argued that they were unstable due to the competition between elites for positions of power and the ability of the constituent district chiefs to operate independently, thus making higher levels of organization dependent on the integrative effectiveness of feasting, rituals, and warfare. On the other hand, Kirch (2001:177–80) observed that there was a remarkable dearth of descriptions of domestic feasting in Hawai'i, which he viewed as a co-option of domestic feasting functions by the elites of complex chiefdoms. Although the role of feasting in complex chiefdoms requires more in-depth investigation, at the level of *simple* chiefdoms, where chiefly authority was maintained by less coercive and less stable means, Junker was absolutely correct, and I was mistaken. My work in Futuna has left little doubt that competition in simple chiefdoms was characteristically rife between both corporate kin groups and villages jockeying for positions of power, alliance, and influence.

There are many other accounts of chiefdoms and chiefly feasts from Indonesia and other parts of Southeast Asia, including Edmund Leach's (1954) cyclical *gumlao* chiefdoms and the accounts of proto-chiefdoms in Indonesia (R. Adams 2004, 2007a,b). In the Chin area, Lehman (1963:142) claimed that chiefdoms were held together through elite polygynous marriages and continuing bride price payments (especially in the form of land rights) that were essentially tribute payments, although he thought that land was acquired by conquest in the past (151). However, space and time preclude the exploration of all these cases. Hopefully, the preceding examples provide a sufficient appreciation for the general character of chiefly feasting in this sector of the world so that we may briefly look at some of the characteristics in other ethnographically documented areas of the world.

The Americas

Large sections of the American Southeast were organized as chiefdoms when Europeans arrived. John Swanton undertook a series of descriptions based on early archives about some of the most important of these groups such as the Caddo and neighboring groups, the Choctaw, and the Creek (see also D. Anderson 1994a:53–7). The early accounts are usually sparse in details on feasting, but the bits that can be gleaned from these early sources appear to be very similar to some of the more detailed descriptions from Polynesia and Southeast Asia.

In the lower Mississippi River drainage, Caddoan chiefs were very powerful and the chiefdoms were among some of the most complex recorded for the Southeastern culture area. Chiefs could have people killed who displeased them, and suttee was practiced for wives and slaves of nobles (Swanton 1911:100–6). Nobles claimed descent from the sun, and this helped to justify elevating chiefs' houses on mounds so that they could be closer to the sun. Nobles abided by laws of their own creation and used a language separate from the common dialect. Chiefs houses could be large enough to hold 4,000 people, and chiefs received the best portions of the harvests, fish, and hunted meat. Administrative officials were appointed by the chiefs.

Feasts were primarily occasions on which tribute was rendered to the chiefs and were generally scheduled when the chief needed provisions. Everyone was required to make contributions (Swanton 1911:110,121). Gibson (1974:98) states that these contributions were returned in part to the general populace at feasts, but only after the chief had appropriated the portion necessary to sustain his own position. Such feasts took place on a regular monthly basis, as well as for occasional special events. An especially important feast was held at the end of July to celebrate the main harvest (Swanton 1911:122). These feasts, as well as celebrations of war victories (and probably feasts to organize raids), were held at or near the chief's house and would last all night (sometimes three days and nights) with many dances. At the first fruits harvest feast, the chief ate first from some of the 350 dishes and then distributed food to others. The floor of his house was covered with meat to a depth of one and a half feet (119). Gifts were presented to guests, and a ball game with 800 players on each side was a main feature. The sister of the chief requisitioned maize for the temple spirits of deceased chiefs, and no one dared to refuse what her emissaries chose to take; everyone made contributions (122). In addition to private cultivated fields, some fields were cultivated in common specifically to supply food for the harvest feasts. The chief's temple, containing the bodies of dead chiefs, was located near his house and on an elevated mound near the main plaza, which measured some 250 by 300 paces. This temple was similarly sustained by food "gifts" every new moon, especially from the first harvest. From these gifts, "the great chief ... makes a distribution of them as he judges best, without any person testifying the least discontent" (166).

The Caddo chiefs were powerful. They had lazy members of the chiefdom whipped and beaten by the chief's officials or enforcers (Swanton 1942:170). The hereditary chiefly title-holders had servants and privileges, such as rights to portions of all feasts whether attended or not. They also had very large houses, and their fields were worked by community members (173). They organized and hosted a number of types of feasts, including feasts for the entire village (or at least all members of importance) and feasts to recruit warriors. As was common elsewhere, funeral feasts appear to have been some of the most grandiose events in Caddo society, with great quantities of food (especially corn) provided so that the departed souls could enter into heaven. Funerals were followed by yearly commemorative feasts at the gravesides and, in some cases, secondary burials in temples (204–210).

The Choctaw chiefdoms of the Mississippi were similarly organized, with a paramount political chief and a war chief (who was only important during war), plus village chiefs and assistant chiefs who arranged ceremonies and feasts and generally succeeded to the positions of village chiefs. Disputes were settled in councils, and the chiefs had warriors to enforce "justice" (Swanton 1931:91–4). Choctaw chiefs seem to have been somewhat more constrained than in neighboring polities by powerful kinship groups and warrior groups whose elders always had to be consulted in decision making. There were feasts throughout the year, but especially in the fall and early winter, with very large gatherings at the midwinter solstice. Green corn (first fruits) feasts appear to have played important roles, and there were healing feasts as well. However, the most elaborately described feasts were the series of funeral feasts that took place a month after the death of an important person, and then 6–13 months after the bones had been defleshed and could be reburied under mounds. The mourning periods essentially provided the surviving kin enough time to kill sufficient game and preserve the meat for the funeral feast that was to follow (183). The final funeral feast was a very large, lavish affair with many kin and visitors and many social activities such as games, dancing, and smoking, all of which took place about 100 meters from the grave site or mortuary house (192).

Less information is available about the early Creek and Seminole Indians. Swanton (1924:555,577) notes that fines were imposed by the chief on individuals who failed to attend feasts. Fines could be in terms of money or the confiscation of a horse or any other animal the offender might have. The major feast was, again, the first harvest of green corn, before which there was a prohibition on eating this and other crops, similar to Polynesian eating taboos before feasts (554–6). Thus, prior to the first fruits feast, there was a period of fasting. Large pots of soup were prepared for the harvest feasts, and dancing continued all night. In the fall, some of these dances involved masked performers who played animal roles in panto-mimes of hunts. As elsewhere in the Southeast, such feasts were held every month. Swanton (1924:551) also recorded a yearly "feast of love" to renew social bonds, which presumably was a village or chiefdom-wide social solidarity feast. At this feast, too, men would mask their faces with large pieces of gourds, paintings, and buffalo horns.

In all, there appears to have been a regular occurrence of monthly or more frequent feasts from early in the spring until late fall. The major dances were purported to keep participants and the tribe in good health. Swanton (1924:548) also refers to the great fasts with ceremonies and medicinals ("black drinks") as a "great unifying element between the several members of the Creek confederacy." This probably refers to intercommunity feasts and a political structure that might have been more like a proto-chiefdom. There were also feasts held after successful hunts and feasts for visiting dignitaries, these latter sometimes being quite lavish displays of chiefly wealth. Apparently, the more important feasts were held in special structures ("banqueting houses") in the main square, where the council house was also located (535).

In addition to the Southeast, some information is also available on the early feasting activities of southern Californian hunter/gatherers that are often cited as examples of hunter/gatherer chiefdoms (Arnold 1993, 1995, 1996; also Ames 2004; L. Gamble 2008; Gamble et al. 2001). Of particular interest are the early Spanish accounts from the region by Boscana (1933) based on his missionary experiences from 1812 to 1831 among the Luiseño Indians. Important for discussions of chief-dom dynamics, and as was common elsewhere, the chief set the dates for feast days (established by astronomical observations), settled disputes with other commun-ities, declared war, and made peace. Feasting and the attendant dancing could last more or less continuously for three to four days or even weeks, eventually making some people feel as though they had been carried to the stars (57), an apparent reference to the achievement of ecstatic states resulting from endless hours of monotone singing and dancing. Alliances were secured with gifts (and presumably feasts), and war was frequently embarked upon, not for territory, but for revenge and trivial causes, as is typical in Beck's "constituent," or simple, chiefdoms. Defaulting on feasting gifts was one common cause for declaring war (69). Special, large, temporary structures were built for some feasts, as for marriages; and condors or eagles were killed for costumes at the major events. Fire walking was also featured (58–9).

Boscana (1933:41) observed installation feasts for new chiefs held in a temple. These events were attended by chiefs from neighboring communities, much as in Polynesia. Guests brought gifts and received gifts, acknowledged or confirmed the new chief as the rightful holder of the title, and feasted on the best available foods for three or four days. Special feasting paraphernalia was used such as turtle shell rattles, whistles, bullroarers, flutes, and feathered boards (42,160). It is not clear if this was in the context of a funeral feast, although mourning ceremonies for chiefs occurred some time after their deaths due to the time needed to amass the food and other resources necessary for the event (Noah 2005:45), and they were similarly attended by all neighboring chiefs (Boscana 1933:41). There were other intervillage feasts that were hosted by villages or groups of wealthy individuals that drew upward of 1,800 people (Blackburn 1976; Noah 2005:48). Early missionaries wrote of the intense rivalry between communities in putting on the best feast, with those not participating becoming targets in warfare, and individuals who did not contribute to feasts sometimes being killed (Noah 2005:46–7,320). This seems similar to village feasts in simple Polynesian chiefdoms, such as those on Futuna that I and Villeneuve documented. In the California chiefdoms, several communities could join together for common memorial feasts for all the recently dead at which property was given away, as in the Iroquois Feast of the Dead and in potlatches (Boscana 1933:191–2; Hudson and Blackburn 1986:53). There were also life stage feasts (at least among the elites), including large child investment feasts when boys attained six or seven years and acquired animal guardian spirits under the influence of datura after fasting, or when girls had their first menstruation, or when the chief's son exhibited his first dance. Given the similarity of the Luiseño with the Chumash, one can surmise that at least the elite boys' guardian spirit initiations may have taken place in the context of secret society initiations. The feasts for arranged marriages and for a woman's first pregnancy appear similar to Northwest Coast marriage alliances (Boscana 1933:41,45–6,48,52–3,60,66,191–2). Individual elite households sponsored feasts for unspecified major events, and announcements were made by criers, similar to the practice among the Gitksan (Beynon 2000). In a review of Chumash ethnographies, Noah (2005:44–5) identified fall harvest feasts, winter solstice feasts, mourning feasts (requiring long preparation times due to their costs), and other large public feasts hosted by villages or groups of rich households. It can probably be assumed that smaller scale solidarity feasts were also a frequent feature of community life.

It is interesting that feast days were determined by the phases of the moon, that the chief was the one who set the precise day, that only the elites knew the calendar, and that the primary function of the calendar was to determine when to feast and commemorate the dead (Boscana 1933:43,65–6) – all characteristics essentially identical to the '*antap* secret society practices of the Chumash. Chumash '*antap* members apparently sponsored major feasts at the winter solstice when they would perform sacred songs, dances, and rituals. Although there was no actual physical building for some of the more important ceremonial feasts, there was a ceremonial dance area and shrine near the chief's house demarcated by a brush fence. Chumash ceremonial features had hearths and feasting areas adjacent to the ceremonial grounds, with each hearth presumably representing one of the various participating social groups. Hearths appear to have been up to 3–4 feet in diameter based on the sketch map in Hudson and Blackburn (1986:56–8).

Farther north, although not technically chiefdoms according to Oberg's definitions, it is worth iterating that the success or importance of Northwest Coast chiefly feasts were in part gauged not only by the value of gifts bestowed, but also by the number of guests and their distance traveled (Tybjerg 1977:193; Cooper 2006:154). This seems typical of transegalitarian and chiefly display feasts with remarkable distances traveled by some Polynesian elites. As seems frequent in chiefdoms, trade in prestige items was controlled by the elite administrators of corporate groups and transferred via marriage wealth/privilege exchanges (Tybjerg 1977:202).

The ethnographic data I have on feasting in Central and South American chiefdoms are sparse, although there are undoubtedly many other ethnohistoric observations. Oberg's (1955) discussion of South American chiefdoms is succinct but does not deal with feasting. Several contributors in Brumfiel and Fox's volume on factional politics in the Americas mention feasting as a component in organizing raids or celebrating victories (Pohl and Pohl 1994:141; Redmond 1994:45–8) or the use of feasts in attracting labor (D'Altroy 1994:175). Otherwise, these authors document many of the same characteristics of chiefdoms that have already been enumerated in this chapter, including the intensive competition within and between chiefdoms resulting in chronic instability (D. Anderson 1994b:66–9), the emphasis on warfare launched not from any scarcity of food or population pressures but for gain (Brumfiel 1994:7; Redmond 1994:53), the use of exotic prestige goods as a means of control within local groups and the vital role that they played in chiefly sociopolitical dynamics (D. Anderson 1994b:71; Helms 1994:58–9; C. Spencer 1994:35–7), the labor and produce provided by the community for chiefs, and the reworking of genealogies to suit political expediencies (C. Spencer 1994:35–7).

As an interesting historical note, Azevedo (2009) reports contact accounts with the Tupinambá that describe chiefdoms held together largely by elite polygynous marriages (typical also of Chin chiefdoms and probably many others) and "hospitality" rituals. These rituals were characterized by binges in which large quantities of fermented beverages made from manioc and maize (products only used at feasts) were consumed. Marriages, rites of passage, mourning rituals for the dead, organizing raids, the undertaking of communal work, and the fêting of important visitors were all occasions for feasting; but the sacrifice and eating of captured enemies were the most important events. The descriptions of these latter feasts are rather graphic, with houses 20–30 fathoms in length packed with people dancing and singing for days and nights on end, recounting many past raids and wars until they entered into ecstatic states and became, in their own minds, supernatural heroes.

In Mesoamerica, J. Eric Thompson (1938:596,603) found early references from Chol Maya communities of special huts used for feasts by "caciques" who obtained delicacies like deer, fish, and honey for the events.

Africa

Africa is another very rich area in the ethnographic literature on chiefdoms and merits much more research than I have been able to devote to it. However, a number of studies should be mentioned, especially those concerning the use of beer in building and running chiefdom political organizations. As Garine (2001:191–2,201) has stated, "there is a strong relationship between drinking and power," "[d]rinking is classically viewed as expressing the social system; in Africa it seems to be creating it. . . . Beer simultaneously creates hierarchy and differential status in some contexts (feasts and ritual . . .) and equality and reciprocity in others . . . beer drinking is social theory." Beer is the "locus of value" for chiefdom groups in Nigeria and elsewhere (Dietler 1990, 2001:81–3; Arthur 2003). Drinking only takes place in social contexts, and alcoholic beverages account for about 33–43% of calorie consumption, or about half a kilogram of millet in the form of beer per day per person mostly consumed in a nonritual fashion at agricultural work party feasts (Garine 2001; Arthur 2003:517). However, beer is an absolute requisite for ancestor cult rituals and for the initiation of boys, at which copious amounts are offered to the ancestors (as their preferred sacrificial food) as well as to friends, allies, and neighbors. Prestige is gained from organizing feasts and distributing large amounts of beer. The Haya "kings" were paid tribute in the form of beer. Marees (1987 [1602]:94–5,111) described early large tribute feasts for the "kings" of the Gold Coast, as well as large feasts to celebrate the anniversaries of their coronations. The fields of the rulers were also worked by their subjects in exchange for work feasts featuring large amounts of palm wine, cooked goats, and many other foods. Here, it is clear that work and tribute feasts underwrote the expenses of rulers. Elsewhere, chiefs were expected to offer their subjects large amounts of beer on important occasions (a practice similar to South American polities), whereas ordinary individuals might only have to prepare large amounts of beer a few times during their lifetimes, such as for the circumcision of their sons. Beer is dependent on surplus production of grain, and, as such, beer is work: work to produce the grain and work to make the beer. In general, only rich families could therefore afford to produce beer. In a kind of circular economic logic, the ability to produce beer created wealth by being directly converted into work and thus into surplus grain, which could then be used to produce more beer or exchanged in reciprocal fashions to create hierarchies. Arthur (2003) reports very similar patterns of beer use in feasts in various parts of Africa. Among the Koma in Cameroon, for example, cattle sacrifice is generally part of beer brewing, and the age-grade ceremonies there require about 500 liters of beer, representing 100 kg of cereal grain, whereas funerals for women required about half that amount.

In some African chiefdoms, such as the Ibo in Nigeria, secret societies (in which chiefs were always high-ranking members) controlled economic markets, dictated laws, judged disputes, and dispensed punishments. Secret society members destroyed houses or even killed offenders when its rules were broken. They demonstrated their power publicly with feasts and rituals that usually included sacrifices of animals or people (Johansen 2004:81). The great harvest festivals were organized and dominated by the secret societies such as the *Ekkpo* among the Ibo. This was a time when effigies were brought out and carried in processions from the secret society building to the public square, and daily sacrifices of fowl and goats were made to the effigies. Tribute for the secret society was collected from all adult males, and human sacrifices were made to the effigies (Johansen 2004:79). Using feasts, chiefs enlisted the help of the secret society members to undertake major projects. Slaves could be sacrificed to ensure the success of a project while at the same time also serving as a dramatic display of the power held by the chief and the secret society. In this way, secret societies and the feasts they organized appear to have played major roles in the creation and exercise of chiefly power in some, and perhaps many, African chiefly societies.

The *Poro* secret society of the Mende in Sierra Leone provides a similar example. The *Poro* controlled most aspects of community life and chiefly politics. The elite council of the *Poro* society (of which the chief was usually a high-ranking member) could even override the wishes of the chief or depose him. The *Poro* council was the real source of power among the Mende. The *Poro* enforced conformity to its rules and culture norms through supernatural authority and periodic use of force. As with the *Ekkpo*, the *Poro* society adjudicated major disputes and determined courses of war. It was essentially an institution whose purpose was to acquire power over the entire community. As Bond (1987:56) has observed of traditional Zambian communities, ambitious people "manipulate the ritual field in pursuit of their own personal interests and social goals."

Eurasia

One of the most graphic descriptions of any chiefly feast in the ethnographic literature was written by Ibn Fadlan Ibn al-Abbas Ibn Rashid Ibn Hammad Faqh in AD 922 when he was sent from Baghdad on a mission to obtain diplomatic ties with the Viking groups that were established as traders on the middle Volga River at Bulghar (Kazan') in what is now the Russian Federation. Ibn Fadlan was able to observe the funeral ceremonies following the death of a chieftain there, and his account constitutes the only eyewitness report of a Viking chief's funeral rituals. The basic outline of the events can be summarized from Montgomery's (2000) translation. These consisted of:

- Temporary burial of the chief for ten days with food and drink offerings by his side, during which there was continuous licentious sex, feasting, and drinking in the community, with pervasive intoxication even to the brink of alcohol-induced mortality. A third of the dead chief's wealth was spent on brewing alcohol for the event. Special burial clothes were made during this period.
- The chief's ship was propped up on shore and people visited it with music and singing. The dead chief's slaves were assembled and a volunteer was requested to accompany the chief. A 15-year-old girl volunteered and was then referred to as the chief's "bride." She was dressed in fine clothes and provided with several servants. She spent the ten days before the burial drinking and feasting and having sex with many men in the community.
- At the end of the ten days, the ship was dragged onto a funeral pyre and a cabin was erected on its deck with a bed of gold brocade inside. The chief was removed from his temporary grave, dressed in his funeral clothes, and placed sitting on his bed. Food and his personal property were laid around the bed.
- Meanwhile the slave girl visited all the tents around the ship and had sex with all the men who considered it their duty to do so. A dog was cut in half and the remains tied to the ship. The chief's weapons were placed in his cabin. Horses, cattle, and chickens were then sacrificed in a brutal fashion. The slave girl was lifted up so that she could look into a doorframe set up in the air and describe her impressions of the afterworld, apparently after drinking a drugged liquid. Her jewelry was then removed and she ascended to the ship's deck by walking on the upraised palms of the men with whom she had had sex. She sang a farewell song. However, on nearing the cabin, she began to scream, at which point she was forced inside by men with staves who pounded the deck to mask her screams. She was then held down on the bed of the dead chief and raped by some of the attending men. They

then held her arms and legs and strangled her while an older woman stabbed her numerous times. Afterward, the attendants left the ship and set fire to it. The remains were buried under a mound.

This account clearly demonstrates the life-and-death power that the elite had over slaves and their very considerable wealth. The ship, by itself, would have been worth a small fortune. However, the elaborate, drawn-out funeral feast forms part of a long tradition begun in transegalitarian societies to advertise the power of the living descendants.

Although nothing quite so lavish is described in the European epic literature, accounts found in early documents like *Beowulf* do describe other types of chiefly feasts among the Anglo-Saxons. These include feasts held in the Mead-Halls (*symbel*'s) where the elites would gather (including women with servants and stewards) at the behest of the chief in order to display his splendor, confer gifts, make speeches, enjoy music, and consume drink served in drinking horns by elite women dressed in finery (Pollington 2003:42). The purpose of these rather structured events appears to have been primarily to display success, create solidarity among the elites, and reaffirm their relative rankings (in seating arrangements, as also occurs in Polynesian men's feasts and kava ceremonies, Northwest Coast potlatches, and probably most other chiefly feasts). There were also wedding feasts, guild feasts, and funeral feasts for elites attended by kin, friends, and followers (60–4). In addition, there is a relatively new kind of feast, called a *gebeorscipe*, which was essentially a rather unruly drinking party hosted by both nonelites or elites. These were presumably to strengthen bonds of friendship and mutual help (53–6).

As in Polynesia, there were "touring feasts" that were held by the chiefs essentially to collect food and tribute to underwrite their administrative costs. In a comparative historical study, Kobishchanow (1987) has shown how common this strategy was (which he called by its Anglo-Saxon epithet, *gafol*). The *gafol* was common not only in chiefdoms, but in early states as well, although some of the "early states" he described would have been considered chiefdoms by many archaeologists. In addition to collecting food and prestige goods, Kobishchanow argued that the *gafol* also strengthened the ruler's power in requiring oaths, suppressing dissent, and introducing or showcasing higher order political elements in constituent communities. When present, the chief or king could settle conflicts, administer justice, and make a show of ritually conferring fertility on the land via sacrificed animals or other means. However, these touring feasts came at a high price for host communities. Large administrative retinues generally accompanied the chief and placed heavy demands on the local resources, sometimes consuming all the fruits of a year's work (109).

ETHNOGRAPHIC SUMMARY

Feasting and the debts that it entailed, both social and economic, appears to have been critical in the formation and existence of simple chiefdoms. There were many similarities in feasting forms and dynamics between simple chiefdoms and trans-egalitarian societies, as might be expected, especially where corporate groups constituted primary social units within chiefdoms that vied with each other for control of the best resources, for titles to political positions, and other benefits. Although there may have been a bit more stability in the power and rank of specific corporate groups than in transegalitarian communities, there were, nevertheless, persisting instabilities and pronounced competition between groups. These became manifest in funeral, marriage, and other competitive corporately supported feasts, where there was often enormous display, consumption, and waste. As with the most competitive Northwest Coast potlatches, Chin challenge feasts, and the *abutu* of the Massim (Chapter 6), some chiefs, such as those in the Philippines, sponsored challenge feasts in attempts to bankrupt their rivals. As was common in transegalitarian communities, defaulting on feasting debts often carried severe consequences, including retribution raids and outright warfare. Chiefs were often deposed or killed as member groups or factions realigned themselves to suit new social, economic, or political conditions. There were continuing powerful pressures to increase production due to competition between social groups for political power, mates, and allies based on feasting and prestige gifts. Therefore, elites frequently initiated new, more productive agricultural techniques such as irrigation, swamp reclamation, and terracing (Earle 1977, 1997:68–72,78,103–4; Urry 1993:62). Feasting at the household and lineage levels probably remained essentially the same as in transegalitarian societies, although most attention has been focused on the larger, more impressive feasts, and little information is available on smaller events. Secret societies persisted or developed from transegalitarian societies into chiefdoms in a number of regions (e.g., in Africa, Melanesia, California, and probably elsewhere). Where this occurred, it might be expected that the feasting patterns associated with secret societies would remain essentially the same, although increases in scale and the amounts of food consumed appear to have characterized chiefly secret society feasts. In fact, the large public feasts typically hosted by secret societies to display their powers may have functioned to garner operating resources from the community and thus have been a precursor to later temple/tribute feasts discussed in Chapter 8. Unfortunately, little information was available on many of these aspects of chiefdom feasting in my survey of the literature, especially concerning specialized structures used by secret societies and regional organizations.

With the new chiefly level of political organization, there were also new feasting elements that were specific to simple chiefdoms and that served to hold the typically fragile political organizations together. These consisted primarily of rotating competitive display feasts sponsored in turn by each member community of the chiefdom. The goal seems to have been to demonstrate to other high-ranking members in the alliance (or to rival chiefdoms) the desirability of having the host community as a member of the chiefdom, to secure their relative position of power within the chiefdom or even, as D. Anderson (1994a) suggests, the potential ability of host villages to assume the role of paramount settlement and chiefdomship.

Similar displays seem to have occurred at "intertribal" or "interchiefdom" gatherings that reportedly involved thousands of participants, whereas the maximum size of the largest transegalitarian feasts generally appear to have involved hundreds of participants. Special neutral or impressive locations were sometimes used for competitive intervillage or interchiefdom feasts. In the few descriptions available, these special locations were several kilometers from host villages and were replete with special huts, stages, and presumably middens (Urry 1993:42–3,73). Enormous waste also characterized these large-scale feasts.

Feasts to celebrate chiefly family rites of passage appear to have been celebrated on a chiefdom-wide basis, at least in some cases (as a politically unifying strategy, as another pretext to obtain resources from the populace, or simply to demonstrate the importance of the chief and his power). It may also have been the case that some chiefly feasts were held primarily for diacritical purposes, although this needs to be critically assessed with more detailed data if they are available.

Another distinctive type of feasting in simple chiefdoms consisted of "touring" and harvest ("first fruits") feasts, in essence a type of tribute feast. Temple feasts also probably served to gather surpluses to underwrite the chiefly administrations. The *symbel* mead hall feasts organized by Anglo-Saxon chiefs appear to have been a regionally distinctive type of chiefly feast, although various of its elements, such as the reaffirmation of elite ranks and the creation of solidarity among elites, occurred in many other regions at chiefly feasts, such as kava drinking feasts held in Polynesia.

In addition, while there may have been occasional instances of human sacrifice or cannibalism as part of some transegalitarian feasts (especially those related to secret societies), human sacrifices and cannibalism seem to have become much more prevalent in chiefdom-level feasting events, both in secret society contexts and other public feasting events such as community fertility rituals, elite feasts, competitive village feasts, victory feasts, and feasts sponsored by chiefs, although specific details are often sparse.

Also related to these new feasting patterns were new patterns of warfare, especially wars in which the goal among simple chiefdoms was not to capture territory or subjugate other populations, but to undermine competitors' abilities to host or repay feasts. Thus, the objective of raids was to destroy rivals' abilities to produce luxury foods such as cocoanuts, bananas, pigs, taro, and yams. It may also be expected that such raids were carried out to procure slaves and sacrificial victims for chiefly feasts, as in the Philippines (Junker 2001:295–8). The classic discussions of chiefdoms portray them as relying exclusively on noncoercive means (benevolence, prestige, kinship, rituals, ideology, economic control, and feasts) to acquire or maintain power. However, even a cursory reading of many ethnographies and early accounts of simple and complex chiefdoms (as well as our own work on Futuna) clearly indicated that chiefs frequently had enforcement cadres that, among simple chiefdoms, used force to obtain compliance from recalcitrant individuals whenever chiefs thought that they could do so with impunity (e.g., see Earle 1977:225).

In addition, chiefly elites appear to have placed much higher values on foods and gifts that they distributed at feasts than on foods and gifts provided by lower ranking families, thus artificially inflating the balance of feast debts strongly in their favor and providing significant economic and political advantages. Therefore, elites specialized in making certain crafts and made special efforts to import exotic raw materials or paraphernalia, typically ones that they monopolistically controlled – presumably to also control the relative value of those goods. Similar tactics may have already been used in transegalitarian feasting, although the practice has not been as well documented and apparently was not as flagrant.

Overall, the new feasting elements in chiefdoms involved much greater scales of the largest feasts accompanied by suitably sized feasting facilities such as plazas and/or large buildings. Chiefs' roles in these societies center predominantly on the organization of ritual feasting events and warfare. These appear to be the glue that holds the chiefly political apparatus together. Both involve the extraction of surpluses from the populace and the creation of debts that obligate various levels of administrators to maintain commitments to the chiefly ritual/feasting/warfare organization. These feasting events provide the means to underwrite the costs of the organization while at the same time binding together those who have decided to play the chiefly political game. It is this group of people who were undoubtedly the first to accept and then to promulgate the many ideological changes that chiefly elites promoted for their own interests, including the taboos on eating valued foods prior to feasts. It is not clear to what extent secondary burial continued to be used. Where it occurred, it may have been used predominantly by elites so as to provide enough time to amass as many resources as possible to hold as grandiose a funeral as possible.

With the development of more complex and larger chiefdoms, some of these patterns may have changed, including the development of true diacritical feasts and a devolution of common household feasts in terms of magnitude and frequency, as in Hawai'i. However, my research has not been able to determine exactly what the nature of such changes could have been, and this should be a focus for future research.

ARCHAEOLOGICAL STUDIES OF CHIEFDOM FEASTS

Although considerable archaeological work has taken place in regions where chiefdoms have existed for centuries or millennia and where feasting was a prominent part of the ethnographic record – especially in Africa and Polynesia – relatively little attention has been devoted to the archaeological interpretation of feasting remains in many of these areas. Much more attention has been paid to the study of feasting remains at the chiefdom level in Neolithic and Bronze Age Europe. The most distinctive archaeological patterns of chiefly feasting to emerge from these studies involve the scale of the largest feasting events, the use of large plaza areas or large earthenworks such as causewayed enclosures as the venues for feasts, and, in some cases, the distinctive nature of feasting remains. In addition, low-level luxury foods should logically have characterized work or solidarity feasts in which participants were from common classes whereas high-level luxury foods or even cannibalized human remains could be expected to have been present at major ritual or elite centers such as the *marae* in Polynesia. On a broader scale, Junker (2001:298), N. Thomas (1990:97,101,104), and Urry (1993:78) have suggested that there appears to be a strong relationship between the occurrence of intensive (competitive) elite feasting activities in archaeological chiefdoms and indications of escalating inter-polity conflicts and human sacrifices. Intensive, long-distance trade (and perhaps the production of local copies of foreign imports), too, appears to have been linked to the expanded feasting activities in chiefdoms (Junker 2001:296).

Polynesia and Southeast Asia

Patrick Kirch (2001; Kirch and O'Day 2003) has probably devoted more attention to the question of archaeological indicators of feasting in Polynesia than anyone else. In the Marquesan Expansion Period (AD 110–1400), he identified the context of feasting events as large rectangular "dance plazas" (up to 26 × 174 m) surrounded by platforms for temples, chiefs' houses, and viewing points for spectators who watched the dances as they feasted – reminiscent of similar arrangements in the historic lower Mississippi chiefdoms. Specialized cookhouse structures roasted the pigs and prepared the food for feasting (Kirch 2001:175). In a more general study of elite versus nonelite protohistoric households on Maui, Kirch and O'Day (2003) demonstrated that elites had much greater access to some animal foods such as

dogs, pigs, birds, large fish and sharks, large limpets and cowries whereas commoner households emphasized shellfish in general, rats, and low-quality cuts of
pork. Sahlins (2003) has also cited a number of archaeological instances of cannibalized human remains that probably represented elite feasts. However, beyond
these observations, relatively little attention seems to have been paid to feasting in
Polynesia.

In Southeast Asia, Laura Junker (2001; Junker et al. 1994) has been the major
voice in developing the importance of feasting for understanding the emergence of
chiefdoms and in documenting evidence of feasting in Philippine archaeological
contexts. This has primarily taken the form of examining elite versus nonelite
households in eleventh- to sixteenth-century assemblages at central places of chiefdoms. Junker has shown that elite households consumed more rice, domestic
animals, and higher valued meat than did other households and also served these
foods on imported Chinese porcelain wares.

North America

The greatest emphasis on identifying and interpreting chiefly feasting remains in
North America appears to involve Mississippian Period sites of the Central and
Eastern United States (c. 1100–1400 CE). Archaeologists sometimes quibble about
whether there were chiefdoms in the Hopewell Period (c. 300 BCE–300 CE), so I
have dealt with the Hopewell sites in Chapter 6. However, the interpretations of
Abrams (Abrams and Le Rouge 2008) indicate that mounds in Ohio were constructed and used for feasts by several smaller surrounding communities. Such
occurrences might be viewed as meeting the archaeological criteria of simple chiefdoms. Knight (2001:327) similarly observed that most communities in the Southeast
lacked mounds and that mound sites were centers of feasting. However, he feels
that these were probably transegalitarian rather than chiefdom-level societies. In
contrast, Gibson (1974) views the relatively elaborate Poverty Point site from 1,000
years earlier as the first clear evidence of a chiefdom in North America (Figure 4.25).

Whereas the level of political organization may be debated for the Hopewell
and earlier cultural traditions, there is widespread agreement on the chiefdom
status of the major Mississippian Period sites. The size of the mounds, the
hierarchical settlement patterns, the developed prestige crafts, the elaborate
elite burials, and the density of populations all constitute convincing indicators
of chiefdom-level organization. Cahokia, in Illinois, was the largest such center,
and Yerkes (2005) has demonstrated that elites consumed substantial amounts of
fish and venison. He has suggested that venison may have been part of the tribute
paid by nonelites to elites. Pauketat and Emerson (2008) have emphasized general models in which rituals (and, by implication, feasts) were created by some

individuals to draw others into participation with commitments to support ever-increasing magnitudes of such events resulting in the construction of the major centers and the creation of elites.

Aside from the evident ceremonialism, the best clear evidence of feasting at Cahokia has been from one large trash pit in the middle of the site that included a series of large-scale events at the principal plaza. The deposits in this pit included sumptuary items (quartz crystals, beads, tobacco, pigments, icons, fine pottery) reflecting elite involvement or sponsorship. There were also very large numbers of domestic cooking vessels, common plants, and faunal remains indicating large numbers of participants who must have included commoners. The estimated minimum number of individuals for this one pit were 68,574 ceramic vessels, 13,238 deer, and 8,313,311 tobacco seeds. Items such as swans, tobacco, and squash indicate ritual elements in the feast (L. Kelly 2001; Pauketat et al. 2002). The analysts have suggested that these feasting events were held to promote community integration, especially between central sites and outlying communities, as well as between the variously ranked segments of the population. High-ranked individuals may have also used such feasts to consolidate their positions. However, I would suggest that, like the first fruits feasts in the North American ethnographies, large-scale feasts such as these may have been used primarily as a means of tribute collection at harvest or other times and/or as a means of establishing patron–client types of relationships and inequalities.

Moundville, in Alabama, is another major Mississippian center that has received considerable attention. Welch and Scarry (1995:413–4) have interpreted unusually high proportions of large flaring-rim bowls as indications that the nobility used food in public presentations involving kin or other groups. They also observed that special serving wares and more abundant remains of the most highly valued animals and joints of meat were associated with higher status residences. Conversely, Jackson and Scott (2003:568) failed to find much evidence of large-scale or easily identifiable feasting associated with mounds that they excavated at Moundville, although they, too, documented elite consumption of a wider variety of animals and perhaps more valued types of meat. Within the Moundville political ambit, Maxham (2000) has concluded that some small sites were used as communal or alliance gathering locations where people shared food in apparent solidarity types of feasts for defense alliances or other common interests of a number of neighboring isolated farmsteads.

In what was probably another chiefly polity near the Moundville chiefdom, Blitz (1993a,b) pioneered some of the techniques used to identify large-group feasting on or near mounds at the Lubbub Creek site. Although decorated pottery occurred in both mound and village residential contexts, larger vessel sizes predominated in the mound contexts, implying for Blitz that food for these feasts was supplied and prepared by mound residents. It also appears that food was stored at mounds and consumed at mounds. The faunal remains were distinctive in the mound contexts. In general, Lindauer and Blitz (1997:186–7) argue that many Mississippian (and earlier) platform mounds were used for large-scale feasting and food storage. This contrasts with the pattern that Potter (2010) has argued should occur with solidarity feasts, in which food preparation should occur at dispersed houses of the participants. Thus, the Lubbub Creek mounds seem to have hosted more centrally organized and competitively oriented feasts so that Blitz's view of them as centers for rituals and feasts seems warranted (Blitz 1993a:73,97,135). Knight (1992; cited in Welch and Scarry 1995) added that each mound was probably the political and ritual center for a different clan that hosted the feasts, which I would presume featured competitive displays. In addition, charnel houses featured meat feasts that were probably also competitive funerary events involving corporate kinship groups (Blitz 1993a:72).

Farther north, in Tennessee, Van Derwarker (1999) documented evidence for feasting at the Toqua site, another Mississippian mound site. She identified feasting remains (rare species, high proportions of preferred deer meat cuts, and large quantities of fish) associated with the primary mound and concluded that feasts were probably sponsored and supplied by elite males and that these events likely created indebtedness among guests (particularly commoners in the form of patron–client relationships). However, she also viewed these large-scale feasts as arenas of political competition and status negotiation between successive hosts, with the highest-ranking guests receiving the preferred cuts of meat. Likewise, Reber (2006:244–5) has argued that maize had a special value in Mississippian societies (see also Fritz and Kidder 1993:9) and that its use in ceremonial feasting contexts played a critical role in the development of social inequalities.

In the Southwest, while many archaeologists view the prehistoric Pueblo remains as transegalitarian communities (as discussed in Chapter 6), there is also a faction of archaeologists who view at least the Chacoan large settlements as chiefdom-like polities, the largest being Pueblo Bonito (Feinman et al. 2000). The great houses that constituted the major centers, often viewed as primarily ritual sites, may be associated with special, large trash deposits (Cameron 2002, although see Plog and Watson 2012). Whether these should be viewed in similar terms to the trash deposits associated with Mississippian mounds (resulting from feasting and corporate kinship ritual activities) is an issue that will have to be dealt with by future research and analysis. I would like to suggest that the great house centers may have been constructed and used as regional centers for secret societies similar to the *katsina* society. However, this, too, would be a topic for future exploration.

Mesoamerica and South America

Not many studies have been made of prehistoric feasting at the chiefdom level in Mesoamerica or South America. As noted in Chapter 5, VanDerwarker and Kruger (2012) allude to the importance of maize for competitive feasts in early coastal lowland sites. However, probably the most extensive treatment in Mesoamerica has been Rosenswig's (2007) analysis of the role of feasting in Middle Formative societies (c. 900–800 BCE) on the Pacific Coast that had adopted Olmec iconography and monumental architecture. Rosenswig identified feasting activities on the basis of high proportions of food serving vessels, including fancy tecomates and decorated dishes, as well as larger serving vessels and a predominance of dogs in the faunal remains. Evidence for feasting was particularly strong in middens associated with elite mound residences. Thus, Rosenswig suggested that the feasts were sponsored by elites in order to more strongly integrate lower classes into the new class social structure of chiefdoms (in the form of patron–client indebtedness) and to manifest elite high status (in the form of diacritical feasts). As Rosenswig states it, "The Conchas phase was thus a time . . . when new political and social differentiation would have required mitigation by increased integrative ritual . . . new feasting behavior would have been required . . . to mitigate the socially divisive forces associated with institutionalizing a higher level of social stratification" (21). Rosenswig concludes that "Competitive feasting would not have served any elites's interests in the Soconusco . . . during the Conchas phase" (22). Although early chiefly elites may have used large-scale feasts to indebt commoners (especially by overvaluing elite contributions and undervaluing commoner contributions), I think there is little support for the idea that elite feasts would not have been competitive. The overwhelming ethnographic documentation of the intensely competitive nature of feasting in simple chiefdoms cautions against such an assumption, although more research may still be required for complex chiefdoms.

In Costa Rica, funerary feasting has been extensively documented at a number of archaeological sites, with smashed vessels probably having been used for drinking maize beer and very large pots for preparing large amounts of food (Snarskis 1984:220; Blanco Vargas et al. 1986; Hoopes and Chenault 1994), all in the context of prehistoric chiefdoms. As is evident from the earlier ethnographic and theoretical discussions, such elaborate funerary feasts form a major part of the competitive dynamics that characterize simple chiefdom. Similar occurrences seem to have taken place in the Brazilian highlands, where large circular enclosures were associated with many ovens and elite burial mounds (Iriarte et al. 2008). Ethnohistorically, periodic feasts were held in the same region at the sites of chiefly cremations with the adjacent preparation of meat in ovens and consumption of maize beer.

Along the Peruvian coast, monumental architecture occurs in the Late Archaic (3000–1800 BCE) and Initial Period/Early Horizon (1500–200 BCE). This architecture is probably associated with chiefdom-level political organizations given the regional size and centrality of the major sites. Dillehay et al (2012:68) state that in the late Archaic construction levels of Huaca Prieta, feasting "appears to have been a primary activity" probably associated with mortuary rituals, a pattern common in other chiefdom contexts. In contrast, Haas and Creamer (2006:755) refer to preliminary analyses of the earliest monumental architectural constructions at Caral indicating that there were work feasts associated with the building of the monuments. They suggest that feasts were used to attract people from the surrounding region to the monumental ritual centers for seasonal ceremonies and building projects. Vega-Centeno (2006) developed similar interpretations from his work at Cerro Lampay, viewing the rituals, feasts, and building events as a means of bonding communities together in the context of weakly developed powers of leaders whom he speculated may not even have been chiefs (contra other researchers). He views the feasting remains associated with repeated building events as contractual work feasts, with the feast provided by elites in exchange for labor to construct the center. This much is probably true. However, Vega-Centeno did not consider these feasts as creating power but only as providing moral authority for exercising power, perhaps within a communitarian framework although this is not explicit. How such large amounts of food could be assembled and controlled has not been addressed in any of the Peruvian studies.

In the Initial and Early Horizon (the Final Formative), a number of regional ritual centers were built mainly in the Highlands, the most notable of which was Chavín de Huántar. Christian Mesia (2013) has documented the occurrence of a large-scale food preparation and midden area lacking monumental architecture (the Wacheqsa sector, immediately north of the monumental core). The refuse included paraphernalia for the consumption of psychoactive substances, prestige items, many camelids, and a few molluscs from the distant coast. He postulates that the actual feasting probably took place in the circular and quadrangular plaza areas and that various regional centers vied with each other to attract supporters using feasts, imposing architecture, psychoactive substances, and impressive rituals. Many of these characteristics bear striking resemblances to secret societies as discussed in Chapters 4 and 6, in which members put on impressive public feasts with demonstrations of their putative supernatural powers, as well as holding more exclusive feasts for initiated members or high-ranking office holders. In addition to the feasting, some of the characteristics at Chavín that resemble secret societies include the limited-access location of the site; the exclusivity of many ritual areas (especially the underground galleries that could only accommodate a few individuals at any one location (Figure 7.12); the iconic emphasis on power animals and fearsome ritual aspects, including transformed humans and the use of darkness (Figure 7.13); the large plaza areas suitable for public displays and costumed

7.12. Underneath the plazas at Chavín de Huántar is a labyrinth of buried tunnels with a few small chambers, such as this one, where the famous "Lanzón" sculpture of a mythical power animal is located. Only a very few people could have squeezed through the passageway to view this sculpture or occupied this chamber at any one time, indicating the highly exclusive nature of some of the ritual activities at the site. (Photograph courtesy of John Rick)

processions, as depicted in the art (Figure 7.13); the attempt to impress initiates and spectators with disorienting settings, sounds, light, psychotropic drugs, and architectonic features so as to create the impression of contacting powerful supernatural forces; the apparent voluntary basis of participation; the control over resources and labor as demonstrated by the scale of construction (which also implies a hierarchical control of the organization by a powerful group with a core strategy that was not systems-serving, but rather self-serving); competition within and between centers to attract support; and the use of "artifice, if not downright deception, in convincing initiates or others about the validity of both the cult and the innate

7.13. The depiction of power and fantastical animals such as that in the Lanzón, together with the portrayal of humans transformed into fearsome half-animals at Chavín, as shown here, indicates that a major ritual focus was on the acquisition of fearsome power at least by the highest ranking, most exclusive group in the cult. These features tend to characterize secret societies. (Photograph courtesy of John Rick)

supernatural connectedness of those orchestrating ritual" (Rick 2008:10,29–34). Thus, as with the case of Göbekli Tepe and perhaps the great houses in the North American Southwest, it seems to me that an argument can be made that these isolated but lavish ritual centers may represent an evolved, elaborated, regional type of secret society, and we can expect that they hosted various kinds of feasts, the remains of which should be sought in future work.

On the Coast during this time period, Ikehara and Shibata (2008) have documented two different scales of feasts (30–55 people vs. 70–113 people) at Cerro Blanco, which they view as serving different functions: repeated work feasts used to construct the centers and reciprocal feasts used by elites to establish and consolidate their power. Like Vega-Centeno (2006), they view Archaic and Formative political power as weakly developed or even absent except for seasonal ceremonials at regional ritual centers with feasting and building activities orchestrated by big

7.14. The large plaza areas at Chavín de Huántar shown in the foreground here were undoubtedly used for impressive rituals and feasting for a larger, lower ranking, and even uninitiated group of spectators. Such public displays of ritual power also characterize secret societies. (Photograph by B. Hayden)

men. This is a scenario that does not differ substantially from the views of simple chiefdoms that I and Villeneuve have developed (2010), although I think the power of Archaic-Formative elites is probably understated. More recently, Ikehara et al. (n.d.) have argued that the unstable chiefdoms in the Middle and Final Formative communities of the Peruvian Coast (contemporary with Chavín) used the costly production of maize to increase their control over labor by producing maize beer that was offered in feasts. The use of this *chichi* beer to marshal labor is suggested to have been critical for the consolidation of elite power and the emergence of subsequent hierarchical sociopolitical organizations, fundamentally continuing as a major strategy of control until the Spanish Conquest.

Europe

In the British Isles and Scandinavia, a great deal of attention has been devoted to chronicling feasting at Neolithic sites, particularly at megalithic tombs and ditched enclosures where feasting and human remains frequently accumulated. Beginning in the Neolithic and continuing on into the Bronze Age, the sheer scale of many megalithic monuments in Western Europe such as Stonehenge, Avebury, and Newgrange (Figure 7.15) implies chiefdom-level polities and populations. In addition, the central place of the major sites and their spacing indicates powerful polities

7.15. Large-scale monuments in the Neolithic and Bronze Age indicate that the societies that constructed them were organized at the chiefdom level. The massive burial chamber at Newgrange (Ireland) shown here must have required many hundreds or thousands of workers to create yet was only used for a limited number of people, presumably a regional chief and his family. (Photograph by B. Hayden)

with, at least, two-level settlement hierarchies. Feasting remains have often been documented associated with human remains (presumably mortuary rituals, but apparently involving human sacrifices as well) at causewayed enclosures, henges, and megalithic tombs (I. Smith 1965; Bradley 1984:5; Hedges 1984:135; Barker 1985:200–1; Sherratt 1991:56; J. Thomas 1991; Patton 1993:109; McOmish 1996:73), but the implications for understanding the dynamics of megalithic societies have often remained unexplored. Oswald et al. (2001:123–5,131) have summarized much of this evidence for causewayed enclosures, noting that some sites exhibit "extravagance in consumption and wastefulness in deposition."

Wainwright and Longworth's 1971 analysis of excavations at Durrington Walls and similar enclosures focused on a number of unusual remains, including indications of human sacrifice; a variety of prestige items including jet, ivory, bone pins, mace heads, axes, ceramic Grooved Wares, and exotic lithics; cult objects, such as phalli and balls; intentionally destroyed wealth items; and feasting remains, including articulated bones and ceramics (202–3,209,218–9, 231–2,266–79). Although they did not pursue the issue (or, in fact, attempt to explain feasting at the site), it seems evident from the scale of this and other sites and from the nature of the remains that competitive feasting among high-status individuals or families was probably a major feature of the political fabric of this Neolithic society. In relation to the intentional destruction of wealth, I have proposed that this only seems to occur in competitive feasting contexts (Hayden 1995), although the universality of this relationship remains to be established. Larsson (2000:101) has also drawn attention to the destruction of wealth in the Neolithic, especially the intentional mass burning or consignment to watery depths of stone axes that has been documented at some sites. These indications of competitive feasting, similar to the competitive funeral feasts documented ethnographically, are reinforced by instances of deliberately broken objects or objects taken out of circulation by burying them and thus essentially destroying them. Such competitive events may well have been sponsored by those who vied for the loyalties of cattle herders in the region. Due to their high mobility, herders could have affiliated themselves with a number of different polities and, thus, one could expect very lavish displays to have been used by chiefs to attract supporters. Competitive feasts, perhaps similar to the Feast of the Dead of the Iroquois, would have probably been most effectively hosted after harvests and summer grazing had ended, thus taking on the additional aspect of harvest and culling feasts, as suggested by Oswald et al.

Subsequent excavations at Durrington Walls by Parker Pearson (Parker Pearson et al. 2006:234–5; Parker Pearson 2007:142) have amply substantiated the large scale, the lavishness, and the competitive nature of feasts at the site. Some of the evidence for feasting that his research team has uncovered may also be related to work feasts for crews while they were erecting the megaliths at nearby Stonehenge. Parker Pearson suggested that a "millenarian zeal in which people from across Britain must have participated in a religiously inspired remodeling of cosmology" motivated people to congregate at Durrington Walls around midwinter and undertake the massive construction of Stonehenge, only 3 kilometers away. However, the abundance of articulated and unfragmented bones seem to indicate a more sanguine interpretation centering on competition between elites to host lavish feasts and build ever more impressive monuments to attract more labor and resources. Indeed, as Parker Pearson himself suggested, Durrington Walls may have been the seasonal habitation area for the Stonehenge locality, the place where most boasting between corporate kin groups or elites took place, as well as the distribution of feast foods to construction workers.

There are other massive Neolithic feasting remains that may have been similar to Durrington Walls, such as the enormous aggregations of pit-hearths at Villeneuve-Tolosane (Haute Garonne, France; Clottes et al. 1979, cited in Gomez de Soto 1993:191). As at Durrington Walls, the Neolithic stone monuments around Carnac in Brittany probably were erected by dispersed groups that seasonally congregated at those sites (e.g., Oswald et al. 2001). Julian Thomas (1991:21–9) has also noted the prevalence of large quantities of feasting remains in the ditches around causewayed enclosures, again emphasizing the importance of choice cuts and articulated limbs of cattle and their primary importance in feasting, as well as constituting the main form of wealth. Yet, despite confirming and extending the earlier documentation, Thomas does not explore any explanatory models for feasting in the Neolithic. Whittle's 1996 overview of the European Neolithic similarly emphasizes these same descriptive points. However, in addition, he proposed the essentials of a model that was being used elsewhere (e.g., J. Hill 1966; Potter 2000) and that would be taken up by Marciniak concerning enclosures and large-scale feasting as "the focus for intensive participatory ceremonialism, which reworked ideas about the integration of separate communities . . . one of the means by which its world was consolidated" (Whittle 1996:274).

Like Thomas (1991:102), who saw Neolithic pottery as used for specialized prestige expressions rather than day-to-day consumption, Whittle viewed the elaboration of pottery that occurred in tandem with the elaboration of ditched enclosures (and where most such pottery was found) as the result of intensifying social interaction, feasts, and social exchanges (Whittle 1996:309,366). My own view is that the grandiose scale of most of these sites and the magnitude of feasting involved went far beyond what one might expect of a simple community integration event. Although community or social group integration was undoubtedly also a prominent feature at such events, competition for political, military, economic, and marital power seems likely to have been the main motive for organizing and producing the required surpluses or prestige items. Ron Adams (2004, 2007) documents just such competitive feasting and displays between wealthy kinship groups vying for power in the ethnographic context of funeral feasting and the raising of megalithic memorials for the dead in Sulawesi and Sumba (Figures 6.12 and 6.13). In his overview of the social foundations of the Neolithic in Britain, Richard Bradley (1984:21,28–9,51,64–5,126,162) observed that large-scale feasting appeared to have taken place primarily at tombs (presumably including ditched enclosures as well as dolmens, long barrows, and passage graves) and that large-scale meat eating was closely associated with prestige objects. This same situation was also documented by R. Adams (2007b:199–205) and was observed by myself in Indonesia. Bradley identified Neolithic feasts by abundant animal bones at sites as well as ceramic serving vessels. The intentional destruction of prestige items such as Grooved Ware ceramics at henge monuments (not to mention the grandiosity of the monuments) noted by Bradley (1984:51) and others is a good indication of intense competition that existed between social groups. Bradley concluded that Neolithic feasts were a means of building personal prestige, including tangible benefits that such prestige entailed, and that feasting was important in the emergence of elites. Ten years later, Sherratt (1995) echoed similar sentiments. These are all interpretations that are relatively close to the political ecology views that I have found useful in understanding the ethnographic aspects of feasting in chiefdom societies. Even Marciniak noted a definite competitive aspect to the Early Neolithic feasts that is critical for understanding their existence.

Our perception of Neolithic feasting is still very biased by the differential visibility of various kinds of sites. Whereas megalithic tombs and ditched enclosures are easily observed, domestic residences and timber halls are much more elusive. Bradley (1984:26–8) suggested that these large central aggregation sites may have been inhabited by elites during most times of the year. Thus, it is extremely useful to find at least one example of a Neolithic timber hall (at Balbridie, Scotland) representing feasting at non-megalithic sites replete with copious quantities (20,000 to date) of charred cereal grains (Fairweather and Ralston 1993). This seems to underline the major role of cereals in feasting contexts in Europe.

Stonehenge itself was most likely reserved almost exclusively for the use of elites (perhaps from Mesolithic times; James 2012) in their monitoring of celestial movements, honoring of their dead ancestors, and feasting. In contrast to Durrington Walls, Stonehenge contained much less feasting debris (as might be expected of smaller, more exclusive groups), and the animal remains were predominantly composed of cattle (vs. pigs at Durrington Walls) with Beaker pottery rather than Grooved Ware ceramics (Parker Pearson et al. 2006:235) – all higher valued prestige items than occurred at Durrington Walls. Parker Pearson et al. view these differences in terms of rituals for the dead (at Stonehenge) versus the living (at Durrington Walls). However, ethnographically, this pattern would seem to make more sense in terms of elite rituals with exclusive participants at Stonehenge versus rituals and feasting (and funeral rituals) for the entire community, commoners and elites, at Durrington Walls. The great effort expended to construct Stonehenge and the astronomical knowledge that the stone arrangements imply are reminiscent of other major constructions, such as Göbekli Tepe and Chavín de Huántar, that were certainly underwritten and used by wealthy elites and may have been the ritual centers for evolved regional secret societies. There can be little doubt that psychologically impressive ceremonies took place at Stonehenge or that its core was used by a relatively small and exclusive group. There can also be little doubt that Stonehenge was meant to impress, whether in the Neolithic or Bronze Age phases of its construction. However, as Gomez de Soto (1993) observed, the magnitude and frequency of animal sacrifices (as part of feasts) became much more pronounced in the metal ages.

Elsewhere in Europe, chiefdom-level feasting has been especially well documented in the Aegean area. The Neolithic site of Makriyalos has already been mentioned in Chapter 6 as possibly representing a chiefly feast at a paramount chiefdom settlement (50 hectares) with massive feasting remains. The Homeric epics that are generally thought to have originated in the Mycenaean Bronze Age provide ample documentation of feasting practices that are discussed in greater detail in Chapter 9. However, many of the polities described may actually have been more like chiefdoms than early city states, and individuals given the epithet of "king" might better have been referred to as "chief."

Although there can be little doubt of the chiefly type of polities that constructed Stonehenge, Avebury, Maes Howe, and Newgrange in the early Bronze Age, other regions in Europe may well have remained organized at the transegalitarian level, as suggested in Chapter 6, especially in parts of Iberia (with the important exception of the copper smelting centers such as Los Millares). In Croatia, chiefdoms seem to have been well established by the end of the Neolithic, replete with human sacrifices accompanying the burials of high-ranking males (*suttee*) and the use of drinking vessels (Milicevic-Bradac 2001).

One of the important feasting developments in the Bronze Age of Europe was the appearance in some locations of enormous feasting middens that appear to represent large chiefly gatherings such as competitive village feasts, first fruits feasts, or intertribal feasts. These large midden sites are known as *Brandopferplatzen* in the Alpine region and are associated with dramatically situated cult locations recalling the impressive locations of ethnographically observed interchiefdom feasts in New Zealand mentioned earlier (Urry 1993:42–3,73). At one Alpine site (Langacker), the debris covered an area 32 meters in diameter and was up to 4 meters in thickness, with an estimated 10–20 large animals on average sacrificed every year for several centuries or perhaps in the course of a few much larger events (Gomez de Soto 1993:192). These large middens were associated with the development of bronze feasting items such as cauldrons, meat hooks, spits, plates, buckets, cups, and dippers that were probably used for reciprocal feasts among elites (Gomez de Soto 1993:192; Armada 2008). On the Salisbury Plain, only 10 kilometers from Stonehenge, but later in date, an even more massive deposit contained 65,000 cubic meters of ceramic, sheep, cattle, pig, deer, human, and coprolite materials resulting from impressive conspicuous consumption events of a competitive nature (McOmish 1996). Lavish and competitive feasts associated with elite funerals also occurred as is evident from the remains of 184 domestic cattle in a single round barrow Beaker burial at Irthlingborough (Northamptonshire, England; Davis and Payne 1993).

Some of the later Iron Age Celtic feasts were mentioned by Roman authors, although few details were recorded. They reported the use of fixed, sometimes enormous, enclosed spaces for feasting, entertainment, jurisprudence, and the recruitment of political followers with offerings of meat, costly drink, grain, and treasure at annual gatherings (Murray 1995:135). These have been identified with Iron Age enclosures known as *Viereckschanzen* and have been interpreted as venues for competitive feasting in establishing or maintaining patron–client relationships in the Celtic political economy, since Celtic sociopolitical organization was strongly based on clientage (Davis and Payne 1993). Dietler (1989, 1990, 1994:130) has argued that the redistribution of prestige goods (mainly at feasts) was used by Hallstatt chiefs to consolidate and expand political power, although items obtained from Etruscans, Greeks, and Romans seem to have been hoarded by the highest ranking elites and only exchanged with chiefs at other polities as part of trade alliances. Both Dietler and Engs (1991) have suggested that the drinking of wine and the vessels associated with it were an integral part of this "international" elite feasting and exchange etiquette. The right and ability to host large feasts was synonymous with the right to rule, presumably at the local or chiefdom level (Dietler and Engs 1991).

In addition to the *Vierechschanzen*, there is at least one Iron Age site with feasting remains on a scale comparable to the feasting middens of the Bronze Age. At Harrow Hill (Sussex), remains of an estimated 1,000 oxen were associated with the hill fort (Davis and Payne 1993:20). Even this pales in comparison to the 4,300 bucrania and entire goats recovered from a single third-millennium BCE burial mound at Kerma (Sudan; Chaix and Grant 1992; Chaix 2002) that probably represents a chiefly burial, or the 360 or more horses sacrificed and buried under chiefly kurgans in the Caucasus (Rolle 1980:45–6). There are several other interpretations of Iron Age archaeological feasting remains, such as the faunal remains at Dún Ailinne (Ireland) that Crabtree argued were part of an elite feast that served to enhance the power and prestige of regional "lords." There are also good indications of competitive chiefly funerary display feasts at sites like Hochdorf (Germany; Biel 1987). In the princely burial chamber in this mound, a 500-liter bronze cauldron containing mead residues was associated with an entire Celtic brewery and five cooking pits used to prepare whole animals for the funeral feast that centered on nine important individuals (represented by nine dinner services in the tomb) and a considerably larger contingent of lower ranking participants (Stika 2005), much like modern Polynesian feasts. Murray (1995:137) views elite funerals as contentious events in which rival versions of sociopolitical reality and power were negotiated using mortuary ritual and feasting, including, of course, copious drink. He argues that it is no coincidence that the *Viereckschanzen* were usually associated with burial monuments.

Feasts at cult sites such as Gournay-sur-Aronde (in northern France) also seem to have been important in establishing political power (Figure 7.16). At this site, the surrounding ditches were repositories for large amounts of animal bones (Bruneaux 2000:130). The enclosing palisade makes it clear that the participants formed an exclusive group, probably elite warriors, either representing the community as a whole (together with allies), a particular kin group, or perhaps even a warrior-based secret society. Méniel (2001:64,68–70,72,77–8,83) discusses other similar examples, including some large enclosures (2,000–4,000 square meters) resembling *Vierechschanzen* with smaller, more exclusive sanctuaries either inside or outside the palisaded enclosures – a pattern of exclusive elite feasting accompanied by (but separate from) large-scale public feasting that should be familiar by now. Most were accompanied by feasting remains that would feed hundreds of people or more, and sometimes by human sacrificial remains. Méniel suggests that these feasts could have served to promote the domination of the rich, to enhance group solidarity, or to establish social ties or alliances. As in Southeast Asia, cattle skulls were put on

7.16. The Celtic temple and enclosure excavated at Gournay-sur-Aronde in France yielded abundant evidence for feasting and the spoils of war deposited in the ditches surrounding the enclosure. The relatively exclusive feasts at this temple undoubtedly cemented pacts of war and celebrated victories, as well as reinforcing debt networks for the establishment of chiefly political power. (Bruneaux 2000:213)

display and horse hides with attached skull and hoofs were sometimes hung above graves. Méniel specifically notes that the vast majority of meat at funeral feasts was consumed by the living instead of accompanying the dead and that animals were used to indicate the richness of funerals rather than grave goods. Bone distributions at the ritual enclosure site of Acy-Romance indicate that guests sat in a circle with the choicest meats going to certain vectors. There also appear to have been some large-scale rural domestic feasts, although the role of these sites is equivocal. The sixth-century BCE cannibalized remains of women and animals found in a cauldron in Byciskala Cave (Bohemia; Green 1997:84) could plausibly represent clandestine secret society feasts held exclusively for initiates.

In contrast, the archaeological feasting remains from Anglo-Saxon times (450–750 CE) are largely represented by the more prosaic competitive funerary feasts (Stoodley 2010), while an example of a medieval chiefly Viking feasting hall has been excavated at Hrísbrú in Iceland (Lucas 2009) where feasts similar to the *symbel* may have taken place. Zori et al. (2013) use the historical sagas to conjure up a chiefly center that competed with others to obtain support from surrounding farmers and create alliances with other chiefs by hosting feasts and gift-giving. These feasts featured difficult to obtain foods, such as beef and beer from barley, which only the rich could afford to import or cultivate (due to the poor returns of barley in Iceland). Attendance by a farmer was considered to be a public declaration of support for a chief, whether at feasts for harvests or Yule, marriages or funerals. Zori et al. (2013:152) suggest that these feasts could have been to create socio-political bonds or to generate or maintain inequalities in the form of patron–role feasts. However, they do not indicate how these might be identified and give no specific interpretations of such feasts.

ARCHAEOLOGICAL SUMMARY

In the European Neolithic, chiefdom-level organizations are represented archaeologically by large megalithic monuments and similar monumental constructions (with few recognizable residential sites) that appear to have been regional central places where large numbers of relatively mobile people gathered seasonally. Chiefly organizations are also indicated by Bronze and Iron Age monumental defenses, mounds, and multitiered settlement hierarchies, not only in Europe but also in Polynesia, eastern North America, Mesoamerica, South America, and undoubtedly in other areas as well. There are good indications of large-scale feasting in chiefdom polities in a number of regions involving deposits in the ditches of causewayed enclosures, in borrow pits (Cahokia and Makriyalos), or in massive Bronze and Iron Age middens. Large open spaces suitable for the gathering of many people, together with large earthen mounds or other constructions, are strongly associated with these locations, which often seem to be central places in the chiefdom settlement hierarchies but may also occur in more marginal (intertribal) locations. The massive structures in at least some regions were foci of seasonal or episodic rituals, feasts, and building activities. However, the scale of the constructions themselves, together with prestige objects, testify to an underlying competitive aspect of gatherings and feasts, probably between competing factions within polities or between contending chiefdoms. From a political ecological perspective, consolidating political power and reciprocal relationships in the chiefly political structure were probably the main motivations for holding these large feasts. Collection of tribute or the amassing of debts and resources to run the chiefly administration were probably additional evident functions if not the main function for large-scale feasts.

Funerary feasts of prominent individuals (especially chiefs, their family members, and high-ranking administrators or heads of corporate groups) continued to be important, as was the case with transegalitarian leaders, and funerals became even more grandiose with the increase of power and control over resources that typified chiefly elites. These were sometimes extraordinary events involving thousands of sacrificed animals. The most elaborate chiefly or corporate burials in Europe were frequently associated with mounds, ditched enclosures, megalithic tombs, and large-scale food remains. Many of these were probably corporate kinship (lineage or clan) burial areas, as were possibly the charnel houses of eastern North America and the Near East. Following Oswald et al. (2001:121–2), it can be suggested that the curiously carefully preserved ditch segments of causewayed enclosures may not only have been constructed by different corporate kin groups, but also reserved for the same group's use in depositing ancestral or trophy skeletal remains, feasting remains, and enacting associated rituals. Of special note was the development in chiefdoms of Bronze Age Europe of specialized bronze feasting cauldrons, meat hooks, spits, and other elite equipment.

In North America, mounds were probably the political and ritual centers for each chiefdom or corporate kinship group within a chiefdom and, like constructions in Europe, constituted competitive material displays in and of themselves, as we can expect the feasts to have been as well, probably replete with a higher diversity of elite foods, serving vessels, and prestige items than usually found in transegalitarian contexts. Food appears to have been stored at some mounds, supplied and prepared by mound owner/residents, as well as consumed at the mounds.

There appears to be some archaeological evidence for secret society feasts in the form of human sacrifices and cannibalism in remote or hidden locations. Elaborate, possibly regional secret societies may also be represented by special ritual sites that may have exhibited both elite and commoner feasting activities. Stonehenge (vs. Durrington Walls), Chavín, Gournay, Caral, Cerro Lampay, Cerro Blanco, the Southwestern Great Houses, and Göbekli Tepe could all be viewed as examples of regional elite cult sites or secret society sites that appear to have been used only on special seasonal occasions according to their excavators. Most of these sites apparently lacked normal residential functions, and in the frameworks of traditional archaeological models, precisely how they dovetailed into other social, political, economic, and ritual aspects of their cultures is not as yet very clear.

These elite-related feasting sites have been proposed as places where diacritical feasts or patron–client feasts were hosted in which overvalued goods were bestowed by elites on nonelites. However, there is little reason to view some sites like Stonehenge or Gournay as including nonelites (who would presumably have been the primary clients or targets at whom diacritical information would be directed). It seems to me that at monumental sites like these, it would make more sense to view feasting activities as promotional displays of success or power used to attract other elite partners in exchange, war, marriage, or ritual, thereby consolidating sociopolitical relationships and reciprocal debts between elites. In my opinion, viewing these locations and their feasts as simple displays to affirm class distinctions or as attempts to indebt lower class clients lacks sufficient causal grit. Sites like Chavín, in particular, with large open spaces suitable for larger numbers of people, seem to have been constructed to demonstrate supernatural power rather than to display any culinary or material distinctiveness in a diacritical fashion. The feasting at Durrington Walls may have entailed patron–client relationships or even some diacritical aspects, but how can this be determined or distinguished from basic work feasts or reciprocal solidarity/alliance feasts meant to hold the chiefdom structure together?

To construct the major mounds, causewayed enclosures, and megalithic monuments in Europe and elsewhere, work feasts could certainly be expected to occur in the archaeological record, and they do at sites like Durrington Walls and the early South American mound constructions like Caral and Cerro Lampay. Of interest are the observations in both areas that these construction events appear to have been scheduled to occur in conjunction with major seasonal events such as harvest festivals or at solstices, thus probably combining seasonal celebrations, ritual activities, and feasting with communal construction activities. As such, they would not have been simply drudge work commitments, but major social and ritual events that could have attracted people from relatively large regions to the ritual centers – people drawn above all by the prospect of abundant rich food and drink. These patterns and principles for organizing people are becoming fairly evident in recent archaeological investigations and plausibly laid the basic foundation for the establishment of the earliest simple city states – a topic to which we now turn.

8

Feasting in Early States and Empires

When Inanna entered the Abzu,
He gave her butter cakes to eat.
He poured cold water for her to drink.
He offered her beer before the statue of the lion.
He treated her respectfully.
He greeted Inanna at the holy table, the table of heaven.
Enki and Inanna drank beer together.
They drank more beer together.
They drank more and more beer together.
With their bronze vessels filled to overflowing,
With the vessels of Urash, Mother of the Earth,
They toasted each other; they challenged each other.

– From Wolkstein and Kramer 1983:13–14

With the emergence of early states, feasting takes on yet grander scales of consumption, sacrifices, pomp, and ceremony. Due to the emergence of writing in tandem with some early states, we also have the first written accounts of feasting from ancient times. In cases such as the Linear B inscriptions on Crete, these accounts are often simple records of the amount of beer, barley, sheep, goats, and other foods being requisitioned, or, in the case of the Shang oracle bones, the human sacrifices being made. However, they also include poetic descriptions of gods like Inanna and Enki having intimate feasts of beer and butter cakes that undoubtedly reflect similar feasts of the Sumerian elites. The early Shang verses also depict worshippers offering ancestors wine, soup, and the first fruits from the paddies:

Abundant is the year, with much millet, much rice...
We make wine, make sweet liquor, We offer it to ancestor, to ancestress,
We use it to fulfill all the rites, To bring down blessings upon each and all.

(Waley 1996:297)

In contrast to those who imagine that the early state apparatus effectively dismantled extended or corporate kinship groups in order to curtail opposition to ruling
factions, here we see the apparent continuation of household, or, more likely,
corporate group feasting in the context of ancestor worship, which is generally
prominent in corporate kinship organizations. At least at the elite (literate) level,
families appear to have functioned as corporate groups with appropriate feasts. It is
more difficult to know what the situation was for most commoners, who left behind
no written accounts. Sumptuous royal feasts, together with smaller scale kinship
feasts, form a pattern that is reported for the New World as well as the Old (e.g.,
Goldstein 2003:165; Hendon 2003:205,207,226; M. Smith et al. 2003:245,259; Ur and
Colantoni 2010; LaTrémolière and Quellier 2012; see Figure 8.1). The tantalizing but
brief and fragmentary early written accounts, supplemented by archaeological
evidence, provide valuable insights into early state-level feasting. However, before
discussing some of this evidence, it will be useful to review a few basic distinctions
between various levels of state organization because there are substantial differences between the early city states, later empires, and contemporary nation states. I
must also beg for some indulgence in my foray into the Classical time periods since
the historic and academic literature becomes exponentially vast with increasing
sociopolitical complexity, and my background in this area is limited. Thus, the
following overviews touch on some notable highlights and are somewhat more
impressionistic or exploratory than the preceding topics.

DEFINITIONS

Many definitions have been advanced in the broad compass of states. Some authors
treat states as synonymous with urban centers, and some make their existence
contingent upon writing, institutionalized social strata, standing armies, craft specialization, interdependent craft productions, or similar criteria. However, from an
archaeological perspective, and to be consistent with the previous definition
of chiefdoms, I focus on the levels of hierarchical integration (three or more
levels) as suggested by H. Wright (1977, 1984). It is possible to divide up the
considerable array of past states into: *simple states,* or city states; *empires;* and
industrial nation states. I limit my discussions here to these rudimentary types,
although other distinctions can be and have been made (e.g., trade vs. subsistence-
based states, theater states, theocratic states, meritocracies, feudal states, primate
center states, contest states, segmentary vs. unitary states, derivative states
[in world systems], and more).

In the scheme used here, simple states, or city states, characterize the earliest
form of state development and typify the Sumerian polities, many Mycenaean and
Minoan states, many Classic and Post-Classic Maya states, small Medieval kingdoms

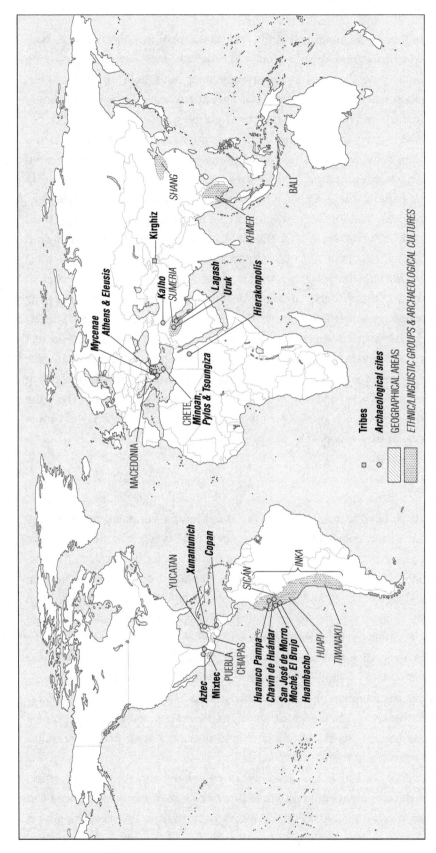

8.1. Locations of key sites, culture areas, ethnic groups, and regions related to feasting in early states and empires.

in Europe, and the historic Balinese states. These states consisted of a single, dominant, typically urban center together with an agriculturally productive hinterland. District and local administrative or service centers, as well as smaller farming villages and hamlets, constituted the second, third, and additional levels of settlement/political hierarchies. By modern standards, the Mycenaean, Mayan, Medieval European, and Balinese examples of paramount political centers in simple states often seem surprisingly small. The urban centers generally held only a few thousand residents, although the total population in the polities was usually in the tens of thousands or more. It is reasonable to assume that within individual simple states the population was relatively homogeneous and shared the same language and cultural background. Therefore, there may have been little need to transform cultural identities or create multiethnic cultural solidarity other than focusing on affiliation with the state polity and emphasizing cooperation between members of different classes or occupations.

In contrast, ancient empires represented very different kinds of polities with different problems and different scales of activity. Empires were expanded to encompass a number of simple states to the point of controlling entire regions and adding additional levels of political settlement hierarchy. Although competition between simple states was often intense, including endemic warfare (e.g., Kramer 1975:18–19), there seems to have been a lack of military, technological, and administrative ability in simple states to be able to integrate large territories in a stable fashion. Remember that, as Rambo demonstrated, there was a cost to complexity. Every increase in political complexity entailed an exponential increase in the cost of maintaining the political structure. These costs involved the establishment of additional cooperative levels of administration, each of which required food surpluses to support personnel and the necessary feasts replete with gifts that made the wheels of government turn. Increasing costs of transportation, communication, and enforcement also had to be underwritten, as well as the increased ostentation of rulers. Empires frequently incorporated a number of different conquered ethnic groups, and this also added to the cost of integrating the polity, or at least its elite levels. Typically, it was the urban dwellers and especially the elites who spoke the language of the conquering rulers and adopted their customs while the rural producers continued to adhere to their own traditions and languages. Examples of past empires include unified Egypt, Ch'in China, Rome, Assyria, Huari, Tiwanaku, and the Mongol, Khmer, Incan, and Aztec states.

Simple states as well as empires continued to exist in favorable environments from about 5000 years ago until about 1700 CE. They generally cycled back and forth between simple states and empires according to variations in economic, climatic, military, and other conditions. The empire level of organization appears to have constituted an absolute ceiling on the level of political and cultural complexity that it was possible to attain given preindustrial technology. This situation changed dramatically with the Industrial Revolution, as clearly chronicled by Hobsbawm (1962, 1968). Industrialization has changed virtually every aspect of traditional life, including family structure, transportation, urbanism, military capabilities, food production, competition, mass production, mass education, ritual, politics, economics, and, of course, feasting. I delve more deeply into this topic in the next chapter, but, for now, it is sufficient to recognize that the nation states that emerged during and after the Industrial Revolution were radically different from traditional simple states and empires.

ETHNOGRAPHIC AND HISTORIC ACCOUNTS OF FEASTING IN SIMPLE STATES

There were few areas in the world where simple states were observed before colonial impacts. However, these included various parts of Southeast Asia, Central Asia, India, Africa, and Mesoamerica. Early written texts from these simple states can help elucidate the role that feasting played in the dynamics of these kinds of polities. From these sources, is possible to distinguish at least five major arenas of state-level feasting: (1) royal feasts, (2) state-sponsored temple/religious feasts and revenue-generating feasts, (3) state-sponsored work feasts, (4) networking feasts, and (5) lineage or family-level feasts. It is apparent that many of the feast types that were common in chiefdom organizations continued to be important in simple states. In fact, the basic political dynamics and feasting types in chiefdoms and simple states may be indistinguishable except in terms of scale and ostentation. Royal funeral feasts provide a good example.

Royal Feasts

Although it may be difficult to imagine elite funerals becoming much more grandiose than the massive kurgan tombs with hundreds or thousands of sacrificed animals, sacrificed people, and food offerings documented in the preceding chapter, some simple states seem to have upped the maximal expressions even more. One of the enhanced manifestations of chiefly practices were the special squads of soldiers or gangs of enforcers that royalty used to carry out arbitrary campaigns of terror and murder to intimidate the governed and obtain acquiescence for their edicts and ideologies (Dickson 2006). In a number of early polities, every action of the king seemed to require the sacrifice of a victim to convey news of his deeds to his ancestors, as with the sacrifices made by Shang royalty in China whenever they consulted oracles. In a perverted form of communitarian ideology, elites justified such actions in terms of strengthening the state and therefore the public good, or simply in terms of demonstrating the power of the elites to potential rivals and the populace at large. As one inquisitor in early Europe was reported to have said, "It doesn't matter whether those we execute are really guilty or not. What matters is that the people are terrified by our trials" (Bobrick 2001:134, cited in Dickson 2006:137). This is a strategy for maintaining power that Dickson (140) associates with complex chiefdoms, as well as with early states throughout the world. It is transparently self-serving for the elites, despite any justifications in terms of the public good.

On the other hand, early state elites, like their chiefly predecessors, also provided entertainment and gustatory delights to their constituents via feasts and ritual displays. They thus used both the stick and the carrot. State rulers frequently employed their own achievements or life passages as suitable pretexts for handing out (as well as receiving) figurative carrots to their populace. Battle victories, installations of rulers or other important figures, and completion of major building projects (especially temples ostensibly erected for the good of the community) all provided good opportunities to vaunt rulers' abilities, power, ideologies, and triumphs.

But of all the royal feasts, and true to preceding practices, funerals were often the most opulent occasions for displaying the destruction of the most property, the sacrifice of the most people, or the construction of the greatest monuments. Royal funerals in some West African kingdoms involved the live burials of servants, concubines, and family members with the deceased, and at annual commemorations of deceased kings large numbers of war captives and criminals were publicly sacrificed to the king's ancestors, along with a large number of female victims sacrificed in private (Dickson 2006:138). In nineteenth-century Bali, royal funerals were attended by 40,000–50,000 spectators who watched as eleven stories (60–70 feet) of wooden pagodas were engulfed by flames that consumed the body of the dead king, followed by the self-immolation of young women to accompany him (Geertz 1980:99–101). Little is said about the feasting at these events, however, it is difficult to conceive of them without large-scale and lavish feasts, certainly for the elites. From these descriptions and Geertz's (117) own analysis, it is evident that these royal funerals were highly competitive "aggressive assertions of status" as part of a "headlong attack in a war of prestige." Of course, "prestige" and "status" can be considered here as synonyms of "power" and "self-interest" on the part of the surviving family and their supporters. Although Geertz (120) thought that rivalry for prestige was the "driving force of Balinese life," it seems likely that what was ultimately at stake were the claims of descendants to close links with powerful predecessors, as well as the revalidation of supporting alliances involved in the succession of a new generation to power and wealth (Oestigaard and Goldhahn 2006). Elaborate funerals were fundamentally used to establish

8.2. Although there no longer are royal funerals in Bali (Indonesia), important and wealthy individuals are still commemorated with large, colorful processions and feasts when they die. This funeral procession was for a wealthy and influential individual. (Photograph by B. Hayden)

continuity in rulership and to maintain the dynastic grip on power. The Balinese funerals were the most dramatic, splendid, large, and expensive of all the royal Balinese displays requiring three months of ceremonies including three days of major events (Figure 8.2). They promoted the ideology that worldly status has a cosmic base and that hierarchy is the governing principle of the universe. Similar events, ideologies, and strategies were probably quite common in early states everywhere.

Networking Feasts

Aside from royal funerals and similar but lesser scale celebrations surrounding life events of royalty (e.g., the investitures, marriages, military victories, and alliance pacts documented in Sumeria; Schmandt-Besserat 2001:397), it is difficult to imagine that there would not have also been networks and entanglements between elites hosting feasts in more private surroundings to secure allies and support. This is probably what the story of Inanna and Enki represents, as depicted in the opening of this chapter, as do a number of ancient Mesopotamian cylinder seals showing elite banqueting (Figures 8.3 and 8.4). The Homeric epics seem to reflect similar elite feasting contexts, as well as a general obsession with elite feasting. Susan Sherratt (2004) has observed that in both the *Iliad* and the *Odyssey*, feasting is the single most frequent activity described aside from fighting. These accounts reflect the

8.3. The "Standard of Ur" depicts Sumerian citizens bringing animals and produce in the lower registers, presumably for the important feast shown in the top register. This may depict an important state-sponsored temple feast held as a means of collecting tribute or perhaps a critical solidarity/alliance feast with regional administrators or elites from other cities. (From *Before Writing* by Denise Schmandt-Besserat, p. 173, figure 104; Austin: University of Texas Press. 1992)

8.4. Cylinder seals used by Sumerians sometimes also depict feasting scenes, presumably involving wealthy or elite individuals. These examples from Ur depict the transport of drink and fish to the relatively intimate feasts in the upper registers where the seated individuals are drinking beer from long straws as is still done in some traditional parts of Africa today. Beer would have only been drunk on special occasions, as indicated in the opening quote for this chapter. Small-scale, more intimate hospitality feasts were undoubtedly used by elites in all early states to secure support and cooperation from key people (Image courtesy of Pierre Amiet, *La Glyptique Mésopotamienne Archaique*, Pl.90:1190–1, CNRS Editions, 1980)

Mycenaean period, when simple city states dominated the Greek political landscape. In the Homeric descriptions, elite feasting is the context for epic poetry, songs, dance, philosophizing, and politics, all of which were used to unify participants in an epic worldview that constituted their collective elite ideology. Gifts such as gold and silver cups were also conferred at these feasts, and it seems evident that these gifts, like prestige objects in general, were being used to forge alliances and maintain loyalties within the city states, as well as to launch cooperative ventures between polities, like the sacking of Troy. For larger venues, elites feasted with each other inside their megarons and courtyards, whereas nonelites feasted outside the palaces (Sherratt 2004). The attempt to build relationships in this way is illustrated in *The Iliad* (9:199–204):

> With this he led them forward, and bade them sit on seats covered with purple rugs; then he said to Patroclus who was close by him,
>
> "Son of Menoetius, set a larger bowl upon the table, mix less water with the wine, and give every man his cup, for these are very dear friends, who are now under my roof."

Linear B inscriptions from that period deal almost exclusively with provisioning palace feasts (Sherratt 2004). The major culinary features of these feasts were meat (with animals bearing gilded horns sometimes transported by boat to the sites), olive oil, wine, and almost certainly bread. Later, *symposia* formed a more exclusive variant of these types of events in which close elite compatriots gathered at a host's house and were entertained by musicians, poetry, dancers, good food and drink, and philosophizing.

A number of scholars have suggested that, like some chiefdom organizations discussed in the preceding chapter, the early states of Southeast Asia and even some of the early empires like the Khmer relied heavily on the personal relationships that rulers were able to forge between themselves and other elites in their realms (Higham 1989:342,352,355). Feasting and lavish displays, both among close affiliates as well as at more public events, therefore were viewed as playing especially critical roles in maintaining the political support networks that constituted the foundation of these states. Geertz (1980) refers to such polities as "theater states." Indeed, royalty often appeared personifying deities in public temple dramas. Under these conditions, political stability was expectedly ephemeral. This may have been a fairly widespread characteristic of the earliest states in many regions, but such issues deserve considerably more research.

In the context of royal and elite network feasts, Bray (2003b:95), Issakidou (2007), Pollock (2003), M. Smith et al. (2003:245), and others have suggested that "haute cuisines" developed to create a visible (diacritical) distinction between social classes (see also Sherratt 2004 on Mycenaean cuisine). However, it is not clear from the written sources whether, as I suspect, the development of fine cuisines was simply a natural consequence of the desire and ability to impress important guests with ever more lavish foods, or whether, as with other sumptuary items, it was really expressly motivated out of a desire to create social distance between the classes. Alternatively, sumptuary items, like monopolies on prestige trade items, may simply have been used to limit competition. What seems to be clear from other discussions of royal feasting (see below) is that special foods were used to bind political supporters together and to run the empire. In all events, detailed accounts concerning the motivations behind the development of fine cuisines seem difficult to come by. The symposia of the Greeks may be an exception, and there are undoubtedly other details of similar banquets in obscure archives of the simple states of Medieval Europe, but this is beyond the scope of this overview.

Temple and Revenue-Generating Feasts

From Mesopotamia to the Aegean, from India to China, and from Mesoamerica to the Andes, early state royalty appear to have frequently organized large-scale feasts requiring large-scale "contributions" for large portions of their populations under the guise of temple or religious events. Why temples should feature so prominently in the governance of early states has always been somewhat of an explanatory conundrum. Many archaeologists and ethnographers concluded that early elites must have gained their power from their control over supernatural knowledge and rituals. However, as illustrated in previous chapters, elites at all levels of sociopolitical organization used a range of more effective strategies to acquire and maintain power. Ideology was only of secondary importance, perhaps only convincing 10–20 percent of the population, but serving to justify elite actions and their demands to the majority (Hayden 2003a:15). Moreover, Flannery (1999:5,7–8,10,14–15) argues that ideological changes occurred *after* states were formed by aggrandizers who appropriated old symbols for their own use.

Early state elites were able to use coercion and intimidation to a far greater extent than in transegalitarian or chiefly societies; however, as Service (1975:270–2) and Earle (1997:110,131) have noted, the use of force by itself is inadequate to hold complex political organizations together for any extended period. Early state elites also used ownership of land and resources (Magness-Gardiner 1994; G. Schwartz 1994; Hayden 1994b:202), together with contractual agreements with tenants, the lure of prestige items, ideological claims, interpolity conflicts, marriages and marriage payments (discussed later), and debts generated by various means to hold state organizations together. Feasts at state (elite) temples can be considered as a new emphasis in the feasting repertory, although it clearly had functional antecedents in chiefly ancestor cults, secret societies, and chiefly temples such as the Polynesian feasts at *marae* and the feasts at Celtic sacred enclosures.

In the amalgam of strategies employed to hold early states together, elites certainly used temples to reinforce their own self-serving ideological constructs of how the cosmos should be constituted: that is, hierarchically, with high kings playing roles similar to high gods if not actually embodying them; mortals as having been created by the gods to serve the gods and give them the gifts they desired; agricultural productivity as controlled by the gods who had to be repaid with feasts, tribute, and ceremonies; worldly status/success being based on supernatural qualities; the power of wealthy ancestors; rewards in the afterlife for warriors; differential values of elite versus agrarian goods; and many other similar "cultural values" or "beliefs." However, beyond the use of temples for ideological propaganda, temples served a number of other good economic and practical political purposes, and feasts were central elements. Temples increased control over the populace and helped to extract goods and labor from citizens and/or control key resources like water, as argued by Hauser-Schäublin (2003).

It is important to recognize that temples were of great use for attracting people. Once gathered, they could be prevailed on or manipulated through feasting and euphoric ambiances to agree to render services, provide goods, agree to commitments, or adopt elite ideologies. But people first had to be attracted to these events. Temples could attract people with large ceremonial performances and feasts hosted in impressive architectural surroundings festooned by colorful textiles, elaborate masks, exotic foods, and entertaining music or dramas. Such periodic allures must have been strong indeed in otherwise fairly drab daily agricultural lives. Like the elite secret societies that may have been ancestral to some of the early state temples, the deity figureheads of the temple were rooted in familiar popular supernatural concepts and would have had an already established appeal for local people. Thus, one practical benefit of temples and temple feasts was their ability to attract people. In fact, it may be that temple feasts were so alluring for many people that those attending willingly provided material or labor contributions for the events. Organizers could then retain a portion of those contributions for their "operating costs."

A second benefit of temple feasts was that the competitive displays and offerings created demands for surplus production, wealth production, and debts that, directly or indirectly, favored increased benefits to elites.

A third economic or practical reason for royalty to establish temples was that, in at least India and probably Indonesia, royal endowments and other "gifts" to the temples were used to intensify agricultural production through the creation of irrigation systems, paddies, raising and renting out plow animals, or similar intensification projects (B. Stein 1960; see also Hauser-Schäublin 2003). Families who benefited from temple agricultural intensification programs were then pressured to make contributions to the temple in compensation, or, as in Greece, temple lands were rented out to agriculturalists. The net recorded rents paid ranged from 140–1,200 tons of barley from estates 300–370 hectares in size. City rulers appear to have granted temples these lands, and city elites retained ultimate control (Ampolo 1992). In other Greek temples, metals and textiles were produced (Hägg 1992), presumably to pay for temple costs and to supply elites with prestige goods or returns on investments. In India, the amassed produce of temples was used (1) to support temple personnel and activities (including general feasts) and (2) to repay the royal founders of the temples or other donors who, in India, received an average of about 10 percent per annum return on their investments (B. Stein 1960:167; see also Morrison 1996:587,596). A similar situation is implied in Bali, where hamlets and villages were tied to specific temples with the general populace making pilgrimages to the temples for their major feast days. The temples "requested" (or required) certain gifts from each village, with the offerings sometimes being considerable amounts of rice, pigs, fish, cocoanuts, salt, water buffaloes, and wealth (Hauser-Schäublin 2003:157,160,164,166ftn). In effect, this was a form of tribute, and the king threatened nonparticipants with punishments (163–4). Those who did not properly honor the deities (presumably with adequate offerings) were also conveniently scapegoated and blamed for crop failures (163–4). As Hauser-Schäublin (2003:177) succinctly states it, "Temples were tax collecting institutions."

A fourth benefit of the establishment of state temples in various districts was their demonstrations of the influence of the ruling personnel (vs. their rivals) in those districts under the guise of religious worship. This kind of political posturing, together with the competition between local elite kin groups to display their prominence, has led B. Stein (1960:171) to observe for South Asia that "the Temple acted more as a place to record political loyalties than as a center of worship." This was also true in Balinese temples, where at the height of the ritual, the king would appear in dazzling attire in the ritual area, standing above the officiating priest like a god incarnate (Hauser-Schäublin 2003:165). Contrary to Geertz and others who viewed the Balinese kingship as all performance and pomp with little power or substance, Hauser-Schäublin (2003:176) argued strongly that pomp served power, not vice versa. The performances were not simply pomp for the king, but material demonstrations of his dominance in the political, economic, and ritual networks that constituted the foundation of his kingdom. The kings sought to control the administration of temples and reserved intimate relationships with the deities for themselves (168). This also seems to have been the case for Sumerian potentates.

A fifth practical reason for royalty to establish temples was that temple administrators, with their higher levels of education and literacy, constituted important links between rural villages and higher political powers, as well as links to state defense forces and trade networks (Wälty 2003). People with concerns or complaints were normally dependent on temple personnel to submit requests to authorities for redress or appropriate action. Thus, elites who controlled temples could exert considerable control over local populations (Figure 8.5). These considerations also provided practical motivations for rural families to support temples with food gifts both at feasts and on a more routine basis so that they would be treated favorably by state officials or helped when in need (Figure 8.6). Temple administrators, in turn, often depicted their gods as being "gourmands" who regularly required a great deal of food (Appadurai 1981:505). In India, three-quarters of such

8.5. Temples became important centers for feasting and other state-related activities that benefited the local populace to some extent, but primarily benefited state elites whether in the major urban centers like Angkor Wat or in rural villages like this Buddhist temple in a Laotian village. (Photograph by B. Hayden)

8.6. Because temple priests were often literate and connected to state elites, the favor of priests was often sought by people who might need support of various kinds from state officials. In this example, a temple priest has been invited to a feast to bless a Balinese household. The host not only could establish a closer rapport with the temple priest and administration, but could also use this opportunity to display his relative wealth and kin support, thereby augmenting his image in the eyes of the priest. Such feasts were essentially promotional in nature, unless there was a specific favor being requested, in which case they would constitute solicitation feasts. (Photograph by B. Hayden)

food gifts were retained by temple personnel for their needs, whereas one-fourth was given to royal or other investors of the temple (B. Stein 1960:172). In all this, the annual temple celebration and feast was a major event at which large amounts of food were conveyed to the temple administration, as well as to participants and pilgrims who attended and contributed to the event. In their fundamentals, these feasting events appear similar in nature to the chiefly sponsored feasts tailored to extract food from the populace under the guise of providing entertainment and food for local constituents.

Another benefit of attracting many people was that events at these locations provided an important venue for local and elite families to show off their wealth and success ("prestige" or "status"), which played such important role in brokering marriage arrangements and economic or political alliances between rural families but was also critical in the political jockeying for power in early states. As Hauser-Schäublin (2003:164,167,169) characterized the situation in Bali, "The temple court was and is an arena for the establishment of political claims" where claims to power were negotiated between competing networks and social groups. The assortment of shrines to ancestors (including the king's ancestors) and deities associated with the temple represented constellations of powerful social groups identified with ruling houses. Thus, rather remarkably, the giving and redistribution of food at temple feasts was a source of conflict and often litigation (Appadurai 1981:506–7).

There are a number of examples of these benefits from the Old World. The Eleusinian "Celebration of Bread" festival at the state-run temples of Eleusis was the "proudest feast of the ancient world" (Jacob 1945:66). Its origins can probably be understood as a form of annual tribute feast for the polity, but the attractions were so alluring that it gained interstate renown. Certainly, many Greeks made generous donations to the temple gods of Eleusis (Demeter and Persephone) with expectations of obtaining ecstatic spiritual experiences, and adorants were encouraged to make similar sacrifices to the temples of many other gods (at Eleusis) who might feel neglected or insulted. As a result, at its height, the temple of Eleusis boasted large granaries overseen by a ten-man financial collegium of shrewd grain merchants who sold grain at good prices for the benefit of the temple treasury, only part of which was used for the costs of the annual feast. A three-man directorate, ultimately taken over by Athenians, oversaw the administration of the temple and had the power to inflict punishments. They ran inns for visitors and undoubtedly profited in many other ways from events and donations (Jacob 1945:66). The yearly celebration of the "mysteries" was a major social and dramatic experience for many citizens of the region and a major economic boon for the priests and polity of Eleusis.

The same basic kinds of arrangements and dynamics observed in the South and Southeast Asian temples discussed earlier may well have characterized early

Sumerian and Mycenaean temples that featured so prominently in the political landscape of the earliest states. Sumerian temples owned, loaned, and managed herds of animals and agricultural lands, taking a generous share of production. According to the analysis by Schmandt-Besserat (2001), inscriptions and depictions show that the Sumerian elites sponsored periodic feasts about once a month at the temples of the main deities in the state pantheon. Like the Hindu temples described earlier, the Sumerian temples organized sensually attractive events replete with pageantry, music, dance, games, drama, and even sacred prostitution that must have drawn people from far and wide and enabled them to parade their own elegance, strength, dexterity, and beauty to attract the attention of others. Royalty would certainly have been lavishly attired. Even the gods descended to earth where they (or their masked impersonators) presided over the feasts and rituals and had special intimate relationships with royalty. "Offerings" from the populace for the feast included grain, animals for sacrifice, fish, oils, and other foods, which were paraded for all to see and probably involved competitive displays. However, standard contributions were strictly mandatory and highly regulated (400–1). A portion of these gifts were offered to the patron deity (temple staff), a portion was allocated to the royal family and administration, and a portion was given back to the populace to enjoy during the feast. Whether at the chiefly level or the early state level, rulers generally seem to have made a big show of their own contributions to these and all official feasts, portraying themselves as the major contributors to communal feasts (Sherratt 2004), but of course they seem to have profited much more from what they received than what they doled out as their contributions.

The quantities consumed could be prodigious: 30,800 kiloliters of barley alone consumed at the inauguration of the temple to Ningirsu in Lagash c. 2500 BCE (Schmandt-Besserat 2001:398). The installation of new priestesses as wives of the principal city deity were promoted as important feasting events as well, with the king and elders presiding over the affair, as described in an early document for a city state of the late second millennium BCE (Falconer 1994:133). When we discuss empires, we will see that feasts in the later Near Eastern empires were even more lavish. Similar arrangements seem to have been established in Mycenaean states if the nine bulls provided by each of nine villages (eighty-one bulls in total) for the Poseidon feast at Pylos is any indication (Sherratt 2004).

Medieval Christian churches with their Passion plays may have served similar functions as the Hindu temples, especially since plows and oxen or horses owned and rented out by the churches were needed by many families to undertake intensive plow agriculture. Although unclear as to whether secular or sacred in nature, Landa (Tozzer 1941:151–65) recorded similar patterns of monthly feasts requiring major contributions among the sixteenth-century Maya of Yucatan, where various sectors of the community served, in turn, as feast sponsors including warriors, fishermen, beekeepers, hunters, curers, the elderly, and parents of children, as well as the community as a whole. In later centuries, the organization of the Maya *cofradia* and cargo system (largely in the areas where clerics were absent) may also have filled a similar role as the temples in early states (especially in providing loans to those in need, having cofradia lands cultivated, and, in some periods, receiving tribute and controlling community surpluses), as well as providing a local supernatural warrant for the exercise of political and economic power (Fariss 1984:324–6,329,333,336–9,340–3). Farther south, in the Inka empire, *ceque* shrines constituted locations at which kin groups were obligated to provide offerings and perform dances over several days on a rotational basis so that food was brought to the shrine on an almost daily basis. Massive amounts of food and *chicha* were consumed and undoubtedly offered to the temple in exchange for a nominal cake served on a silver or gold plate, ostensibly given to them by the Sun (Coben 2004).

Thus, the focus on religious institutions such as temples, far from being rooted in putative spiritual qualities of royalty or the religious fervor of the populace, appears to have largely been an expedient practical strategy for increasing production, obtaining revenues from investments, entangling local populations in debts and sociopolitical webs, and promoting the self-interests of the elites and those with ambitions, all under the guise of religious needs or mitigating the material consequences of failure to adequately honor the gods. The elaboration of temples with permanent staffs may be a characteristic that distinguishes states from chiefdoms, although this issue requires more careful scrutiny. Nor is it clear whether harvest or first fruits feasts continued to exist as state-run revenue generating events separate from temple feasts or whether temple feasts had completely absorbed these functions.

The "touring" feasts, or *gafol*, documented in Chapter 7 for chiefdoms, were sometimes less reliant on religious justifications or manipulations for the extraction of surpluses than were temple feasts. Kobishchanow (1987) observed that touring feasts were commonly used in many early states to obtain tribute and assurances of political loyalties, particularly in Medieval Europe, but elsewhere as well. Although temples could not exhibit royal personages at every event, they had the advantage of being permanently fixed on the landscape, in contrast to ambulatory royalty with their peripatetic appearances and *gafol* visits. Although there does not appear to be any record of touring feasts among the Yucatec Maya of the sixteenth century, they did have a functional equivalent of bringing elites from outlying centers to the main towns for warrior feasts (Tozzer 1941:165). It is reasonable to suggest that this was to maintain contact and the fidelity of the military and administrative organizations within the states' jurisdictions.

Work Feasts and Alliance Feasts

There are few ethnographic or historic accounts of actual work feasts in early states, although Sumerian accounting documents make it clear that state laborers were given beer and bread for their work. Feasts given to raise armies might also be considered a type of work or alliance feast. As Odysseus relates, after he armed nine boats and gathered a crowd, he feasted his faithful companions for six days and covered all the expenses needed to offer sacrifices to the gods and provision the feasts (*The Odyssey* XIV, 248–51). All early states undoubtedly used work feasts to one extent or another to recruit manpower for their many construction or other projects; however, it is among the Inca of South America that this practice is best documented historically. Although this documentation is from a later empire rather than an early state, we have seen in the preceding chapter that this practice seems to extend back in time to early polities in the region, possibly even being used in some early chiefdoms. Whether the large-scale use of *chicha* to underwrite armies and state production or surpluses was a development only in later empires or occurred even earlier than the initial simple states is an open question that will be interesting to investigate in the future.

Kinship Feasts

Some researchers have argued that state-level administrators attempted to curtail the existence or power of extensive kinship groups such as clans either because they limited the power of the king or to prevent powerful rival factions from disrupting centralized rule (e.g., Earle 1997:6). As Sahlins (1968:93) phrased it, "Where kinship is king, the king is in the last analysis only kinsman, and something less than royal." Hence, strong kinship groups were thought to be antithetical to the political central-ization of large groups. However, it is apparent that, at least at the level of elites, kinship and kin-based corporate groups continued to play an important role in the inheritance or acquisition of wealth and power well into the development of empires (as exemplified by the exploits of the Juliani to which Julius Caesar belonged). Elite kin helped each other in economic and political maneuvers, and they often formed corporate lineages, as evidenced by the corporate precincts that lasted for many generations in Teotihuacan, Classic Mayan sites, Bronze Age Mesopotamian cities, and Roman villas (Millon 1967; L. Brown 2001; Ur and Colantoni 2010). Feasting certainly must have continued to play a key role in maintaining cooperation between members of such corporate kinship groups and in negotiating advantageous economic and political relationships with other cor-porate kin groups. Therefore, funerals, in particular, continued to be important events (Figure 8.2 & 8.7). Even in rural areas of Southeast Asia, lineage houses continued

8.7. The importance of funeral feasts and lineages in Minoan early state societies is clearly illustrated in this depiction from the Hagia Triada sarcophagus (Crete). Celebrants can be seen bringing to a tomb with an ancestral statue before it drink (probably wine), undetermined foods, and calves to be sacrificed. Note the exclusive and predominantly elite status of the participants. (Permission granted by the Scuola Archeologica Italiana di Atene)

to be constructed and used to hold lineage feasts that reified the power of lineage heads and the land resources that they controlled (Freedman 1965, 1970) (Figure 6.17).

Although corporate kinship groups may not have been eliminated in most early states, their relative strength may have waxed and waned in relation to the strength of centralization in the polity. For instance, in Imperial China, lineages came into being to protect resources, especially in contexts of uncertainty, competition, and change. The growth of lineage landholdings increased dramatically during periods of weakened state control (Rankin and Escherick 1990:317). It has also been argued that strong lineages could more effectively evade taxes and limit the state's ability to act in local affairs (Gates 1996:107). If this is a general pattern, the magnitude of corporate kinship feasting may provide an important barometer of centralized power in state-level organizations. However, much more research is required to establish this relationship as reliable and to monitor it archaeologically. One might also wonder if strong lineages were the result of weak centralized control or the cause of it.

Some of the most graphic descriptions of elite corporate kinship feasts come from India, where they have even been characterized as "Hindu potlatches." This alludes to the competitive nature of these feasts for "prestige," which is, in this case, explicitly linked to power, influence, success, supporters, social networks, social credit, and a group's rank in all these dimensions compared to others (Hanchett 1975:42,48). Both Hanchett and Appadurai (1981) focus on marriages as the most extreme expression of kinship-based feasting in India. Such feasts serve to define networks of support and to bind supporters to factions. They also define caste boundaries, establish possible future marriage arrangements (entailing access to land, education, and wealth), open paths to careers, and display overall socio-economic and political power. As such, marriage feasts are intensely competitive events, with many of the characteristics that have been previously noted at the level of corporate kinship feasting: the contractual basis of reciprocity, the extreme generosity, ongoing affinal exchanges, the cultivation of important officials as guests, and the straining of family finances to the maximum in order to impress guests sometimes to the point of courting financial disaster (Hanchett 1975:35,39,41,47–8). Even ambitious individuals in the lowest ranked groups use this strategy in attempts to improve their conditions. In this system, the large debt loads assumed by lower ranked families generally benefit higher ranked families who have surpluses and wealth to loan out (typically at high rates of interest) thus pushing surplus production to its maximum and establishing important sources of power and sources of labor (39). Failure to perform adequately at whatever social level is considered a humiliation and defeat of one's endeavors (39,48–50), similar to becoming a "rubbish man" in transegalitarian societies.

Among the sixteenth-century Maya of the Yucatan, strictly reciprocal feasts and gifts were organized by elites and carried corporate responsibilities. The return of the invitations and gifts transcended particular individuals who, upon death, passed on their obligations and debts to their descendants (Tozzer 1941:92). In the Andean region, Hastorf (2003) has similarly emphasized the ongoing importance of corporate kinship feasts within state or empire organizations. In this case, the focus is more on ancestors than on marriage, although a number of occasions, such as marriages, funerals, ancestral ceremonies, and house embellishments, typically are used to varying degrees to promote family or lineage prospects through competitive displays. We can probably also expect that other, albeit less grandiose, kin-based feasts were common in early states, similar to the birth, coming-of-age, or tattooing feasts observed in chiefdoms and transegalitarian societies. Harvest feasts, hosted for group solidarity at the household, corporate kinship, or village level (rather than state-organized events), may also have been common in early states, as historical texts indicate for early Greek city states (Nilsson 1940:25–8).

Thus, overall, it is possible to view the feasting complex of early states, like the chiefdoms before them, as basically incorporating many feasting practices of previous sociopolitical organizational types and sometimes transforming them. Feasting at the family, corporate kinship, and village levels of transegalitarian or chiefdom societies seem to continue to be vibrant and important among elites in early states, and especially in segmentary states in which the lower order settlements had considerable autonomy. Even in the major urban centers and lower order settlements of unitary states, we can probably expect these types of feasts to be important at least at the elite level and perhaps to some extent at the poorer ends of the spectrum. The socioeconomic safety networks that they create become ever more important with increasingly extralocal political entanglements in individual lives, as demonstrated in rural China by Yan (1996). These traditional feasting and gift-giving networks could be used to exert influence and obtain favorable decisions at higher political levels of governance.

In addition to these kinship and family-based feasts, continuities of feast types from chiefdoms to early states include the touring feasts used by chiefs, the secret society-*cum*-temple feasts, the ancestral feasts of leaders, the work feasts, the fidelity bonding of elite factions or supporters through feasting, and the city- or polity-wide feasts, including celebrations of the life stages in the ruler's family. The only new feasting features in early states appear to be the magnitude of the feasts, the institutionalization of temple tribute feasts, and the increasingly ostentatious polity-wide celebrations of royal achievements or life events.

The basic principles on which many early states were organized also exhibit strong continuities with chiefdoms, especially the use of ritual and ancestral institutions to construct the political framework of the state through displays of success, power, and wealth, together with economic investments. As Hauser-Schäublin (2003:168), Geertz (1980), and others have observed, the Balinese state was not so much a territorial unit as a network of temples and affiliated local elites with their supporters or dependents. Loyalties and affiliations with higher political levels were constantly shifting and being contested by rivals. Conversely, there were some distinctive changes from chiefdoms in the dynamics of early state organizations including the increased use of terror. States are partly defined by some researchers as having standing armies. Thus, it is worth contemplating the possible emergence of new types of feasting events for soldiers as well as other specialist, guild-like organizations since early states were also supposed to be characterized by increased specialization. However, I am not aware of any historical evidence for such profession-specific feasts, although there is likely to be some documentation for guild feasts in empires. It is also possible to view some of the transegalitarian or chiefly secret society feasts as having strong warrior components. This, too, would be an interesting avenue to investigate.

ARCHAEOLOGICAL FEASTS IN EARLY STATES

It seems that the greatest amount of archaeological interest in early state feasting has concentrated in the Mycenaean city states, the Middle Eastern centers, and the Andean areas. These areas will therefore serve as the focus for our discussion.

Minoan and Mycenaean Feasting

PALACE FEASTS

The archaeological literature on Mycenaean feasting is substantial. However, a relatively comprehensive recent overview volume on the topic has been edited by James Wright (2004a). As might be expected, the greatest attention has been spent on elite feasting in the palaces. On the basis of Linear B inscriptions, pottery, and fauna, Stocker and Davis (2004) and Palaima (2004) concluded that the larger palace feasts at Pylos involved small groups of about twenty-two elite participants in the palace feasting room (where bronze vessels were used) with a much larger group of lower ranking participants in the palace courtyards and vicinity (where coarse ceramic wares were used) and a third, or middle, group in the palace who used fine ceramic cups (Bendall 2004). Isaakidou et al. (2002; Halstead and Isaakidou 2004) concluded that at least nineteen cattle were sacrificed for these types of events, enough to feed hundreds or even thousands of people, and they, too, think that the limited number of special cups inside the palace probably represents a more exclusive group of feasters inside the palace, although Borgna (2004:137,149) indicates that a number of rooms in the palaces were used for banquets on different social/ritual occasions so that the situation is undoubtedly somewhat more complex.

Isaakidou et al. suggest that the Bronze Age use of small exclusive rooms may represent a change from *in*clusive types of feasts in the Late Neolithic (as represented at Makriyalos) to more *ex*clusive feasting events in the Bronze Age. Girella (2007:152–3) and Borgna (2004:136,146) suggest a similar difference between the Minoan (more communal feasting) and the Mycenaean (more exclusive feasting) periods. However, due to the vicissitudes of archaeological recovery and changes in material use and visibility, this may be more of an apparent than real change. As noted in Chapter 6, most large feasts in ethnographic transegalitarian societies have separate, more exclusive eating areas (often in domestic structures) for lineage heads or other important participants in feasts, while the lower ranking lineage members and other guests eat outside (Figures 6.9 and 6.11). In addition to these large feasts, lineage heads (even in transegalitarian societies) are frequently involved in much more exclusive, small-scale feasts of a political, ritual, or planning nature attended only by themselves. This was also probably the way feasts were organized at Çatal Höyük. The same pattern may well characterize most Neolithic and Bronze Age feasts at the chiefdom and simple state levels, with the material expression of the highest ranking feasters simply becoming more distinctive and archaeologically identifiable as increasing architectural elaboration and political complexity developed in tandem with increasing levels of wealth.

According to Mycenaean inscriptions, at least one palatial feast was for the installation of a new king, perhaps involving similar dynamics as the installation feasts of chiefs discussed in Chapter 7. Key aspects probably involved the demonstration of economic and organizational ability, as well as the warranting of the new title and position by key power holders in the region. Other feasts were larger, and Halstead and Isaakidou suggest that very large feasts may not only have served to attract allies and supporters, or reinforce social solidarity in the polity, but also to promote the prestige of the palace administration and naturalize sharp socioeconomic inequalities within the society (see also Halstead 1998–9:187). This appears to follow the ideas enunciated by Hamilakis (1999a:40,45,49; 1999b:58–60) about feasts serving to transform wealth into power, especially under highly competitive sociopolitical and economic conditions. Similarly, Borgna (2004:127,134–5) and Girella (2007:157) view large Minoan palace-sponsored feasts as serving to create, affirm, or legitimize hierarchies of power and dependencies (Dietler's patron–role types of feasts), as well as to promote certain ideologies and political strategies, all the while enhancing the social bonding and political unity of dispersed groups. In this view, Minoan feasts are essentially political tools.

Halstead and Isaakidou point out that the invocation of the (elite) gods during the sacrifice of the animals for the feast conceptually ensured participation of those deities and legitimized the elite social ideology that they represented. Feasting contributions from dependents and supporters were justified by representing the goods as given to the gods in exchange for the use of their lands (Halstead 1998–9:168). By attending the feast and accepting highly valued foods from the sacrifices, participants tacitly acknowledged or acquiesced to the ritual and social scenarios being promulgated by the elite organizers. Isaakidou et al. (2002:90) point out that virtually all feasts involved sacrifices in the name of the gods, who received their portion (some of the blood, bones, the tail, and the gall bladder), while mortals feasted upon the meat and fat.

All the functions (alliance building, solidarity, political power, patron–client relationships, palace promotion, naturalizing inequalities, promulgating ideologies) that various authors propose for palace feasts may have been pursued simultaneously at large palace events, although perhaps not in the same locations or with the same emphasis in all instances. Still to be considered by Aegean archaeologists is the possibility that large palace feasts (and they were large if the 4,000 cups recorded on the Linear A tablets at Ayia Triada and the thousands of cups recovered from modest palaces like Petras are any indication; Girella 2007:147) may have functioned like the monthly large-scale Sumerian feasts held primarily for collecting resources to underwrite the elite administration, although these, too, undoubtedly served to promote many auxiliary goals such as those just listed. Interestingly, Athens, too, held ritual animal sacrifices and feasting every month, and the largest of their public sacrifices, the Panathenaia, was explicitly to display Athenian power to official visitors from other polities, especially other members of the Delian League, as well as to reward the loyalty of officials working for Athenian interests outside of the homeland (Palaima 2004:101–2). Hundreds of oxen were sacrificed at Athena's temple at the largest of these events, and it can be wondered whether these events were not also essential means of collecting tribute or conscripting services and goods under the pretext of necessary celebrations for the gods.

Palaima argues that the same dynamic was in play during Mycenaean times when palatial elites struggled to maintain control over member communities and to outdo competitors in displays of power and the ability to provide feasts. Halstead (1998–1999:167,187; Halstead and Isaakidou 2011:91; see Bendall 2004 as well) also observes that individuals were obligated to contribute to the large palace feasts at Pylos, which seems to echo the Sumerian practice of imposing feast contributions on citizens in order to collect food and other items to sustain the political administration. There can be little doubt that for many people attending temple feasts, the receipt of some food, together with the pomp and ceremony and social interactions, all contributed to feelings of identity with the sponsoring polities – or, "social solidarity," although this was likely to have been an advantageous side-benefit for the organizers that they were also fully aware of and did what they could to promote. All of these suggested functions seem to me to be more reasonable than the claims that palatial feasts were essentially diacritical in nature; that is, meant to differentiate the ruling elite from everyone else, as suggested by Isaakidou (2007), Halstead (2007:42), Bendall (2004), and others.

NONPALACE ELITE FEASTS

James Wright (2004) alludes to a wide range of other types of feasts that may have occurred inside palaces, as well as elsewhere. However, with some notable exceptions such as Eleusis, not as much archaeological or historical work has been directed to documenting or interpreting other feast types. Hamilakis (1999b:59) refers to drinking parties that essentially constituted work feasts, perhaps much as household work parties in contemporary urban societies often feature copious beer supplied by the host. Hamilakis notes that work parties were one means of using surpluses to achieve other ends, including increasing inequalities on the part of the rich.

Borgna (2004) and Girella (2007) have discussed other types of feasts in greater detail than most authors. Borgna (2004:143–9) remarks on the apparent complexity of feasting patterns in a variety of Minoan contexts, from cemeteries, to caves, to peak sanctuaries, and in palace rooms that varied from small dark chambers to huge banquet halls. Most nonpalace feasts appear to have been sponsored by corporate ("communal") groups in which individual hosts are difficult to detect unless identified with individual house remains.

Borgna (2004:134,138) has investigated feasting in elite households where wine mixing kraters were used in contexts outside of the palaces. These events are viewed as quite competitive between rival elites with the aim of acquiring political authority largely via the creation or strengthening of ties with supporters. Halstead (2007:42) also interpreted faunal remains in terms of the use of meat gifts to create reciprocal debts and negotiate social relationships between households and probably lineages. The use of prestige items as gifts and the desire to maintain alliances for marriage purposes or to access resources makes good sense within this framework (Borgna 2004:135). These interpretations seem very reasonable to me. It is less clear that these events would be of a patron–client nature or that they were motivated by redistributive concerns, as postulated by Borgna. Reciprocal feasts of support or rivalry seem more likely. Some of these events apparently also entailed larger groups of participants outside the houses (as might be expected of promotional marriage or funeral feasts) because the number of cups recovered from some elite households greatly exceeded the number of people that could fit into the indoor spaces (135).

FUNERAL FEASTS

Exclusive participation certainly seems to have been important in certain contexts, such as some funerals and some palace events – a pattern established well before the Palatial period. Hitchcock (2011) views exclusive feasting events as having played a key role in the early creation of socioeconomic stratification involving the construction of monumental tombs as well as the lavish rituals associated with them (Figure 8.7). Hamilakis (1998:118) also views the controlled access to sacred space (as exemplified by funeral rituals and feasting) as a source of social power. Girella (2007:152–3) concurs but argues for some important changes over time from larger corporate-sponsored funerary feasts to more exclusive banqueting within rock-cut tombs, although one must wonder again if lower ranking participants were not also banqueting outside.

Although Early Palatial period cemetery feasts may have been characterized by limited access to tombs, there were huge numbers of cups and serving or consuming vessels in the cemetery areas (Hamilakis 1998:137) indicating yet again, a select number of high-ranking participants in privileged areas, as well as large numbers of lower ranking participants in open areas – the same organizational pattern that occurs in most ethnographic studies of chiefdoms and transegalitarian societies.

SANCTUARY FEASTS

Peak sanctuaries (Figure 8.8) exhibit similar large numbers of feasters drawn from regional communities, leading to the suggestion that feasting in these locations was primarily a communal event of aggregated rural people from the entire region who

8.8. The remains of a temple or shrine structure in the foreground at the important Minoan peak sanctuary of Youchtas. The largest religious feast of the year still takes place at this site, although the rituals are now held in the church in the background. (Photograph courtesy of Andonis Vasilakis)

gathered to enhance social solidarity and stability (Borgna 2004:137). Although solidarity within the group hosting these feasts may have been enhanced, the underlying motive of the organizers was more likely to have been the promotion of individual or possibly corporate benefits and political control, as discussed previously.

Given the writing and the prestige items found at peak sanctuaries, together with the limited access to building interiors at peak sanctuaries in the Palatial Period (Kyriakidis 2005:86–9,116,118), it would appear that elites were participants, and likely organizers or hosts, in feasts and rituals at peak sanctuary sites. Haggis (1999:78–81) argues that chiefly elites also organized peak sanctuary feasts and rituals in *Pre*palatial times as a means to spread their ideologies throughout the entire region, as a means of extracting surpluses and labor from people in the region, and as a means of affirming sociopolitical structures. Kyriakidis (2005:113–4) concurs, viewing peak sanctuaries from their beginnings as:

ideal semi-neutral places for higher-ranking persons of chiefdoms (such as chiefs, wealthier individuals, local spiritual leaders, and so on) to meet and create what Stanish calls 'pan regional elite alliances' with their equals from other villages . . . a second link between peers from different communities appears over the existing link between those belonging to the same community. . . . The potential political value of these sites, therefore, would have dated back to the very beginning of their ritual use. . . . They are bound to have been the arena for local political competition . . . nodes of tension, competition and mediation between agents, factions or towns.

This description bears a strong resemblance to characteristics of secret societies. Haggis goes further and suggests that Minoan peak sanctuaries were similar to pre-Sumerian (Ubaid) temples. Both were possibly similar to the roles of Buddhist/ Hindu temples of South and Southeast Asia described previously. In light of these observations, in-depth analyses of feasting remains at both peak and cave sanctuaries seem critical, including determining the costs of offerings, costs of construction and ritual paraphernalia, size of gatherings, and other important characteristics discussed in Chapter 1. Kyriakidis (2005:86–9,131–2) has already taken the first step in this direction by examining the number of cups and figurines (in the tens of thousands at some sites), which indicate large numbers of participants who gathered periodically, perhaps similar to the large feasts and ceremonies that secret societies periodically host to demonstrate their spirit power for the general populace and to indebt, or at least impress, them through patron–client types of feasts.

In addition to the occurrence of common cups and feasting or food preparation wares, Kyriakidis (2005) has also compiled the evidence for elite presences at peak sanctuary rituals, including fine wares, weapons, metal containers or other items (double axes, gold jewelry, and gold overlays), stone vessels, scripts, and other items. The investment in sophisticated architecture, leveling bedrock, and ritual paraphernalia of later Cretan peak sanctuaries, as well as the practice of human sacrifices (per Sakellaraki and Sapouna-Sakellaraki 1981) seem consistent with elite-sponsored events such as those that secret society members typically hold for a populace, as well as the more exclusive clandestine rituals and feasts held out of view of the populace. Despite the large number of common vessels and the large gathering grounds at peak sanctuaries, there is clearly more that transpired, especially from the Protopalatial period onward, than the often proposed communal rural events that were thought to be popularly organized (Marinatos 1993:116). In fact, Girella (2007:149–51,157) interprets peak, as well as cave, sanctuary feasts as being linked to the palaces and as serving to legitimize elite power in the context of divine displays and feasting gifts to the general populace – essentially, the patron–role model of feasting. On the other hand, Kyriakidis (2005:117,126) portrays peak sanctuaries as institutions independent of the palaces, cross-cutting political boundaries and adding another tier of complexity to the political organization of Crete, perhaps, I would again suggest, similar to the kind of political role that secret societies generally play together with their public feasts and displays of supernatural powers or connections. In this respect, they may have been a key component in the consolidation of political power in emerging chiefdoms, only to come into conflict with the aspirations of later palace elites trying to forge state types of political networks, after which peak sanctuaries were abandoned. In this fashion, peak and cave sanctuary feasts may have been created by elites to attract support for the political centers of the region. Some cave deposits have yielded hundreds of cooking vessels. In any case, it seems very probable that peak sanctuaries with large feasts, as well as cave sanctuaries, played critical roles in the evolution of political centralization in Minoan times and should provide very fertile ground for future research. In a similar vein, Steel (2004:177) has argued that the Bronze Age ceramic and faunal assemblages in sanctuaries on Cyprus represent ritual feasting by a religious hierarchy.

DISTRICT FEASTS

Elsewhere, in other contexts, excavations at the relatively small settlement of Tsoungiza indicate that it was a regional center for feasting (associated with a temple to Zeus) involving the sacrifice of cattle, with an estimated 1,400–2,100 pottery vessels in a single refuse dump, probably tying together the regional political structure and involving all individuals of importance from the surrounding area (Dabney et al. 2004). Such large-scale feasts at surprisingly small settlements may have rotated among settlements in the same tier of the political hierarchy (with Mycenae dominating the hierarchy), perhaps on a decadal or similar basis, much as the proto-chiefdom district feasts did in the Torajan areas discussed in the preceding chapter. Similar alliance feasts between rural communities in Classical Greek times have been reported by Gernet (1981; cited by Hamilakis 1999b:60).

In fact, with the collapse of the palaces on Crete in Late Minoan times, Borgna (2004:136,150–1) considers political organization to have reverted to the chiefdom level, with the locus of large feasts shifting from palaces to elite households involving more exclusive inner circles and more emphasis on individuals than on corporate socioeconomic groups, as tended to be the case on the Mycenaean mainland in Greece as well. Determining whether these political organizations constituted chiefdoms or states is beyond the limits of this analysis, but I have opted to include them in this discussion given their historical origins from palace-centered state organizations in the Minoan period.

From the perspective of identifying feasting behavior archaeologically, it is noteworthy that the Aegean area has provided multiple lines of evidence for feasts that enable archaeologists to arrive at reliable conclusions about feasting by employing "triangulation" based on several different kinds of evidence. These include the faunal analyses of Halstead and others; the ceramic analyses of numbers and types of vessels (e.g., *kraters* and drinking cups or bowls), including the identification of prestige wares, such as Kamares ware, used exclusively for feasting (Day and Wilson 1998:356); prestige or costly plant products such as olive oil, wine, and pomegranates (Hamilakis 1999a); architecture; feasting-associated prestige items; inscriptions; and graphic depictions. The largest feasts were organized by the palace and elites, including feasts for funerals, accessions, victories, and peak and cave worship. However, more exclusive feasts among elites also occurred within palaces and outside palaces (and undoubtedly among nonelite agriculturalists in villages, although these have not been recognized archaeologically). Temple feasts appear to have been new venues that were probably used to obtain food, services, and resources.

Mesopotamia and Egypt

A similar range of material indicators of feasting exists for early Mesopotamian states, which is probably not unexpected given the exchanges and interactions between these early centers and the states in the Aegean. However, with a few notable exceptions, feasting seems to have featured to a far less extent in Near Eastern archaeological interpretations than in the Aegean area, which seems surprising since historic accounts depict festivals occurring every day in Uruk with dancing in the streets and priestesses providing sex as a connection with divinity and as a lure to support temple feasts (Mitchell 2004:14,81). Bottéro (1994) has examined feasting in the Near East from more different angles than perhaps anyone else. Utilizing the historic accounts, he documents the use of feasts to seal contracts in a ritual fashion, to ratify alliances between states, to solidify support of those individuals critical to the rule of the king, to celebrate completion of large works, and as monthly honoring of family ancestors (at the new moon) with the entire society celebrating the king's ancestors. He also alludes to a fictional historical novel on Sumerian life in order to discuss feasts for marriages as well as to defend family or factional interests; to celebrate successes from which all concerned would benefit (e.g., battle victories such as depicted on the Standard of Ur; Pollock 2003:24); to take on political, administrative, or ritual roles; to involve people in new relationships; to obtain things or services from others; to publicly recognize undertakings or roles; and to have a good meal and discuss matters with friends. Most of these purposes are familiar from our discussions of transegalitarian and chiefdom feasting. It is interesting to note again the strong continuing emphasis on kinship organizations and ancestor worship, which also characterized Far Eastern and South American early states as well as later empires. Ur and Colantoni (2010):57,68) even portray household feasting rooms and storage facilities as the major feasting venues for the Bronze Age cities of northern Mesopotamian, although the largest of these households seem to have been attached to temples or other institutions, whereas there was no large-scale storage in the temples or palaces themselves. It is worth iterating that why strong kinship organizations should continue to be important, how their strength varied under changing political conditions, and how the tensions that must have arisen between such groups and central authorities were mitigated should provide good fodder for future analysis.

Surprisingly absent from Bottéro's overview is any mention of funeral feasts. Yet, these are documented in considerable detail for the very lavish Sumerian royal funerals represented in the archaeological record (Baadsgaard et al. 2011:9). Scaled-down versions of these funeral feasts probably also characterized lesser elite and even commoner funerals, especially given the existence of strong kinship groups featuring ancestor worship and elaborate marriage feasts. The tens or hundreds of crude bowls and food remains recovered from funeral contexts indicate a range of sizes of funeral feasts, as do the use of metal or stone vessels (vs. crude bowls) for funerals of the more important or wealthy people (Pollock 2003:26). Nor are work feasts or tribute feasts explicitly mentioned by Bottéro (but see Crawford 1981:110–1; Eyre 1987:25; Joffe 1998:304–5; Mitchell 2004:183–4; Neumann 2004). Joffe also provides an overview of the use of alcohol (in feasts) as an important element in the emergence of early states in Western Asia and elsewhere. He focuses primarily on its use in underwriting craft production; providing compensation for labor; establishing political power; fueling competition among temples, palaces, and corporations for dependents (clients, workers, and administrators); creating acceptance or acquiescence of elite ideologies and symbols; and altering gender roles. Geller (1992:24) also suggests that beer making in predynastic Egypt was "a dominant elite-building and maintaining industry" on the basis of a large brewery discovered at Hierkonopolis. Collon (1987) observed that early second-millennium Syrian seals appear to depict feasting beverages consumed in the context of intercity rivalry and were probably being used to establish alliances and attract supporters.

More than anyone else, Denise Schmandt-Besserat (2001) has drawn attention to the role of the monthly Sumerian feasts organized by the temples nominally held to honor various patron deities (and probably royal ancestors, real or fictitious). However, the underlying motive for organizing these temple feasts appears to have been the garnering of tribute from the populace. Feasting was the "leitmotif" of ancient Near Eastern art, and, at the state level, it provided a relatively painless, or at least more acceptable, fashion of contributing to the "common good" in the form of the state administration – perhaps not too dissimilar to the strategies used by big men in transegalitarian societies to get others to produce surpluses and hand control over to feast organizers for "good causes" such as defense, allies, or other forms of the common good.

In Sumeria, the king reviewed the major gifts brought in processions (Figure 8.3), and records were certainly kept, but the texts are silent concerning the consequences of failures to contribute to temple feasts or to contribute enough. These feasts were also ideal venues for promulgating the elite versions of myths and self-serving ideological concepts, especially among a slightly intoxicated citizenry. The elites did not fail to insist that mortals had been created by the gods in order to maintain the deities who required food, jewelry, and ritual paraphernalia – all, of course, managed by the royal entourage and temples. Mortals had to produce surpluses in order to give the gods what the gods purportedly needed (Schmandt-Besserat 2001:398). As noted earlier, for the inauguration of the temple of Ningirsu in Lagash, the king boasted of providing 30,800 kiloliters of barley, alone! Falconer (1994) showed that prestige animals were consumed almost exclusively at temples in smaller Mesopotamian temples located in relatively autonomous rural hamlets within the orbit of Bronze Age city states. This indicates that many of the same strategies were employed in rural areas as in the urban centers, albeit at a much reduced scale and with appropriate modifications. These temples may well have functioned like the rural village temples described at the beginning of this chapter.

At the major centers, the elaborate pageantry, music, drama, dance, games, sacred prostitution, ceremonialism, and impressive appearance of the king and the gods (descended to earth for the event) cannot have failed to attract many people (as the performances were meant to) or to impress them. Anyone who had pretensions for improving their sociopolitical standing could have used such opportunities to vaunt their abilities and success in public. Temple feasts were undoubtedly major social arenas for participants and spectators alike, just as they are today in India, Indonesia, and many other parts of the traditional world. And for such events, large courtyards or plazas were required to host the multitude of participants, although elites undoubtedly continued to feast inside. Thus, temple precincts generally encompassed large open areas, whether in Sumer, Egypt, South America, Mesoamerica, or other areas with early states.

Despite Bottéro's relatively pragmatic list of reasons for feasting, he concludes that feasts were essentially organized primarily to experience a collective life and establish a common identity (Bottéro 1994:13), thus placing the motivating force for feasting in the symbolic and ideological or phenomenological realm which I think is unrealistic. Pollock (2003:26,33) also views the driving force behind Sumerian feasting as symbolic and ideological, although her specific interpretation of it is diametrically opposed to Bottéro's. In place of creating a common identity, she proposes that feasts organized by the early states were "principally a means to distinguish exclusive contexts and styles of consumption" or to promote exclusivity. Bray (2003a:9) similarly emphasizes the use of feasts to promote class distinctions (or to differentiate members of social groups), although she also recognizes that other motivations may have played a role, such as the creation of debts and the acquisition of political power. Pollock's views of Sumerian feasts would seem to fit the description of diacritical feasts proposed by Dietler. However, as Schmandt-Besserat has shown, these were not really redistributive events (although redistribution did occur during them), but taxation events, with some "tax rebate" in the form of the alcohol and food consumed. It is again difficult to imagine such huge expenditures and efforts made simply for the purpose of distinguishing exclusive styles of consumption or to promote exclusivity. The fundamental logic of feasts is not to break social bonds but to create them, although by the nature of any social gathering, some people at some level will be excluded. Nevertheless, the creation of ingroup versus outgroup distinctions may certainly have been a secondary, even desired, effect.

South America

The archaeology of early South American states rivals the Aegean for its discussion of feasting in state-level societies. Although most attention has been devoted to occurrences in later empires, some discussion has also taken place about the role of feasting in emergent state societies. As noted in Chapter 1, there is a wide range of opinions concerning the level of sociopolitical integration of earlier prehistoric societies in the area. For heuristic purposes, I consider some centers from the Early Horizon (800–200 BCE) and the Early Intermediate Period (200 BCE–700 CE) as early state-level societies.

At the earlier end of the spectrum, the work of David Chicoine (2010, 2011) at the Early Horizon site of Huambacho in the Nepeña Valley of coastal Peru is probably the most detailed. This was a regional center that appears to have been subordinate to a larger contemporaneous site in the valley (Caylán), thus indicating a degree of complexity approaching statehood. Chicoine also views the feasting structures as reflecting institutionalized hierarchies of control, both in terms of their size, their spatial layouts, and the restricted occurrence of prestige items probably made by craft specialists. As Chicoine (2011:450) summarizes the situation, these societies "were complex and . . . socially stratified systems, marked by political hierarchies, centralized religious structures, labor specialization, and large-scale public projects." One of the more interesting aspects of his analysis is the identification of two large enclosed plazas (up to 6,000 square meters; see Figure 8.9) with decorated raised colonnaded benches (apparently for the seating of elites while lower ranking people gathered and ate below in the open), as well as a range of smaller sized colonnaded patios for smaller more exclusive feasts (Figure 8.10; Chicoine 2011:439–40). Similar large courtyards (for patron–client or tribute types of feasts with commoners) and smaller feasting rooms (for exclusive elite feasts) probably

8.9. At the Early Horizon district center of Huambacho, on the coastal plain of Peru, the large open courtyards, one of which is shown here, were used for periodic feasting by the general populace, while the colonnaded periphery was probably reserved for elite participants who benefited from the shade. (Photograph courtesy of David Chicoine)

8.10. Much smaller patio and room complexes at Huambacho also appear to have been used for feasting, but for smaller groups of participants probably consisting exclusively of elites. (Photograph courtesy of David Chicoine)

also characterized Late Intermediate centers such as the ramped palaces at Pachacamac. These examples are strikingly reminiscent of Minoan and Mycenaean large banquet halls, together with smaller rooms used for a variety of other feast sizes and compositions. Large temple courtyards for feasting and ceremonies also typify Sumerian, Egyptian, and Polynesian states and chiefdoms and perhaps many others. They certainly seem to be common at this level of political organization.

As in the Minoan case, archaeological attention has primarily focused on the large-scale feasts rather than on the smaller, more exclusive events, although Chicoine acknowledges that the smaller venues were probably for elite participants and served a variety of purposes, with smaller patio complexes ranging from a mere 44 square meters to 1,200 square meters. He views the large feasts in the plazas as serving a range of functions: diacritical, patron–role, community solidarity, work (construction), and tribute collection. Elites are portrayed as organizing these feasts to justify demands for producing the surpluses that were surrendered to them – reminiscent of Sumerian "taxation" feasts. To attract as many willing producers as possible, South American elites, like their Near Eastern counterparts, developed techniques to make feasts as emotionally, aesthetically, and gustitorily appealing as they could by providing food, drink, ritual, and entertainment, notably with music and undoubtedly drama and dance in a multisensorial spectacle, all experienced in impressive architectural settings that may well have been constructed to enhance acoustic, lighting, and even psychotropic effects (Chicoine 2011:447). John Rick (2008:32–4), in particular, has emphasized the use of such effects by elites to make their claims of access to alternate worlds believable via the manipulation and deception of participants in ritual events at Chavín de Huantar. It is telling that some ritual spaces could only have been occupied by very small numbers of individuals (Figure 7.12). To make credible the power of emerging authorities, fearsome half human/half animals were among the entities that confronted celebrants (Figure 7.13). Rick argues that these were highly competitive rituals that did not serve the common interest but rather the interests of the organizers. In a similar vein, Chicoine (2011:450) inferred that "Elites benefited from these events and manipulated the emotional aspects of feasts to intensify local production and muster greater material surpluses ... these transformations were part of the political strategies of community leaders competing for local support and authority. The success of these new elites was materialized in the capacity to sponsor various building projects."

Although it cannot be doubted that community solidarity was enhanced as a by-product of these feasts (Delibes and Barragán 2008:114) or that status differences were reaffirmed, it seems unlikely that these objectives by themselves would have provided sufficient reason for building such elaborate feasting structures or undertaking the complex organizational activities required to host feasts with thousands of people probably attending. Of particular interest in this time period is the adoption of maize and its predominant use in feasts, especially by political competitors who appear to have used maize beer to attract as many people to the events as possible and make them want to partake in, and contribute to, large feasts. Chicoine and others (Murra 1960; Burger and van der Merwe 1990; Gummerman 1994; see also Clark and Blake 1994:25 for similar observations in Mesoamerica) emphasize that the use of maize was primarily as a prestige food, and its primary use was for brewing *chicha*, presumably undertaken on a relatively large scale to improve the allure of feasts. The use of maize beer (either provided at a limited scale to elites or on a larger scale to all adult feast participants) may have played a large role in motivating the sociopolitical and material transformations that characterize the changes from the Initial Period to the Early Horizon on the coast.

In the Early Intermediate Period, a number of local states established or extended their hegemony. One of the most notable of these states was centered on the coast at Moche, and George Gummerman IV has perhaps done the most detailed analysis of feasting practices associated with this polity. In a series of conference papers, publications, and presentations, Gummerman (1994, 2004, 2010) has focused on the importance of funerary feasts and, within these, the importance of maize. At the site of El Brujo, he recovered a large kitchen with several massive hearths (two more than 4 meters long) and many large storage jars on a funerary platform adjacent to two cemeteries with rich burials indicating funerary feasting. How much of the food that was prepared was destined to accompany the defunct person and how much was destined for consumption by participants in the funerary feast is difficult to determine. However, Gummerman emphasizes that, except for rulers, funerary rituals were surprisingly limited in scale, probably on the scale of corporate kin-based participants. Even at the capital, Moche, he notes that there is no clear evidence of much large-scale feasting or storage.

Gummerman similarly concluded that evidence of work party feasts at Moche sites indicates small-scale events such as might be hosted by a household or lineage, a far cry from the massive work feasts organized by the Incan empire. Even evidence for feasts in elite compounds (postulated to have been held to reward agricultural laborers) are inferred to have been small on the basis of the associated room sizes. However, as repeatedly pointed out, ethnographically, interior rooms are generally only for the high-ranking participants of feasts, with lower ranking members feasting outside and often eating off of perishable dishes such as large leaves or woven fronds. On the basis of archaeological feasting evidence, Gummerman infers a relatively decentralized political structure with extended households and lineages as the most significant socioeconomic and political factions in Moche society. Given the widespread importance of funerary feasting among other early states and chiefdoms, or even transegalitarian societies and the occurrence of large feasts in most of these societies, the small scale claimed for Moche feasting seems somewhat aberrant. One wonders if this is not perhaps due to sampling and recovery biases (a caveat expressed by Gummerman) or even obliviousness to the significance of feasting remains on the part of earlier excavators. In contrast to Gummerman's interpretations, Delibes and Barragán (2008:106,112,114–5) describe "intense activity related to the celebration of fiestas and rituals" for elite funerals in the Mochica site of San José de Moro. Without estimating the sizes of groups, they write of large-scale competitive preparations and consumption of *chicha* at the site by many elite people from different settlements of the region. Gummerman's conclusions also contrast markedly with Gero's study of feasting at other Early Intermediate Period sites such as Queyash Alto in the highlands, where she sees high degrees of political competition leading to a more ranked society and the consolidation of power in the hands of fewer individuals (cited in Renfrew & Bahn 1996:208). On the other hand, if Gummerman's interpretation does prove to be robust (as perhaps indicated by the work of Ur and Colantoni [2010] in Mesopotamia), this would add a new dimension to our models of the structural variability of early states.

Mesoamerica

Despite some lavish depictions of banquets and elaborate ritual spectacles among the Maya and other Mesoamerican groups, comparatively little archaeological analysis has focused on feasting among early, or simple, states in Mesoamerica. This is all the more surprising since Peten polychromes appear to have been the equivalent of the fine china dinner sets of modern Industrial households, which no self-respecting household would be without (LeCount 2001:947). We can probably assume that periodic feasts were held to honor the kings and queens buried within Temples I–V in Tikal, as well as in the temples at Palenque and other sites, but no study of feasting behavior has been undertaken in these contexts that I know of. Lisa LeCount (2001) has probably undertaken the most comprehensive discussion of feasting in Maya states to date. Based in part on early Spanish accounts, she distinguishes between elite and commoner feasts as well as private versus public, small-scale versus large-scale, and inclusive versus exclusive feasts (the latter being viewed as diacritical in nature; LeCount 2001). Following Brumfiel's and Randsborg (1982:135) lead, she also suggests that in competitive political situations (such as Blanton's network-based political economies), consumption of prestige goods and foods should flourish, whereas in more placid political milieux (such as Blanton's corporate political organizations), ostentatious displays and feasts should be more subdued. The widespread distribution of feasting wares both spatially and economically in households at Xunantunich and elsewhere (LeCount 2001, Gonlin 1994) would seem to imply a more network-oriented feasting and political organization perhaps similar to that proposed for Southeast Asia and other areas.

In addition, LeCount (2001:937) thinks that festival feasting to celebrate harvests, solstices, or other events with special foods were a type of diacritical feast, presumably because it helped to establish local or polity identities and inclusiveness while at the same time displaying and celebrating elite prerogatives. As in previous examples, one must wonder exactly how the large public festivals were funded and whether there were not ulterior motives for organizing large feasts, such as the collection of tribute or goods to run the administrative components of early states, as may have been the case especially at harvest festivals, year-end ceremonies celebrating the departure of Kukulcan, and at annual rain ceremonies dedicated to Chac and Itzamna (943–4). But little is known about these aspects of feasting in Maya states, and we must wonder whether there were any dominant diacritical motives behind either public or private feasts. Certainly, the widespread distribution of the Peten polychromes used in feasting seems inconsistent with diacritical motives for hosting feasts but make good sense in terms of establishing reciprocal political alliances.

It is clear from Landa's sixteenth-century accounts that elites held feasts in which return payments for food and gifts by guests was mandatory. M. Smith et al. (2003:246), following work by Pohl (1998, 1999, 2003), view the elaborate polychrome vessels in the Mixteca-Puebla Postclassic city states as having been used in feasts to create or maintain alliances between simple state polities, probably similar to Landa's descriptions. There is no reason to believe the situation was much different during Classic times. There were also more open, large-scale, inclusive feasts that did not involve the obligatory return of gifts by guests (except probably for some specially invited individuals). LeCount interprets these, respectively, as competitive and diacritical in nature. Drinking cacao and/or *chicha*, and eating meat (a rare item in daily foods) were key components of ethnohistoric feasts. Hendon (2003:225–7) seems to have evidence of such feasting in the remains at Classic period Copan as well as small-scale feasting in rural households, although, here again, she imputes the motive behind such feasts as attempts by elites to define themselves by excluding commoners (207).

One of the most unusual occurrences of feasting remains among these early states were the food remains associated with Maya ball courts (Figure 8.11), which illustrates the remarkably versatile nature of feasts in the use of pretexts. As reported by J. Fox (1996:484,493), the use of ball game competitions between factions or villages was a widespread context for competitive displays including feasting, competitive gift exchanges, and displays involving slaves, jewelry, elaborate ritual clothing, and expensive exotic paraphernalia. Although the nominal

8.11. Ball courts such as this example at Mixco Viejo (Guatemala) were important feasting sites in Mesoamerica. They combined sports, betting, ostentatious displays of wealth, and sometimes human sacrifices in a unique constellation of co-occurring feasting activities. It would seem that the eating was as competitive as the sports. (Photograph by B. Hayden)

justification for holding these events may have been to celebrate harvests and ensure good future crops, the activities involved clearly indicate that political gamesmanship was the underlying motive: to wit, displays of power, success, and triumphs that were meant to impress potential or current allies, dissuade rivals, and create indebted relationships in volatile political contexts. Warren Hill (1999; Hill and Clark 2001) has dealt with this topic in even greater detail and from the broader overall perspective of competitive sports, including the Maya ball game and the modern Olympics. In his view, competitive sports bear many similarities to feasting as an aggrandizer strategy. He points out that elites, by their very nature, are high-roller high-risk takers who create large debts, gamble, host feasts, and risk everything in waging wars. Competitive sports can combine all of these features, even to the extent of being a means to acquire territory or losing lives. Although this is a fascinating field to explore, it would take us far away from our primary focus on feasting. However, in cases like the Maya ball game, feasting and competitive sports intersect and occur as part of the same event. Hill (1999) has documented the use of competitive sports and feasting beginning in the Early Formative of the Chiapas coastal region, thus extending this strategy or tactic back to early chiefdom levels of organization. Other chiefdoms, like the Kirghiz of Afghanistan, sometimes have highly competitive but loosely organized sports (Nairn 1981). However, in general, it may be that organized competitive intercommunity sports became particularly prominent with the development of early states. Other competitive sports events, such as the original Classic Olympic games, may have featured prominent feasting as well. Aside from these accounts, there is also evidence for state-level feasting in some Mayan caves (Moyes, 2013), possibly indicating feasts held by secret societies.

SUMMARY OF SIMPLE STATES

Early, simple states developed from chiefly political organizations and shared a great deal in common with chiefdoms, both in terms of politics and feasting dynamics. Both chiefdoms and early states were probably ethnically uniform and did not face the challenges of integrating linguistically and culturally diverse factions into a single political organization. If ostentation is any barometer of political organizations based on personal relationships involving feasting (vs. polit-ical power based on control of resources), then relationship-based states may have been surprisingly common in both chiefdoms and early states. Changes in emphasis and new developments included the greater use of coercion; the expanded impor-tance of polity-wide celebrations held in honor of rulers' accomplishments, ancestors, or life stages (sometimes including competitive sports events); and an expanded and institutionalized use of temple festivals for tribute collection. These develop-ments are all amenable to archaeological detection, especially with epigraphic commemorations. There appear to have been five fundamental types of feasts in early states: (1) royal events, (2) regular temple tribute and other revenue-generating feasts, (3) state corvée work, (4) political network support, and (5) corporate kinship and possibly guild events (Scullard 1981:122).

Kinship-based feasts may have varied in strength under changing degrees of political centralization, and, like royal celebrations, they should be amenable to agent-based analyses if feasting remains can be identified with specific households. The more exclusive elite gatherings for intimate political support may also be susceptible to detection and agency analysis at the household level. Multiple lines of evidence can be brought to bear on these issues using "triangulation" techniques. These include epigraphy and iconography; ceramic, stone, and metallic serving wares; special architectural, storage, and cooking features; faunal and floral remains; human remains and burial materials; prestige items; and special locations (especially caves, mountain peaks, cemeteries, temples, palaces, and sports facili-ties). Of particular interest are widespread occurrences of large gathering areas (courtyards, plazas, or halls) often associated with temples or palaces. Alcoholic beverages like beer also frequently feature as a major element in attracting people to feasts for work, alliances, or tribute collection.

There is a tendency among archaeologists to interpret the appearance of exclu-sive feasting facilities (special rooms and wares) as evidence of a fundamental shift from communal to more individual or exclusive commensal behavior. This theme appears when dealing with the transition from Megalithic to Bronze Age burials and feasting, as well as in early versus later states in the Andean area and in the Aegean. However, on the basis of ethnoarchaeological research (Chapters 6 and 7), it would appear that there have always been small (c. 10–20 people) exclusive feasts involving the highest ranking individuals of communities, whether transegalitarian or more complex. And, at larger feasts, privileged guests and hosts have probably always segregated themselves (usually eating inside hosts' houses) from the lower ranking participants (usually eating outside houses). Thus, the appearance of what seem to be exclusive elite feasting facilities and wares probably simply reflects the increasing wealth of elites in more complex societies that enabled them to build special rooms for their feasting cronies and buy specialty wares to serve them with while the majority of participants ate and drank in open venues with more common, often perishable, wares. Thus, the material visibility of these feasts has probably varied greatly as a consequence of the wealth available for such purposes. I doubt that there was any major change in feasting dynamics from inclusive to exclusive participation as frequently postulated.

Similarly, the common notion that early state feasts were often organized for the primary purpose of distinguishing elite classes from the hoi polloi is, I think, a misrepresentation of the fundamental driving forces behind the exorbitant expenditures for many feasts. Certainly, hosting the major state feasts was prompted by a number of mutually reinforcing factors or motives, but diacritical concerns seem to pale in comparison to the other more practical motives and benefits, such as tribute collection.

One of the more intriguing problems of early states is the nature of the dialectic between centralized political power and decentralized corporate kinship power as reflected in the relative magnitude of feasts sponsored by kinship versus royal groups. Another interesting issue involves the near universal central importance of temples in political organizations. Temples, of course, are highly visible archaeologically, and understanding the reasons for investing huge amounts of resources in their construction and establishing the practical benefits that elites derived from promulgating these institutions is central to understanding the nature of early states. There are clearly precedents among chiefdoms and even transegalitarian societies, but early state temples seem to develop new levels of entanglements involving attempts to attract the populace to events, extracting surpluses as tribute, developing arable resources as investments, charging interest on loans, displaying sociopolitical rank and control, and as a liaison or monitor of the elites for local affairs. Further exponential escalation of the state use of temples and administrative costs continued with the emergence of empires with new problems of social integration to solve, issues to which we now turn.

EMPIRES

Although written and graphic accounts from early simple states often provide tantalizing titbits of information about feasting, the art of writing was usually in a fairly rudimentary state of development, and one is left with snippets of allusions even to the most important events, although written accounts from later written epics like *The Iliad* or from medieval kingdoms sometimes do provide fairly detailed feasting descriptions. With the emergence of empires and their need for keeping accounts, documents, and records of important events, writing and visual depictions of events tended to become much more elaborate (with some exceptions, such as the Inca and Teotihuacan empires, which left no written records although they did use other accounting and recording techniques). In fact, the textual material from some of these empires, such as the Roman, Shang, and later empires is often overwhelming, and I only briefly touch on some of the more salient aspects here. With the emergence of empires, the field of feasting simply becomes too vast to deal with in any thorough fashion for an analysis such as this one. Roman food and dining alone form the focus of numerous books and articles. However, there are some remarkable historical accounts from empires that should at least be mentioned in passing, as well as a few archaeological analyses that I would like to draw attention to. Thus, this discussion will be short but hopefully illustrative of some of the changes in feasting behavior that occur with the emergence of empires. As stated at the beginning of this chapter, empires operate at new scales of political and administrative organization. They have new problems of integrating multiethnic groups and dealing with urban anomie and unruly behavior/social unrest. Thus, we might well expect new developments in feasting as well.

The Mediterranean Empires

One of the most obvious developments is in the sheer opulence of the elite feasts and the sheer magnitude of the major events open to the public, such as the Roman "triumphs." An account of a more intimate elite marriage feast from third-century BCE Macedonia hosted by Caranus (a relation of a companion of Alexander the Great) provides a taste of the new levels of wealth and power that could be attained in empires and subsequently used in feasting:

Caranus celebrated his marriage with a banquet at which the number of men invited to gather was twenty; no sooner had they taken their places on the couches, than they were presented with silver cups, one for each, to keep as their own. Each guest had been crowned before he entered with a gold tiara. And after they had emptied their cups, they were each given a bronze platter containing a loaf as wide as the platter; also chickens and ducks, and ring doves too, and a goose and an abundance of such viands piled high; and each guest took his portion, platter and all, and distributed among the slaves who stood behind him. Following which came a second platter of silver, on which again lay a huge loaf, and geese, hares, young goats and curiously moulded cakes besides, pigeons, turtledoves, partridges and other fowl in plenty. This also they presented to the slaves, and when they had had enough food they washed their hands. Then numerous chaplets were brought in, made of all kinds of flowers, and in addition gold tiaras, equal in weight to the first chaplet. Then they proceeded to drinking toasts and when they had at last pleasantly taken leave of all sobriety, there entered flute girls and singers and some Rhodian Sambuca players. The girls looked quite naked, but some said they had on tunics. Then came in other girls carrying each two jars fastened together with a gold band and containing perfume; one jar was silver, the other gold, and held half a pint. These also they gave to each guest. After that there was brought in a fortune rather than a dinner, namely a silver platter gilded all over to no little thickness, and large enough to hold a whole roast pig – a big one too – which lay on its back upon it. Roasted inside it were thrushes, ducks and warblers in unlimited number, peas puree poured over eggs, oysters and scallops; all of which towering high, was presented to each guest, platters and all. After this they drank, and then received a kid, piping hot, again upon a platter as large as the last, with spoons of gold. Caranus then ordered baskets and bread racks made of plaited ivory strips to be given the guests to contain their gifts. Then more crowns again, and a double jar of gold and silver containing perfume, equal in weight to the first. Then trooped in men, Ithyphallic dancers, clowns and some naked female jugglers who performed tumbling acts among swords and blew fire from their mouths. After they had finished their attention was given to a warm and almost neat drink of three wines and very large gold cups were given each guest. After this draught they were all presented with crystal platters about two cubits in diameter, lying in a silver receptacle and full of a collection of all kinds of baked fish. Then they washed their hands again and put on crowns, again receiving gold tiaras twice the size of the former ones, and another double jar of perfume.

They then each drank a six-pint bowl of Thasian wine and after this a chorus of one hundred entered singing tunefully a wedding hymn (for this was a marriage feast); then came in dancing girls, some attired as Nereids, others as Nymphs. They then threw open the room, which had been curtained all about with white linen, and when this curtain was drawn back it disclosed Cupids, Dianas, Pans and Hermae holding lights in silver brackets. While admiring this artistic device, boars were served to each guest, on silver platters rimmed with gold; they were skewered with silver spears. The slaves then stuffed their happy baskets full until the customary signal for concluding the banquet was sounded on the trumpet. After more drinking in small cups there came in the concluding courses; that is dessert in ivory baskets, and flat cakes of every variety. Then they arose and took leave, quite sober – the gods be their witness! – because they were apprehensive for the safety of the wealth they took with them. They had carried away a fortune from Caranus's banquet and were now looking for houses, or lands, or slaves to buy. (Hippolochus: Athenaeus *Deipnosophistae* IV.128; in Bullitt 1969:56–8)

Other descriptions of feasts include Trimalchio's feast, in which live birds flew out of the stomach of a roasted boar and an astrological globe provided foods related to each sign of the zodiac (J. Renfrew 2004:47–52). The banquet described by the poet Martial featured a pool that served as the table on which dishes floated (Capasso 2005:36). These accounts pale, however, in comparison to Caranus's wedding feast and the feast given by Cleopatra, said to be the most expensive event of all time (Renfrew 2004:47). As described by Lucan, her banqueting hall was a jewel in itself with gold plating and precious stones on the ceiling, pillars of agate, walls of marble, an onyx floor, doors of tinted tortoise shell and emeralds framed by ebony posts. The couches were jewel-studded with coverlets of purple embroidered in gold and red cochineal. The tables were supported by gleaming elephant tusks. The wine goblets were of jasper, and the servers represented a variety of races. The guests poured cinnamon and cardamom oils on their hair and washed their hands from ewers of rock crystal. Cleopatra was weighed down by necklaces of pearls, although not so much that her white breasts could not be observed through her diaphanous silk clothes. Caesar had never seen anything as impressive. She offered him every kind of flesh, fowl, and fish available, and every delicacy, including the finest aged wines, almost certainly to impress him with her wealth, her power, and her desirability as a political and amorous ally (Graves 1957: Book X). The fate of her empire hung on her ability to establish a close relationship with Caesar. Any diacritical effects must have been an afterthought, if they even entered her thoughts at all. As can be seen from these accounts, high cuisine certainly constituted a major feature of elite feasting in empires and most likely in early states as well, if not in chiefdom societies.

The development of elite cuisines has been a preoccupation of a number of authors (Bray 2003b; M. Smith et al. 2003:245; Isaakidou 2007; Hastorf 2008), especially as diacritical elements of feasts. The Romans (like the medieval French potentates) even published cookbooks and etiquette books on how to prepare foods and host important feasts (e.g., Edwards 1984; and Athenaeus' *Deipnosophistae*; see also Scully 1986). However, as indicated earlier, I think it is more parsimonious simply to view distinctive elite cuisines as natural outgrowths of competitive feasting and attempts to indebt individuals by constantly raising the culinary bar as well as the lavishness of gifts. From Hippolochus's description, it is difficult to imagine that Caranus went to such great effort and expense simply to diacritically distinguish himself and his friends from the hoi polloi. It seems much more likely to me that the goal of the lavishness of this feast was to forge strong political alliances with his twenty guests, putting them in his debt and obtaining their support for future undertakings or enterprises. Can there be any doubt that the fate of participating in the rule over entire empires could justify the expense of such feasts? Julius Caesar, like other Roman leaders, held his triumph celebrations and feasts to win the support of the key decision makers (the Senate), the troops, and the general populace (Scullard 1981:213–8), all part of a strategy to consolidate his hold on political power. Fine cuisine was simply one of the useful features of this strategy. It was also a feature of the Roman *convivia* and *symposia* – essentially private dinners or drinking parties among close associates, sometimes including those from lower social levels, presumably to assess their suitability for promotion to higher level roles. Like the more ostentatious events, and like contemporary Western dinner parties, these Roman events were probably hosted to solidify social, political, and economic support networks.

In terms of more routine feasts, the Romans celebrated Saturnalia and the Kalends with gifts and feasting among family and friends, at least for the elites and their imitators and perhaps for all classes. There were Saturnalia feasts in all communities and in the countryside, with local feasts for senators and knights that were open to the local citizens (Scullard 1981:205–7). Neighbors and friends continued to be fêted following the Saturnalia at the Compitalia feasts with pig sacrifices, street dancing, games, and general jollity (59). Class distinctions were supposed to be minimized or even dissolved at the Saturnalia, with mock kings creating social chaos (Scullard 1981; Miles 1990:165–9), apparently in attempts to reduce tensions and unrest due to the complex ethnic composition and inequalities of most empires. A wide range of temples were devoted to different deities to accommodate different ethnic groups, a characteristic of many empires. Other institutions were established that often cross-cut ethnic differences. These included the sports organizations, circuses or coliseum spectacles, and many of the mystery cults of the Roman era with their celebratory feasts, including the early Christian "love feast." The mystery cults, in particular, provided many benefits to their members and helped to consolidate the imperial social fabric which, by many accounts, was often frayed, if not torn. Other divisions in Roman society and politics were represented by major feasts such as the thirty *curia* with their assembly halls for feasting on holy days (Scullard 1981:73). Guilds, too, probably hosted feasts (122) to maintain a united front for prospective apprentices and clients. Other professions, such as the military, also hosted feasts for legion deities (Henig 1982:218).

At the family level, ancestral or household deity (*Lares*) feasts were often held at gravesides or around the house (MacMullen 1981:39; Henig 1982:220; Scullard 1981:74–5). However, for larger festive gatherings (from groups of nine to large crowds), many houses did not have adequate facilities. Thus, in order to host parties and cement relationships with friends or others, temples were frequently used. Family and kin who wanted to celebrate various events could do so in the presence of the gods and in cultured, agreeable settings. In *lectisternia* celebrations, the icon of the god was brought out from the temple and laid on a dining couch beside the celebrants while suitable sacrifices, music, surroundings, and rituals were provided. The god was considered as an honored guest or even the host of the feast being held in his or her house (MacMullen 1981). Invitations were sent out by priests in the name of the deity, e.g., "Dionysius asks you to dine . . ." The temple itself was a repository of culture, not only in art and architecture, but also housing antiquities, aviaries, zoological parks, and presenting public lectures, features not found elsewhere in most communities. There were kitchens, animal pens for the sacrifices, and dining rooms (up to twenty-five separate rooms) or tents around the sacral areas, including inns for those who remained overnight. There were butchers, bakers, chefs, sommeliers, cupbearers, dancers, and musicians available to serve the feasting parties. Meat and a surfeit of wine with excessive indulgence characterized such sacred feasts – features not typical of normal meals. Temple priests obtained a share of all the animals sacrificed at the temple altars and were able to sell any excess. Indeed, the great bulk of meat eaten in the Roman Empire was probably consumed at temple feasts. It should therefore not come as a surprise to learn that considerable deposits of animal bones have been reported from a number of Roman temple excavations (MacMullen 1981:39–41). These temple feasts must have been costly affairs and were likely hosted by those who were relatively well off in Roman society to establish or cement important social and political relationships, as with other networking feasts.

The devotees of particular temples also hosted feasts at the temples, and the priests hosted annual citywide celebrations with banquets open to all, undoubtedly to promote the miracles that occurred at the temples and to promote the advantages of feasting at their temples (MacMullen 1981:47), just as a modern-day hotel promoter might advertise the benefits of staying at his establishment rather than a competitor's. Such displays also recall the yearly feasts and displays hosted by many secret societies even in transegalitarian and chiefdom societies. The temples in Roman times thus seem to have been more economic institutions (which had to obtain licenses from the government) than religious ones.

The Near East

In some instances, Roman poets and historians have left graphic accounts of the most outstanding examples of elite and public feasts; however, there appears to have been minimal attention devoted to other levels and kinds of feasting that undoubtedly took place. In addition, classical archaeologists dealing with empires seem to have focused heavily on monumental constructions, temples, documents, and prestige items rather than documenting feasting remains in much detail. This situation is not much different when dealing with Near Eastern empires. However, Bottéro (1994:11) does refer to a "Pantaguelesque" feast given by the Assyrian emperor Assurnasirpal II in 870 BCE for all his support personnel, including everyone who helped restore his capital, Kalhu (Nimrud) and all the inhabitants of that city: 69,574 people in all, as commemorated on a stela itemizing the dizzying array of food served, including 300 oxen, 1,000 calves, 15,000 sheep, 1,000 lambs, 500 deer, 500 gazelles, 10,000 eggs, 10,000 loaves of bread, 10,000 jars of beer, 10,000 skins of wine, 10,000 measures of chick peas, and much more (Schmandt-Besserat 2001:398) – perhaps the largest feast of the ancient world, and undoubtedly meant, like Egyptian pyramids and modern Olympic games, to advertise the host's political power and successes in order to attract workers, allies, supporters, and trade partners. Intercity feasting rivalries, presumably to establish trade and military alliances and to attract support from other polities, also seem to have been depicted on Syrian seals of the early second millennium BCE, especially featuring beverages (presumably beer; Teissier 1984:63–4, nos. 352–9; Collon 1987:27).

Pinnock (2004:19) reports a New Year's Festival in Neo Babylonian times that was in preparation for the sacred marriage between the king and a goddess or her representative. This may have been similarly used to promote the desirability of partnerships with the empire as well as another opportunity to demand resources from the populace. And, as in earlier states, there were also special feasts to inaugurate new buildings, presumably either work-based feasts to compensate laborers, but probably also promotional feasts hosted to vaunt the power of the polity elites and to have the undertaking officially recognized or sanctioned, much as feasts to install new house features functioned in transegalitarian societies (Chapter 6).

The use of beer and bread to attract and compensate workers on imperial construction or other projects seems fairly widespread in the Near East, from Mesopotamia to Dynastic Egypt, where large complexes with two-story ovens used in the production of large quantities of beer and bread have been unearthed (H. Crawford 1981:110–1; Eyre 1987:25; Joffe 1998:304–5). This appears to extend back into predynastic (early state) times, when fermented beer and wine are viewed as predominantly an "elite-building and maintaining industry" (Geller 1992:24). As in other empires, evidence of more intimate elite feasts continues to exist, probably involving the core members of political factions or kinship groups (Joffe 1998:304).

South America

Together with the eastern Mediterranean, the empires of the Andes have attracted especially intense archaeological investigations into feasting (see Kaulicke, 2005, Kaulicke and Dillehay, 2005, and Rosenfeld, 2012 for overviews), and much of the attention has focused on the role of *chicha* beer in imperial dynamics. Following Murra (1960), Craig Morris (1979, 1988) was perhaps the strongest early archaeological advocate to draw attention to the critical role that maize and *chicha* played in running pre-Hispanic empires like the Incan state. Morris documented this aspect archaeologically at Huánuco Pampa, an Incan district administrative center. Morris

(1979, 1988) emphasized the high prestige of maize *chicha* and also the inflated value of gifts from the Inca or his representatives versus the low value attributed to the obligatory "gifts" in return from subjects. Morris (1979) cites the 1556 testimony from Cristóbal Payco, a coastal chief, to the effect that "the main reason that the people obey their leaders here, is through the custom that they [the leaders] have to give the people drink . . . and if they do not oblige by giving the people drink neither will the people plant their crops for them." This seems to follow the tradition of using beer to obtain labor, feasting tribute, and goods for administrative or elite purposes in the early South American states discussed previously, as well as similar uses of beer in early Near Eastern states and empires.

Jennings (2005) and others have continued the study of maize beer production and consumption in the running of the Incan state. As Jennings (2005:243) summarizes the situation, "the Inca was able not only to fulfill his reciprocal duties for the labor service rendered to the state but also to reaffirm his position of power by putting laborers in his debt by the sheer quantity of food and *chichi* that he provided." In addition, the Inca provided huge quantities of food and *chicha* to guests at various feasts throughout the year – on average about 12 liters of *chicha* per person. One can only surmise that the guests were other elites or people of power whom the Inca wanted to put in his debt or with whom he wanted to establish alliances, thereby consolidating his power base. As Morris (1979:32) expressed it, the Inca had to entertain and provide *chicha* to state officials or workers. "It was central to keeping his armies on the move, preventing revolt, and maintaining the storehouse filled. Feasting and *chicha* were critical elements in keeping the Incan state functioning."

The same political strategy has been detected in other, pre-Incan, Andean empires. Maize was the economic foundation of the Huari empire (beginning c. 800 CE), and archaeologists have noted an overall good correlation between intensive maize agriculture and sociopolitical complexity (Finucane 2009:535). Large Huari breweries, with capacities of up to 1,800 liters, have been documented archaeologically (Joffe 1998:308; Moseley et al. 2005). In addition to the positive inducements to acquiesce to imperial rule that feasting and *chicha* consumption provided, there were also imperial strategies of dividing and relocating ethnic groups in order to curtail political opposition. However, as appears to have been the case in early states, no concerted effort seems to have been made to dismantle the strong kinship-based corporate groups that could form important factions within the empire and challenge the rule of emperors. Among others, Hastorf (2003) and George Lau (2002) have documented the persistent importance of ancestor worship into the Huari empire, at least among elites, and even up until the present among peasant land-holding groups (see also Rosenfeld 2012:151,157). Corporate kinship ancestral cults involved enormous expenditures of wealth for burials, funeral feasts, and recurring memorial feasts focused on key kinship figures. However, Lau does note a change in scale of ancestor feasts over time, perhaps corresponding to the broadly based use of clan ancestors by chiefs in early periods versus the more restricted use of ancestors by later elites. Rankin and Escherick (1990:317) document relative increases in lineage landholdings, and presumably power, during times of devolving state power in Imperial China, and this provides at least one possible explanatory model for changes over time in the scale of Andean corporate kinship feasting displays.

Farther north, on the coast, Shimada et al. (2004) envision very large-scale public feasting and consumption of *chicha* in plazas associated with the burials of the highest ranking elites during the Middle Sicán expansion (c. 900 CE), which overtook earlier more localized states like Moche. Perhaps these large-scale memorial events represent deified imperial ancestral worship, not unlike the pyramid complexes of the Egyptian pharaohs and Maya temples. As before, elites appear to have continued the tradition of using small-scale, more intimate feasts to secure local support for labor and military requirements (Joffe 1998:308) and to establish reciprocal support with other elites in the ambiance of more secluded patios, as interpreted by Cook and Glowacki for Huari rulers (2003:195). Rosenfeld (2012:151,157) documents funerary feasts within lineage compounds at Conchopata, a second- or third-tier Huari settlement about 10 kilometers from Huari. She interprets these as diacritical feasts; however, given the strong pattern of using funerary feasts to consolidate alliances, this seems unlikely. On the other hand, she also documents the use of large patios (c. 40 × 60 meters) for larger scale feasting, viewed as patron-role in function. This seems more likely, although simple work feasts or tribute feasts should also be considered. A more provocative conclusion is that, in contrast to the Inca practice, the Huari imperial elite probably did not directly finance these larger feasts, but they continued to be organized and underwritten by local elites. In contrast, Cook and Glowacki emphasize the use of beer to obtain corvée labor (as reflected in the abundance of mass-produced bowls) and they propose this as a fundamental element in the imperial Huari expansion, one that was effectively copied by the Inca who replaced the Huari political apparatus. Huari elites may have emphasized the use of feasting to establish patron–client relationships in the form of work feasts, with the elites providing beer in exchange for labor and goods. As an aside, Cook and Glowacki lament the limited information on feasting from historic documents and most Incan archaeology.

Goldstein (2003) is one of the few to deal with feasting in the Tiwanaku empire, which was a major rival of the Huari empire. He extends earlier interpretations on the importance of maize to claim that the Tiwanaku expansion was associated with a new and greater emphasis on the drinking of *chicha*. In fact, he suggests that the Tiwanaku expansion was driven by a "mania for maize beer" (144). Goldstein uses isotopes to show that before Tiwanaku influence on the coast, maize only made up 3–18 percent of the diet, whereas with Tiwanaku control, 46–76 percent of the diet consisted of maize or maize products like beer (163). Apparently, the widespread distribution of *chicha*, together with newly introduced feasting practices, placed people in such a blissful state that they readily accepted Tiwanaku rule without putting up much resistance! Thus, the empire spread in the wake of bliss without the need to conquer other polities. If this seems somewhat difficult to swallow, the claim that chiefly feasts (in earlier and imperial periods) were driven by the desire to empower elites with symbolic capital (146) is equally difficult. That the state-level feasts that Goldstein discusses were used primarily to establish patron–client relationships and debts seems more credible. The pattern of feasting that he argues spread with the Tiwanaku polity (little large-scale imperial-based feasting, but considerable feasting at the corporate and household levels) is certainly interesting and seems to be quite different from the large-scale imperial works and celebratory feasts of the Huari and Inca but reminiscent of Gummerman's interpretation of Moche political organization. One might even conceive of Tiwanaku as a confederation of independent polities or kin groups allied for the main purpose of stopping Huari expansion. In fact, D'Altroy (2001) and Hastorf (2001) have concluded that in Wanka II times, prior to the Incan expansion, the polities on the central coast of Peru were composed of small-scale competing political units where feasting occurred mainly in elite households. With the Incan incursions into the area, there was an abrupt and staggering "leap of scale," with the new imperial Incan center hosting feasts for "great throngs of people" in "vast open plazas" approaching 17 hectares in size (Figure 8.12).

Tamara Bray (2003b) also emphasizes the critical role of maize in consolidating political power, with maize and meat constituting highly esteemed "food of the gods" that was consumed on special occasions rather than for quotidian meals. She focuses on the development of a fine cuisine among the Incan elite, viewing its development as due to the desire to establish "visible differences between social classes" (95). Once again, I am sure that it did have this effect, but I am more skeptical that this was the real motivating force behind the development of high-brow cuisine.

Other Areas

In other areas, it is worth noting that the Aztec emperors invited subject and enemy kings to major Aztec events such as coronations, imperial funerals, and temple dedications, all accompanied by large-scale human sacrifices (M. Smith et al. 2003:245). There can be little doubt that these were high-level promotional feasts meant to suitably impress and intimidate rivals or potential rival factions within the

8.12. The Inca established huge spaces for periodic large gatherings of their subjects, which undoubtedly included large-scale feasting. This example of an Incan plaza is at Pachacamac, the most important ritual site on the Peruvian coast at the time of conquest. The plaza extends between the low mounds on the sides (c. 100 meters) and almost to the tree line on the far horizon (c. 300 meters) (Photograph by B. Hayden)

empire. There were certainly some large-scale events involving many people, as attested to by the deposit of 1,000 ceramic vessels near the Templo Mayor in the Aztec capital (254). These may have been for some of the large feasts, described by Sahagun, that rulers gave for the general populace to pacify any discontent (Anderson and Dibble 1981:96–8). As in Sumeria, "pleasure girls" (courtesans) were used to attract people to the events, although they reportedly only took the hands of nobles and warriors. The ball courts, too, continued to be used as venues for feasting, predominantly by elites and as an element in political strategies. In addition, there were many temple feasts at which commoners made food offerings especially upon the "arrival of the god." Contributors sometimes received some food back as part of a feast (Anderson and Dibble 1981:7,16,21–3,29,36,97,128,149,153,159–62), again indicating that Aztec temple feasts may have been used for gathering tribute as an effective revenue-producing strategy similar to strategies used elsewhere. If that did not suffice, there were also occasions when priests performed dances at houses and expected to be given food, or they went from house to house to request food, with maize going to the temple granary (62–4,84). Sahagun reports a surprising number of household-based feasts celebrated by "everyone," especially events at which neighbors, kin, and close friends exchanged tamales and invited each other to share food, including at the new year festivities (84,153,167). There were also more lavish household-based feasts such as to celebrate the piercing of children's ears, with feasts both in the household and at the local temple at which everyone drank pulque, even children (165) – events that appear remarkably similar to Polynesian coming of age feasts described in Chapter 7. However, the most extravagant household feasts, with blood relatives as hosts, were undoubtedly those to celebrate the capture of an enemy at which the captive constituted the main course (49). There were also marriage feasts and feasts for various professions. Smith et al. (2003) emphasize that feasting was important at all social levels, as indeed it appears to have been, from commoner feasts for funerals or the sacrifice of captured enemies, to the high "lords' feasts" which Smith et al., like others, view as hosted to serve diacritical functions (i.e., to reinforce class differences) – a view to which I demur.

In the Far East, I have already mentioned the funerary and ancestor feasts described in the Shang Hymns: the "soup well seasoned, well prepared, well mixed," the "clear wine" brought for the ancestors (and participants) so that victory, blessings, and prosperity would be conferred upon descendants (Waley 1996:319). From the same or even earlier period, the Yi Ching counsels rulers to use "great sacrificial feasts and sacred rites" as the means to unite men (i.e., to gain allies) (Trigram 59, in Wilhelm 1967:227). There are also numerous archaeological examples of bronze and ceramic wine containers (*lei*) and spouted serving vessels dating back to the Zhou empire (1122–756 BCE). At a considerably later period, Charles Higham (1989:342) has interpreted competitive feasting as a major component of political organization in the Khmer empire. He interprets the political structure as having been based largely on relationship networks not unlike the political dynamics characteristic of chiefdoms in the Philippines documented by Laura Junker in the previous chapter or the "theater states" discussed earlier in this chapter.

SUMMARY

With the emergence of empires, there do not appear to be any major changes in feasting strategies or dynamics, although there are clearly differences in scale, uses of prestige resources, and attempts made to integrate diverse ethnic groups into a coherent sociopolitical framework. I am struck by the enormous potential of archaeological feasting remains to inform us about the nature of the political organizations and dynamics of both early states and empires, particularly in terms of tribute collection and the relative importance of centralized rule versus decentralized power centers such as corporate kinship groups. The apparent recurrence of groups of twenty for intimate feasts (in Mycenae and Macedonia) is an interesting possible pattern in early states and empires, and perhaps earlier political organizations, that may be of some interest in developing future models. I am also struck by our ability to trace a continuous tradition of feasting strategies, dynamics, and purposes from the initial appearance of feasts in transegalitarian societies to their use in empires with, of course, suitable adjustments along the way (reviewed in the next chapter). It is a story of changes in emphasis, staging, foods, scale, rituals, and strategies. In contrast, a fundamental shift in the world order was ushered in by the advent of the Industrial Revolution. This entailed a radical restructuring of the basic premises on which traditional feasting systems were built, so that feasts in contemporary nation states bear only a superficial resemblance or relevance to what existed previously. This constituted the most dramatic development since the advent of competitive or promotional types of feasts in the Upper Paleolithic. It is to this remarkable transformation that we now turn in approaching the end of our inquiry.

9

Industrial Feasting

> By any reckoning this was probably the most important event in world
> history ... since the invention of agriculture and cities.
>
> – Hobsbawm 1962:29

Indeed, the Industrial Revolution was an earth-shaking development for human cultures. As Hobsbawm notes, it was a revolution in the true sense of the word. It completely transformed almost every aspect of society and environment from economics to education, ideology, politics, family relations, religions, and, of course, feasting. The first signs of change began to appear in Britain, and slightly later in Europe, in the 1780s, attaining a significant influence on society and governments by the 1840s with the building of the railways and construction of massive heavy industry in Britain. After this time, revolutionary changes in society became a constant feature of life continuing into the present with nuclear and computer developments.

Prior to the Industrial Revolution, no previous society had been able to break through the productive barrier created by traditional technology, transport, and social structures. Slave-based empires were the maximum expression of political and cultural complexity that could be achieved, and these summits of achievement stretched capabilities to the limit; they were anything but stable. They generally collapsed after only a few hundred years of existence. What the Industrial Revolution achieved for the first time in human history was a seemingly unlimited ability to produce goods, services, and manpower (in machine form) on a constant around-the-clock output basis, coupled with a voracious ability to find, develop, and use new resources. Profit became the dominant credo, and no amount of human suffering deterred its pursuit until Luddite saboteurs and others began to destroy the means of production and tried to overturn the ruling order. Some of the most serious consequences of the Industrial Revolution were social (Hobsbawm 1962:38). Rural families were driven off their lands for new agribusinesses and to provide cheap and mobile labor for the new factories. Families that had provided mutual assistance in agricultural villages were divided and scattered. Rural skills and work habits were antithetical to industrial production; labor had to be trained and educated appropriately. The demise of slavery and the rise of democracies were inevitable long-term outcomes of industrialization. In ideological terms, the influence of churches had to be curtailed while money had to be seen as the major goal in work and life – a requirement for all of life's needs or desires. Every human activity, including knowledge, production, and reproduction, grew exponentially (297). Everything became a superlative in relation to what had gone before. The European nation state, born of commercial middle-class interests during the Renaissance, gave way to the Industrial state and Industrial empires.

The study of feasting during the Renaissance and early Industrial periods falls more in the domain of the historian than the prehistorian. Given the vast amount of written documentation, it is challenging to chronicle changes in feasting behavior during these turbulent years or those that came after. Therefore, I leave these developments for others to undertake. However, it may be interesting to examine some of our own feasting practices in light of the observations from traditional cultures described in preceding chapters. We are on relatively familiar ground in dealing with the outcome of Industrial changes. Indeed, most of us can easily recognize many kinds of feasts that we ourselves have attended as denizens of Industrial communities. We also have some sense as to what motivates people to organize and host our feasting events, even though such things are almost entirely implicit and unspoken. The rationales for our feasts seem to have sunk into a sort of collective cultural unconscious and become only dimly recognized even by hosts, if motives are thought about at all. But this has probably always been somewhat the case, even in tribal societies. However, now, it seems that we are even less conscious of these things than before. In fact, we follow many cultural traditions without a very conscious comprehension of why we perform acts like Thanksgiving or Christmas dinners or gift exchanges. We engage in these and many other aspects of cultural rituals because it makes us feel good, or because it is expected of us or is customary, or because we have accepted the superficial reasons given us (e.g., to celebrate the birth of Christ). Nevertheless, a little reflection should reveal much stronger and deeper reasons for engaging in most of these enduring traditions, a topic to be discussed shortly.

To appreciate and understand the complexity of contemporary Industrial feasting, it will be useful to contrast some of the basic Industrial dynamics with those of the traditional societies that we have been dealing with in previous chapters. Above all else, the development of the individual as an independent entity has revolution-ized, and is revolutionizing, human society, including its feasting foundations. As has been repeatedly demonstrated in the preceding chapters, people in traditional societies are highly dependent on each other for succor in the event of poor harvests, accidents, floods or other disasters, sickness, accusations or attacks from others, and overpowering debts, as well as for raising houses or financing marriages and funerals.

With an ever-increasing standard of living (made accessible to the majority of people through salaried employment), we have reached a state at which the individual, rather than the family or lineage or other support network, has become the basic economic unit, capable of garnering all the resources that he or she needs to sustain life and even reproduce (Ensor 2011). For *most* people, health is covered by employers' insurances or national health systems, as is welfare, periods of unemployment, police protection, basic education, and other critical aspects of life. Money is now the key to overcoming adversity, not social connections; money and welfare programs are the keys to survival. If there are some people who fall between the cracks of Industrial societies or are incapable of dealing with the slings and arrows of misfortune, they are often ignored by the majority and by governments who consider them the authors of their own plights and do little to help.

The advent of the computer and the internet have taken the Industrial trend toward independence and individualization to even greater extremes. It is no longer necessary to deal with other people face-to-face to obtain information, make purchases, deal with bureaucracies, or even sometimes to work. "Friendships" are formed at a distance on the computer with no face-to-face contact. Children's worlds are increasingly dominated by interactions with computers rather than other people. New generations are increasingly self-centered, introspective, individualists. Under these conditions, marriages become less stable, children become more alienated, and birth rates plummet. Individuals have less time for each other as they pursue their own materialist goals promulgated by Industrial powers rather than pursing dyadic or a collective bonding experiences. Religion has become, above all, a relationship between *the individual* and supernatural powers rather than a communal often ecstatic experience as it was in the past. Education is the key to higher salaries, higher levels of consumption, and greater technical expertise for competitive industries. Universal education was an inevitable outcome of Industrialization, and this, in turn, made universal suffrage inevitable.

Mixed into this tsunami of change, feasting has been unable to escape fundamental changes. But, however transformed or eroded, feasting is still one of the few avenues for preserving the social fabric of the human species. Feasting cannot be replaced by computer alternatives because feasting entails, by its very nature, eating with other people. As we have seen in Chapter 2, over the millennia, feasting has been built on a number of innate characteristics found in the majority of human populations. Millennia of feasting and the natural selective advantages that feasting has provided in terms of marriages, offspring, and survival have probably ingrained in our genes an even greater attraction to feasting and the creation of special bonds with others through sharing food and experiencing various euphoric states together. Nevertheless, there have been strong Industrial pressures to thwart these tendencies so that, for many people, there has been a shift in feasting behavior toward more self-centered sources of individual pleasure consisting of lonely gourmet eating or isolated drinking of fine alcohols versus the previous use of these things exclusively in important social contexts. In-person social networking has frequently become depauperate. For many people today, feasts are largely viewed as psychologically gratifying events that appeal to the unabashedly self-indulgent sybaritic side of our nature rather than important social tools for achieving specific goals, as in the past. Thus, there is a tendency to view modern feasts as nonessential entertainment, fun epiphenomena, or peripheral amusements to the more serious domains of economics, politics, and personal success. In our Industrial culture consciousness, feasts are not portrayed in serious terms as pathways to establishing the most basic relationships in society, although perhaps some wealthy elites and recent immigrants who still adhere to earlier traditions may use feasts in these more traditional ways.

The fundamental reasons for hosting feasts may have become submerged in the mists of our collective cultural unconscious, our dimly remembered heritage. Yet, the innate propensity to seek out social relationships and to create networks of assistance are still there. Nor has the Industrial world yet found a way to make everyone completely self-reliant. We may have many of our basic needs taken care of through salaried employments and government programs, but there are still many people who do not fit the molds and many more who find a need on occasion for a helping hand, whether it is for household moving, building projects, safety, repairs, or other minor affairs of life. Companies and industries still need people to run them, and mutually supportive cadres of workers or administrators make far more effective producers than do disinterested, alienated workers or administrators. Feasting provides a powerful tool for creating the desired esprit du corps in these contexts, as well as in nonindustrial contexts. Promotional displays are also still key to corporate success, and feasting plays an important role here especially in recruitment and garnering contracts. Thus, at various levels, the earlier dynamics and logic of feasting can sometimes still be expected to operate in modern Industrial societies.

Aside from some of the more obvious corporate applications, does a study of feasting in traditional societies have any practical benefits for the average Industrial citizen? Given the massive social changes wrought by industrialization, can studies of traditional feasting help us today in our own endeavors? The answer, I think, is, "Yes." But, as we have done previously, in order to unravel the intrinsic meaning and dynamics of our own feasts, we must follow certain methodological procedures to achieve these insights. It will be useful to review some of these before proceeding, in order to adopt an appropriate perspective and avoid ethnocentric biases – the tendency to see through the charades of other cultures while maintaining that our own privileged beliefs and views are unassailable truths. Thus, here are some rules to follow in interpreting our own feasting practices:

First: We must *emphasize observable behavior* rather than what people say about what they are doing:

- How many people are attending a feast?
- What is their relationship to the hosts?
- Have they provided any support (food, gifts, money)? Is food potluck or provided by the host?
- Is alcohol involved?
- Are children present, or the elderly, or both sexes?
- Are their any ostentatious displays or speeches?
- How are people dressed?
- Has the house (or facility) been carefully cleaned beforehand? How large and lavish is it?
- What is the quality of the serving vessels and tableware?
- What is the cost of the food provided? How much time has been involved in preparation?
- Are there any exceptional kinds of food or preparations?
- What gifts are given? What is their value? Is reciprocity expected? What are the consequences of nonreciprocity?
- Are there any particularly prominent guests who are otherwise not related to the hosts?
- Have some or all guests been invited because they have hosted previous feasts to which the current host was invited?
- Are future reciprocal invitations expected from guests, or certain guests? What are the consequences of not reciprocating?

Second: *Do not confuse symbolic reasons* for holding feasts with the practical underlying reasons. Christmas may symbolically fête the birth of Christ, but this does not explain why people have lavish Christmas dinners or exchange gifts. Nor does it explain why these exact same activities took place well before the birth of Christ in Roman times. From a behavioral point of view, Christmas is fundamentally a ritual to reaffirm and strengthen social and emotional bonds between family members (as well as close kin and friends), to increase family solidarity, if you like – to make the family an effective socioeconomic unit for a range of reasons including reproduction and old age security. In the same fashion, tribal funeral feasts are not really held because the dead require them. The dead don't care. The lavish feasts given in the name of the dead are really held for the living kin. The same is true of house enhancement feasts, marriage feasts, curing feasts, and most other feasts that are often explained in terms of cultural "customs."

Third: To understand underlying practical dynamics, we must only look at general trends. There is certainly a very wide range of idiosyncratic behavior that characterizes all human populations, especially in the symbolic and feasting realms (Hayden and Cannon 1982, 1984:191–4). Individual behavior can be heavily influenced by ideology, personal values, other charismatic individuals, and personal histories or insecurities. Our contemporary cultural values also promote festive, self-indulgent, and sybaritic experiences for their ability to provide self-gratification. In some cases, such factors may dominate the behavior of specific individuals, but they do not explain the overall trends and patterns exhibited by most people most of the time that are the essential grist of cultural evolution and archaeological study.

OUR FEASTS

If we follow these guidelines, what can we infer about the Industrial society feasts of the modern North American continent? We can group our feasting events into broadly similar functions.

Christmas Dinners, Thanksgiving Dinners, Sunday Dinners, Wedding Anniversaries, Small Adult Birthday Parties

At a very basic level, all these feasts (Figures 9.1 and 9.2) appear to maintain family (nuclear or extended) identity, cooperation, emotional bonding, and general family solidarity primarily involving nuclear families, but often extending out to include two or three generations and sometimes close friends. Being absent from such events is a serious matter if no valid excuse is offered. There is usually no *individual*-centered ostentation or display at Christmas feasts. Frequently, everyone in the family contributes to help in preparations. Good tableware, food, and dress may indicate the desire to convey the specialness of the event or the rewards of family socioeconomic strategies and membership, but excessive jewelry and very formal evening dress are normally considered inappropriate. Everyone is served equally, although sometimes in order of age. Where hierarchical ranks are emphasized, it is usually to underline the family hierarchy of authority involving control over the family resources and how important they are. No reciprocity is necessary or expected.

9.1. Fundamental to the Industrial social and economic structure is the nuclear family unit and, to varying extents, extended families as well. A variety of feasting occasions predictably serve to reinforce the cooperation, social structure, and group identity of the family such as this relatively traditional mid-century wedding anniversary celebration of an extended family.

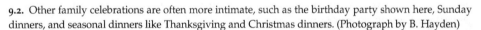

9.2. Other family celebrations are often more intimate, such as the birthday party shown here, Sunday dinners, and seasonal dinners like Thanksgiving and Christmas dinners. (Photograph by B. Hayden)

Business Parties and Receptions

As one of the most fundamental socioeconomic units in contemporary Industrial society, it would be surprising if feasts did not play a prominent role in business organizations and dynamics. Business parties, dinners, conference parties, receptions, and company New Year's or Christmas parties fill the bill (Figure 9.3). At the larger end of the scale, events such as company Christmas parties are meant to impress upon all guests (employees and others) how successful the organization is (whether a business, academic department, or other) and how desirable it is to be part of the organization. Such large events entail both solidarity aspects as well as promotional and recruitment motives. Rival organizations often compete to outdo each other in the lavishness of such major feasts. Food and drinks are generally paid for by the organization, the party is identified with the organization, and typically there is a formal speech by the figurehead of the organization, usually extolling the merits and accomplishments of the organization and its personnel. Distribution of food is usually equitable. Dress, whether casual or formal, tends to be whatever is considered "in" for the host organizations.

At the smaller, more familiar, end of the scale, dinners or lunches for coworkers or department personnel constitute important means of reducing the sometimes intense personal conflicts among coworkers that can be detrimental to effective

9.3. Businesses, corporations, and institutions constitute other fundamental socioeconomic organizations in Industrial societies. Another major class of contemporary Industrial feasts, such as the formal dinner shown here, consists of events to promote organization status (success and power) and solidarity within the organization. (Photograph courtesy of Greg Ehlers)

operations in the workplace. In some industrial countries like Japan, such events may occur fairly frequently, and attendance may be a criterion for advancement. In the Occident, such meals are usually only held a few times a year.

Marriage and Funeral Feasts

In today's societies, these are some of the more difficult types of feasts to understand from a practical political ecological framework. This is so, in part, because there is so much variation in these "symbolically" defined categories according to ethnic traditions, social class, individual preferences, and wealth. Both marriages and funerals run the gamut from very small, essentially nuclear family or individual affairs to enormous feasting events involving hundreds or thousands of people.

My unsystematic observations of practices in Industrial communities are that many of the larger feasts are held by wealthy families (or those aspiring to become wealthy) or by immigrant families who have continued to use coping strategies designed to deal with adverse economic conditions in their original homeland. Weddings in many impoverished homelands are a means of pooling resources of the parental socioeconomic networks so as to improve newlyweds' chances of establishing themselves and progressing to a higher standard of living (from which the parents also hope to benefit). The resulting support networks between parental generation families serve as socioeconomic safety nets, mobility contacts, and investments in children. They are strongly reciprocal, if not between nuclear families within a kindred, then certainly between lineages or kindreds.

In Industrial contexts, maintaining kinship or other contacts in distant locations can be a very effective strategy for acquiring help, especially when individuals or families want to relocate or become established in new environments such as new cities. Kin or fictive kin in these networks often provide initial places to live as well as some economic and subsistence support, transport, and useful contacts for new arrivals who may not speak the language of their host country or who may experience discrimination difficulties and might benefit from others who know the system or who have useful connections. As a result, guests often travel considerable distances to attend funeral and marriage feasts of other people in a support network even if they are sometimes only distantly related. Cross-culturally, marriages and funerals provide some of the most compelling and important emotional pretexts for reaffirming such networks – a topic addressed by Dietler (2001) and Hayden (2009a).

These expansive network traditions may fade as subsequent generations become increasingly self-reliant economically and succeed in increasing their personal standard of living. On the other hand, if individuals achieve very wealthy elite standings, then marriage and funeral feasts become forums for ostentatious promotional displays of success. At this level, they are instrumental in forming alliances of influence and power between elites. Guests are generally eager to attend such elite marriages and funerals (and to provide impressive support through gifts) because they seek to reinforce or establish relationships with the rich and powerful. Therefore, there tends to be considerable competition among guests in dress, gifts, manners, conversation, and demonstrated knowledge of many sorts. From the perspective of the wealthy hosts, these feasts can also serve as testing grounds for choosing relationships that they deem to be desirable or beneficial.

Children's Birthday Parties

In terms of my own childhood, these were some of the most mystifying feasts I have witnessed (Figure 9.4). They were ostensibly held for the benefit of children who enjoyed them well enough in prepubescent years, but shunned them soon after. However, I later became convinced that young children, like Christ's birth, were fundamentally pretexts for underlying adult agendas. It is important to recognize that the birthday parties I knew were promoted and organized by adults, not by the attending children. What was critical at children's birthday parties was the interaction between the mothers of the children who were partic- ipating. Fathers were rarely, if ever, present. Mothers with young children had a wide variety of common problems, including infant sicknesses, suburban social isolation, mobility impediments, and child care constraints. In my youth, in order to cope with these problems, young mothers developed networks of mutual support with women in similar situations; that is, with other women who had young children and who lived in the neighborhood. For most suburban and urban young mothers, members of their extended families lived too far away or were too preoccupied with salaried jobs to be able to help when needed, sometimes urgently. Mothers of young children could establish or reinforce these support networks with reciprocal invitations to birthday parties. Gifts were contributed to the feast not for the benefit of the child who had the birthday, but as tokens of mutual support between the mothers and perhaps as a means of motivating the child to participate. It was the mothers who bought gifts and wrapped them, not the children. Solidarity was exhibited among all who attended by the equal distribution of food and sometimes gifts for guests. Specialty foods (cake and ice cream) were provided to entice children to participate. Today, similar parties are sometimes held among parents who have children enrolled in daycare facilities.

9.4. Children's birthday parties, often beginning from the time that infants are one year old, may help to socialize children; however, a more certain benefit undoubtedly is obtained by the mothers who organize such events. As shown here (a party from the mid-century United States), mothers typically create mutual help and information networks that are very valuable in the early parenting years. (Photograph by F. Douglas Hayden)

Dinner/Cocktail Parties

Perhaps equally enigmatic are the dinner parties that individual households host (see Figure 1.1). In some cases, the guests are coworkers, and, in these situations, one may surmise that the hosts are generally members of the workforce who seek support from others or may even have aspirations to achieve higher positions. In other cases, dinner parties seem to be composed of friends or people with whom one might be interested in forming stronger friendship or mutual helping relationships. In Industrial societies, where kin typically live at some distance, friendships often fill the void of mutual help relationships that were previously occupied by kinship networks. Many people feel that friendships are crucial when help is needed due to sickness, accidents, security concerns, or labor-demanding tasks such as moving, or simply to explore new aspects of one's world. These are usually the people who are invited to dinner parties, whether small or large. In the case of large parties, perhaps a wider net is cast so as to include a number of people who might potentially be considered for a more formal mutual helping relationship. Dinner parties are prime arenas for exploring the desirability of further developing many such relationships and for consolidating those that already exist. A favorable reaction between host and guest at a large party event may lead to a subsequent invitation to a smaller, more intimate dinner, as well as to suggestions to get together for other mutual projects.

Teenage Parties

Teenagers hold some of the wildest, drunkest, and noisiest parties in contemporary society. Why do they do that? To get off on the experience, to be sure. However, between hormonal storms raging in immature bodies and brains and the confused array of roles promoted for teenagers in our rapidly changing social and technological environments, it is not surprising that many teens attempt to make names for themselves as people who can put on large, impressive, wild parties. The emphasis is on reputation among peers. Peers are those invited, and the more the better. Size signals success. Quantity takes precedence over quality. Food and drink, too, are notable in terms of quantity, not quality. Renown is gauged by size, noise, and extreme behavior. The residue of such events settles on the host and the network of friends with which he or she is most closely allied. One of the main targets of hosting such events undoubtedly is to ultimately draw attention to the organizer from the opposite sex and thereby enhance his or her courtship and mating potential. More proximately, however, successful party hosting also results in larger numbers of friends, reciprocal invitations to fun events and parties, inclusion in teams or projects, and simply greater popularity and attention.

Other Common Feasts

Feasts with obvious practical benefits include work parties, romantic dinners, and smaller intimate dinners between two or more friends or visitors.

APPLYING THE LESSONS

Here, I would like to provide some useful tips for successful feasting and point out some of the underlying dynamics of our feasts. If we are conscious of these aspects, we should be able to make all our feasting-related endeavors more effective. Sometimes we become unconscious of exactly why we are engaging in activities such as cleaning the house before a party, or setting out the best china, or expending our available cash on prime cuts of meat, shrimp, avocados, cheeses, wines, and pastries to offer our guests. It simply becomes the thing that we should do for a proper party. Yet if we stop and think about it for a minute, we do these things, of course, *to impress our guests* with our good qualities and our ability to provide such things for them. We want to make as favorable an impression on them as possible so as to be able to develop or enhance desirable relationships with our guests. We want to satisfy our own needs, which may simply involve sharing mutually pleasurable experiences or perhaps of developing romantic relationships or even more practical relationships. In traditional societies, the practical benefits overwhelmingly dominate the motivations behind hosting feasts. In our society, with its greater emphasis on leisure, affluence, and the individual, self-gratification or mutual enjoyment relationships seem to play much more significant roles. This aspect of our own culture has undoubtedly colored our understanding of feasting activities in traditional societies in which people are more frequently confronted with calamities, misfortunes, and shortfalls that carry more dire consequences.

There may be readers who decry the preceding kind of analysis, maintaining that the analytical dissection of our traditions removes the humanity from our behavior and reduces it to cold calculations directed by self-interest – that it kills the charm of our traditions. I would argue, quite the contrary, that by recognizing the underlying purpose of our half-conscious behaviors we render them far more meaningful. Moreover, we no longer become slaves to patterns of behavior that we learned from our parents or peers and never really understood. With more penetrating perceptions we can use our feasting (and other) behavior with purpose and intention to help achieve goals that we strive for. By making our intentions and techniques conscious, we can avoid making many faux pas and anticipate the appropriate responses in given situations. We should view social conventions the same way that we view technology. Feasts and other social conventions are fundamentally a kind of social technology made up of social tools for achieving certain goals and for dealing with social problems. If we know how to use those tools properly, they can make our lives much more enjoyable and easier. This should no more diminish the enjoyment or humanness of these events than the scientific knowledge of an oenologist concerning the chemistry of wine should diminish his gustatory appreciation of drinking the wine. Nor should a botanist's knowledge of a flower's structure detract from his ability to enjoy the beauty of a flower.

That being said, here are a few suggested feasting guidelines derived from my ethnoarchaeological observations of traditional feasts to assist both hosts and guests at feasting events in the Industrial world.

Feasting Guidelines:

1. *Clearly establish the purpose of the feast* in your mind and choose appropriate levels of dress, food, venue, guests, and auxiliary events.
2. *Formally invite people who you especially want to come.* Even send formal invitations via regular or e-mail.
3. To establish favorable social relationships is the main goal of most feasts. To do this, you need to *make a good impression.*
4. *Don't be stingy* or overly demanding of your guests.
5. *Clean the house or premises* thoroughly.
6. If you are a guest, *show your support* with work contributions (cleanup, washing dishes or other help) or impressive food contributions. Don't be stingy.
7. If you are a host, always *make sure that there is more than enough food and drink* and *provide some outstanding delicacies,* especially meats and alcohols.
8. *Be attentive to all your guests' needs.* The feast is for them, and your needs should be of less importance. Traditional hosts often take on self-effacing roles even to the point of not eating during the feast themselves.
9. *Hold promotional and networking feasts in as impressive an environment* as possible. Special decorations always enhance the atmosphere.
10. *For promotional or networking feasts, try to add interesting features* such as singing, dancing (group or invited performance), fireworks, bonfires, social games, round robin stories or riddles, or other imaginative fun features.
11. *In networking and promotional feasting, reciprocity is essential.* If you are no longer interested in maintaining social contact with an individual or family, don't reciprocate their invitations. Don't offer support. But be prepared to have made an enemy. This was expressed by one writer in Ann Landers's column of advice who complained bitterly about the lack of reciprocal gifts at the feast given for his children's marriage. Landers's (1999) upbraided him for being petty, but the promotional aspect of the marriage was obviously

more important to her than traditional reciprocity. I am sure her inquirer remained antagonistic toward his nonreciprocating guests. The moral is: if you want to avoid social rupture and antagonisms, reciprocate.

12. *When the goal is to create solidarity within a group, sharing the costs (potlucking) and workload is critical.*
13. *Use ostentation when trying to impress rivals, prospective allies, employees,* or individuals who are considering associating with you, especially if you are in competition with someone else.
14. *Excessive ostentation is not appropriate in creating solidarity* among equals.
15. *In work feasts, the quality of the food and drink will determine the number and quality of helpers* that will come to your aid (all other things being equal).
16. *Follow up with reinforcement.* Contact the host or guests to express gratitude within a reasonable period after the feast in situations where you have a particular interest in developing a relationship.

Ultimately, in this Industrial Age, why do we want to impress other people, or even our own children? There are many reasons. But most of them involve the fact that we still need help from other people from time to time. We may not need them all the time or as much of the time as in traditional societies, since impersonal, business-like institutions now dominate so many aspects of our lives. But, at some points, we all need other people to live even in our technological and highly structured social system. We need people when we are confronted with problems, difficulties, accidents, and calamities. We need people to procreate. We need people for help to obtain positions and to advance our careers. We need people to defend our interests, and the more powerful and wealthy those people are, the better we will be able to defend our interests.

In the past, kinship networks provided humanity with an important means for enlisting help from others when needed. Mutual participation in rituals also helped to create helping bonds between individuals. Primordial food sharing and, much later, surplus-based feasting has provided yet another major axis for creating close emotional bonds and mutual helping relationships in the panoply of social technology that is distinctly human. Over several million years, it seems that we have acquired an innate yearning for friendship, companionship, and partners because this was adaptive. These are still vibrant parts of our human heritage, and we should use them knowingly and wisely.

CONCLUSION

I have been on a quest for more than twenty years to try to understand why people in traditional cultures spend so much of their resources, time, and effort to throw gigantic and not-so-gigantic feasts. Taking on crippling debts for many years in order to outfeast others is commonplace in Southeast Asian and many other tribal communities. In some events, large amounts of food were left to rot because no one could eat it all, and this, too, was considered a sign of greatness (Young 1971). Feasts are still the biggest, most spectacular, most costly events in the cultural repertories of many traditional communities. They epitomize all that is important in these cultures and contain the distilled essences of these cultural traditions. They are showpieces for the most splendid rituals, foods, costumes, jewelry, dance perform-ances, songs, and decor. Copious amounts of intoxicants, freshly slaughtered meat, and food flow across feasting landscapes. Feasts can be viewed as the source of all the world's pleasures and delights and the cause of all of its woes given the competition, conflicts, and debts that lie beneath the enticing pleasures and the superficial expressions of joy.

For some government administrators and ethnographers, these are economi-cally irrational behaviors. However, the research that I and my students have conducted using a political ecology approach has demonstrated that there are very real, very tangible, and very practical benefits that the hosts of these traditional feasts hope to derive from their efforts and investments. Political ecology, as conceived of by ethnoarchaeologists (in contradistinction to applied anthropolo-gists who study modern elite abuses in exploiting resources), assumes that activities that consume large amounts of time, energy, and resources convey practical bene-fits to those engaged in them. The feasting benefits that we can identify include the establishment of socioeconomic safety nets, the establishment of political power within communities, the enhancement of economic advantages, the consolidation of socioeconomic differentials by forcing disadvantaged households into debt, the acquisition of desirable (and multiple) mates, the creation of military alliances for defense or aggression, and the exchange of wealth involving investments.

We have ranged far and wide over a vast panoply of feasts in the quest to understand what they are about and how they functioned at a variety of levels of organization. In closing, I would like to iterate some of the more fundamental observations that have emerged over the course of this inquiry. We have seen how feasts generally appear to be a critical element for holding together social and political groups, whether at the transegalitarian level, the chiefdom level, or the state level. Above all, feasts are predicated on surplus production. They require surpluses and constitute a way to transform surplus production into other desirable relationships or services, including political power, reproduction, and comfortable lifestyles. Because of the importance of these outcomes for survival and reproduc-tion, feasts generally become competitive to varying degrees and in varying ways. Competition, in turn, drives the need to increase surpluses and devise new ways to impress others using food, prestige technologies, rituals, or performances. This is a powerful new cultural dynamic based on food production that did not previously exist in the world and that only began to appear in a few places during the Upper Paleolithic with the advent of transegalitarian societies. This cultural dynamic became much more widespread with "Mesolithic" technologies that increased surpluses and laid the foundation for more transegalitarian community organizations. It became even more widespread with subsequent abilities to produce food and increase surpluses in the Neolithic. Given competitive feasting contexts, there could never be enough rice or wheat or animals or other desirable foods to be assured of gaining the desired benefits from feasts. Ethnographer after ethnographer has observed that the driving force behind the intensified production of food in transegalitarian societies (whether complex hunter/gatherers or horti-culturalists) is not hunger, but the use of food in competitive feasts to attain political and social goals. They describe how people often go deeply into debt and half starve themselves for months before and after a feast for the sole purpose of giving away ever more impressive amounts or qualities of food and other gifts at key feasts. I am convinced that feasts have played critical roles in the intensification of food production and in devising more efficient food processing technologies, as well as in developing a range of prestige technologies used to impress guests or create debts. As part of this complex, feasting pressures can be linked to the domestication of plants and animals. The motivation for intensification in transegalitarian societies is not need, but greed. Given the constant pressures of ambitious, aggressive, aggrandizer, triple-A personality types, and the competition between them, the rate of cultural change as well as population increases could be expected to have accelerated exponentially since the advent of feasts. This acceleration has been documented archaeologically (Cotterel and Kamminga 1990). It can be argued that feasting has relentlessly pushed the productive and innovative capacities of many societies to their limits over the past 20,000 years or more.

The feasting models developed in this book also help to account for the development of socioeconomic inequalities, heterarchies (composed of rival corporate kin groups, each with internal hierarchies), and the increasing development of political centralization. Increased intensities of warfare developed in tandem with these developments and can be causally linked to them. Feasting was essential in organizing support for war parties in many traditional societies, whereas warfare was also sometimes provoked in order to galvanize communities into producing more for alliance feasts, peacemaking feasts, and casualty compensations. The inevitable defaulting on feasting debts due to the desire to outcompete others may have been important causes of increased warfare as well. The emergence of interaction spheres for the acquisition of prestige goods and foods, changes in gender roles, the development of social or cultural identities, and some of the first public architecture can also be related to feasting developments (Hayden and Villeneuve 2011b).

Many archaeologists prefer to see the driving force behind feasting (as well as increasing artistic or ritual complexity) in terms of the need to create social solidarity, ease social tensions, or confront common problems via communitarian organization, or as the desire to acquire prestige or, more rarely, as a means to adjust consumption to variable resources. Other suggestions are that feasts are simply "costly signaling" (neglecting the powerful role of debts accrued via feasts) or that the lavish feasts of the elites were primarily given in order to diacritically distinguish between elites and others or to create "symbolical capital." From my experiences in traditional communities and reading others' ethnographies, I am convinced that these explanations, although they may all contain a germ of truth, have missed the mark. The enduring and widespread cultural institutions, above all the costly ones, that have been chronicled in the preceding chapters testify to major benefits being acquired via feasting, with select members benefiting to a far greater extent than the ordinary or junior members of the communities. To me, it is difficult to understand how such privileged customs come to be part of cultural traditions without recourse to the role of individuals seeking to promote their own self-interests above the community – individuals who have the means to leverage their desired behavior into the status of accepted cultural norms or at least tolerated behaviors. These are the aggrandizers who are, and always have been, present in all cultures and who forever push their cultural traditions into new configurations only made possible by the production and deployment of surplus foods in manipulative strategies to obtain acceptance or acquiescence.

RECAPITULATION

To briefly summarize the developmental trajectory of feasts as I currently understand it, we can begin with the tentative observation that simple foragers seem to lack the most salient features of many feasts: amassing surpluses, lavish displays, and food-based competition. At most, it appears that what might be considered solidarity feasts occurred, although others might argue that big game kills in general were displays of prowess and were used to augment hunters' social positions. However, more research is required in these areas.

Many of the classic feast types become clearly established with the emergence of transegalitarian societies, initially among complex hunter/gatherers, and then among horticulturalists and pastoralists. With the ability to produce relatively reliable surpluses, aggrandizers began to develop strategies to use this potential for their own benefit. Thus, we see in the archaeological record technology for extracting, processing, and storing abundant resources; larger, more sedentary communities (but lacking settlement hierarchies); denser populations; the emergence of prestige technologies and procurement of exotic materials; new technologies related to prestige foods (brewing, lipid extraction, cultivation, bread making); high value placed on children (for marriage exchanges); social and economic inequalities (in graves); secondary burials (to permit time for the amassing of maximum possible resources for lavish funerals); exclusive ritual organizations (especially secret societies that cross-cut corporate kinship groups); and high levels of violence (the result of competition).

Feasting probably provided the means for luring many people into binding agreements of support under a wide variety of pretexts and constituted an essential tool in the deployment of other strategies and the development of socio-economic inequalities. Small-scale family or kindred feasts for alliances or promotion constitute one end of the spectrum, and most typically are represented in domestic refuse by broken or lost prestige items, sometimes prestige serving vessels, unusually large hearths or food preparation vessels, remains of domesticated animals, and sometimes special structures or sections of structures. In exceptional cases, high-status seating platforms and trophy parts of feasting animals occur in household architecture. Typically, with lip service paid to egalitarian ethics but behavior revealing many inequalities, ostentation could not be too overtly expressed by individuals, so that any bold promotional displays had to be masked. Thus, the most ostentatious (promotional) displays were nominally held for the sake of others, especially the dead and newly married couples or house improvements to honor ancestors. The largest feasts therefore often occurred at burial locations, at the individual or corporate lineage houses, or (in the case of military alliances with other villages or community-wide feasts) around the household of the principal community administrator, although this latter case has yet to be demonstrated. The size (number of animals killed) of the largest funeral or marriage feasts that occur in a community seem to be useful as rough proxy measures for the ability of social groups to produce and amass surpluses, especially considering that these events are always underwritten by extensive borrowing and debts that extend to larger portions of the community.

Other feasting developments in many transegalitarian societies include work feasts (sometimes identifiable especially in construction projects) and exclusive feasts of ritual organizations that may have included anthropophagy in some instances. Another facies of the feasts held by exclusive ritual organizations was often the holding of public feasts (at dance grounds, clearings, corporate houses, or designated structures) to demonstrate the supernatural and corporal power of these organizations – essentially a religious kind of patron-client or tribute feast. Restitution feasts for social or ritual transgressions of a wide array of proscribed types of behavior are also distinctive feasting features of most transegalitarian societies.

With the emergence of chiefdoms, this same array of feasting features generally seems to have continued. I have argued that feasting was an essential social glue that, together with warfare, held the chiefly organizations together. However, the hierarchical regional settlement organization of chiefdoms required more administrative personnel, more and larger feasts, and more prestige goods. Thus, the cost of maintaining the polity was probably an order of magnitude higher than the cost of maintaining transegalitarian polities (independent villages). Indeed, chiefdoms only seem to have been viable where surplus food production could be increased accordingly. Whereas the largest feasts recorded for transegalitarian communities involved hundreds of animals, the largest feasts recorded for chiefdoms involved thousands of animals. The increase in the maximum size of chiefly feasts is often reflected in special architecture, such as temples associated with large plazas.

Competition between corporate kinship factions within chiefdoms was generally extreme, resulting in unstable reigns and lavish feasting displays. Highly competitive feasts between villages within chiefdoms were new elements in the feasting repertory, as were "intertribal" feasts in which members of rival chiefdoms congregated for lavish displays often in special, "neutral" locations. Massive feasting middens recorded from Bronze Age Europe very likely represent the remains of such feasts, whereas refuse from village feasts sometimes accumulated near temple or plaza areas. First fruits (harvest) feasts held at the paramount chief's village and "touring" feasts at constituent villages of a chiefdom appear to be additional new types of feasts designed by chiefs to acquire surpluses needed for their administrations. Another new pretext for demanding yet more contributions from chiefdom constituents was the community-wide celebration of life events of the chief or his family (births, marriages, deaths, victories). If some households were reluctant to contribute to these or other chiefly endeavors, enforcement cadres were often used to obtain compliance.

With the emergence of simple state organizations, the same suite of feasting features continued to be used. However, periodic feasts at the state temples with large courtyards or plazas tended to become the primary venues for gathering in surpluses, perhaps derived from traditions of secret society public feasts. In most archaeological cases, it is difficult to tell whether harvest or touring feasts continued to be used to collect tribute. Temples also often served a number of other important economic functions for elites. In some areas like Crete and the Maya area, cave or mountain peak sanctuaries may have been predecessors of state temples and served essentially as ritual centers for elite regional secret societies. Empires continue this same pattern, but on an even more lavish scale, holding feasts at which tens of thousands of animals were consumed. Feasts for occupational specialists also seem to emerge with empires, and probably for sports and popular religious organizations as well. To what extent corporate kinship organizations and their feasts may have remained active or may have been subsumed by other state organizations is not clear; however, at least at the elite levels, corporate kinship groups seem to have retained strong social, political, and economic roles.

FUTURE DIRECTIONS

I have consistently been surprised at the range and depth of topics that a feasting perspective seems capable of opening up in archaeological inquiries about the past. At every turn, there appear to be new potential insights into fundamental issues, but it is often frustrating to try to pursue these topics from the literature because of the lack of basic observations about the relevant topics. Nevertheless, from the small amount of research that I have been able to conduct on feasting in tradition societies, I have become convinced of the unusual theoretical power that feasting models bring to the discipline. Although the broad outlines of feasting research seem a bit clearer after the preceding overview, there are still many issues to be clarified and investigated. What are some of the most glaring topics that require more research? A number of these have been mentioned in previous chapters. Some of these include:

- The nature of feasting among simple hunter/gatherers and whether there is anything that really qualifies as a feast
- Investigations into the cross-cultural occurrence of key personality types, such as aggrandizers, and their prevalence in various types of societies
- Investigations into the prevalence of acceptance versus skepticism concerning claims to ritual knowledge or power (see, for example, the prevalence of anger toward God as documented by Exline et al. [2011])
- Further assessments of feasting's role in the domestication process
- Identifying the role of beer in political control prior to state formation (was beer used exclusively by elites prior to early states?)
- Conditions under which special structures are built for feasting
- Conditions under which prestige serving vessels or eating vessels are developed for feasting
- Documenting the marginalization process of families that do not participate in reciprocal feasting
- Determining whether there were major shifts from inclusive to exclusive feasts that characterized various periods (e.g., Neolithic to Bronze Age Western Europe; Minoan to Mycenaean; simple chiefdoms to complex Hawaiian chiefdoms)
- Determining the role of wealth and the proliferation of material items with increasing wealth in the material visibility of feasts

- Documenting the range of household variation within communities of feasting involvement and magnitudes of expenditures over long terms (e.g., ten-year periods).
- Improved documenting and understanding the variable rates of interest charged on loans
- Understanding why large portions of inheritable wealth were often consumed upon the death of the owner
- Documenting penalties for nonparticipation or defaulting on feasting debts
- Determining whether feasts are generally organized for the communal good or whether they are ultimately organized for the self-interests of the organizers, and developing material correlates for these outcomes
- Identifying the conditions under which the destruction of prestige objects or foods takes place at feasts
- Examining variations in the basis of power (war, staple finance, prestige item exchange, temples, or other strategies of control) of chiefdoms and early states, as well as variations in the primary loci of power (corporate kin groups vs. elite hierarchies); were the small size of Moche feasts aberrant, a product of limited sampling, or part of normal early state variation?
- Determining whether sizes of kin group feasts are suitable indicators of political decentralization. If so, how were conflicts with central powers mitigated?
- Documenting the role of feasting in governing and financing simple states
- Determining how feasting in complex chiefdoms differs from simple chiefdoms
- Examining claims for diacritical feasting more critically
- Determining the role of feasting at major ritual sites like Gobekli Tepe, Chavin, Minoan sanctuaries, and Southwestern Great Houses and whether they constituted secret society ritual centers
- Investigating the role of Minoan peak sanctuaries and caves in ritual and feasting as related to political organization

In addition, and above all, it is imperative to carry out additional ethnoarchaeological fieldwork on traditional feasting. I would suggest that a political ecological investigative framework is one of the most productive approaches for generating new theoretical insights in such studies. In future ethnoarchaeological research, the internal dynamics of the *full range* of feasting activities need to be documented and accounted for. Today, traditional societies are being transformed at a dizzying speed; however, there are still a number of remote areas of the world where former traditions of feasting are maintained or at least where details of such events are remembered. Complex hunter/gatherers in Siberia, pastoral nomads in Africa and the Near East, peasant Mediterranean or Andean villages, Amazonian or insular

Southeast Asian tribes, and many others all hold on to age-old feasting traditions or memories of them. Similarly, the historic or ethnographic literature bears much more careful culling for observations on feasting. Historic accounts and archives from Roman times to the Medieval and Renaissance periods in Europe should be particularly rewarding. It may be too late to record feasting-like behaviors of traditional simple foragers; however, the existing literature should be combed, region by region, for any relevant details and synthesized. The work in this volume represents only an initial step in such research.

Archaeologically, techniques, methods, and standards need to be oriented toward recovering, documenting, and interpreting feasting remains. Quantified data, in particular, is sorely missing from many vague descriptions of "dense bone accumulations" that appear likely to have been feasting remains. Roasting pits need to be examined in light of the scale of food prepared and possible roles in feasts. Greater care in the analysis of hearths and fire-cracked rocks is required for inferences concerning their size, temperatures, and frequencies of use. The role of pottery, mortars, grinding stones, fire-cracked rocks, and prestige serving vessels needs to be more carefully documented, especially with residue analyses to determine the types of foods that were prepared and the probable frequency or scale of preparation. Ethnographers have been particularly remiss in failing to document on any maps the precise location and size of actual feasting events, food preparation features for feasts, or any special locations or structures used for feasting, not to mention hearth sizes and numbers, food serving vessels and food preparation tools or vessels (numbers, sizes, ownership, and storage locations), prestige items displayed or destroyed, or disposal of wastes. In fact, most ethnographies contain no community or household maps at all. In general, we require a much better understanding of the material correlates of feasting behavior, a topic that Michael Dietler and I considered using as the basis for another workshop or conference on feasting.

In particular, the types of foods and food preparations in feasts need to be documented more carefully both ethnographically and archaeologically. We need to develop a better theoretical foundation for identifying feasting foods and how special they or their preparations might be, as well as a better understanding of when and why mundane foods were prepared in unusual quantities for feasts (abundance often being a luxury in itself) as noted by Hastorf (2003, 2008) and van der Veen (2003). We know that lipids, meat, and fermented beverages were highly valued. However, there is still considerable debate about the role of cereals and other starches. What are the costs and benefits of ground seeds over boiled whole seeds? What are the benefits and costs of cereals transformed into bread or beer? Nutrition-based studies of costs and benefits need to be carried out. How have various technological innovations like mortars, sickles, irrigation, or domestication changed the availability and value of various foods over time? Today, with industrialization, we have taken the most sacred foods of the past (the bull, the wheat, the rice, the maize, the cacao) and turned them into profane banalities (the supermarket breads, fast food hamburgers, TV beers, and dollar chocolates). Did similar kinds of transformations take place in earlier times?

Some time ago, Sahlins (1958) made the general observation that political complexity in Polynesia was strongly related to island productivity and the frequency of feasting. However, what is sorely missing in most cases is a better understanding of the constraints on production, as well as on the accumulation and use of surpluses. In particular, the relationships among wealth, surplus production, and political power require more careful investigation and documentation, as do other ways in which surpluses can be used to increase self-benefits for individuals.

In an ideal ethnoarchaeological study, it would be possible to determine for each study community information on the location of each household's agricultural fields (or resource extraction areas); on their annual production over a ten-year period; the total surplus produced by each household and how that surplus is used; how much is stored (and where); the political power of the household residents (and the support networks that they are part of); the costs of participating in feasting/support networks; a profile of their feasting behavior over a ten-year period (both attending or contributing to feasts and hosting them); and what immediate and long-term benefits resulted from or were hoped to result from those activities. I think it is useful to view feasting investments the same way that stock market investors view their investments, especially since both seek to obtain benefits from the use of their surplus resources. Work feasts are essentially short term investments with low risks. Middle term investments can be expected to provide some returns or benefits within a few months or years, such as reciprocal help and support from participating in lineage feasts. There may be some risk due to intervening circumstances, but the benefits can usually be counted upon and should not be difficult to monitor in ethnographic studies. However, the benefits from long term feasting investments are much more difficult to track and probably involve much greater risks due to changing fortunes and relationships. Thus, the outcomes of investments in promotional feasts, funeral feasts with reciprocal gift giving, and feasts to enhance the marriage value of children may not be known for years after the feasting investments and the outcomes can be very uncertain and difficult to track. This poses important methodological problems for field studies and documenting the benefits of feasting.

Of particular importance, we need a clearer understanding of reciprocal wealth transfers, such as a pig given to support a marriage feast with the understanding that an almost identical pig should be returned to the donor for a subsequent marriage feast at his household. There appears to be no net economic benefit unless it is simply the storage of wealth or labor (as documented by Monaghan 1990) or perhaps the prospect of acquiring additional resource or other rights in the case of large, defaulted repayments. If putting resources in a bank is an appropriate analogy, some feasting networks would be banks that paid zero percent interest, but could possibly guarantee a payback; whereas if producers held onto their surpluses, they would be at a high risk of losing them due to normal decay, animal mortality or disease, theft, or accident. Alternatively, as Monaghan (1990) has argued, these arrangements allowed hosts to call in many more resources for an event than they could provide on their own due to labor or other logistical bottlenecks such as the limited ability to keep animals or to make fresh tortillas, cooked rice, or other specialty foods. However, in many societies, there existed a range of interest rates for lending stock or grain, typically from 0 to 100 percent. We still have a poor understanding of how such systems with variable interest rates operate and of the consequences of defaulting on loans to various kinds of people. Nor do we understand very well why large proportions of a person's accumulated animal or other wealth is often consumed or destroyed at their funeral feasts rather than large portions of it being passed on to inheritors.

We also have a poor understanding of the proportion of households in communities that do not participate in feasts – and why they do not participate or do so only minimally. Similarly, we need to know who contributes most to feasts and what advantages they derive, or hope to derive, since outcomes are never certain and there are always risks of not attaining desired goals. Extending these lines of inquiry, it would be useful to develop theoretical models to explain why some aspects of traditional feasts were abandoned in the face of modern industrial contacts and why others persisted or were transformed.

On more mundane material levels, it would be nice to be able to trace all the food removed from feasts in the form of gifts or by other means and where all the bones from feasts end up as deposits in the ground. We know that large amounts of meat were often given to guests to take home with them and that bones were often tossed into the toft or bush areas around such homes, but we lack detailed information on any bones that were specifically tagged or any detailed documentation of large accumulations of bones left at the principal feasting sites. Similarly, it would be useful to be able to tag and follow the origin and post-feasting repository of any pots or other items used at a particular feast. Borrowing and pooling of materials used in large feasts appears to have been a common practice in many traditional villages, and this could blur material signatures for such activities on a household basis, as can the dominant role of lineages as the main competitive units in many societies. In fact, in general, what archaeologists require for a good understanding of these material and politico-economic systems is individual household data, as well as data for lineages or corporate kin groups for a large proportion of the households in any given community. This is the only reliable way of documenting the community and feasting dynamics with the full range of variation and an understanding of who hosts feasts and why. This household interview and inventory approach is one that I and my students have found to be invaluable in our own ethnographic work on feasting in traditional communities.

Finally, we need to refine our theoretical models at all levels: the overarching *metatheories*; the *middle range theories* that deal with such relationships as those between feasting and war, domestication, or the creation of chiefdom polities; and the *lower range theories* that deal with material assemblage formation and deposition processes. Indeed, this volume constitutes only a first-generation analysis, part heuristic and part substantive. It is meant to initiate the process of general theory development rather than create any definitive solutions. Virtually all topics treated herein merit much more research, including the changes that took place in Medieval, Renaissance, and Industrial times and that are taking place today. Archaeologically, feasting models can rarely be developed on the basis of single excavations at sites or even single sites. Rather, regional synthetic approaches including the full range of settlements, specialized structures, and households are needed to develop comprehensive models of feasting and cultural systems. Given the limitations of archaeological excavation techniques, this cannot be achieved without taking a regional perspective (e.g., Hayden 2011b). However, ultimately, I am convinced that if archaeologists can describe a culture's feasting behavior, they will hold an invaluable key to understanding a remarkable range of important features of the past 30,000 years of prehistory. In view of the observations in this book, we may well ask ourselves where we would be without feasts? It can be argued that we would still be simple hunter/gatherers.

References Cited

Abrams, Elliot M. 2000. Adena ceremonialism in anthropological perspective. Paper presented at 65th Annual Society for American Archaeology meeting, Philadelphia.

Abrams, Elliot, and Mary Le Rouge. 2008. Political complexity and mound construction among the early and late Adena of the Hocking Valley, Ohio. In *Transitions: Archaic and Early Woodland Research in the Ohio Country*, eds. Martha Otto and Brian Redmond, 214–31. Athens: Ohio University Press.

Abrams, H. L. 1987. The preference for animal protein and fat: A cross-cultural survey. In *Food and Evolution*, eds. Marvin Harris and Eric Ross, 207–23. Philadelphia: Temple.

Adams, John. 1973. *The Gitksan Potlatch*. Toronto: Holt, Rinehart, and Winston.

Adams, Ron. 2001. *Ethnoarchaeology of Torajan Feasts*. M.A. thesis, Simon Fraser University, Archaeology Department.

    2004. An ethnoarchaeological study of feasting in Sulawesi, Indonesia. *Journal of Anthropological Archaeology* **23**: 56–78.

    2005. Ethnoarchaeology in Indonesia illuminating the ancient past at Çatalhöyük? *American Antiquity* **70**: 181–8.

    2007a. Maintaining cohesion in house societies of West Sumba, Indonesia. In *The Durable House: House Society Models in Archaeology*, ed. Robin Beck Jr., 344–62. Carbondale: Southern Illinois University Press.

    2007b. *The Megalithic Tradition of West Sumba*, Indonesia. Ph.D. dissertation, Simon Fraser University.

Adams, Ron, and Ayu Kusumawati. 2011. The social life of tombs in West Sumba, Indonesia. *Archaeological Papers of the American Anthropological Association* **20**: 17–32.

Aikens, C. Melvin, and Takayasu Higuchi. 1982. *Prehistory of Japan*. New York: Academic Press.

Albion, Deborah. 2005. Approaches to the study of children, food and sweet eating. *Early Childhood and Care* **175**: 407–17.

Aldenderfer, Mark. 2010. Gimme that old time religion: Rethinking the role of religion in the emergence of social inequality. In *Pathways to Power: New Perspectives on the Emergence of Social Inequality*, eds. G. Feinman and T. D. Price, 77–94. New York: Springer.

Alexander, Diana. 1992. A reconstruction of prehistoric land use in the Mid-Fraser River area based on ethnographic data. In *A Complex Culture of the British Columbia Plateau*, ed. Brian Hayden, 99–176. Vancouver: University of British Columbia Press.

Allen, Michael J., and Barbara Applin. 1996. The story of the buckskin barrow. *Current Archaeology* **13**(2): 52–6.

Alvard, M. 2012. Human sociality. In *Evolution of Primate Societies*, ed. J. C. Mitani, 585–603. Chicago: University of Chicago Press.

Ames, Kenneth. 1994. The Northwest Coast: Complex hunter-gatherers, ecology, and social evolution. *Annual Review of Anthropology* **23**: 209–29.

    1995. Chiefly power and household production on the Northwest Coast. In *Foundations of Social Inequality*, eds. T. D. Price and G. Feinman, 155–87. New York: Plenum.

    2004. Supposing hunter-gatherer variability. *American Antiquity* **69**: 364–74.

    2008. Slavery, household production, and demography on the southern Northwest Coast. In *Invisible Citizens: Captives and Their Consequences*, ed. Catherine Cameron, 138–58. Salt Lake City: University of Utah Press.

Amiet, Pierre. 1980. *La glyptique mésopotamienne archaïque*. Paris: CNRS Editions.

Ampolo, Carmine. 1992. The economics of the sanctuaries in Southern Italy and Sicily. In *Economics of Cult in the Ancient Greek world*, eds. Tullia Linders and Brita Alroth, 25–8. Uppsala: Academiae Ubsaliensis.

Andel, Tjeerd van, and Curtis Runnels. 1988. An essay on the "emergence of civilization" in the Aegean world. *Antiquity* **62**: 234–47.

Anderson, Arthur, and Charles Dibble. 1981. Florentine codex. Vol. **2**, *The Ceremonies*. Santa Fe, NM: School of American Research.

Anderson, David. 1994a. *The Savannah River chiefdoms*. Tuscaloosa: University of Alabama Press.

    1994b. Factional competition and the political evolution of Mississippian chiefdoms in the Southeastern United States. In *Factional Competition and Political Development in the New World*, eds. Elizabeth Brumfiel and John Fox, 61–76. Cambridge: Cambridge University Press.

    2002. The evolution of tribal social organization in the Southeastern United States. In *The Archaeology of Tribal Societies*, ed. W. Parkinson, 246–77. Ann Arbor, MI: International Monographs in Prehistory.

    2004. Archaic mounds and the archaeology of Southeastern tribal societies. In *Signs of Power: The Rise of Cultural Complexity in the Southeast*, eds. J. Gibson and P. Carr, 270–99. Tuscaloosa: University of Alabama Press.

    2010. The end of the Southeastern Archaic. In *Trend, Tradition, and Turmoil: What Happened to the Southeastern Archaic?*, eds. David Thomas and Matthew Sanger, 273–302. New York: American Museum of Natural History, Anthropological Papers.

Anderson, Leslie. 1994. *The Political Ecology of the Modern Peasant*. Baltimore: Johns Hopkins.

Anderson, Patricia. 1999. Experimental cultivation, harvest, and threshing of wild cereals. In *Prehistory of Agriculture*, ed. P. Anderson, 118–44. Los Angeles: Institute of Archaeology, University of California.

Appadurai, Arjun. 1981. Gastro-politics in Hindu South Asia. *American Ethnologist* **8**: 494–511.

Aranda, Gonzalo. 2008a. Introducción: Somos lo que comemos. El significado social del consumo de alimentos y bebidas. *Cuadernos de Prehistoria y Arqueología De La Universidad De Granada* **18**: 11–16.

    2008b. Cohesión y distancia social. *Cuadernos de Prehistoria y Arqueología De La Universidad De Granada* **18**: 107–23.

Aranda, Gonzalo, and José Antonio Guerrero Esquivel. 2007. Poder y prestigio en las sociedades de la cultura de El Argar. el consumo communal de bovidos y ovicapridos en los rituals de enterramiento. *Trabajos De Prehistoria* **64**(2): 95–118.

Aranda, Gonzalo, and Sandra Montón-Subías. 2011. Feasting death: Funerary rituals in the Bronze Age societies of South-eastern Iberia. In *Guess Who's Coming to Dinner*, eds. Gonzalo Aranda, Sandra Montón-Subías, and Margarita Sánchez, 130–57. Oxford: Oxbow Books.

Aranda, Gonzalo, Sandra Montón-Subías, and Margarita Sánchez (eds.). 2011. *Guess who's coming to dinner*. Oxford: Oxbow Books.

Aranda, Gonzalo, and José Antonio Esquivel. 2006. Ritual funerario y comensalidad en las sociedades de la edad del bronce del sureste peninsular: La cultura de El Argar. *Trabajos De Prehistoria* **63**: 117–33.

Armada Pita, Xose-Lois. 2008. *Carne, Drogas O Alcohol? Calderos Y Banquetes En El Bronce Final De La Peninsula Iberica*. Ph.D. dissertation, Instituto de Estudios Gategos Padre Sarmiento. San Roque, Santiago de Compostela.

Arnold, Bettina. 1999. "Drinking the feast": Alcohol and the legitimation of power in Celtic Europe. *Cambridge Archaeological Journal* **9**: 71–93.

Arnold, Jeanne. 1993. Labor and the rise of complex hunter-gatherers. *Journal of Anthropological Archaeology* **12**: 75–119.

    1995. Transportation, innovation, and social complexity among maritime hunter-gatherer societies. *American Anthropologist* **97**: 733–47.

    1996. The archaeology of complex hunter-gatherers. *Journal of Archaeological Method and Theory* **3**: 77–115.

    2001. The Channel Islands project. In *The Origins of a Pacific Coast Chiefdom: The Chumash of the Channel Islands*, ed. Jeanne Arnold, 21–52. Salt Lake City: University of Utah Press.

Arthur, John W. 2003. Brewing beer: Status, wealth and ceramic use alteration among the Gamo of South-western Ethiopia. *World Archaeology* **34**(3): 516–28.

Asouti, Eleni, and Dorian Fuller. 2013. A contextural approach to the emergence of agriculture in Southwest Asia. *Current Anthropology* **54**: 299–345.

Axtell, James. 1981. *The Indian Peoples of Eastern America*. New York: Oxford University Press.

Azevedo, Joao Fernandes. 2009. Feast and sin: Catholic missionaries and native celebrations in early colonial Brazil. *Social History of Alcohol and Drugs* **23**: 111–27.

Baadsgaard, Aubrey, Janet Monge, Samantha Cox, and Richard Zettler. 2011. Human sacrifice and intentional corpse preservation in the royal cemetery of Ur. *Antiquity* **85**: 27–42.

Bahn, Paul. 1980. Crib-biting: Tethered horses in the Paleolithic? *World Archaeology* **12**: 212–17.

Bahuchet, Serge, and J. M. Thomas. 1985. Conservation des ressources alimentaires en forêt tropicale humide: Chasseurs-cueilleurs et proto-agriculteurs d'Afrique centrale. In *Les techniques de conservation des grains a long terme, 3, fasc. 1.*, 15–31. Paris: Editions Du CNRS.

Balter, Michael. 2007. Seeking agriculture's ancient roots. *Science* **316**: 1830–5.

Baldwin, James. 1990. Muruk, dok, pik, kakaruk: Prehistoric implications of geographical distributions in the Southwest Pacific. In *Pacific Production Systems*, eds. D. Yen and J. Mummery, 231–257. Canberra: Australian National University.

Bamforth, Douglas. 2011. Origin stories, archaeological evidence, and post-Clovis Paleoindian bison hunting on the Great Plains. *American Antiquity* **76**: 24–40.

Barbeau, Marius, and William Beynon. 1987. *Tsimshian narratives 2: Trade and warfare*. Ottawa: Canadian Museum of Civilization.

Barbier, Jean Paul. 1988. A stone rider of the Bstak of Sumatra. In *Islands and Ancestors: Indigenous Styles of Southeast Asia*, eds. Jean Paul Barbier and D. Newton, 50–65. New York: Te Neues.

Barker, Graeme. 1985. *Prehistoric Farming in Europe*. Cambridge: Cambridge University Press.
   1992. Animals as wealth in the African Iron Age: The origins of status? *Anthropozoologica* **16**: 47–52.

Barlow, K., and Renée Heck. 2002. More on acorn eating during the Natufian. In *Hunter-Gatherer Archaeology*, eds. S. Mason and J. Hather, 128–45. London: Institute of Archaeology, University College London.

Barnard, Alan, and James Woodburn. 1988. Property, power and ideology in hunter-gatherer societies. In *Hunters and Gatherers 2*, eds. Tim Ingold, David Riches, and James Woodburn, 4–31. New York: Berg.

Barnett, H. 1955. *The Coast Salish of British Columbia*. Eugene: University of Oregon Press.

Barth, Fredrik. 1967. Economic spheres in Darfu. In *Themes in Economic Anthropology*, ed. R. Firth, 149–74. New York: Travistock.

Bar-Yosef, Ofer. 1999. From sedentary foragers to village hierarchies: The emergence of social institutions. *Proceedings, British Academy* **100**:61–77.

Bar-Yosef, Ofer, and Anna Belfer-Cohen. 2002. Facing environmental crisis: Societal and cultural changes at the transition from the Younger Dryas to the Holocene in the Levant. In *The Dawn of Farming in the Near East*, eds. R. Cappers and S. Bottema, 55–66. Berlin: Ex Oriente.

Beaune, Sophie A. de. 1995. *Les hommes au temps de Lascaux*. Paris: Hachette.

Beck, Robin Jr. 2003. Consolidation and hierarchy: Chiefdom variability in the Mississippian Southeast. *American Antiquity* **68**: 641–61.

Bégouën, R., and J. Clottes. 1981. Nouvelles fouilles dans la salle des morts de la caverne d'Enlène, à Montesquieu-Avantès (Ariège). *Congès préhistorique de France*, **21**: 33–57.

Beidler, Lloyd. 1982. Biological basis of food selection. In *The Psychobiology of Human Food Selection*, ed. L. Barker, 3–15. Chichester, UK: England Ellis Horwood.

Bendall, L. 2004. Fit for a king? Hierarch, exclusion, aspiration and desire in the social structure of Mycenaean banqueting. In *Food, Cuisine, and Society in Prehistoric Greece*, eds. P. Halstead and J. Barrett, 105–35. Oxford: Oxbow Books.

Bender, Barbara. 1978. Gatherer-hunter to farmer, a social perspective. *World Archaeology* **10**: 204–22.
   1985. Emergent tribal formations in the American midcontinent. *American Antiquity* **50**: 52–62.

Benedict, Ruth. 1934. *Patterns of Culture*. Boston: Houghton Mifflin.

Benz, Bruce, and John Staller. 2006. The antiquity, biogeography, and culture history of maize in the Americas. In *Histories of Maize*, eds. J. Staller, R. Tykot, and B. Benz, 665–73. London: Elsevier.

Berndt, Ronald, and Catherine Berndt. 1970. *Man, Land and Myth in North Australia*. East Lansing: Michigan State University Press.

Beteille, A. 1981. The idea of natural inequality. In *Social Inequality*, ed. G. Berreman, 59–80. New York: Academic Press.

Beynon, William. 2000. *Potlatch at Gitsegukla*. Vancouver: University of British Columbia Press.

Biel, Jorg. 1987. A Celtic grave in Hochdorf, Germany. *Archaeology* **40**(6): 22–9.

Binford, Lewis. 1985. Human ancestors: Changing view of their behavior. *Journal of Anthropological Archaeology* **4**: 292–327.

Birket-Smith, Kaj. 1967. *Studies in Circumpacific Culture Relations*. Det kongelige danske videnskabernes selskab historisk-filosofiske meddelelser 42,3. Copenhagen: Kommissinar: Munksgaard.

Bishop, Charles A. 1987. Coast-interior exchange: The origins of stratification in Northwestern North America. *Arctic Anthropology* **24**: 72–83.

———. 1998. The politics of property among northern Algonquians. In *Property in Economic Context*, ed. Antonio Gilman and Robert C. Hunt, 247–67. Lanham, MD: University Press of America.

Blackburn, Thomas. 1976. Ceremonial integration and social interaction in aboriginal California. In *Native Californians: A Theoretical Retrospective*, ed. Lowell J. Bean and Thomas Blackburn, 225–43. Ramona: Ballena Press.

Blake, Michael. 1974. Ollie Site (EeRk 9) Final Report. (Report on File, Archaeology Branch, British Columbia Provincial Government, Victoria).

Blake, Michael, and John Clark. 1999. The emergence of hereditary inequality: The case of Pacific Coastal Chiapas, Mexico. In *Pacific Latin America in Prehistory: The Evolution of Archaic and Formative Cultures*, ed. M. Blake, 55–73. Pullman: Washington State University Press.

Blanco Vargas, Aida, Juan Vicente Guerrero Miranda, and Silvia Salgado González. 1986. Patrones funerarios del policromo medio en el sector sur de gran nicoya. *Vínculos* **12**: 135–58.

Blanton, Richard, and Jodi Taylor. 1995. Patterns of exchange and the social production of pigs in Highland New Guinea. *Journal of Archaeological Research* **3**: 113–45.

Bliege Bird, Rebecca, Douglas W. Bird, Eric Alden Smith, and Geoffrey C. Kushnick. 2002. Risk and reciprocity in Meriam food sharing. *Evolution and Human Behavior* **23**: 297–321.

Bliege-Bird, Rebecca, and Eric Smith. 2005. Signaling theory, strategic interaction and symbolic capital. *Current Anthropology* **46**: 221–48.

Blinman, Eric. 1989. Potluck in the protokiva: Ceramics and ceremonialism in Pueblo I villages. In *Architecture of Social Integration in Prehistoric Pueblos*, eds. W. Lipe and M. Hegmon, 113–24. Cortez, CO: Crow Canyon Archaeological Center.

Blitz, John. 1993a. Big pots for big shots: Feasting and storage in a Mississippian community. *American Antiquity* **58**: 80–96.

———. 1993b. *Ancient Chiefdoms of the Tombigbee*. Tuscaloosa: University of Alabama Press.

Bloch, Maurice, and Dan Sperber. 2002. Kinship and evolved psychological dispositions. *Current Anthropology* **43**: 723.

Blurton Jones, N. G. 1984. A selfish origin for human food sharing: Tolerated theft. *Ethology and Sociobiology* **5**: 1–3.

Blurton Jones, N. 1987. Tolerated theft, suggestions about the ecology and evolution of sharing, hoarding, and scrounging. *Social Science Information* **26**: 31–54.

Boas, Franz. 1921. *Ethnology of the Kwakiutl*. Bureau of American Ethnology, 35th Annual Report, pts. 1 and 2. Washington, DC: Government Printing Office.

———. 1934. *Geographical Names of the Kwakiutl Indians*. New York: Columbia University Press.

———. 1966. *Kwakiutl Ethnography*. Chicago: University of Chicago Press.

Boesch, C. 1994. Cooperative hunting in wild chimpanzees. *Animal Behavior* **48**: 653–67. doi: 10.1006/anbe.1994.1285.

Boesch, C., and H. Boesch-Achermann. 2000. *The Chimpanzees of the Taï Forest: Behavioral Ecology and Evolution.* Oxford: Oxford University Press.

Bogaard, A., M. Charles, K. Twiss, A. Fairbairn, N. Yalman, D. Filipovic, G. Demirergi, F. Ertug, N. Russell, and J. Henecke. 2009. Private pantries and celebrated surplus: Storing and sharing food at Neolithic Çatalhöyük, Central Anatolia. *Antiquity* **89**: 649–68.

Bogucki, Peter. 1999. *The Origins of Human Society.* Malden, MS: Blackwell.

Bond, George. 1987. Ancestors and Protestants: Religious coexistence in the social field of a Zambian community. *American Ethnologist* **14**: 55–72.

Borgna, Elisabetta. 2004. Aegean feasting: A Minoan perspective. In *The Mycenaean Feast*, ed. James C. Wright, 127–60. Princeton, NJ: American School of Classical Studies in Athens.

Boscana, Geronimo. 1933 (1978 reprint). *Chinigchinich: Historical account of the belief, usages, customs, and extravagancies of the Indians of this mission of San Juan Capistrano called the Acagchemem tribe.* Banning, CA: Malki Museum Press.

Bottéro, J. 1994. Boisson, banquet et vie sociale en Mésopotamie. In *Drinking in Ancient Societies*, ed. Lucio Milano, 3–14. Padova: Sargon srl.

Bowles, Sam. 2011a. Cultivation of cereals by the first farmers was not more productive than foraging. *Proceedings of the National Academy of Sciences* **108**: 4760–5.

2011b. History lesson from the first farmers. *New Scientist* **211**(2823): 26–7.

Boyd, Donna. 1996. Skeletal correlates of human behavior in the Americas. *Journal of Archaeological Method and Theory* **3**: 189–251.

Boyd, Matthew, and Clarence Surette. 2010. Northernmost precontact maize in North America. *American Antiquity* **75**: 117–33.

Bradley, Richard. 1984. *The Social Foundations of Prehistoric Britain.* London: Longman.

Braidwood, Robert. 1953. Symposium: Did man once live by bread alone? *American Anthropologist* **55**: 515–26.

Bray, Tamara. 2003a. The commensal politics of early states and empires. In *The Archaeology and Politics of Food and Feasting in Early States and Empires*, ed. Tamara Bray, 1–16. New York.: Kluwer/Academic/Plenum.

2003b. To dine splendidly: Imperial pottery, commensal politics, and the Inca state. In *The Archaeology and Politics of Food and Feasting in Early States and Empires*, ed. Tamara Bray, 93–142. New York: Kluwer Academic/Plenum.

Brookes, Samuel. 2004. Cultural complexity in the Middle Archaic of Mississippi. In *Signs of Power: The Rise of Cultural Complexity in the Southeast*, eds. J. Gibson and P. Carr, 97–113. Tuscaloosa: University of Alabama Press.

Brookfield, H. C. 1972. Intensification and disintensification in Pacific agriculture: A theoretical approach. *Pacific Viewpoint* **13**: 30–48.

1984. Intensification revisited. *Pacific Viewpoint* **25**: 15–44.

Brown, James. 1983. Summary. In *Archaic Hunters and Gatherers in the American Midwest*, eds. J. Philips and J. Brown. New York: Academic Press.

Brown, James, and Robert Vierra. 1983. What happened in the Middle Archaic? In *Archaic Hunters and Gatherers in the American Midwest*, eds. J. Philips and J. Brown, 1–17. New York: Academic Press.

Brown, Linda. 2001. Feasting on the periphery: The production of ritual feasting and village festivals at the Ceren site, El Salvador. In *Feasts: Archaeological and Ethnographic Perspectives* on Food, Politics, and Power, eds. Michael Dielter and Brian Hayden, 368–90. Washington, DC: Smithsonian Institution Press.

Brumfiel, Elizabeth. 1976. Regional growth in the Eastern Valley of Mexico: A test of the "population pressure" hypothesis. In The Early Mesoamerican Village, ed. K. Flannery, 234–47. New York: Academic Press.

1994. Factional competition and political development in the New World: An introduction. In Factional Competition and Political Development in the New World, eds. Elizabeth Brumfiel and John Fox, 3–15. Cambridge: Cambridge University Press.

Bruneaux, Jean-Louis. 2000. Les religions gauloises. Paris: Errance.

Bryant, Raymond. 1992. Political ecology: An emerging research agenda in third world studies. Political Geography 2(1): 12–36.

Builth, Heather. 2002. The Archaeology and Socioeconomy of the Gunditjmara. Ph.D. dissertation, Flinders University of South Australia.

2006. Gunditjmara environmental management. In Beyond Affluent Foragers, eds. Colin Grier, Jangsuk Kim, and Junzo Uchiyama, 4–23. Oxford: Oxbow.

Bullitt, Orville. 1969. Search for Sybaris. London: J. M. Dent & Sons.

Bullinger, Anke, Judith M. Burkart, Alicia P. Melis, and Michael Tomasello. 2013. Bonobos, Pan paniscus, chimpanzees, Pan troglodytes, and marmosets, Callithrix jacchus, prefer to feed alone. Animal Behavior 85: 51–60.

Burch, Ernest S. Jr. 1988. Modes of exchange in North-west Alaska. In Hunters and Gatherers 2: Property, Power, and Ideology, ed. Tim Ingold, David Riches, and James Woodburn, 95–109. New York: Berg Publishers Ltd.

Burger, R., and N. van der Merwe. 1990. Maize and the origin of highland Chavín civilization: An isotopic perspective. American Anthropologist 92: 85–95.

Burley, David. 1980. Marpole: Anthropological Reconstructions of a Prehistoric Northwest Coast Culture Type. Burnaby, BC: Archaeology Department, Simon Fraser University.

Cail, Hannah. 2011. Feasting on Fido: Dogs as a delicacy at Bridge River. Paper presented at the Annual Meetings of the Society for American Archaeology, Sacramento.

Cameron, Catherine M. 2002. Sacred earthen architecture in the northern Southwest: The Bluff Great House berm. American Antiquity 67(4): 677–95.

Campbell, Joseph. 1983. Historical Atlas of World Mythology, Vol. 1: The Way of the Animal Powers. San Francisco: Harper and Row.

Cannon, Aubrey. 1989. The historical dimension in mortuary expressions of status and sentiment. Current Anthropology 30: 437–58.

1992. Conflict and salmon on the Interior Plateau of British Columbia. In A Complex Culture on the British Columbia Plateau, ed. B. Hayden, 506–24. Vancouver: University of British Columbia Press.

Capasso, Gaetano. 2005. Journey to Pompeii. Ottaviano: Capware.

Carlson, Roy. 2011. The religious system of the Northwest Coast of North America. In The Oxford handbook of the archaeology of ritual and religion, ed. Timothy Insoll, 639–55. Oxford: Oxford University Press.

Carlson, Roy, and Philip Hobler. 1993. The Pender Island excavations and the development of Coast Salish culture. B.C. Studies 99(Autumn): 25–50.

Carneiro, Robert L. 1981. The chiefdom: Precursor of the state. In The Transition to Statehood in the New World, ed. Grant Jones and R. R. Kautz. Cambridge: Cambridge University Press.

Carrasco, Pedro. 1961. The civil-religious hierarchy in Mesoamerican communities. *American Anthropologist* **63**: 483–97.

Cashdan, Elizabeth A. 1980. Egalitarianism among hunters and gatherers. *American Anthropologist* **82**: 116–20.

Cauvin, Jacques. 1978. *Les premiers villages de Syrie - Palestine du IXème au VIIème millénaire avant J. C.* Paris: Maison de l'Orient.

Chagnon, Napoleon, and Timothy Asch. 1970. *The feast.* VHS VideoInsight Media.

Chagnon, Napoleon A. 1968. *Yanomamo: The Fierce People.* New York: Holt, Rinehart, and Winston.

1979. Is reproductive success equal in egalitarian societies? In *Evolutionary Biology and Human Social Behavior*, eds. N. Chagnon and W. Irons, 374–401. North Scituate, MA: Duxbury Press.

2000. Manipulating kinship rules: A form of male Yanomamo reproductive competition. In *Adaptation and Human Behavior*, eds. Lee Cronk, Napoleon Chagnon, and William Irons, 115–29. New York: Aldine De Gruyter.

Chaix, Louis. 2002. Omniprésence du cuir à Kerma (Soudan) au IIIe millénaire av. J.-C. In *Le travail du cuir de la préhistoire à nos jours*, eds. F. Audoin-Rouzeau, S. Beyries, 31–40. Antibes: Editions APDCA.

Chaix, Louis, Anne Bridault, and Regis Picavet. 1997. A tamed brown bear (Ursus arctos L.) of the late Mesolithic from la Grande-Rivoire (Isère, France). *Journal of Archaeological Science* **24**: 1067–74.

Chaix, Louis, and Annie Grant. 1992. Cattle in ancient Nubia. *Anthropozoologica* **16**: 61–5.

Chapman, Robert. 1995. Urbanism in Copper and Bronze Age Iberia? *Proceedings of the British Academy* **86**: 29–46.

1996. Problems of scale in the emergence of complexity. In *Emergent Complexity: The Evolution of Intermediate Societies*, ed. Jeanne E. Arnold, 35–49. Ann Arbor, MI: International Monographs in Prehistory.

Charles, D., and J. Buikstra. 1983. Archaic mortuary sites in the Central Mississippi drainage. In *Archaic Hunters and Gatherers in the American Midwest*, eds. J. Philips and J. Brown, 117–46. New York: Academic Press.

Chicoine, David. 2010. Elite strategies and ritual settings in coastal Peru during the first millennium B.C. In *Comparative Perspectives on the Archaeology of Coastal South America*, eds. R. Cutright, E. Lopez-Hurtado, and A. Martoin, 191–212. Pittsburgh: Center for Comparative Archaeology, University of Pittsburgh.

2011. Feasting landscapes and political economy at the Early Horizon center of Huambacho, Nepeña Valley, Peru. *Journal of Anthropological Archaeology* **30**: 432–53.

Claassen, Cheryl. 2010. *Feasting with Shellfish in the Southern Ohio Valley.* Knoxville: University of Tennessee Press.

Clark, John, and Mike Blake. 1989. The Emergence of Rank Societies on the Pacific Coast of Chiapas, Mexico. Paper presented at the Circum-Pacific Prehistory Conference, Seattle.

1994. The power of prestige: Competitive generosity and the emergence of rank societies in lowland Mesoamerica. In *Factional Competition and Political Development in the New World*, eds. Elizabeth Brumfiel and John Fox, 17–30. Cambridge: Cambridge University Press.

Clark, John, and Denis Gosser. 1995. Reinventing Mesoamerica's first pottery. In *The Emergence of Pottery*, eds. William Barnett and John Hoopes, 209–11. Washington, DC: Smithsonian Institution Press.

Clark, Sharri. 2009. Material matters: Representations and materiality of the Harappan body. *Journal of Archaeological Method and Theory* **16**: 231–61.

Clarke, Michael. 1998. *Feasting among the Akha of Northern Thailand*. M.A. thesis. Burnaby, BC: Department of Archaeology, Simon Fraser University.

2001. Akha feasting: An ethnoarchaeological perspective. In *Feasts: Archaeological and Ethnographic Perspectives on Food, Politics, and Power*, eds. Michael Dielter and Brian Hayden, 144–17. Washington and London: Smithsonian Institution Press.

Clermont, Norman. 1980. Le contrat avec les animaux bestiaire sélectif des indiens nomades du Québec au moment du contact. *Recherches Amérindiennes Au Québec* **10**(1–2): 91–109.

Coben, Lawrence. 2006. Other Cuzcos: Replicated theaters of Inka power. In *Theaters of Power and Community: Archaeology of Performance and Politics*, eds. Takeshi Inomata and Lawrence Coben, 223–59. Walnut Creek, CA: AltaMira Press.

Codding, B., and T. Jones. 2007. Man the showoff? Or the ascendance of a just-so-story. *American Antiquity* **72**: 349–57.

Codere, Helen. 1950. *Fighting with Property*. Seattle: University of Washington Press.

Cohen, David. 2011. The beginnings of agriculture in China. *Current Anthropology* **52**(Supplement 4): S273–94.

Cohen, Mark. 1977. *The Food Crisis in Prehistory*. New Haven, CT: Yale University Press.

2009. Introduction: Rethinking the origins of agriculture. *Current Anthropology* **50**: 591–5.

Collon, Dominique. 1987. *First Impressions: Cylinder Seals in the Ancient Near East*. Chicago: University of Chicago Press.

Coltrain, Joan Brenner, and Steven Leavitt. 2002. Climate and diet in Fremont prehistory: Economic variability and abandonment of maize agriculture in the Great Salt Lake Basin. *American Antiquity* **67**(3): 453–85.

Condominas, Georges. 1977. *We Have Eaten the Forest*. New York: Hill & Wang.

Conkey, Margaret. 1980. The identification of prehistoric hunter/ gatherer aggregation sites: The case of Altamira. *Current Anthropology* **21**: 609–30.

Connolly, Bob, and Robin Anderson. 1987. *First Contact: New Guinea's Highlanders Encounter the Outside World*. New York: Penguin.

Cook, Anita, and Mary Glowacki. 2003. Pots, politics, and power: Huari ceramic assemblages and imperial administration. In *The Archaeology and Politics of Food and Feasting in Early States and Empires*, ed. Tamara Bray, 173–202. New York: Kluwer Academic/ Plenum.

Cooper, H. Kory. 2006. Copper and social complexity: Frederica de Laguna's contribution to our understanding of the role of metals in native Alaskan society. *Arctic Anthropology* **43**: 148–63.

Cotterell, Brian, and Johan Kamminga. 1990. *Mechanics of Pre-Industrial Technology*. Cambridge: Cambridge University Press.

Cowan, C., and Patty Jo Watson. 1992. Some concluding remarks. In *The Origins of Agriculture*, eds. C. Cowan and P. Watson, 207–12. Washington, D.C.: Smithsonian Institution Press.

Cowgill, George L. 1975. On causes and consequences of ancient and modern population changes. *American Anthropologist* **77**: 505–25.

1979. Teotihuacan, internal militaristic competition, and the fall of the Classic Maya. In *Maya Archaeology and Ethnohistory*, eds. Norman Hammond and Gordon Willey, 51–62. Austin: University of Texas Press.

1996. Population, human nature, knowing actors, and explaining the onset of complexity. Paper presented at Proceedings of the 26th Annual Chacmool Conference, Calgary, Alberta.

1998. Comment. *Current Anthropology* **39**(1): 122–3.

Craig, O., H. Saul, A. Lucquin, Y. Nishida, K. Taché, L. Clarke, A. Thompson, et al. 2013. Earliest evidence for the use of pottery. *Nature*, doi:10.1038/nature12109.

Crawford, Gary. 1992. Prehistoric plant domestication in East Asia. In *The Origins of Agriculture*, eds. C. Cowan and P. Watson, 7–38. Washington, DC: Smithsonian Institution Press.

2006. East Asian plant domestication. In *Archaeology of Asia*, ed. Miriam Stark, 77–95. Oxford: Blackwell.

2011. Advances in understanding early agriculture in Japan. *Current Anthropology* **52**(Supplement 4): S331–46.

Crawford, Harriet. 1981. Some fire installations from Abu Salabikh, Iraq. *Paléorient* **7**: 105–14.

Crellin, David. 1994. *Is there a dog in the house?: The cultural significance of prehistoric domesticated dogs in the Mid Fraser River region of British Columbia*. M.A. thesis, Simon Fraser University.

Crellin, David, and Ty Heffner. 2000. The cultural significance of domestic dogs in prehistoric Keatley Creek society. In *The Ancient Past of Keatley Creek*, ed. B. Hayden, 151–64. Burnaby, BC: Archaeology Press.

Cronk, Lee. 1991. Wealth, status, and reproductive success among the Mukogodo of Kenya. *American Anthropologist* **93**:345–60.

Curet, L., and W. Pestle. 2010. Identifying high-status foods in the archeological record. *Journal of Anthropological Archaeology* **29**:413–31.

Cybulski, Jerome. 1992. Culture change, demographic history, and health and disease on the Northwest Coast. In *In the Wake of Contact*, eds. G. Milner and C. Larsen, 75–87. New York: Wiley-Liss.

Dabney, Mary K., Paul Halstead, and Patrick Thomas. 2004. Mycenaean feasting on Tsoungiza at ancient Nemea. In *The Mycenaean Feast*, ed. James C. Wright, 77–96. Princeton: American School of Classical Studies in Athens.

Dalton, George. 1971. Tradtional, tribal, and peasant economies: An introductory survey of economic anthropology. In *McCaleb Modules in Anthropology*. Reading, MA: Addison-Wesley.

1977. Aboriginal economies in stateless societies. In *Exchange Systems in Prehistory*, eds. Timothy Earle and J. Ericson, 191–212. New York: Academic Press.

D'Altroy, Terence. 1994. Factions and political development in the Central Andes. In *Factional Competition and Political Development in the New World.*, eds. Elizabeth Brumfiel and John Fox, 171–87. Cambridge: Cambridge University Press.

2001. From autonomous to imperial rule. In *Empire and Domestic Economy*, eds. T. D'Altroy and C. Hastorf, 325–9. New York: Kluwer Academic/Plenum.

Darby, Melisssa. 2005. The intensification of wapato (*Sagittaria latifolia*) by the Chinookan people of the lower Columbia River. In *Keeping It Living*, eds. D. Deur and N. Turner, 194–217. Seattle: University of Washington Press.

Davenport, Sue, Peter Johnson, and Yuwali. 2005. *Cleared Out: First Contact in the Western Desert*. Canberra: Australian Studies Press.

Davis, S., and F. Valla. 1978. Evidence for the domestication of the dog 12,000 years ago in the Natufian of Israel. *Nature* **276**: 608–10.

Davis, Simon, and Sebastian Payne. 1993. A barrow full of cattle skulls. *Antiquity* **67**: 12–22.

Dawson, George. 1880. *Report on the Queen Charlotte Islands, 1878*. Montreal: Dawson Bros.

Day, Peter M., and David E. Wilson. 1998. Consuming power: Kamares ware in Protopalatial Knossos. *Antiquity* **72**: 350–8.

De Laguna, Frederica. 1972. *Under Mount Saint Elias*. Washington, DC: Smithsonian Institution Press.

DeBoer, Warren. 1986. Pillage and production in the Amazon. *World Archaeology* **18**: 231–46.
  2001. The big drink: Feast and forum in the upper amazon. In *Feast Archaeological and Ethnographic Perspectives on Food, Politics, and Power*, eds. M. Dielter and B. Hayden, 215–39. Washington and London: Smithsonian Institution Press.

Delibes, Rocío, and Alfonso Barragán. 2008. El consumo ritual de chicha en San José de Moro. In *Arqueología Mochica, nuevas enfoques*, eds. L. Castillo and H. Bernier, 105–17. Lima: Fondo Editorial PUCP, IFEA.

Detlef, Gronenborn. 1999. A variation on a basic theme: The transition to farming in southern Central Europe. *Journal of World Prehistory* **13**: 123–210.

Deur, Douglas. 2002. Rethinking precolonial plant cultivation on the Northwest Coast of North America. *Professional Geographer* **54**(2): 140–57.
  2005. Tending the garden, making the soil: Northwest Coast estuarine gardens as engineered environments. In *Keeping It Living: Traditions of Plant Use and Cultivation on the Northwest Coast of North America*, eds. D. Deur and N. Turner, 296–330. Seattle: University of Washington Press.

de Waal, F. B. M. 1997. The chimpanzee's service economy: Food for grooming. *Evolution and Human Behavior* **18**: 375–86.

Dickson, D. Bruce. 2006. Public transcripts expressed in theatres of cruelty: The royal graves at Ur in Mesopotamia. *Cambridge Archaeology Journal* **16**: 123–44.

Diehl, Michael. 1996. The intensity of maize processing and production in upland Mogollon pithouse villages A.D. 200–1000. *American Antiquity* **61**: 102–15.

Dietler, Michael. 1989. Greeks, Etruscans and thirsty barbarians. In *Centre and Periphery Comparative Studies in Archaeology*, ed. T. Champion, 128–41. London: Unwin Hyman.
  1990. Driven by drink: The role of drinking in the political economy and the case of early Iron Age France. *Journal of Anthropological Archaeology* **9**: 352–406.
  1994. Quenching Celtic thirst. *Archaeology* **47**:45–8.
  2001. Theorizing the feast: Rituals of consumption, commensal politics, and power in African contexts. In *Feasts: Archaeological and Ethnographic Perspectives on Food, Politics, and Power*, eds. Michael Dielter and Brian Hayden, 65–114. Washington DC: Smithsonian Institution Press.

Dietler, Michael, and Brian Hayden, eds. 2001. *Feasts: Archaeological and Ethnographic Perspectives on Food, Politics and Power*. Washington, DC: Smithsonian Institution Press.

Dietler, Michael and Ingrid Herbich. 2001. Feasts and labor mobilization: Dissecting a fundamental economic practice. In *Feasts: Archaeological and Ethnographic Perspectives on Food, Politics, and Power*, ed. Michael Dielter and Brian Hayden, 240–65. Washington and London: Smithsonian Institution Press.

Dietrich, O., M. Heun, J. Notroff, K. Schmidt, and M. Zarnkow. 2012. The role of cult and feasting in the emergence of Neolithic communities. New evidence from Göbekli Tepe, South-eastern Turkey. *Antiquity* **86**: 674–95.

Dillehay, Tom, D. Bonavia, S. Goodbred, M. Pino, V. Vasquez, T. Tham, W. Conklin, J. Splitstoser, D. Piperno, and J. Iriarte. 2012. Chronology, mound-building and environment at Huaca Prieta, coastal Peru, from 13 700 to 4000 years ago. *Antiquity* **86**: 48–70.

Dillehay, Tom, Patricia Netherly, and Jack Rossen. 1989. Middle preceramic public and residential sites on the forested slope of the Western Andes, Northern Peru. *American Antiquity* **54**: 733–59.

Donald, L., and D. Mitchell. 1975. Some correlates of local group rank among the Southern Kwakiutl. *Ethnology* **14**:325–46.

Doran, Glen H. 2002. Introduction to wet sites and Windover (8BR246) investigations. In *Windover Multidisciplinary Investigations of an Early Archaic Florida Cemetery*, ed. G. Doran, 13–204. Gainesville: University Press of Florida.

Douaire-Marsaudon, F. 1998. *Les premiers fruits*. Paris: Editions CNRS/Editions de la Maison des Sciences de l'Homme.

Drennan, Robert. 1983. Ritual and ceremonial development at the hunter gatherer level. In *The Cloud People: Divergent Evolution of the Zapotec and Mixtec Civilizations.*, 30–2. New York: Academic Press.

Drucker, Philip. 1941. Kwakiutl dancing societies. *University of California Publications in Anthropological Records*.

1951. *The Northern and Central Nootkan tribes*. Vol. **144**. Washington, DC: Smithsonian Institution, Bureau of American Ethnology, Bulletin. 1941.

Dubuc, Constance, Kelly D. Hughes, Julie Cascio, and Laurie R. Santos. 2012. Social tolerance in a despotic primate: Co-feeding between consortship partners in rhesus macaques. *American Journal of Physical Anthropology* **148**: 73–80.

Dunbar, R. 2003. The social brain: Language and society in evolutionary perspective. *Annual Review of Anthropology* **32**: 163–81.

Duncan, Neil A., Deborah Pearsall, and Robert Benfer Jr. 2009. Gourd and squash artifacts yield starch grains of feasting foods from Preceramic Peru. *Proceedings of the National Academy of Science* **106**(32): 13202–6.

Durrenberger, E. 1989. Lisu ritual, economy, and ideology. In *Ritual, Power and Economy*, ed. S. Russell, 103–20. Dekalb: Northern Illinois University Press.

Earle, Timothy. 1977a. Aboriginal economies in stateless societies. In *Exchange Systems in Prehistory*, ed. T. Earle and J. Ericson, 191–212. New York: Academic Press.

1977b. A reappraisal of redistribution: Complex Hawaiian chiefdoms. In *Exchange Systems in Prehistory*, eds. T. Earle and J. Ericson, 213–29. New York: Academic Press.

1978. *Economic and Social Organization of a Complex Chiefdom*. Anthropology Paper No. 63. Ann Arbor: University of Michigan Museum of Anthropology.

1987. Chiefdoms in archaeological and ethnohistorical perspective. *Annual Review of Anthropology* **16**: 279–308.

1989. The evolution of chiefdoms. *Current Anthropology* **30**:84–8.

1997. *How Chiefs Come to Power: The Political Economy in Prehistory*. Stanford, CA: Stanford University Press.

2001. Economic support of Chaco Canyon society. *American Antiquity* **66**: 26–35.

Eaton, S. Boyd, Marjorie Shostak, and Melvin Konner. 1988. *The Paleolithic Prescription*. New York: Harper and Row.

Edwards, John. 1984. *The Roman Cookery of Apicius*. Vancouver: Hartley and Marks.

Eliade, Mircea. 1958. *Patterns in Comparative Religion*. Cleveland: World Publishing.

Elmendorf, W., and A. Kroeber. 1960. *The Structure of Twana Culture with Comparative Notes on the Structure of Yurok Culture*. Seattle: University of Washington Press.

Emmerson, Thomas, and Timothy Pauketat. 2008. Historical-processual archaeology and culture making: Unpacking the Southern Cult and Mississippian religion. In *Belief in the Past*, eds. K. Hays-Gilpin and D. Whitley, 167–88. Walnut Creek, CA: Left Coast Press.

Engs, Ruth. 1995. Do traditional Western European drinking practices have origins in antiquity? *Addiction Research* 2: 227–39.

Ensminger, Jean, and Jack Knight. 1997. Changing social norms common property, bride-wealth, and clan exogamy. *Current Anthropology* 38(1): 10–70.

Ensor, Bradley. 2011. Kinship theory in archaeology. *American Antiquity* 76: 203–27.

2013. *The archaeology of kinship*. Tucson: University of Arizona Press.

Erickson, C. 2006. Intensification, political economy, and the farming community. In *Agricultural Strategies*, eds. J. Marcus and C. Stanish, 334–63. Los Angeles: Cotzen Institute of Archaeology.

Erickson, Philippe. 1987. De l'apprivoisement à l'approvisionnement: Chasse, alliance et familiarisation en Amazonie Amérindienne. *Techniques et Cultures* 9:105–40.

Esaka, Teruya. 1986. The origins and characteristics of Jomon ceramic culture. In *Windows on the Japanese Past*, ed. Richard Pearson, 223–8. Ann Arbor: Center for Japanese Studies, University of Michigan.

Exline, J., C. Park, J. Smyth, and M. Carey. 2011. Anger toward god: Social-cognitive predictors, prevalence, and links with adjustment to bereavement and cancer. *Journal of Personality and Social Psychology* 100: 129–48.

Eyre, Christopher. 1987. Work and organization of work in the Old Kingdom. In *Labor in the Ancient Near East*, ed. M. Powell, 5–48. New Haven, CT: American Oriental Society.

Fagan, Brian, D. Grenda, D. Maxwell, A. Keller, and R. Ciolek-Torrello. 2006. *Life on the Dunes*. Technical series 88. Redlands, California: Statistical Research Inc.

Fages, P. 1937. (Translated by H. Priestly. (orig. 1775). *A Historical, Political, and Natural Description of California*. Berkeley: University of California Press.

Fairweather, Alan, and Ian Ralston. 1993. The Neolithic timber hall at Balbridie, Grampian region, Scotland: The building, the date, the plant macrofossils. *Antiquity* 67: 313–23.

Falconer, Steven. 1994. Village economy and society in the Jordan Valley: A study of Bronze Age rural complexity. In *Archaeological Views from the Countryside*, eds. Glenn Schwartz and Steven Falconer, 121–42. Washington, DC: Smithsonian Institution Press.

Falk, Pasi. 1991. Homo culinarius. *Social Science Information* 30:757–89.

Falvey, Leslie. 1977. *Ruminants in the Highlands of Northern Thailand*. Chiang Mai: Thai-Australian Highland Agronomy Project, Tribal Research Institute, Chiang Mai University, Thailand.

Farriss, Nancy. 1984. *Maya Society under Colonial Rule*. Princeton, NJ: Princeton University Press.

Fehr, Emst, and Bettina Rockenbach. 2003. Detrimental effects of sanctions on human altruism. *Nature* 422: 137–40.

Feil, Daryl. 1987. *The Evolution of Highland Papua New Guinea Societies*. Cambridge: Cambridge University Press.

Feinman, Gary, and Jill Neitzel. 1984. Too many types: An overview of prestate societies in the Americas. *Advances in Archaeological Method and Theory* **7**: 39–102.

Feinman, Gary M., Kent G. Lightfoot, and Steadman Upham. 2000. Political hierarchies and organizational strategies in the Puebloan Southwest. *American Antiquity* **65**(3): 449–70.

Fibiger, L., T. Ahlstrom, P. Bennike, and R. Schulting. 2013. Patterns of violence-related skull trauma in Neolithic southern Scandinavia. *American Journal of Physical Anthropology* **150**: 190–202.

Finucane, Brian. 2009. Maize and sociopolitical complexity in the Ayacucho Valley, Peru. *Current Anthropology* **50**:535–45.

Firth, Raymond. 1951. *Elements of Social Organization*. London: Watts.

1959 (1929). *Economics of the New Zealand Maori*. Wellington, NZ: R. E. Owen.

1983. Magnitudes and values in Kula exchange. In *The Kula.*, eds. J. Leach and E. Leach, 89–105. Cambridge: Cambridge University Press.

Fischer, Anders. 2002. Food for feasting? In *The Neolithisation of Denmark.*, eds. A. Fischer and K. Kristiansen, 341–94. Sheffield: J. R. Collis.

Fitzhugh, Ben. 2003. *The Evolution of Complex Hunter-Gatherers*. New York: Kluwer/Plenum Publishing.

Flannery, Kent. 1968. Olmec and the Valley of Oaxaca. In *Dumbarton Oaks Conference on the Olmec.*, ed. Elizabeth Benson, 79–110. Washington, DC: Dumbarton Oaks.

1969. Origins and ecological effects of early domestication in Iran and the Near East. In *The Domestication and Exploitation of Plants and Animals*, eds. Peter Ucko and George Dimbleby, 73–100. Chicago: Aldine.

1973. The origins of agriculture. *Annual Review of Anthropology* **2**: 271–310.

1986a. The research problem. In *Guilá Naquitz: Archaic Foraging and Early Agriculture in Oaxaca, Mexico.*, ed. K. Flannery, 3–18. Orlando, FL: Academic Press.

1986b. A visit to the master. In *Guilá Naquitz: Archaic Foraging and Early Agriculture in Oaxaca, Mexico.*, ed. K. Flannery, 511–19. Orlando, FL: Academic Press.

1986c. Food procurement area and preceramic diet at Guilá Naquitz. In *Guilá Naquitz.*, ed. K. Flannery, 303–17. Orlando, FL: Academic Press.

1999. Process and agency in early state formation. *Cambridge Archaeological Journal* **9**: 3–21.

Ford, Clellan. 1968 (1941). *Smoke from Their Fires: The Life of a Kwakiutl Chief (Charles Nowell)*. Hamden, CT: Archon Books.

Ford, Richard. 1985. The process of plant food production in prehistoric North America. In *Prehistoric Food Production in North America*, ed. R. Ford, 1–18. Ann Arbor: Museum of Anthropology, University of Michigan.

Formicola, Vincenzo. 2007. From the Sunghir children to Romito dwarf. *Current Anthropology* **48**: 446–53.

Fox, John G. 1996. Playing with power: Ballcourts and political ritual in Southern Mesoamerica. *Current Anthropology* **37**: 483–509.

Fox, William. 1988. The Elliott Village: Pit of the dead. *Ontario Archaeological Society KEWA Newsletter, London Chapter* **88**(4): 2–9.

1997. Constructing archaeological expectations from Meswaki ritual. *The Michigan Archaeologist* **43**: 3–25.

Fox, William A., and Robert Salzer. 1999. Themes and variations: Ideological systems in the Great Lakes. In *Taming the Taxonomy: Toward a New Understanding of Great Lakes Archaeology*, eds. Ronald Williamson and Christopher Watts, 236–57. Toronto: Eastend Books.

Frayser, Suzanne. 1985. *Varieties of Sexual Experience*. New Haven, CT: Human Relations Area Files.

Freedman, Maurice. 1965. *Lineage Organization in Southeastern China*. New York: Athlone Press.

—— 1970. Ritual aspects of Chinese kinship and marriage. In *Family and Kinship in Chinese Society*, ed. M. Freedman, 164–79. Stanford, CA: Stanford University Press.

Fretheim, S. 2009. Feast in the forest. In *Mesolithic Horizons.*, eds. S. McCartan, R. Schulting, G. Warren, and P. Woodman, 378–84. Oxford: Oxbow.

Fried, Morton. 1967. *The Evolution of Political Society: An Essay in Political Anthropology*. New York: Random House.

Fried, Morton H. 1960. On the evolution of social stratification and the state. In *Culture in History: Essays in Honor of Paul Radin.*, ed. S. Diamond, 714–31. New York: Columbia University Press.

Friedman, Jonathan. 1975. Tribes, states, and transformations. In *Marxist Analysis and Social Anthropology*, ed. M. Bloch, 161–202. New York: Wiley.

Friedman, J., and M. Rowlands. 1977. Notes towards an epigenetic model of the evolution of "civilization." In *The Evolution of Social Systems*, eds. J. Friedman and M. Rowlands, 201–76. London: Duckworth.

Frimigacci, D. 1990. *Aux temps de la terre noire*. Paris: Editions CNRS.

Fritz, G., and T. R. Kidder. 1993. Recent investigations into prehistoric agriculture in the Lower Mississippi Valley. *Southeastern Archaeology* 1: 1–14.

Fruth, B., and G. Hohmann. 2002. How bonobos handle hunts and harvests: Why share food? In *Behavioural Diversity in Chimpanzees and Bonobos*, eds. C. Boesch, G. Hohmann, and L. F. Marchant, 231–43. Cambridge: Cambridge University Press.

Fry, Douglas. 2006. *The Human Potential for Peace*. New York: Oxford University Press.

Fuller, Dorian, Emma Harvey, and Ling Qin. 2007. Presumed domestication? Evidence for wild rice cultivation and domestication in the fifth millennium BC of the Lower Yangtze region. *Antiquity* **81**: 316–31.

Fuller, Dorian, L. Qin, Y. Zheng, A. Zhao, X. Chen, L. Hosoya, and S. Sun. 2009. The domestication process and domestication rate in rice: Spikelet bases from the Lower Yangtze. *Science* **323**: 1607–10.

Gamble, Clive. 1999. *The Paleolithic Societies of Europe*. Cambridge: Cambridge University Press.

Gamble, Lynn. 2008. *The Chumash World at European Contact*. Berkeley: University of California Press.

Gamble, Lynn, Phillip Walker, and Glenn Russell. 2001. An integrative approach to mortuary analysis: Social and symbolic dimensions of Chumash burial practices. *American Antiquity* **66**: 185–222.

Garcea, Elena. 2001. Cultural adaptations at Uan Tabu from the Upper Pleistocene to the Late Holocene. In *Uan Tabu*, ed. Elena Garcea, 219–51. Florence: Edizeoni All'Insegna del Giglio.

—— 2004. An alternative way towards food production: the perspective from the Libyan Sahara. *Journal of World Prehistory* **18**:107–54.

—— 2006. Semi-permanent foragers in semi-arid environments of North Africa. *World Archaeology* **38**: 197–219.

2008. Sahara, eastern. In *Encyclopedia of Archaeology*, ed. Deborah Pearsall. Vol. 1, 56–61. New York: Academic Press.

Garine, Eric. 2001. An ethnographic account of the many roles of millet beer among Duupa agriculturalists (Poli Mountains) Northern Cameroon. In *Drinking: An Anthropological Approach*, eds. Igor de Garine and Valerie de Garine, 191–204. New York: Berghahn.

Garrido-Pena, Rafael. 2006. Transegalitarian societies: An ethnoarchaeological model for the analysis of Copper Age Bell Beaker using groups in Central Iberia. In *Social Inequality in Iberian Late Prehistory*, eds. Pedro Diaz-del-Rio and Leonardo García, 81–96. Oxford: Hadrian Books.

Garrido-Pena, Rafael, Manuel Rojo-Guerra, Iñigo García-Martínez de Lagrán, and Cristina Tejedor-Rodríguez. 2011. Drinking and eating together: The social and symbolic context of commensality rituals in the Bell Beakers of the Interior of Iberia (2500–2000 cal BC). In *Guess Who's Coming to Dinner*, eds. Gonzalo Aranda, Sandra Montón-Subías, and Margarita Sánchez, 109–29. Oxford: Oxbow Books.

Garrod, Dorothy, and Danielle Bate. 1930. *The Stone Age of Mount Carmel*. Vol. 1. Oxford: Clarendon Press.

Gat, Azar. 2000. The human motivational complex. *Anthropological Quarterly*: 20–15.
2006. *War in Human Civilization*. Oxford: Oxford University Press.

Gates, Hill. 1996. *China's Motor: A Thousand Years of Petty Capitalism*. Ithaca, NY: Cornell University Press.

Geertz, Clifford. 1980. *Negara*, Princeton, NJ: Princeton University Press.

Geller, Jeremy. 1992. From prehistory to history: Beer in Egypt. In *The Followers of Horus*, eds. R. Friedman and B. Adams, 19–26. Oxford: Oxbow.

Gilby, I. C. 2006. Meat sharing among the Gombe chimpanzees: Harassment and reciprocal exchange. *Animal Behavior* **71**: 953–63.

Gilman, Antonio. 1981. Stratification in Bronze Age Europe. *Current Anthropology* **22**: 1–24.

Girella, Luca. 2007. Forms of commensal politics in Neopalatial Crete. *Creta Antica* **8**: 135–68.

Goldman, Irving. 1970. *Ancient Polynesian Society*. Chicago and London: University of Chicago Press.

Goldschmidt, Walter R., and Harold E. Driver. 1943. The Hupa White Deerskin Dance. *American Archaeology & Ethnology* **35**: 103–31.

Goldstein, Paul. 2003. From stew-eaters to maize-drinkers: The chicha economy and the Tiwanaku expansion. In *The Archaeology and Politics of Food and Feasting in Early States and Empires*, ed. Tamara Bray, 143–72. New York: Kluwer Academic/Plenum.

Gomes, C. M., and C. Boesch. 2009. Wild chimpanzees exchange meat for sex on a long-term basis. *PLoS One* **4**: 5116. doi: 10.1371/journal.pone.0005116.

Gomez de Soto, José. 1993. Cooking for the elite: Feasting equipment in the Late Bronze Age. In *Trade and Exchange in Prehistoric Europe.*, eds. C. Scarre and F. Healy. Oxford: Oxbow Books.

Gonlin, Nancy. 1994. Rural household diversity in Late Classic Copan, Honduras. In *Archaeological Views from the Countryside*, eds. Glenn Schwartz and Steven Falconer, 177–97. Washington, DC: Smithsonian Institution Press.

Goodall, J. 1986. *The Chimpanzees of Gombe*. Cambridge, MA: Belknap Press.

Gopnik, Alison. 2009. *The Philosophical Baby*. New York: Farrar, Straus and Giroux.

Goring-Morris, Nigel, and Anna Belfer-Cohen. 2011. Evolving human/animal interactions in the Near Eastern Neolithic: Feasting as a case study. In *Guess Who's Coming to*

Dinner: Feasting Rituals in the Prehistoric Societies of Europe and the Near East, eds. Gonzalo Aranda, Sandra Montón-Subías, and Margarita Sánchez, 64–72. Oxford: Oxbow Books.

Goring-Morris, Nigel, and Liora Horwitz. 2007. Funerals and feasts during the Pre-pottery Neolithic B of the near east. *Antiquity* **81**: 1–17.

Gould, Richard. 1966. The wealth quest among the Tolowa Indians of Northwestern California. *American Philosophical Society Proceedings* **110**(1): 67–89.

Graves, Robert (trans.). 1957. *Pharsalia (Civil War)*. Manchester, UK: Carcanet Press.

Graves, William M., and Scott Van Keuren. 2004. What feast? Communalism and the social context of food presentation and consumption in the Late Prehispanic Southwest. Paper presented at the Annual Meetings, Society for American Archaeology, Montreal.

Green, Miranda. 1997. *The World of the Druids*. London: Thames and Hudson.

Gregg, Susan. 1988. *Foragers and Farmers: Population Interaction and Agricultural Expansion in Prehistoric Europe*. Chicago: University of Chicago Press.

Gregory, C. A. 1982. Gifts and commodities. In *Studies in Political Economy*, ed. John Eatwell, 18–25. New York: Academic Press.

Gremillion, Kristen. 1996. The paleoethnobotanical record for the Mid-Holocene Southeast. In *Archaeology of the Mid-Holocene Southeast*, eds. Kenneth Sassaman and D. Anderson, 99–114. Gainesville: University of Florida Press.

———. 2004. Seed processing and the origins of food production in Eastern North America. *American Antiquity* **69**(2): 215–33.

Grier, Colin. 2010. Probables pasados y posibles futuros: Sobre la reconstrución de cazadores-recolectores complejos de la NWC. In *La excepción y la norma: Las sociedades indígenas de la costa noroeste de norteamérica desde la arqueología*, eds. Assumpció Vila and Jordi Estévez, 147–66, 228–30. Madrid: Consejo Superior de Investigaciones Científicas.

Griffin, Bion. 1998. An ethnographic view of the pig in selected traditional Southeast Asian societies. In *MASCA Research Papers in Science and Archaeology*, ed. Sarah Nelson, 28–37. Philadelphia: University of Pennsylvania Museum of Archaeology and Anthropology.

Grimstead, Deanna, and Frank Bayham. 2010. Evolutionary ecology, elite feasting, and the Hohokam. *American Antiquity* **75**: 841–64.

Gummerman, George IV. 1994. Corn for the dead: The signification of Zea mays in Moche burial offerings. In *Corn and Culture in the Prehistoric New World*, eds. S. Johannessen and C. Hastorf, 399–410. Boulder, CO: Westview Press.

———. 2004. Local lords and local feasts: Moche feasting on the north coast of Peru. Paper presented to the Pre-Columbian Society of Washington, DC.

———. 2010. Big hearths and big pots: Moche feasting on the North Coast of Peru. In *Inside Ancient Kitchens*, ed. Elizabeth Klarich, 111–32. Boulder, CO: University of Colorado Press.

Gurven, M. 2004. To give and to give not: The behavioral ecology of human food transfers. *Behavioral and Brain Sciences* **27**: 543–83.

Gurven, M., W. Allen-Arave, K. Hill, and M. Hurtado. 2000b. "It's a wonderful life": Signaling generosity among the Ache of Paraguay. *Evolution and Human Behavior* **21**: 263–82.

Gurven, M., M. Borgerhoff, P. Hooper, H. Kaplan, R. Quinlan, R. Sear, E. Schniter, et al. 2010. Domestication alone does not lead to inequality. *Current Anthropology* **51**: 49–64.

Gurven, M., K. Hill, H. Kaplan, A. Hurtado, and R. Lyles. 2000a. Food transfers among Hiwi foragers of Venezuela: Tests of reciprocity. *Human Ecology* **28**: 171–218.

Haaland, R. 2007. Porridge and pot, bread and oven: Food ways and symbolism in Africa and the Near East from the Neolithic to the present. *Cambridge Archaeological Journal* **17**(2): 165.

Haas, Jonathan, and Winifred Creamer. 2006. Crucible of Andean civilization: The Peruvian Coast from 3000 to 1800 BC. *Current Anthropology* **47**: 745–60.

Habu, Junko. 2004. *Ancient Jomon of Japan*. Cambridge: Cambridge University Press.

Habu, Junko, M. Kim, M. Katayama, and H. Komiya. 2001. Jomon subsistence-settlement systems at the Sannai Maruyama site. *Bulletin of the Indo-Pacific Prehistory Association* **21**: 9–21.

Hägg, Robin. 1992. Sanctuaries and workshops in the Bronze Age Aegean. In *Economics of Cult in the Ancient Greek World*, eds. Tullia Linders and Brita Alroth, 29–32. Uppsala: Academiae Ubsaliensis.

Haggis, Donald. 1999. *Staple Finance, Peak Sanctuaries, and Economic Complexity in Late Prepalatial Crete*, ed. A. Chaniotis, 53–85. Stuttgart.

Hahn, Eduard. 1896. *Die haustiere and ihre beziehungen zur wirtschaft des menschen*. Leipzig: Duncker and Humblot.

1909. *Die entstehung der pflugkultur*. Heidelbert: Winter.

Haimi, A. 1960. Archaeology. *Israel Year Book* **10**:113–22.

Hakansson, N. Thomas. 1994. Grain, cattle, and power: Social processes of intensive cultivation and exchange in Precolonial Western Kenya. *Journal of Anthropological Research* **50**: 249–76.

1995. Irrigation, population pressure, and exchange in Precolonial Pare, Tanzania. *Research in Economic Anthropology* **16**: 297–323.

2010. History and the problem of synchronic models. *Current Anthropology* **51**: 105–7.

Halpern, Georges M. 2000. The case for pleasure. *Century Premier Journal* **2000**: 10–18.

Halstead, Paul. 1989. The economy has a normal surplus. In *Bad Year Economics*, eds. P. Halstead and J. O'Shea, 68–80. Cambridge: Cambridge University Press.

1990. Waste not, want not: Traditional responses to crop failure in Greece. *Rural History* **1**: 147–64.

1998–9. Texts, bones and herders: Approaches to animal husbandry in Late Bronze Age Greece. *Minos* **33**–4:149–89.

2007. Carcasses and commensality: Investigating the social context of meat consumption in Neolithic and Early Bronze Age Greece. In *Cooking up the Past*, eds. Christopher Mee and Josette Renard, 25–48. Oxford: Oxbow.

Halstead, Paul, and Valasia Isaakidou. 2004. Faunal evidence for feasting: Burnt offerings from the Palace of Nestor at Pylos. In *Food cuisine and society in prehistoric Greece*, ed. Paul Halstead and J. Barrett, 136–54. Oxbow: Oxford.

2011. Political cuisine: Rituals of commensality in the Neolithic and Bronze Age Aegean. In *Guess Who's Coming to Dinner*, eds. Gonzalo Aranda, Sandra Montón-Subías, and Margarita Sánchez, 91–108. Oxford: Oxbow.

Halstead, Paul, and John O'Shea. 1982. A friend in need is a friend indeed: Social storage and the origins of social ranking. In *Ranking, Resources and Exchange*, eds. Colin Renfrew and Stephen Shennan, 92–9. Cambridge: Cambridge University Press.

1989. Introduction: Cultural responses to risk and uncertainty. In *Bad Year Economics: Cultural Responses to Risk and Uncertainty*, eds. P. Halstead and J. O'Shea, 1–7. Cambridge: Cambridge University Press.

Hamilakis, Yannis. 1998. Eating the dead: Mortuary feasting and the politics of memory in the Aegean Bronze Age societies. In *Cemetery and Society in the Aegean Bronze Age*, ed. Keith Branigan, 115–32. Sheffield: Sheffield Academic Press.

———. 1999a. Food technologies/technologies of the body: The social context of wine and oil production and consumption in Bronze Age Crete. *World Archaeology* **31**: 38–54.

———. 1999b. The anthropology of food and drink consumption and Aegean archaeology. In *Palaeodiet in the Aegean*, eds. Sarah Vaughan and W. Coulson, 55–63. Oxford: Oxbow Books.

Hampton, O. W. 1999. *Culture of Stone*. College Station: Texas A&M University Press.

Hanchett, Suzanne. 1975. Hindu potlatches. In *Competition and Moderization in South Asia*, ed. H. Ullrich, 27–59. New Delhi: Abhinav Publications.

Hare, Robert. 1993. *Without Conscience*. New York: Guilford Press.

Harkin, Michael. 2007. Swallowing wealth: Northwest coast beliefs and ecological practices. In *Native Americans and the Environment*, eds. M. Harkin and D. Lewis, 211–32. Lincoln: University of Nebraska Press.

Harlan, Jack. Views on agricultural origins. 2006. Available from http://www.hort.purdue.edu/newcrop/history/lecture03/r_3-1.html.

Harris, David. 1989. An evolutionary continuum of people-plant interactions. In *Foraging and Farming: The Evolution of Plant Exploitation*, eds. D. Harris and G. Hillman, 11–26. London: Unwin, Hyman.

Harris, Marvin. 1979. *Cultural Materialism*. New York: Vintage.

Hastorf, Christine. 2001. The Xauxa Andean life. In *Empire and Domestic Economy*, eds. T. D'Altroy and C. Hastorf, 315–24. New York: Kluwer Academic/Plenum.

———. 2003. Andean luxury foods: Special food for the ancestors, deities, and the elite. *Antiquity* **77**: 545–54.

———. 2008. Food and feasting, social and political aspects. In *Encyclopedia of Archaeology*, ed. Deborah Pearsall, 1386–95. Orlando, FL: Academic Press.

Hauser-Schäublin, Brigitta. 2003. The Precolonial Balinese state reconsidered. *Current Anthropology* **44**: 153–82.

Hawkes, Kristen. 1991. Showing off: Tests of an hypothesis about men's foraging goals. *Ethology and Sociobiology* **2**: 29–54.

———. 1992. Sharing and collective action. In *Evolutionary Ecology and Human Behavior*, eds. E. Smith and B. Winter Halder, 269–300. New York: Aldine de Gruyter.

Hawkes, Kristin, and Rebecca Bird. 2002. Showing off, handicap signaling, and the evolution of men's work. *Evolutionary Anthropology* **11**: 58–67.

Hawkes, Kristin, James O'Connell, and Nic Blurton-Jones. 2001. Hunting and nuclear families. *Current Anthropology* **42**: 681–709.

Hayden, Brian. 1975. Dingoes: Pets or producers? *Mankind* **10**: 11–15.

———. 1981. Subsistence and ecological adaptations of modern hunter/gatherers. In *Omnivorous Primates: Gathering and Hunting in Human Evolution*, eds. Geza Teleki and Robert Harding, 344–421. New York: Columbia University Press.

———. 1986. Resources, rivalry, and reproduction: The influence of basic resource characteristics on reproductive behavior. In *Culture and Reproduction*, ed. Penn Handwerker, 176–95. Boulder, CO: Westview Press.

———. 1990. Nimrods, piscators, pluckers, and planters: The emergence of food production. *Journal of Anthropological Archaeology* **9**: 31–69.

1992a. Conclusions: Ecology and complex hunter/gatherers. In *A Complex Culture of the British Columbia Plateau*, ed. B. Hayden, 525–63. Vancouver: University of British Columbia Press.

1992b. Models of domestication. In *Transitions to Agriculture in Prehistory*, eds. Anne Gebauer and T. Price, 11–19. Madison, WI: Prehistory Press.

1993. The cultural capacities of Neanderthals: A review and re-evaluation. *Journal of Human Evolution* **24**: 113–46.

1994a. Competition, labor, and complex hunter-gatherers. In *Key Issues in Hunter-Gatherer Research*, eds. E. Burch Jr. and L. Ellanna, 223–39. Oxford: Berghahn.

1994b. Village approaches to complex societies. In *Archaeological Views from the Countryside*, eds. Glenn Schwartz and Steven Falconer, 198–206. Washington, DC: Smithsonian Institution Press.

1995. Pathways to power: Principles for creating socioeconomic inequalities. In *Foundations of Social Inequality*, eds. T. D. Price and G. Feinman, 15–85. New York: Plenum Press.

1997. *The Pithouses of Keatley Creek*. Fort Worth, TX: Harcourt Brace.

1998. Practical and prestige technologies: The evolution of material systems. *Journal of Archaeological Method and Theory* **5**: 1–55.

2000. On territoriality and sedentism. *Current Anthropology* **41**: 109–12.

2001a. Fabulous feasts: A prolegomenon to the importance of feasting. In *Feasts: Archaeological and Ethnographic Perspectives on Food, Politics and Power*, eds. M. Dietler and B. Hayden, 23–64. Washington, DC: Smithsonian Books.

2001b. Richman, poorman, beggerman, chief: The dynamics of social inequality. In *Archaeology at the Millennium: A Sourcebook*, eds. G. Feinman and T. Price, 231–72. New York: Kluwer Academic Plenum Publishers.

2001c. The dynamics of wealth and poverty in the transegalitarian societies of Southeast Asia. *Antiquity* **75**: 571–81.

2003a. *Shamans, Sorcerers, and Saints: The Prehistory of Religion*. Washington, DC: Smithsonian Books.

2003b. Hunting and feasting: Health and demographic consequences. *Before Farming* **4**: 166–76.

2003c. Were luxury foods the first domesticates? ethnoarchaeological perspectives from Southeast Asia. *World Archaeology* **34**: 458–69.

2004. Sociopolitical organization in the Natufian: A view from the Northwest. In *The Last Hunter- Gatherer Societies in the Near East.*, ed. Christophe Delage, 263–308. Oxford: BAR International Series.

2008. *L'homme et l'inégalité*. Paris: CNRS Editions.

2009a. Funerals as feasts: Why are they so important? *Cambridge Archaeological Journal* **19**: 29–52.

2009b. Forward. In *Ceramics before Farming.*, eds. Peter Jordan and Marek Zvelebil, 19–26. Walnut Creek, CA: Left Coast Press.

2009c. The proof is in the pudding: Feasting and the origins of domestication. *Current Anthropology* **50**: 597–601, 708–9.

2011a. Big man, big heart? the political role of aggrandizers in egalitarian and transegalitarian societies. In *For the Greater Good of All: Perspectives on Individualism, Society, and Leadership.*, eds. Donald Forsyth and Crystal Hoyt, 101–18. New York: Palgrave Macmillan.

2011b. Feasting and social dynamics in the Epipaleolithic of the Fertile Crescent. In *Guess Who's Coming to Dinner: Feasting Rituals in the Prehistoric Societies of Europe and the Near East.*, eds. Gonzalo Aranda, S. Montón-Subías, and M. Sánchez Romero, 30–63. Oxford: Oxbow.

2011c. Rice: The first Asian luxury food? In *Why Cultivate?*, eds. G. Barker and M. Janowski, 73–91. Cambridge: McDonald Institute Monographs.

Hayden, Brian, and Ron Adams. 2004. Ritual structures in transegalitarian communities. In *Complex Hunter-Gatherers: Evolution and Organization of Prehistoric Communities on the Plateau of Northwestern North America*, eds. William Prentiss and Ian Kuijt, 84–102. Salt Lake City: University of Utah Press.

Hayden, Brian, and Aubrey Cannon. 1982. The corporate group as an archaeological unit. *Journal of Anthropological Archaeology* 1:132–58.

1984. *The Structure of Material Systems: Ethnoarchaeology in the Maya Highlands.* Washington DC: Society for American Archaeology Papers No. 3.

Hayden, Brian, Neil Canuel, and Jennifer Shanse. 2012. What was brewing in the Natufian? An archaeological assessment of brewing technology in the Epipaleolithic. *Journal of Archaeological Method and Theory* 20: 102–50.

Hayden, Brian, and Rob Gargett. 1990. Big man, big heart? A Mesoamerican view of the emergence of complex society. *Ancient Mesoamerica* 1: 3–20.

Hayden, Brian, and Sara Mossop Cousins. 2004. The social dimensions of roasting pits in a winter village site. In *Complex Hunter-Gatherers: Evolution and Organization of Prehistoric Communities on the Plateau of Northwestern North America*, eds. William Prentiss and Ian Kuijt, 140–54. Salt Lake City: University of Utah Press.

Hayden, Brian, and Suzanne Villeneuve. 2010. Who benefits from complexity? A view from Futuna. In *Pathways to Power*, eds. T. D. Price and G. Feinman, 95–146. New York: Springer.

2011a. Astronomy in the Upper Paleolithic? *Cambridge Archaeological Journal* 21: 331–55.

2011b. A century of feasting studies. *Annual Review of Anthropology* 40: 433–49.

Hedges, John. 1984. *Tomb of the Eagles.* London: John Murray.

Hefner, Robert. 1983. The problem of preference: Economic and ritual change in Highlands Java. *Man* 18: 669–89.

Helms, June. 1999. Political ideology in complex societies. In *Complex Polities in the Ancient Tropical World*, eds. E. Bacus and L. Lucero, 195–200. Arlington, VA: American Anthropological Association.

Helms, Mary. 1994. Chiefdom rivalries, control, and external contacts in lower Central America. In *Factional Competition and Political Development in the New World*, eds. Elizabeth Brumfiel and John Fox, 55–60. Cambridge: Cambridge University Press.

Hendon, Julia. 2003. Feasting at home. In *The Archaeology and Politics of Food and Feasting in Early States and Empires*, ed. T. Bray, 203–34. New York: Kluwer/Plenum.

Henig, Martin. 1982. Seasonal feasts in Roman Britain. *Oxford Journal of Archaeology* 1: 213–23.

Herskovits, Melville. 1940. *Economic Anthropology.* New York: W. W. Norton.

Heyman, Marjorie, Elliot M. Abrams, and AnnCorinne Freter. 2005. Late Archaic community aggregation and feasting in the Hocking Valley. In *The Emergence of the Moundbuilders: The Archaeology of Tribal Societies in Southeastern Ohio*, eds. E. M. Abrams and A. Freter, 67–81. Athens: Ohio University Press.

Higham, Charles. 1989. *The Archaeology of Mainland Southeast Asia.* Cambridge: Cambridge University Press.

2011. The bronze age of Southeast Asia: New insight on social change from Ban Non Wat. *Cambridge Archaeological Journal* **21**: 365–89.

Hildebrandt, William, and Kelley McGuire. 2002. The ascendance of hunting during the California Middle Archaic: An evolutionary perspective. *American Antiquity* **67**: 231–56.

Hildebrandt, William, and Jeffrey Rosenthal. 2009. Shellfish transport, caloric return rates, and prehistoric feasting on the Laguna De Santa Rosa, Alta California. *California Archaeology* **1**:55–78.

Hill, J. 1984. Prestige and reproductive success in man. *Ethology and Sociobiology* **5**: 77.

Hill, James. 1966. A prehistoric community in Eastern Arizona. *Southwestern Journal of Anthropology* **22**: 9–30.

Hill, Kim, and Hillard Kaplan. 1993. On why male foragers hunt and share food. *Current Anthropology* **34**: 701–10.

Hill, K. R., R. Walker, M. Bozicevic, J. Eder, T. Headland, B. Hewlett, A. Hurtado, F. Marlowe, P. Weissner, and B. Wood. 2011. Coresidence patterns in hunter-gatherer societies show unique human social structure. *Science* **331**: 1286–9.

Hill, Warren. 1999. *Ballcourts, competitive games, and the emergence of complex society*. Ph.D. dissertation, University of British Columbia.

Hill, Warren, and John Clark. 2001. Sports, gambling, and government: America's first social compact? *American Anthropologist* **103**: 331–45.

Hillman, Gordon. 2000. The plant food economy of Abu Hureyra 1 and 2: The Epipaleolithic. In *Village on the Euphrates*, eds. A. Moore, G. Hillman, and A. Legge, 327–98. Oxford: Oxford University Press.

Hillman, Gordon, R. Hedges, A. Moore, S. Colledge, and P. Pettitt. 2001. New evidence of late glacial cereal cultivation at Abu Hureyra on the Euphrates. *The Holocene* **11**: 383–93.

Hitchcock, Louise. 2011. Monumentalizing hierarchy: The significance of architecture in the emergence of complexity on Minoan Crete. Tenth International Cretan Congress (Khania) **A2**:85–102.

Ho, Pin-Ti. 1969. The loess and the origin of Chinese agriculture. *American Historical Review* **75**: 1–36.

Hobsbawm, Eric. 1962. *The Age of Revolution*. New York: Vintage Random House.

Hockings, K., T. Humle, J. Anderson, D. Biro, C. Sousa, G. Ohashi, and T. Matsuzawa T. 2007. Chimpanzees share forbidden fruit. *PLoS ONE* **2**: 886.

Hodder, Ian. 1990. *The Domestication of Europe*. London: Basil Blackwell.

2006. *The Leopard's Tale*. London: Thames and Hudson.

Hodder, Ian, and C. Cessford. 2004. Daily practice and social memory at Çatalhöyük. *American Antiquity* **69**: 17–40.

Hodder, Ian, and Lynne Meskell. 2012. Symbolism, feasting, and power at Çatalhöyük. *Current Anthropology* **53**:128–9.

Hoffman, Walter. 1891. The Mide'wiwin or "Grand Medicine Society" of the Ojibwa. *Bureau of American Ethnology, Annual Report for the Years 1885–1886* **7**: 143–300.

1896. The Menominee Indians. *Bureau of American Ethnology, Annual Report for 1892–1893* **14**: 3–328.

Hoopes, J., and M. Chenault. 1994. Excavations at Sitio Bolivar. In *Archaeology, Volcanism, and Remote Sensing in the Arenal Region, Costa Rica*, eds. P. Sheets and B. McKee, 87–105. Austin: University of Texas Press.

Hudson Travis, and Thomas C. Blackburn. 1986. *The Material Culture of the Chumash Interaction Sphere*. Vol. **IV**. Socorro: Ballena Press.

Hull, Kathleen, John Douglass, and Andrew York. 2013. Recognizing ritual action and intent in communal mourning features on the Southern California Coast. *American Antiquity* **78**: 24–47.

Humle T., K. Hockings, G. Ohashi, and T. Matsuzawa. 2008. Plant-food and tool sharing in wild chimpanzees. Paper presented at the XXII Congress of the International Primatological Society, Edinburgh, Scotland.

Hunn, Eugene. 1990. *Nch'i-Wana, The Big River: Mid-Columbian Indians and Their Land*. Seattle: University of Washington Press.

Huntington, R., and P. Metcalf, eds. 1979. *Celebrations of Death*. Cambridge: Cambridge University Pres.

Ikehara, Hugo, and Koichiro Shibata. 2008. Festines e integracón social en el Periodo Formativo. *Boletín de Arqueología PUCP* **9**:123–59.

Ikehara, Hugo, J. Fiorella Paipay, and Koichiro Shibata. (N.d.) Cuisine, feasts and leadership: The intensification of *Zea mays* use during the Late Formative in the Andean North Coast.

Iriarte, Jose, J. Christopher Gillam, and Oscar Marozzi. 2008. Monumental burials and memorial feasting: An example from the Southern Brazilian Highlands. *Antiquity* **82**: 947–61.

Isaac, Erich. 1962. On the domestication of cattle. *Science* **137**(3525): 195–98.

Isaac, Glynn. 1978. Food-sharing and human evolution. *Journal of Anthropological Research* **34**: 311–25.

Isaakidou, Valasia. 2007. Cooking in the labyrinth: Exploring "cuisine" at Bronze Age Knossos. In *Cooking and Culinary Practices in the Neolithic and Bronze Age Aegean*, ed. Josette Renard Christopher Mee, 5–24. Oxford: Oxbow Books.

Isaakidou, Valasia, Paul Halstead, Jack Davis, and Sharon Stocker. 2002. Burnt animal sacrifice at the Mycenaean "Palace of Nestor," Pylos. *Antiquity* **76**: 86–92.

Izikowitz, Karl. 1951. *Lamet: Hill Peasants in French Indochina*. Uppsala: Goteborg.

Jackson, H. 1991. The trade fair in hunter-gatherer interaction: The role of intersocietal trade in the evolution of Poverty Point culture. In *Between Bands and States*, ed. Susan Gregg, 265–86. Carbondale: Southern Illinois University Press.

Jackson, H. Edwin, and Susan L. Scott. 2003. Patterns of elite faunal utilization at Moundville, Alabama. *American Antiquity* **68**(3): 552–72.

Jacob, H. E. 1945. *Six Thousand Years of Bread*. Garden City, NY: Doubleday, Doran.

Jaeggi, A. V., J. Burkhart, and C. van Schaik. 2010. On the psychology of cooperation in humans and other primates: Combining the natural history and experimental evidence of prosociality. *Philosophical Transactions of the Royal Society B* **365**: 2723–35.

Jaeggi, A. V., M. van Noordwijk, and C. van Schaik. 2008. Begging for information: Mother-offspring food sharing among wild Bornean orangutans. *American Journal of Primatology* **70**: 533–41.

Jaeggi, A., and C. van Schaik. 2011. The evolution of food sharing in primates. *Behavioral Ecology and Sociobiology* **65**: 2125–40.

James, N. 2012. Stonehenge: New contexts ancient and modern. *Antiquity* **86**:922–3.

Jefferies, Richard. 1997. Middle Archaic bone pins: Evidence of Mid-Holocene regional-scale social groups in the Southern Midwest. *American Antiquity* **62**: 464–87.

2004. Regional-scale internation networks and the emergence of cultural complexity along the northern margins of the Southeast. In *Signs of Power: The Rise of Cultural*

Complexity in the Southeast, eds. J. Gibson and P. Carr, 71–85. Tuscaloosa: University of Alabama Press.

Jennbert, K. 1984. Den produktiva gavan. tradition och innovation i Sydskandinavien for omkring 5300 ar sedan. *Acta Archaeologica Ludensia* 4: 16–25.

1985. Neolithisation: A Scanian perspective. *Journal of Danish Archaeology* 4: 196–7.

1987. Neolithisation processes in the Nordic area. *Swedish Archaeology 1981–1985*: 21–35.

1998. "From the inside": A contribution to the debate about the introduction of agriculture in Southern Scandinavia. In *Harvesting the Sea, Farming the Forest the Emergence of Neolithic Societies in the Baltic Region.*, eds. Marek Zvelebil, Lucyna Domanska, and Robin Dennell, 31–5. Sheffield: Sheffield Academic Press.

Jennings, Justin. 2005. La chichera y el patron: Chicha and the energetics of feasting in the prehistoric Andes. *Archaeological Papers of the American Anthropological Association* 14: 241–59.

Jennings, Justin, Kathleen Antrobus, Sam Atencio, Erin Glavich, Rebecca Johnson, German Loffler, and Christine Luu. 2005. "Drinking beer in a blissful mood" alcohol production, operational chains, and feasting in the ancient world. *Current Anthropology* 46: 275–304.

Jensen, K., B. Hare, J. Call, and M. Tomasello. 2006. What's in it for me? Self-regard precludes altruism and spite in chimpanzees. *Proceedings of the Royal Society B* 273: 1013–21.

Jerardino, Antonieta. 2011. Integrating hunter-gatherer resource intensification and feasting along the West Coast of South Africa. Paper presented at the Annual Meetings of the Society for American Archaeology, Sacramento.

Jewitt, John. 1974. *The Adventures and Sufferings of John R. Jewitt, Captive among the Nootka, 1803–1805*. Toronto: McClelland and Stewart.

Jilek, Wolfgang. 1982. *Indian Healing*. Surrey, BC: Hancock House.

Jochelson, Waldemar. 1908. *Jesup North Pacific Expedition. The Koryak*. Memoir 6. New York: American Museum of Natural History.

Jochim, Michael. 2002. The implications of inter-group food exchange for hunter-gatherer affluence and complexity. In *Beyond Affluent Foragers*, eds. Colin Grier, Jangsuk Kim, and Junzo Uchiyama, 80–92. Oxford: Oxbow Books.

Joffe, Alexander H. 1998. Alcohol and social complexity in ancient Western Asia. *Current Anthropology* 39: 297–322.

Johannessen, Sissel. 1993. Food, dishes, and society in the Mississippi Valley. In *Foraging and Farming in the Eastern Woodlands*, ed. Margaret Scarry, 182–205. Gainesville: University Press of Florida.

Johansen, Shirley. 2004. *Prehistoric secret societies*. M.A. thesis, Simon Fraser University, Archaeology Department.

Johnson, Steven. 2003. Are we finally getting good enough at biochemistry to understand the mystery-and magic-of romance? *Discover* 24(5): 71–6.

Jordan, Peter. 2001. The materiality of shamanism as a "world-view." In *The Archaeology of Shamanism*, ed. Neil Price, 87–104. London: Routledge.

2003. *Material Culture and Sacred Landscape: The Anthropology of the Siberian Khanty*. Walnut Creek, CA: Rowman and Littlefield.

Jordan, Richard. 1994. Aqsqiluteng: Feasting and ceremonialism among the traditional Koniag of Kodiak Island, Alaska. In *Anthropology of the North Pacific Rim*, eds.

W. Fitzhugh and V. Chaussonet, 147–73. Washington, DC: Smithsonian Institution Press.

Joyce, A., and M. Winter. 1996. Ideology, power, and urban society in Pre-Hispanic Oaxaca. *Current Anthropology* **37**: 33–45.

Joyce, Rosemary, and John Henderson. 2007. From feasting to cuisine: Implications of archaeological research in an early Honduran village. *American Anthropologist* **109**: 642–53.

Junker, Laura Lee. 1999. *Raiding, Trading, and Feasting: The Political Economy of the Philippine Chiefdoms.* Honolulu: University of Hawai'i Press.

— 2001. The evolution of ritual feasting systems in prehispanic Philippine chiefdoms. In *Feasts Archaeological and Ethnographic Perspectives on Food, Politics, and Power*, eds. M. Dielter and B. Hayden, 267–310. Washington and London: Smithsonian Institution Press.

Junker, Laura Lee, Karen Mudar, and Marla Schwaller. 1994. Social stratification, household wealth, and competitive feasting in 15th/16th- century Philippine chiefdoms. *Research in Economic Anthropology* **15**: 307–58.

Junker, Laura, and Lisa Niziolek. 2010. Food preparation and feasting in the household and political economy of Pre-Hispanic Philippine chiefdoms. In *Inside Ancient Kitchens: New Directions in the Study of Daily Meals and Feasts*, ed. Elizabeth Klarich, 17–54. Boulder: University of Colorado Press.

Kaberry, Phyllis. 1942. Law and political organization in the Abelam tribe, New Guinea. *Oceania* **12**: 79–95.

— 1971. Political organization among the Northern Abelam. In *Politics in New Guinea*, eds. R. Berndt and P. Lawrence, 35–73. Nedlands: University of Western Australia Press.

Kaelas, Lili. 1981. Megaliths of the Funnel Beaker culture in Germany and Scandinavia. In *The Megalithic Monuments of Western Europe*, ed. Colin Renfrew, 77–90. London: Thames and Hudson.

Kaner, Simon. 2009. *The Power of Dogu*. London: British Museum.

Kansa, Sarah, and Stuart Campbell. 2002. Feasting with the dead? A ritual bone deposit at Domuztepe, Southeastern Turkey (c. 5550 cal BC). In *Behavior Behind Bones*, ed. Sharyn O'Day, 2–13. Oxford: Oxbow.

Kaplan, Hillard, and Kim Hill. 1985. Food sharing among Ache foragers: Tests of explanatory hypotheses. *Current Anthropology* **26**: 223–45.

Katz, Solomon, and Mary Voigt. 1986. Bread and beer: The early use of cereals in the human diet. *Expedition* **28**(2): 23–34.

Kaulicke, Peter. 2005. Las fiestas y sus residuos. *Boletín De Arqueología PUCP* **9**: 387–402.

Kaulicke, Peter, and Tom Dillehay, eds. 2005. *Boletín de arqueología PUCP, encuentros: Identidad, poder y manejo de espacios públicos*. Vol. **9**. Lima: Universidad Catolica del Peru, Departamento de Humanidades.

Keane, Webb. 1997. *Signs of Recognition: Powers and Hazards of Representation in an Indonesian Society*. Berkeley: University of California Press.

Keeley, Lawrence. 1995. Protoagricultural practices among hunter-gatherers. In *Last Hunters-First Farmers*, eds. T. Douglas Price and Anne Gebauer, 243–72. Santa Fe, NM: School of American Research Press.

— 1996. *War before Civilization*. New York: Oxford University Press.

Keen, Ian. 2006. Constraints on the development of enduring inequalities in Late Holocene Australia. *Current Anthropology* **47**: 7–35.

Kelly, Lucretia S. 2001. A case of ritual feasting at the Cahokia site. In *Feasts: Archaeological and Ethnographic Perspectives on Food, Politics, and Power*, eds. Michael Dielter and Brian Hayden, 334–67. Washington and London: Smithsonian Institution Press.

Kelly, Raymond. 2000. *Warless Societies and the Origin of War*. Ann Arbor: University of Michigan Press.

Kelly, Robert. 1995. *The Foraging Spectrum*. Washington, DC: Smithsonian Institution Press.

Kennedy, John G. 1978. Tarahumara of the Sierra Madre: Beer, ecology, and social organization. In *Worlds of Man: Studies in Cultural Ecology*, ed. Walter Goldschmidt, 97–223. Arlington Heights, IL: AHM Publishing Corporation.

Kessler, David. 2009. *The End of Overeating*. Rodale, NY: Emmaus.

Keswani, Priscilla. 1994. The social context of animal husbandry in early agricultural societies. *Journal of Anthropological Archaeology* **13**: 255–77.

Kidder, T., A. Ortmann, and L. Arco. 2008. Poverty Point and the archaeology of singularity. *SAA Archaeological Record* **8**: 9–12.

Kim, Seung-Og. 1994. Burials, pigs, and political prestige in Neolithic China. *Current Anthropology* **35**(2): 119–33.

Kirch, Patrick. 1975. *Cultural adaptation and ecology in Western Polynesia*. Ph.D. dissertation, Yale University.

1990. Production, intensification, and the early Hawaiian kingdom. In *Pacific Production Systems: Approaches to Economic Prehistory*, eds. D. Yen and J. Mummery, 190–209. Canberra: Department of Prehistory, Research School of Pacific Studies, Australian National University.

1991. Chiefship and competitive involution: The Marquesas Islands of Eastern Polynesia. In *Chiefdoms: Power, Economy, and Ideology*, ed. Timothy Earle, 119–45. Cambridge: Cambridge University Press.

1994. *The Wet and the Dry: Irrigation and Agricultural Intensification in Polynesia*. Chicago: University of Chicago Press.

2000. *On the Road of the Winds: An Archaeological History of the Pacific Islands before European Contact*. Berkeley: University of California Press.

2001. Polynesian feasting in ethnohistoric, ethnographic, and archaeological contexts: A comparison of three societies. In *Feasts: Archaeological and Ethnographic Perspectives on Food, Politics, and Power*, ed. Michael Dielter and Brian Hayden, 168–84. Washington and London: Smithsonian Institution Press.

Kirch, Patrick, and Roger Green. 2001. *Hawaiki, Ancestral Polynesia*. Cambridge: Cambridge University Press.

Kirch, Patrick V., and Sharyn Jones O'Day. 2003. New archaeological insights into food and status: A case study form pre-contact Hawaii. *World Archaeology* **34**(3): 484–97.

Kirch, Patrick V., and Marshall Sahlins. 1994. *Anahulu: The Anthropology of History in the Kingdom of Hawaii*. Chicago: University of Chicago Press.

Kirsch, A. 1973. *Feasting and Social Oscillation*. Southeast Asia Program Data Paper 92, Department of Asian Studies. Ithaca, NY: Cornell University Press.

Kirkby, Anne. 1973. *The Use of Land and Water Resources in the Past and Present, Valley of Oaxaca, Mexico*. Memoir 5. Ann Arbor: University of Michigan, Museum of Anthropology.

Klarich, Elizabeth A. ed. 2010a. *Inside Ancient Kitchens: New Directions in the Study of Daily Meals and Feasts*. Boulder: University of Colorado Press.

Klein, Michael J. 1997. The transition from soapstone bowls to Marcey Creek ceramics in the Middle Atlantic region: Vessel technology, ethnographic data, and regional exchange. *Archaeology of Eastern America* **25**: 143–58.

Klein, Richard. 1989. *The Human Career*. Chicago: University of Chicago Press.

Kloos, Peter. 1969. Role conflicts in social fieldwork. *Current Anthropology* **10**: 509–12.

Knauft, Bruce M. 1990. Melanesian warfare: A theoretical history. *Oceania* **60**: 250–310.

Knight, Vernon James. 2001. Feasting and the emergence of platform mound ceremonialism in Eastern North America. In *Feasts: Archaeological and Ethnographic Perspectives on Food, Politics, and Power*, eds. Michael Dielter and Brian Hayden, 311–33. Washington and London: Smithsonian Institution Press.

Knuckey, Graham. 1991. *Dispute settlement and community conflict in prehistoric Australian Aboriginal populations*. B.A. Honours thesis, University of New England.

Kobishchanow, Yurii M. 1987. The phenomenon of gafol and its transformation. In *Early State Dynamics.*, eds. Henri Claessen and Pieter Van de Velde. Vol. **2**, 108–28. Leiden: E. J. Brill.

Koch, Eva. 1998. *Neolithic Bog Pots*. Copenhagen: Det Kongelige Nordiske Oldskriftselskab.

Kohler, T., D. Cockburn, P. Hooper, K. Bocinsky, and Z. Kobti. 2012. The coevolution of group size and leadership. *Advances in Complex Systems* **15**. doi: 10.1142/S0219525911003256.

Kottak, Conrad. 1999. The new ecological anthropology. *American Anthropologist* **101**: 23–35.

Kramer, Samuel. 1975. *Sumerian Culture and Society: The Cuneiform Documents and Their Cultural Significance*. Cummings Module in Anthropology, no. 58. Menlo Park, CA: Cummings.

Krause, Aurel. 1956. *The Tlingit Indians*. Seattle: University of Washington Press.

Kroeber, A. L. 1925. *Handbook of the Indians of California*. Vol. Bulletin **78**. Washington, DC: Smithsonian Institution, Bureau of American Ethnology.

1953. *Handbook of the Indians of California*. Berkeley: California Book Company, Ltd.

Kuhn, Steven, and Mary Stiner. 2001. The antiquity of hunter-gatherers. In *Hunter-Gatherers: An Interdisciplinary Perspective*, eds. Catherine Panter-Brick, Robert Layton, and Peter Rowley-Conwy, 99–129. Cambridge: Cambridge University Press.

Kunstadter, Peter. 1966. Residential and social organization of the Lawa of North Thailand. *Southwestern Journal of Anthropology* **22**: 61–84.

Kurland, J., and S. Beckerman. 1985. Optimal foraging and hominid evolution: Labor and reciprocity. *American Anthropologist* **87**: 73–93.

Kyakas, Alome, and Polly Wiessner. 1992. *From inside the Women's House*. Brisbane: Robert Brown.

Kyriakidis, Evangelos. 2005. *Ritual in the Bronze Age Aegean*. London: Duckworth.

Larsson, Lars. 2000. Axes and fire – contacts with the gods. In *Form, Function, & Context: Material Culture Studies in Scandinavian Archaeology*, eds. Deborah Olausson and Helle Vandkilde, 93–103. Stockholm: Almquist & Wiksell International.

LaTrémolière, Elisabeth, and Florent Quellier. 2012. *Festins de la renaissance*. Paris: Picard & Epona.

Lau, George F. 2002. Feasting and ancestor veneration at Chinchawas, North Highlands of Ancash, Peru. *Latin American Antiquity* **13**(3): 279–304.

Law, R. G. 2000. Pits long, large and prestigious: Recognition of varieties of Maori kumara storage pits in Northern New Zealand. *New Zealand Journal of Archaeology* **21**(1999): 29–45.

Leach, Edmund. 1954. *Political Systems of Highland Burma*. Boston: Beacon Press.

Leach, Helen. 1999. Intensification in the Pacific: A critique of the archaeological criteria and their application. *Current Anthropology* **40**(3): 311–39.

———. 2003. Did East Polynesians have a concept of luxury foods? *World Archaeology* **34**(3): 447–54.

Leacock, Eleanor. 1954. *The Montagnais "Hunting Territory" and the Fur Trade*. Memoir 78, American Anthropological Association.

LeCount, Lisa J. 2001. Like water for chocolate: Feasting and political ritual among the Late Classic Maya at Xunantunich, Belize. *American Anthropologist* **103**(4): 935–53.

Lee, Richard. 1979. *The Dobe !Kung*. New York: Holt, Rinehart and Winston.

Lee, Richard, and Irven Devore, eds. 1968. *Man the Hunter*. Chicago: Aldine de Gruyter.

Legge, A. J., and P. Rowley-Conwy. 2000. The exploitation of animals. In *Village on the Euphrates. From Foraging to Farming at Abu Hureyra*, eds. A. M. Moore, G. Hillman, and A. Legge, 424–71. Oxford: Oxford University Press.

Legras, Jean-Luc, Dider Merdinoglu, Jean-Marie Cornuet, and Francis Karst. 2007. Bread, beer and wine: *Saccharomyces cerevisiae* diversity reflects human history. *Molecular Ecology* **16**: 2091–2102.

Legros, Dominique. 1985. Wealth, poverty and slavery among the 19th-century Tutchone Athapaskans. *Research in Economic Anthropology* **7**: 37–64.

Lehman, F. K. 1963. *The Structure of Chin Society*. Urbana: University of Illinois Press.

———. 1989. Internal inflationary pressures in the prestige economy of the feast of merit complex. In *Ritual, Power and Economy*, ed. Susan Russell, 89–102. DeKalb: Northern Illinois Press.

Lemonnier, Pierre. 1990. *Guerres et festins*. Paris: Maison des Sciences de l'Homme.

Levi-Strauss, Claude. 1969. *The Elementary Structure of Kinship*. Boston: Beacon Press.

Lewin, Roger. 1986. Self-interest in politics earns a Nobel Prize. *Science* **234**: 941–2.

Lewis-Williams, David, and David Pearce. 2005. *Inside the Neolithic Mind*. London: Thames and Hudson.

Lewthwaite, James. 1986. The transition to food production: A Mediterranean perspective. In *Hunters in Transition*, ed. Marek Zvelebil, 53–66. Cambridge: Cambridge University Press.

Lidén, Kersten. 1995. Megaliths, agriculture, and social complexity: A dietary study of two Swedish megalithic populations. *Journal of Anthropological Archaeology* **14**: 404–17.

Lightfoot, Kent, and Gary Feinman. 1982. Social differentiation and leadership development in early pithouse villages in the Mogollon region of the American Southwest. *American Antiquity* **47**: 64–85.

Lindauer, Owen, and John Blitz. 1997. Higher ground: The archaeology of North American platform mounds. *Journal of Archaeological Research* **5**(2): 169–207.

Liverani, Mario. 2006. *Uruk: The First City*. London: Equinox.

Loeb, Edwin. 1926. Pomo folkways. *University of California Publications in American Archaeology and Ethnology* **19**: 152–410.

———. 1936. The distribution and function of money in early societies. In *Essays in Anthropology Presented to A. L. Kroeber*, ed. Robert Lowie, 153–68. Berkeley: University of California Press.

Logan, A., C. Hastorf, and D. Pearsall. 2012. "Let's drink together": Early ceremonial use of maize in the Titicaca Basin. *Latin American Antiquity* **23**: 235–58.

Longacre, William. 1964. Archaeology as anthropology: A case study. *Science* **144**: 1454–5.

López, Gabriel, and Federico Restifo. 2012. Middle Holocene intensification and domestication of camelids in North Argentina, as tracked by zooarchaeology and lithics. *Antiquity* **86**: 1041–54.

Loring, Stephen. 1989. Une réserve d'outils de la periode intermédiaire sur la côte du Labrador. *Recherches Amerindiennes Au Quebec* **19**: 45–57.

1992. *Princes and princesses of ragged fame: Innu archaeology and ethnohistory in Labrador.* Ph.D. dissertation, University of Massachusetts.

Lorrain, Claire. 2000. Cosmic reproduction, economics and politics among the Kulina of Southwest Amazonia. *Journal of the Royal Anthropological Institute* **6**: 293–310.

Lourandos, Harry. 1980. Change or stability? Hydraulics, hunter-gatherers and population in temperate Australia. *World Archaeology* **11**: 245–64.

1985. Intensification and Australian prehistory. In *Prehistoric Hunter-Gatherers: The Emergence of Complexity*, eds. T. Price and J. Brown, 427–35. New York: Academic Press.

1988. Paleopolitics: Resource intensification in Aboriginal Australia and Papua New Guinea. In *Hunters and Gatherers*, eds. Tim Ingold, David Riches, and James Woodburn. Vol. **1**, 148–60. New York: Berg.

Love, J. R. B. 1936. *Stone-Age Bushmen of Today.* London and Glasgow: Blackie & Son Ltd.

Lu, Tracey. 2006. The occurrence of cereal cultivation in China. *Asian Perspectives* **45**: 129–58.

Lucas, Gavin, ed. 2009. *Hofstathir: Excavations of a Viking Age Feasting Hall in North-eastern Iceland.* Reykjavik: Institute of Archaeology, Iceland.

MacDonald, George. 1989. *Kitwanga Fort Report.* Ottawa: Canadian Museum of Civilization.

MacDonald, James. 2005. Cultivating in the Northwest: Early accounts of Tsimshian horticulture. In *Keeping It Living*, eds. D. Deur and N. Turner, 240–73. Seattle: University of Washington Press.

Mace, Ruth. 1993. Transitions between cultivation and pastoralism in Sub-Saharan Africa. *Current Anthropology* **34**: 363–87.

MacMullen, Ramsay. 1981. *Paganism in the Roman Empire.* New Haven: Yale University Press.

Magness-Gardiner, Bonnie. 1994. Urban-rural relations in Bronze Age Syria. In *Archaeological Views from the Countryside*, eds. Glenn Schwartz and Steven Falconer, 37–47. Washington, DC: Smithsonian Institution Press.

Maher, L., E. Banning, and M. Chazan. 2011. Oasis or mirage? Assessing the role of abrupt climate change in the prehistory of the Southern Levant. *Cambridge Archaeological Journal* **21**: 1–29.

Mainfort, Robert. 1985. Wealth, space, and status in a historic Indian cemetery. *American Antiquity* **50**(3): 555–79.

Mainland, Ingrid, and Paul Halstead. 2002. The diet and management of domestic sheep and goats at Neolithic Makriyalos. In *Diet and Health in Past Animal Populations*, ed. J. Davies, M. Fabis, I. Mainland, M. Richards, and R. Thomas, 104–12. Oxford: Oxbow Books.

Marciniak, Arkadiusz. 2001. Scientific and interpretive components in social zooarchaeology. The case of early farming communities in Kujavia. *Archaeologia Polona* **39**: 87–110.

2004. Everyday life at the LBK settlement: A zooarchaeological perspective. In *LBK Dialogues: Studies in the Formation of the Linear Pottery Culture*, eds. Alena Lukes and Marek Zvelebil, 129–41. Oxford: Archaeopress (BAR International Series 1304).

2005. *Placing Animals in the Neolithic: Social Zooarchaeology of Prehistoric Farming Communities.* London: UCL Press.

Marees, Pieter de. 1987 (orig. 1602). *Description and Historical Account of the Gold Kingdom of Guinea*. Oxford: Oxford University Press.

Makarewicz, Cheryl. 2012. The Younger Dryas and hunter-gatherer transitions to food production in the Near East. In *Hunter-Gatherer Behavior: Human Responses during the Youner Dryas*, ed. M. Eren, 195–230. Walnut Creek, CA: Left Coast Press.

Marinatos, Nanno. 1993. *Minoan Religion*. Charlotte: University of South Carolina Press.

Marlowe, Frank. 1999. Showoffs or providers? The parenting effort of Hadza men. *Evolution and Human Behavior* **20**: 391–404.

Marrinan, Rochell. 2010. Two Late Archaic period shell rings, St. Simon's Island, Georgia. In *Trend, Tradition and Turmoil: What Happened to the Southeastern Archaic?*, eds. D. Thomas and M. Sanger, 71–102. New York: American Museum of Natural History.

Marshall, Fiona, and Elisabeth Hildebrand. 2002. Cattle before crops: The beginnings of food production in Africa. *Journal of World Prehistory* **16**: 99–143.

Marshall, Yvonne. 2002. Transformations of Nuu-chah-nulth house. In *Beyond Kinship: Social and Material Reproduction in House Societies*, eds. Rosemary A. Joyce and Susan D. Gillespie, 73–102. Philadelphia: University of Pennsylvania Press.

Martin, John. 1827. *Tonga Islands: William Mariner's Account (Reprint)*. Tonga: Vava'u Press.

Martin, Louise. 1999. Mammal remains from the Eastern Jordanian Neolithic, and the nature of caprine herding in the steppe. *Paléorient* **25**(2): 87–104.

Matsui, A., N. Ishiguro, H. Hongo, and M. Minagawa. 2002. Wild pig? or domesticated boar? An archaeological view on the domestication of Sus scrofa in Japan. In *The First Steps of Animal Domestication*, eds. J.-D Vigne, J. Peters, and D. Helmer, 148–59. Oxford: Oxbow.

Mauss, Marcel. 1924. *The Gift*. New York: Free Press.

Maxham, Mintcy D. 2000. Rural communities in the Black Warrior Valley, Alabama: The role of commoners in the creation of the Moundville landscape. *American Antiquity* **65**(2): 337–54.

Maxwell, David. 2003. Using faunal remains to recognize and interpret prehistoric ceremonial deposits: An example from San Nicolas Island, California. In *Transitions in Zooarchaeology*, eds. Kathlyn Stewart and Frances Stewart, 103–13. Ottawa: Canadian Museum of Nature.

McAnany, Patricia. 1994. *Living with the Ancestors*. Austin: University of Texas Press.

McGovern, Patrick. 2003. *Ancient Wine: The Search for the Origins of Viniculture*. Princeton: Princeton University Press.

McGovern, Patrick E., Juzhong Zhang, Jogen Tang, Zhiqing Zhang, Gretchen Hall, and R. Moreau. 2004. Fermented beverages of pre- and proto-historic China. *Proceedings of the National Academy of Science* **101**(51): 17593–8.

McGrew, William. 1996. Dominance status, food sharing, and reproductive success in chimpanzees. In *Food and the Status Quest: An Interdisciplinary Perspective*, eds. P. Wiessner and W. Schiefenhovel, 39–45. Oxford: Berghahn Books.

McGuire, Kelly R., and Hildebrandt William R. 2005. Re-thinking Great Basin foragers: Prestige hunting and costly signaling during the Middle Archaic period. *American Antiquity* **70**(4): 695–712.

McIlwraith, T. 1948. *The Bella Coola Indians*. Toronto: University of Toronto Press.

McOmish, David. 1996. East Chisenbury: Ritual and rubbish at the British Bronze Age-Iron Age transition. *Antiquity* **70**: 68–76.

Mead, Margaret. 1937. *Cooperation and Competition among Primitive Peoples.* 1961 reprint ed. Boston: Beacon Press.

Meiklejohn, C., J. Wyman, K. Jacobs, and M. Jackes. 1997. Issues in the archaeological demography of the agricultural transition in Western and Northern Europe. In *Integrating Archaeological Demography*, ed. Richard Paine, 311–26. Carbondale: Center for Archaeological Investigations, Southern Illinois University.

Meillassoux, C. 1981. *Maidens, Meal and Money.* Cambridge: Cambridge University Press.

Melis, Alicia, Anna-Claire Schneider, and Michael Tomasello. 2011. Chimpanzees, *Pan troglodytes*, share food in the same way after collaborative and individual food acquisition. *Animal Behavior* **82**: 485–93.

Mellaart, James. 1967. *Çatal Hüyük: A Neolithic Town in Anatolia.* London: Thames and Hudson.

Méniel, Patrice. 2001. *Les gaulois et les animaux.* Paris: Errance.

Mesia, Christian. 2013. Feasting and power during the Andean Formative. Paper presented at the Annual Meetings of the Society for American Archaeology. Honolulu.

Meurers-Balke, Jutta, and Jens Lüning. 1999. Some aspects and experiments concerning the processing of glume wheats. In *Prehistory of Agriculture*, ed. Patricia Anderson, 238–53. Los Angeles: Institute of Archaeology, University of California.

Midgley, Magdalena S. 1992. *TRB Culture the First Farmers of the North European Plain.* Edinburgh: Edinburgh University Press.

Miles, Clement. 1990 (orig. 1912). *Christmas in Ritual and Tradition, Christian and Pagan.* Detroit: Omnigraphics.

Milicevic-Bradac, Marina. 2001. Treatment of the dead on the Eneolithic site of Vucedol, Croatia. In *The Archaeology of Cult and Religion*, eds. Peter F. Biehl and Francois Bertemes with Harald Meller, 209–15. Budapest: Archaeolingua Alapitvany.

Milisauskas, Sarunas, and Janusz Kruk. 1993. Archaeological investigations on Neolithic and Bronze Age sites in Southeastern Poland. In *Case Studies in European Prehistory*, ed. Peter Bogucki, 63–94. Boca Raton, FL: CRC Press.

Miller, Bruce, and Daniel Boxberger. 1994. Creating chiefdoms. *Ethnohistory* **41**: 267–93.

Millon, René. 1967. Teotihuacán. *Scientific American* **216**(6): 38–48.

Mills, Antonia. 2005. *"Hang onto These Words": Johnny David's Delamuukw Evidence.* Toronto: University of Toronto Press.

Mills, Barbara J. 2004. The establishment and defeat of hierarchy: Inalienable possessions and the history of collective prestige structures in the Pueblo Southwest. *American Anthropologist* **106**(2): 238–51.

    2007. Performing the feast: Visual display and suprahousehold commensalism in the Puebloan Southwest. *American Antiquity* **72**: 210–39.

Minagawa, M., A. Matsui, and N. Ishiguro. 2005. Patterns of prehistoric boar sus scrofa domestication, and inter-islands pig trading across the East China Sea. *Chemical Geology* **218**: 91–102.

Miracle, Preston. 2002. Mesolithic meals form Mesolithic middens. In *Consuming Passions and Patterns of Consumption*, eds. Miracle Preston, and Nicky Milner, 65–88. Cambridge: McDonald Institute.

Mitani, J. C. 2006. Reciprocal exchange in chimpanzees and other primates. In: *Cooperation in Primates: Mechanisms and Evolution*, eds. P. M. Kappeler and C. P. van Schaik, 101–13. Heidelberg: Springer-Verlag.

Mitani, J., and D. Watts. 1999. Demographic influences on the hunting behavior of chimpan-zees. *American Journal of Physical Anthropology* **109**: 439–54.

Mitani, John C., and David P. Watts. 2001. Why do chimpanzees hunt and share meat? *Animal Behavior* **61**: 915–24.

Mitchell, Stephen. 2004. *Gilgamesh*. New York: Free Press.

Modjeska, Nicholas. 1982. Production and inequality: Perspectives from central New Guinea. In *Inequality in New Guinea Highlands Societies*, ed. Andrew Strathern, 50–108. Cambridge: Cambridge University Press.

Monaghan, John. 1990. Reciprocity, redistribution, and the transaction of value in the Mesoamerican fiesta. *American Ethnologist* **17**: 758–74.

Montgomery, James. 2000. Ibn Fadln and the Riyyah. *Journal of Arabic and Islamic Studies* **3**: 1–25.

Moore, A. M., G. Hillman, and A. Legge. 2000. *Village on the Euphrates*. Oxford: Oxford University Press.

Moore, J. 1984. The evolution of reciprocal sharing. *Ethology and Sociobiology* **5**: 5–14.

Morgan, Christopher. 2012. Modeling modes of hunter-gatherer food storage. *American Antiquity* **77**:714–36.

Morris, Craig. 1979. Maize beer in the economics, politics, and religion of the inca empire. In *Fermented Food Beverages in Nutrition*, eds. Clifford Gastineau, William Darby, and N. Turner, 21–35. New York: Academic Press.

   1988. A city fit for an Inka. *Archaeology* **41**(5): 43–9.

Morrison, Kathleen D. 1996. Typological schemes and agricultural change. *Current Anthropology* **37**(4): 583–608.

Moyes, Holley. 2013. *Sacred Darkness: A Global Perspective on the Ritual Use of Caves*. Boulder: University Press of Colorado.

Muir, Robert, and Jonathan Driver. 2002. Identifying ritual use of animals in the Northern American Southwest. In *Behaviour Behind Bones*, ed. Sharyn O'Day, 128–43. Oxford: Oxbow.

Munro, Natalie. 2006. The role of the turkey in the southwest. In *Handbook of North American Indians: Environment, Origins, and Population*, ed. Douglas Ubelaker. Vol. **3**, 463–70. Washington, DC: Smithsonian Institution Press.

Munro, Natalie, and Leore Grosman. 2010. Early evidence (ca. 12,000 B.P.) for feasting at a burial cave in Israel. *National Academy of Science, Proceedings* **107**: 15362–6.

Munro, Neil. 1963. *Ainu Creed and Cult*. New York: Columbia University Press.

   1970. *Iyomande: Ainu Bear Festival*. 16 mm. film, DVD. Berkeley: University of California Extension Media Center.

Murra, J. 1960. Rite and crop in the Inca state. In *Culture in History*, ed. S. Diamond, 393–407. New York: Columbia University Press.

Murray, Matthew. 1995. Viereckschanzen and feasting: Socio-political ritual in Iron-Age Central Europe. *Journal of European Archaeolocy* **3**(2): 125–51.

Nairn, Charlie. 1981. *Kirghiz of Afghanistan*. DVD. London: PBS Video.

   1991. *Ongka's Big Moka (Kawelka)*. London: Image Media Services, Granada Television.

Nakamura, Carolyn, and Lynn Meskell. 2009. Articulate bodies: Forms and figures at çatalhöyük. *Journal of Archaeological Method and Theory* **16**: 205–30.

Nash, June. 1970. *In the Eyes of the Ancestors*. New Haven, CT: Yale University Press.

Nassaney, Michael S. 1992. Communal societies and the emergence of elites in the prehistoric American Southeast. *Archaeological Papers of the American Anthropological Association* **3**: 111–43.

Neitschmann, B. 1973. *Between Land and Water: The Subsistence Ecology of the Mosquito Indians.* New York: Seminar Press.

Netting, Robert. 1977. *Cultural Ecology.* Menlo Park, CA: Cummings.

Neumann, H. 2004. Beer as a means of compensation for work in Mesopotamia during the Ur III period. In *Drinking in Ancient Society,* ed. L. Milano, 321–31. Padova: Sargon srl.

Niblack, Albert. 1890. *The Coast Indians of Southern Alaska and Northern British Columbia.* Report for 1888. Washington, DC: U.S. National Museum.

Nicholas, George. 2007. Prehistoric hunter-gatherers in wetland environments. In *Wetland Archaeology and Environments,* eds. Malcolm Lillie and Stephen Ellis, 245–72. Oxford: Oxbow.

Nilsson, Martin. 1940. *Greek Folk Religion.* Philadelphia: University of Pennsylvania Press.

Nishida, T. 1970. Social behavior and relationship among wild chimpanzees of the Mahali Mountains. *Primates* **11**: 47–87.

Nishida, T., T. Hasegawa, H. Hayaki, Y. Takahata, and S. Uehara. 1992. Meat-sharing as a coalition strategy by an alpha male chimpanzee? In *Topics in Primatology,* eds. T. Nishida, W. C. McGrew, P. Marler, M. Pickford, and F. B. M. de Waal, 159–74. Tokyo: University of Tokyo Press.

Noah, Anna. 2005. *Household economies: The role of animals in a historic period chiefdom on the California coast.* Ph.D. dissertation, University of California, Los Angeles.

Oberg, Kalervo. 1955. Types of social structure among the lowland tribes of South and Central America. *American Anthropologist* **57**: 472–87.

——— 1973. *The Social Economy of the Tlingit Indians.* Seattle: University of Washington Press.

Oestigaard, Terje, and Joakim Goldhahn. 2006. From the dead to the living: Death as transactions and re-negotiations. *Norwegian Archaeological Review* **39**: 25–38.

Ohnuki-Tierney, Emiko. 1974. *The Ainu of the Northwest Coast of Southern Sakhalin.* Prospect Heights, IL: Waveland Press.

Oliva, Martin. 2000. Gravettienska sidliste U Dolnich Vestonic: Les sites gravettiens près de Dolni Vestonice. *Acta Mus.Moraviae, Sci.Soc.* **85**: 29–108.

Oliver, D. 1974. *Ancient Tahitian Society.* Honolulu: University of Hawai'i Press.

Olson, Ronald L. 1954. Social life of the Owikeno Kwakiutl. *Anthropological Records* **14**(3): 213–60.

Ostapkowicz, Joanna. 1992. *The visible ghosts: The human figure in Salish mortuary art.* B.A. Honours Thesis, Simon Fraser University, Archaeology Department.

Oswald, Alastair, Carolyn Dyer, and Barber Martyn. 2001. *The Creation of Monuments: Neolithic Causewayed Enclosures in the British Isles.* London: English Heritage.

Otterbein, Keith. 2004. *How War Began.* College Station: Texas A&M Press.

Overmann, Karenleigh. 2013. Material scaffolds in numbers and time. *Cambridge Archaeological Journal* **23**: 19–23.

Owens, D'Ann, and Brian Hayden. 1997. Prehistoric rites of passage: A comparative study of transegalitarian hunter-gatherers. *Journal of Anthropological Archaeology* **16**: 121–61.

Owens-Celli, Morgyn Geoffry. 1997. *Wheat Weaving and Straw Craft.* Asheville, NC: Lark Books.

Özkaya, Vecihi, and Aytaç Coskun. 2009. Körtik tepe, a new Pre-pottery Neolithic A site in South-eastern Anatolia. *Antiquity Online Project Gallery* http://antiquity.Ac.uk/proj gall/ozkaya/, 83.

Palaima, Thomas G. 2004. Sacrificial feasting in the Linear B documents. In *The Mycenaean Feast*, ed. Wright James C., 97–126. Princeton, NJ: American School of Classical Studies in Athens.

Pappa, Maria, Paul Halstead, Kostas Kotsakis, and Duska Urem-Kotsou. 2004. Evidence for large-scale feasting at Late Neolithic Makriyalos, N. Greece. In *Food, Cuisine and Society in Prehistoric Greece.*, eds. Paul Halstead and John Barrett, 16–44. Oxford: Oxbow Books.

Parker Pearson, M., J. Pollard, C. Richards, J. Thomas, C. Tilley, K. Welham, and U. Albarella. 2006. Materializing Stonehenge: The Stonehenge Riverside Project and new discoveries. *Journal of Material Culture* 11: 227–61.

Parker Pearson, Mike. 2007. The Stonehenge Riverside Project: Excavations at the east entrance of Durrington Walls. In *From Stonehenge to the Baltic.*, eds. Mats Larsson and Mike Parker Pearson, 125–44. Oxford: BAR International 1692.

Parkes, Peter. 1992. Reciprocity and redistribution in Kalasha prestige feasts. *Anthropozoologica* (16): 37–46.

Pastore, Ralph. 1985. Excavations at Boyd's Cove: The 1985 field season. In *Archaeology in Newfoundland & Labrador 1985.*, eds. Jane Sproull Thomson and Callum Thomson, 218–32. St. John's: Newfoundland Museum.

1992. *Shanawdithit's People*. Newfoundland: Atlantic Archaeology Ltd.

Patton, Mark. 1993. *Statements in Stone: Monuments and Society in Neolithic Brittany*. London: Routledge.

Pauketat, T., and T. Emerson, eds. 1997. *Cahokia: Domination and Ideology in the Mississippian World*. Lincoln: University of Nebraska Press.

Pauketat, Timothy R., Lucretia S. Kelly, Gayle J. Fritz, Neal H. Lopinot, Scott Elias, and Eve Hargrave. 2002. The residues of feasting and public ritual at early Cahokia. *American Antiquity* 67(2): 257–79.

Peacock, Sandra. 1998. *Putting down roots: The emergence of wild plant food production on the Canadian Plateau*. Ph.D. dissertation, University of Victoria.

2002. Perusing the pits: Evidence for pre-historic geophyte processing on the Canadian Plateau. In *Hunter-Gatherer Archaeobotany*, eds. S. Mason and J. Hather, 45–63. London: Institute of Archaeology.

Peacock, Sandra, and Nancy Turner. 2000. "Just like a garden": Traditional resource management and biodiversity conservation on the Interior Plateau of British Columbia. In *Biodiversity and Native America.*, eds. Paul Minnis and Wayne Elisens, 133–79. Norman: University of Oklahoma Press.

Peebles, Christopher, and Susan Kus. 1977. Some archaeological correlates of ranked societies. *American Antiquity* 42: 421–48.

Perlès, Catherine. 1992. Systems of exchange and organization of production in Neolithic Greece. *Journal of Mediterranean Archaeology* 5(2): 115–64.

1996. Les stratégies alimentaires dans les temps préhistoriques. In *Histoire de l'alimentation*, eds. J.-L. Flandrin and M. Montanari, 29–46. Paris: Fayard.

2001. *The Early Neolithic of Greece*. Cambridge: Cambridge University Press.

Perloff, Richard. 2003. *The Dynamics of Persuasion*. Mahway, NJ: Erlbaum.

Perodie, James R. 2001. Feasting for prosperity: A study of southern Northwest Coast feasting. In *Feasts Archaeological and Ethnographic Perspectives on Food, Politics, and Power*, eds. Michael Dielter and Brian Hayden, 185–214. Washington and London: Smithsonian Institution Press.

Perrot, Jean. 1957. Le Mesolithique de Palestine et les récentes découvertes à Eynan. *Antiquity and Survival* **2**(2/3): 90–9.

Perrot, J., and D. Ladiray. 1988. *Les hommes de Mallaha (Eynan) Israel*. Paris: Association Paléorient.

Peters, Joris, and Klaus Schmidt. 2004. Animals in the symbolic world of Pre-pottery Neolithic Göbekli Tepe, South-eastern Turkey. *Anthropozoologica* **39**: 179–221.

Peterson, Nicolas. 2006. Comment on I. Keen. *Current Anthropology* **47**: 23–4.

Pinnock, Frances. 2004. Considerations on the "banquet theme" in the figurative art of Mesopotamia and Syria. In *Drinking in Ancient Society*, ed. L. Milano, 15–26. Padova: Sargon srl.

Piperno, Dolores. 2011. The origins of plant cultivation and domestication in the New World tropics. *Current Anthropology* **52** (Supplement 4): S453–70.

Pita, Xose-Lois Armada. 2008. *Carne, drogas O alcohol? Calderos Y banquetes en el Bronce Final de la Peninsula Iberica*. Instituto de Estudos Galegos Padre Sarmiento.

Plog, Stephen, and Adam Watson. 2012. The Chaco pilgrimage model: Evaluating the evidence from Pueblo Alto. *American Antiquity* **77**: 449–77.

Pluckhahn, Thomas, J. Compton, and Mary Theresa Bonhage-Freund. 2006. Evidence of small-scale feasting from the Woodland Period site of Kolomoki, Georgia. *Journal of Field Archaeology* **31**: 263–84.

Pohl, John. 1998. Themes of drunkenness, violence, and factionalism in Tlaxcalan altar paintings. *RES: Anthropology and Aesthetics*: 184–207.

1999. The lintel paintings of Mitla and the function of the Mitla palaces. In *Mesoamerican Architecture as a Cultural Symbol.*, ed. Jeff Kowaslki, 176–97. Oxford: Oxford University Press.

2003. Ritual and iconographic variability in Mixteca-Puebla polychrome pottery. In *The Postclassic Mesoamerican World.*, eds. Michael Smith and Frances Berdan, 201–6. Salt Lake City: University of Utah Press.

Pohl, Mary, and John Pohl. 1994. Cycles of conflict: Political factionalism in the Maya Lowlands. In *Factional Competition and Political Development in the New World*, eds. Elizabeth M. Brumfiel and John W. Fox, 138–57. Cambridge: Cambridge University Press.

Pollington, Stephen. 2003. *The Mead-Hall: Feasting in Anglo-Saxon England*. Hockwold-cum-Wilton: Anglo-Saxon Books.

Pollock, Susan. 2003. Feasts, funerals, and fast food in early Mesopotamian states. In *The Archaeology and Politics of Food and Feasting in Early States and Empires*, ed. Tamara Bray, 17–38. New York: Kluwer Academic/Plenum.

Post, Richard. 1938. The Sinkaietk or Southern Okanagon of Washington: The subsistence quest. In *The Sinkaietk or Southern Okanaglon of Washington: General series in anthropology no. 6, contributions from the laboratory of anthropology, 2.*, ed. Leslie Spier, 11–34. Menasha, WI: George Banta.

Potter, James M. 1997. Communal ritual and faunal remains: An examples from the Dolores Anasazi. *Journal of Field Archaeology* **24**:353–64.

2000. Pots, parties, and politics: Communal feasting in the American Southwest. *American Antiquity* **65**(3): 471–92.

2010. Making meals matter. In *Inside Ancient Kitchens*, ed. E. Klarich, 241–53. Boulder: University Press of Colorado.

Potter, James M., and Scott Ortman. 2004. Community and cuisine in the Prehispanic American Southwest. In *Identity, Feasting, and the Archaeology of the Greater Southwest*, ed. Barbara Mills, 173–91. Boulder: University Press of Colorado.

Powdermaker, Hortense. 1932. Feasts in New Ireland: The social function of eating. *American Anthropologist* **34**: 236–47.

Price, Barbara. 1972. The burden of the cargo. In *Mesoamerican Archaeology: New Approaches*, ed. N. Hammond, 445–66. Austin: University of Texas Press.

Price, T. D., and Ofer Bar-Yosef. 2011. The origins of agriculture: New data, new ideas. *Current Anthropology* **52**(Supplement 4):S163–74.

Price, T. D., and J. Brown, eds. 1985. *Prehistoric Hunter-Gatherers*. Orlando, FL: Academic Press.

Pruetz, Jill, and Stacy Lindshield. 2012. Plant-food and tool transfer among savanna chimpanzees at Fongoli, Senegal. *Primates* **53**: 133–45.

Rambo, A. Terry. 1991. Energy and the evolution of culture: A reassessment of White's Law. In *Profiles in Cultural Evolution*, eds. A. Terry Rambo and Kathleen Gillogly. Ann Arbor: Museum of Anthropology, University of Michigan.

Randsborg, Klavs. 1982. Rank, rights and resources: An archaeological perspective from Denmark. In *Ranking, Resource and Exchange*, eds. Colin Renfrew and Stephen Shennan, 132–40. Cambridge: Cambridge University Press.

Rankin, Mary, and Joseph Esherik. 1990. Concluding remarks. In *Chinese Local Elites and Patterns of Dominance*, eds. J. Esherik and M. Rankin, 305–45. Berkeley: University of California Press.

Rappaport, Roy. 1968. *Pigs for the Ancestors*. New Haven, CT: Yale University Press.
   1999. *Ritual and Religion in the Making of Humanity*. Cambridge: Cambridge University Press.

Rathje, William. 1972. Praise the gods and pass the metates: A hypothesis of the development of lowland rainforest civilization in Mesoamerica. In *Contemporary Archaeology*, ed. Mark Leone, 365–92. Carbondale: Southern Illinois University Press.

Rautman, Alison E. 1998. Hierarchy and heterarchy in the American Southwest: A comment on McGuire and Saitta. *American Antiquity* **63**(2): 325–33.

Rawlings, T., and J. Driver. 2010. Paleodiet of domestic turkey, Shields Pueblo (5MT3807), Colorado. *Journal of Archaeological Science* **37**: 2433–41.

Reay, Marie. 1959. *The Kuma: Freedom and Conformity in the New Guinea Highlands*. Melbourne: Melbourne University Press.

Reber, Eleanora. 2006. A hard row to hoe: Changing maize use in the American Bottom and surrounding areas. In *Histories of Maize*, eds. J. Staller, R. Tykot, and B. Benz, 235–48. San Diego: Academic Press.

Redmond, Elsa. 1994. External warfare and the internal politics of Northern South American tribes and chiefdoms. In *Factional Competition and Political Development in the New World*, eds. Elizabeth Brumfiel and John Fox, 44–54. Cambridge: Cambridge University Press.

Renfrew, Colin, and Paul Bahn. 1996. *Archaeology: Theories, Methods and Practice*. London: Thames and Hudson.

Renfrew, Jane. 2004. *Roman Cookery Recipes and History*. London: English Heritage.

Rick, John. 2008. The architecture of the temple at Chavín de Huántar I. In *Chavín: Art, Architecture, and Culture*, eds. William Conklin and Jeffrey Quilter, 3–34. Los Angeles: Cotsen Institute of Archaeology, UCLA.

Rindos, David. 1984. *The Origins of Agriculture*. London: Academic Press.

Ritzenthaler, Robert. 1978. Southwestern Chippewa. In *Handbook of North American Indians: Northeast*, ed. Bruce Trigger. Vol. **15**, 743–59. Washington, DC: Smithsonian Institution.

Robinson, Brian. 2008. "Archaic period" traditions of New England and the Northeast. *The SAA Archaeological Record* **8**(5): 23–6.

Rohner, Ronald, and Evelyn Rohner. 1970. *The Kwakiutl*. New York: Holt, Rinehart and Winston.

Rojo-Guerra, Manuel Angel, Rafael Garrido-Pena, Inigo Garcia-Martinez-De-Lagran, Jordi Juan-Treserras, and Juan Carlos Matamala. 2006. Beer and Bell Beakers: Drinking rituals in Copper Age Inner Iberia. *Proceedings of the Prehistoric Society* **72**: 243–65.

Rolle, Renate. 1980. *The World of the Scythians*. London: B. T. Batsford.

Romanoff, Steven. 1992. The cultural ecology of hunting and potlatches among the Lillooet Indians. In *A Complex Culture of the British Columbia Plateau*, ed. Brian Hayden, 470–505. Vancouver: University of British Columbia Press.

Roscoe, Paul. 2000. Costs, benefits, typologies, and power: The evolution of political hierarchy. In *Hierarchies in Action: Cui bono?*, ed. M. Diehl, 113–33. Carbondale: Southern Illinois University Press.

2002. Comment. *Current Anthropology* **43**: 259–60.

2009. Social signaling and the organization of small-scale society: The case of contact-era New Guinea. *Journal of Archaeological Method and Theory* **16**: 69–116.

2012. Before elites: The political capacities of big men. In *Before Elites*, eds. T. Kienlin and A. Zimmerman, 41–54. Bonn: Rudolf Habelt.

(n.d.) Great Men, Big Men, Prestige and Power. Unpublished ms. on file with the author.

Rosenberg, Danny, and Dani Nadel. In press. The sounds of pounding: Boulder mortars and their significance to Natufian burial customs. Current: Anthropology.

Rosenberg, Michael. 1994. Hallan Çemi Tepesi: Some further observations concerning stratigraphy and material culture. *Anatolica* **20**: 121–40.

1998. Cheating at musical chairs: Territoriality and sedentism in an evolutionary context. *Current Anthropology* **39**: 653–81.

Rosenberg, Michael, and Davis, Michael. 1992. Hallan Çemi Tepesi, an Early Aceramic Neolithic site in Eastern Anatolia. *Anatolica* **18**: 1–18.

Rosenberg, Michael, and Robert Redding. 2000. Hallan Çemi and early village organization in Eastern Anatolia. In *Life in Neolithic Farming Communities*, ed. I. Kuijt, 39–61. New York: Kluwer.

Rosenbert, D. 2008. Serving meals making a home: The PPNA limestone vessel industry of the Southern Levant and its importance to the Neolithic revolution. *Paléorient* **34**: 23–32.

Rosenfeld, Silvana. 2012. Animal wealth and local power in the Huari Empire. *Nawpa Pacha: Journal of Andean Archaeology* **32**:131–64.

Rosenswig, Robert M. 2007. Beyond identifying elites: Feasting as a means to understand early Middle Formative society on the Pacific Coast of Mexico. *Journal of Anthropological Archaeology* **26**: 1–27.

Rosman, A., and P. Rubel. 1971. *Feasting with Mine Enemy*. Prospect Heights, IL Waveland Press.

Ross, Anne. 2006. Comment on I. Keen. *Current Anthropology* **47**: 24–5.

Roth, H. Ling. 1899. *The Aborigines of Tasmania*. Halifax, England: F. King & Sons.

Rousseau, Jerome. 1979. Stratification and chiefship. In *Challenging Anthropology. A Critical Introduction to Social and Cultural Anthropology*, eds. David H. Turner, and Gavin A. Smith, 229–44. Toronto: McGraw-Hill.

Rowley-Conwy, Peter, and Keith Dobney. 2007. Wild boar and domestic pigs in Mesolithic and Neolithic Southern Scandinavia. In *Pigs and Humans*, eds. U. Albarell, K. Dobney, A. Ervynck, and P. Rowley-Conwy, 131–55. Oxford: Oxford University Press.

Runnels, Curtis, and Tjeerd van Andel. 1988. Trade and the origins of agriculture in the eastern Mediterranean. *Journal of Mediterranean Archaeology* 1(1): 83–109.

Russell, Nerissa. 1993. *Hunting, Herding and Feasting: Human Use of Animals in Neolithic Southeast Europe*. Berkeley: University of California Press.

2012. Social Zooarchaeology: Humans and Animals in Prehistory. Cambridge: Cambridge University Press.

Russell, Nerissa, and Louise Martin. 2005. Catal Höyük mammal remains. In *Inhabiting catalhöyük: Reports from the 1995–99 Seasons*, ed. Ian Hodder, 33–97. Ankara: British Institute of Archaeology.

Russell, Nerissa, Louise Martin, and Hijlke Buitenhuis. 2005. Cattle domestication at Çatalhöyük revisited. *Current Anthropology* 46: 101–8.

Russo, Michael. 2004. Measuring shell rings for social inequality. In *Signs of Power: The Rise of Cultural Complexity in the Southeast*, eds. Jon Gibson and Philip Carr, 26–70. Tuscaloosa: University of Alabama Press.

2008. Late Archaic shell rings and society in the Southeast U.S. *SAA Archaeological Record* 8(5): 18–22.

Russo, M., and G. Heide. 2001. Shell rings of the southeast US. *Antiquity* 75: 491–2.

Ruyle, Eugene. 1973. Slavery, surplus, and stratification on the Northwest Coast: The ethno-energetics of an incipient stratification system. *Current Anthropology* 14: 603–17.

Sadr, K. 2005. From foraging to herding: The West Coast of South Africa in the first millennium AD. *Human Evolution* 20: 217–30.

Sahlins, Marshall. 1958. *Social Stratification in Polynesia*. Seattle: University of Washington Press.

1968. *Tribesmen*. Englewood Cliffs, NJ: Prentice-Hall.

1972. *Stone Age Economics*. Chicago: University of Chicago Press.

2003. Artificially maintained controversies: Global warming and Fijian cannibalism. *Anthropology Today* 19: 3–5.

Saitta, Dean. 1997. Power, labor, and the dynamics of change in Chacoan political economy. *American Antiquity* 62: 7–26.

1999. Prestige, agency, and change in middle-range societies. In *Material Symbols: Culture and Economy in Prehistory*, ed. J. Robb, 135–49. Carbondale: Southern Illinois University Press.

Saitta, D., and A. Keene. 1990. Polities and surplus flow in communal societies. In *The Evolution of Political Systems*, ed. S. Upham, 203–24. Cambridge: Cambridge University Press.

Sakaguchi, Takashi. 2009. Storage adaptations among hunter-gatherers: A quantitative approach to the Jomon period. *Journal of Anthropological Archaeology*. 28: 290–330.

Sakellaraki, Y., and E. Sapouna-Sakellaraki. 1981. Drama of death in a Minoan temple. *National Geographic* 159(2):205–22.

Salzer, Bob. 1998. Ho-chunk offer radar to explore mysteries of the Southeast cornber. *Newsletter of the Gottschall Rock Art Project* 14: 1–8.

Samuels, Stephan. 2005. Ozette household production. In *Household Archaeology on the Northwest Coast*, eds. E. Sobel, D. Gahr, and K. Ames, 200–44. Ann Arbor, MI: International Monographs in Prehistory.

Sánchez, Margarita. 2008. El consumo de alimento como estrategia social: Recetas para la construcción de la memoria y creación de identidades. *Cuadernos De Prehistoria y Arqueología De La Universidad De Granada* **18**: 17–39.

　　2011. Commensality rituals: Feeding identities in prehistory. In *Guess Who's Coming to Dinner*, eds. Gonzalo Aranda, Sandra Montón-Subías, and Margarita Sánchez, 8–29. Oxford: Oxbow Books.

Sand, Christophe. 1999. Comment. *Current Anthropology* **40**: 329–30.

Sandarupa, Stanislaus. 1996. *Life and death in Toraja.* 21 Computer: Ujung Pandang, Sulawesi.

Sanders, William, and Barbara Price. 1968. *Mesoamerica: The Evolution of a Civilization.* New York: Random House.

Sassaman, Kenneth. 2010. Getting from the Late Archaic to Early Woodland in three middle valleys. In *Trend, Tradition and Turmoil: What Happened to the Southeast Archaic?*, eds. David Thomas and Mathew Sanger, 229–36. New York: American Museum of Natural History.

Sassaman, Kenneth, Meggan Blessing, and Asa Randall. 2006. Stallings island revisited. *American Antiquity* **71**: 539–65.

Satterthwait, Leonn. 1987. Socioeconomic implications of Australian Aboriginal net hunting. *Man* **22**: 613–36.

Saulieu, Geoffroy de. 2004. *Art rupestre et statues-menhirs dans les Alpes.* Paris: Errance.

Saunders, Joe. 2004. The stratigraphic sequence at the Rollins Shell Ring: Implications for ring function. *Florida Anthropologist* **57**: 249–68.

　　2010. Late Archaic? What the hell happened to the Middle Archaic? In *Trend, Tradition and Turmoil: What Happened to the Southeastern Archaic?*, eds. D. Thomas and M. Sanger, 237–46. New York: American Museum of Natural History.

Saunders, Joe, R. Mandel, C. Sampson, C. Feathers, K. Gremillion, C. Hallmark, H. Jackson, J. Johnson, R. Jones, R. Saucier, G. Stinger, and M. Vidrine. 2005. Watson Brake, a Middle Archaic mound complex in Northeast Louisiana. *American Antiquity* **70**:595–630.

Scarborough, Vernon, and William Burnside. 2010. Complexity and sustainability: Perspectives from the ancient Maya and the modern Balinese. *American Antiquity* **75**: 327–63.

Schachner, Gregson. 2010. Corporate group formation and differentiation in Early Puebloan villages of the American Southwest. *American Antiquity* **75**: 473–96.

Schaepe, David. 2006. Rock fortifications. *American Antiquity* **71**: 671–705.

Schlegel, Alice. 1991. Status, property, and the value of virginity. *American Ethnologist* **18**: 719–34.

Schmandt-Besserat, Denise. 1992. *Before Writing.* Austin: University of Texas Press.

　　1996. *How Writing Came About.* Austin: University of Texas Press.

　　2001. Feasting in the ancient Near East. In *Feasts: Archaeological and Ethnographic Perspectives on Food, Politics, and Power*, eds. Michael Dielter and Brian Hayden, 391–403. Washington and London: Smithsonian Institution Press.

Schnitger, Friedrich. 1939. *Forgotten Kingdoms in Sumatra.* Leiden: E. J. Brill.

Schulting, Rick. 1994. The hair of the dog: The identification of a Coast Salish dog-hair blanket from Yale, British Columbia. *Canadian Journal of Archaeology* **18**: 57–76.

　　1996. Antlers, bone pins and flint blades: The Mesolithic cemeteries of Teviec and Hoedic, Brittany. *Antiquity* **70**: 335–50.

Schwadron, Margo. 2010. Prehistoric landscapes of complexity: Archaic and Woodland period shell works, shell rings, and tree islands of the everglades, South Florida.

In *Trend, Tradition and Turmoil: What Happened to the Southeast Archaic?*, eds. David H. Thomas and Matthew Sanger, 113–46. New York: American Museum of Natural History.

Schwartz, Glenn. 1994. Rural economic specialization and early urbanization in the Khabur Valley, Syria. In *Archaeological Views from the Countryside*, eds. Glenn Schwartz and Steven Falconer, 19–36. Washington, DC: Smithsonian Institution Press.

Schwartz, Marion. 1997. *A History of Dogs in the Early Americas*. New Haven, CT: Yale University Press.

Schwarz, Frederick. 1994. *Archaeological Investigations at the Bank Site, Terra Nova National Park, Bonavista, Bay, Newfoundland*. Report prepared for the Archaeology Branch, Atlantic Regional Office, Canadian Parks Service, Halifax, N.S.

1996. Recent Indian communal feasting structures in Newfoundland and Labrador. Paper presented at Canadian Archaeological Association Annual Meeting Abstracts, Halifax.

Scullard, H. 1981. *Festivals and Ceremonies of the Roman Republic*. London: Thames and Hudson.

Scully, Terence. 1986. *Chiquart's "on Cookery": A Fifteenth-Century Savoyard Culinary Treatise*. New York: Peter Lang.

Seeman, Mark F. 1979. Feasting with the dead: Ohio Hopewell charnel house ritual as a context for redistribution. In *Hopewell Archaeology, the Chllicothe Conference*, eds. David Brose and N. Greber, 39–46. Kent, OH: Kent State University Press.

1986. Adena houses and their implications for Early Woodland settlement models in Ohio Valley. In *Early Woodland Archaeology*, eds. Kenneth Farnsworth and Thomas Emerson, 564–80. Kampsville, IL: Center for American Archaeology Press.

Serpell, James. 1996. *In the Company of Animals*. Cambridge: Cambridge University Press.

Service, Elman. 1962. *Primitive Social Organization*. New York: Random House.

1971. *Primitive Social Organization: An Evolutionary Perspective*. New York: Random House.

1975. *Origins of the State and Civilization*. New York: W. W. Norton.

Seymour, Deni. 1994. Peripheral considerations: Defining the spatial and physical correlates of storage behavior in Hohokam structures. *Kiva* **59**:377–94.

Sharp, Henry. 1994. Inverted sacrifice. In *Circumpolar Religion and Ecology*, eds. T. Irimoto and T. Yamada, 253–71. Tokyo: University of Tokyo Press.

Sheehan, Glenn. 1985. Whaling as an organizing focus in northwestern Alaskan Eskimo societieis. In *Prehistoric Hunter-Gatherers*, eds. T. D. Price and J. Brown, 123–54. Orlando, FL: Academic Press.

1989. In the belly of the whale. *Archaeology* **42**: 52–64.

Shennan, Stephen. 1986. Central Europe in the third millennium B.C. *Journal of Anthropological Archaeology* **5**: 115–46.

Sherman, D. George. 1990. *Rice, Rupees, and Ritual Economy and Society among the Samosir Batak of Sumatra*. Stanford, CA: Stanford University Press.

Sherratt, Andrew. 1991. Sacred and profane substances: The ritual use of narcotics in later Neolithic Europe. In *Sacred and Profane*, eds. P. Garwood, D. Jennings, R. Skeates, and J. Toms. Vol. **32**, 50–64. Oxford: Oxford University Committee for Archaeology Monographs.

1995. Alcohol and its alternatives. In *Consuming Habits: Drugs in History and Anthropology*, eds. J. Goodman, P. Lovejoy, and A. Sherratt, 11–46. London: Routledge.

Sherratt, Susan. 2004. Feasting in Homeric epic. In *The Mycenaean Feast*, ed. James C. Wright, 181–213. Princeton, NJ: American School of Classical Studies at Athens.

Shimada, Izumi, Ken-ichi Shinoda, Julie Farnum, Robert Corruccini, and Hirokatsu Watanabe. 2004. An integrated analysis of pre-historic mortuary practices. *Current Anthropology* **45**(3): 369–86.

Shinichiro, Takakura. 1960. The Ainu of Northern Japan. *American Philosophical Society, Transactions.* **50**(4): 1–88.

Shnirelman, V. A. 1990. Class and social differentiation in Oceania. In *Culture and History in the Pacific*, ed. Jukka Siikala. Vol. **27**. Helsinki: Suomen Antropologinen Seura; The Finnish Anthropological Society.

1992. Complex hunter-gatherers: Exception or common phenomenon? *Dialectical Anthropology* **17**: 183–96.

Shryock, Andrew. 1987. The Wright Mound reexamined. *Midcontinental Journal of Archaeology* **12**: 243–68.

Silk, J. B., S. Brosnan, J. Vonk, J. Henrich, D. Povinelli, A. Richardson, S. Lambeth, J. Mascaro, and S. Schapiro. 2005. Chimpanzees are indifferent to the welfare of unrelated group members. *Nature* **437**: 1357–9.

Silk, Joan, Sarah Brosnan, Joseph Henrich, Susan P. Lambeth, and Steven Shapiro. 2013. Chimpanzees share food for many reasons: The role of kinship, reciprocity, social bonds and harassment on food transfers. *Animal Behavior* **85**: 941–7.

Silk, J., and B. House. 2011. The evolutionary foundations of human moral sentiments. *Proceedings of the National Academy of Sciences* **108**: 10910–7.

Sillitoe, Paul. 1978. Big men and war in New Guinea. *Man* **13**: 252–71.

Simeone, William. 1995. *Rifles, Blankets, and Beads: Identity, History, and the Northern Athapaskan Potlatch*. Norman: University of Oklahoma Press.

Simmons, Alan. 2004. The earliest residents of Cyprus: Ecological pariahs or harmonious settlers? Paper presented at the Annual Meeting of the Society for American Archeology, Montreal.

2007. *The Neolithic Revolution in the Near East*. Tucson: University of Arizona Press.

Simoons, Frederick. 1968. *Mithen: A Ceremonial Ox*. Madison: University of Wisconsin Press.

1994. *Eat Not This Flesh*. Madison: University of Wisconsin Press.

Skibo, James. 1999. *Ants for Breakfast*. Salt Lake City: University of Utah Press.

Smalley, John, and Michael Blake. 2003. Sweet beginnings: Stalk sugar and the domestication of maize. *Current Anthropology* **44**: 675–704.

Smith, Bruce. 2001a. The transition to food production. In *Archaeology at the Millennium*, eds. Gary Feinman and T. Douglas Price, 199–230. New York: Kluwer Academic Plenum Publishers.

2001b. Low-level food production. *Journal of Archaeological Research* **9**: 1–43.

2007. Niche construction and the behavioral context of plant and animal domestication. *Evolutionary Anthropology* **16**: 188–99.

Smith, Bruce, and Richard Yarnell. 2009. Initial formation of an indigenous crop complex in Eastern North America at 3800 B.P. *Proceedings, National Academy of Science* **106**: 6561–6.

Smith, Eric, and Bruce Winterhalder, eds. 1992. *Evolutionary Ecology and Human Behavior*. New York: Aldine de Gruyter.

Smith, Isobel. 1965. *Windmill Hill and Avebury*. Oxford: Clarendon Press.

Smith, Michael, Jennifer Wharton, and Jan Marie Olson. 2003. Aztec feasts, rituals, and markets. In *The Archaeology and Politics of Food and Feasting in Early States and Empires*, ed. Tamara Bray, 235–70. New York: Kluwer Academic/Plenum.

Smith, Monica. 2012. Networks of provision, networks of disposition: The potential for feast failure. Paper presented at Annual Meetings, Society for American Archaeology, Memphis.

Snarkis, M. 1984. Central America: The Lower Caribbean. In *The archaeology of Lower Central America*, eds. F. Lange and D. Stone, 195–232. Albuquerque: University of New Mexico Press.

Snyder, Lynn, and Jennifer Leonard. 2006. Dogs. In *Handbook of North American Indians, vol. 3, Environment, Origins, and Population*, ed. Douglas Ubelaker, 452–62. Washington, DC: Smithsonian Institution Press.

Soffer, Olga. 2000. Gravettian technologies in social contexts. In *Hunters of the Golden Age*, eds. Wil Roebroeks, M. Mussi, J. Svoboda, and Kelly Fennema, 59–75. Leiden: University of Leiden.

Solecki, R., R. Solecki, and A. Agelarakis. 2004. *The Proto-Neolithic Cemetery in Shanidar Cave*. College Station: Texas A&M University Press.

Speck, Frank. 1935. *Naskapi. The Savage Hunters of the Labrador Peninsula*. Norman: University of Oklahoma Press.

Speiser, F. 1996. *Ethnology of Vanuatu: An Early Twentieth Century Study*. Honolulu: University of Hawai'i.

Spencer, Charles. 1994. Factional ascendance, dimensions of leadership, and the development of centralized authority. In *Factional Competition and Political Development in the New World*, eds. Elizabeth Brumfiel and John Fox, 31–43. Cambridge: Cambridge University Press.

Spencer, R. 1959. *The North Alaskan Eskimo: A Study in Ecology and Society*. Washington, DC: Bureau of American Ethnology: Bulletin 17.

Speth, John. 1990. Seasonality, resource stress, and food sharing in so-called "egalitarian" foraging societies. *Journal of Anthropological Archaeology* 9: 148–88.

Speth, John, and Katherine Spielmann. 1983. Energy source, protein metabolism, and hunter-gatherer subsistence strategies. *Journal of Anthropological Archaeology* 2: 1–31.

Spindler, Louise. 1978. Menominee. In *Handbook of North American Indians: Northeast.*, ed. Bruce Trigger. Vol. 15, 708–24. Washington, DC: Smithsonian Institution.

Spriggs, Mathew. 1986. Landscape, land use, and political transformation in Southern Melanesia. In *Island Societies*, ed. Patrick Kirch, 6–19. Cambridge: Cambridge University Press.

——— 1990. Why irrigation matters in Pacific prehistory. In *Pacific Production Systems: Approaches to Economic Prehistory*, eds. D. Yen and J. Mummery, 174–85. Canberra: Department of Prehistory, Research School of Pacific Studies, The Australian National University, Canberra.

Stafford, Michael. 1999. *From Forager to Farmer in Flint: A Lithic Analysis of the Prehistoric Transition to Agriculture in Southern Scandinavia*. Aarhus: Aarhus University Press.

Stahl, Peter. 2003. Pre-Columbian animal domestication at the edge of empire. *World Archaeology* 34:470–83.

Staller, John. 2006. The social, symbolic, and economic significance of zea mays L. in the Late Horizon period. In *Histories of Maize*, eds. J. Staller, R. Tykot, and B. Benz, 449–67. Amsterdam: Elsevier.

Stanford, Craig B. 2001. A comparison of social meat-foraging by chimpanzees and human foragers. In *Meat Eating and Human Evolution*, eds. Craig B. Stanford and Henry T. Bunn, 122–40. Oxford: Oxford University Press.

Stanford, Craig, and Henry Bunn. 1999. Meat eating and hominid evolution. *Current Anthropology* **40**: 726–8.

Stannish, Charles. 1994. The hydraulic hypothesis revisited: Lake Titicaca basin raised fields in theoretical perspective. *Latin American Antiquity* **5**: 312–32.

Starin, E. D. 1978. Food transfer by wild titi monkeys (Callicebus torquatus torquatus). *Folia Primatologica* **30**: 145–51.

Stasch, Rupert. 2012. The semiotics of world-making in Korowai feast longhouses. *Language and Communication* **23**: 359–83.

Steel, Louise. 2004. A goodly feast . . . A cup of mellow wine: Feasting in Bronze Age Cyprus. In *The Mycenaean Feast*, ed. James C. Wright, 161–80. Princeton, NJ: American School of Classical Studies at Athens.

Stein, Burton. 1960. The economic function of a Medieval South Indian temple. *Journal of Asian Studies* **19**:163–76.

Stevens, C. 1996. *The Political Ecology of a Tongan village*. University of Arizona.

Stevens, J. R. 2004. The selfish nature of generosity: Harassment and food sharing in primates. *Proceedings of the Royal Society of London, Series B* **21**: 451–6. doi: 10.1098/rspb.2003.2625.

Stevens, Jeffrey, and Ian C. Gilby. 2004. A conceptual framework for nonkin food sharing: Timing and currency of benefits. *Animal Behavior* **67**: 603–14.

Stevens, J. R., and D. Stephens. 2002. Food sharing: A model of manipulation by harassment. *Behavioral Ecology* **13**: 393–400.

Stevenson, H. N. C. 1943. *The Economics of the Central Chin Tribes*. Bombay: Times of India Press.

Steward, Julian. 1938. *Basin-Plateau Aboriginal Sociopolitical Groups*. Washington, DC: Smithsonian Institution: Bureau of American Ethnology Bulletin 120.

   1955. *Theory of Culture Change*. Urbana: University of Illinois Press.

Stika, Hans-Peter. 2005. Comment. *Current Anthropology* **46**:296.

Stiner, Mary, Natalie Munro, and Todd Surovell. 2000. The tortoise and the hare. *Current Anthropology* **41**: 39–68.

Stocker, Sharon R., and Jack L. Davis. 2004. Animal sacrifice, archives, and feasting at the Palace of Nestor. In *The Mycenaean Feast*, ed. James C. Wright, 59–76. Princeton, NJ: American School of Classical Students at Athens.

Stoodley, Nick. 2010. Feasting with the dead: Food and drink in Anglo-Saxon burial rituals. *Journal of English and Germanic Philology* **109**: 227–30.

Stordeur, Danielle, and F. Abbès. 2002. Du PPNA au PPNB: Mise en lumière d'une phase de transition à Jerf el Ahmar (Syrie). *Bulletin, Société Préhistorique Française* **99**: 563–95.

Stordeur, Danielle, and George Willcox. 2009. Indices de culture et d'utilisation des céréales à Jerf el Ahmar. In *De mediterranée et D'ailleurs . . .*, 693–710. Toulouse: Archives d'Ecologie Prehistorique.

Stothert, Karen E. 1985. The preceramic Las Vegas culture of coastal Ecuador. *American Antiquity* **50**(3): 613–37.

Stott, Philip, and S. Sullivan, eds. 2001. *Political Ecology*. London: Edward Arnold.

Strathern, Andrew. 1971a. Pig complex and cattle complex. *Mankind* **8**: 129–36.

1971b. *The Rope of Moka*. Cambridge: Cambridge University Press.

Suttles, Wayne. 1958. Private knowledge, morality, and social classes among the Coast Salish. *American Anthropologist* **60**: 497–507.

1968. Coping with abundance: Subsistence on the Northwest Coast. In *Man the Hunter*, eds. R. Lee and I. Devore, 56–68. Chicago: Aldine de Gruyter.

1987. Private knowledge, morality, and social classes among the Coast Salish. In *Coast Salish Essays*, ed. W. Suttles, 3–14. Seattle: University of Washington Press.

Swanton, John R. 1911. Indian tribes of the Mississippi Valley and adjacent coast of the Gulf of Mexico. *Smithsonian Institution Bureau of American Ethnology Bulletin*(43).

1924 (printed 1928). Religious beliefs and medical practices of the Creek Indians. *Bureau of American Ethnology Annual Report* **1924**/1925: 473–672.

1931. Source material or the social and ceremonial life of the Choctaw Indians. *Smithsonian Institution Bureau of American Ethnology Bulletin*(103).

1942. Source material on the history and ethnology of the Caddo Indians. *Smithsonian Institution Bureau of American Ethnology Bulletin*(132).

Tabarev, A. V. 2007. On oysters and archaeologists (the notion of "aquaculture" in Far Eastern archaeology). *Archaeology, Ethnology & Anthropology of Eruasia* **4**(32): 52–9.

Taché, Karine. 2008. *Structure and regional diversity of the Meadowood Interaction Sphere*. Ph.D. dissertation, Burnaby: Simon Fraser University.

2011. *Structure and Regional Diversity of the Meadowood Interaction Sphere*. Museum of anthropology publications, memoir 48. Ann Arbor: University of Michigan.

Taché, Karine, and O. Craig. n.d. Cooperative harvesting of aquatic resources triggered the beginning of pottery production in Nortyheastern North America. Ms. prepared for publication submission.

Taché, Karine, Daniel White, and Sarah Seelen. 2008. Potential functions of Vinette I pottery. *Archaeology of Eastern North America* **36**: 63–90.

Tainter, John A. 1988. *The Collapse of Complex Societies*. Cambridge: Cambridge University Press.

Talbot, Amaury. 1923. *Life in Southern Nigeria*. New York: Barnes and Noble.

Tannahill, R. 1973. *Food in History*. London: Eyre Methuen.

Tanner, Adrian. 1979. *Bringing Home Animals: Religious Ideology and Mode of Production of the Mistassini Cree Hunters*. St. John's: Institute of Social and Economic Research Memorial University of Newfoundland.

Tchernov, E., and F. Valla. 1997. Two new dogs, and other Natufian dogs. *Journal of Archaeological Science* **24**: 65–95.

Teissier, Beatrice. 1984. *Ancient Near Eastern Cylinder Seals from the Marcopoli Collection*. Berkeley: University of California Press.

Teit, James. 1900. *The Thompson Indians of British Columbia*. Memoir. Vol. **2**(4). New York: American Museum of Natural History.

1906. *The Lillooet Indians*. Leiden: E. J. Brill.

1909. The Shuswap. In *American Museum of Natural History Memoirs*. Vol. **2**(7), 447–789. New York: American Museum of Natural History.

Teleki, G. 1973. *The Predatory Behavior of Wild Chimpanzees*. Lewisburg, PA: Bucknell University Press.

Terrell, J., J. Hart, S. Barut, N. Cellinese, and A. Curet. 2003. Domesticated landscapes: The subsistence ecology of plant and animal domestication. *Journal of Archaeological Method and Theory* **10**: 323–68.

Testart, Alain. 1982. The significance of food storage among hunter-gatherers. *Current Anthropology* **23**: 523–37.

Thomas, Julian. 1991. *Rethinking the Neolithic*. Cambridge: Cambridge University Press.

Thomas, Nicholas. 1990. *Marquesan Societies*. Oxford: Clarendon Press.

Thompson, J. Eric. 1938. Sixteenth and seventeenth century reports on the Chol Maya. *American Anthropologist* **40**: 584–604.

Thompson, Victor, and C. Fred Andrus. 2011. Evaluating mobility, monumentality, and feasting at the Sapelo Island shell ring complex. *American Antiquity* **76**: 315–44.

Tooker, Elizabeth. 1964. *An Ethnography of the Huron Indians*. Bulletin 190. Washington, DC: Bureau of American Ethnology.

Townsend, Patricia. 1974. Sago production in a New Guinea economy. *Human Ecology* **2**: 217–36.

Tozzer, Alfred. 1941 (reprinted 1966). *Landa's relación de las cosas de Yucatan*. Cambridge, MA: Peabody Museum, Harvard University.

Trenholm, Sarah. 1989. *Persuasion and Social Influence*. Englewood Cliffs, NJ: Prentice Hall.

Trigger, Bruce. 1969. *The Huron, Farmers of the North*. New York: Holt, Rinehart, Winston.

1976. *The Children of Aataentsic, A History of the Huron people to 1660*. Montreal: McGill-Queen's University Press.

Trinkaus, K. 1995. Mortuary behavior, labor organization, and social rank. In *Regional Approaches to Mortuary Analysis*, ed. L. Beck, 53–75. New York: Plenum.

Trivers, R. L. 1971. The evolution of reciprocal altruism. *Quarterly Review of Biology* **46**: 35–57.

Tuck, James. 1976. *Newfoundland and Labrador Prehistory*. Ottawa: National Museum of Man.

Turnbull, David. 2002. Performance and narrative, bodies and movement in the construction of places and objects, spaces and knowledges. *Theory, Culture and Society* **19**: 125–43.

Turner, Nancy, and Harriet Kuhnlein. 1982. Two important "root" foods of the Northwest Coast Indians. *Economic Botany* **36**: 411–32.

1983. Camas (camassia spp.) and riceroot (fritillaria spp): Two liliaceous "root" foods of the Northwest Coast Indians. *Ecology of Food and Nutrition* **13**: 199–219.

Turner, Nancy, and Sandra Peacock. 2005. Solving the perennial paradox: Ethnobotanical evidence for plant resource management on the Northwest Coast. In *Keeping It Living: Traditions of Plant Use and Cultivation on the Northwest Coast of North America*, eds. D. Deur and N. Turner, 101–50. Seattle: University of Washington Press.

Twiss, Katheryn. 2008. Transformations in an early agricultural society: Feasting in the Southern Levantine Pre-pottery Neolithic. *Journal of Anthropological Archaeology* **27**: 418–42.

2012. The archaeology of food and social diversity. *Journal of Archaeological Research*. doi: 10.1007/s10814-012-9058-5.

Tybjerg, Tove. 1977. Potlatch and trade among the Tlingit Indians of the American Northwest Coast. *Temenos*(**13**): 189–204.

Tykot, Robert, and John Staller. 2002. The importance of early maize agriculture in coastal Ecuador: New data from La Emerenciana. *Current Anthropology* **43**: 666–77.

Tyler, Stephen. 1973. *India: An Anthropological Perspective*. California: Goodyear Publishing Company.

Ubelaker, D. H., M. Katzenberg, and J. Doyon. 1995. Status and diet in Precontact Highland Ecuador. *American Journal of Physical Anthropology* **97**: 403–11.

Ugan, Andrew. 2005. Does size matter? body size, mass collecting and their implications for understanding prehistoric foraging behavior. *American Antiquity* **70**: 75–89.

Ur, Jason, and Carlo Colantoni. 2010. The cycle of production, preparation and consumption in a Northern Mesopotamian city. In *Inside Ancient Kitchens: New Directions in the Study of Daily Meals and Feasts*, ed. Elizabeth Klarich, 55–82. Boulder: University Press of Colorado.

Urry, Katherine. 1993. *Te hakari: Feasting in Maori society and its archaeological implications*. M.A. thesis, University of Auckland.

van der Sanden, Wijnand. 1996. *Through Nature to Eternity*. Amsterdam: Batavian Lion International.

Van der Veen, M. 2003. When is food a luxury? *World Archaeology* **34**: 405–27.

Vander Wall, Stephen. 1990. *Food Hoarding in Animals*. Chicago: University of Chicago Press.

Van Derwarker, Amber M. 1999. Feasting and status at the Toqua site. *Southeastern Archaeology* **18**(1): 11–24.

VanDerwarker, Amber, and Robert Kruger. 2012. Regional variation in the importance and uses of maize in the early and middle formative olmec heartland. *Latin American Antiquity* **23**: 509–32.

van Gijn, Annelou, and Marek Zvelebil. 1997. Stone age, ideology and scaling the ladder of inference. *Analecta Praehistorica Leidensia* **29**: 3–11.

van Noordwijk, Maria, and Carel van Schaik. 2009. Intersexual food transfers among orangutans. *Behavior Ecology and Sociobiology* **63**: 883–90.

Vason, George. 1840. *Life of the Late George Vason of Nottingham*. London: John Snow.

Vaughn, Kevin J. 2005. Crafts and the materialization of chiefly power in Nasca. *Archaeological Papers of the American Anthropological Association* **14**: 113–30.

Vayda, Andrew. 1967. Pomo trade feasts. In *Tribal and Peasant Economies*, ed. George Dalton, 494–500. New York: Natural History Press.

1976. *War in Ecological Perspective*. New York: Plenum Press.

Vega-Centeno, R. 2006. Construction, labor organization, and feasting during the late Archaic Period in the Central Andes. *Journal of Anthropological Archaeology* **25**: 1–22.

Vigne, Jean-Denis, Isabelle Carrère, François Briois, and Jean Guilaine. 2011. The early process of mammal domestication in the Near East: New evidence from the Pre-Neolithic and Pre-Pottery Neolithic in Cyprus. *Current Anthropology* **52**(Supplement 4):S255–72.

Waddell, Eric. 1972. *The Mound Builders*. Seattle: University of Washington Press.

Wadley, Greg, and Angus Martin. 1993. The origins of agriculture? A biological perspective and a new hypothesis. *Australian Biologist* **6**: 96–105.

Wainwright, G., and I. Longworth. 1971. *Durrington Wall, Excavations 1966–1968*. London: Society of Antiquaries.

Webster, G. 1990. Labor control and emergent stratification in prehistoric Europe. *Current Anthropology* **31**: 337–66.

Walens, S. 1981. *Feasting with Cannibals*. Princeton, NJ: Princeton University Press.

Waley, Arthur. 1996. *The Book of Songs*. New York: Grove Press.

Walker, Harlan, ed. 2003. *The Fat of the Land*. New York: Footwork.

Walker, P. 1989. Cranial injuries as evidence of violence in prehistoric Southern California. *American Journal of Physical Anthropology* **80**: 313–23.

Wälty, Samuel. 2003. Comment on Hauser-Schäublin. *Current Anthropology* **44**: 173–4.

Wason, Paul. 1994. *The Archaeology of Rank*. Cambridge: Cambridge University Press.

Watanabe, Hitoshi. 1972. *The Ainu Ecosystem*. Seattle: University of Washington Press.

Watkins, Trevor. 1992. The beginning of the Neolithic: Searching for meaning in material culture change. *Paléorient* **18**(1): 63–75.

　　2010. Changing people, changing environments: How hunter-gatherers became communities that changed the world. In *Landscapes in Transition*, eds. B. Finlayson and G. Warren, 106–14. Oxford: Oxbow.

Watters, R. 1960. The nature of shifting cultivation. *Pacific Viewpoint* **1**: 59–99.

Webb, Malcolm C. 1998. Chiefdom as church. *Current Anthropology* **39**(5): 742–4.

Webb, S., and P. Edwards. 2002. The Natufian human skeletal remains from Wadi Hammeh 27 (Jordan). *Paléorient* **28**: 103–24.

Webster G. 1990. Labor control and emergent stratification in prehistoric Europe. *Current Anthropology* **31**: 337–266.

Weiner, Annette. 1988. *The Trobrianders of Papua New Guinea*. New York: Holt, Rinehart and Winston.

Weinstein-Evron, Mina. 2009. *Archaeology in the Archives: Unveiling the Natufian Culture of Mount Carmel*. Boston: Brill.

Weiss, Ehud, Mordecai Kisleve, and Anat Hartmann. 2006. Autonomous cultivation before domestication. *Science* **312**: 1608–10.

Weiss, Ehud, and Daniel Zohary. 2011. The Neolithic Southwest Asian founder crops. *Current Anthropology* **52**(Supplement 4):S237–54.

Welch, Paul D. and Margaret Scarry. 1995. Status-related variation in foodways in the Moundville chiefdom. *American Antiquity* **60**(3): 397–419.

Wells, Peter. 1984. *Farms, Villages, and Cities*. Ithaca, NY: Cornell University Press.

White, C. 2001. Isotopic evidence for Maya patterns of deer and dog use at Preclassic Colha. *Journal of Archaeological Science* **28**: 89–107.

Whittle, Alisdair. 1994. The first farmers. In *The Oxford Illustrated Prehistory of Europe*, ed. Barry Cunliffe, 136–66. Oxford: Oxford University Press.

　　1996. *Europe in the Neolithic*. Cambridge: Cambridge University Press.

Widgren, M. 2007. Pre-colonial landesque capital. In *Rethinking Environmental History*, eds. A. Hornborg, J. Martineq-Alier, and J. McNeill. Walnut Creek, CA: AltaMira.

Wiessner, Polly. 1982. Risk, reciprocity and social influences on !Kung San economics. In *Politics and History in Band Societies*, eds. E. Leacock and R. Lee, 61–84. Cambridge: Cambridge University Press.

　　1989. Style and changing relations between the individual and society. In *The Meaning of Things*, ed. Ian Hodder, 56–63. New York: Harper Collins.

　　1996. Leveling the hunter: Constraints on the status quest in foraging societies. In *Food and the Status Quest*, eds. P. Wiessner and Wulf Schiefenhovel, 171–92. Providence: Berghahn.

　　2001. Of feasting and value: Enga feasts in a historical perspective (Papua New Guinea). In *Feasts: Archaeological and Ethnographic Perspectives on Food, Politics, and Power*, eds. Michael Dielter and Brian Hayden, 115–43. Washington and London: Smithsonian Institution Press.

　　2002a. Hunting, healing, and hxaro exchange. A long-term perspective on !Kung (Ju/'hoansi) large-game hunting. *Evolution and Human Behavior* **23**: 407–36.

　　2002b. The vines of complexity. *Current Anthropology* **43**: 233–69.

Wiessner, Polly, and Akii Tumu. 1998. *Historical Vines*. Washington, DC: Smithsonian Institution Press.

Wilcox, D., R. McGuire, and C. Sternberg. 1981. *Snaketown Revisited*. Archaeology series, no. 155. Tucson: Arizona State Museum, University of Arizona.

Wilhelm, Richard. 1967. *The I Ching*. Princeton, NJ: Princeton University Press.

Wilk, Richard. 1983. Little house in the jungle. *Journal of Anthropological Archaeology* 2: 99–116.

Willcox, George. 1996. Evidence for plant exploitation and vegetation history from three early Neolithic Pre-pottery sites on the Euphrates. *Vegetation History and Archaeobotany* 5: 143–52.

—— 1998. Archaeobotanical evidence for the beginnings of agriculture in Southeast Asia. In *The Origins of Agriculture and Crop Domestication the Harlan Symposium.*, eds. A. Damania, J. Valkoun, G. Willcox, and C. Qualset, 25–38. Damascus: ICARDA, IPGRI, FAO, GRCP.

—— 1999. Agrarian change and the beginnings of cultivation in the Near East. In *The Prehistory of Food*, eds. Chris Gosden and Jon Hather, 478–500. London: Routledge.

—— 2005. The distribution, natural habitats, and availability of wild cereals in relation to their domestication in the Near East. *Vegetation History and Archaeobotany* 14: 534–41.

—— 2007. The adoption of farming and the beginnings of the Neolithic in the Euphrates Valley. In *The Origins and Spread of Domestic Plants in Southwest Asia and Europe.*, eds. S. Colledge and J. Conolly, 21–36. Walnut Creek, CA: Left Coast Press.

—— 2011. Searching for the origins of arable weeds in the Near East. *Vegetation History and Archaeobotany*. doi: 10.1007/s00334-011-0307-1.

Willcox, G., S. Fornite, and L. Herveux. 2008. Early Holocene cultivation before domestication in Syria. *Vegetation History and Archeobotany* 17: 313–25.

Williams, E. 1988. *Complex Hunter-Gatherers: A Late Holocene Example from Temperate Australia.* Vol. 423. London: BAR International.

Williams, Judith. 2006. *Clam Gardens: Aboriginal Mariculture on Canada's West Coast.* Vancouver: Transmontanus-New Star Books.

Williams, Nancy, and Eugene Hunn. 1982. *Resource Managers: North American and Australian Hunters and Gatherers.* Boulder, CO: Westview Press.

Williams, Patrick, Donna Nash, Michael Moseley, Susan deFrance, Mario Ruales, Ana Miranda, and David Goldstein. 2005. Los encuentros y las bases para la administración política Wari. *Boletín De Arqueología PUCP* 9: 207–32.

Wilson, Norman, and Arlean Towne. 1978. Nisenan. In *Handbook of North American Indians, California.*, ed. R. Heizer. Vol. 8, 387–97. Washington, DC: Smithsonian Institution Press.

Wilson, Robert, and Catherine Carlson. 1980. *The Archaeology of Kamloops*. Burnaby, BC: Department of Archaeology, Simon Fraser University.

Winterhalder, Bruce. 1996a. A marginal model of tolerated theft. *Ethology and Sociobiology* 17: 37–53.

—— 1996b. Social foraging and the behavioral ecology of intragroup resource transfers. *Evolutionary Anthropology* 5: 46–57.

Winterhalder, Bruce, and C. Goland. 1997. An evolutionary ecology perspective on diet choice, risk, and plant domestication. In *People, Plants, and Landscapes: Studies in Ethnobotany*, ed. K. Gremillion, 123–60. Tuscaloosa: University of Alabama Press.

Wittfogel, Karl. 1957. *Oriental Despotism*. New Haven, CT: Yale University Press.

Wohlt, P. 1978. *Ecology, agriculture and social organization: The dynamics of group composition in the Highlands of Papua New Guinea.* Ph.D. dissertation, University of Minnesota.

Wolf, Eric. 1972. Ownership and political ecology. *Anthropological Quarterly* **45**: 201–5.

Wolkstein, Diane, and Noah Kramer. 1983. *Inanna, Queen of Heaven and Earth*. New York: Harper and Row.

Wood, Brian. 2006. Prestige or provisioning? A test of foraging goals among the Hadza. *Current Anthropology* **47**: 383–87.

Wood, Brian, and Kim Hill. 2000. A test of the "showing-off" hypothesis with Ache hunters. *Current Anthropology* **41**: 124–5.

Woodburn, James. 1966. *The Hadza*. Vol. **16** mm. film. London School of Economics.

1982. Egalitarian societies. *Man* **17**: 431–51.

1988. African hunter-gatherer social organization: Is it best understood as a product of encapsulation? In *Hunters and Gatherers 1: History, Evolution and Social Change*, eds. Tim Ingold, David Riches, and James Woodburn. Vol. **1**, 31–64. New York: Berg.

Woodward, Mark. 1989. Economy, polity, and cosmology in the Ao Naga mithan feast. In *Ritual, Power, and Economy: Upland-Lowland Contrasts in Mainland Southeast Asia*, ed. Susan Russell, 121–42. DeKalb: Northern Illinois University Press.

Woodward, Mark, and Susan Russell. 1989. Introduction: Transformations in ritual and economy in upland and lowland Southeast Asia. In *Ritual, Power, and Economy: Upland-Lowland Contrasts in Mainland Southeast Asia*, ed. Susan Russell, 1–26. DeKalb: Northern Illinois University Press.

Wrangham, R. W. 1975. *Behavioural ecology of chimpanzees in Gombe National Park, Tanzania*. Ph.D. thesis, Cambridge University.

1996. *Chimpanzee Cultures*. Cambridge, MA: Harvard University Press.

Wright, Henry. 1977. Recent research on the origin of the state. *Annual Review of Anthropology* **6**: 379–97.

1984. Prestate political formations. In *On the Evolution of Complex Societies*, ed. T. Earle, 43–77. Malibu, CA: Undena Press.

Wright, James C., ed. 2004. *The Mycenaean Feast*. Athens/Princeton: American School of Classical Studies.

Wright, Katherine I. 1994. Ground-stone tools and hunter-gatherer subsistence in Southwest Asia: Implications for the transition to farming. *American Antiquity* **59**: 238–63.

Wymer, DeAnne. 1994. The social context of early maize in the Mid-Ohio Valley. In *Corn and Culture in the Prehistoric New World*, eds. Sissel Johannessen and Christine Hastorf, 411–26. Boulder, CO: Westview Press.

Wynne-Edwards, V. 1962. *Animal Dispersion in Relation to Social Behavior*. Edinburgh: Oliver and Boyd.

Yacobaccio, Hugo. 2004. Social dimensions of camelid domestication in the southern Andes. *Anthropozoologica* **39**: 237–47.

Yamamoto, S., and M. Tanaka. 2010. The influence of kin relationship and reciprocal context on chimpanzees' other-regarding preferences. *Animal Behavior* **79**: 595–602.

Yan, Yunxiang. 1996. *The Flow of Gifts*. Stanford, CA: Stanford University Press.

Yanagisako, Sylvia. 1979. Family and household: The analysis of domestic groups. *Annual Review of Anthropology* **8**: 161–205.

Yartah, T. 2005. Les batîments communautaires de tell 'Abr 3 (PPNA, Syrie). *Neo-Lithics* **1**: 3–9.

Yasuda, Y. 2002. Origins of pottery and agriculture in East Asia. In *Origins of Pottery and Agriculture*, ed. Y. Yasuda, 119–42. New Delhi: Roli Books.

Yengoyan, Aram. 1976. Structure, event, and ecology in Aboriginal Australia. In *Tribes and Boundaries in Australia*, ed. N. Peterson, 121–32. Canberra: Australian Institute of Aboriginal Studies.

Yerkes, Richard W. 2005. Bone chemistry, body parts, and growth marks: Evaluating Ohio Hopewell and Cahokia Mississippian seasonality, subsistence, ritual, and feasting. *American Antiquity* **70**(2): 241–65.

    2006. Middle Woodland settlements and social organization in the Central Ohio Valley. In *Recreating Hopewell*, eds. Douglas K., Charles Buikstra, and Jane Buikstra, 57–61. Gainesville: University Press of Florida.

Yeshurun, Reuven, Guy Bar-Oz, and Dani Nadel. 2013. The social role of food in the Natufian cemetery of Raqefet Cave, Mount Carmel, Israel. *Journal of Anthropological Archaeology* **32**: 511–26.

Yoffee, N. 1993. Too many chiefs? In *Archaeological Theory: Who Sets the Agenda?*, eds. N. Yoffee and A. Sherratt, 60–78. Cambridge: Cambridge University Press.

    2005. *Myths of the Archaic State*. Cambridge: Cambridge University Press.

Young, Michael. 1971. *Fighting with Food*. Cambridge: Cambridge Press.

Zahavi, A., and A. Zahavi. 1997. *The Handicap Principle*. New York: Oxford University Press.

Zeder, Melinda A. 2001. *Feast or forage, the transition to agriculture in the Near East*. Paper presented at the Society for American Archaeology Annual Meeting, New Orleans.

Zeder, Melinda, and Bruce Smith. 2009. A conversation on agricultural origins: Talking past each other in a crowded room. *Current Anthropology* **50**: 681–93.

Zori, D., J. Byock, E. Erlendsson, S. Martin, T. Wake, and K. Edwards. 2013. Feasting in Viking age Iceland: Sustaining a chiefly political economy in a marginal environment. *Antiquity* **87**: 150–65.

Zvelebil, Marek. 1994. Plant use in the Mesolithic and its role in the transition to farming. Paper presented at Proceedings of the Prehistoric Society, London.

    1995. Hunting, gathering, or husbandry? Management of food resources by the Late Mesolithic communities of temperate Europe. *MASCA Research Papers in Science and Archaeology* **12**(1995 Supplement): 79–104.

    2006. Mobility, contact, and exchange in the Baltic Sea Basin 6000–2000 BC. *Journal of Anthropological Archaeology* **25**: 178–92.

Index

CPSIA information can be obtained
at www.ICGtesting.com
Printed in the USA
LVHW100811140419
614090LV00007B/90/P

9 781107 617643